"Expanding the canonical book *The Zionist Idea, The Zionist Ideas* clarifies the wealth of rich ideas regarding the Jewish people's sovereign national home in the land of Israel. This book will help flip today's destructive 'dialogue of the deaf' into a thoughtful, constructive conversation—perhaps from which a new shared vision for Jewish nationalism will emerge."

—RUTH CALDERON, member of Knesset 2013–15 and author of *A Bride for One Night: Talmud Tales*

"As the story of Zionism continues to unfold in the twenty-first century, Gil Troy provides those who wish to understand its past, present, and future this invaluable guide. Building on Hertzberg's seminal volume, *The Zionist Ideas* expands our range of vision, exploring Zionism in its political, religious, and cultural dimensions as imagined by Zionists both in Israel and the Diaspora. With expertly curated selections and his own penetrating analysis, Troy accompanies us on a tour of Zionism's evolution from the ideology of a fledgling, yet ancient, national movement to the philosophical underpinning of its own manifestation: the miracle of statehood for the Jewish people. Embracing the diversity of views about an ideology come to life, he offers clues to Zionism's next chapters as Israel matures, struggles, and strives to keep faith with its founders' vision."

—DANIEL B. SHAPIRO, former U.S. ambassador to the State of Israel

"This work promises to be an important contribution to Jewish historiography. I highly recommend it."

—HOWARD SACHAR, professor emeritus of history and international affairs at George Washington University

"Gil Troy is ideally situated to update this classic: as an outstanding scholar and historian, community leader, and one of today's most inspiring and influential Zionist thinkers and commentators. The result is a must-read—a Zionist Bible for the twenty-first century—comprehensive and compelling. The impressive range of thinkers, from yesterday to today, from pioneers to torchbearers, from left to right, illuminated by Professor Troy's extraordinary commentary, attests to and affirms the enduring character of the Zionist idea."

—IRWIN COTLER, former minister of justice and attorney general of Canada, and human rights activist

"This is an incredible collection—so very well thought out and conceptualized!"

—CSABA NIKOLENYI, director of the Azrieli Institute of Israel Studies at Concordia University

The Zionist Ideas

In loving memory of our mother and grandmother, Rosalie "Chris" (Laks) Lerman, who blessed us with a passionate love for Israel and Judaism.

And in loving tribute to our teacher, Mel Reisfield, a life-changing Zionist educator who energized generations of American Jewish youth to understand the centrality of Israel to Jewish life.

Rosalie "Chris" (Laks) Lerman was born in Starachowice, Poland, in 1926 to Isaak and Pola Laks. Isaak and Pola were modern Jews and committed Zionists. They taught their three daughters Hebrew, Torah-driven values, and Jewish history. They raised their children to visualize—and hoped they would experience—a world in which Jews were restored to a national homeland in Israel.

The Nazi invasion of Poland upended their lives. Pola perished in the first death-camp deportations. Isaak died in Auschwitz months before the war ended. Miraculously, the Laks daughters survived Auschwitz and the death march to Ravensbruck.

Despite these experiences, Rosalie believed in the ability of the world to repair, and in the power of light over darkness and love over hate. She, along with our father and grandfather, Miles Lerman, spent a lifetime working to create a world of trust, understanding, and mutual respect among all people.

Rosalie felt privileged to experience the miracle of modern Israel. She celebrated Israel's successes and was candid in acknowledging its flaws. She viewed Israel as a "work in progress," knowing we still have much to do before the Zionist dream of a Jewish homeland thriving in peace and harmony with its neighbors is realized.

May the courage and optimism of Rosalie "Chris" (Laks) Lerman and the vision and passionate teaching of Mel Reisfield inspire us all.

—DAVID LERMAN, SHELLEY WALLOCK, BROOKE LERMAN, JULIA LERMAN, *and* TED LERMAN

The Jewish Publication Society expresses its gratitude for
the generosity of the primary sponsors of this book:

David Lerman and Shelley Wallock, in memory of our mother,
Rosalie Lerman, and in honor of our teacher Mel Reisfield,

and for the additional support of:

Morrie I. Kleinbart, in memory of my beloved parents,
David and Dora Kleinbart, z"l.

JPS ANTHOLOGIES
OF JEWISH THOUGHT

University of Nebraska Press
Lincoln

THE
ZIONIST IDEAS

Visions for the Jewish Homeland—
Then, Now, Tomorrow

GIL TROY

Foreword by Natan Sharansky

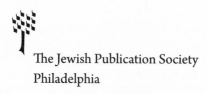

The Jewish Publication Society
Philadelphia

Acknowledgments for the use of copyrighted material
appear on pages 503–17, which constitute an extension
of the copyright page. "Zionism: A Jewish Feminist-
Womanist Appreciation" © Einat Ramon.

Library of Congress Cataloging-in-Publication Data
Names: Troy, Gil, editor. | Scharansky, Anatoly,
writer of foreword.
Title: The Zionist ideas: visions for the Jewish
homeland—then, now, tomorrow /
[edited by] Gil Troy; foreword by Natan Sharansky.
Description: Lincoln: University of Nebraska Press,
[2018] | Series: JPS anthologies of Jewish thought |
"Published by the University of Nebraska Press as a
Jewish Publication Society book."
Identifiers: LCCN 2017052567
ISBN 9780827612556 (pbk: alk. paper)
ISBN 9780827613980 (epub)
ISBN 9780827613997 (mobi)
ISBN 9780827614253 (pdf)
Subjects: LCSH: Zionism—History—Sources. | BISAC:
RELIGION / Judaism / History. | SOCIAL SCIENCE /
Jewish Studies. | HISTORY / Middle East / Israel.
Classification: LCC DS149 .Z6752 2018 |
DDC 320.54095694—dc23 LC record available at
https://lccn.loc.gov/2017052567

Set in Arno Pro by Mikala R Kolander.

Contents

5. *Pioneers*: Cultural Zionism   103

6. *Pioneers*: Diaspora Zionism   125

PART TWO. *Builders*: Actualizing and Modernizing the Zionist Blueprints

9. *Builders*: Revisionist Zionism

10. *Builders*: Religious Zionism

11. *Builders*: Cultural Zionism   267

PART THREE. *Torchbearers*: Reassessing, Redirecting, Reinvigorating

14. *Torchbearers*: Labor Zionism 363

17. *Torchbearers*: Cultural Zionism

18. Torchbearers: Diaspora Zionism

Foreword

Natan Sharansky

The Zionist idea gave me—and millions of others—a meaningful identity. In June 1967, when I was nineteen, the call from Jerusalem—"The Temple Mount Is in Our Hands"—penetrated the Iron Curtain. Democratic Israel's surprising victory in the Six-Day War, defeating Arab dictatorships threatening to destroy it, inspired many of us all over the world to become active participants in Jewish history. This notion that the Jews are a people with collective rights to establish a Jewish state in our ancient homeland, the Land of Israel, connected us to something more important than simple physical survival. Forging a mystical link with our people, we discovered identity, or as we call it, "peoplehood." Suddenly we Soviet Jews, Jews of silence, robbed of our heritage by the Soviet regime, realized there is a country that called us its children.

As thousands of us applied to immigrate to Israel, roused by that cry from our distant past, anticipating a more hopeful future even while knowing the cost we would have to pay in the present, we found meaning in the Zionist idea.

The rediscovery of my identity, my community, my people, gave me the strength to fight for my rights, for the rights of other Jews, and for the rights of others, allying me with dissidents fighting communist tyranny. I discovered that this synthesis of the universal, the democratic, with the particularist, the nationalist, is central to the Zionist idea.

When the Soviet court sentenced me, and I said to my people, to my wife, Avital, "Next Year in Jerusalem!" but told the judges, "To you I have nothing to say," I found strength in the Zionist idea.

When a Prisoner of Zion incarcerated next to me in the Gulag, Yosef Mendelevitch, informed me by tapping in code that by his calculations the Memorial Day siren was sounding in Jerusalem, and we both stood in silence, separated by thick oppressive walls, but each sensing the beating of hearts thousands of kilometers away, we were united by the Zionist idea.

When millions of Jews wore those bracelets with Soviet Jewish names on them, twinned their bar and bat mitzvahs with Soviet Jewish kids they had never met, marched in rallies, and shouted "Let my people go," they championed the Zionist idea.

Years later, in 1991 when I went to Ethiopia amid its raging civil war and witnessed Operation Solomon, Israel sending huge planes to bring Ethiopian Jews home to Israel, we all felt this amazing connection through the Zionist idea.

And today, as the head of the Jewish Agency, transitioning the organization from a Zionism of survival to a Zionism of identity and mutual exchange, we are introducing a new generation of Jews to the Zionist idea—and modern Zionist ideas.

That shift explains why today, nearly sixty years after Arthur Hertzberg's *The Zionist Idea* was published in 1959, and seventy years after Israel's establishment in 1948, we desperately need a new edition. We need a modern book celebrating, as Professor Gil Troy notes, the Zionist *ideas*: the many ways to make Israel great—and the many ways individuals can find fulfillment by affiliating with the Jewish people and building the Jewish state.

When I arrived in Jerusalem in 1986, I had lived the Zionist idea but did not know Hertzberg's classic anthology. Nine years later, while starting the New Immigrants' Party, I wondered whether having a separate political party for Jews from the former Soviet Union contradicted basic Zionist ideals of unity. A friend recommended Hertzberg's book for a crash course on the history of Zionism.

Reading the impressive range of Zionist thinkers, I finally understood how people with such different views, from communists and socialists to pious rabbis and liberal capitalist Revisionists, could also be Zionist. This pluralism inspired our party's move away from the cookie-cutter approach to nation building. Eventually, our new party, Yisrael BaAliyah, encouraged a mosaic of cultures and traditions whereby an individual does not need to sacrifice personal identity for an all-consuming ideology.

That experience proved what this successor to Hertzberg's book demonstrates: We now live in a world of Zionist ideas, with many different ways to help Israel flourish as a democratic Jewish state.

I first met Gil Troy in print, in 2003, when my cabinet portfolio included Diaspora Jewish affairs, and he had just published his best-selling Zionist manifesto, *Why I Am a Zionist: Israel, Jewish Identity, and the Challenges of Today*. In that path-breaking book, and his many eloquent columns, he went beyond defending Israel and combating antisemitism. He also articulated a positive vision of "Identity Zionism" that resonates with Jews today, young and old, in Israel and in the Diaspora.

When we met in 2008, I was struck by the fact that despite coming from different generations, despite having been born into very different political systems and Jewish experiences, both of us are *defending identity* as an anchor in today's world. As lovers of democracy and human rights, we both appreciate the importance of retaining particular cultural, national, ethnic, and religious heritages in a world that dismisses nationalism, often endorsing a selfish individualism or a simplistic, universalist cosmopolitanism that communism's abuses should have discredited.

I am thrilled that the Jewish Publication Society commissioned Gil Troy to update Hertzberg's *The Zionist Idea*. He is the right person for this most right project at the absolute right time. And this magnificent work, his magnum opus, is the perfect follow-up to Hertzberg's work.

Combining, like Hertzberg, a scholar's eye and an activist's ear, Troy has done this classic justice. The book provides just enough selections from the original, supplemented by important Pioneer voices Hertzberg missed. It then escorts us into the Builders' era and up to today, the time of the Torchbearers. Subdividing each time period into six schools of Zionist thought, Troy traces the many Zionist ideas—Political, Revisionist, Labor, Religious, Cultural, and Diaspora—as they developed, all of these Zionisms committed, in different ways, to establishing, and now perfecting, Israel as a democratic Jewish state.

Today, while celebrating Israel's seventieth anniversary, Jews in Israel and beyond are reassessing their own identities—reappraisals that can lead to stronger Jewish identity as we rediscover what makes our people exceptional. In its first seventy years, Israel often served as a refuge, a shelter from oppression, absorbing more than three million Jews fleeing persecution. This book shows that now we can become a beacon of opportunity, appealing to Jews seeking not only a high standard of living, but a meaningful quality of life. A revived Zionist conversation, a renewed Zionist vision, can create a Jewish state that reaffirms meaning for those already committed to it while addressing the needs of Jews physically separated from their ancestral homeland, along with those who feel spiritually detached from their people.

To survive, every nation needs a glue that binds it together. For some it is history, for others language, and for others a creed. Our strongest glue is our Judaism, whether it be understood as a nationality, a faith, a response to antisemitism, or peoplehood. But no matter how we relate to our Judaism, one thing is clear: If the Zionist idea is to flourish, we must allow our nation to continue being exceptional, to continue representing the deep connection between the desire of people to belong and to be free.

How lucky we are to have this new book, filled with old-new ideas, Theodor Herzl–style, to guide this important and timely conversation, so that Israel, in middle age, can inspire our young and our old, the Jewish nation, and the world.

Acknowledgments

Although I first absorbed the Zionist idea in the home of my parents, Elaine and Bernard Dov Troy, I first encountered Arthur Hertzberg's book *The Zionist Idea* at Camp Tel Yehudah, the summer home of Young Judaea, America's largest Zionist youth movement. While steeping us in Zionist thought back when we loved arguing Zionism—and life—into the night, the book taught me and my peers that conversations about Zionism often bubble over: exploring Jewish civilization, interpreting Jewish history, confronting modernity, critiquing society, understanding nationalism.

At the time, we did not know that Emanuel Neumann, who initiated the book, helped found Young Judaea in 1909. Then too I never would have dared imagine that decades later the Jewish Publication Society would honor—and challenge—me with updating this classic. And I never would have predicted that this successor edition's generous sponsor, David Lerman, himself a Young Judaean, would dedicate the book to the man to whom I also wish to dedicate it: my friend and mentor, Mr. Tel Yehudah, Mel Reisfield. Mel and his wife Yaffa have blessed me with their friendship for more than four decades. With this dedication, I thank them both in the names of thousands.

Young Judaea's expansive, thoughtful spirit suits this volume. As the centrist, pluralistic Zionist youth movement, it celebrates learning—and arguing—about Zionism from left to right, from Ber Borochov to Ze'ev Jabotinsky. In fact, Mel Reisfield introduced me to the schools of Zionist thought this volume explores, using camp props: a black beard for Theodor Herzl, a pitchfork for A. D. Gordon, a clenched fist for Jabotinsky, a white beard for Rav Kook, and a wheel for Ahad Ha'am.

These thinkers are my intellectual godparents, especially given that I'm a link in a chain of Zionist youth movement intermarriages. My father led the Revisionist Betar movement; my mother attended the first Labor Zionist Habonim Year-in-Israel Workshop (her Yiddishist

Bundist camp mentor stopped speaking to her when she went to Israel).
I married Linda Adams, from the Socialist Zionist HaShomer HaTzair
youth movement. Her parents, Annie z"l and Marcel Adams, crossbred
HaShomer with the centrist Hanoar Hatzioni. Today, our kids belong
to the Religious Zionist B'nai Akiva.

I thank this extraordinary family for their love—and enduring me
book after book. Special love to Linda, whom we all acknowledge as the
real Zionist in the family—as well as our artist and muse.

This book proved particularly complicated. Fortunately, I was blessed
with amazing research assistants, especially Viktoria Bedo, Adam Bellos,
Kinneret Belzer, R'nana Goldenhersh, Rachel Greenspan, Hadar Ahiad
Hazony, Yair Leibler, Yehudah Leibler, Kendra Meisler, Elie Peltz, Gidon
Schreiber, Brian Teitelbaum, Samantha Viterbi, Aaron Weinberg, Zemira
Zahava Wolfe, Ari Zackin—as well as my four children, Lia, Yoni, Aviv,
and Dina, who assisted in multiple ways.

These assistants helped realize a broader vision shaped by the smart-
est, most passionate Zionists I know and could consult, including Gur
Alroey, Adi Arbel, Yonatan Ariel, Peter Beinart, Jeremy Benstein, Gor-
don Bernat-Kunin, Dganit Mazouz Biton, Erez Biton, Nir Boms, David
Breakstone, Meir Buzaglo, Jeffrey Cahn, David Cape, Alan Caplan, Barry
Chazan, Anita Besdin Cooper, Eitan Cooper, Scott Copeland, Ariela
Cotler, Irwin Cotler, Rachel Sharansky Danziger, Tamar Darmon, Mark
Dratch, Noah Efron, David Ellenson, Rachel Fish, Don Futterman, Tony
Fyne, Elon Gold, Micha Goodman, Daniel Gordis, Steve Greenberg, Jon-
athan Gribetz, Robbie Gringras, Danny Hakim, Hillel Halkin, Donniel
Hartman, Yossi Klein Halevi, Yoaz Hendel, Sara Hirschorn, Benjamin
Ish Shalom, Simon Klarfeld, Jen Klor, Justin Korda, Alex Levine, Linda
Lovitch, David Makovsky, Yisrael Medad, Gidi Mark, Michael Oren,
Daniel Polisar, Einat Ramon, Zohar Raviv, Iris Rosenberg, Limor Rubin,
Jonathan Sarna, Theodore Sasson, Leonard Saxe, Elli Schor, Eli Schul-
man, Eilon Schwartz, Natan Sharansky, Bill Slott, David Starr, Chaim
Steinmetz, Alon Tal, Shmuel Trigano, Ilan Troen, Josh Weinberg, David
Weinstein, Leon Wieseltier, Thea Wieseltier, Orit Yitzhak, and Noam
Zion. My two brothers Daniel Troy and Tevi Troy continue to bless me
with advice, insight, feedback—and enduring friendship.

I am also grateful to supportive institutions, especially McGill University, the Shalom Hartman Institute, the University of Haifa's Ruderman Program for American Jewish Studies, and the Interdisciplinary Center in Herzliya.

I wish to honor the memory of another great Zionist, Arthur Hertzberg, who set a dauntingly high standard with a work I have grown to appreciate even more with each round of researching and writing. His majestic introduction remains the classic historiographical and philosophical evaluation of the Zionist idea—and achievement. And his choice of texts proved impressively resonant today. Two-thirds of the introductions in this book's first "Pioneers" section are edited versions of his preambles, representing a unique collaboration between us bridging six decades. Some spelling and grammatical matters in the excerpts have been changed to conform to the *Chicago Manual of Style* and JPS style.

Fifty-nine years after Hertzberg thanked the man who initiated his project, Emanuel Neumann, as "goad and guide," I am thrilled to thank the visionary who initiated this update that metamorphosed into its own book: the JPS director Rabbi Barry Schwartz. He too has been a model "goad and guide." Joy Weinberg, the JPS managing editor, edited with a keen eye for inconsistencies, a trained ear for infelicities, a sharp mind that improved every entry, and a big heart that made it a delight to learn from her. Heather Stauffer secured dozens of permissions diligently and gracefully. They and the impressive Jewish Publication Society–University of Nebraska Press team—including the fabulous copyeditor Brian King—labored valiantly to publish the book in time to help us all celebrate Israel's seventieth anniversary by reexamining the meaning of Zionism—and liberal nationalism—today.

As a scholar, I want readers to appreciate Zionism in historical context, understanding its origins, achievements, and challenges then, now, and tomorrow. As a Zionist activist and educator, I want Jews and non-Jews concerned about the Jewish future to join this rousing conversation about this grand Jewish experiment. Together, we can help the Jewish homeland that fulfilled its founding mission as a refuge so magnificently reach its full potential as an old-new dreamland: a model Jewish democracy.

Introduction

How Zionism's Six Traditional Schools of Thought Shape Today's Conversation

In the beginning was the idea, the Zionist idea. In 1959, when the rabbi, historian, and Zionist leader Arthur Hertzberg published what would become the classic Zionist anthology in English, the State of Israel was barely a decade old. The Zionist idea, recognizing the Jews as a people with rights to establish a state in their homeland, *Eretz Yisra'el,* was still relatively new. True, Zionism had biblical roots. True, Jews had spent 1,878 years longing to rebuild their homeland after the Romans destroyed the Second Temple. True, Europeans had spent more than a century debating "the Jewish problem"—what to do with this unassimilable and often-detested people. Still, it was hard to believe that the Wandering Jews had returned home.

Building toward Israel's establishment in 1948, the Zionist movement had to convince the world—and the skeptical Jewish supermajority—of the fundamental Zionist logic. The European Enlightenment's attempts to reduce Judaism just to a religion failed. The Jewish people always needed more than a synagogue as communal space. In modern times, Jews' unique national-religious fusion earned them collective rights to statehood, somewhere. Next, the Land of Israel, the ancestral Jewish homeland, was the logical, legitimate, and viable place to relaunch that Jewish national project. Finally, restoring Jewish sovereignty there was a pressing priority, to save the long-oppressed Jews—and let them rejuvenate, spawning a strong, proud, idealistic New Jew.

After realizing this primal Zionist idea in 1948, Zionism evolved. The Jewish national liberation movement now sought to defend and perfect the state—understanding, as the Israeli author A. B. Yehoshua writes, that "A Zionist is a person who accepts the principle that the State of Israel doesn't belong solely to its citizens, but to the entire Jewish people." As

Israel's builders steadied the state, this second-stage Zionism revolved around the question, What kind of nation should Israel be?

In today's third stage, with Israel safe, prosperous, thriving, yet still assailed, Zionism's torchbearers find themselves defending three politically unpopular assumptions: First, the Jews' status as what the philosopher Michael Walzer calls "an anomalous people," with its unique religious and national overlap, does not diminish Jews' collective rights to their homeland or the standard benefits enjoyed by every nation-state, particularly security and legitimacy. Second, the Palestinians' contesting land claims—whatever one thinks of them, from left to right—do not negate the Jewish title to Israel. Third, Israel has a dual mission: to save Jewish bodies and redeem the Jewish soul.

Zionists, therefore, recognize the Jewish people as a nation not just a religion, who, having established the Jewish state in their national homeland *Eretz Yisra'el*, now seek to perfect it. As Israel's first prime minister David Ben-Gurion said, "Israel cannot just be a refuge. . . . it has to be much, much more." Now, nearly sixty years after *The Zionist Idea* debuted, and as Israel celebrates its seventieth birthday, this successor anthology chronicles these Zionist challenges and opportunities—presenting different Israeli and Diaspora visions of how Israel should flourish.

The Zionist Ideas Today

Since 1959, *The Zionist Idea* has been the English speaker's Zionist Bible, the defining text for anyone interested in studying the Jewish national liberation movement. *The Zionist Idea* was so authoritative it took me decades before I realized that all the Zionist voices I heard in my head spoke in English, when few actually had.

Arthur Hertzberg's classic invited readers into sprawling conversations about Judaism, Jewish history, modernity, and industrialization, about nationalism's meaning and sovereignty's potential. Readers jumped from thinker to thinker, savoring the famous Zionists—Herzl, Ahad Ha'am, Gordon—while encountering unfamiliar ones—the Berdichevskys, Katznelsons, Brenners.

To some academics and activists, Hertzberg's tome was such a foundational work that any update is like digitizing the Mona Lisa or colorizing *Casablanca*. As an avowed enthusiast, I can well understand this perspective. Nonetheless, history's affirmative answer—"Yes!"—to the first edition's fundamental question—is a Jewish state viable?—does necessitate a new volume. In the ensuing decades, political, religious, and social progress transformed the Zionist conversation. Israel's 1967 Six-Day War triumph stirred questions Hertzberg never imagined, especially how Israel and the Jewish people should understand Zionism when the world perceives Israel as Goliath not David. The Revisionist Likud's victory under Menachem Begin in 1977 generated new dilemmas regarding how increasingly left-wing, cosmopolitan Diaspora Jews should relate to an increasingly right-wing, nationalist Israel. And Israel's emergence as a high-tech powerhouse vindicated Zionism, even as some feared capitalism's corruptions.

Six decades of arguments, dreams, frustrations, and reality checks also intruded. Deciding what enduring historic selections merited inclusion in a new edition and which others were outdated required comparing the finalists with hundreds of other texts. What I thought would be a quick attempt to modernize *The Zionist Idea* blossomed into a major overhaul.

In contemplating what *The Zionist Ideas* should be, I returned to the original mandate. In 1955, Emanuel Neumann of the Theodor Herzl Foundation invited Arthur Hertzberg to publish, in English, the key Zionist texts showing "the internal moral and intellectual forces in Jewish life" that shaped this "idea which galvanized a people, forged a nation, and made history." As Neumann noted: "Behind the miracle of the Restoration lies more than a century of spiritual and intellectual ferment which produced a crystallized Zionist philosophy and a powerful Zionist movement."[1]

The golden age of Zionist manifesto writing is over. But the rich payload of ideas in this volume—and those left behind on my cutting room floor—testify to the Zionist debate's ongoing vitality. Readers will discover significant writings that advance our understanding of what Zionism achieved, sought to achieve, or still seeks to achieve. No reactive or headline-driven op-eds appear here—only enduring visions. Respecting Hertzberg's dual sensibility as scholar and activist, I sought only defining, aspirational, programmatic texts. The expanded Zionist debate as Zionism went from marginal to mainstream warranted including many more essays, even if only excerpted briefly. Using this criteria, I reduced Hertzberg's thirty-seven thinkers to twenty-six. To reflect the burgeoning conversation since, I multiplied the number of entries to 169, while respecting the publisher's mandate to shorten the text to approximately 180,000 words—Hertzberg's was 240,000.

Of course, no volume could contain every significant Zionist essay, any more than the argumentative Jewish people could ever agree on a Zionist canon. Nevertheless, all these pieces help assemble the larger Zionist puzzle—an ever-changing movement of "becoming" not just "being," of saving the world while building a nation. Together, these texts help compare what key thinkers sought and what they wrought, while anticipating the next chapters of this dynamic process.

Non-Jewish voices do not appear here. There's a rich history of non-Jews defending Zionism eloquently—from George Eliot to Winston Churchill, from Martin Luther King Jr. to Daniel Patrick Moynihan, from President John Kennedy to the Reverend John Hagee. Moynihan's United Nations Speech in 1975, for example, galvanized Americans to defend democracy and decency when the General Assembly singled out one form of nationalism, Zionism, as racist. However, most such texts by non-Jews are defensive or explanatory rather than personal or visionary. Beyond this, including non-Jews would detract from the focus on how the Jewish conversation about Jewish nationalism established and now influences Israel. This book gives Jewish Zionists their say—demonstrating how their Zionist ideas evolved.

Like Abraham's welcoming shelter, the book's Big Tent Zionism is open to all sides, yet defined by certain boundaries. Looking left, staunch critics of Israeli policies belong—but not anti-Zionists who reject the Jewish state, universalists who reject Jewish nationalism, or post-Zionists who reject Zionism. Looking right, Religious Zionists who have declared a culture war today against secular Zionists fit. However, the self-styled "Canaanite" Yonatan Ratosh (1908–81), who allied with Revisionist Zionists but then claimed Jews who didn't live in Israel abandoned the Jewish people, fails Zionism's peoplehood test. Similarly, Meir Kahane (1932–90), whose party was banned from the Knesset for "incitement to racism," fails Zionism's democracy and decency tests. All the visions included preserve Zionism's post-1948 principle of Israel as a Jewish democracy in the Jewish homeland—inviting debate regarding what Israel means for Israelis, the Jewish people, and the world.

The original work excluded female thinkers, overlooking Henrietta Szold the organizer, Rachel Bluwstein the poet, Rahel Ben Zvi the pioneer, and Golda Meir, the Labor leader. It bypassed the *Mizrahi* dimension. Given his Labor Zionist bias, writing two decades before Likud's 1977 victory, Hertzberg approached Ze'ev Jabotinsky as a fighter asserting Jewish rights but not as a dreamer envisioning a liberal nationalist state.

This new volume also reframes the Zionist conversation within six Zionist schools of thought which this introduction defines and traces: Political, Labor, Revisionist, Religious, Cultural, and Diaspora Zionism. Most histories of Zionism track the ideological ferment that shaped the first five. Diaspora Zionism, the sixth stream, has changed significantly. Zionism began, mostly, with European Jews debating their future individually and collectively; American Zionists checked out from the personal quest but bought in—gradually—to aid the communal state-building project. Today, most Diaspora Jews seek inspiration, not salvation, from Israel.

Organizing the debate around these six schools makes sense because most Zionisms were hyphenate Zionisms—crossbreeding the quest for Jewish statehood with other dreams regarding Judaism or the world. Historians must often be zoologists, categorizing ideas and individuals resistant to being forced tidily into a box. The French historian Marc Bloch—a Jew the Nazis murdered in 1944—explained in his classic *The Historian's Craft* that history should not just generate a "disjointed, and . . . nearly infinite enumeration." Worthwhile history delivers "a rational classification and progressive intelligibility."[2] This insight suits the Zionist narrative.

Refracting Zionism through the lens of these six visions places today's debates in historical context, illustrating the core values of each that sometimes united, sometimes fractured, the perpetually squabbling Zionist movement. Seeing how various ideas cumulatively molded broader ideological camps illuminates Zionist history—and many contemporary Jewish debates.

Some may question the choice to associate certain thinkers who seemingly defy categorization with particular schools of thought. Admittedly, great thinkers often demonstrate greatness through their range. Yet this general categorization locates the texts historically and ideologically, even if a particular Zionist thinker never waved that particular ideological banner. Putting these thinkers into conversation with one another can prove clarifying. For example, placing the philosopher Eliezer Schweid among Revisionists does not make this capacious thinker a Revisionist. Yet his analyses of the ongoing Zionist mission and the Promised Land's cosmic power explain certain directions of modern Revisionist thought. Similarly, the Jerusalem Platform, the vision statement of Herzl's Zionist Organization, later of the World Zionist Organization, defines Zionism broadly, embracing Political Zionism, saluting Cultural Zionism. Still, its multidimensionality best illustrates the many ways Diaspora Zionists engage Zionism today. Moreover, these six intellectual streams never came with membership cards, even though some of these schools of thought spawned some Israeli political parties.

Purists may thus insist that Labor Zionism has become left-wing Zionism and Revisionist Zionism, right-wing Zionism. Using the original terms contextualizes the ideologies, spotlighting how each faction perpetuates—or abandons—its historic legacy. Words like "Religious" in "Religious Zionism" risk fostering incorrect assumptions; some non-Orthodox Jews express a Religious Zionism, meaning their Zionism also stems from faith. Including them emphasizes that no one can monopolize or too narrowly define any one tendency.

The Zionist Ideas catalogues the thinkers within the six schools over these three major phases of Zionism:

1. Pioneers: Founding the Jewish State—until 1948: How dreamers like Theodor Herzl and A. D. Gordon, Ze'ev Jabotinsky and Rav Kook, Ahad Ha'am and Louis Brandeis, conceived of Jewish nationalism and a Jewish state;
2. Builders: Actualizing and modernizing the Zionist blueprints— from 1948 until 2000: How leaders like David Ben-Gurion, Golda

Meir, and Menachem Begin, along with thinkers as diverse as Naomi Shemer, Ovadia Yosef, and Yitz Greenberg built Israel.

3. Torchbearers: Reassessing, redirecting, reinvigorating in the twenty-first century: How heirs to Israel's dreamers and builders reconcile what Professor Ilan Troen calls the Zionism of Intention with the realities of modern Israel—and the Diaspora.

Although, history's progress always tweaks historians' periodization schemes, this division follows a compelling logic. The year 1948 divides the movement that might have failed—until the British mandate's final moments—from the movement that executed a stunning historical feat. Pivoting at 2000 satisfies our bias toward half-century and century markers to shape this splash of time. It also marks a shift in the Zionist conversation, as the campaign to delegitimize Zionism intensified just as Zionists recognized a more stable, prosperous, capitalist yet controversial Israel coexisting with a more confident yet identity-challenged Diaspora.

Sadly, the most frequent question non-Israeli Jews have asked me about this book is, "Will you include anti-Zionists, too?" When feminist anthologies include sexists, LGBT anthologies include homophobes, and civil rights anthologies include racists, I will consider anti-Zionists. This Jewish need to include our enemies when telling our own story tells its own story.

No volume can be everything to all readers. This edition, like the original, addresses English speakers. While sensitive to the Israeli conversation, the selection process reflects a Diaspora sensibility. Israelis need a Hebrew translation—keeping many texts, and adding others.

Zionism: The Prehistory

In his majestic introduction to *The Zionist Idea*, Arthur Hertzberg called Zionism the "twice-born movement," noting that by the 1860s, the dream Moses Hess and others had envisioned was "stillborn" because hopes of "assimilation and religious Reform" still dominated.[3] Antisemitism had yet to disillusion that first generation.

Actually, the Bible spawned the Zionist idea, making Zionism a thrice-born idea. That first premodern birth reflected the Jewish homeland's centrality to Judaism. The second mid-nineteenth-century attempt emphasized peoplehood—that Jews are distinct not only religiously but sociologically and thus politically. The third incarnation succeeded by creating a movement that established a modern democratic state for this distinct people on their ancestral homeland.

Some start the Jewish story with Abram becoming Abraham in the Bible. Others note the archaeological evidence of neighboring villages in northern Israel: one left behind eaten pig bones, the other did not. Judaism's foundation, however, begins with a holy triangle: In the Land, the People fulfill God's vision.

While every homeland has historical and cultural landmarks, the Promised Land adds moral, and spiritual, dimensions. Jewish heroes— Deborah the poetess, Samuel the prophet, Samson the strongman— flourished in this greenhouse for great collective Jewish enterprises. Such leaders imparted abiding messages mixing pride in the Jewish peoplehood narrative with the universal moral quest for equality and freedom.

Jewish history crests toward David the charismatic founding the national capital, Jerusalem, and Solomon the wise building the magnificent Holy Temple, embodying Jewish piety, probity, and power. Kings I reports that King Solomon merited honors and riches because the justice he dispensed reflected his caring for the people. The Zionist movement sought to restore this glorious history brimming with spiritual and moral potential.

Although the wandering Jewish people could not always remain on the land, their land remained in their hearts. After the Second Temple's destruction in 70 CE and the mass dispersion of Jews, culminating with the infusion of Muslims after the Muslim conquest in 636, Jews nevertheless remained tethered to the Land of Israel. Jews always prayed toward Jerusalem, one of the four "holy cities," along with Safed, Tiberias, and Hebron, where Jewish communities maintained footholds. In considering themselves "exiled," Jews defined themselves by their homeland not their temporary homes.

While kept apart from Israel, the children of Israel remained a people apart. That idiosyncratic Jewish mix of religion and peoplehood kept the Jews in a true exilic condition, East and West. Jewish laws and communal institutions encouraged self-government. In the West, after the eleventh century, most Ashkenazic Jews lived in *kehillot*, independent communities. As long as the community paid taxes and obeyed the external laws, Jews could maintain their rabbinical hierarchy, schools, social services, and community funds. They could be ethnically, nationally, ethically, and religiously Jewish, mastering democratic skills that would be useful centuries later. Their Judaism was so integrated they lacked a word for "religion." The modern Hebrew word for religion, *dat*, borrows the Persian word for law.

In the East—North Africa, the Middle East, and Asia—*Mizrahi* Jews also were detached. Islam imposed a second-class "dhimmi" status on Jews, Christians, and other minorities. This theoretical protection actually degraded non-Islamic peoples. Still, *Mizrahi* Jews' instinctive distinctiveness generated praise when the formal Zionist movement emerged in Europe. As "born Zionists" forever dreaming of the Land of Israel, these *Mizrahim* always were ready to return home.

Origins of the Zionist Movement

The nineteenth century resurrected the Zionist idea. Europe had emerged from the Middle Ages into an age of "isms," powerful modernizing movements. Rationalism celebrated the mind, trusting logic and science to advance humanity technologically and socially. Liberalism celebrated the individual, recognizing every individual's basic rights—a notion derived from biblical notions of equality. And nationalism celebrated the collective, organizing governments along ethnic, historical, Romantic, geographic connections—and shared destiny.

These movements revolutionized Jewish life. The Enlightenment, the modernizing movement of rationalism, liberalism, and individualism, promised to secure respect for Jews as equals in society. The Emancipation promised to grant Jews basic political rights. The Jews' version of the Enlightenment, melting their ghetto world, was the Haskalah. From the Hebrew root *s-k-l* for brain, the movement's name reflected its faith that reason would liberate the Jews.

The *maskilim*, the Enlightened Jews, wanted normalization, while valuing their Jewish heritage. In the 1700s, the philosopher Moses Mendelssohn advised: "be a cosmopolitan man in the street and a Jew at home." In 1862 the socialist philosopher Moses Hess further infuriated his former comrade Karl Marx by toasting Judaism's duality: "my nationality," he proclaimed, "is inseparably connected with my ancestral heritage, with the Holy Land and the Eternal City, the birthplace of the belief in the divine unity of life and of the hope for the ultimate brotherhood of all men." Fifteen years later, Peretz Smolenskin, born in Russia, living in Vienna, claimed Judaism survived exile because Jews "always regarded" themselves "as a people—a spiritual nation" with Torah "as the foundation of its statehood." These and a few other thinkers mapped out Zionism's core ideas, paralleling Jewish nationhood to the other European nations then coalescing. But history was not yet ready for Zionism.

European nationalism did not tolerate Jewish distinctiveness. In 1789, riled by French Revolutionary nationalism and egalitarianism, the liberal deputy Count Stanislas Adélaide de Clermont-Tonnerre, thinking he was defending Jews' basic human rights, proclaimed: "We must refuse everything to the Jews as a nation and accord everything to Jews as individuals." Then, in 1806 Napoleon Bonaparte convened an Assembly of Jewish Notables, christening it as the venerable Jewish tribunal, the Sanhedrin. Pushing French nationalism, the emperor posed twelve menacing questions probing Jewish stances on intermarriage, polygamy, divorce, and usury—testing whether Jews were French first. Telling Napoleon what he demanded to hear, calling themselves "Frenchmen of the Mosaic persuasion," these Jews unraveled three millennia of an integrated Jewish identity.

Six decades later, when Enlightenment and Emancipation spread from French and German Jewish elites to Eastern Europe, the Russian Jewish poet J. L. Gordon urged his fellow Russian Jews: "Raise your head high, straighten your back, And gaze with loving eyes open" at your new "brothers." Gordon echoed Moses Mendelssohn's formula for the new, double-thinking non-Zionist Jew: "Be a person on the street and a Jew at home."[4] He articulated the Haskalah's promise: an updated yet traditional Judaism at home, but acceptance, normalcy, outside in Europe.

Alas, that old-fashioned affliction—Jew hatred—combined with many Jews' submissive approach to assimilationism, soured other Jews on the

Enlightenment. Symbolic punches culminated with the big blow from 1881 to 1884: pogroms, more than two hundred anti-Jewish riots unleashing mass hooliganism and rape. "The mob, a ravenous wolf in search of prey," Smolenskin wrote, "has stalked the Jews with a cruelty unheard of since the Middle Ages."

The pogroms annihilated Jews' modern messianic hope of redemption via universal acceptance. Some sulked back into the despairing ghetto. Some began what became the two-million-strong immigration to America. Some escaped into socialism's class-based promise of universalism. And a determined, marginal minority sought salvation through nationalism. "We have no sense of national honor; our standards are those of second-class people," Smolenskin smoldered. "We find ourselves . . . exulting when we are tolerated and befriended."

The great optimism these modern "isms" stirred—rationalism, secularism, liberalism, socialism, communism—had also helped breed that virulent, racial "ism": antisemitism. Enlightenment fans and critics embraced this all-purpose hatred. Antisemites hated Jews as modernizers and traditionalists, rich and poor, capitalists and communists. Blood-and-soil nationalists said the Jews would never fit in and should stop trying to belong; liberal nationalists said the Jews weren't trying hard enough to fit in and should stop sticking out.

Antisemitism represented European blood-and-soil nationalism gone foul; perfuming it with lofty liberal nationalist rhetoric intensified the betrayal. The Russian Jewish physician Leon Pinsker, whose very profession epitomized Enlightenment hopes, diagnosed this European disease, writing, "the Jews are ghosts, ethereal, disconnected." He predicted: "This pathological Judaeophobia will haunt Europe until the Jews have a national home like all other nations."

This European double cross crushed enlightened Jews' pipedreams and helped launch a state-oriented Zionism. The "thrice-born" old-new movement finally took, at least among a small band who believed the Jews were a nation; assimilation could never overcome antisemitism, and a reconstituted Jewish national home offered the only hope.

That said, the Zionist backstory is more complex than antisemitism serving as the (unkosher) yeast fermenting Jewish nationalism. The philosopher Jean Paul Sartre erred when claiming the antisemite makes the Jew. Similarly, antisemitism marks but does not make Zionism: the persecution of Jews has legitimized and popularized the Zionist movement without defining it. Zionism is and always was more than anti-antisemitism.

In 1878 three years before the Russian pogroms, religious Jews established Petah Tikvah, the Gates of Hope, as Palestine's first modern Jewish agricultural settlement. In 1882 members of the group BILU, intent on cultivating the Holy Land, responded to the pogroms with hopes that transcended those crimes, articulating what would be the First Aliyah's communal vision: "HEAR O ISRAEL! The Lord is our God, the Lord is one, and our land Zion is our only hope."

In 1890 the Viennese anti-religious rebel Nathan Birnbaum coined the terms "Zionist" and "Zionism." Birnbaum translated the name of the coalition of post-pogrom organizations in Russia, "Hovevei Zion," sometimes "Hibbat Zion," "lovers of Zion," into German as "Zionismus," which quickly became Zionism.

By then, the stubborn linguist most responsible for reviving Hebrew was already at work. Born in 1858 in Lithuania, Eliezer Ben-Yehuda arrived in Palestine in that turning-point year of 1881, understanding that a national revival required a land—Israel, only Israel—and a language—Hebrew, only Hebrew. Forever experimenting, cannibalizing, hijacking, synthesizing, Ben-Yehuda called a tablecloth "mappah," from the Talmudic term; ice cream "glidah" from "galid," the Mishnaic word for frost; and socks "garbayim" from "jawrab," Arabic for sock—or possibly "gorba," Aramaic for leg garment. In waves of intellectual creativity, Ben-Yehuda modernized the language. With steady cultural leadership, he peddled it to the people. On November 29, 1922, when the British authorities mandated Hebrew as the Palestinian Jews' language, this early Zionist miracle achieved official sanction.

Zionist Solutions to "The Jewish Problem"

Movements often romanticize their founding moments, overemphasizing epiphanies supposedly launching their crusade. One oversimplification claims that publishing Betty Friedan's *The Feminine Mystique* in

1963 triggered modern feminism. Similarly, many mistakenly point to Theodor Herzl's Zionist "aha" moment. A cultivated, assimilated Middle European, Herzl was a frustrated playwright, lawyer, and journalist covering the divisive 1894 treason trial of a French army captain, Alfred Dreyfus. Legend has it that Herzl's Jewish identity awakened—and his Zionist vision emerged—when the crowds shouted "Death to the Jews" rather than "Death to the Traitor," a particularly reprehensible Jew-hating indulgence because Dreyfus had been framed. Two years later, in 1896, Herzl published his manifesto, *Der Judenstaat* (The Jewish state).

Herzl's breakthrough is also overstated. Like Friedan's feminism, Zionism had been simmering for decades. And Herzl wasn't such a non-Jewish Jew. Some of his Jewish nationalist musings predated the Dreyfus trial.

Still, Herzl's impact shouldn't be understated. As the nineteenth century ended amid intellectual chaos, fragmenting identity, great anticipation, and sheer Jewish anguish, his vision resonated. Herzl's mid-course correction for the Jewish people in their flight from ghetto to modernity reoriented their messianic hopes from oblivion toward Zion. The model Jewish society Zionism now envisioned would heal the "Jewish Problem" of antisemitism and the Jews' problem of assimilation while—added bonus—inspiring the Western world too.

More than the mugged Jew, the reluctant Zionist, Herzl was the balanced Jew, the model Zionist. He had one foot in the past and one in the present, one in European "isms" and one in Judaism, one in nineteenth-century Romantic liberal nationalism and one in a centuries-old Jewish religio-nationalism. Herzl embodied the thrice-born Jewish nationalist movement's two main streams: he grafted its Jewish character onto a Western national liberation movement.

Herzl was also the great Jewish doer. He could be grandiose, trying to build a state top down through white-tie-and-tails diplomacy, rubbing elbows not sullying hands or straining muscles. But, like a fairy godmother, he turned Jewish fantasies into realities: a Zionist Congress; a World Zionist Organization; a Zionist newspaper, *Die Welt* (The world); a Zionist novel, *Altneuland* (Old-new land); a Zionist fundraising machine, the Jewish National Fund; and, eventually, a Jewish state. If David Ben-Gurion was the Jewish revolution's King David—magnetic leader and

Spartan statesman—Theodor Herzl was its Moses, delivering the core ideas without reaching the Promised Land.

Herzl's defining axiom testified to his magic: "If you will it, it is no dream." Before Herzl there were various Zionist initiatives. When he died, there was not just *a* Zionist movement but *the* Zionist Movement, building toward a Jewish state for the Jewish people.

Many remember Herzl as garrison Zionist not dream fulfiller, largely because Asher Ginsberg, writing under the pen name Ahad Ha'am, attacked Herzl as Jewishly ignorant and politically grandiose. Worrying about Judaism more than the Jews, Ahad Ha'am doubted a state was "attainable." For a people oppressed by persecution and seduced by assimilation, he prescribed a national cultural renaissance in the Jewish homeland.

The spread of nationalism and antisemitism, combined with the Zionist movement's surprising momentum, made most Zionists Herzlian. Nevertheless, Ahad Ha'am's Cultural Zionism—thanks especially to Eliezer Ben-Yehuda—steeped the movement in enduring Jewish values, folk practices, and redemptive aspirations. Ben-Yehuda's linguistic revolution bridged Political and Cultural Zionism. He understood that without an independent political infrastructure in its homeland, the Jewish body politic would never heal, but without a thriving culture in its historic language, the Jewish soul would never revive. Today, we are Herzl when we flash our passports to enter or exit the Jewish state he envisioned—a flourishing political and economic entity that saved Jews. We are Ben-Yehuda when we speak Hebrew. We are Ahad Ha'am when we enjoy an Israeli song, movie, book, sensibility, personality quirk. And we are all of them when we push Israel to redeem Judaism and improve the world.

In short, Zionism was a Jewish response to the crisis of modernity. Herzl, whose political Zionism is now remembered as pragmatic and unromantic, envisioned that with a Jewish state, "We shall live at last as free people on our own soil, and in our own homes peacefully die." Yet he could also be prophetic. Imagining this new home of the Jews, he wrote: "The world will be liberated by our freedom, enriched by our wealth, magnified by our greatness."

While rooted in Jewish tradition, while inhaling Herzl's utopian yet European spirit, Zionism was also radical. In the early 1900s, the Hebrew novelist and yeshiva dropout Micah Joseph Berdichevsky flipped the rabbinic warning against being distracted by nature when studying holy books. Insisting that Israel will "be saved" only when Jews notice trees not texts, he cried: "Give us back our fine trees and fine fields! Give us back the Universe!"

This cry went beyond returning to the land. It called for purifying, electrifying revolution. The socialist and Political Zionist, David Ben-Gurion, thus described Zionism's double challenge: While rebelling against external powers, akin to the American, French, and Russian Revolutions, Zionism also rejected the internal, beaten, ghetto-Jewish personality. Zionism sought to spawn New Jews to form an *Am Segula*, an enlightened nation inspiring other nations—another revamped biblical concept.

Many entwined this personal Jewish revolution with the return to nature. Zionism's secular rebbe, Aharon David Gordon, preached that "a life of labor" binding "a people to its soil and to its national culture" would return Jews to "normal," finally acting, looking, feeling, working, and earning like other nations. The bearded, intense Gordon modeled this principle by moving from Russia to Palestine in 1904 at age forty-eight and eventually, awkwardly, wielding a shovel at Kibbutz Degania Aleph. His insistence on workers' dignity spurred today's Labor social justice activism, while his mystical love of the land inspired today's religious and Revisionist settlers.

As an enlightened movement disdaining ghetto Judaism, Zionism in extreme form mirror imaged Reform Judaism, with some Zionists jettisoning religious not national identity. Some Herzlian Zionists reasoned that, freed from antisemitism, Jews could flourish as cultivated Europeans away from Europeans. This quest for "normalcy" misread Jewish history and civilization: Zionism doesn't work as a de-Judaized movement or a movement lacking big ideas. It's as futile as trying to cap a geyser; Jewish civilization's intellectual, ideological, and spiritual energy is too great.

The symbol of this extreme was Herzl's consideration of the British offer of a homeland in Uganda—technically the Kenya highlands. Reeling from the Kishinev pogroms that spring, Herzl endorsed this immediate intervention to alleviate Jewish suffering. The proposal almost killed the movement. Recognizing the danger, Herzl concluded the divisive Sixth

Zionist Congress in August 1903, by saying, in Hebrew: "If I forget thee, O, Jerusalem, may my right hand forget its cunning"—reaffirming his commitment to the homeland.

The traditionalists' fury taught the territorialists how central Zion was to Zionism. It also underlay Chaim Weizmann's classic exchange with Lord Balfour—whose 1917 declaration validated modern Zionism officially, internationally. "Mr. Balfour, suppose I was to offer you Paris instead of London, would you take it?" Weizmann asked. "But Dr. Weizmann, we have London," Balfour replied, prompting Weizmann's line: "True, but we had Jerusalem when London was a marsh."[5]

The territorialists' defeat was defining. Zionism was a Western national movement seeking political independence and what German theorists called *Gewaltmonopol des Staates*, the monopoly on the legitimate use of violence within that political entity. Yet this Western hybrid, steeped in Jewish lore, needed the language to be Hebrew, the flag and national symbols to be Jewish, the land to be Israel, and the mission to be messianic. Zionism was Davidic in its pragmatism—kingly—and Isaiahan in its sweep—high-minded; this cosmic element was essential to its success. In loving the land and people, Zionism—at its most secular—remained a passionate, Romantic, religious movement. Most early secular Zionists could not take the Zion out of Zionism, or divorce the Jews and their future state from Judaism. (Similarly, today's "secular" Israelis denounce religion while living by the Jewish religious calendar, speaking the holy language, and often knowing Jewish texts better than many of their "religious" American cousins.)

The Zionist revolution also defied the twentieth-century trend toward individualism and the Jewish trend toward sectarianism. "Judaism is fundamentally national," Ahad Ha'am insisted, "and all the efforts of the 'Reformers' to separate the Jewish religion from its national element have no result except to ruin both the nationalism and the religion." "Hatik-vah," the national anthem, rhapsodized about *the* one, ancient, enduring hope—and, like so many Jewish prayers, spoke of abstractions as singular, but the people as collective: *The* Jewish spirit sings as *the* eyes seek Zion, but *our* hope of two thousand years is to be a free nation in *our* land. Decades later, Rabbi David Hartman would compare Zionism's rebellion against religion to the rebel teenager's loud vow to run away from home—without actually leaving.

Thus began a glorious exercise in state building, and nationalist myth making. The hearty *halutzim*, the pioneers, came to the land *"livnot u'le-hibanot bah,"* to build and be personally rebuilt. Their sweat irrigated the national revival. They drained swamps, paved roads, founded kibbutzim. They revitalized old cities, especially Jerusalem, and established new cities, most famously Tel Aviv, the rejuvenating "hill of spring." They put the passionate, land-loving words of writers such as Rachel Bluwstein to stirring, land-building melodies. And they fought like good New Jews—and ancient Israelites. They battled the elements. They skirmished with some Arab neighbors, while cooperating with others. They resisted despair. And as they created a bronzed, self-confident, battle-tested farmer-soldier, a New Jew, they quarreled ideologically with the intensity of their ghettoish Talmudist selves.

January 4, 1925, marked a milestone in national development: the founding of Hebrew University in Jerusalem. Opening a university reflected Zionism's rationalist, scientific side, its understanding that a true cultural revolution included what the national poet Hayyim Nahman Bialik called "all elements of life, from the lowest to the most sublime," and a certain confidence. If you can stop draining swamps temporarily to launch lasting cultural institutions, you're on your way to building a sophisticated nation-state.

Bialik, the poet who rejected exile, now offered prose of liberation. Standing on Mount Scopus with its view of Jerusalem's historic walls, he welcomed this new university into a long line of "nationalist schools in all its forms" that had started with the lowly *heder,* a one room Torah school for young Eastern European boys. He celebrated the union of the rough, secular pioneers with their ethereal religious cousins—the "Earthly Jerusalem" the youth were building alongside the traditional "Heavenly Jerusalem" of their parents' and grandparents' dreams.

Pioneers: Founding the Jewish State

Bialik's address marked a rare ceasefire amid the Zionist movement's characteristic factionalism—clashing schools of thought that illustrated Zionism's vitality. The early Zionist movement was indeed a many-splendored thing: a rollicking conversation synthesizing Judaism, nationalism, liberalism, idealism, rationalism, socialism, and capitalism. These visionary, sometimes doctrinaire, intellectual pioneers tackled the world's problems—often while toiling to make the desert bloom.

The Zionist idea of creating a Jewish state united them. Thinkers in all six intellectual streams viewed the Jews as a people, Israel as its homeland, and the state as having an essential role in saving Jews and Judaism. All struggled with the despair antisemitism induced without ever burying *Hatikva*, the hope of making their Jewish state a model state too.

Political Zionism: Theodor Herzl's pragmatic yet utopian Zionism, his nineteenth-century Romantic liberal nationalism harnessed toward establishing a democratic Jewish state in Palestine, the Jewish homeland, prioritizing securing a state to save Jewish lives. Yet, "Jewish normalcy" would also help Jews cultivate their enlightened and traditional selves, saving the world—and perhaps even saving Judaism.

Labor Zionism: The utopian yet pragmatic Zionism of the kibbutz and the moshav championed rebuilding the Jewish self by working the land. Thinkers such as A. D. Gordon and Berl Katznelson grounded the intellectual, urbanized, ghettoized European Jew in the challenging practicalities of agriculture, while injecting dollops of Marxism and universalism. Although passionately secular, Labor Zionism fostered an enduring love for *Eretz Yisra'el*, the Land of Israel. Kibbutznikim became Bible-quoting amateur archaeologists.

At the same time, the socialists among these Laborites harnessed the prophetic tradition, the messianic impulse, fostering social justice, envisioning the New Jews as a socialist vanguard. The socialist political theorist Nahman Syrkin said the "tragic element" of Jews' "historic fate," meaning antisemitism, could free them to fulfill a "unique historic mission": being the first to realize socialism's "basic principles of peace, co-operation, and cultural progress." Like the secular Marxist Bundists, Labor Zionists were too conscious of antisemitism's toxicity to expect class consciousness to unite all workers magically. Instead, they commissioned their virtuous people to create a socialist exemplar. By saving the world, they could save Judaism and Jews.

Revisionist Zionism: Ze'ev Jabotinsky's pragmatic, passionate, yet classically liberal democratic Zionism. Revisionists considered themselves Herzl's purest followers, accentuating the political goal of achieving a Jewish state as soon as possible to save as many Jews as possible. "Eliminate the Diaspora, or the Diaspora surely will eliminate you," Jabotinsky warned bluntly, characteristically, in 1937. Two "m's" characterized his approach: what Jabotinsky called "monism," excluding big theories about culture, economy, religion, or society to stress the immediate political mission of state-building; and "militancy," a gruff uncompromising strategy mixed with a martial style that occasionally flirted with fascism.

Although caricatured as a result as lacking in vision, these European Romantics were passionate about peoplehood, their common past, and their homeland. Their politics absorbed A. D. Gordon's love of land with Ahad Ha'am's nationalist cultural revivalism. Their secularism incorporated dashes of pride in their religious traditions too.

Certain Revisionists took Jabotinsky's discipline and land love to an extreme, stirring an ultranationalism. This monist zeal made some devotees very aggressive and others deeply depressed when the post-1948 state began with Jerusalem divided. Eventually, though, Jabotinskyite purists, steeped in his individualistic liberalism, would help Israel privatize, capitalize, modernize, and prosper.

Religious Zionism: This spiritual Zionism, harmonizing "Orthodoxy" and Zionism, rooted Zionism in Judaism's traditional land-based nationalism. According to adherents such as Abraham Isaac Kook, Jews could only fulfill all the mitzvot, commandments, in the homeland. Seeing the political state as the pathway to mystical salvation, religious Zionists accepted their secular allies. As Kook taught: "The state is not the supreme happiness of man." The typical nation-state is about as mystical or inspirational as "a large insurance company." The State of Israel, by contrast, "is ideal in its foundation . . . the foundation of God's throne in the world." By saving Judaism, they could save Jews and the world.

Cultural Zionism: Ahad Ha'am's more secular spiritual Zionism called for cultivating the Jewish homeland as a national cultural center to revive Judaism and Jewish pride. Ahad Ha'am dismissed Herzl's state-building plans as chimerical. Also, as a Russian Jew, he instinctively mistrusted all governments, doubting that even a Jewish state could be virtuous.

This aloofness toward sovereignty anticipated contemporary Israel-Diaspora relations. With a literate Eastern European Jew's love of Jewish culture, Ahad Ha'am envisioned Israel as the Jewish people's spiritual, intellectual, cultural, and religious center. Israel would be the center of the wheel, connected to each Diaspora community by spokes. Palestine's blossoming Jewish culture would ennoble the Diaspora Jew. Trusting in this new Hebrew culture's redemptive richness, the poet Hayyim Nahman Bialik rejoiced in 1932: "Everything that is created in the Land of Israel by Jews becomes culture."

Diaspora Zionism: Louis Brandeis and Henrietta Szold developed this philanthropic, support-oriented Zionism reconciling American patriotism with Jewish nationalism. They emphasized Zionism's liberal democratic character while broadening the definition of a Zionist to include supporters of the Zionist idea. European Zionists were transforming themselves into New Jews; Diaspora Zionists were rescuing distressed fellow Jews. Initially, Jews migrated by the millions to America and by the thousands to Palestine. In the Diaspora, Zionism offered—and often became—a recipe for Jewish renewal the American migration lacked.

Builders: Actualizing—and Modernizing—the Zionist Blueprints

They had done it. They established a state. The Nazi's butchering of six million Jews had settled the ideological argument for most Jews and much of the world. And the death of six thousand more Jews fighting to establish a 600,000-person state in 1948's Independence War settled the practical question. Ahad Ha'am was half-wrong: a state emerged despite his doubts. Theodor Herzl was half-right: the state existed, but it was more Jewish and surprisingly Eastern, not just European, especially after 850,000 Jewish refugees from Arab lands arrived.

Proving again that this state was not like any other, politicians and rabbis, novelists and poets, diplomats and soldiers, in Israel and globally, debated its mission. Political Zionism continued underscoring the state's survival, and significance. Political theorists, including Isaiah Berlin, Albert Memmi, and Emmanuel Levinas, assessed the meaning of a Jewish state after millennia of suffering and toasted this model of liberal nationalism. Jewish heroes, including Jerusalem's bridge-building mayor Teddy Kollek and the martyred anti-terrorist fighter Yoni Netanyahu, the eloquent Holocaust survivor Elie Wiesel, and the heroic Soviet refusenik Natan Sharansky, offered old-new lessons about Jewish values, Zionist grit, and communal idealism. Israel's 1967 Six-Day War triumph, overcoming fears of a second Auschwitz, brought moral clarity and renewed energy to Political Zionism, the Jewish people's protector. By 2000, the scrappy yet still controversial Zionist movement had outlived communism, fascism, Sovietism, and Nazism.

The most revolutionary Zionism experienced a most revolutionary change. After being dethroned in 1977, the Labor Party absorbed the global, post-1960s human-rights revolutions' sensibilities, becoming more committed to women's rights, sexual liberation, gay rights, and Palestinian rights. Labor stopped being the socialist, collectivist, "Knesset-and-kibbutz" party of "us"; instead this party of "you and I" balanced individual rights and social responsibility. The transformed party built national pride through self-actualization and protection of individual rights, while still demanding social justice—and, increasingly, defining itself by insisting on ceding territory for peace.

Revisionist Zionists gained power in 1977, after nearly three decades in opposition, with their charismatic, Jabotinskyite leader Menachem Begin updating Revisionist ideology. As the liberal democratic and nationalist party, Likud competed with the rival Labor Party, juggling Jabotinsky's collectivist nationalism with his individualism. Laborites trusted the government's ability to address economic and social matters. Likud's formula trusted individuals to prosper with less government supervision and ownership—yet trusted national security policies and national control of culture.

Menachem Begin's rise confused Zionists, right and left. The right-wing territorial maximalists who had spent the 1950s bemoaning the loss of Old Jerusalem and the rise of a socialist Zionist state could grumble no longer: Revisionists were now leading a post-1967 "Greater Land of Israel" movement, settling the West Bank, Gaza Strip, Golan Heights, and Sinai Peninsula—the areas Israel captured in 1967. Yet Begin's emergence in 1979 as the first Israeli leader to swap land for peace—with Egyptian President Anwar Sadat—rocked the Zionist Right. Simultaneously, Begin's emergence as a populist peacemaker and social welfare liberal beloved by Israel's neglected *Mizrahim* rocked the Zionist left, which considered itself more committed to social justice.

The Six-Day War repurposed Religious Zionism. Pre-state Religious Zionists, epitomized by the elder Rav Abraham Isaac Kook, loved secular pioneers, seeing beyond their rebellion into their Jewish souls. By contrast, post-1967 Religious Zionists, epitomized by the younger Rav Zvi Yehudah Kook, loved the biblical land so much they prioritized settling the newly conquered land over uniting the people. Resulting movements, such as Gush Emunim, the Bloc of the Faithful, seeking to reestablish Jewish settlements in the ancient Jewish heartland, despite Palestinian resistance and global opposition, radicalized much of National Religious society. Once-fanciful spiritual fantasies now spawned militant plans. This mobilization—and the rise of the Jabotinskyite right—also mainstreamed religious nationalists professionally and politically. The once-quiescent community became more central, powerful, and prosperous in Israel—sociologically and ideologically.

Other Religious Zionisms blossomed. Reform Jewry Zionized. These once universalist believers that Judaism was just a religion imbibed the Zionist faith when the Holocaust proved that oppressed Jews needed a homeland. Subsequently, the Reform rabbi Richard Hirsch and others recognized the Jewish state's theological significance. Traditional Religious Zionists, including Professor Eliezer Berkovits, started mining the Jewish state's ethical, religious, spiritual, even halakhic—legal—potential.

Meanwhile, Israel's dynamic culture vindicated Ahad Ha'am's Cultural Zionism. A distinctive culture in Hebrew, high and low, in literature and song, radiated throughout the Jewish world. Israel often provided a vivid triptych for Jewish lives: a rousing soundtrack, inspiring Jewish images, and a rich vocabulary for Jewish meaning. The New Jew was celebrated, mass marketed, and often mimicked throughout the Jewish world. Even as songwriters like Naomi Shemer delighted in "Jerusalem of Gold," poets like Yehuda Amichai emphasized a treasured new normalcy: the Jerusalemite shopper carrying his groceries whom tourists should photograph instead of the city's ancient ruins.

Like Reform Zionism, Diaspora Zionism buried its ambivalences, demonstrating a new American Jewish focus on supporting Israel—while benefitting culturally and spiritually from the Jewish state. Initially, Rabbi Arthur Hertzberg worried in 1949 that the movement was "now in search of a program" as American Jewish Committee president Jacob Blaustein demanded that David Ben-Gurion stop negating the Diaspora, pushing *aliyah*, and presuming to speak for American Jews. However, the euphoria after the Six-Day War and Entebbe Rescue "miracles," exorcising widespread Jewish fears of Israel's annihilation in May 1967, then October 1973, confirmed Israel's importance to most Jews, including those increasingly assimilated in the Diaspora.

Zionism brought "profound changes" to Diaspora Jewry, particularly in the United States the historian Jonathan Sarna notes, from strengthening the Jewish body to stretching the Jewish soul. Throughout the Jewish world, Israel instilled a sense of peoplehood and renewed Jewish pride. It inspired the teaching of Hebrew and the revitalizing of camps and Hebrew schools while religiously invigorating America's Conservative and Reform movements. Diaspora Jews in democracies learned how to mobilize politically, democratize their leadership, and galvanize generations of Israel-oriented fundraisers.[6]

Jews didn't only ask what they could do for their country; Diaspora Zionism became Identity Zionism as Jews realized what their country could do for them, religiously, culturally, and personally. Writers like the passionate American immigrant to Israel, Hillel Halkin, and the ambivalent Upper West Side Jewish liberal, Anne Roiphe, endorsed Israeli Judaism, Israeli life, and Zionist values as healthy, non-materialistic alternatives to Western selfishness and American Jewish superficiality.

At the same time, by Israel's fiftieth anniversary in 1998, a new ambivalence seeped into the discourse: worries that modern Israel didn't measure up to history's now mythic heroism or Zion's lofty ideals. This disappointment had been building, especially after Menachem Begin shifted the country right in 1977, then led Israel into the 1982 Lebanon War, resulting in the Sabra and Shatila massacre Christian Phalangist soldiers perpetrated against Palestinians. Israel was no longer above criticism.

In 1973 the liberal rabbi Arnold Jacob Wolf blasted Israel's attitudes toward the Palestinians, the poor, the ultra-Orthodox, the rabbinate, and the Jewish left. Many jeremiads would follow. For a movement that considered itself exemplary, Zionism suffered as the Palestinian issue in particular muddied its self-image. Even as the worldwide obsession with the Palestinian issue reinforced paranoid Zionists' fears that "the world hates the Jews," the difficulties of a democracy depriving people of basic rights—no matter how justified by security threats—dimmed idealistic Zionists' hopes that Israel would be that light unto the nations. Dismissing generations of blue-and-white oversimplifications, Israel's great novelist Amos Oz bluntly admitted: "My Zionism is hard and complicated." Repudiating the settlement movement, Oz added: "I am a Zionist in all that concerns the redemption of the Jews, but not when it comes to the redemption of the Holy Land."

Torchbearers: Reassessing, Redirecting, Reinvigorating

By the twenty-first century, it had become fashionable in academic circles to declare Zionism irrelevant, anachronistic, racist, colonialist, imperialist, evil. Post-Zionist cynicism spread within Israel as a delegitimization campaign blackened the state's international reputation and the high hopes of the Oslo Peace Process collapsed into the deep dread of Palestinian terrorists' suicide bombings. Often the Zionist response was too defensive, reducing Zionism solely to Israel advocacy.

Eventually, a modern, mature, Zionist conversation emerged, weighing big questions about Jewish peoplehood and statehood, Jewish political power and religious influence, Jewish democracy and spirituality, Jewish traditions and universal ideals: How should a Jewish national liberation movement welcome Arabs who constitute 20 percent of Israel's citizenry? How should a Jewish democratic movement address anti-democratic voices? How should a liberal nationalist movement striving for perfection accommodate ugly realities—and failures? And how do you tend your own particular Jewish cocoon while soaring forth into the world with high ideals?

Although many thinkers often crossed wires, the six streams of Zionist discourse remain discernable. Each Zionist "school" has a characteristic institution or symbol. Political Zionism has the Knesset, Israel's temple of sovereignty and democracy. The kibbutz still embodies Labor Zionism's highest ideals. Revisionist Zionism's capitalist revolution has launched thousands of start-ups. Religious Zionism prizes the Western Wall's national and religious significance. Cultural Zionism, disseminated through the innovative *ulpan* method of Hebrew teaching, is today broadcast through *ulpanim*, television studios, among other media. And Taglit-Birthright Israel has epitomized Diaspora Zionism's new mutual, inspirational, identity-based approach to connecting Israeli and Diaspora Jewry.

Delving into the transformations:

Political Zionism: Increasingly sensitive to the attacks against Israel, Political Zionists now explain how a Jewish state can be democratic too. They press Israel to extend Herzl's founding vision beyond survival, applying Jewish and Western ethics to morally complex situations, from fighting asymmetric wars against terrorists hiding among civilians to achieving economic fairness without sacrificing prosperity.

Labor Zionism: Even as communism's collapse discredited socialism and Israel's culture of abundance led most kibbutzim to privatize, the desire to make the Zionist state epitomize liberal ideals with a Jewish twist persisted. The Israeli leftists who emerged were often more urbanized, more individualistic, than their ideological forbears. Nevertheless, the Labor Zionist dream of an equitable Israeli society persisted. Even as many leftists repudiated Israel, Israel's liberal legacy could not be ignored. As some liberal Zionists countered: "Progressive Zionism is not an Oxymoron."

Israelis on the left have embraced the human-rights agenda, juggling individualism with liberal communal ideals advocating exchanging land for peace and pursuing social justice. The novelists David Grossman, Amos Oz, and A. B. Yehoshua, among others, have refused to let the settler movement define their Zionism, demanding a Zionism that respects Palestinian and Jewish rights. Especially after the Social Protests of 2011 against pricey cottage cheese and astronomical rent, the Labor Party became the voice of activists like Stav Shaffir. She and her peers speak about preserving *Hatikvah*, "the Hope," to synchronize egalitarianism with Zionism.

Revisionist Zionism: Years in power made many Revisionists fear that the necessary compromises governing entails trumped Jabotinsky's enduring principles. Yet Jabotinsky's proactive approach to fighting antisemitism and asserting Jewish pride spurred his heirs to treat the delegitimization campaign against Israel and Zionism as strategic threats. And while some right-wing Knesset members occasionally floated undemocratic proposals, Revisionist Zionist purists continued tempering their nationalism with Jabotinskyite liberalism, championing individual rights for all. As a result, Revisionists like Benny Begin and Reuven Rivlin now bring to Israeli politics a passionate patriotism combining a maximalist approach to the territories, with demands of equality for Israeli Arabs.

Religious Zionism: Post-1967 war triumphalism propelled Religious Zionism into a best-of-times, worst-of-times scenario. Religious Zionists have flourished as observant Jews in the Jewish state, far more than their grandparents imagined. Yet, Religious Zionism has been divided and demoralized. Those on the right, including

Rabbis Zvi Tau and Eli Sadan, often attack the government for being too secular and accommodating of Palestinian demands. The alienation peaked following the Gaza disengagement in 2005, which many called "the Expulsion"—heavy Jewish historical overtones intended. Meanwhile, those leaning toward the center or the left, from Rabbi Benjamin Lau to Leah Shakdiel, disdain their camp's triumphalism, rigidity, and occasional harshness toward others. Still, Religious Zionists seek a robust Judaism in the democratic State of Israel. If Political Zionists usually justify the Israeli experiment in modern Western terms, Religious Zionists usually explain it with traditional Jewish language.

Cultural Zionism: While the initial Zionist conversation revolved around addressing the core needs of the Jewish people and the state, today, with the Jewish refuge having become the hi-tech "Start-Up Nation," more personal and tribal concerns proliferate. Many Zionists today are hyphenate Zionists, in modern identity parlance rather than classical ideological terms: articulating Queer Zionism, Feminist Zionism, *Mizrahi* Zionism. Thus Cultural Zionism has also become Identity Zionism. In this way the Zionist idea has helped Diaspora Jews navigate what Taglit-Birthright Israel leaders call "their own Jewish journeys," individual quests for meaning.

Within the Jewish homeland, questions now arise about Israel's cultural mission: Should Israelis seek a generic normalcy or a particular Jewish identity? Should Israelis emphasize their membership in a globalizing world or a still healing and rebuilding Jewish one? And how does being steeped in full-time, total Jewish culture affect Israelis' conversation with their fellow Jewish worldwide?

Diaspora Zionism: Two demographic revolutions have recast the American Zionist debate. The Holocaust made the American Jewish community the world's largest. Then by 2013, Israel's Jewish community had outstripped American Jewry, a result of American Jewry's escalating intermarriage rate and Israel's thriving Jewish birth rate—even among secular Israelis.

Beyond supporting Israel, Diaspora Zionists found inspiration in Israel's integrated, authentic, 24–7 3-D people-powered Judaism. At the same time, many American Jewish intellectuals began negating the notion that the Diaspora was "exile." Some rejected the notion of a "Diaspora" with Jewish communities dispersed around Israel the center. Demanding mutuality, they reconceived of global Jewry with what Simon Rawidowicz of Brandeis University called two ellipses—Israel and North America. This reorientation sparked discussions about how Israel helps the Jewish people—and how the Jewish people help Israel.

Meanwhile, another, more controversial, institution—the settlement—defines Israel for millions. Originally, Political and Labor Zionists treasured settlements as the country's building blocks. Today, Political Zionists divide over the issue. Most Labor Zionists oppose most settlements. Nonetheless, the vast majority of Israelis endorse maintaining sovereignty over key Jerusalem neighborhoods and the five consensus suburban "Settlement Blocs." Negev land swaps could balance this potentially negotiable terrain, cumulatively comprising ninety square miles, housing about 200,000 people. Revisionist and Religious Zionism have thrived, partially by expanding settlements throughout the lands Israel acquired in 1967. These different perceptions of the same phenomenon emphasize the challenge the Palestinian problem poses to Zionist unity, purity, and popularity.

Controversies, Challenges, and Dreams

Inevitably, critics claim that Zionism's identity anomalies invalidate the movement. Such harsh verdicts show that Israel is targeted for special, obsessive condemnation as "the Jew among the nations"—in the Canadian academic and politician Irwin Cotler's phrase. Each of the world's 196 countries represents some kind of identity cocktail mixing religion and ethnicity. Yet only the Jewish mix is deemed toxic.

In fact, Zionism's seeming paradoxes highlight the legitimacy of the Zionist mission to establish a Jewish democratic state for the long-suffering Jewish people in their traditional homeland. Judaism, as uniquely both a religion and a nation, allows individuals to convert to Judaism, then join the Jewish people—a biologically permeable, non-racist form of nationalism. Both the Zionist movement and the idea of nationalism formally began in Europe. Slightly less than half of the world's Jews live in the Jewish state today, but more Italians live outside of Italy and there are seven times more Irish Americans than Irish citizens. The Jews and the Palestinians assert rival claims to the same land, just as other nations have conflicting land claims without invalidating one another's essential claims to nationhood. Nationalism isn't an exclusive land deed; it's an identity-building process based on a shared past or present.

These exceptions demonstrate the Zionist idea's resilience—and Jewish civilization's post-1948 renaissance. Zionism was the great miracle maker. It reestablished Jewish sovereignty in the Jewish homeland as Israel cumulatively welcomed three million refugees from the Holocaust, the Arab expulsion, Soviet persecution, Ethiopian dislocation. It returned the Jews to history, transforming the world's perma-victims into robust actors on history's stage, with rights and responsibilities. It established a Western-style democracy in the hostile Middle East with a significant minority of Arabs and a majority of Jews, mostly from undemocratic countries. It started a Jewish cultural revolution: reviving Hebrew, modernizing the Holy Tongue into a language for blessing—and cursing. And while facilitating ultra-Orthodox and Orthodox revivals, it generated creative religious inspiration that revitalized Jewish life worldwide and offered the most viable home for perpetuating secular Jewish identity.

Today's Israel is robust. These miracles have become routine realities in a high-tech, science, and pharma behemoth; a breeding ground for do-gooding civil society NGOs; and a laboratory for creative Jewish living whose population has grown ten-fold, as its gross domestic product has multiplied thirty-fold—per capita.

Yet today's Zionist conversation is fragile. The anti-Zionist campaign against Israel has distorted the discussion. On the left, opponents of Israel's policies toward the Palestinians frequently join the delegitimization derby—sometimes consciously, sometimes not—emboldening those who escalate from criticizing Israeli policy to rejecting Zionism. Some trendsetting intellectuals purport to reject all nationalisms. Yet somehow they favor politically correct nationalisms like the Palestinians' while disfavoring "First World" ones, with an obsessive disdain for Zionism. Even some Zionists, like Ari Shavit, speak about "Zionism" as a force compelled to displace and demean Palestinians.

On the right, Israel's defenders often become so defensive, they quash the open, critical discourse all democracies—and ideological movements—need to mature. Denying any wrongdoing, even any dilemmas, has alienated Zionist critics of Israeli policy, polarizing the community unnecessarily. Many on the right try monopolizing the word "Zionist"; many on the left oblige, abandoning Zionism. In 2014, Israel's center-left coalition called itself the Zionist Union to restore Zionist pluralism. However, beyond Israel, especially on Western university campuses, even some Israel advocates avoid the "Z-word" because "it doesn't poll well."

Retreating from "Zionism," which has inspired and empowered millions over generations, just because enemies target it, violates Zionism's main mission of nurturing Jewish dignity. Such submissiveness disregards the feminist example of "taking back the night." In weighing "the strange career" of the "troublesome" N-word, the Harvard Law professor Randall Kennedy, an African American, observes that "targets of abuse can themselves play significant roles in shaping the terrain of conflict and thus lessen their vulnerability through creative, intelligent, and supple reactions."[7]

If in Hertzberg's day, Zionist triumphalism overlooked Israeli imperfections, a creative, intelligent, supple Zionist conversation today should acknowledge problems—and tap Zionist ideas to fix them. To a West increasingly skeptical about liberal nationalism, Zionism might model its constructive form of democratic nationalism—that nations should stand for something, bound by a sense of the past that enriches the present and builds a better future. To a West that increasingly regards particularism as merely selfish, Zionism might model its understanding of particularist national identities as value anchors and launching pads for communal good works to benefit others.

A mere six decades but eons ago in terms of Jewish potency, dignity, and stability, the philosopher Sir Isaiah Berlin looked at his scattered, tattered, shattered people and praised the miracle of Israel at its most basic. "The creation of the State of Israel has rendered the greatest service that any human institution can perform for individuals," he avowed. Israel "has restored to Jews not merely their personal dignity and status as human beings, but what is vastly more important, their right to choose as individuals how they shall live." Today, even as Israel still faces lethal threats, Jews are stronger, prouder, safer—indeed freer.

If Zionism originally provided communal protection, most Zionists today would acknowledge that the Zionist future depends on helping to elevate the Israel that has been established. Traditionally, most Jews struggled to survive; today, most Jews seek meaning. Israel, a laboratory of authentic Jewish living, may offer the Jewish communal answer to individual ennui. In Israel, many Jews feel whole; they have integrated their "Jewish" and "modern," "secular" and "spiritual" selves; they live by a Jewish calendar; they are rooted in the Jewish home.

In this book, many Zionists share a dream for Israel to become a vast *tikkun olam* project: a noble experiment in democratic nationalism synthesizing the best of Jewish and Western teachings, a Jewish force for universal good. In pushing Israel to be a "Values Nation," Zionism activates what Israel's president Shimon Peres called the Jewish dissatisfaction gene—that predisposition to see what isn't right, then fix it.

Achieving this goal requires engaging Jews from right to left, in Israel and the Diaspora, in debate about why Jews need a Jewish state today—and what that state's character ought to be. In marrying the traditional Zionist sources with recent texts bearing new ideas, *The Zionist Ideas* can help reinvigorate this conversation. I submit *The Zionist Ideas* as a tool to reclaim the discussion from polarizing political wars into a robust, substantive debate about the meanings of Zionism, the missions of Judaism, and the value of liberal nationalism. Diverse texts spanning the political and religious spectrums invite ever more people of different backgrounds and beliefs to consider what Israel is, how it should grow, and how it addresses the contemporary debate about national identities—

especially when that debate roiling the Western world about how we organize and see ourselves has turned so venomous.

To help ignite this new Zionist conversation, readers can visit www .zionistideas.com. There they will find the discussion guides to this volume and can sign up, as many already have, to host Zionist salons— thoughtful, text-based discussions examining Zionist dreams, values, and visions of about the Zionism of yesterday, today, and tomorrow.

With such open-ended discussions in mind, there is no one, right way to read this book. While its logical, chronological flow lends itself to reading it "English style," from start to finish, others may find it more compelling to read it "Hebrew style," from right to left, meaning from today to yesterday. Still others may prefer a free-style reading, sampling thinkers, akin to how I read Hertzberg as a youth.

These quintessentially Zionist teachings can help guide all readers— scholars, teachers, students, religious leaders, members, activists, spectators, critics. As the 1944 Nobel laureate in physics, Isidor I. Rabi, recalled, he became a scientist because his mother never asked what he learned in school. Instead, she always queried: "Izzy, did you ask a good question today?"[8] Modern Zionists would best turn some exclamation points into question marks—while preserving some exclamation points. Second, in 1914 Henrietta Szold's protégé Jessica Sampter launched Hadassah's School of Zionism, because "knowledge is the only safe foundation for ideals." Considering Zionist education "our most important work," Szold agreed, cautioning, "A nation cannot be made by instinctive, vague, misty feeling, however fine the instinct may be. . . . We must bring emotion out of its obscurity into the clarification of thought."[9] Finally, the American Supreme Court justice Louis Brandeis observed: "The great quality of the Jews is that they have been able to dream through all the long and dreary centuries. . . ." At last, Zionism gives the Jews "the power to realize their dreams."[10]

The Zionist idea succeeded: it exists, it works. Today's mission involves questioning, studying, dreaming, and fulfilling different Zionist ideas. The challenge is to look back accurately—with a dash of romance— and to look forward creatively—with a touch of rigor—weighing what Zionism can mean and become, today and tomorrow.

Notes

1. Emanuel Neumann, foreword, in *The Zionist Idea: A Historical Analysis and Reader,* ed. Arthur Hertzberg (Philadelphia: Jewish Publication Society, 1959, 1997), 13.
2. Marc Bloch, *The Historian's Craft* (New York: Vintage, 1953), 10.
3. Arthur Hertzberg, ed., *The Zionist Idea: A Historical Analysis and Reader* (Philadelphia: Jewish Publication Society, 1959, 1997), 32–33.
4. J. L. Gordon, "Awake My People" (1866), in *The Jew in the Modern World: A Documentary History,* ed. Paul Mendes-Flohr and Jehuda Reinharz (Oxford: Oxford University Press, 1995), 384.
5. Chaim Weizmann, *Trial and Error: The Autobiography of Chaim Weizmann* (Philadelphia: Jewish Publication Society, 1949), 115, 144.
6. Jonathan Sarna, "The Future of Diaspora Zionism," *Avar ve'Atid: A Journal of Jewish Education, Culture and Discourse,* October 1997, 75–76.
7. Randall Kennedy, *Nigger: The Strange Career of a Troublesome Word* (New York: Penguin, 2002), 147.
8. *New York Times,* January 19, 1988.
9. Rebecca Boim Wolf, "Jessie Sampter and the Hadassah School of Zionism," in *The Women Who Reconstructed American Jewish Education, 1910–1965,* ed. Carol K. Ingall (Lebanon NH: Brandeis University Press, 2010), 47, 49.
10. Louis Brandeis, *Brandeis on Zionism: A Collection of Addresses and Statements* (New York: Zionist Organization of America, 1942), 37–38.

The Zionist Ideas

PART ONE

Pioneers

Founding the
Jewish State

1

Pioneers

Political Zionism

Political Zionism identified the fundamentals that still define the Zionist project. As the Russian Jewish novelist Peretz Smolenskin exclaimed, "We are a people"—the Jews share national ties, not merely religious ones. Beyond that, as the Zionist pioneer Leon Pinsker and others proclaimed, this people, like all peoples, needed and deserved a state: "Since the Jew is nowhere at home, nowhere regarded as a native, he remains an alien everywhere." Finally, as Theodor Herzl discovered by the mass Jewish rejection of his Kenya Highlands–Uganda proposal in 1903, Jews must return to the Jewish homeland, *Eretz Yisra'el*, the Land of Israel.

Beyond these tenets, all Zionists assumed that creating a Jewish state would solve the Jewish Problem. Yet, as the following selections demonstrate, even the first Political Zionists differed regarding just what was *the* Jewish Problem. While most specified antisemitism, others addressed the drift toward assimilation, the shame of accommodation, the ongoing humiliation.

In short, Zionism arose from the dashed hopes of Emancipation, the European movement promising that Jews would be recognized fully as equal citizens communally and individually. The pogroms, the ranting and ravings of Jew haters, the continued toadying of Jews who wanted so badly to be accepted, all this tormented—and dispirited—many Jews.

The Haskalah, the enlightened Jewish intellectual movement, sought to reconcile tradition and modernity. In the early 1860s, a century after the German Jewish philosopher Moses Mendelssohn first started imagining it, the Russian Jewish poet J. L. Gordon articulated the sentiment exquisitely, endorsing "being a person on the street and a Jew at home." Although that model works for millions in the Diaspora today, Zionists ultimately concluded that Jewish pride, dignity, and integrity required living on a Jewish street in a Jewish state.

Although Theodor Herzl is the central figure of this first founding phase of Political Zionism, other contemporaries offered similar diagnoses. After his death at age forty-four, the movement was blessed with worthy successors who took Herzl's dream and improvised a blueprint for a functional state—even if, as the Israeli writer Natan Alterman warned, it wouldn't be delivered on a silver platter.

Peretz Smolenskin (1842–85)

Yes, we are a people!

HaToeh BeDarchei HaChayim (The wanderer in life's ways) is the title of Peretz Smolenskin's autobiographical novel describing the adventures of an orphan who wanders through all of contemporary Jewish life until he dies defending his people in a Russian pogrom. This tale summarized not only Smolenskin's life but his generation's journey. This most widely read book of modern Hebrew letters in the 1870s depicted the painful halfway house many enlightened Jews lived in, between the ghetto and modernity.

Like his protagonist, Smolenskin was born in the Russian Pale of Settlement, the western provinces of the tsarist empire, which were alone open to the Jewish population. At the age of twenty he migrated to Odessa, the great Black Sea port that hosted Russia's most modern Jewish community. He spent five years there studying music and languages while earning his keep by teaching Hebrew—and writing.

In 1868 Smolenskin settled in Vienna. He and a collaborator founded a monthly publication, *HaShahar* (The dawn), which he issued until his death from tuberculosis in Meran, Austria, in 1885.

Smolenskin is modern Hebrew literature's transition figure between the "Enlightenment," which ended with the Russian pogroms of 1881, and the return to nationalist moorings. Until his last "Zionist" novel, written in the 1880s following the pogroms, his work in belles lettres expressed the usual notions that modernizing Jewish life was desirable and inevitable. Even then, however, he was no uncritical admirer of modernity. His novels emphasized a countertheme: the assimilation of the Jew would not necessarily yield acceptance by society or personal happiness.

In the aftermath of the pogroms, Smolenskin abandoned his theorizing about Jewish national culture and the definition of Jewry as a spiritual nation. Instead he endorsed the evacuation of Eastern Europe. He asked its Jews not to repeat the woeful cycles of their history by emigrating to America or to any other lands of exile. There was only one answer—Zionism.

The excerpts which follow are from a volume he published as a series of articles in his own *HaShahar* in the years 1857–77: from an essay reacting to the pogroms of 1881, which expressed his later Zionism of complete exodus; and from a late piece critiquing Reform Judaism and the Haskalah, which he regarded as the immediate enemies.

It Is Time to Plant (1875–77)

The Jewish people has outlived all others because it has always regarded itself as a people—a spiritual nation. . . . Yes, we are a people. We have been a people from our beginnings until today. We have never ceased being a people, even after our kingdom was destroyed and we were exiled from our land, and whatever may yet come over us will not eradicate our national character. But we are not today a people like all others, just as we were not a people like the others even when we dwelt in our own land. The foundation of our national identity was never the soil of the Holy Land, and we did not lose the basis of our nationality when we were exiled. We have always been a spiritual nation, one whose Torah was the foundation of its statehood.

From the start our people has believed that its Torah took precedence over its land and over its political identity. We are a people because in spirit and thought we regard ourselves bound to one another by ties of fraternity. Our unity has been conserved in a different way, through forms different from those of all other peoples, but does this make us any the less a people?

Let Us Search Our Ways (1881)

Calamity after calamity and disaster after disaster have afflicted the Jews of Russia. In many communities not a stone has been left standing. The shops of our brethren have been pillaged and looted, and whatever the mob could not carry off, it has utterly destroyed. Many Jews have been murdered and the wounded are without number. The mob, a ravenous wolf in search of prey, has stalked the Jews with a cruelty unheard of since the Middle Ages. Perhaps most shocking of all, many supposedly decent people appeared among the makers of the pogroms. There is no end to the affliction that has already struck so many tens of thousands. . . .

We have no sense of national honor; our standards are those of second-class people. We find ourselves rejoicing when we are granted a favor and exulting when we are tolerated and befriended. . . .

The Haskalah of Berlin (1883)

The Haskalah of Berlin rested on this keystone: to imitate the gentiles, to abandon our own traditions, to disdain our own manners and ideas, and to conduct ourselves both at home and without—in the synagogue, within our families, everywhere—in imitation of others. As a reward for such a great achievement, so these upright and wise teachers assured us, our children, or our children's children, or their children, would be accepted as equals.

The consequences of this doctrine were: first, the destruction of the sentiment which is the unifying principle and strongest foundation of the House of Israel—that we are a nation; and, second, the abandonment of the hope of redemption. . . .

A false doctrine, that religion is the keystone of the House of Israel, was substituted. But this stone, too, crumbled into dust; the very people who paid all this lip service to religion condemned it and spurned all religious customs and laws because they were different from the ways of the gentiles. . . .

In assuring us that, as a reward for "Enlightenment," we would be able to establish our homes wherever we happened to be, they have told us to abandon all hope of returning to our own land and living there in dignity, as all peoples do. And we, having seen that all this did not get us anywhere, and that it did not even help us secure the love we sought—we declare: Only a dog neither has nor wants a home. A man who chooses to live his whole life as a transient, without a thought for the establishment of a permanent home for his children, will forever be regarded as a dog. And we must seek a home with all our hearts, our spirit, our soul. . . .

Leon Pinsker (1821–91)

**Autoemancipation: Judeophobia! Since the Jews are
nowhere at home, they remain aliens everywhere. . . .**

Leon Pinsker was the most assimilated among the Russian Jews who
turned Zionist under the impact of the events of 1881. A passionate
patriot, he had believed the Russian regime would liberalize itself
into a constitutional monarchy in which all people would be equals.
Because he had staked his faith in Russia and had relatively little Jewish affiliation, he was even more disillusioned by the pogroms than
most of his contemporaries.

Alongside an impressive medical career, after 1860 Pinsker took a
considerable interest in Jewish affairs. He wrote for the two earliest
Jewish weeklies in the Russian language and was active in the affairs
of the Society for the Spread of Culture among the Jews of Russia,
founded in 1863. Rejecting the "Enlighteners" who wrote in Hebrew,
he believed the Russian language and culture should dominate the
inner life, even the religion, of the Jew.

Outbreaks of violence were familiar phenomena in the life of Russian Jews. Why, then, did the 1881 pogroms constitute an emotional
crisis for so many, Pinsker among them, and a break in modern Jewish
history? There are two major reasons: their extent, and the composition of the mobs. The assassination of Tsar Alexander II in March 1881
(ironically as he was about to grant a liberal constitution) triggered
violence in nearly two hundred cities and villages. These, moreover,
were not lynchings carried out by an illiterate rabble. Leading newspapers whipped up the frenzy. Men of education and position participated in the attacks. And the government abetted the pogromists.

Pinsker left the Society for the Spread of Culture, declaring that
"new remedies, new ways" would have to be found. He went to central and western Europe to advance his new ideas about concentrating the bulk of Jewry in a national state. Alas, he found no adherents.
Returning to Russia, he published his views anonymously in German
in a pamphlet entitled *Auto-Emancipation*.

Like Herzl fifteen years later, Pinsker was sufficiently outside the influence of the traditional emotions centering around the Holy Land not to argue that a Jewish state had to be only in Zion. Palestine was preferable, but any land suitable for a national establishment would do.

Pinsker's pamphlet was greeted with vociferous indignation in many circles. The Orthodox regarded the author, who did not remain anonymous for long, as lacking in religion. The liberals, especially those outside Russia, attacked him as a traitor to the faith in humanity's ultimate victory over prejudice and hatred.

Nevertheless, the personal prestige of the man and the intellectual impact of the pamphlet propelled Pinsker to the foreground of the ferment toward creating a Jewish nationalist organization. Pinsker became the leader of the new Hibbat Zion movement, also known as Hovevi Zion. These groups of "lovers of Zion," believing the best reaction to the pogroms was to establish agricultural settlements in Palestine, convened in a founding conference in 1884. Pinsker's "Auto-Emancipation" is the first great statement of the anguish of the Jew driven to assert his own nationalism because the wider world rejected him. The theme would recur in Theodor Herzl's writing.

Auto-Emancipation: An Appeal to His People by a Russian Jew (1882)

That age-old problem, long called the Jewish Question, yet again provokes discussion. . . .

This is the kernel of the problem as we see it: the Jews comprise a distinctive element among the nations under which they dwell, and as such can neither assimilate nor be readily digested by any nation.

Hence the solution lies in finding a means of readjusting this exclusive element to the family of nations, so that the essential reason for the Jewish Question will be permanently removed. . . .

The Jewish people lacks most of the essential attributes which define a nation. It lacks that authentic, rooted life which is inconceivable without a common language and customs and without geographic cohesion. The

Jewish people has no fatherland of its own, though many motherlands; no center of focus or gravity, no government of its own, no official representation. The Jews are home everywhere, but are nowhere at home. . . .

Among the living nations of the earth the Jews as a nation are long since dead.

With the loss of their country, the Jewish people lost their independence, and fell into the kind of decay that would suck the life out of any healthy organism. The state was crushed before the eyes of the nations. But after the Jewish people had ceased to exist as an actual state, as a political entity, they nevertheless resisted total annihilation—they lived on spiritually as a nation.

In this people the world saw the uncanny form of one of the dead walking among the living. The ghostlike apparition of a living corpse, of a people without unity or organization, without land or other bonds of unity, no longer alive, and yet walking among the living—this spectral form without precedence in history, unlike anything that preceded or followed it, was doomed to haunt the imagination of the nations. . . .

Judeophobia is a psychic aberration. As a psychic aberration it is hereditary, and as a disease transmitted for two thousand years it is incurable.

This fear of ghosts, the mother of Judeophobia, has evoked this pure—I might say Platonic—hatred. As a result, the whole Jewish nation is often blamed for the real or supposed misdeeds of its individual members; it is libeled in so many ways—and buffeted about so shamefully. . . .

Since the Jews are nowhere at home, nowhere regarded as a native, they remain aliens everywhere. . . .

To sum up then: to the living, the Jew is a corpse; to the native, a foreigner; to the homesteader, a vagrant; to the proprietary, a beggar; to the poor, an exploiter and a millionaire; to the patriot, a man without a country; for all, a hated rival. . . .

Consequently, we are duty-bound to devote all our remaining moral force to reestablishing ourselves as a living nation, so that we may ultimately assume a more fitting and dignified role among the family of the nations. . . .

In order to build a secure home, end our endless life of wandering, and rise to the dignity of a nation in our own eyes and in the eyes of the world, we must, above all, not dream of restoring ancient Judaea. . . . We shall take with us the most sacred possessions which we have saved from the shipwreck of our former country, the God-idea and the Bible. It is these alone which have made our old fatherland the Holy Land, and not Jerusalem or the Jordan. Perhaps the Holy Land will again become ours. If so, all the better, but, first, we must determine—and this is the crucial point—what country is accessible to us, and at the same time suitable to offer the Jews of all lands who must leave their homes a secure and undisputed refuge, capable of flourishing. . . .

The people's consciousness is awake. The great ideas of the eighteenth and nineteenth centuries have not passed us by without leaving a trace. We feel not only as Jews; we feel as people. As human beings, we, too, wish to live and be a nation as the others. And if we seriously desire that, we must first of all extricate ourselves from the old yoke, and rise courageously to our full height. We must first of all desire to help ourselves and then the help of others is sure to follow. . . .

Let "Now or never" be our watchword. Woe to our descendants, woe to the memory of our Jewish contemporaries, if we let this moment pass by! . . .

Help yourselves, and God will help you!

Theodor Herzl (1860–1904)

> We are one people. . . . We are strong enough to
> form a State, and, indeed, a model State.

Theodor Herzl was born on May 2, 1860, in Budapest, Hungary, the second child and only son of a rich merchant. He received his preliminary education in a technical school and high school in Budapest. When he was eighteen, the family moved to Vienna after his sister's death from typhoid. Herzl enrolled in the University of Vienna's law school. After gaining his doctorate in 1884, Herzl practiced for a year as a minor civil servant but soon gave up the law to devote himself to writing. With relative ease he won regard as a feuilletonist, a familiar essayist, the favorite form of central European journalism, and as a writer of light, fashionable plays. In 1892 he was appointed to the staff of the *Neue Freie Presse*, the most important Viennese newspaper. Later that year Herzl arrived in Paris as its resident correspondent.

On the surface of his consciousness Herzl shared the conventional view of the westernized Jewish intellectual in the late nineteenth century—progress was on the march and complete assimilation was desirable and inevitable. Nonetheless, the emotional explosion that was soon to take place in his life and result in his Zionism had its roots in his earlier life. His Jewish education had been skimpy, but his grandfather, Simon Loeb, a congregant of the proto-Zionist rabbi Yehudah Alkalai, visited Budapest regularly. While still at the university Herzl encountered antisemitism in its new, theoretical, pseudoscientific form as racism in the writings of Eugen Dühring. He withdrew from his fraternity because it had participated in a memorial meeting for the German nationalist composer Richard Wagner that had degenerated into an antisemitic rally.

When he arrived in Paris, Herzl confronted antisemitism again, as a rising phenomenon of French life. He wrote a long account of it for his paper, suggesting that hatred of the Jew was serving as a lightning rod to draw the masses' revolutionary life away from society's real woes.

The Jewish problem was now in the forefront of his attention. The result of two years of pondering, of intellectual and emotional zigzagging, was his 1893 play, *The New Ghetto*. Its hero, Dr. Jacob Samuel, is Herzl. Samuel ultimately dies in a duel, crying out that he wants to get "out of the ghetto." Herzl demonstrated that even the most assimilated Jews are in an invisible ghetto in a gentile world.

In 1894 Alfred Dreyfus, a Jewish captain on duty with the French general staff, was accused of spying for Germany. Herzl provided his Vienna paper with regular accounts of the Dreyfus trial and its effect on French public life. He was present at the Ecole Militaire when Dreyfus was stripped of his epaulets and drummed out the gate in disgrace. For Herzl this moment was a hammer blow. The howling of the mob outside the gates of the parade ground, shouting "*A bas les Juifs*"—"down with the Jews"—fully transformed him into a Zionist.

In the early days of May 1895 Herzl requested an interview with Baron Maurice de Hirsch, the founder of Jewish colonization in Argentina, to pitch his idea of a Jewish national state. Baron de Hirsch was not receptive. Herzl soon hoped that perhaps the Rothschilds would listen to him. In five days of feverish writing he poured into his diary a sixty-five-page pamphlet—essentially outlining his Jewish state—which he entitled "Address to the Rothschilds." "I have the solution to the Jewish question," he wrote. "I know it sounds mad; and at the beginning I shall be called mad more than once—until the truth of what I am saying is recognized in all its shattering force." Finally, after much reworking and some difficulty in finding a publisher, his "Jewish State" appeared in February 1896.

While Herzl continued to work as literary editor of the *Neue Freie Presse* to support his family, he spent the last eight years of his life in feverish, superhuman Zionist activity. In August 1897, more than two hundred delegates from all over the Jewish world answered his call to come to Basel, Switzerland, to found the World Zionist Organization. Here, its purpose was proclaimed: "Zionism seeks to secure for the Jewish people a publicly recognized, legally secured, home in Palestine." The delegates on August 30, 1897, endorsed what became "The Basel Program," emphasizing the push for a "home in Palestine" and the broader mission of revitalizing the Jewish people. Succeeding congresses, six in Herzl's lifetime, finalized the movement's organizational infrastructure—and culture.

In 1902 Herzl finished his utopian novel *Altneuland (Old New Land)*. This European fantasy showcased Herzl's idealism, romanticism, and liberalism. His Jewish state was Western but Jewish. Demonstrating this global vision, one character proclaimed, following "the restoration of the Jews, I should like to pave the way for the restoration of the Negroes. . . ." The character, expressing Herzl's commitment to social justice, then explained how national pride engenders world peace: "All human beings ought to have a home. Then they will be kinder to one another. Then they will understand and love one another more."

For Herzl, the most important aspect of his work was diplomacy—he negotiated with the sultan of Turkey, Kaiser Wilhelm, the king of Italy, and Pope Pius X. Ironically, his one great success in the international arena almost wrecked the Zionist movement. In 1903 the British government offered him a large tract of land in Uganda, East Africa, for a Jewish self-governing settlement. That year, Herzl proposed to the World Zionist Congress that the offer be accepted as a "temporary haven," one that seemed urgently needed after the brutal pogrom in Kishinev, Russia. Yet the Zionists of Russia, led by the young Chaim Weizmann, among others, blocked him.

A Jewish state in Uganda was not meant to be in any case; the British government withdrew the offer a year or so later. The scenes of high drama that attended the discussion are, however, of crucial importance in the history of Zionism, for the seal was set on its devotion to a territorial state in Zion, and only in Zion.

Worn out by his exertions, Herzl died not far from Vienna on July 3, 1904. Forty-five years later, on August 17, 1949, an airplane flying the blue-white flag of the new State of Israel brought his remains to the country of which he was the principal architect.

The Jewish State (1896)

The idea which I have developed in this pamphlet is an ancient one: It is the restoration of the Jewish State.

The world denounces the Jews resoundingly, thus reawakening this once-dormant idea. . . .

The decisive factor is our propelling force. And what is that force? The plight of the Jews. . . . The world needs the Jewish State; therefore it will come to be. . . .

The Jewish Question still exists. It would be foolish to deny it. . . .

I think the Jewish Question is more than a social or religious one, notwithstanding that it sometimes takes these and other forms. It is a national question which can only be resolved by making it a political world-question to be discussed and settled by the civilized nations of the world in council.

We are a people—one people.

We have honestly endeavored everywhere to merge ourselves into the social life of surrounding communities and to preserve the faith of our fathers. We are not permitted to do so. In vain are we loyal patriots, our loyalty in some places running to extremes; in vain do we make the same sacrifices of life and property as our fellow-citizens; in vain do we strive to increase the fame of our native land in science and art, or her wealth by trade and commerce. In countries where we have lived for centuries we are still denounced as strangers, and often by those whose ancestors were not yet domiciled in the land where Jews had already started suffering. . . .

No human being is wealthy or powerful enough to transplant a nation from one habitat to another. An idea alone can achieve that and this idea of a state may have the requisite power to do so. The Jews have dreamt this kingly dream all through the long nights of their history. "Next year in Jerusalem" is our old phrase. It is now a question of showing that the dream can be converted into a living reality. . . .

Everything tends, in fact, to one and the same conclusion, which is clearly enunciated in that classic Berlin phrase: "*Juden Raus*" (Out with the Jews!)

I shall now put the question in the briefest possible form: Are we to "get out" now and where to?

Or, may we yet remain? And, how long? . . .

We are one people—our enemies have made us one without our consent, as repeatedly happens in history. Distress binds us together, and, thus united, we suddenly discover our strength. Yes, we are strong enough to form a state, and, indeed, a model state. We possess all human and material resources necessary for the purpose. . . .

Let sovereignty be granted us over a portion of the globe large enough to satisfy the rightful requirements of a nation; the rest we shall manage for ourselves.

The creation of a new state is neither ridiculous nor impossible. We have in our day witnessed the process in connection with nations which were not largely members of the middle class, but poorer, less educated, and consequently weaker than ourselves. The governments of all countries blighted by antisemitism will be keenly interested in assisting us to obtain the sovereignty we want. . . .

Palestine is our ever-memorable historic home. The very name of Palestine would attract our people with a force of marvelous potency. . . .

Here it is, fellow Jews! Neither fable nor deception! . . .

Therefore I believe that a wondrous generation of Jews will spring into existence. The Maccabeans will rise again.

Let me repeat once more my opening words: The Jews who wish for a state will have it. We shall live at last as free people on our own soil, and die peacefully in our own homes.

The world will be liberated by our freedom, enriched by our wealth, magnified by our greatness.

And whatever we attempt there to accomplish for our own welfare, will react powerfully and beneficially for the good of humanity.

From the Diaries of Theodor Herzl
(Begun in Paris, around Pentecost, 1895)

When did I actually begin to concern myself with the Jewish Question? Probably ever since it arose; certainly from the time that I read [Eugen] Dühring's [antisemitic] book, [*The Parties and the Jewish Question* (1881)]. . . . As the years went on, the Jewish Question bored into me and gnawed at me, tormented me, and made me very miserable. In fact, I kept coming back to it whenever my own personal experiences— joys and sorrows—permitted me to rise to broader considerations. . . .

At first, the Jewish Question grieved me bitterly. There might have been a time when I would have liked to get away from it—into the Christian fold, anywhere. But in any case, these were only vague desires born of youthful weakness. For I can say to myself with the honesty inherent in this diary—which would be completely worthless if I played the hypocrite with myself—that I never seriously thought of becoming baptized or changing my name. This latter point is even attested to by an incident. When as a green young writer I took a manuscript to the *Vienna Deutsche Wochenschrift*, Dr. Friedjung advised me to adopt a pen-name less Jewish than my own. I flatly refused, saying that I wanted to continue to bear the name of my father and I offered to withdraw the manuscript. Friedjung accepted it anyway.

I then became a writer of sorts, with little ambition and petty vanities. . . .

In Paris I was in the midst of politics—at least as an observer. I saw how the world is run. I also stood amazed at the phenomenon of the crowd—for a long time without comprehending it.

Here too I reached a higher, more disinterested view of antisemitism, from which at least I did not have to suffer directly. In Austria or in Germany I must constantly fear that someone will shout "Hep, hep!" after me. But here I pass through the crowd unrecognized.

In Paris, then, I gained a freer attitude toward antisemitism which I now began to understand historically and make allowances for.

Above all, I recognized the emptiness and futility of efforts to "combat antisemitism." Declamations made in writing or in closed circles do no good whatever; they even have a comical effect. It is true that in addition to careerists and simpletons there may be very stalwart people serving on such "relief committees." These resemble the "relief committees" formed after—and before—floods, and they accomplish about as much. . . .

Antisemitism has grown and continues to grow—and so do I.

Third Letter to Baron Hirsch (Paris, June 3, 1895)

I spoke of an army, and you already interrupted me when I began to speak of the (moral) training necessary for its march. . . . I know all the things it involves: money, money, and more money; means of transportation; the provisioning of great multitudes (which does not mean just food and drink, as in the simple days of Moses); the maintenance of manly discipline; the organization of departments; emigration treaties with the heads of some states, transit treaties with others, formal guarantees from all of them; the construction of new, splendid dwelling places. Beforehand, tremendous propaganda, the popularization of the idea through newspapers, books, pamphlets, talks by travelling lecturers, pictures, songs. Everything directed from one center with sureness of purpose and with vision.

But I would have had to tell you eventually what flag I will unfurl and how. And then you would have asked mockingly: A flag, what is that? A stick with a rag on it?—No, sir, a flag is more than that. With a flag one can lead men wherever one wants to, even into the Promised Land.

For a flag men will live and die; it is indeed the only thing for which they are ready to die in masses, if one trains them for it; believe me, the policy of an entire people—particularly when it is scattered all over the earth—can be carried out only with imponderables that float in thin air. Do you know what went into the making of the German Empire? Dreams, songs, fantasies, and black-red-and-gold ribbons—and in short order. Bismarck merely shook the tree which the visionaries had planted.

What? You do not understand the imponderable? And what is religion? Consider, if you will, what the Jews have endured for the sake of this vision over a period of two thousand years. Yes, visions alone grip the souls of men. . . .

Max Nordau (1849–1923)

Antisemitism has also taught many educated Jews the way back to their people.

Max Nordau was Herzl's most important colleague and disciple. In 1896 when he accepted Herzl's Zionist faith, Nordau was much the more famous of the two. He already possessed a European-wide reputation as an avant-garde writer and critic of society.

Like Herzl, Nordau was born in Budapest and received a comparable education under German cultural influence. He began to write in his adolescence. By 1873 his literary gifts were sufficiently well regarded to earn him the post of Viennese correspondent of Budapest's important German language newspaper, the *Pester Lloyd*. By 1880 he was permanently domiciled in Paris, practicing as a doctor, writing for a number of newspapers, and publishing a succession of popular books.

As an old friend, Nordau was one of the first to whom Theodor Herzl came to expound his Zionist ideas. There is even a perhaps apocryphal story that Herzl came to Nordau to consult him as psychiatrist in the fear that he was out of his mind. After several days of conversation Nordau supposedly stretched out his hand to Herzl to say: "If you are crazy, so am I." Nordau, at any rate, had also been present at the degradation of Dreyfus and was similarly deeply affected by the antisemitic outcries.

Nordau's adherence to Zionism gave it the stamp of approval as "advanced" thought and helped attract younger Jewish intellectuals to the new cause. A master of rhetoric, Nordau delivered an opening address on the state of Jewry at the First Zionist Congress and repeated this performance at every one until the tenth.

However, within a few years after Herzl's death, Nordau found himself estranged from the new leadership of the Zionist movement. He remained an uncompromising "messianist"—seeking a dramatic solution to the Jewish problem. That made him contemptuous both of philanthropic Zionism, the social work Zionism of the Americans helping their poor European cousins, and Cultural Zionism, with its focus on revitalizing Jewish culture more than building a state. The organization, however, was now in the hands of the "practical" Zionists who believed the ultimate political aim of the movement should be subordinated to the immediate work of building up the Jewish settlement in Palestine.

Nordau returned to the Zionist scene in 1919. He disdained the careful phraseology of the 1917 Balfour Declaration, in which the British foreign secretary declared "His Majesty's government views with favor the establishment in Palestine of a national home for the Jewish people, and will use their best endeavors to facilitate the achievement of this object, it being clearly understood that nothing shall be done which may prejudice the civil and religious rights of existing non-Jewish communities in Palestine, or the rights and political status enjoyed by Jews in any other country."

Nordau kept demanding not merely "a Jewish National Home in Palestine," but the immediate establishment of a Jewish state. The border war among the Poles, Ukrainians, and Russians was then raging, resulting in the murder of tens of thousands of Jews. Though Nordau knew that conditions in Palestine were not ripe to absorb mass immigration, he demanded that such be done. In his view, which approached the position of the young Vladimir Jabotinsky, the fast-tracked Jewish majority in Palestine that would result was considerably more important than careful colonization. In 1920 Nordau returned to Paris, where he died, on January 23, 1923. Three years later his remains were transferred to Tel Aviv.

Zionism (1902)

Zionism is the result of two impulses which came from without: first, the principle of nationality, which dominated thought and sentiment in Europe for half a century and determined the politics of the world; second, antisemitism, from which the Jews of all countries suffer to some degree.

The principle of nationality has awakened a sense of their own identity in all the peoples; it has taught them to regard their unique qualities as values and has given them a passionate desire for independence. . . .

Antisemitism has also taught many educated Jews the way back to their people. . . . But, in the case of most Zionists, the effect of antisemitism was only to force them to reflect upon their relationship to the nations of the world, and their reflection has led them to conclusions which would endure in their minds and hearts if antisemitism were to disappear completely. . . .

Whoever maintains and believes that the Jews are not a nation can indeed not be a Zionist; he cannot join a movement which has as its sole purpose the desire to normalize a people which is living and suffering under abnormal conditions. He who is convinced to the contrary that the Jews are a people must necessarily become Zionist, as only the return to their own country can save the Jewish nation which is everywhere hated, persecuted, and oppressed, from physical and intellectual destruction. . . .

The Zionists know that they have undertaken a work of unparalleled difficulty. Never before has the effort been made to transplant several million people peacefully and in a short space of time, from various countries; never has the attempt been made to transform millions of physically degenerate proletarians, without trade or profession, into farmers and herdsmen; to bring town-bred hucksters and tradesmen, clerks and men of sedentary occupation, into contact again with the plough and with Mother Earth. It will be necessary to get Jews of different origins to adjust to one another, to train them practically for national unity, and at the same time to overcome the superhuman obstacles of differences of language, cultural level, ways of thought, and varying prejudices of people who will come to Palestine from all the countries of the world. . . .

Muskeljudentum, Jewry of Muscle (1903)

For too long, all too long, we have been engaged in the mortification of our own flesh.

Or rather, to put it more precisely—others did the killing of our flesh for us. Their extraordinary success is measured by hundreds of Jewish corpses in the ghettos, in the churchyards, along the highways of medieval Europe. We ourselves would have gladly done without this "virtue." We would have preferred to develop our bodies rather than kill them or to have them—figuratively and actually—killed by others. . . .

In the narrow Jewish street our poor limbs soon forgot their gay movements; in the dimness of sunless houses our eyes began to blink shyly; the fear of constant persecution turned our powerful voices into frightened whispers, which rose in a crescendo only when our martyrs on the stakes cried out their dying prayers in the face of their executioners. But now, all coercion has become a memory of the past, and at least we are allowed space enough for our bodies to live again. Let us take up our oldest traditions; let us once more become deep-chested, sturdy, sharp-eyed men. . . .

For no other people will gymnastics fulfill a more educational purpose than for us Jews. It shall straighten us in body and in character. It shall give us self-confidence, although our enemies maintain that we already have too much self-confidence as it is. But who knows better than we do that their imputations are wrong. We completely lack a sober confidence in our physical prowess.

Our new muscle-Jews [*Muskeljuden*] have not yet regained the heroism of our forefathers who in large numbers eagerly entered the sport arenas to take part in competition and to pit themselves against the highly trained Hellenistic athletes and powerful Nordic barbarians. But morally, even now the new muscle-Jews surpass their ancestors, for the ancient Jewish circus fighters were ashamed of their Judaism and tried to conceal the sign of the Covenant by means of a surgical operation, ... while the members of the Bar Kokhba [Association] loudly and proudly affirm their national loyalty.

May the gymnastic club flourish and thrive and become an example to be imitated in all the centers of Jewish life!

Jacob Klatzkin (1882–1948)

**Strip Zionism of the territorial principle
and you have destroyed its character.**

Jacob Klatzkin was the most temperate stylist and yet perhaps the most devastating anti-traditionalist of all the rebels within Zionism. In Zionist literature he has been known chiefly as the most radical denier of any possibility of a future Jewish life in the Diaspora. He is the most important Zionist thinker to affirm that a third-rate, normal, national Jewish state and culture in Palestine would be enough.

Like Berdichevski and Ahad Ha'Am, Klatzkin was born within the ghetto aristocracy of Russia. His father was a distinguished rabbi. Klatzkin's first published book, in 1902 when he was but twenty, belonged to the genre of traditional rabbinic scholarship. He was, however, already attracted to secular culture and Zionism. After a few years of study in Western Europe, his transformation was complete. From 1909 to 1911 he served the World Zionist Organization as the editor of its official organ, *Die Welt*, founded by Theodor Herzl, and then directed the main office of the Jewish National Fund. Concurrently Klatzkin crystallized his own views in a number of essays in Hebrew that were collected in 1914 under the title *Tehumim* (Boundaries).

Klatzkin based his Zionist position on his general definition of nationalism. What makes a nation, he asserted, is land and language. Therefore, the Jews needed to reacquire their land and again speak their language—Hebrew. Let there be no talk of spiritual uniqueness, of destiny and mission for all this is a mark of the diseased abnormality of an un-nation. Moreover, he insisted, all Jews must, with deliberate speed, either immigrate to Palestine or disappear by intermarriage. There can be neither a middle ground nor an alternative.

When Hitler came to power in 1933, Klatzkin left for Switzerland, and in 1941 he arrived in the United States. After World War II he returned to Europe. He died in Switzerland in 1948.

Boundaries: Judaism Is Nationalism (1914–21)

To be a Jew means the acceptance of neither a religious nor an ethical creed. We are neither a denomination nor a school of thought, but members of one family, bearers of a common history. Denying the Jewish spiritual teaching does not place one outside the community, and accepting it does not make one a Jew. In short, to be part of the nation one need not believe in the Jewish religion or the Jewish spiritual outlook. . . .

The national definition, too, requires an act of will. It defines our nationalism by two criteria: partnership in the past and the conscious desire to continue such partnership in the future. There are, therefore, two bases for Jewish nationalism—the compulsion of history and a will expressed in that history. A Jew who no longer wishes to belong to the Jewish people, who betrays the covenant and deserts his fellows in their collective battle for redemption, has thereby abandoned his share in the heritage of the past and seceded from his people. . . .

The assimilated Jews claim that we have ceased being a nation in the Diaspora. Jewish nationalists must reply: We are a nation even in the Diaspora, so long as our goal is to be redeemed from it, so long as we labor for the rebirth of our land and our language. . . .

What is really new in Zionism is its territorial-political definition of Jewish nationalism. Strip Zionism of the territorial principle and you have destroyed its character and erased the distinctions between it and the preceding periods. This is its originality—that Judaism depends on form and not on content. For it the alternatives are clear: Either the Jewish people shall redeem the land and thereby continue to live, even if the spiritual content of Judaism changes radically, or we shall remain in exile and rot away, even if the spiritual tradition continues to exist. . . .

Zionism began a new era, not only for the purpose of making an end to the Diaspora but also in order to establish a new definition of Jewish identity—a secular definition. I am certain that the builders of our land will in the future sacrifice themselves for national forms, for land and language, as our ancestors accepted martyrdom for the sake of the religious content of Judaism. . . .

Assimilation is infecting ever greater segments of our people and its impact is becoming ever more profound. It has not yet obscured our national identity nor has it solved the Jewish problem, but this is no proof that it will not come to that. Assimilation is still in mid-career. And yet even in its earlier stages it has managed to disfigure and impoverish our people. . . .

The Judaism of the *galut* is not worthy of survival. . . . The *galut* falsifies our national character. . . .

Perhaps our people can maintain itself in the *galut*, but it will not exist in its true dimensions—not in the prime of its national character. *Galut* can only drag out the disgrace of our people and sustain the existence of a people disfigured in both body and soul—in a word, of a horror. At the very most it can maintain us in a state of national impurity and breed some sort of outlandish creature in an environment of disintegration of cultures and of darkening spiritual horizons. The result will be something neither Jew nor gentile—in any case, not a pure national type. . . .

The *galut* is corrupting our human character and dignity. . . .

It is no accident that Zionism arose in the West and not in the East. Herzl appeared among us not from the national consciousness of a Jew but from a universal human consciousness. Not the Jew but the man in him brought him back to his people. He recognized the moral collapse of assimilation and its disgrace. There is a moral-aesthetic power throbbing in every one of his Zionist speeches; it is he who said to the assimilationists: We must begin by creating decent people. He told us nothing new, but everything he said was new. A new spirit found utterance in him, the spirit of a person restoring his human dignity . . . for Zionism is an aspiration toward morality and beauty. It has come, as one of its chief purposes, to redeem the man in us. . . .

Chaim Weizmann (1874–1952)

We have the right to build our home in *Eretz Yisra'el*, harming no one, helping all.

To write a brief biography of Chaim Weizmann is impossible, for his was the central career of Jewish history in the first half of the twentieth century. As he reminded a thousand audiences, Weizmann's roots were in the old ghetto of the Russian Pale of Settlement. He was born in the village of Motol, near the city of Pinsk, and received the usual pious early training. He attained a doctorate from the University of Geneva in 1900 and remained in the city to teach chemistry there for the next four years.

Weizmann moved to England in 1904. After some months in Manchester, he was appointed to the university faculty. During the First World War, he transferred to London to direct a special laboratory that the British government had created for his important work on the production of acetone, a vital ingredient of naval gunpowder. Weizmann remained at this post until after the war, when he became almost totally involved in Zionism. Nonetheless, throughout his life, he continued, with some fraction of his time, to work as a research chemist. During the Second World War he again pursued chemical research of military importance, both in England and the United States.

Weizmann's Zionism was a natural outgrowth of his early upbringing. He adhered to the movement announced by Herzl at the very beginning and was already a delegate to the Second Zionist Congress in 1898. He was never in complete sympathy with Herzl, whom he faulted for not loving Judaism as much as he loved Jews, although he understood that "Had Herzl been to a *heder* [religious school], never would the Jews have followed him. He charmed the Jews because he came to them from the European culture."

From the beginning of his days in England, Weizmann was busy as a Zionist making contacts and converts in the highest political circles. He led the complex negotiations in London that resulted in the Balfour Declaration. After the British general Edmund Allenby occupied southern Palestine, Weizmann headed the Zionist Commission, which went out to advise the British military government on behalf of Jewish national interest in the country.

In 1919 Weizmann was among the delegation leaders who appeared before the Versailles Peace Conference to present the case for Zionist aspirations in Palestine.

At the London Zionist Conference of 1920, Weizmann was elected president of the World Zionist Organization; he would retain this office, with an interruption from 1931 to 1935, until 1946. As the responsible leader of Zionism, he had to deal with many internal rows. Moreover, in political crisis after crisis he had to defend the Zionist position before the world and often had to induce his followers to swallow bitter pills. For example, in the emotional speech excerpted here, he asked them to accept the Peel Commission's partition proposal as at least a beginning for negotiation.

At the first Zionist Congress after the Second World War, Weizmann was not reelected to the presidency. Abba Hillel Silver and David Ben-Gurion both stood against him in favor of a more active policy of resistance to the British. Nonetheless, his personal eminence was unchallenged. When the state was declared, Weizmann was immediately invited to be president of its Provisional Government Council. Then, from 1949 to his death in 1952, he was the first president of Israel.

On the Report of the Palestine Commission
(Twentieth Zionist Congress, Zurich, August 4, 1937)

I say to the Mandatory Power: You shall not outrage the Jewish nation. You shall not play fast and loose with the Jewish people. Say to us frankly that the National Home is closed, and we shall know where we stand. But this trifling with a nation bleeding from a thousand wounds must not be done by the British whose Empire is built on moral principles— that mighty Empire must not commit this sin against the People of the Book. Tell us the truth. This at least we have deserved.

[Here Weizmann broke down and wept, and then continued after a pause.]

Permit me, at this historic juncture, to say a word to the Arab people. We know that the Mufti [of Jerusalem, Haj Amin al-Husseini] and [another Nazi collaborator Fawzi al-] Kawkaji are not the Arab nation. In the present world those who have bombs and revolvers at command wield political power. But in the history of a nation their life is like one day, even if it extends over years.

There is an Arab nation with a glorious past. To that nation we have stretched out our hand, and do so even now—but on one condition. Just as we wish them to overcome their crisis and to revert to the great tradition of a mighty and civilized Arab people, so must they know that we have the right to build our home in *Eretz Yisra'el*, harming no one, helping all. When they acknowledge this we shall reach common ground, and I hope for the time when we shall once more recognize each other. . . .

I consider that two criteria have to be applied in appraising such a principle. The first—does it offer a basis for a genuine growth of Jewish life? I mean both in quality and in volume; does it offer a basis for the development of our young Palestinian culture, of which the Report speaks with true respect? Does this principle afford a basis for building up such a Jewish life as we picture, for rearing true men and women, for creating a Jewish agriculture, industry, literature, etc.—in short, all that the ideal of Zionism comprises?

This is one test. For our great teacher, Ahad Ha'Am, who is with us no longer, it might have been the only one. But times have changed, and Jewish history, which, alas! for the most part, is not ours to mold, faces us with a tragic problem. We must, therefore, apply yet another test. Does the proposal contribute to the solution of the Jewish problem, a problem pregnant with danger to ourselves and to the world? . . .

Natan Alterman (1910–70)

The silver platter Zionist

The great Zionist poet Natan Alterman was born in Warsaw in 1910 and moved to Mandatory Palestine in 1925. While honing his literary talents, Alterman also wrote a weekly column, first for *Ha'aretz* starting in 1934, and after 1943, for the Histadrut Labor Federation daily, *Davar*. Alterman's lyricism and nationalism, often linked to current events as the State of Israel emerged, made him, in David Ben-Gurion's words, "The Conscience of the Nation."

In 1934 his poem, "Shir Moledet" (Song of the homeland), expressed the simple love of homeland sharpened by working the land. Eleven years later, his song "Kalaniot" (Anemones), celebrating the joy even one such flower blooming can bring for generations, became a classic. Jewish underground fighters sang it to warn one another when British soldiers were around; then in 1948 the singer Shoshana Damari made it her signature song—and that founding generation's anthem.

In 1936 Alterman's bitter poem, "Horgai HaSadot" (The killers of the fields), contextualized the fears of the Yishuv, the Jewish residents of Mandatory Palestine, within the broader sweep of Jewish history. Describing marauders emerging "like massive-jawed raptors / At a desert crawl," he concluded: "For ancient destiny has not let go, no he hasn't. / For amid her tranquility and the songs of her tents, / He's been holding her in a headlock since Vespasian, / And brandishing his whip."

Alterman's anguish during the Shoah had him penning sarcastic mockeries of the prayers, writing, "Praised are You . . . who has chosen us out of all the nations" in 1942. But Alterman refused to become a traumatized, isolationist Jew. A year later, on October 8, 1943, in "The Swedish Tongue," he thanked the Swedes for welcoming the Danish Jews, while bashing the rest of Europe for erecting lethal barriers with fancy legal terms and politicized fears.

In 1947 Alterman achieved Zionist immortality with his poem "Magash HaKesef" (The silver platter). During the difficult debate over whether or not to accept the November 29, 1947, United Nations Partition Plan that divided Palestine and internationalized Jerusalem, Chaim Weizmann had warned, "The state will not be given to the Jewish people on a silver platter." Alterman's weekly posting, "The Seventh Column," in *Davar*, on December 19, 1947, captured the sense of sacrifice that would be necessary to create the state. These words became among the most famous in the Zionist lexicon and are still read throughout Israel, especially on Remembrance Day.

Once the state was declared, this iconoclast ranged widely in his political beliefs. He assailed the Israeli military regime controlling Israeli Arabs until November 1966 and championed equal rights among all Israelis, both Jews and Arabs. Yet after 1967, once Israel had captured the Gaza Strip, the Sinai Peninsula, the West Bank, and the Golan Heights in the Six-Day War, Alterman joined other literary figures to endorse the Greater Land of Israel Movement, which called for the Israeli government to maintain the captured areas and settle them with Jews.

Shir Moledet (Song of the homeland) (1935)

On the mountains the sun already blazes
And in the valley the dew still shines
We love you, homeland,
With joy, with song and with toil.
From the slopes of Lebanon to the Dead Sea
We shall crisscross you with ploughs
We shall yet cultivate and build you
We shall yet beautify you.

We will dress you in a gown of concrete and cement
And lay for you a carpet of gardens,
On the soils of your redeemed fields
The harvest will chime with bells.
The desert wilderness, we will cross,
The swamps, we will drain.
What we give is for your glory and satisfaction,
What has not yet been given, we shall give.

In the hills, in the hills our light shined,
We will climb the mountain.
We will leave yesterday behind,
Although the path to tomorrow remains long.

Even if the difficult path is treacherous,
And even if some of us may fall,
We will love you, our homeland, forever,
We are yours in battle and in toil.

Magash HaKesef (The silver platter) (1947)

And the land quiets, the crimson sky slowly dimming over smoking
  frontiers
And the nation arises, heartbroken but breathing,
To receive the miracle, the only one, there is no other. . . .

As the ceremony approaches, it will rise amid the moon, standing
  erect in terror and joy. When across from it a young man and
  woman emerge and slowly, slowly march toward the people.

Dressed in battle gear, dirty,
Shoes heavy with grime, they climb the path quietly.
They didn't change their clothes, they didn't wipe their brows,
Still bone weary from days and nights in the battlefield

Interminably exhausted, abstainers from rest,
Yet wearing their youth like dew glistening on their head.
Silently, the two approach and stand immobile at attention, giving
  no sign of living or dying.

Then, enveloped in tears and wonder, the nation will ask: "Who
  are you?"
And the two reply quietly, "We are the silver platter on which the
  Jewish state was given."

This they will say and fall back encased in shadows
And the rest will be told in Israel's chronicles.

Albert Einstein (1879–1955)

Jewish nationalism as necessary nationalism.

Albert Einstein was a most reluctant Zionist. Born in Germany in 1879 to a secular family, Einstein wanted to live in a world without borders—and in some ways intellectually he did. But his internationalism and discomfort with nationalism were no match for German antisemitism. By 1919 a decade and a half before Adolf Hitler and the Nazis dismissed Einstein's groundbreaking scientific work as "Jewish Physics" and a "Jewish perversion," the already legendary physicist would proclaim: "I am as a human being, an opponent of nationalism. But as a Jew, I am from today a supporter of the Zionist effort." Einstein wrote to one friend: "One can be an internationalist without being indifferent to members of one's own tribe. . . . The Zionist cause is very close to my heart. . . . I am glad that there should be a little patch of earth on which our kindred brethren are not considered aliens."

Acting on his Zionist impulses, Einstein visited Palestine, fundraised for Hebrew University, and endorsed Zionism before, during, and after World War II. His worldwide fame and his Jewish pride made him, as his biographer Walter Isaacson wrote, "a living patron saint for Jews." But as a pacifist, Einstein feared the impact a Jewish state would have on the Palestinian Arabs—then, on the Jewish soul. In 1946 he testified before the Anglo-American Committee of Inquiry, saying, "The state idea is not according to my heart. I cannot understand why it is needed." While endorsing the development of a Jewish homeland in Palestine, he preferred to see a bi-national state at best.

Partisans on all side of the issue would seek the approval of the man reputed to be the greatest intellect of his time, whom *Time* magazine had crowned as the "person of the century," the master scientist in an age of science. Indeed, anti-Zionists still quote Einstein's testimony and other sayings to try to delegitimize Israel. But for all his ambivalence, Einstein endorsed the Jewish claim to Palestine. He saw Jewish anti-Zionists as engaged in "a pitiable attempt to obtain favor and toleration from our enemies by betraying true Jewish ideals."

Once the Jewish state was established, Einstein supported Israel. On the symbolically significant date of November 29, 1949, two years after the United Nations General Assembly voted to endorse a Jewish state and partition Palestine, Einstein delivered an NBC radio address lauding Israelis' self-sacrifice in absorbing hundreds of thousands of Jewish refugees from East and West who had nowhere else to go. "The Jews of Palestine did not fight for political independence for its own sake," he insisted, "but they fought to achieve free immigration for the Jews of many countries where their very existence was in danger."

When Chaim Weizmann died, David Ben-Gurion offered Einstein the presidency of the State of Israel. Einstein turned down the offer elegantly, saying he was too independent for politics; Ben-Gurion, aware of Einstein's iconoclasm, was relieved.

Yet in refusing, Einstein added: "I am the more distressed over these circumstances, because my relationship to the Jewish people has become my strongest human bond, ever since I became fully aware of our precarious situation among the nations of the world." Raised to be what Isaac Deutscher called a non-Jewish Jew, Albert Einstein felt forced by the world to be the always Jewish Jew, and the reluctant Zionist.

Palestine, Setting of Sacred History of the Jewish Race (with Erich Kahler, April 14, 1944)

Even if we put aside the spiritual, religious and cultural ties making Palestine the only place in the world which persecuted Jews could consider their home and develop with all the devotion a homeland inspires— there is not even any other country acceptable to human beings which the numerous refugee conferences were able to offer to this hounded people. The Jews are prepared for extreme sacrifices and hardest work to convert this narrow strip which is Palestine into a prosperous country and model civilization. . . .

For the true source of Arab resistance and hostility toward a Jewish Palestine is neither religious nor political, but social and economic. . . . The big Effendis fear the example and the impulse which the Jewish colonization of Palestine presents to the peoples of the Near East, they resent the social and economic uplift of the Arabian workers in Palestine. They act as all fascist forces have acted: they screen their fear of social reform behind nationalistic slogans and demagoguery. . . .

The purpose of this statement is not a nationalistic one. We do not, and the vast majority of Jews does not, advocate the establishment of a state for the sake of national greed and self-glorification, which would run counter to all the traditional values of Judaism and which we consider obsolete everywhere. In speaking up for a Jewish Palestine, we want to promote the establishment of a place of refuge where persecuted human beings may find security and peace and the undisputed right to live under a law and order of their making. The experience of many centuries has taught us that this can be provided only by home rule and not by a foreign administration. This is why we stand for a Jewish controlled Palestine, be it ever so modest and small.

We do not refer to historic rights, although if there exists something like a historic right on a country, the Jews, at least as well as the Arabs, could claim it on Palestine. We do not resort to threats of power, for the Jews have no power; they are, in fact, the most powerless group on earth. If they had had any power they should have been able to prevent the annihilation of millions of their people and the closing of the last door to the helpless victims of the Nazi. What we appeal to is an elementary sense of justice and humanity. . . .

2

Pioneers

Labor Zionism

Labor Zionism envisioned a Jewish working class settling in Palestine and constructing a progressive Jewish society—treating Political Zionism as the start, not the end, of the journey. These left-wing Zionists were sufficiently realistic—and scarred—to reject Marxism's faux cosmopolitanism, the delusion that class solidarity transcended Europe's addiction to ethnic, religious, and national hatreds. Nevertheless, they did not just want to solve the Jewish Problem, or fashion a strong and self-sufficient New Jew. They wanted to save the world by creating a new model for humanity. They believed that founding an old-new Jewish state in the ancient Jewish homeland enabled the Jewish people to bring alive a realistic socialism—one that acknowledged tribalism and respected differences, while still seeking equality and social justice.

In fact, many Labor Zionists wanted to use the solidarity fostered by Jewish national ties—and suffering—to eradicate the usual boundaries between the haves and have-nots. The proto-Zionist and comrade of Karl Marx, Moses Hess, recognized that just as "nature produces specific and unique plant and animal types," history produces "folk types." Zionism could teach how to bridge socialism and nationalism; communal solidarity could in turn serve to motivate the achievement of distributive justice, the just allocation of goods in society. As a result, A. D. Gordon and others rejected the socialist movement's class-obsessed hostility to nationalism, making it more appropriate to call this school of thought "Labor Zionism."

Remarkably, this strain of Zionism dominated in the years prior to the state's founding—and during Israel's first thirty years. Labor Zionism produced one of the most successful and democratic institutional expressions of socialism in the world—the kibbutz. Institutions such as the Histadrut labor union reflected a communal and internationalist sensibility. Thus, Labor Zionists demonstrated that it was indeed possible to balance universalism and particularism.

The Jewish people will participate in the great historical movement of present-day humanity only when it will have its own fatherland.

Moses Hess lived in the midst of the intellectual ferment and political turmoil of the nineteenth century. Though almost entirely self-educated, he, along with Heinrich Heine and a host of other thinkers, were the first generation of German Jews to grow up within Western culture. By temperament, though, he was an outsider, an enemy not only of the established order but also of many values of the very political left with which he was associated.

Hess was born in Bonn, Germany. When his parents moved to Cologne in 1821, they left nine-year-old Moses behind, having deemed the Jewish educational opportunities in Cologne insufficient. He remained in the charge of his grandfather, a rabbi by training though not by profession, who taught him enough Hebrew so that when he returned to Jewish interests after thirty years of neglect, Hess was able to tap strong emotional and intellectual roots in the tradition. As he first entered maturity, however, Hess abandoned his Jewish concerns.

Like other advanced intellectuals of the milieu, among whom Karl Marx and Friedrich Engels were to become the most famous, Hess went from philosophy to ideological politics. By 1840, after some wanderings, he turned up in Paris, where he was active in socialist circles. Even though Hess was sufficiently active in the German revolution of 1848 to earn the sentence of death, the *Communist Manifesto* that year sealed the break that had been developing between him and Marx and Engels. Hess never accepted their materialistic determinism, the idea that human beings are what they are because of something material outside or inside of them. His socialism was of the ethical variety, expressing a romantic love for humanity. Karl Marx took pains to mock Hess for this in the *Manifesto*.

By 1853 Hess was back in Paris, where he remained for the rest of his days. There he devoted himself to scientific studies. As he delved into anthropology, he became convinced that the future world order needed to be organized as a harmonious symphony of national cultures, each expressing in its own way the ethical socialism that remained his quasi-religious faith.

A rekindled interest in the faith and fate of his own people brought him back to Jewish studies, resulting in the 1862 publication of "Rome and Jerusalem." This diffuse short volume contains echoes of all his ideas, including his general theory of national socialism for all peoples. Its major importance lies in his statement of Jewish nationalism, which anticipated many of Zionism's central themes.

Rome and Jerusalem (1862)

After twenty years of estrangement I have returned to my people. . . .

A sentiment which I believed I had suppressed beyond recall is alive once again. It is the thought of my nationality, which is inseparably connected with my ancestral heritage, with the Holy Land and the Eternal City, the birthplace of the belief in the divine unity of life and of the hope for the ultimate brotherhood of all men. . . .

Because of the hatred that surrounds him on all sides, the German Jew is determined to cast off all signs of his Jewishness and to deny his race. No reform of the Jewish religion, however extreme, is radical enough for the educated German Jews. . . .

As long as the Jew denies his nationality, as long as he lacks the character to acknowledge that he belongs to that unfortunate, persecuted, and maligned people, his false position must become ever more intolerable. What purpose does this deception serve? The nations of Europe have always regarded the existence of the Jews in their midst as an anomaly. We shall always remain strangers among the nations. . . .

The really dishonorable Jew is not the old-type, pious one who would rather have his tongue cut out than utter a word in denial of his nationality, but the modern kind who, like the German outcasts in foreign countries, is ashamed of his nationality because the hand of fate is pressing heavily upon his people. The beautiful phrases about humanity and enlightenment which he uses so freely to cloak his treason, his fear of being identified with his unfortunate brethren, will ultimately not protect him from the judgment of public opinion. These modern Jews hide in vain behind their geographical and philosophical alibis. You may mask yourself a thousand times over; you may change your name, religion, and character; you may travel through the world incognito, so that people may not recognize the Jew in you; yet every insult to the Jewish name will strike you even more than the honest man who admits his Jewish loyalties and who fights for the honor of the Jewish name....

The national character of Judaism does not exclude universalism and modern civilization; on the contrary, these values are the logical effect of our national character. If I nonetheless emphasize the national root of Judaism rather than its universalist blooms, that is because in our time people are all too prone to gather and deck themselves out with the pretty flowers of the cultural heritage rather than to cultivate them in the soil in which they can grow.

Judaism is the root of our whole contemporary universalist view of life. There is nothing in the moral teaching of Christianity, in the scholastic philosophy of the Middle Ages, or in modern humanitarianism— and, if we add the latest manifestation of Judaism, Spinozism—there is nothing even in modern philosophy, which does not stem from Judaism....

Nature does not produce flowers and fruits or plants and animals which are all exactly alike because they represent some generalized form; on the contrary, nature produces specific and unique plant and animal types. By the same token the creative power in history produces only folk types....

A common, native soil is a precondition for introducing healthier relations between capital and labor among the Jews. The social man, just like the social plant and animal, needs a wide, free soil for his growth and development; without it, he sinks to the status of a parasite, which feeds at the expense of others....

The Jewish people will participate in the great historical movement of present-day humanity only when it will have its own fatherland. As long as the great Jewish masses remain in their position of inequality, even the relatively few Jews who have entirely surrendered their Jewish identity in

the vain attempt to escape individually from the fate of the Jewish people, will be more painfully affected by the position of the Jews than the
masses who feel themselves only unfortunate but not degraded. Hence,
no Jew, whether Orthodox or not, can refrain from co-operating with
the rest in the task of elevating all Jewry. Every Jew, even the converted,
should cling to the cause and labor for the regeneration of Israel. . . .

BILU (1882)

**The Lord is our God, the Lord is one, and
our land Zion is our only hope.**

Although only fourteen young Russian Jews landed in Palestine as
the first wave of immigrants from this organization devoted to agricultural settlement in the Land of Israel—and six of them left pretty
quickly—BILU embodies the Zionist pioneering idea. The group's
members—the first settlers coming to Israel for nationalist and socialist reasons—helped found the city of Rishon LeTzion in 1882, then
the town of Gedera in 1884. They articulated the despondency of the
Russian intellectuals—the *maskilim*—who watched the pogroms of
1881 through 1884 kill their dreams of equality. And they pioneered
the greater movement of young idealists who built the country, of
zealous communitarians who would create the kibbutzim, and of
committed Zionists who would rally around Theodor Herzl fifteen
years later. Ultimately, one Biluimnik, Menashe Meirovitz, would
survive long enough to witness Israel's establishment, dying in 1949
at age eighty-nine.

These New Jews are remembered as secular revolutionaries. Yet
the movement's name and manifesto encapsulate Zionism's mixed
message about the past. BILU is an acronym based on the verse in Isaiah (2:5): "*Beit Ya'akov Lechu VeNelkha*, House of Jacob, come let us
go." Its rhetoric captures what the group's leader Israel Belkind called
the members' commitment to "move there ourselves," not just send
others—and demonstrates their fluency in traditional texts.

BILU Manifesto (1882)

To our brothers and sisters in exile!
"If I do not help myself, who will help me?"

Nearly two thousand years have passed since, in an evil hour, after an heroic struggle, the glory of our Temple vanished in fire and our kings and chieftains exchanged their crowns and diadems for the chains of exile. We lost our country where our beloved ancestors had lived. Into the Exile we took with us, of all our glories, only a spark of the fire by which our Temple, the abode of the Great One, was engirdled, and this little spark kept us alive while the towers of our enemies crumbled into dust, and this spark leapt into the celestial flame and illuminated the heroes of our race and inspired them to endure the horrors of the dance of death and the tortures of the autos-da-fe.

And this spark is again kindling and will shine for us, a true pillar of fire going before us on the road to Zion, while behind us is a pillar of cloud, the pillar of oppression threatening to destroy us.

Are you asleep, O our nation? What have you been doing until 1882? Sleeping and dreaming the false dream of assimilation. Now thank God, you have waked from your slothful slumber. The pogroms have awakened you from your charmed sleep. Your eyes are open to recognize the obscure and delusive hopes. Can you listen in silence to the taunts and mocking of your enemies? . . .

Where is your ancient pride, your old spirit? Remember that you were a nation possessing a wise religion, a law, a constitution, a celestial Temple whose wall is still a silent witness to the glories of the past. . . .

Your state in the West is hopeless: the star of your future is gleaming in the East. Deeply conscious of all the foregoing, and inspired by the true teaching of our great master, Hillel, "If I do not help myself, who will help me?" we propose to form the following society for national ends:

The society will be named "BILU," according to the motto, "House of Jacob, come let us go." . . .

We want:

... A home in our country. It was given to us by the mercy of God; it is ours as registered in the archives of history. ...

Greetings dear brothers and sisters!

Hear O! Israel! The Lord is our God, the Lord is one, and our land Zion is our only hope.

God be with us!

The Pioneers of BILU.

Joseph Hayyim Brenner (1881–1921)

Workers' settlements—this is our revolution. The only one.

Joseph Hayyim Brenner's first novel, *BaHoref* (In the winter), ends with his autobiographical hero, Feierman, put off a train because he has no ticket, left stranded beside a snow-covered road in the middle of nowhere. By other names, Feierman (i.e., Brenner) is the protagonist of all his succeeding novels, and his destiny is always the same: abortive beginnings, unrealized strivings, and bitterness against himself and the world.

Both in his art and his personal life, Brenner wandered between the blackest pessimism and qualified affirmation. His childhood and youth were conventional—born in the Ukraine, educated in the usual orthodoxy, then a break to general studies—but there seems to have been an extra dimension of poverty and personal suffering. He matured in the 1890s during a particularly hopeless period for Russia and Russian Jewry. All thought of accommodation with the tsarist regime had ended; there were only three alternatives—to labor for a revolution, to migrate westward, or to turn Zionist and go to Palestine. In turn, Brenner attempted each of these solutions.

In his late teens Brenner was attracted by the Bund, the newly formed group of revolutionary Jewish socialists violently opposed to Jewish nationalism—they wanted the workers of all peoples to unite. After three years of working illegally for the party, he drifted out of that movement to reaffirm his Jewish loyalties through Zionism. From 1902 to 1903 he served in the Russian army—depicting this period of his life in a novella, *Shanah Ahat* (One year)—then escaped to London.

His experiences in England made him no happier. The new East European immigrants were packed tight in its Whitechapel section, London's East Side, living in indescribable misery, eking out their existence in sweatshops.

In 1909 he left for Palestine, where he led the then small labor and pioneer groups. He also taught in Tel Aviv's first high school while editing and writing. A dozen years later, he was found dead, murdered near Tel Aviv during the Arab outbreaks against the Jews in May 1921.

When Brenner had begun to write in the 1890s, he found inspiration in Russian literature, particularly Dostoyevsky and Tolstoy, Russian masters who offered uncompromising criticisms of society and treated convention as a sham. Brenner was also influenced by Mendele Moher Sefarim (Shalom Jacob Abramovitz), the greatest nineteenth-century novelist writing in both Hebrew and Yiddish, who targeted the disintegrating Russian ghetto. Invoking a conscious proletarian perspective, Brenner repeated this social criticism with greater vehemence.

The considerably shortened excerpt is from Brenner's essay, "Ha'arachat Azmenu be-Sheloshet Ha-Krahim" (The estimate of ourselves in three volumes). While he reviews a collected edition of Mendele's works, he comments upon his own hatred of the Jewish past, both its culture and its society, and his faith that a new, sound, healthy Jew could be made to arise only if he were to begin over again in Zion.

Self-Criticism (1914)

Yes, indeed, we have survived, we live. True, but what is our life worth? We have no inheritance. Each generation gives nothing of its own to its successor. And whatever was transmitted—the rabbinical literature—were better never handed down to us. In any case, by now it is more and more certainly passing away. Everything we know about our lives tells us that there are only masses of Jews who live biologically, like ants, but a living Jewish people in any sociological sense, a people each generation of which adds a new stratum to what preceded it and each part of which is united with the other—such a people hardly exists any longer. . . .

A "living" people whose members have no power but for moaning, and hiding a while until the storm blows over, turning away from their poorer brethren to pile up their pennies in secret, to scratch around among the goyim, make a living from them, and complain all day long about their ill will—no, let us not pass judgment upon such a people, for indeed it is not worth it. . . .

It would be a sign of steadfastness and power, of productive strength, if the Jews would go away from those who hate them and create a life for themselves. That I would call heroic sacrifice. . . .

History! History! But what has history to tell? It can tell that wherever the majority population, by some fluke, did not hate the Jews among them, the Jews immediately started aping them in everything, gave in on everything, and mustered the last of their meager strength to be like everyone else. . . . Even when the yoke of ghetto weighed most heavily upon them—how many broke through the walls? How many lost all self-respect in the face of the culture and beautiful way of life of the others! How many envied the others! How many yearned to approach them!

. . . Yes, our environment is crumbling. This is nothing new, for this environment has never been stable; it has always lacked a firm foundation. We never had workers, never a real proletariat. What we had and have are idle poor. Basically nothing has changed, but now the very forms of life have dissolved. . . .

We have to start all over again, to lay down a new cornerstone. But who will do that? Can we do it, with our sick character? This is the question.

This is the question: In order that our character be changed as much as possible, we need our own environment; in order to create such an environment ourselves—our character must be radically changed. . . .

Our urge for life says: All this is possible. Our urge for life whispers hopefully in our ear: Workers' Settlements, Workers' Settlements.

Workers' Settlements—this is our revolution. The only one.

Nahman Syrkin (1868–1924)

A classless society and national sovereignty are the only means of solving the Jewish problem completely.

The first great Zionist writer, Moses Hess, had combined socialism and nationalism, but his work was forgotten. That such a combination would be made again, when Herzlian Zionism appeared, was inevitable, for in the 1890s, socialism was the greatest single influence on the thought of young Jewish intellectuals. Socialist Zionism arose out of the misery and ferment of Russian Jewry, as the life of Nahman Syrkin demonstrates.

He began that life within a pious family in Mohilev. By temperament a rebel, he finished school in Minsk, where he joined a group of Hibbat Zion while becoming involved in the revolutionary underground. By 1888 he was in Berlin, starving but studying economics and socialist theory at one of the German and Swiss universities full of Russian Jewish students who, like himself, had been barred by the Russian universities. Syrkin would later recall that it took all the inner certainty and skill in argument he could muster to stand alone, at war with the entire intelligentsia within which he moved when he first announced his Socialist Zionism. He first published his thesis in a pamphlet in 1898, *Die Judenfrage und der sozialistische Juden-staat* (The Jewish problem and the socialist Jewish state), excerpted below.

Syrkin had attended the First Zionist Congress the year before, and he remained in the organization until 1905. For four years he was a territorialist, believing that a Jewish state should be founded on any available land, not necessarily in Palestine. He returned to Zionism as a representative of the newly formed Poale Zion (Workers of Zion) party, which professed that a Jewish proletariat would emerge in the Land of Israel and then participate in the class struggle. In 1907 he moved to the United States to continue serving as an often-controversial official of the Labor Zionist movement. Syrkin died in New York in 1924.

Syrkin's socialism was not Marxist but ethical and utopian; it was rooted, like Hess's, in love of humanity and the ideals of biblical prophecy. Society, both Jewish and general, was, in his view, dominated by the class interests of the bourgeoisie, which ran counter to Jewish nationalism, or even to the French, German, and other nationalisms that the wielders of power professed. Nor could Syrkin have unqualified faith in a socialist new order, because he forecast that the Jew would still be prey to exclusion as a member of a minority. Hence, the only true bearers of Jewish nationalism were the masses, and the only true socialism would have to include a Zionist solution to the Jewish problem.

The Jewish Problem and the Socialist Jewish State (1898)

For a Jewish state to come to be, it must, from the very beginning, avoid all the ills of modern life. To evoke the sympathetic interest of modern man, its guidelines must be justice, rational planning, and social solidarity. . . . The Jewish state can come about only if it is socialist; only by fusing with socialism can Zionism become the ideal of the whole Jewish people—of the proletariat, the middle class, and the intelligentsia. All Jews will be involved in the success of Zionism, and none will be indifferent. The messianic hope, which was always the greatest dream of exiled Jewry, will be transformed into political action. The Jewish people, presently living in misery, will gain lofty content. . . .

Because the Jews are placed in an unusual situation, that they are forced to find a homeland and establish a state, they therefore have been presented with the opportunity to be the first to realize the socialist vision. This is the tragic element of their historic fate, but it is also a unique historic mission. What is generally the vision of a few will become a great national movement among the Jews; what is utopian in other contexts is a necessity for the Jews.

The Jews were historically the nation which caused division and strife; it will now become the most revolutionary of all nations. From the humblest and most oppressed of all peoples it will be transformed to the proudest and greatest. The Jews will derive their moral stature from their travail, and out of the pain of their existence will come a pattern of noble living. The Jew is small, ugly, servile, and debased when he forgets and denies his great character. He becomes distinguished and beautiful in the moral and social realms when he returns to his true nature.

Israel is to be compared to a sleeping giant, arising from the slough of despair and darkness and straightening up to his infinite height. His face is rimmed by rays of glory of the pain of the world which he has suffered on his own body. He knows his task, to do justice and proclaim truth. His tragic history has resulted in a high mission. He will redeem the world which crucified him.

Israel will once again become the chosen of the peoples!

Ber Borochov (1881–1917)

Zionism can be realized only if proletarian Zionism can be realized.

Within a decade after their movement launched in 1897, various Zionists had synthesized Jewish national thought with almost every major contemporary thinker—except for Karl Marx.

For Zionism, "scientific socialism" was the most unassimilable of all outlooks, for it pronounced nationalism to be, like religion, an opiate of the masses, a force capitalists employed to divert the proletariat from its true interests. Both Jewish and non-Jewish Marxists had always denied with special vehemence the existence of any specific Jewish problem; the socialist revolution of the future, they asserted, would put an end to antisemitism and the Jews would disappear into the proletariat. To be sure, Syrkin had argued against these ideas as a humanitarian and utopian socialist, but he was not effective among the Marxists. A theory of Zionism that was expressed solely in terms of dialectical materialism was still lacking. Propelled by antisemitism, Ber Borochov, who helped found and led the Poale Zion (Workers of Zion) party, provided it.

We are today too remote from the mood of Russia in the last days of tsarism, when Marxist faith that revolution was inevitable so permeated the young, to appreciate Borochov's impact. By the same token,

Marx's thought is no sacred canon to us, and so we are not moved by a theory of Zionism that evolved like a geometrical theorem from "prooftexts" in *Das Kapital*. Nonetheless, in and for that time and place, Borochov's construction was a brilliant intellectual achievement. It remains significant today as well: an important minority element in the Israeli labor movement continued to be Marxist in outlook and draw upon Borochov's early theories well into the 1970s.

Borochov was born in the Ukraine. His "Enlightened" parents provided him with a first-class formal education, to which he added considerably with his own readings. Upon graduation from the local high school, he resolved not to go to university; he had already encountered enough antisemitism in his high-school teachers. He worked for a year in the Social Democratic Party until he was expelled as a Zionist deviationist. From that point forward, his life's work became Jewish national activity in workers' groups and refining his Marxist Zionist thought.

In December 1906, the Russian Poale Zion group crystallized, and Borochov wrote its platform, aided by another brilliant young theoretician, Yitzhak Ben-Zvi—eventually the non-Marxist, very mildly socialist, and almost universally beloved president of Israel. After 1907 difficulties with the Russian police forced Borochov to leave. He traveled all over Europe as a party functionary.

With the outbreak of World War I, Borochov came to America. He continued his careers as ideologist and propagandist. In March 1917, he returned to his native land. He died in Kiev that December, at the young age of thirty-six.

This selection from the platform he wrote for Poale Zion revolves around Borochov's equally original, and in part prophetic, ideas that antisemitism made Jewish nationalism necessary until communism would truly triumph, that only Palestine would remain open to large Jewish immigration, and that an inevitable (he called it "stychic," from the Greek word for "elementary") process would bring Jews there.

Our Platform (1906)

Antisemitism is becoming a dangerous political movement. Antisemitism flourishes because of the national competition between the Jewish and non-Jewish petty bourgeoisie and between the Jewish and non-Jewish proletarized and unemployed masses. Antisemitism menaces both the poor helpless Jews and the all-powerful Rothschilds. . . .

Capitalistic economy has reached the stage where no revolutionary changes are possible without the participation of the working masses and especially of the organized sections of the proletariat. The emancipation of the Jewish people either will be brought about by Jewish labor, or will not be attained at all. But the labor movement has only one weapon at its command: the class struggle. The class struggle must assume a political character if it is to lead to a better future. . . .

Political territorial autonomy in Palestine is the ultimate aim of Zionism. For proletarian Zionists, this is also a step toward socialism.

The broadening and consolidation of Jewish economic and cultural positions in Palestine will proceed at a rapid pace along with the above-mentioned processes. Parallel with the growth of economic independence will come the growth of political independence. The ideal of political autonomy for the Jews will be consummated by political territorial autonomy in Palestine.

Aaron David Gordon (1856–1922)

What we need is zealots of labor!

If Herzl was Zionism's president in exile and Ahad Ha'am its secular rabbi, Aaron David Gordon was the movement's secular mystic and saint. In 1904 he came, unknown and unannounced, to Palestine, to do physical labor by the side of the much younger handful of Zionist idealists who were already there or would soon arrive—and almost immediately he became their central personality. In his lifetime he was revered; since his death he has become a legend.

He was born in a village in the province of Podolia to a family of notable piety and learning related to Baron Horace Günzburg, one of Russia's great magnates. His childhood and youth were spent in a farming village on an estate that his father managed for the Günzburgs. After Gordon's marriage, he served these wealthy relatives by managing a large tract of land they had rented for farming. Here he spent twenty-three years (1880–1903), until the lease ran out.

Now forty-seven, with a wife and two almost grown children, Gordon had to find a new job. After months of indecision, he gave his family whatever money he had—enough to provide for a while, until, he hoped, he could have them join him—and left for Palestine.

Middle-aged, a white-collar worker all his days, and physically weak, he nevertheless insisted that he must be a laborer on the land. The redemption of humanity as a whole, and of the Jew in particular, could come, he believed, only through physical labor.

After initial difficulties, Gordon found day labor in the vineyards and wineries of Petah Tikva. He worked there for five years and worked three more nearby after he had brought over his wife and daughter (his wife died almost immediately). He then spent ten years at various places in the Galilee. His last days were spent in Degania, one of the earliest kibbutzim (collective farming settlements) of the Labor Zionist movement.

Gordon's outlook and career parallel the later life of Leo Tolstoy—the Russian writer also left his family to live among the peasants in true communion with nature and his soul. Behind them both stands the romantic idealization of the natural man, the notion that people are inherently good but corrupted by society.

Gordon, in particular, also emerged from a preceding century of criticism of the Jewish ghetto as a spiritual ruin because of its stunted economy. Let the Jews cease concentrating on livelihoods earned by their wits and return to farming, so this argument went; let them acquire a "normal" economic profile, engaging in proper proportion in all levels of production rather than figuring so overwhelmingly as middlemen. Some founders of Religious Zionism, such as Samuel Hayyim Landau (1892–1928), insisted: "Torah cannot be reborn without labor, and labor, as a creative and nation-building force, cannot be reborn without Torah." Most of these labor zealots, of course, were avowedly secular.

As substratum to these notions, even though he was no longer a practicing religious Jew in the last period of his life, Gordon anchored his outlook in a mystique about the metaphysical bond between the Jew and the Land of Israel that derived from the classical religious tradition with some kabbalistic overtones. Nations, he asserted, are cosmic phenomena, the result of man's interaction with nature in its particular expression in one place by which the unique soul and history of the nation is formed. No matter what may happen to a nation after it is created—even if, like the Jews, a nation is exiled—both its corporate soul and the souls of its individuals are stunted until they return to their true habitat. There they can become whole again by living the life of nature. Hence, physical labor, the renewal of the true self in reverent harmony with the cosmos, is religion.

People and Labor (1911)

The Jewish people has been completely cut off from nature and imprisoned within city walls these two thousand years. We have become accustomed to every form of life, except to a life of labor—of labor done at our own behest and for its own sake. It will require the greatest effort of will for such a people to become normal again. We lack the principal ingredient for national life. We lack the habit of labor—not labor performed out of external compulsion, but labor to which one is attached in a natural and organic way. This kind of labor binds a people to its soil and to its national culture, which in turn is an outgrowth of the people's soil and the people's labor. . . .

We are a people without a country, without a living national language, without a living culture—but that, at least, we know and it pains us, even if only vaguely, and we seek ways and means of doing what needs must be done. But we seem to think that if we have no labor it does not matter—let Ivan, or John, or Mustapha do the work, while we busy ourselves with producing a culture, with creating national values, and with enthroning absolute justice in the world. . . .

What are we seeking in Palestine? Is it not that which we can never find elsewhere—the fresh milk of a healthy people's culture? What we are come to create at present is not the culture of the academy, before we have anything else, but a culture of life, of which the culture of the academy is only one element. We seek to create a vital culture out of which the cream of a higher culture can easily be evolved. We intend to create creeds and ideologies, art and poetry, and ethics and religion, all growing out of a healthy life and intimately related to it; we shall therefore have created healthy human relationships and living links that bind the present to the past. What we seek to create here is life—our own life—in our own spirit and in our own way. . . .

We need a new spirit for our national renaissance. That new spirit must be created here in Palestine and must be nourished by our life in Palestine. It must be vital in all its aspects, and it must be all our own.

What we need is zealots of Labor—zealots in the finest sense of the word.

Our Tasks Ahead (1920)

There is a cosmic element in nationality which is its basic ingredient. That cosmic element may best be described as the blending of the natural landscape of the Homeland with the spirit of the people inhabiting it. This is the mainspring of a people's vitality and creativity, of its spiritual and cultural values. . . .

We have no country of our own, we have no living national language, but instead a number of vernaculars borrowed from others. Religion? But our religion is on the wane, and it certainly cannot be the answer for those who are not religious. What, then, is that elusive, unique, and persistent force that will not die and will not let us die? . . .

That answer is that there is a primal force within every one of us which is fighting for its own life, which seeks its own realization. This is our ethnic self, the cosmic element of which we spoke, which, combined with the historic element, forms one of the basic ingredients of the personality of each and every one of us. The ethnic self may be described as a peculiar national pattern of mental and physical forces which affects the personality of every individual member of the ethnic group. . . .

Jewish life in the Diaspora lacks this cosmic element of national identity; it is sustained by the historic element alone which keeps us alive and will not let us die, but it cannot provide us with a full national life. What we have come to find in Palestine is the cosmic element. . . .

It is life we want, no more and no less than that, our own life feeding on our own vital sources, in the fields and under the skies of our Homeland, a life based on our own physical and mental labors; we want vital energy and spiritual richness from this living source. We come to our Homeland in order to be planted in our natural soil from which we have been uprooted, to strike our roots deep into its life-giving substances, and to stretch out our branches in the sustaining and creating air and sunlight of the Homeland. Other peoples can manage to live in any fashion, in the homelands from which they have never been uprooted, but we must first learn to know the soil and ready it for our transplantation. . . .

We are engaged in a creative endeavor the likes of which is not to be found in history: the rebirth and rehabilitation of a people that has been uprooted and scattered to the winds. It is a people half dead, and the effort to recreate it demands the exclusive concentration of the creator on his work. . . . Here, in Palestine, is the force attracting all the scattered cells of the people to unite into one living national organism. The more life in this seed, the greater its power of attraction.

It is our duty, therefore, to concentrate all our strength, all our thinking, all our mind and heart, on this central spot. We must not ever, even for a moment, let our minds wander from it. We must shun political activity as destructive of our highest ideals; otherwise we become unwitting traitors to the principle of our true self which we have come here to bring back to life. Nor must we tie ourselves to the world proletariat, to the International, whose activities and whose methods are basically opposed to ours. We must draw our inspiration from our land, from life on our own soil, from the labor we are engaged in, and must be on guard against allowing too many influences from outside to affect us. What we seek to establish in Palestine is a new, recreated Jewish people, not a mere colony of Diaspora Jewry, not a continuation of Diaspora Jewish life in a new form. It is our aim to make Jewish Palestine the mother country of world Jewry, with Jewish communities in the Diaspora as its colonies—and not the reverse. We seek the rebirth of our national self, the manifestation of our loftiest spirit, and for that we must give our all....

Rachel Bluwstein (1890–1931)

O, my Kinneret. Did you exist, or did I dream a dream?

Aiding the profound thinkers, sublime poets expressed the love of the land and the joy in making it bloom. One verbal virtuoso, the Hungarian-born kibbutznik and World War II fighter, Hannah Szenes, would epitomize Zionist pioneering, poetry, and patriotism. Her thirteen-word ode to Israel's beauty—"My Lord, make these eternal: sand, sea, rushing waters, crashing heavens, and human prayers"— was immortalized following her execution by Nazi firing squad at age twenty-three. Before Szenes, Rachel Bluwstein, known simply as Rachel the poetess, brought to life A. D. Gordon's vision that reconnecting the people with their land would trigger a cultural renaissance as part of the national renaissance.

Raised in Russia and the Ukraine, Rachel visited Palestine in 1909 when she was nineteen, on her way to study art and philosophy in Italy. Inspired, she stayed, learning Hebrew by listening to kindergarten children chattering. Like most of the early pioneers, she suffered in Palestine but loved her new home. When she moved to Kvutzat Kinneret by the shores of the Galilee, she met A. D. Gordon, to whom she dedicated her first Hebrew poem. Years later, she also lived in Kibbutz Degania, linking her to two iconic early kibbutzim and solidifying her identity as the bard of the flourishing Galilee.

Many of Rachel's poems were set to music and are still sung, making her one of the first to shape the Zionist soundtrack of the twentieth century. Among many favorites, thanks to her beloved poem "Ve'ulai," "Perhaps," generations of Israelis sang longingly, lovingly, "HaKineret Sheli," O, my Sea of Galilee. Did you exist, or did I dream a dream?"

Stricken by tuberculosis and exiled from Degania, whose members feared contagion, she wandered between Jerusalem and Tel Aviv, earning money by giving private Hebrew lessons. When she died an early death in 1931, the Yishuv mourned, a testament to the cultural and ideological impact of her short, lyrical poetry created in her short, tragic life.

Rachel was buried in the Kinneret cemetery overlooking her cherished Sea of Galilee. This cemetery for the original pioneers remains a Zionist pilgrimage spot for those wishing to honor Rachel and others who built not only the state's infrastructure, but its mythology.

My Country (1926)

I have not sung you, my country,
not brought glory to your name with the great deeds of a hero
or the spoils a battle yields.
But on the shores of the Jordan
my hands have planted a tree,
and my feet have made a pathway through your fields.

Modest are the gifts I bring you.
I know this, mother.
Modest, I know, the offerings of your daughter:
Only an outburst of song
on a day when the light flares up,
only a silent tear
for your poverty.

Berl Katznelson (1887–1944)

**A renewing and creative generation does not throw
the cultural heritage of ages into the dustbin. It
examines and scrutinizes, accepts and rejects.**

The generation that was born in Russia in the 1880s and came to Palestine in their early adulthood. The group known as the Second Aliyah, quickly became the leadership of the new Zionist settlement. The movement these mostly socialist Zionists fashioned dominated the government of Israel throughout the first decades of its existence. David Ben-Gurion and Yitzhak Ben-Zvi became its highest officers.

Berl Katznelson was their contemporary and, until his death in 1944, a central figure of Socialist Zionism. While still an adolescent in Bobruisk, the White Russian city of his birth, he entered the whirlpool of ideologies and parties that was then the predominant concern of advanced young Russian Jews. Always a lover of the Hebrew language and emotionally a Zionist, he nonetheless wandered among the parties of the left for a few years without committing to any particular doctrine. After turning twenty he decided to go to Palestine and prepared himself in several skills, including blacksmithing.

In 1909, at age twenty-two, he arrived in Jaffa. Like the older A. D. Gordon and his near contemporary Joseph Hayyim Brenner, who became his friends, Katznelson started his life in Palestine as a day laborer on the farm—and a labor organizer. He led a strike, founded a traveling library for farm workers, helped create a labor exchange for newcomers, and wrote frequently for the periodicals of the Labor Zionist movement.

During World War I, Katzenelson remained in Palestine. When the British army conquered its southern part, he enlisted in 1918 in its newly formed battalion of Palestinian Jews. After 1920 he became a front-rank official of Palestinian Jewry and the World Zionist movement. He remained consistently at the center of Labor Zionist affairs and spoke frequently before international bodies and Jewish communities abroad until his death in Jerusalem in 1944.

Katznelson's major importance, however, was not in politics, but in journalism and cultural affairs. In 1925 he founded the Tel Aviv newspaper *Davar* as the organ of the trade union organizations, the Histadrut. He remained its editor until his death. Am Oved, the publishing house of the Histadrut, was also his creation; indeed, he influenced the entire cultural program of Palestinian labor.

Revolution and Tradition (1934)

We like to call ourselves rebels—but may I ask, "What are we rebelling against?" Is it only against the "traditions of our fathers"? If so, we are carrying coals to Newcastle. Too many of our predecessors did just that. Our rebellion is also a revolt against many rebellions that preceded ours. We have rebelled against the worship of diplomas among our intelligentsia. We have rebelled against rootlessness and middlemanship, and not only in the forms in which they appeared in the older Jewish way of life; we have rebelled against their modern version as well, against the middlemanship and rootlessness of some of the modern Jewish nationalist and internationalist intellectuals, which we find even more disgusting than all the earlier manifestations of these diseases. We have rebelled against the assimilationist utopia of the older Jewish socialist intelligentsia. We have rebelled against the servility and cultural poverty of the Bund. We are still faced with the task of training our youth to rebel against "servility within the revolution" in all its forms—beginning with those Jews who were so much the slaves of the Russian Revolution that they even distributed proclamations calling for pogroms in the name of the revolution, and including the Palestinian Communist Party of our day, which is acting in alliance with the pogromists of Hebron and Safed.

There are many who think of our revolution in a much too simple and primitive manner. Let us destroy the old world entirely, let us burn all the treasures that it accumulated throughout the ages, and let us start anew—like newborn babes! There is daring and force of protest in this approach. Indeed, there really were many revolutionaries who thus pictured the days of the Messiah. But it is doubtful whether this conception, which proceeds in utter innocence to renounce the heritage of the ages and proposes to start building the world from the ground up, really is revolutionary and progressive, or whether there is implicit within it a deeply sinister reactionary force. History tells of more than one old world that was destroyed, but what appeared upon the ruins was not better worlds, but absolute barbarism. . . .

People are endowed with two faculties—memory and forgetfulness. We cannot live without both. Were only memory to exist, then we would be crushed under its burden. We would become slaves to our memories, to our ancestors. Our physiognomy would then be a mere copy of preceding generations. And were we ruled entirely by forgetfulness, what place would there be for culture, science, self-consciousness, spiritual life? Arch-conservatism tries to deprive us of our faculty of forgetting, and pseudo-revolutionism regards each remembrance of the past as the "enemy." But had humanity not preserved the memory of its great achievements, noble aspirations, periods of bloom, heroic efforts, and strivings for liberation, then no revolutionary movement would have been possible. The human race would have stagnated in eternal poverty, ignorance, and slavery.

Primitive revolutionism, which believes that ruthless destruction is the perfect cure for all social ills, reminds one, in many of its manifestations, of the growing child who demonstrates his mastery of things and curiosity about their structure by breaking his toys. . . .

A renewing and creative generation does not throw the cultural heritage of ages into the dustbin. It examines and scrutinizes, accepts and rejects. At times it may keep and add to an accepted tradition. At times it descends into ruined grottoes to excavate and remove the dust from that which had lain in forgetfulness, in order to resuscitate old traditions which have the power to stimulate the spirit of the generation of renewal. If a people possesses something old and profound, which can educate man and train him for his future tasks, is it truly revolutionary to despise it and become estranged from it? . . .

The Jewish year is studded with days which, in depth of meaning, are unparalleled among other peoples. Is it advantageous—is it a goal—for the Jewish labor movement to waste the potential value stored within them? The assimilationists shied away from our Jewish holidays as obstacles on the road to their submergence among the majority because they were ashamed of anything which would identify them as a distinct group—but why must we carry on their tradition? Did not bourgeois assimilationism and Enlightenment, and even the Jewish socialism which followed in their wake, discard many valuable elements of social uplift which are contained in our tradition? If we really are Zionist Socialists, it does not befit us to behave like dumb animals following every stupid tradition, just because it calls itself "modern" and is not hallowed by age. We must determine the value of the present and of the past with our own eyes and examine them from the viewpoint of our vital needs, from the viewpoint of progress toward our own future.

Let us take a few examples: Passover. A nation has, for thousands of years, been commemorating the day of its exodus from the house of bondage. Throughout all the pain of enslavement and despotism, of inquisition, forced conversion, and massacre, the Jewish people has carried in its heart the yearning for freedom and has given this craving a folk expression which includes every soul in Israel, every single downtrodden, pauperized soul! . . . I know no literary creation which can evoke a greater hatred of slavery and love of freedom than the story of the bondage and the exodus from Egypt. I know of no other remembrance of the past that is so entirely a symbol of our present and future as the "memory of the exodus from Egypt."

And Tishah b'Av. Many nations are enslaved, and many have even experienced exile. . . . Israel knew how to preserve the day of its mourning, the date of its loss of freedom from oblivion. . . . Our national memory was able, with these very simple means, to make every Jewish soul, all over the world, feel heavy mourning at the same day and the same hour. . . .

I am not setting specific rules as to the form our holidays should assume. Suitable forms will grow from a living feeling within the heart and an upright and independent spirit. . . . As long as Israel is dispersed and is prey to persecution and hatred, to contempt and to forced conversion, as in Yemen in Asia, Algiers in Africa, and Germany in Europe—or even though they enjoy emancipation purchased through assimilation in capitalistic France and communistic Russia—I shall never forget, I shall never be able to forget, the most fearful day in our destiny—the day of our destruction.

Rahel Yanait Ben-Zvi (1886–1979)

Work in the settlement was a joy.

Labor Zionists sought to redeem the Jewish people and the world simultaneously. They believed that working the Land of Israel with their hands would free them from the exile's despair and the industrialized world's inequities. Among the purists of the Second Aliyah, the wave of idealists who imported and then synthesized Russian revolutionary ideas with Zionism, were Golda Lishansky and Isaac Shimshelevich (1884–1963).

Lishansky was born into a Hasidic family. When she made *aliyah* from the present-day Ukraine in 1908, she took the name Rahel Yanait, honoring Alexander Yannai, the king from the Second Temple who had expanded the boundaries of the Land of Israel. In 1918 she married Shimshelevich, who by then was called Yitzhak Ben-Zvi.

The Ben-Zvis became the power couple of the Second Aliyah—those pioneers who came between 1904 and 1914, establishing Ahuzat Bayit, which became Tel Aviv, and the first kibbutz, Degania, among other accomplishments. For all their love of agriculture—expressed in the selection that follows—the Ben Zvis settled in Jerusalem, embracing "its antiquities . . . envisioning and dreaming about the future of our nation in the homeland," she would later recall.

Known as Haverah (comrade) Rahel, she helped found the Hebrew Gymnasium, the self-defense organization HaShomer, the Zionist Pioneer Women of America, and the Meshek Ha-Poalot—the Working Women's Farm in Talpiot, outside Jerusalem. As the selection—from the famous 1931 Zionist text, *The Plough Woman: Records of the Pioneer Women in Palestine*—recounts, she viewed this farm as one of many redemptive instruments initiated by the Labor Zionists. While crusading for equality—and refusing to settle for second-class status—she articulated the pioneers' faith that their hard work would create a Jewish state inspiring the world.

Yitzhak Ben-Zvi served as Israel's second president from 1952 to 1963. In those years and until her death in 1979, Rahel Yanait Ben-Zvi continued to embody the pioneers' idealism—and to celebrate the heritage of the *Mizrahi* Jews (Jews descended from Middle Eastern communities), the beauties of Jerusalem, and the importance of the new generations of Israelis walking the Land of Israel and loving it just as passionately as the founding generation.

The Plough Woman (1931)

The Meshek HaPolalot has a distinct purpose: to prepare the woman worker for the general *meshek* [farm settlement]. But at first it had an additional purpose: it was a larger school of life. There was an educational value in the dividing up of the work, the sharing of responsibility and the adaptation of the individual to the group life. The *meshek* had to take up all its economic problems. In such surroundings the character of the *haverah* [comrade] set firm; she developed the necessary independence and initiative. We were amazed sometimes to see the difference which one year made in a woman. Helpless at first, she was at the end of this period an intelligent cooperator, participating in the management and showing a thorough understanding of the complicated economic and administrative problems of the settlement.

Work in the settlement was a joy. Steeped as we were in our labors, the hours of the long day slipped by uncounted and unnoticed. But the purest and most supreme joy was in the tree nurseries—our pioneer contribution to the country. . . .

With our own hands we raised, on our soil, tens and hundreds of thousands of shoots, and a kind of bond was created between our fruitful little corners and the wild, bare hills around us. We were participating in the great task of re-afforesting the country. . . .

[Still,] in no form of Palestinian life does the woman play her proper role economically, culturally, and spiritually. The road that lies before the women in *Eretz Yisra'el* is still a long one, but its direction already seems to be clear: however strong our desire to broaden the basis of woman's life in village and town, so as to make it all-inclusive, the directive principle is and must remain, for the women worker's movement, agricultural.

3

Pioneers

Revisionist Zionism

Treating Revisionist Zionism simply as a reaction to the moderation of Political Zionism and the leftism of Labor Zionism is like considering the winter merely the absence of the heat of summer and the colors of fall. Shaped by the fertile, farseeing, flamboyant mind of Vladimir Ze'ev Jabotinsky, honed—and sometimes distorted—by his followers, Revisionist Zionism fully envisioned who the New Jew should be and what the Jewish state should and should not do.

Beyond demanding a more aggressive state-building timetable, Revisionist Zionism juggled individual rights with communal needs, while synthesizing Jewish tradition and Western liberalism. Jabotinsky and his followers tempered a strong nationalist impulse with a commitment to individual dignity and free enterprise they felt their socialist rivals lacked. Similarly, the modernist, rationalist Jabotinsky nevertheless shared the mystical faith of Ahad Ha'am, A. D. Gordon, and Abraham Yitzhak Kook in the Jewish nation's creative power when returning to its homeland.

Tragically, the fight over establishing the state, along with the hostility of their triumphal Labor rivals, embittered many Revisionists. In 1947 when David Ben-Gurion accepted the United Nations Partition Plan, settling for his "half a loaf," this pragmatism negated the Revisionists' both-sides-of-the-Jordan-River territorial maximalism, leaving many ideologues demoralized. Moreover, their rage at Ben-Gurion's heavy-handed tactics led many Revisionists to feel they were in internal exile, even as the millennial dreams of reestablishing a Jewish state came true.

Finally, some purists among them, celebrating the "Hebrew" dimension of the national character—or the naturalistic "Canaanite" character of the return to the land—rejected a defining tenet of Zionism: that the Jews were one people, whether they lived in the Promised Land or in the Diaspora.

The Union of Zionists-Revisionists (1925)

The aim of Zionism is the creation of a Jewish commonwealth that is, above all, a Jewish majority in Palestine.

Revisionist Zionism is remembered as reactive because it began in 1925 in rebellion against the moderate Zionist leadership of the Anglophile Chaim Weizmann. It resulted, a decade later, in a formal withdrawal from the Zionist Organization and the launching of the NZO, the New Zionist Organization. The 1925 Declaration of the Zionists-Revisionists—forged in frustration after the Fourteenth Zionist Congress in Vienna—shows that the Revisionists disdained the mainstream movement's passivity, servility, and "complete bankruptcy of ideas." Beyond this, Revisionists like Julius Brutzkus blasted Socialist Zionism for romanticizing settlement, leading the movement down an "agrarian blind alley." Joseph Schechtman and other Revisionists mocked the Cultural Zionists' cultural and spiritual fetishism as neglecting pressing Jewish needs.

The Zionist-Revisionists also had particular aims: a Jewish majority in Palestine, more support from British Colonial authorities, Jewish settlement on both sides of the Jordan, more effective self-defense, and a faith in what they called "Hebraism."

Declaration of the Central Committee of the Union of Zionists-Revisionists (Paris, November 1925)

The Fourteenth Congress brought out two points in the present state of Zionism: on the one hand an expansion and deepening of the movement resulting from the growing desire of the Jewish masses to emigrate to Palestine, and on the other a great decline of the Zionist Organization, a weakening of its spiritual foundation, and a complete bankruptcy of ideas on the part of the leadership. . . .

For the last four years both the tactics and the principles of the official leaders of the Zionist Organization have mainly expressed themselves in denial of the aims and methods of political Zionism, servile passiveness where there should have been a worthy stand against the infringement of our rights, worship of finance presented as the chief factor in the nation's reconstruction, the minimizing of national consciousness, a cringing before England as if she had given us a refuge out of compassion, and before the Jewish plutocracy as if the deliverance of our people depended on them.

Against this doctrine which was born in the old ghetto and leads to a new ghetto, Revisionism sets up an entirely different conception. *The aim of Zionism is the creation of a Jewish commonwealth that is, above all, a Jewish majority in Palestine....*

Our relations with Great Britain should be, and, in our own view, could be based on a foundation of mutual loyalty.... There is no question here of charity or alms; it is a case of mutual obligations and mutual benefits. And if the activity or the inactivity of the British Administration in Palestine prove harmful to us, our fight against it is justified, and we are firmly convinced that by our struggle for a full-blooded policy of transforming Palestine into the Land of Israel we render a great service also to British interests in the East....

The struggle for the consolidation of our political achievement is at the same time an indispensable preliminary condition for the consolidation of our economic position in Palestine: for the inclusion of Transjordan within the frontiers of Palestine and the area of Jewish settlement... and an effective defense of the *Yishuv* and of its productive work....

We want to have law and order in Palestine. But to ensure this law and order there must be a special body which has the necessary authority and power....

In the Palestine of the future, under the aegis of a Jewish majority, its various peoples, we trust, will co-operate peacefully on the basis of equality of rights and mutual respect. Moreover, we consider the economic welfare of the non-Jewish population one of the fundamental conditions for the welfare of the country. This determines our attitude towards the Arabs in Palestine. We want peace, friendly and neighborly relations. But in the main question of our right to the gradual transformation of Palestine into the Land of Israel, there can be no concessions....

Ze'ev Jabotinsky (1880–1940)

The aim of Betar is very simple though difficult: to create a "normal," "healthy" citizen for the Jewish nation.

While no man in Zionism's history except Herzl was as adored by his disciples, few Zionists were hated as intensely as Vladimir Ze'ev Jabotinsky. His followers rallied to him as the Garibaldi of the Jewish revolution; his foes reviled him as its would-be Mussolini. Obviously, he was an extraordinary man.

Jabotinsky was born in Odessa when it flourished as the great center of Jewish life on the Black Sea. Nevertheless, his generation was raised much more on Russian than on Jewish culture. He became an active Zionist in 1903, when he helped organize a Jewish self-defense corps in Odessa against a threatening pogrom. Already a great orator, he put this talent, as well as his pen, to the use of Zionist propaganda thereafter. A working journalist, he traveled widely all over Russia and Europe before 1914.

Jabotinsky concluded that Zionism could mean only a bold, Herzlian political struggle for a state. He rejected the Zionist establishment's assumption that either the Turks, who then ruled Palestine, or the Arabs would accept Zionism any more easily if it de-emphasized its final aims or even abandoned them. In his view, colonization depended on political achievements—and, therefore, ultimately on power.

When the First World War began, Jabotinsky roved around Europe as a correspondent for a liberal Moscow daily. Once Turkey joined Germany in battle in October 1914, Jabotinsky decided the future of Jewish aspirations in Palestine rested with the Allies. Almost single-handedly, he won British consent to the formation of three Jewish battalions, the first of which, the 38th Fusiliers, fought with General Edmund Allenby in the 1918 Palestine campaign.

After the war, Jabotinsky was the least hopeful of all the Zionists that the British would provide real support or smooth relations with the Arabs during the expected period of mass immigration. During the Arab riots of 1920, he organized a self-defense corps in Jerusalem. The British military administration sentenced him to fifteen years for illegal possession of arms—instigating a storm. He was soon pardoned and the conviction subsequently revoked.

Jabotinsky's reputation was now at its height. He was elected to the Zionist Executive in 1921, but he and Chaim Weizmann clashed. Jabotinsky believed in rapid mass immigration to Palestine and in mobilizing Jewish military and police units; Weizmann called for careful colonization and trusted the British. Within two years Jabotinsky resigned, charging that his colleagues' policies would result in the loss of Palestine.

Jabotinsky returned to Zionist work in 1925, when he organized a new Zionist party, the Revisionists. "The aim of Zionism is a Jewish state," he proclaimed after touring the Baltics in 1924. "The territory—both sides of the Jordan. The system—mass colonization. The solution of the financial problem—a national loan. These four principles cannot be realized without international sanction. Hence the commandment of the hour—a new political campaign and the militarization of Jewish youth in *Eretz Yisra'el* and the Diaspora."

His group left the movement in 1935 to found the New Zionist Organization. Groups under his influence oversaw illegal Jewish immigration into Palestine during the 1930s as well as direct action by the Irgun (Zionist paramilitary organization) against the British—all conducted with special daring and elan.

Jabotinsky's vision was detailed and compelling. In founding the youth movement Betar, he championed the New Jew, proud of a rich past but ready for current challenges. In testifying before the British Royal Commission on Palestine of 1937, known also as the Peel Commission, he justified the birth of a new state. And in his famous, still-controversial essay, "The Iron Wall," he demonstrated a realistic respect for Arab nationalism without apologizing for his assertive Jewish nationalism.

The Fundamentals of the Betarian World Outlook (1934)

1. The mission of Betar: The duty and aim of Betar is very simple though difficult: to create that type of Jew which the nation needs in

order to better and quicker build a Jewish state. In other words, to create a "normal," "healthy" citizen for the Jewish nation. The greatest difficulty is encountered because, as a nation, the Jews today are neither "normal" nor "healthy" and life in Diaspora affects the intelligent upbringing of normal and healthy citizens. . . .

2. The Jewish state: The basis of the Betarian viewpoint consists of one idea: the Jewish state. In this simple idea however, lies a deep meaning indeed. What do the nations of the world symbolize? They symbolize that every nation must contribute its own share to the common culture of humanity, a share which is distinguished by its own specific spirit. . . . For this purpose, every nation must possess its own "laboratory," a country wherein the nation alone is master and can freely suit the common life in accordance with its own conception of good and evil. . . .

3. The Jewish majority in *Eretz Yisra'el:* What then is, practically speaking, a Jewish "State"? When can it truly be said that our country has ceased to be "Palestine" and become *Eretz Yisra'el?* Only then, when there will be more Jews than non-Jews; for the first condition of a national state is national majority. . . .

After attaining a majority in Palestine and being enabled to govern upon broad democratic principles, we will have before us even a more important task: *Shivat Tzion* (the return to Zion). By this we mean the creation of such conditions which would enable every Jew who is unwilling or unable to live in the Diaspora to settle in the Jewish state and earn a livelihood there. . . .

Afterward will come probably the most important task of all: to make *Eretz Yisra'el* the leading state of the civilized world, a country the customs and laws of which are to be followed by the whole universe. . . .

4. The Hebrew language: Betar recognizes Hebrew as the only and eternal language of the Jewish people. In Palestine it must become the only language in all phases of life; in the Diaspora it must, at least, be the language of the Jewish educational system, starting with the kindergarten and ending with high school (later on perhaps college too, if we shall ever have Jewish universities in the Diaspora). . . .

5. *HadNess:* . . . This is the one fundamental which distinguishes Betar from all other Zionist Youth movements. The latter have the characteristic

tendency to "coordinate" two ideals like Zionism and socialism serving both simultaneously. As a result, there is a confusion which renders impossible a clear-cut relationship toward Zionism and the Jewish state. . . .

This admixture of various ideals which Betar absolutely rejects we may call biblically, "*schaatnez*" [the prohibition against mixing wool and linen]. . . . The euphonistic stand of Betar may be termed in Hebrew "*HadNess*" (one banner). . . . Everything which disturbs the upbuilding of the Jewish state, whether in connection with private interests or with a group or class must, without preconditions, bow to the one banner, to the command of the highest, the supreme ideal: to the Jewish state. . . .

6. Class struggle: Especially distinct is the difference between Betar and other youth organizations regarding the idea of class struggle in Palestine. . . . In Palestine, higher and mightier than class interests, the common interest of rebuilding the Jewish state rules supreme. . . .

7. The Legion: The Betari is steadfast concerning Legionism: it demands of its members as well of the Jewish youth generally that they fully train in the technique of utilizing firearms, and that they be in readiness always to answer personally the call of self-defense or, time being opportune, of a new Jewish army. The Betari holds that a pioneer who did not prepare himself for this task is useless and unsuitable for Palestine and "*Hachsharat haGarin*" (military training) is the first and most important of all other requisites. . . .

9. *Hadar Betari*: *Hadar* is a Hebrew word which hardly is at all translatable into another language: It combines various conceptions such as outward beauty, respect, self-esteem, politeness, faithfulness. The only suitable "translation" into the language of real life must be the Betari—in all dealings, actions, speech and thought. Naturally, we are all as yet removed from such a state of things, and in one generation cannot be achieved. Nevertheless, *Hadar Betar* must be the daily goal of each one of us: our every step, gesture, word, action and thought must always be strictly executed from the *Hadar* viewpoint. . . .

Hadar consists of a thousand trifles which collectively form everyday life. . . .

More important is moral *Hadar*. You must be generous, if no question of principle is involved. Do not bargain about trivialities, you, rather should give something instead of exacting it from somebody else. Every word of yours must be a "word of honor," and the latter is mightier that steel. A time must eventually arrive when a Jew desiring to express his highest appreciation of human honesty, courtesy, and esteem will not say, as now: "He is a real gentleman!" but "He is a real Betari!"

Evidence Submitted to the Palestine Royal Commission (House of Lords, February 11, 1937)

The cause of our suffering is the very fact of the Diaspora, the bedrock fact that we are everywhere a minority. It is not the antisemitism of men; it is, above all, the antisemitism of things, the inherent xenophobia of the body social or the body economic under which we suffer. . . .

I want you to realize this: The phenomenon called Zionism may include all kinds of dreams—a "model community," Hebrew culture, perhaps even a second edition of the Bible—but all this longing for wonderful toys of velvet and silver is nothing in comparison with that tangible momentum of irresistible distress and need by which we are propelled and borne.

We are not free agents. We cannot "concede" anything. Whenever I hear the Zionist, most often my own Party, accused of asking for too much— Gentlemen, I really cannot understand it. Yes, we do want a State; every nation on earth, every normal nation, beginning with the smallest and the humblest who do not claim any merit, any role in humanity's development, they all have States of their own. That is the normal condition for a people. Yet, when we, the most abnormal of peoples and therefore the most unfortunate, ask only for the same condition as the Albanians enjoy, to say nothing of the French and the English, then it is called too much. I should understand it if the answer were, "It is impossible," but when the answer is, "It is too much," I cannot understand it. I would remind you (excuse me for quoting an example known to every one of you) of the commotion which was produced in that famous institution when Oliver Twist came and asked for "more." He said "more" because he did not know how to express it; what Oliver Twist really meant was this: "Will you just give me that normal portion which is necessary for a boy of my age to be able to live."

I assure you that you face here today, in the Jewish people with its demands, an Oliver Twist who has, unfortunately, no concessions to make. What can be the concessions? We have got to save millions, many millions. I do not know whether it is a question of rehousing one-third of the Jewish race, half of the Jewish race, or a quarter of the Jewish race; I do not know; but it is a question of millions. Certainly the way out is to evacuate those portions of the Diaspora which have become no good, which hold no promise of any possibility of a livelihood, and to concentrate all those refugees in some place which should not be Diaspora, not a repetition of the position where the Jews are an unabsorbed minority within a foreign social, or economic, or political organism. Naturally, if that process of evacuation is allowed to develop, as it ought to be allowed to develop, there will very soon be reached a moment when the Jews will become a majority in Palestine.

I am going to make a "terrible" confession. Our demand for a Jewish majority is not our maximum—it is our minimum. . . .

I have the profoundest feeling for the Arab case, in so far as that Arab case is not exaggerated. This Commission have already been able to make up their minds as to whether there is any individual hardship to the Arabs of Palestine as men, deriving from the Jewish colonization. We maintain unanimously that the economic position of the Palestinian Arabs, under the Jewish colonization and owing to the Jewish colonization, has become the object of envy in all the surrounding Arab countries, so that the Arabs from those countries show a clear tendency to immigrate into Palestine. I have also shown to you already that, in our submission, there is no question of ousting the Arabs. On the contrary, the idea is that Palestine on both sides of the Jordan should hold the Arabs, their progeny, and many millions of Jews. What I do not deny is that in that process the Arabs of Palestine will necessarily become a minority in the country of Palestine.

What I do deny is that that is a hardship. It is not a hardship on any race, any nation, possessing so many National States now and so many more National States in the future. One fraction, one branch of that race, and not a big one, will have to live in someone else's State. . . .

There is only one way of compromise. Tell the Arabs the truth, and then you will see the Arab is reasonable, the Arab is clever, the Arab is just; the Arab can realize that since there are three or four or five wholly Arab States, then it is a thing of justice which Great Britain is doing if Palestine is transformed into a Jewish state. Then there will be a change of mind among the Arabs, then there will be room for compromise, and there will be peace.

The Iron Wall (*Jewish Herald,* November 26, 1937 [original 1923])

The author of these lines is considered to be an enemy of the Arabs, a proponent of their expulsion, etc. This is not true. My emotional relationship to the Arabs is the same as it is to all other peoples—polite indifference. My political relationship is characterized by two principles. First: the expulsion of the Arabs from Palestine is absolutely impossible in any form. There will always be two nations in Palestine—which is good enough for me, provided the Jews become the majority. Second: I am proud to have been a member of that group which formulated the Helsingfors Program [in 1906]. We formulated it, not only for Jews, but for all peoples, and its basis is the equality of all nations. I am prepared to swear, for us and our descendants, that we will never destroy this equality and we will never attempt to expel or oppress the Arabs. Our credo, as the reader can see, is completely peaceful. But it is absolutely another matter if it will be possible to achieve our peaceful aims through peaceful means. This depends, not on our relationship with the Arabs, but exclusively on the Arabs' relationship to Zionism. . . .

Individual Arabs may perhaps be bought off, but this hardly means that all the Arabs in *Eretz Yisra'el* are willing to sell a patriotism that not even Papuans will trade. Every indigenous people will resist alien settlers as long as they see any hope of ridding themselves of the danger of foreign settlement. That is what the Arabs in Palestine are doing, and what they will persist in doing as long as there remains a solitary spark of hope that they will be able to prevent the transformation of "Palestine" into the "Land of Israel." . . .

This colonization can, therefore, continue and develop only under the protection of a force independent of the local population—an iron wall which the native population cannot break through. This is, in toto, our policy towards the Arabs. To formulate it any other way would only be hypocrisy. . . .

In the first place, if anyone objects that this point of view is immoral, I answer: It is not true; either Zionism is moral and just or it is immoral and unjust. But that is a question that we should have settled before we became Zionists. Actually we have settled that question, and in the affirmative. We hold that Zionism is moral and just. And since it is moral and just, justice must be done. . . .

All this does not mean that any kind of agreement is impossible, only a voluntary agreement is impossible. As long as there is a spark of hope that they can get rid of us, they will not sell these hopes, not for any kind of sweet words or tasty morsels, because they are not a rabble but a nation, perhaps somewhat tattered, but still living. A living people makes such enormous concessions on such fateful questions only when there is no hope left. Only when not a single breach is visible in the iron wall, only then do extreme groups lose their sway, and influence transfers to moderate groups. Only then would these moderate groups come to us with proposals for mutual concessions. And only then will moderates offer suggestions for compromise on practical questions like a guarantee against expulsion, or equality and national autonomy.

I am optimistic that they will indeed be granted satisfactory assurances and that both peoples, like good neighbors, can then live in peace. But the only path to such an agreement is the iron wall, that is to say the strengthening in Palestine of a government without any kind of Arab influence, that is to say one against which the Arabs will fight. In other words, for us the only path to an agreement in the future is an absolute refusal of any attempts at an agreement now.

Saul Tchernichovsky (1875–1943)

All of Israel is sainted, you are the Maccabee!

Saul Tchernichovsky was a poet and a doctor—a Zionist Chekhov!— who embodied many of the qualities Jabotinsky sought in an ideal Betari. A passionate nationalist and a classicist, Tchernichovsky was an elegant translator who rendered in Hebrew many of the West's greatest works, from Homer to Shakespeare. He was also a passionate naturalist, loving the land, which associated him with the nationalistic Canaanite movement of the 1940s. Believing that much of the Middle East had been a Hebrew-speaking civilization in antiquity, the Canaanites worked to revive it. The "Hebrew" nation they envisioned would also welcome the Middle East's Arab population.

But, as the two poems that follow demonstrate, Tchernichovsky loved all the Jewish people. Thus, unlike Yonatan Ratosh and other Canaanites who repudiated Jews in the Diaspora as not belonging to the same people, Tchernichovsky remained within the Zionist camp. Some European Jews sang his famous poem "I Believe," better known by its first two words, "*Sachki, Sachki,*" on their way to the gas chambers. Others now propose that song as an alternative national anthem to "Hatikvah." The faith in national redemption to redeem individuals and humanity captures liberal nationalism at its best, just as his poem, "They Say There's a Land," guides the reader elegantly from the universal to the particulars of the Jewish people's homeland.

Born in present-day Ukraine in 1875, trained in medicine at Heidelberg and Lausanne, Tchernichovsky arrived in Palestine in 1931. A member of the Committee of the Hebrew Language who helped develop a modern medical vocabulary in the Holy Language, Tchernichovsky was a beloved doctor in Tel Aviv. He died suddenly in 1943.

I Believe (1892)

Laugh, laugh, at my dreams,
I the dreamer now speak.
Laugh—while knowing I still believe in humanity,
Because I still believe in you.
Because my soul still thirsts for freedom
I haven't sold out for a golden calf.
Because I will still believe in humanity,
In its spirit, its powerful, empowerment.

That spirit will pulverize binding chains
It will raise us up, with heads held high
No worker will die of hunger
Souls will be nourished with freedom, the poor people with bread.
Laugh, but know I also believe in friendship
I'll believe—I will still find a heart
A heart of my hopes, and of another's hopes,
That will feel joy, and understand anguish.
I will also believe in the future
Even if redemption day seems far away
But when it does come, it will bring peace
And a blessing from nation to nation.
Then, my people will also flourish
And in the land a new generation will arise
One that shakes off its iron shackles.
And eye after eye will see light.
It will live, love, work, prosper
A generation living in its land.
Not in the future, not in heaven—
And its spirit shall be eternal.
And then a poet shall sing a new song
With a heart pulsing full of profound beauty
To him, the young one, hovering above my grave,
As flowers blossom into a wreath.

They Say There's a Land (1923)

They say: There is a land, a land drenched with sun.
Wherefore is that land? Where is that sun?
They say: There is a land, its pillars are seven, seven planets,
    blossoming on every hill.
Where is that land, the stars of that hill?
Who shall guide our way, tell me my path?

Already have we passed several deserts and oceans,
Already have we crossed several, our strengths are waning.
How did we err? That we have not been left alone yet?
That same land of sun, that one we have not found.
A land which will fulfill what every individual hoped for,
Everyone who enters, had encountered Akiva.
Peace to you, Akiva! Peace to you, The Rabbi! Where are the saints?
Where is the Maccabee?
Akiva answers; the Rabbi answers: All of Israel is holy, you are
the Maccabee!

The Irgun (1939)

**Our right to a Jewish state is not only an historical and human
right. . . . We are prepared to back it with military force.**

The tensions over economics, politics, and ideology within the Zionist Movement eventually boiled over into fights over military tactics and strategy. Following the Arab riots of 1929, some of those active in defending the Jews of Jerusalem became frustrated, perceiving that Jewish passivity and dependence upon British protection was encouraging Arab terrorism. In 1931 they broke off from the Haganah, the main Zionist self-defense organization, and founded the Irgun Zvai Leumi (IZ"L), the National Military Organization. Although many of the founders eventually returned to the Haganah, the IZ"L became the Revisionists' army.

In 1939 with war in Europe looming, oppression of Jews intensifying, and the British White Paper limiting Jewish immigration to Palestine, the Irgun was fighting both the British and the Arabs. The following proclamation, issued three months before Germany invaded Poland, captures the overall vision that would define the Irgun during the war years and in the fight for independence. The Irgun did stop fighting the British when World War II formally erupted.

Proclamation of the Irgun Zvai Leumi (June 1939)

1. The historical fact is that the reclaiming of a homeland, independence and liberty of an oppressed nation never succeeds without the support of an adequate military force ready to stand up to threat and challenge.

2. The troubles in Palestine of 1920, 1921, and 1929 have proved conclusively that the Arabs use armed violence as a recurrent means to obstruct the establishment of the Jewish state, and that the passive attitude of the Jews in face of this violence is only encouraging Arab terrorists to continue.

3. We cannot depend on the Mandatory Power to check Arab violence and keep Palestine in a state of peace, which is the preliminary condition of the development of a Jewish state. The British Administration in Palestine is outspokenly anti-Zionist and anti-Jewish. . . .

4. Assuming even that we are free from British hostility in Palestine, it is essential in the present state of world affairs, that we prove to the world that our right to a Jewish state is not only an historical and human right but that we are ready and prepared to back it with military force, rather than relying on British bayonets.

5. In the event of war Palestine will be a most precious strategical point in the Near East, of the greatest concern to the Western European Democracies. . . . Purely rational and sentimental claims of Jewry to Palestine will be even less respected by Great Britain in case of war than they are in times of peace. Only as an armed force of sufficient strength to assure the defense of Palestine shall we be able to attain a bargaining position which will induce Britain to agree to the creation of the Jewish state. . . .

Since the publication of the White Paper in the beginning of May 1939, the Organization is engaged in active resistance against Britain and the Arabs with the aim to defy the new Ukases. . . . For us it is a battle for death or life. . . .

It is a God-given right of the Jews to return to Palestine as free men to their fatherland. This right dates from times immemorial and was again asserted, in modern times, by the whole civilized world, in the Mandate for Palestine. Britain's action in closing the doors of Palestine for persecuted Jews is an act of black treason against a people with its back to the wall, as well as a cynical repudiation of a solemn international obligation. . . .

If England is not willing to help us, notwithstanding her solemn obligation to do so, the Jews will fight for their rights without England's help. . . .

To the defeatists among us we say: Thanks for the lesson of "pacifism at any price." You have brought us to where we are now. But tens of thousands of Jewish youth, young sturdy men with a desire to live like free men, are being organized and well trained: they are being prepared for the decisive battle that will be fought in Palestine and which will decide the fate of our people and country. We have learned the lesson of Round Table conferences based on the ideas of begging for justice and going unheeded, but tens of thousands, only the beginning, have not forgotten that theirs was a nation of warriors, and like the Maccabees are ready to fight in order to reconquer the Land of Israel for Israel and their children. They are ready to fight as the English, French, or Americans would have done in case their country were to be under enemy yoke, and as the Czechs are preparing to do now. . . .

Avraham (Yair) Stern (1907–42)

There is no sovereignty without the redemption of the land, and there is no national revival without sovereignty.

Jabotinsky's decision to declare a truce with England to fight Hitler split the Irgun. The charismatic classicist, poet, and militarist Avraham Stern led a breakaway faction eventually called Lechi, Lochamei Herut Yisra'el, the Freedom Fighters of Israel. Critics, however, disparaged the group as zealots and called them "The Stern Gang."

Born in Poland in 1907, Stern, whose nom de guerre was Yair, arrived in Israel in 1925 and defended Jewish Jerusalem during the 1929 riots. In 1933 he turned from studying the Greek and Roman classics to fighting full time for his homeland.

Stern had written an anthem for the Irgun—"Unknown Soldiers"— that reflected the ferocity of a generation of fighters ready to die but hoping to live as free Jews in their homeland. It became the Lechi anthem after the split. As the fight against the British intensified, Stern's words rang louder, as the Jewish warriors sang: "In days red with slaughter, destruction and blood, Nights black with pain and despair, Over village and town our flag we'll unfurl, Love and freedom the message 'twill bear. . . . And if we must die our people to free, We are willing our lives to surrender."

Stern also articulated eighteen principles to guide Lechi.

On February 12, 1942, two years after Lechi's founding, British soldiers raided Stern's hideout and killed him.

Eighteen Principles of Rebirth (1940)

1. The Nation: The Jewish people is a covenanted people, the originator of monotheism, formulator of the prophetic teachings, standard bearer of human culture, guardian of glorious patrimony. The Jewish people is schooled in self-sacrifice and suffering; its vision, survivability, and faith in redemption are indestructible.

2. The Homeland: The homeland in the Land of Israel within the borders delineated in the Bible ("To your descendants, I shall give this land, from the River of Egypt to the great Euphrates River." Genesis 15:18) This is the land of the living, where the entire nation shall live in safety.

3. The Nation and Its Land: Israel conquered the land with the sword. There it became a great nation and only there it will be reborn. Hence Israel alone has a right to that land. This is an absolute right. It has never expired and never will.

4. The Goals: 1. Redemption of the land. 2. Establishment of sovereignty. 3. Revival of the nation. There is no sovereignty without the redemption of the land, and there is no national revival without sovereignty. These are the goals of the organization during the period of war and conquest.

5. Education: Educate the nation to love freedom and zealously guard Israel's eternal patrimony. Inculcate the idea that the nation is master to its own fate. Revive the doctrine that "The sword and the book came bound together from heaven" (Midrash Vayikra Rabbah 35:8).

6. Unity: The unification of the entire nation around the banner of the Hebrew freedom movement. The use of the genius, status, and resources of individuals, and the channeling of the energy, devotion, and revolutionary fervor of the masses for the war of liberation.

7. Pacts: Make pacts with all those who are willing to help the struggle of the organization and provide direct support.

8. Force: Consolidate and increase the fighting force in the homeland and in the Diaspora, in the underground and in the barracks, to become the Hebrew army of liberation with its flag, arms, and commanders.

9. War: Constant war against those who stand in the way of fulfilling the goals.

10. Conquest: The conquest of the homeland from foreign rule and its eternal possession. These are the tasks of the movement during the period of sovereignty and redemption.

11. Sovereignty: Renewal of Hebrew sovereignty over the redeemed land.

12. Rule of Justice: The establishment of a social order in the spirit of Jewish morality and prophetic justice. Under such an order no one will go hungry or unemployed. All will live in harmony, mutual respect, and friendship as an example to the world.

13. Reviving the Wilderness: Build the ruins and revive the wilderness for mass immigration and population increase.

14. Aliens: Solve the problem of alien population by exchange of population.

15. Ingathering of the Exiles: Total ingathering of the exiles to their sovereign state.

16. Power: The Hebrew nation shall become a first-rate military, political, cultural, and economical entity in the Middle East and around the Mediterranean Sea.

17. Revival: The revival of the Hebrew language as a spoken language by the entire nation, the renewal of the historical and spiritual might of Israel. The purification of the national character in the fire of revival.

18. The Temple: The building of the Third Temple as a symbol of the new era of total redemption.

Haim Hazaz (1898–1973)

A people that does not live in its own land
and control its own fate has no history.

If David Ben-Gurion taught Zionists the importance of surviving, no
matter what the price, Haim Hazaz chronicled the psychic cost of that
survival. Zionists learned in the twentieth century just how mild the
ugly nineteenth-century antisemitism that originally triggered their
movement was compared to the horrors of Auschwitz. The scale of
the Holocaust was so unfathomable, the assault on body and soul so
complete, perhaps only a great novelist could capture the despair it
engendered. Haim Hazaz insightfully described the philosophical
challenge Jew hatred posed to the Jewish people, and the emotional
challenge its resulting crimes posed to individual Jews.

Born in 1898 in Siderovitchi, in the region of Kiev, Hazaz grew up in
the Ukrainian countryside. After fearing the chaos of the Russian Revolution and suffering the loneliness of the exiled writer in Istanbul, Paris,
and Berlin, Hazaz arrived in Palestine in 1930. Displaying dazzling range,
Hazaz rendered the exotic world of Yemenite Jews living in Jerusalem
as vividly as the more familiar universe of Eastern European Jewry. His
only son, Nahum Zuzik Hazaz, a twenty-year-old artist and writer, died
in an attack on Mount Scopus during the 1948 war. Zuzik's mother, the
poetess Yocheved Bat-Miriam, never wrote another poem again.

Hazaz's most famous work, *HaDerisha*, flirts with the nihilism of
Jewish history and of Zionism amid the profound hatred Jews endured.
The protagonist, Yudka, translated as "Little Judah" or "Jew," sees Zionism and Israel as such a break with the passivity of *galut* suffering, he
fears a mass vertigo will result.

Hazaz's story was written in 1942, when word of the Holocaust was
just emerging, revealing a surprising sensitivity to the Hitlerian evil
that not everyone shared. The ideological struggles Yudka posed, won-
dering about the fallowness and perversity of Diaspora life as well as
the novelty and confusion of Israel, anticipated much of the Zionist
agenda in the ensuing decades.

The Sermon (1942)

"You already know," Yudka began, coughing an uncertain apology in his throat, "that I object to Jewish history. Have a little patience with me and I'll explain why.... In the first place, I must say that we really don't have a history at all. That's a fact. And that's also ... how shall I put it? ... in a word, that's where the skeleton tumbles out of the closet. You see, we never made our own history, the Gentiles always made it for us. Just as they turned out the light for us and lit the stove for us and milked the cow for us on the Sabbath, so they made history for us the way they wanted and we took it whether we liked it or not. But it wasn't ours, it wasn't ours at all! ...

"You see, it isn't just that we accept our suffering. It's that we love our suffering, all suffering ... we actually want to suffer, we long for it ... we can't do without it. Suffering is what protects and preserves us ... without it we'd have nothing to live for. Have you ever heard of a group of Jews that didn't suffer? I never have. A Jew who didn't suffer would be a freak of nature, half a Gentile, not a Jew at all ... which is why I say that such heroism has been our greatest vice. Suffering, suffering, and more suffering! Everything wallows around it ... not in it, mind you, but around it. There's an enormous difference there. Yes, everything wallows around it: Jewish history, Jewish life, Jewish manners, Jewish literature, Jewish culture, Jewish folksong ... Jews taken singly and Jews taken en masse ... everything! ...

"This much is clear: Zionism is not a continuation of a cure for a disease. That's nonsense! It's an act of destruction, a negation of what's come before, an end ... I believe that what we have in Palestine today is no longer Judaism already, to say nothing of what we will have in the future. After all, we haven't begun to see the end of it. I'm talking about Zionism's inner essence, its hidden power—yes, I am....

"Well, it's known that Jews in this country are ashamed to speak Yiddish, as though it were somehow a disgrace. They don't hate it, they're not afraid of it, they don't refuse to speak it, they're simply ashamed. But Hebrew ... and oddly enough, with a Sephardic accent, which is foreign to most of them ... that they speak with their heads held high, with a kind of self-esteem, even though it's much harder for them than Yiddish and has none of this liveliness, none of the juiciness, none of the fresh, spontaneous earthiness that Yiddish has. What is behind this? Can it be that they prefer to make life more difficult for themselves, just like that? No, it's very simple: Hebrew is not a continuation, it's different, it's a case in itself, there's practically nothing Jewish about it. . . . The main thing is that it sounds different, not Jewish, so that they can feel proud of it. . . .

"I'm finishing: in a nutshell, the purpose. A different people, one above all that makes its own history by and for itself, rather than having it made for it by others. . . . A real history, that is, and not some communal ledger in the archives . . . that's what it's all about! Because a people that does not live in its own land and control its own fate has no history. . . ."

4

Pioneers

Religious Zionism

Although many Zionists rejected rabbinic authority and strictures, the Zionist movement was deeply, quintessentially Jewish. Religious Jews had been building a case for a Jewish return to the homeland long before Theodor Herzl in the 1890s—or Moses Hess in the 1860s. Religious Zionists sought heavenly redemption and national redemption. Among the early leading Religious Zionists, some paralleled the emerging Zionist conversation yet remained distant; others worked within the Zionist movement itself.

Whereas most major secular Zionist ideologues hailed from Europe, some of the most passionate, naturalistic expressions of Religious Zionism came from Jews living in the East. These Jews were of Sephardic, Spanish heritage or of Eastern, *Mizrahi* heritage, rooted in the Arab or Persian worlds. They were "born Zionist." Living in Arab countries that mostly resisted European Enlightenment, many more were "born" nationalist and religious, with fewer of the ideological gymnastics that divided Europe's Ashkenazic Jews.

Abraham Yitzhak Kook, a Torah scholar respected East and West, became the great matchmaker between religion and Zionism. Accepting the Zionist idea if not the Zionist movement, he articulated the religious yearning for a revitalized homeland. He shared a cosmic love of the land with secular thinkers like A. D. Gordon and longed for national liberation with the secular Zionist pioneers. Despite the pioneers' rebellion against religious ritual, Kook blessed them for redeeming the land and the Jewish people. "That which is holy will become renewed and that which is new will become holy," he said. Visiting the settlement of Poriah in 1913, Kook told a Jewish watchman wearing a Bedouin robe: "Let's exchange. I'll take your 'rabbinical cloak,' and you'll take mine." Modeling Jewish unity at its best, Kook proclaimed: "I wore your clothes, and you wore mine. So it should also be on the *inside*—together in our hearts!"

Kook's synthesis helped Religious Zionists embrace these revolutionaries while helping the rebels embrace the traditionalist continuities that gave the Zionist movement legitimacy, focus, and gravitas.

Kook died in 1935. Although he lacked an army of followers when he was alive, his words still shape Religious Zionism.

Yehudah Alkalai (1798–1878)

We, as a people, are properly called Israel only in the Land of Israel.

Yehudah Alkalai was born in 1798 in Sarajevo. He spent his boyhood in Jerusalem. In 1825 he was called to serve as rabbi in Semlin, the capital of Serbia. Not far away, the Greeks had recently won their national war of independence, and the other nationalities of the Balkans, including the Serbs among whom he lived, were each beginning to rise against their Turkish overlord. Hence ideas of national freedom and restoration came easily to Alkalai.

The turning point in Alkalai's life happened in 1840. The Jews of Damascus faced the Blood Accusation, the resurrected Medieval libel that they had slaughtered a gentile and used his blood to prepare unleavened bread for Passover. Alkalai became convinced that for security and freedom the Jewish people must look to a life of its own within its ancestral home.

After 1840 books and pamphlets pouring from Alkalai's pen explained his program of self-redemption. Much of his pleading addressed Jewish notables like the English financier Moses Montefiore and the French politician Adolph Cremieux. Alkalai's schemes for carrying out this great work included convoking a "Great Assembly," floating a national loan, and creating one national fund to purchase land, with another to receive tithes. Such ideas reappeared later in Herzl's writing and would be realized through the Zionist movement.

Alkalai ended his days in the city of his visions, Jerusalem, in 1878. Simon Loeb, Theodor Herzl's grandfather, was one of Alkalai's few disciples. And one of Alkalai's granddaughters was among the delegates to the First Zionist Congress.

The Third Redemption (1843)

It is written in the Bible: "Return, O Lord, unto the tens and thousands of the families of Israel."

We, as a people, are properly called Israel only in the Land of Israel. . . .

There are two kinds of return: individual and collective. Individual return means that each of us should turn away from our evil personal ways and repent; the way of such repentance has been prescribed in the devotional books of our religious tradition. This kind of repentance is called individual, because it is relative to the particular needs of each one. Collective return means that all Israel should return to the land which is the inheritance of our fathers, to receive the Divine command and to accept the yoke of Heaven. This collective return was foretold by all the prophets; even though we are unworthy, Heaven will help us, for the sake of our holy ancestors. . . .

I wish to attest to the pain I have always felt at the error of our ancestors, that they allowed our Holy Tongue to be so forgotten. Because of this our people was divided into seventy peoples; our one language was replaced by the seventy languages of the lands of exile. . . . We must redouble our efforts to maintain Hebrew and to strengthen its position. It must be the basis of our educational work.

Samuel Mohilever (1824–98)

The Torah, which is the Source of our life, must be the foundation of our regeneration in the land of our fathers.

Religious Zionism—not mere traditional piety about the Holy Land but a conscious blending of Orthodoxy in religion with modern Jewish nationalism—was an important, albeit minority stream of Zionist thought. Rabbi Samuel Mohilever, the seminal figure in its development, helped launch pre-Herzlian Russian Zionism, the Hibbat Zion movement—and lived long enough to announce his adherence to Herzl.

Mohilever was born in 1824 in a village near Vilna, the intellectual center of Lithuanian Jews. He was so brilliant a talmudist that he was ordained a rabbi at age eighteen. In 1883 already notable not only as a scholar but as a communal leader, he was elected to the prestigious rabbinic post in Bialystok, Poland, which he then occupied for fifteen years, until his death in 1898.

The refugee crisis following the pogroms of 1881 mobilized Mohilever. Attending a conference of Jewish leaders in Lemberg, the capital of Galicia, he suggested—without effect—that the refugees be diverted to Palestine. On this journey Mohilever also visited Warsaw, where he organized that city's first Hibbat Zion chapter. Mohliver's decision to work with avowed agnostics on founding agricultural settlements in Palestine turned out to be the crucial turn in the history of Religious Zionism. It determined its future as an organized "party," often caught between ultra-Orthodox contempt and secular neglect.

In 1893 ongoing tensions between Mohilever and the secularists in Hibbat Zion's headquarters in Odessa led to the movement's decision to create another center that would work within the Orthodox community. This office, which he headed, was given the Hebrew name Mizrachi, the Hebrew word for "eastern," as well as the abbreviation of *merkaz ruhani*, or "spiritual center." When Rabbi Jacob Reines and other Mohilever disciples refounded that still-formidable Zionist organization in 1902, they continued the name, the spirit, and the stance.

Mohilever also labored on behalf of colonization in Palestine. His greatest service in this field came early in 1882 when he met the young Baron Edmond de Rothschild in Paris and convinced Rothschild to support the struggling settlers in the Holy Land. This is the note Mohilever sounded in his message to the First Zionist Congress he sent through his grandson.

Message to the First Zionist Congress (1897)

All "Sons of Zion" must be completely convinced and must believe with a perfect faith that the resettlement of our country—i.e., the purchase of land and the building of houses, the planting of orchards and the cultivation of the soil—is one of the fundamental commandments of our Torah. Some of our ancient sages even say that it is equivalent to the whole Law, for it is the foundation of the existence of our people. . . .

In conclusion, I lift up my voice to my brethren: Behold, it is now two thousand years that we await our Messiah, to redeem us from our bitter exile and to gather our scattered brethren from all corners of the earth to our own land, where each shall dwell in security, under his vine and under his fig tree. This faith, strong within us, has been our sole comfort in the untold days of our misery and degradation. And even though in the last century some have arisen in our midst who have denied this belief, tearing it out of their hearts and even erasing it from their prayers, the masses of our people hold fast to this hope, for the fulfillment of which they pray morning, noon, and night, and in which they find balm for their suffering. . . .

Our hope and faith has ever been, and still is, that our Messiah will come and gather in all the scattered of Israel, and instead of our being wanderers upon the face of the earth, ever moving from place to place, we shall dwell in our own country as a nation, in the fullest sense of the word. Instead of absorbing the contempt and mockery of the nations, we shall be honored and respected by all the peoples of the earth. This is our faith and hope, as derived from the words of our prophets and seers of blessed memory and to this our people clings! . . .

Isaac Jacob Reines (1839–1915)

A special people, with a special faith and a special religion, can only be construed if they have a special land.

Rabbi Isaac Jacob Reines took Rabbi Samuel Mohliver's mission further, mainstreaming religious Jews within the formal Zionist movement. Reines was born in Karolin, Poland, in 1839 to a father who decades earlier had moved to Safed, only to see Arab riots destroy his livelihood. A star student at the Volozhin Yeshiva and then at Eishishok, in 1883 Reines became the rabbi in Lida, Lithuania, present-day Belarus. A principled iconoclast, he fought to have secular studies incorporated into the local yeshiva.

Despite inheriting a deep love of Zion, Reines studied the Zionist movement carefully before concluding that "it is the duty and obligation of every Jew to join." He then attended the Zionist Congress. In 1902 he helped found the Mizrachi movement, which viewed Torah as the center of Zionism, seeing Jewish nationalism as a means to achieve religious objectives. He also published a Zionist manifesto, *Or Chadash al Tzion* (A new light on Zion).

Reines opposed religious anti-Zionists and anti-religious Zionists. He explained: "The Zionists say that every Jew who is not a Zionist is not a Jew. I say that every Zionist who is not a Jew is not a Zionist." Yet, seeking a kind of unity, Reines explained that the Zionist movement linked "free thinkers" and Orthodox Jews in a common project, "helping an entire nation," thereby bestowing a holy task on the supposedly secular Jewish community. He reasoned that anyone involved in building Palestine was engaging in "one of the greatest and most exalted mitzvot," because "the improvement of the majority is more important than the improvement of the individual."

The Mizrachi movement continues to perpetuate Reines's legacy. Its B'nai Akiva youth movement, founded in 1929, champions the ideal of what the Polish Hasidic Zionist leader Rabbi Samuel Landau called *Torah v'Avodah*: learning Torah while understanding secular work as honoring God too. Today, through its religious schools, kibbutzim, and political parties, Mizrachi continues to shape Israel.

A New Light on Zion (1902)

A fundamental basis of faith is to believe in the return of the people of Israel in their land. We cannot forge a unique people that will forever be dispersed and scattered among the nations, without a land of their own. Nationalism, then, is the central foundation of Jewish faith, and even when the Jews are scattered among the nations, they are known as a special people because of their hope to return to their land. A special people, with a special faith and a special religion, can only be construed if they have a special land, or a hope to return to their land, because a religion and a faith emanating from the Holy One, Blessed be He, will not command a people to suffer everlastingly. On this assumption, then, we conclude that faith in general and faith in redemption will be joined together, since one cannot exist without the other. . . .

The belief that Israel will return to its own land originates with the inherent relationship between Israel and the land and with the promise that the Holy One, Blessed be He, will give the land to His children. Such a belief instills a strong feeling of belonging between Israel and the land.

Each and every Jew should consult his heart and recall all that has passed and occurred to our fathers in this land and how they sacrificed their lives and their blood was spilled like water upon it; can such things not light his soul like burning coals and his heart with fire?

One should always desire to spread his tent in the Holy Land and through this he will see Eden and gain satisfaction to no end. . . .

Abraham Isaac Kook (1865–1935)

Eretz Yisra'el is part of the very essence of our nationhood; it is bound organically to its very life and inner being.

Modern Zionist thought is the creation of a gallery of extraordinary leaders, but even among them a few stand out as originals. Abraham Isaac Kook is one. Kook cannot be explained from the outside in—if he can be explained, at all—by listing the facts of his life, the influences that touched him, and the antecedents of his thought. The essence of Kook is within. He was a mystic whose career was determined by experiences of inner illumination. He was a religious Zionist engaged not in defending the ritual observances—though he practiced them with unique fervor—but in living out an approaching "end of days."

His view of Zionism, and his most important acts as the first chief rabbi of Palestine during the British mandate, make sense only if we understand his certainty, from foretold prophecy, that the present generation would experience the coming of the Messiah. He could therefore prepare himself to become priest of the restored cult in the Temple in Jerusalem and accept all builders of Palestine, heretics included, as unwitting instruments of the ever more manifest Redemption.

Even as a child, maturing in a small town in Latvia, Kook was known for unusual endowments of mind. But what distinguished him wherever he studied in adolescence were his fervor in prayer and his sense of the immediacy of God. When he arrived at the yeshiva in Volozhin at age nineteen, Kook had distinguished himself in another regard:

He loved to speak Hebrew—then usually a sign of at least incipient heresy—without evincing any change in his rapturous piety.

At twenty-three Kook assumed the post of rabbi in the village of Zimel, where he remained for six years, until 1894. His next call was to the much larger city of Boisk, Lithuania. There, he published his first essay on Zionism in which he accepted modern Jewish nationalism, even at its most secular, as an expression of the divine endowment within the Jewish soul and as a forerunner of the Messiah. In the summer of 1904, he arrived in the Holy Land to serve as chief rabbi of Jaffa and the agricultural colonies nearby.

The years in Jaffa constituted the crucial period of Kook's career. He increased his scope as a writer and a communal leader, laboring ever more self-consciously for a renaissance of Orthodox Judaism. In 1909 he championed leniency in a controversy over the biblical law of letting the Holy Land lie fallow on the seventh year. As Zionism splintered Orthodoxy, Kook tried keeping the peace—only to be attacked violently by many ultra-Orthodox Jerusalemites.

In the summer of 1914, Kook visited Europe—and found himself stranded when World War I began. Eventually he served as rabbi in London, from 1916 to 1919—amid the negotiations and controversy surrounding the Balfour Declaration of November 2, 1917. From that perch he urged British Jews to support a Jewish national home while denouncing anti-Zionists. As he proclaimed: "The entire debate whether it is our national or our religious heritage that preserves and sustains us [as Jews] is a bitter mockery."

In 1919 Kook returned to Palestine to serve as chief rabbi of the Ashkenazi Jews in Jerusalem. Two years later he was elected as the Ashkenazi head of the new rabbinic court of appeals, becoming, in effect, the Ashkenazi chief rabbi of Palestine—an office he held until his death in 1935.

The Land of Israel (1910–30)

Eretz Yisra'el is not something apart from the soul of the Jewish people; it is no mere national possession serving as a means of unifying our people and buttressing its material, or even its spiritual, survival. *Eretz Yisra'el* is part of the very essence of our nationhood; it is bound organically to its very life and inner being. Human reason, even at its most sublime, cannot begin to understand the unique holiness of *Eretz Yisra'el*; it cannot stir the depths of love for the land that are dormant within our people. What *Eretz Yisra'el* means to the Jew can be felt only through the Spirit of the Lord which is in our people as a whole, through the spiritual cast of the Jewish soul, which radiates its characteristic influence to every healthy emotion. This higher light shines forth to the degree that the spirit of divine holiness fills the hearts of the saints and scholars of Israel with heavenly life and bliss.

To regard *Eretz Yisra'el* as merely a tool for establishing our national unity—or even for sustaining our religion in the Diaspora by preserving its proper character and its faith, piety, and observances—is a sterile notion; it is unworthy of the holiness of *Eretz Yisra'el*. A valid strengthening of Judaism in the Diaspora can come only from a deepened attachment to *Eretz Yisra'el*. The hope for the return to the Holy Land is the continuing source of the distinctive nature of Judaism. The hope for the Redemption is the force that sustains Judaism in the Diaspora; the Judaism of *Eretz Yisra'el* is the very Redemption.

Jewish original creativity, whether in the realm of ideas or in the arena of daily life and action, is impossible except in *Eretz Yisra'el*. On the other hand, whatever the Jewish people creates in *Eretz Yisra'el* assimilates the universal into characteristic and unique Jewish form, to the great benefit of the Jewish people and of the world. The very sins which are the cause of our exile also pollute the pristine wellspring of our being, so that the water is impure at the source. Once the unique wellspring of Israel's individuality has become corrupt, its primal originality can express itself only in that area of loftiest universal creativity which belongs to the Jew—and only in the Diaspora, while the Homeland itself grows waste and desolate, atoning for its degradation by its ruin. While the life and thought of Israel is finding universal outlets and is being scattered abroad in all the world, the pristine well of the Jewish spirit stops running, the polluted streams emanating from the source are drying up, and the well is cleansing itself, until its original purity returns.

When that process is completed, the exile will become a disgust to us and will be discarded.... The creativity of the Jew, in all its glory and uniqueness, will reassert itself, suffused with the all-encompassing riches of the spirit of the greatest giant of humanity, Abraham, whom the Almighty called to be a blessing to humanity.

Jews cannot be as devoted and true to our own ideas, sentiments, and imagination in the Diaspora as we can be in *Eretz Yisra'el*....

This is the meaning of the Jew's undying love for *Eretz Yisra'el*—the Land of Holiness, the Land of God—in which all of the Divine commandments are realized in their perfect form. This urge to unfold to the world the nature of God, to raise one's head in His Name in order to proclaim His greatness in its real dimension, affects all souls, for all desire to become as one with Him and to partake of the bliss of His life. This yearning for a true life, for one that is fashioned by all the commandments of the Torah and illumined by all its uplifting splendor, is the source of the courage which moves Jews to affirm, before all the world, their loyalty to the heritage of their people, to the preservation of its identity and values, and to the upholding of its faith and vision....

The Rebirth of Israel (1910–30)

It is a grave error to be insensitive to the distinct unity of the Jewish spirit, to imagine that the Divine stuff which uniquely characterizes Israel is comparable to the spiritual content of all the other national civilizations. This error is the source of the attempt to sever the national from the religious element of Judaism. Such a division would falsify both our nationalism and our religion, for every element of thought, emotion, and idealism that is present in the Jewish people belongs to an indivisible entity, and all together make up its specific character....

Lights for Rebirth (1910–30)

Apart from the nourishment it receives from the life-giving dew of the holiness of *Eretz Yisra'el*, Jewry in the Diaspora has no real foundation and lives only by the power of a vision and by the memory of our glory, i.e., by the past and the future. But there is a limit to the power of such a vision to carry the burden of life and to give direction to the career of a people—and this limit seems already to have been reached. Diaspora Jewry is therefore disintegrating at an alarming rate, and there is no hope for it unless it replants itself by the wellsprings of life, of inherent sanctity, which can be found only in *Eretz Yisra'el*. Even one spark of this real life can revive great areas of the kind of life that is but a shadow of a vision. The real and organic holiness of Jewry can become manifest only by the return of the people to its land, the only path that can lead to its renascence. Whatever is sublime in our spirit and our vision can live only to the degree that there will be a tangible life to reinvigorate the tiring dream....

Many of the adherents of the present national revival maintain that they are secularists. If a Jewish secular nationalism really were imaginable, then we would, indeed, be in danger of falling so low as to be beyond redemption. But Jewish secular nationalism is a form of self-delusion: the spirit of Israel is so closely linked to the spirit of God that a Jewish nationalist, no matter how secularist his intention may be, must, despite himself, affirm the divine. An individual can sever the tie that binds him to life eternal, but the House of Israel cannot. All of its most cherished national possessions—its land, language, history, and customs—are vessels of the spirit of the Lord.

How should people of faith respond to an age of ideological ferment which affirms all of these values in the name of nationalism and denies their source, the rootedness of the national spirit, in God? To oppose Jewish nationalism, even in speech, and to denigrate its values is not permissible, for the spirit of God and the spirit of Israel are identical. What they must do is work all the harder at the task of uncovering the light and holiness implicit in our national spirit, the divine element which is its core. The secularists will thus be constrained to realize that they are immersed and rooted in the life of God and bathed in the radiant sanctity that comes from above....

The claim of our flesh is great. We require a healthy body. We have greatly occupied ourselves with the soul and have forsaken the holiness of the body. We have neglected health and physical prowess, forgetting that our flesh is as sacred as our spirit. We have turned our backs on physical life, the development of our senses, and all that is involved in the tangible reality of the flesh, because we have fallen prey to lowly fears, and have lacked faith in the holiness of the Land. "Faith is exemplified by the tracate Zeraim (Plants)—man proves his faith in eternal life by planting."

Moshe "Kalphon" HaCohen (1874–1950)

And it came to pass that the spirit of the Lord settled in the heart of a hero. . . . Herzl was his name.

By blessing the late Theodor Herzl in 1920 as a "hero and warrior who fought ferociously for our brethren," Tunisia's great rabbinic scholar, Moshe "Kalphon" HaCohen, disproved two common caricatures about Zionism. He showed that some religious Jews loved Herzl, despite the Zionist rebellion against religion. And he showed that many *Mizrahi* Jews were Zionist, even as most Herzlian Zionists ignored them.

Based in the southern Mediterranean island of Djerba, with a priestly pedigree tracing back to Ezra the Scribe, Moshe "Kalphon" HaCohen was famed for his scholarly rigor, piety, and modesty. Invited to join the Bet Din, the rabbinical court, when he was twenty-five, he only accepted the position, reluctantly, eighteen years later. A studious sort, he produced eighty volumes of widely respected, religiously conservative, commentaries, including the nine-volume classic, *Shoel v'Nishal.*

HaCohen supported Herzl's call for Zionism enthusiastically. One book, *Zechut Moshe* (*Moses's Good Fortune*), praised secular Zionists for their emancipation from the Enlightenment. HaCohen wrote: "There were many from among our brethren, the Jewish people, who had not grown up with the blessings of Judaism, the Torah, and the commandments, and were like a baby wandering innocently among the non-Jews. Despite this, a national feeling stirred in their breasts, a passion to reestablish a Jewish state that would stand out from among the other nations in the world."

To HaCohen, the Balfour Declaration of 1917, and the San Remo Conference in 1920 of Allied powers endorsing a Jewish national home, heralded "the *atchalta degeulah,* the first stirrings of the redemption."

He celebrated San Remo with a communal service, blowing the shofar and reciting the *Hallel* prayer for thanksgiving—one of many ways this rabbinic giant offered religious validation to what many religious people dismissed as a secular enterprise. Similarly, by blessing Herzl in his 1920 book, *Mateh Moshe (Moses's Headquarters)*, this Tunisian rabbi emerged as the *Mizrahi* Rav Kook.

HaCohen had considered moving to Palestine in 1898, but the then-twenty-four-year-old's rabbi father calculated that the Messiah was coming imminently and persuaded him to wait. Five decades later, in 1949, he prepared once again to settle in what was now the new state whose birth his community had celebrated for three full days. This time, illness intervened. He died a year later. In 2006 the Israeli government undertook complicated diplomatic maneuverings to inter the bones of this still-revered, deeply Zionist, rabbinic sage in Jerusalem.

Mateh Moshe (Moses's Headquarters) (1920)

And it came to pass that the spirit of the Lord settled in the heart of a hero and warrior who fought ferociously for our brethren. Herzl was his name. He himself had almost been submerged and lost among the nations. Instead, his was a thunderous presence. He was a man of transcendent virtues. When he invested heart and soul for the good of the Jewish people, he became a man of war, engaged in a battle of advice and ideas, to see how and in what way to reclaim the Land of Israel. He developed some lofty ideas and inscribed them on the sheets of various newspapers. . . .

Some say that with great regret that all of Israel is desolate. . . . In that spirit, I clarified the words of the prophet (Isaiah 60:15): "Whereas thou hast been forsaken and hated, so that no one passed through thee, I will make thee an eternal excellency, a joy of many generations." It is well known that among enlightened cities, some places are particularly famous for their glory and wonder, such as the exalted capital of Paris, and the equally exalted cities of London and New York. Given that they keep updating these cities in the spirit of the time, when they were recently renovated, they had to spend several hundred million dollars to demolish all the ugly buildings that accumulated over several centuries.

That is not the case in the Land of Israel. Neither built up nor sophisticated, it lacks a large population. Thus, there is nothing preexisting to think about. It will be easy to build and repair the country on a grand scale as has occurred in no other city or country. Because that which is existing in our country now is not worthy. It is indeed forsaken and abandoned, and people don't pass through. And the text teaches that by being forsaken and abandoned it will be easy for your children and your builders to make you become a light of the world and the delight of generations.

Meir Bar-Ilan (Berlin) (1880–1949)

When we have a state, should anyone try to separate church and state, this will represent not a separation but a contradiction.

The Zionist revolution against rabbinic passivity inspired a new generation of rabbinic activists—leaders who absorbed the Zionist genius for applying Jewish ideas to contemporary problems and implemented solutions politically, diplomatically, even physically. The model scholar-statesman of religious Zionism from the 1920s through the 1940s was Meir Berlin.

Berlin was born into Lithuania's most eminent rabbinic family, absorbing his father's love of Torah—and dream of a rebuilt Israel. Lionized by his acronym as "the Netziv," his father, Rabbi Naphtali Zevi Judah Berlin, headed the legendary Volozhin Yeshiva. "Our Zionism is not a forty-year-old innovation, but rather an expression of national desire developed over a period of thousands of years," the young Berlin declared at the 1937 World Zionist Congress. "For us the building of *Eretz Yisra'el* . . . is a necessity, part of the internal soul of Judaism."

Berlin championed "*torah v'avodah*," religious and secular excellence. He perpetuated the family's scholarly legacy by eventually launching the *Encyclopedia Talmudit*. By leading the Mizrachi movement in the United States and Israel, he helped synthesize Zionism and Orthodoxy.

While attending his first Zionist Congress, Berlin spearheaded the Religious Zionist opposition to Herzl's Uganda plan. Eventually coining the Mizrachi slogan "The land of people for the people of Israel according to the Torah of Israel," Berlin envisioned a truly Jewish state that did not ghettoize religion. Instead, the "spirit of Torah" would resonate "in the thoroughfare, on the street, upon the masses and within the state."

After a decade of leading Mizrachi in the United States—launching over one hundred chapters there—Berlin immigrated to Palestine in 1926. Now heading international Mizrachi, he opposed partitioning Palestine, established the Religious Zionist newspaper *HaTzofeh*, and appeared before the U.S. Congress lobbying to save the Jews of Europe in the 1940s. Throughout, he affirmed the Torah as relevant to "church" and "state" while trying to prevent the growing *kulturkampf* between religious and secular Zionists. A diligent immigrant, he Hebraicized "Berlin" to Bar-Ilan.

Stricken ill in his sixties, he died in 1949, able to see the state he helped create but unable to mold it. Nevertheless, today the Religious Zionist mainstream follows the example of this scholarly statesman, living in the secular and religious worlds. This approach is embodied in Israel's leading religious institution of higher education, which now bears his name, Bar Ilan University.

What Kind of Life Should We Create in *Eretz Yisra'el*? (1922)

Both our people, as a whole, and our religion, in specific, are totally different from all others. Among the nations of the world, statecraft is kept separate from religion. The foundations of each derive from different realms of the spirit, and there is a wide gap between the forms in which each expresses itself. The state does not impinge upon the sphere of religion, and religion does not concern itself with the conduct of the state....

When we have a state, should anyone try to separate church and state, this will represent not a separation but a contradiction. Should someone say: "Let the religious concern themselves with religious matters and stay out of the affairs of the state," it will be as if he were saying: "Let us divide the Torah into sections; the minor portions, dealing with moral and spiritual matters, we shall accept, but the rest, dealing with custom and daily action, we shall eliminate and replace with other laws. . . ."

It is our conviction that "there can be no substitute for the Torah," that the only means to unite all sects and factions of the Jewish people into one homogenous state is by regenerating every aspect of our life on the basis of our heritage of Torah. This does not mean that we should scoff at and ignore the values and customs of this generation. Even if these values and customs are in contradiction to the laws of our Torah, we must modify them gradually. . . .

In sum: The question of the right way of life in our homeland is a question of education and influencing the community. . . . We must, therefore, teach the people, young and old, to respect and know the Torah. . . .

5

Pioneers

Cultural Zionism

To those who assume the Jewish national home must be a Jewish state, Ahad Ha'am may be the most enigmatic Zionist. The Hebrew essayist and founder of Cultural Zionism Asher Zvi Ginsberg chose the Hebrew pen name Ahad Ha'am, meaning "one of the nation," to emphasize his Zionist faith that pairing this long-exiled people with its long-longed-for land would revolutionize both. Yet he harbored the *galut* Jew's doubts that this crazy scheme to reestablish Jewish sovereignty could succeed.

It takes greatness to be so wrong yet so right. Ahad Ha'am's Cultural Zionism quickly became more about his optimism than his pessimism, more about culture, history, language, and learning reviving the nation than about his doubting the nation could reestablish a state. Today, we hail Cultural Zionism's cavalcade of successes: from grand projects including Eliezer Ben-Yehudah's resurrecting the Hebrew language and Hayyim Nahman Bialik's enlivening Hebrew culture, to the efforts of every new immigrant to learn the new language, sing the new songs, master the new culture. Despite its ethereal goals, Cultural Zionism was strikingly practical and productive, shaping this national renaissance.

Eliezer Ben-Yehudah (1858–1922)

**The Hebrew language can live only if we revive
the nation and return it to its fatherland.**

Eliezer Ben-Yehudah will be remembered longest for his crucial role in
the revival of modern Hebrew as a language of everyday speech. He was
the first to state, and to incarnate in a significant career, a main "messianic" theme of Zionism—the notion that the Jews must end their
peculiar history by becoming a modern, secular nation. However, he
realized the Jews "cannot become a living nation—*am chai*—without
returning to their ancestral language—*lashon ha'avot"* and using that
language "in everyday discourse, from old to young . . . in all facets of
life, at all hours, days and night." This insight taught all nationalists
the significance of sovereignty and culture—what he called "the land
and the language"—in uniting a people.

Ben-Yehudah was born as Eliezer Perlman in Lushki, within the
Lithuanian province of the Russian empire. He received the traditional
ghetto education. At age fifteen he left the yeshiva to enter a scientific
high school in Dvinsk. Amid the swirl of revolutionary and nationalist
thoughts then spinning around most Russian schools, young Perlman
had his epiphany, committing to "the Jews' revival in the homeland."
He decided to migrate to Paris to study medicine, to be useful when
he then settled in Palestine.

A bout of tuberculosis in France doomed Ben-Yehudah's medical ambitions. Nevertheless, the nationalist fervor there triggered
his second epiphany: that the Jews cannot unite without a common
language. Identifying Hebrew as the Jew's only language, he rejected
Yiddish and all other substitutes. He Hebraized his name in 1879
when signing his first published essay. Still, he wondered, Will the
Jewish people embrace this linguistic revival, and can the Hebrew
language handle it?

After recuperating in the warmer climate of Algiers, in 1881 he moved
to Palestine, where he lived until his death in 1923, except for four years
in America during the First World War. Settling in Jerusalem, he and
his wife established the first household in which only modern Hebrew

was spoken. This resolve, from which neither abuse nor abject poverty could swerve him, had him searching the classic Hebrew literature for terms to be used in everyday life and inventing what he could not find.

The result was Ben-Yehudah's greatest work: a modern multivolume Hebrew dictionary, *The Complete Dictionary of Ancient and Modern Hebrew* (five volumes appeared during his lifetime). As a natural corollary of these labors, he cofounded, and became the first president, of the Academy for the Hebrew Language (Va'ad HaLashon).

A Letter of Ben-Yehudah (1880)

29 KISLEV, 5641, ALGAZIR

It is plain for all to see, sir, that our youth is abandoning our language— but why? Because in their eyes it is a dead and useless tongue. All our efforts to make them appreciate the importance of the language to us, the Hebrews, will be of no avail. Only a Hebrew with a Hebrew heart will understand this, and such a person will understand even without our urging. Let us therefore make the language really live again! Let us teach our young to speak it, and then they will never betray it!

But we will be able to revive the Hebrew tongue only in a country in which the number of Hebrew inhabitants exceeds the number of gentiles. Therefore, let us increase the number of Jews in our desolate land; let the remnants of our people return to the land of their fathers; *let us revive the nation and its tongue will be revived, too!* . . .

True, the Jewish nation and its language died together. But it was not a death by natural causes, not a death of exhaustion, like the death of the Roman nation, which therefore died forever! The Jewish nation was murdered twice, both times when it was in full bloom and youthful vigor. . . .

The Hebrew language can live only if we revive the nation and return it to its homeland. . . . The Jewish religion will, no doubt, be able to endure even in alien lands; it will adjust its forms to the spirit of the place and the age, and its destiny will parallel that of all religions! But the nation? The nation cannot live except on its own soil; only on this soil can it revive and bear magnificent fruit, as in days of old!

Introduction to *The Complete Dictionary of Ancient and Modern Hebrew* (1908)

I realized that without two essential components, the Jews can never revive as a nation and they are: the land and the language. . . . But is it realistic? That was the big question facing me.

And as I scrutinized the question it branched into two:

Are the people up for it? Is the language up for it?

Regarding the people: can a community, be it large or small, speak the language it abandoned centuries ago? And can a language which stopped being spoken by any community, be it large or small, centuries upon centuries ago, revive as the regular language of everyday discourse for a community, be it large or small?

Regarding the first question. . . . I understood that the public is just a collective of individuals. . . . I realized that ultimately, it all depends on the national will, and I fully believed in our nation's willpower.

But that second question! . . . The more I endeavored to speak Hebrew, the more I expanded my conversational boundaries, the more suffocated I started to feel. My vocabulary was the rabbinic vocabulary of any *yeshiva bucher*, who learned in *heder* in Lithuania. . . . It's a lovely language for spiritual matters . . . but . . . when we hit more trivial and vulgar matters, we were struck mute! . . .

Then, with the simple logic of adolescence, I came to this simple conclusion: If the only thing missing for us to speak Hebrew . . . is the simple, natural language of everyday life . . . that gap must be filled. . . . From that day forward, I decided to fill it. Thus was born the idea to write this dictionary.

Ahad Ha'am (Asher Zvi Ginsberg) (1856–1927)

From this center, the spirit of Judaism will radiate to the great circumference to inspire them with new life and to preserve the over-all unity of our people.

Ahad Ha'am was born as Asher Zvi Ginsberg in Skvira, in the Russian Ukraine, on August 18, 1856. His family was part of the very highest aristocracy in the Hasidic Jewish community. Ginsberg's formal education was so pious that his teacher was forbidden to instruct him in the Russian alphabet, lest this lead to heresy.

Nonetheless, Ginsberg taught himself to read Russian at age eight, from storefront signs. Gradually, he progressed to the "forbidden books" of the modern Hebrew Enlightenment. By age twenty he reached the wider horizons of literature and philosophy in Russian and German. The family moved to Odessa in 1886, under the constraint of a new tsarist ukase forbidding Jews to lease land.

At thirty-three Ginsberg published his first article. Not regarding himself as a writer, he signed it as Ahad Ha'am, i.e., "one of the people." Although from then on he became known by the pen name, he was far from populist. The moniker did, however, express his faith in the creative Jewish people power he hoped Jewish nationalism would restore.

Becoming an official of the Wissotzsky Tea Company, he traveled throughout Russia on its behalf for four years. He moved to London in 1907 when his firm opened a branch there and continued his writing and activism.

More worried about assimilation than antisemitism, Ahad Ha'am championed the cultural revival and modernization of the Jewish people through the agency of a carefully chosen few. "A complete national life involves two things," he preached, "first, full play for the creative faculties of the nation in a specific national culture of its own, and, second, a system of education whereby the individual members of the nation will be thoroughly imbued with that culture, and so molded by it that its imprint will be recognizable in all their way of life and thought."

Most Zionists rejected his views as elitist and defeatist, especially in light of Theodor Herzl's vision of political rebirth that electrified the masses and ultimately launched the State of Israel. Still, many Jews in Palestine embraced this "spiritual" or "cultural" Zionism, understanding that a Jewish state without a rich spiritual and cultural life would be like a person without a soul.

Ultimately, Ahad Ha'am's fight against assimilation, demoralization, and boorishness helped ensure that Zionism was not merely a defensive movement against antisemitism but an expansive one—building an old-new Jewish culture for the New Jew. He fought to ensure that the cultural aspirations of the People of the Book survived the much-needed revolution against excessive bookishness. And, as an oppressed Russian Jew, his inbred skepticism about state power made him among the first Zionists to warn of the moral challenges dealing with the neighboring Arab population would pose.

When Ahad Ha'am settled in Tel Aviv in 1921, Mayor Meir Dizengoff had the street on which he lived named after him and even closed it to traffic during his afternoon rest hours. In his sunset years this agnostic reached his apotheosis as the secular rabbi—indeed, almost the secular Hasidic rebbe—of a wide circle within the growing Jewish settlement in Palestine. When he died on January 2, 1927, all Tel Aviv attended his funeral.

On Nationalism and Religion (Baden-Baden, September 18, 1910)

TO DR. J. L. MAGNES (NEW YORK)

What we have to do is to revert to the system which our ancestors adopted in days gone by and to which we owe our survival: We have to make the Synagogue itself the House of Study, with Jewish learning as its first concern and prayer as a secondary matter. Cut the prayers as short as you like, but make your Synagogue a haven of Jewish knowledge, alike for children and adults, for the educated and the ordinary folk. . . . But learning—learning—learning: that is the secret of Jewish survival.

Then you say you want "to propagate national religion and religious nationalism." I must confess that this formula is not altogether clear to me. "National religion"—by all means: Judaism is fundamentally national, and all the efforts of the "Reformers" to separate the Jewish religion from its national element have had no result except to ruin both the nationalism and the religion. Clearly, then, if you want to build and not to destroy, you must teach religion on the basis of nationalism, with which it is inseparably intertwined. But when you talk of propagating "religious nationalism," I do not know what you mean (unless you are simply saying the same thing in other words). Do you really think of excluding from the ranks of the nationalists all those who do not believe in the principles of religion? If that is your intention, I cannot agree. In my view our religion is national—that is to say, it is a product of our national spirit—but the reverse is not true. If it is impossible to be a Jew in the religious sense without acknowledging our nationality, it is possible to be a Jew in the national sense without accepting many things in which religion requires belief. . . .

The Jewish State and the Jewish Problem (1897)

The truth is bitter, but with all its bitterness it is better than illusion. We must admit to ourselves that the "ingathering of the exiles" is unattainable by natural means. We may, by natural means, someday establish a Jewish State; it is possible that the Jews may increase and multiply within it until the "land is filled with them"—but even then the greater part of our people will remain scattered on foreign soils. . . . Thus we are driven to the conclusion that the real and only basis of Zionism is to be found in another problem, the spiritual one.

The western Jew, having left the ghetto and having sought acceptance by the gentile majority, is unhappy because his hope of an open-armed welcome has been disappointed. Perforce he returns to his own people and tries to find within the Jewish community that life for which he yearns—but in vain. The life and horizon of the Jewish community no longer satisfy him. He has already grown accustomed to a broader social and political life, and on the intellectual side the work to be done for our Jewish national culture does not attract him, because that culture has played no part in his earliest education and is a closed book to him. In this dilemma he therefore turns to the land of his ancestors and imagines how good it would be if a Jewish state were reestablished there—a State and society organized exactly after the pattern of other States. Then he could live a full, complete life within his own people, and he could find at home all that he now sees outside, dangled before his eyes but out of reach. Of course, not all the Jews will be able to take wing and go to their State; but the very existence of the Jewish state will also raise the prestige of those who remain in exile, and their fellow citizens will no longer despise them and keep them at arm's length, as though they were base slaves, dependent entirely on the hospitality of others. . . .

The eastern form of the spiritual problem is absolutely different from the western. In the West it is the problem of the Jews; in the East, the *problem of Judaism*. The first weighs on the individual; the second, on the nation. The one is felt by Jews who have had a European education; the other, by Jews whose education, has been Jewish. The one is a product of antisemitism, and is dependent on antisemitism for its existence; the other is a natural product of a real link with a millennial culture, and it will remain unsolved and unaffected even if the troubled Jews all over the world attain comfortable economic positions, are on the best possible terms with their neighbors, and are admitted to the fullest social and political equality.

It is not only the Jews who have come out of the ghetto; Judaism has come out, too. For the Jews the exodus from the ghetto is confined to certain countries and is due to toleration; but Judaism has come out (or is coming out) of its own accord wherever it has come into contact with modern culture. This contact with modern culture overturns the inner defenses of Judaism so that it can no longer remain isolated and live a life apart! The spirit of our people desires further development; it wants to absorb the basic elements of general culture which are reaching it from the outside world to digest them and to make them a part of itself, as it has done before at various periods of its history. But the conditions of its life in exile are not suitable for such a task. In our time culture expresses itself everywhere through the form of the national spirit, and the stranger who would become part of culture must sink his individuality and become absorbed in the dominant environment. In exile, Judaism cannot, therefore, develop its individuality in its own way. When it leaves the ghetto walls, it is in danger of losing its essential being or—at very least—its national unity; it is in danger of being split up into as many kinds of Judaism, each with a different character and life, as there are countries of the dispersion.

Judaism is, therefore, in a quandary: It can no longer tolerate the *galut* form which it had to take on in obedience to its will to live when it was exiled from its own country; but without that form, its life is in danger. So it seeks to return to its historic center where it will be able to live a life developing in a natural way, to bring its powers into play in every department of human culture, to broaden and perfect those national possessions which it has acquired up to now, and thus to contribute to the common stock of humanity in the future as it has in the past, a great national culture, the fruit of the unhampered activity of a people living by the light of its own spirit.

For this purpose Judaism can for the present content itself with little. It does not need an independent state, but only the creation in its native land of conditions favorable to its development: a good-sized settlement of Jews working without hindrance in every branch of civilization, from agriculture and handicrafts to science and literature. This Jewish settlement, which will grow gradually, will become in course of time the center of the nation, wherein its spirit will find pure expression and develop in all its aspects to the highest degree of perfection of which it is capable.

Then, from this center, the spirit of Judaism will radiate to the great circumference, to all the communities of the Diaspora, to inspire them with new life and to preserve the over-all unity of our people. When our national culture in Palestine has attained that level, we may be confident that it will produce men in the Land of Israel itself who will be able, at a favorable moment, to establish a State there—one which will be not merely a state of Jews but a really Jewish state. . . .

The secret of our people's persistence is . . . that at a very early period the Prophets taught it to respect only the power of the spirit and not to worship material power. Therefore, unlike the other nations of antiquity, the Jewish people never reached the point of losing its self-respect in the face of more powerful enemies. As long as we remain faithful to this principle, our existence has a secure basis, and we shall not lose our self-respect, for we are not spiritually inferior to any nation. But a political ideal which is not grounded in our national culture is apt to seduce us from loyalty to our own inner spirit and to beget in us a tendency to find the path of glory in the attainment of material power and political dominion, thus breaking the thread that unites us with the past and undermining our historical foundation. Needless to say, if the political ideal is not attained, it will have disastrous consequences because we shall have lost the old basis without finding a new one. But even if it is attained under present conditions, when we are a scattered people not only in the physical but also in the spiritual sense—even then, Judaism will be in great danger. . . .

In sum: Hibbat Zion, no less than "Zionism," wants a Jewish state and believes in the possibility of the establishment of a Jewish state in the future. But while "Zionism" looks to the Jewish state to furnish a remedy for poverty and to provide complete tranquility and national glory, Hibbat Zion knows that our state will not give us all these things until "universal Righteousness is enthroned and holds sway over nations and States"—it looks to a Jewish state to provide only a "secure refuge" for Judaism and a cultural bond to unite our nation. "Zionism," therefore, begins its work with political propaganda; Hibbat Zion begins with national culture, because only *through* the national culture and *for its sake* can a Jewish state be established in such a way as to correspond with the will and the needs of the Jewish people.

Hayyim Nahman Bialik (1873–1934)

Come, with one voice, shoulder to shoulder,
to the aid of the people.

Hayyim Nahman Bialik's early life was similar to Ahad Ha'am's. He was born in a village near Zhitomir, in the Russian province of Volhynia, as the eighth and youngest child of poor parents. At age seventeen he was given reluctant consent to leave for the yeshiva of Volozhin. There, he began to write—even poetry as early as 1890—and took a further step toward intellectual emancipation by joining a secret students' organization of Hibbat Zion.

In 1891 he left the yeshiva for Odessa, the then home of Ahad Ha'am and a galaxy of intellectual leaders engaged in the national revival in Hebrew. Marrying the daughter of a lumber merchant, he settled in a small town for four years to work in his father-in-law's business. It was among the future poet's foibles that he imagined himself to possess a talent for business but lost his money in this first venture. By 1897 he turned to the traditional occupation of Hebrew writers: teaching the language to the young.

Bialik's intellectual emancipation from Orthodox faith was not fully rationalist. His romantic love of the Jewish past even included the recent ghetto. He felt—keenly and sentimentally—the imperative to preserve the treasures of classical Hebrew literature as a "usable past" for the Zionist national revival. His labors as publisher and editor, from which he would make his living until his death, were largely devoted to this aim.

This old-new synthesis helped catapult two of his poems into youth movement anthems: From "Techezakna" ("Be Strengthened"), the people sang, "May they grow strong, the hands of our gifted brothers. . . . Come with one voice, shoulder to shoulder to the aid of the people." And from "Shir Ha'avoda Vehamelacha" ("The Song of Work and Labor"), they sang, "To whom our thanks? To whom our blessing? To work and labor."

For all his love of tradition, Bialik also detested the *galut* weakness the tradition reinforced. His poem, "The City of Slaughter," is the Jewish *Guernica*, a powerful blending of art and reportage detailing the devastation of the Kishinev pogrom. Some of his Zionist vision was forged in fury against such antisemitic brutality.

He also became one of Hebrew University's most enthusiastic boosters. There, he believed, the old and the new, the Jewish and the supranational, would fuse, revitalizing contemporary and traditional Hebrew culture. Under pressure from the Russian writer and political activist Maxim Gorky, Russia's communist rulers permitted Bialik to emigrate in 1921. After three years in Berlin he settled in Tel Aviv, on a street the municipality called by his name. He died in 1934 in Vienna, where he had gone for an operation, and was buried in Tel Aviv.

The City of Slaughter (1903)

Arise and go now to the city of slaughter;
Into its courtyard wind thy way;
There with thine own hand touch, and with the eyes of
thine head,
Behold on tree, on stone, on fence, on mural clay,
The spattered blood and dried brains of the dead. . . .
Come, now, and I will bring thee to their lairs
The privies, jakes and pigpens where the heirs
Of Hasmoneans lay, with trembling knees,
Concealed and cowering,—the sons of the Maccabees!
The seed of saints, the scions of the lions!
Who, crammed by scores in all the sanctuaries of their shame,
So sanctified My name!
It was the flight of mice they fled,
The scurrying of roaches was their flight;
They died like dogs, and they were dead! . . .
I grieve for you, my children. My heart is sad for you.
Your dead were vainly dead; and neither I nor you
Know why you died or wherefore, for whom, nor by what
laws;
Your deaths are without reason; your lives are without cause.

At the Inauguration of the Hebrew University (January 4, 1925)

Ladies and Gentlemen! You all know what has become of our old spiritual strongholds in the Diaspora in recent times. . . . For all their inner strength, and for all the energy the nation had expended upon creating and preserving these centers, they stood not firm on the day of wrath; by the decree of history they are crumbled and razed to the foundations and our people is left standing empty-handed upon their ruins. This is the very curse of the *galut*, that our undertakings do not, indeed cannot, prosper. . . . Through cruel and bitter trials and tribulations, through blasted hopes and despair of the soul, through innumerable humiliations, we have slowly arrived at the realization that without a tangible homeland, without private national premises that are entirely ours, we can have no sort of a life, either material or spiritual.

Without *Eretz Yisra'el*—*Eretz* means land, literally land—there is no hope for the rehabilitation of Israel anywhere, ever. Our very ideas about the material and intellectual existence of the nation have also meanwhile undergone a radical change. We no longer admit a division of the body and the spirit, or a division of the man and the Jew. . . . A people that aspires to a dignified existence must create a culture; it is not enough merely to make use of a culture—a people must create its own, with its own hands and its own implements and materials, and impress it with its own seal. Of course our people in its "diasporas" is creating culture; I doubt whether any place in the world where culture is being produced is entirely devoid of Jews. But as whatever the Jew creates in the Diaspora is always absorbed in the culture of others, it loses its identity and is never accounted to the credit of the Jew. Our cultural account in the Diaspora is consequently all debit and no credit. . . .

Better a little that is undisputedly my own than much that is not definitely either mine or somebody else's. Better a dry crust in my own home and on my own table than a stall-fed ox in the home of others and on the table of others. Better one little university but entirely my own, entirely my handiwork from foundations to coping stones, than thousands of temples of learning from which I derive benefit but in which I have no recognized share. Let my food be little and bitter as the olive, if I may but taste in it the delicious flavor of a gift from myself.

It was in this frame of mind that we took refuge in this land. We are not come here to seek wealth, or dominion, or greatness. How much of these can this poor little country give us? We wish to find here only a domain of our own for our physical and intellectual labor. We have not yet achieved great things here. We have not had time to wash the dust of long wanderings from our feet and to change our patched garments. Undoubtedly many years have yet to pass until we have healed this desolate land, of the leprosy of its rocks and the rot of its swamps. For the present there is only a small beginning of upbuilding; yet already the need has been felt for erecting a home for the intellectual work of the nation. Such has ever been the nature of our people: it cannot live for three consecutive days without Torah. Already at this early hour we experience cultural needs that cannot be postponed and must be satisfied at once. . . .

May we succeed in raising the science and learning that will issue from this house to the moral level to which our people raised its Torah! . . .

Ladies and Gentlemen! Thousands of our youth, obeying the call of their hearts, are streaming from the four corners of the earth to this land for the purpose of redeeming it from desolation and ruin. . . . They are plowing rocks, draining swamps, and building roads amid singing and rejoicing. These young people know how to raise simple and crude labor—physical labor—to the level of highest sanctity, to the level of religion. It is our task to kindle such a holy fire within the walls of the house which has just been opened upon Mount Scopus. Let those youths build the Earthly Jerusalem with fire and let them who work within these walls build the Heavenly Jerusalem with fire, and between them let them build and establish our House of Life. "For Thou, O Lord, didst consume it with fire, and with fire Thou wilt rebuild it."

Micah Joseph Berdichevski (1865–1921)

We must cease to be Jews by virtue of an abstract Judaism and become Jews in our own right, as a living and developing nationality.

"I love and I hate," the Roman poet Catullus wrote about the lady he could neither be happy with nor abandon. In essence Micah Joseph Berdichevski's many volumes embroider this theme, except his was a love-hate relationship with Judaism and Jewish tradition. He described this state of soul as the mark of his generation: "the rent in the heart" that inevitably attended the passage from the religious faith of the ghetto to secular values of modern European civilization.

In their syntheses, both Ahad Ha'am and Hayyim Nahman Bialik found some peace in cultural Zionism. For Berdichevski, Ahad Ha'am's greatest Zionist adversary, such a peace was not real or possible: He saw only tension and affirmed only revolt. In his eyes, tradition—whether in Jewish history or the history of civilization—was an illusion, and balance between the old and new a figment of closet philosophers' imaginings. True, primal values were created by rebels who arose to challenge all conventional life and thought; therefore, a valid Jewish national revival was not to be found in books but in the proud human dignity of those who were not enslaved, even by a great past.

And yet, from Berdichevski's pen we possess some of the most poignant appreciations of the very tradition he professed to condemn and also unsurpassed volumes opening Talmudic legend, morality, and Hasidism to modern readers.

Berdichevski was born in the middle of the nineteenth century into a family of notable rabbinic lineage. His family lived in Medzhybizh, Ukraine, the birthplace of Hasidism. By age seventeen, when a suitable match with an heiress was arranged for him, he was already well known as a phenomenal scholar. In secret, however, he was reading modern, "Enlightened" works. When his pious father-in-law caught him in this "crime," he was thrown out on the street and forced to divorce his young bride.

In 1890 Berdichevski left for Western Europe, studying at the University of Breslau and at its academy for painting. Within two years a radically different writer emerged—one who spoke now of the vagueness of much debated great values, like Jewish tradition, culture, and nationalism, and of the neglect of the individual. He soon adopted a key Nietzschean idea—the need for "transvaluation of values" (reevaluation of all values)—as the slogan for his radical attack on Jewish tradition.

In the later years of his life Berdichevski was concurrently producing collections of Talmudic and post-Talmudic legends and preparing a major study that asserted that nature worship and idolatry, not biblical monotheism, had been the real religion of ancient Israel. His writings in Hebrew filled twenty volumes.

From 1911 Berdichevski lived in Berlin, supporting himself as a dentist, devoted to his scholarly writings and belles lettres and secluded from public affairs. He sought no disciples. Still, after his death in

1921 he left a legacy which still lives on. Fewer and fewer Israelis may know his name, but more and more live out his grand contradiction—embracing tradition and modernity passionately, even if paradoxically.

Wrecking and Building (1900–1903)

After the destruction of the Temple our political status declined and our independence came to an end. We ceased to be a people actively adding to its spiritual and material store and living in unbroken continuity with its earlier days. As our creativity diminished, the past—whatever had once been done and said among us, our legacy of thoughts and deeds—became the center of our existence, the main supports of our life. The Jews became secondary to Judaism. . . .

We must cease to be Jews by virtue of an abstract Judaism and become Jews in our own right, as a living and developing nationality. The traditional "credo" is no longer enough for us. . . .

It is not reforms but transvaluations that we need—fundamental transvaluations in the whole course of our life, in our thoughts, in our very souls. . . .

Such a choice promises us a noble future; the alternative is to remain a straying people following its erring shepherds. A great responsibility rests upon us, for everything lies in our hands! We are the last Jews—or we are the first of a new nation.

In Two Directions (1900–1903)

Is it any wonder that there arose among us generation after generation despising Nature, who thought of all God's marvels as superfluous trivialities?

Is it surprising that we became a non-people, a non-nation—non-men, indeed?

I recall from the teaching of the sages: Whoever walks by the way and interrupts his study to remark, How fine is, that tree, how fine is that field, forfeits his life!

But I assert that then alone will Judah and Israel be saved, when another teaching is given unto us, namely: Whoever walks by the way and sees a fine tree and fine field and a fine sky and leaves them to think on other thoughts—that man is like one who forfeits his life!

Give us back our fine trees and fine fields! Give us back the Universe.

On Sanctity (1899)

A beaten, tortured, and persecuted people is unable to be holy. If we have no national livelihood, if we do not eat the fruit of our soil, but only toil on the lands of strangers, how can we be exalted in the spirit? If we are at war with ourselves in everything we do and think and are, how shall we attain elevation of soul and find the way to purification? A holy people must surely be a living people.

Martin Buber (1878–1965)

> Our only salvation is to become Israel again, to become a whole, the unique whole of a people and a religious community; a renewed people, a renewed religion, and the renewed unity of both.

Though born in Vienna, Martin Buber was by earliest experience a Galician Jew. Until age fourteen he was raised in Lemberg in the "Enlightened" house of his grandfather, Solomon Buber, a wealthy aristocrat and distinguished figure in modern, "scientific" Talmudic scholarship. The then dominant milieu of Galician Jewry, Hasidism, was later to become decisive in his development.

In 1896 Buber left for the University of Vienna, and during the next four years, he studied in Leipzig, Zurich, and Berlin. By 1898 launching a lifelong quest to see how authentic Jewish religious experiences could reconcile modern politics with the unique Jewish religious-national synthesis, he founded the Zionist organization in Leipzig. He then worked under Herzl in Vienna as editor of *Die Welt*, the official organ of Zionism, but by the end of 1901 he left the editorship. Breaking from Herzl, a staunch political Zionist, Buber was becoming ever more a cultural and spiritual Zionist.

Buber, Chaim Weizmann, and others were instrumental in founding the "Democratic Fraction" in cultural opposition to Herzl at the

Fifth Zionist Congress. Buber soon joined several of this group in founding a publishing house to encourage a renaissance of Jewish spiritual creativity.

In 1904 Buber withdrew from public activity to return to his studies. He began writing on Hasidism and investigating the philosophy of religion. His interests in mysticism—Christian, Eastern, and Jewish— prepared himself for his crucial book in religious philosophy, *I and Thou* (1923).

During the 1920s Buber and Franz Rosenzweig founded a renowned school of adult Jewish studies in Frankfurt. In 1938 Buber immigrated to Palestine, where he occupied the chair in social philosophy at Hebrew University until his retirement in 1951.

Upon his arrival in Palestine, Buber soon joined with Judah Magnes and others, many of them his disciples from central Europe, in advocating a binational Jewish-Arab state, avowing that the Jewish people should proclaim "its desire to live in peace and brotherhood with the Arab people and to develop the common homeland into a republic in which both peoples will have the possibility of free development."

Buber's notion that one's deeper self is reached ultimately only in relationship to a group was the basis for this larger philosophy. Both he and Berdichevski took to heart Nietzsche's vision of a new society to be created by men of superior capacity, dreaming of a new morality and a new age. As Jews who knew Judaism's classical tradition, they took the obvious step of asserting that the Land of Israel was uniquely fit for greatness and that the Jewish people was by nature peculiarly capable of rising to unparalleled heights. They diverged in that Berdichevski imagined the supermen and the superculture of Zionism as perhaps toying with might, while Buber sought heroism in the dimension of morality—of answering the greatest demands that God can make on humans.

Hebrew Humanism (1942)

Israel is not a nation like other nations, no matter how much its representatives have wished it during certain eras. Israel is a people like no other, for it is the only people in the world which, from its earliest beginnings, has been both a nation and a religious community. In the historical hour in which its tribes grew together to form a people, it became the carrier of a revelation. The covenant which the tribes made with one another and through which they became "Israel" takes the form of a common covenant with the God of Israel. . . . Israel was and is a people and a religious community in one, and it is this unity which enabled it to survive in an exile no other nation had to suffer, an exile which lasted much longer than the period of its independence. He who severs this bond severs the life of Israel. . . .

It remained for our time to separate the Jewish people and the Jewish religious community which were fused from earliest beginnings, and to establish each as an independent unit, a nation like unto other nations and a religion like unto other religions. Thanks to the unparalleled work in Palestine, the nation is on the rise. The religion, however, is on a steep downward fall, for it is no longer a power which determines all of life; it has been confined to the special sphere of ritual or sermons. But a Jewish nation cannot exist without religion any more than a Jewish religious community without nationality. Our only salvation is to become Israel again, to become a whole, the unique whole of a people and a religious community; a renewed people, a renewed religion, and the renewed unity of both.

According to the ideas current among Zionists today, all that is needed is to establish the conditions for a normal national life, and everything will come of itself. This is a fatal error. We do, of course, need the conditions of normal national life, but these are not enough—not enough for us, at any rate. We cannot enthrone "normalcy" in place of the eternal premise of our survival. If we want to be nothing but normal, we shall soon cease to be at all.

The great values we have produced issued from the marriage of a people and a faith. We cannot substitute a technical association of nation and religion for this original marriage, without incurring barrenness. The values of Israel cannot be reborn outside the sphere of this union and its uniqueness. . . .

An Open Letter to Mahatma Gandhi (1939)

You, Mahatma Gandhi, who know of the connection between tradition and future, should not associate yourself with those who pass over our cause without understanding or sympathy.

But you say—and I consider it to be the most significant of all the things you tell us—that Palestine belongs to the Arabs and that it is therefore "wrong and inhuman to impose the Jews on the Arabs." . . .

I belong to a group of people who from the time Britain conquered Palestine have not ceased to strive for the concluding of a genuine peace between Jew and Arab. . . .

We considered it a fundamental point that in this case two vital claims are opposed to each other, two claims of a different nature and a different origin which cannot objectively be pitted against one another and between which no objective decision can be made as to which is just, which unjust. We considered and still consider it our duty to understand and to honor the claim which is opposed to ours and to endeavor to reconcile both claims. We could not and cannot renounce the Jewish claim; something even higher than the life of our people is bound up with this land, namely its work, its divine mission. But we have been and still are convinced that it must be possible to find some compromise between this claim and the other, for we love this land and we believe in its future; since such love and such faith are surely present on the other side as well, a union in the common service of the land must be within the range of possibility. Where there is faith and love, a solution may be found even to what appears to be a tragic opposition.

In order to carry out a task of such extreme difficulty—in the recognition of which we have had to overcome an internal resistance on the Jewish side too, as foolish as it is natural—we have been in need of the support of well-meaning persons of all nations, and have hoped to receive it. But now you come and settle the whole existential dilemma with the simple formula: "Palestine belongs to the Arabs."

What do you mean by saying a land belongs to a population? Evidently you do not intend only to describe a state of affairs by your formula, but to declare a certain right. You obviously mean to say that a people, being settled on the land, has so absolute a claim to that land that whoever settles on it without the permission of this people has committed a robbery. But by what means did the Arabs attain the right of ownership in Palestine? Surely by conquest, and in fact a conquest with intent to settle. You therefore admit that as a result their settlement gives them exclusive right of possession; whereas the subsequent conquests of the Mamelukes and the Turks, which were conquests with a view to domination, not to settlement, do not constitute such a right in your opinion, but leave the earlier conquerors in rightful ownership. Thus settlement by conquest justifies for you a right of ownership of Palestine; whereas a settlement such as the Jewish—the methods of which, it is true, though not always doing full justice to Arab ways of life, were even in the most objectionable cases far removed from those of conquest—does not justify in your opinion any participation in this right of possession. . . .

Our settlers do not come here as do the colonists from the Occident to have natives do their work for them; they themselves set their shoulders to the plow and they spend their strength and their blood to make the land fruitful. But it is not only for ourselves that we desire its fertility. The Jewish farmers have begun to teach their brothers, the Arab farmers, to cultivate the land more intensively; we desire to teach them further: together with them we want to cultivate the land—to "serve" it, as the Hebrew has it. The more fertile this soil becomes, the more space there will be for us and for them. We have no desire to dispossess them: we want to live with them. We do not want to dominate them: we want to serve with them. . . .

6

Pioneers

Diaspora Zionism

With more than half of today's Jewish population living in Israel, it is hard to see Zionism in historical proportion. From 1880 to 1920, as two million Eastern European Jews moved to America, barely 115,000 moved to Palestine. Yet despite being so marginal demographically, Zionism threatened American Jewry ideologically: American Jews had arrived in the Golden Medina; they did not want to feel caught between dueling Promised Lands.

Steeped in liberal ideals and committed to helping other Jews, American Zionism resolved the ideological dilemma. Both Louis Brandeis, a lawyer and U.S. Supreme Court justice, and Henrietta Szold, the founder of Hadassah: The Women's Zionist Organization of America, understood how menacing pure Zionism could be to the American Jewish dream—yet how essential American Jewish support was to fulfill the Zionist dream. Thanks to them, American Jewry became Zionized just enough to support the Jews in Palestine, without feeling pressed to move there.

While creating an emotional, financial, technical, and political pipeline for the Jewish national project, early American Zionists improvised enough of a positive feedback mechanism to make the relationship feel mutual. Invariably American Jews drew pride and power from their support for the Jewish national project.

Initially, this "Social Work" or Philanthropic Zionism was mostly an American phenomenon; European Zionism focused on fulfilling "my" Zionist revolution not facilitating "yours." Eventually, all Western Diaspora communities—situated in free democracies—embraced this openhearted, hands-off Americanized approach. Diaspora Zionists proclaim "We are one" with Israel—while remaining at home away from the homeland.

Solomon Schechter (1847–1915)

Zionism ... The great bulwark against assimilation.

Although Solomon Schechter never led the organized Zionist movement, he nonetheless became a central figure in its development in America. Schechter was born in Romania, probably in 1847; his small birthplace lacked accurate birth records. After a traditional education, he went to Vienna, then Berlin, then England, quickly becoming a notable stylist in English and a great interpreter of Judaism to the English-speaking world.

In 1902 Schechter came to America to head a reorganized Jewish Theological Seminary, the Conservative movement's flagship. Gradually, he fashioned this institution to represent many of his views, among them emphasizing the religious nationhood of the Jew. He accepted Political Zionism as a spiritual rebuff to assimilation, and the indispensable tool for saving Jews. In his non-mystical, modern way, Schechter shared with Rav Kook the idea that anything creative within Jewry can help achieve the divine aims inherent in the Jewish people.

Schechter's credo, a reinterpretation of Ahad Ha'am, helped Americanize Cultural Zionism, distinguishing between a healthy Americanization balanced with Judaism and an unhealthy assimilation abandoning Judaism. As Conservative Judaism's master builder, intellectually and institutionally, Schechter instilled a Zionist temper within the movement, emphasizing Jewish peoplehood and pride. Conservative Judaism became the most overwhelmingly Zionist of America's three major Jewish religious groupings, with Reform initially ambivalent about Zionism and Orthodoxy marginal demographically.

Zionism: A Statement (1906)

To me personally, after long hesitation and careful watching, Zionism recommended itself as the great bulwark against assimilation. By assimilation I do not understand what is usually understood by Americanization: namely, that every Jew should do his best to acquire the English language;

that he should study American history and make himself acquainted with the best productions of American literature; that he should be a law-abiding citizen, thoroughly appreciating the privilege of being a member of this great commonwealth, and joyfully prepared to discharge the duties of American citizenship.

What I understand by assimilation is loss of identity; or that process of disintegration which, passing through various degrees of defiance of all Jewish thought and of disloyalty to Israel's history and its mission, terminates variously in different lands. . . .

It is this kind of assimilation, with the terrible consequences indicated, that I dread most; even more than pogroms. To this form of assimilation, Zionism in the sense defined will prove, and is already proving, a most wholesome check. . . . Zionism declares boldly to the world that Judaism means to preserve its life by not losing its life. It shall be a true and healthy life, with a policy of its own, a religion wholly its own, invigorated by sacred memories and sacred environments, and proving a tower of strength and of unity not only for the remnant gathered within the borders of the Holy Land, but also for those who shall, by choice or necessity, prefer what now constitutes the *galut*. . . .

It is a tragedy to see a great ancient people, distinguished for its loyalty to its religion, and its devotion to its sacred law, losing thousands every day by the mere process of attrition. It is a tragedy to see sacred institutions as ancient as the mountains, to maintain which Israel for thousands of years shrank from no sacrifice, destroyed before our very eyes and exchanged for corresponding institutions borrowed from hostile religions. It is a tragedy to see the language held sacred by all the world, in which Holy Writ was composed, and which served as the depository of Israel's greatest and best thought, doomed to oblivion and forced out gradually from the synagogue. It is a tragedy to see the descendants of those who revealed revelation to the world and who developed the greatest religious literature in existence, so little familiar with real Jewish thought, and so utterly wanting in all sympathy with it, that they have no other interpretation to offer of Israel's scriptures, Israel's religion, and Israel's ideals and aspirations and hopes, than those suggested by their natural opponents, slavishly following their opinions, copying their phrases, repeating their catchwords, not sparing us even the taunt of tribalism and Orientalism. . . .

The rebirth of Israel's national consciousness, and the revival of Israel's religion, or, to use a shorter term, the revival of Judaism, are inseparable. When Israel found itself, it found its God. When Israel lost itself, or began to work at its self-effacement, it was sure to deny its God.

Louis Dembitz Brandeis (1856–1941)

Let no American imagine that Zionism is inconsistent with patriotism. Multiple loyalties are objectionable only if they are inconsistent.

Louis Dembitz Brandeis was the most distinguished figure in American life to become a Zionist. He served for twenty-two years on the U.S. Supreme Court, and his opinions reoriented constitutional law toward social and economic realism.

Brandeis was born to Jewish immigrants in Louisville, Kentucky, in 1856. By his twenty-first birthday, he had already graduated from Harvard Law School at the head of his class. After achieving financial independence at the bar in Boston, he devoted himself ever more to public causes.

Brandeis grew up without any formal religion. Until age fifty-four, he avoided appreciable contact with the Jewish community. He met its newest segment in 1910 when he was called to help settle a strike in New York's Jewish-dominated garment industry. The poor, pious Eastern European Jews' progressive yet traditional values jump-started this aristocratic Bohemian Jew's Zionist journey.

When the First World War broke out, the Zionist movement's central office was in Berlin. The responsibility to support the Jewish settlement in Palestine suddenly fell on American Jewry. A Provisional Executive Committee for General Zionist Affairs was organized in New York, and Brandeis accepted unanimous election to be its head. Serving in this office from 1914 to 1918, Brandeis became the active leader of American Zionism. He reconciled his Jewish loyalties with his American patriotism particularly eloquently when addressing the conference of Reform rabbis in 1915. Brandeis equated Zionism with progressivism, ethnic pride with Americanism, and the pioneers with the Pilgrims. These parallels domesticated Zionism, sanitizing it, Americanizing it, popularizing it.

Brandeis also played an influential role in the negotiations that preceded the 1917 Balfour Declaration. Having been appointed to the Supreme Court in 1916 by his friend President Woodrow Wilson, Brandeis legitimized the fledgling movement as patriotic and significant.

Brandeis's approach to Zionism, however, proved controversial. He advocated putting all Zionist effort into the businesslike building of Palestine, enlisting the aid of certain individuals who were not ideologically Zionist to do so. The European Zionists, headed by Chaim Weizmann, disagreed. A formal breach at an international Zionist meeting in London in 1920 carried the fight to America. Brandeis and his followers lost at the convention in Cleveland in 1921 and he resigned office—though he retained Zionist membership, lending advice and support during the mounting crises of Palestinian Jewry, to the end of his life in 1941.

The Jewish Problem and How to Solve It (1915)

Zionism seeks to establish in Palestine, for such Jews as choose to go and remain there, and for their descendants, a legally secured home, where they may live together and lead a Jewish life, where they may expect ultimately to constitute a majority of the population, and may look forward to what we should call home rule. The Zionists seek to establish this home in Palestine because they are convinced that the undying longing of Jews for Palestine is a fact of deepest significance; that it is a manifestation in the struggle for existence by an ancient people which has established its right to live, a people whose three thousand years of civilization has produced a faith, culture, and individuality which will enable it to contribute largely in the future, as it has in the past, to the advance of civilization; and that it is not a right merely but a duty of the Jewish nationality to survive and develop. They believe that only in Palestine can Jewish life be fully protected from the forces of disintegration; that there alone can the Jewish spirit reach its full and natural development; and that by securing for those Jews who wish to settle there the opportunity to do so, not only those Jews, but all other Jews will be benefited, and that the long perplexing Jewish problem will, at last, find solution. . . .

This land, treeless a generation ago, supposed to be sterile and hopelessly arid, has been shown to have been treeless and sterile because of man's misrule. It has been shown to be capable of becoming again a land "flowing with milk and honey." Oranges and grapes, olives and almonds, wheat and other cereals are now growing there in profusion. . . .

Our Jewish Pilgrim Fathers have laid the foundation. It remains for us to build the superstructure.

Let no American imagine that Zionism is inconsistent with Patriotism. Multiple loyalties are objectionable only if they are inconsistent. A man is a better citizen of the United States for being also a loyal citizen of his state, and of his city; for being loyal to his family, and to his profession or trade; for being loyal to his college or his lodge. Every Irish American who contributed toward advancing home rule was a better man and a better American for the sacrifice he made. Every American Jew who aids in advancing the Jewish settlement in Palestine, though he feels that neither he nor his descendants will ever live there, will likewise be a better man and a better American for doing so. . . .

There is no inconsistency between loyalty to America and loyalty to Jewry. The Jewish spirit, the product of our religion and experiences, is essentially modern and essentially American. Not since the destruction of the Temple have the Jews in spirit and in ideals been so fully in harmony with the noblest aspirations of the country in which they lived. . . .

Indeed, loyalty to America demands rather that each American Jew become a Zionist. For only through the ennobling effect of its strivings can we develop the best that is in us and give to this country the full benefit of our great inheritance. The Jewish spirit, so long preserved, the character developed by so many centuries of sacrifice, should be preserved and developed further, so that in America as elsewhere the sons of the race may in the future live lives and do deeds worthy of their ancestors. . . .

Henrietta Szold (1860–1945)

The Jew and his Judaism can be perpetuated only by their repatriation in the land of the fathers.

Through the organization she founded, Hadassah, the Women's Zionist Organization of America, Henrietta Szold shaped what she called "practical Zionism," a Zionism that, every year to this day, mobilizes hundreds of thousands of American women and serves millions of Israelis.

Born in Baltimore in 1860, Szold was educated in secular and religious studies by her erudite parents, Rabbi Benjamin and Sophie Szold. This trained her for her first historical contribution, as a master essayist, translator, teacher, and editor. In 1893 she became the first editor of the Jewish Publication Society.

In 1909 she and her mother visited Palestine—changing her life and transforming history. Deeply moved by the poverty, disease, starvation—along with the idealism, communal spirit, and determination—she and some friends soon founded Hadassah. A verse from Jeremiah—*Aruhat Bat Ami*: the healing of the daughter of my people—became their motto.

Szold's initial goal was quite modest: to send two nurses to Palestine. By 1918 Hadassah had sent forty-five medical professionals. Today, the organization runs two modern hospitals in Jerusalem, the jewels in the crown of Israeli medicine. And this miracle-making organization has mobilized millions of American Jews to donate billions of dollars—and hours—to build the Jewish state.

Szold essentially offered a template for American Zionism that reconciled American nationalism with Jewish nationalism, while helping non-Zionists and even anti-Zionists support the Jewish national project in Palestine. The following letter to Augusta Rosenwald, whose husband Julius Rosenwald owned Sears Roebuck, illustrates how expertly Szold navigated those ideological shoals.

Szold's second historic initiative was establishing Youth Aliyah, which eventually rescued twenty-two thousand refugee children during World War II, and subsequently thousands of others facing oppression around the world. If Louis Brandeis was the individual most responsible for showing American Jews how to reconcile their Zionist and American identities, Szold was most responsible for teaching American Jews that Zionism entails doing not just cheering.

Letter to Augusta Rosenwald (January 17, 1915)

However, the paramount consideration is that you are advancing the cause of Palestine. From my point of view, as I need not tell *you*, that is the cause of the Jew and, most important of all, of Judaism. In many respects the war catastrophe has left me bewildered and uncertain. In one respect I see more clearly than ever—that is, in respect to Zionism, the anomalous situation of the Jew everywhere—the distress, misery and in part degradation (witness Poland!) of seven millions, more than half, of our race; the bravery of the Jews who are serving in all of the armies; the size of the contingent we are contributing to every front— means to me that the Jew and his Judaism must be perpetuated and can be perpetuated only by their repatriation in the land of the fathers.

It is a miracle that, though we Zionists were not hitherto able to bring many to our way of thinking, nevertheless many in these days of stress think with pity of our little sanctuary. They have come to us and said: "Even if we do not see eye to eye with you, we are going to help you save the sanctuary you have established." Perhaps they feel that it will yield sanctuary, refuge, and protection in the days of readjustments soon to dawn, we hope.

If you succeed, in your appeal to the Federation of Temple Sisterhoods, in conveying to the Jewish women of America the need of such a sanctuary for the Jew, the need of a center from which Jewish culture and inspiration will flow, and if you can persuade them to set aside one day of the year as a Palestine Day, on which thoughts and means are to be consecrated to a great Jewish world-organizing purpose, you will have accomplished a result that will bring immediate blessing to those now in distress and in terror of life, and a blessing for all future times redounding to the benefit not only of those who will make use of their sanctuary rights in Palestine, but also those who like ourselves remaining in a happy, prosperous country, will be free to draw spiritual nourishment from a center dominated wholly by Jewish traditions and the Jewish ideals of universal peace and universal brotherhood.

Horace Mayer Kallen (1882–1974)

The outcome of the Haskala . . . is the recovery of the idea of Jewish nationality on a secular and civil basis, as the peer of other European nationalities.

Throughout his career, Horace Mayer Kallen toggled between the academic life of a professor of philosophy and his activism as an organizational leader and thinker in Jewish affairs—the latter an application of the pragmatic philosophy he formed under the influence of his teacher, William James.

Kallen was born in Germany in 1882 and brought to the United States as a child. After both undergraduate and graduate training at Harvard (PhD, 1908), he taught philosophy there for three years. Positions at Clark College and the University of Wisconsin were further preambles to his appointment to New York's new New School for Social Research in 1918.

Kallen wrote many books on education, art, politics, and religion. He followed James in affirming that human experience cannot be reduced to conformity to a single way, for it varies in different traditions and cultures, all of which have equal rights to self-expression. Consequently, he held, the basis of democratic life was secular; and the absolute of any social group should not predominate over that of another. Today Kallen is recognized as the father of multiculturalism, helping Americans appreciate their society as a salad bowl and not a melting pot.

A lifelong Zionist, Kallen believed that the modern Jewish experience had led to "the recovery of the idea of Jewish nationality on a secular and civil basis, as the peer of other European nationalities." The Zionist movement affirmed a Jewish loyalty centering around group and culture rather than religion—and the creation of such a secularized Jewish society in Palestine excited him. This excerpt exemplifies how he reconciled his nationalist understanding of Judaism with modern liberal ideas.

Zionism and Liberalism (1919)

The nationalist philosophy of Zionism is an extension of the assumptions of liberalism from the individual to the group. . . . Democracy and nationalism made up a single engine of liberalism; they were together against the oppressor. The prophet and philosopher of this nationalism is . . . [Giuseppe] Mazzini, and the sum of his teaching might be uttered in a slight modification of the Declaration of Independence: all nationalities are created equal and endowed with certain inalienable rights; among these rights are life, liberty, and the pursuit of happiness.

This is the whole Zionist ideology. . . . The Zionists have said: "The Jews are a historic people among other peoples, neither better nor worse. They have their national qualities which their past attests and which afford some indication of the future. They are entitled equally with any other to express their qualities freely and autonomously as a group, making such contribution to the co-operative enterprise of civilization as their qualities as a group promise." . . .

Whether races or nationalities are of "pure" breed or not, they exist as associations deriving from a real or credited predominant inheritance, an intimate sameness of background, tradition, custom, and aspiration. Genuine liberalism requires for them the same freedom of development and expression as for the individual. Indeed, in requiring it for the individual, it must necessarily require it for them. They are the essential reservoirs of individuality. Zionism might be described as aiming to conserve and strengthen, under far more favorable than ghetto conditions, the values of such a type of reservoir. . . . It is slander to attribute to the Zionists anything beyond the wish for international service through national freedom.

Stephen S. Wise (1874–1949)

Justice to the Jew, freedom for the Jew, Jewish equality, with all the free people of the earth.

Even as President Franklin D. Roosevelt complained that the quarreling Jews didn't have a pope, in the 1930s and 1940s, American Jewry had the next best thing—Rabbi Stephen S. Wise. The founding rabbi of the Free Synagogue in New York, heading both the American Jewish Congress and the World Jewish Congress, Wise was American Jewry's leading spokesman—and the country's leading Zionist. He fought Tammany Hall corruption in his youth, helped found the National Association for the Advancement of Colored People in middle age, and helped American Jews reconcile their Zionism with their Americanism.

A dramatic orator, Wise explained that his Zionism was natural, inherited from his father—and reinforced by meeting Theodor Herzl at the Second Zionist Congress in 1898 when he was twenty-four years old. Wise said Jews had been American for a few generations—but Jews for four thousand years.

Early on, Wise recognized Adolf Hitler as a mortal threat to European Jewry, which redoubled his efforts to establish a Jewish homeland. Indeed, it took the Holocaust to popularize Zionism in America. By 1942 American Jews were ready to let solidarity and sympathy eclipse their ideological concerns.

The Biltmore Conference in New York that year captured the shift. While reaching out to the Arabs of Palestine, the conference declared: "The new world order that will follow victory cannot be established on foundations of peace, justice, and equality, unless the problem of Jewish homelessness is finally solved." The conference endorsed opening immigration to Palestine and establishing "a Jewish Commonwealth integrated in the structure of the new democratic world. . . . Then and only then will the age old wrong to the Jewish people be righted."

Having reached that conclusion earlier, Wise was frustrated by "Jewish cowards" who ignored the threat antisemitism imposed and the opportunities Zionism offered. In October 1945, denouncing the "timidity" of Jews "greatly disturbed and alarmed over [the] Jewish resort to arms," he proclaimed: "A people that will not resort to self-defense and to all that resistance means in order to save itself from enslavement and shame is not fit to survive."

Under his leadership—and shaken by the Holocaust—American Jews overcame fears of dual loyalty to support a Jewish state whole-heartedly. Like Brandeis and Szold, Wise knew how to make this new American Zionist consensus "safe" by being altruistic, but it was revolutionary nonetheless.

Challenging Years (1949)

1935: Zionism means infinitely more than the building or rebuilding of the Jewish National Home. It means the Jewish will to live Jewishly versus the wish to survive. . . .

1944: Zionism means the reconstituting of the Jewish people as a people in the Jewish Homeland. I have only to add that it will come as one of the moral triumphs of the global war. . . .

The Jew owes it to himself to insist upon a free and democratic Jewish National Home. The Christian world owes to the Jew reparation for all the centuries of wrong and hurt and humiliation—reparation for the awful and tragic Hitler years. . . . A free and democratic Jewish Commonwealth means nothing more than justice to the Jew, freedom for the Jew, Jewish equality, with all the free people of the earth.

1948: Laugh, at those who speak of dual loyalties and divided allegiance. We have an allegiance to the spiritual heritage of a great and imperishable people. We have another allegiance to the people of our great country, of whom we are a part. There is no divided allegiance. There is a transcending allegiance crowning and glorifying both.

If men say to you, ask of you, "Are you a citizen of the State of Israel?" or "Are you a citizen of the American Republic and teacher of its people?" answer them: "The memories, the traditions, the hopes, the dreams, the sufferings, the sorrows of four thousand years have not sundered me from the blood and the race of the people of Israel. I am one of them. As a citizen I belong wholly to America. America is my country and I have none other. To it I give the utmost of my loyalty, the deepest of my love, the truest of my service."

Milton Steinberg (1903–50)

I am impelled to Zionism by the needs of my own spirit.

Milton Steinberg's enthusiasm for the Zionist movement was even greater than that of his mentor Mordecai Kaplan—and his prose was even more accessible. An extraordinary American-born writer, Steinberg put his PhD in philosophy from Columbia University and his Conservative rabbinic degree from the Jewish Theological Seminary to good use. In 1933 he became rabbi of New York's Park Avenue Synagogue. Six years later came the publication of his historical novel about the struggle over faith, *As a Driven Leaf,* which became a classic.

Steinberg embraced the inspirational possibilities the great Jewish state-building adventure afforded. Ahead of his time, he emphasized what American Jews get ideologically and emotionally from the Jewish state rather than what they give politically, diplomatically, and financially. This push from a Zionism of necessity to a Zionism of choice anticipated the Identity Zionism of the late twentieth century, launching thousands of pilgrimages to Israel and expressions of support for Israel—for American Jews' sake, not just for Israel's.

Steinberg died of a heart attack in 1950. He was only forty-six years old.

The Creed of an American Zionist (1945)

It is not true that I am a Zionist because I am not content to be an American, or because I doubt America's future. This land, I am deeply convinced, is on its way to new horizons of freedom and justice. In other words, it is not the fact that, pessimistic about the Jewish prospect in America, I have one eye cocked on Palestine—just in case. . . .

I am a Zionist in the first place because I am a religious Jew. From my Judaism I have derived a God faith, an ethical code, personal and social, a pattern of observances, but also, interwoven with these, a love for Palestine and the yearning that at least a part of the House of Israel be restored to its soil. That aspiration is written deep in the Bible. It is inscribed boldly in the whole rabbinic tradition, ancient and medieval. And it pervades Jewish ritual. My religious heritage, then, makes me a Zionist. . . .

But my thinking on Zionism is not altogether so high-flown. I advocate Zionism as the most immediate and practicable answer to a vast, terrible, and very tangible need. Long ago, in the halcyon days of the nineteenth century, Herzl and his associates already perceived the incipient pressure of political reaction, economic constriction, and psychic mass embitterment. . . .

And has not the Old World House of Israel been trampled into blood-drenched splinters? And in the grim devastation, does not Jewish Palestine shine as a joy-bringing, hope-dispensing beacon? What is more, the need of a haven of refuge will in the future be more, not less, acute. No Jew, no Zionist, no person of good will and democratic persuasion, can tolerate the thought of any Jew's being denied residence and equality status in the land of his birth or citizenship. For this objective, among others, the present great war is being waged. . . .

But I am impelled to Zionism by a more personal consideration, by the needs of my own spirit. No tradition can coast along merely on past momentum. Every religion and culture must for its health be constantly regenerated with new elements fashioned after its genius but stamped in the mold of the day.

Now, though Judaism is extraordinarily rich in accumulated resources, it too requires infusions of the fresh, novel, and contemporaneous. Yet it is everywhere a minority religion and culture; even its most devoted adherents expend themselves mainly in the larger civilization. To Judaism they come with the remainder of their time and energy. But people are not normally creative under such circumstances, as the state of Judaism demonstrates.

Hence there must be a place where Hebraism will be a first culture, where it can flourish without hindrance, and whence transfusions of new values may emanate.

Nor is this abstruse verbiage. The brilliant renaissance in Palestine, the revival there of Jewish music, art, letters, folkways, the theaters and the Hebrew tongue have invigorated, stimulated, and enriched every Jewry in the world. That too is why I am a Zionist; because, while I would remain a Jew without Jewish Palestine, my Judaism, by virtue of it, is more meaningful to me and my Jewish fellows.

There are other reasons for my Zionism, over which I cannot pause: the contribution it has made to Jewish self-respect at a time when so many forces conspire to break it down; the promise inherent in the social experiments afoot in the Jewish homeland. But tempting as such themes are, I must forego them to deal with another matter closer to our line of inquiry: How, if all I have said is true, can any Jew be anti-Zionist? . . .

Judaism, religion and culture alike, needs Jewish Palestine for its fulfillment. Wherefore considerations of universalism, far from negating Zionism, endorse it. For only when enriched and stimulated by a Jewish homeland will Jewry be equal to its destiny. . . .

PART TWO

Builders

Actualizing and
Modernizing the
Zionist Blueprints

7

Builders

Political Zionism

Political Zionism was never just about survival, although it often looked that way. Political Zionism was the home of Israel's realists, first in their sober assessment of European antisemitism, then in their defense against Israel's Arab neighbors. Nevertheless, Theodor Herzl's romantic, utopian, European liberal nationalism animated this realism with idealism. As the State of Israel found its footing, its leaders remembered that Zionism was the Jewish people's national liberation movement, charged with developing a nation-state that could be a light unto the nations.

In Israeli political terms, May 14, 1948, answered the essential question of Political Zionism: Will we have a Jewish state? Still, a new challenge emerged: surviving.

The ongoing fight for Israel's existence then entailed repeated restatements of the essential Zionist idea. As the state developed amid crushing conditions—facing wars, international repudiation, terrorism, hostile internal populations, and waves of mass migration—leaders kept updating the Zionist vision for war and peace, for democracy and prosperity. Underlying all this was the question Herzl never fully resolved: Should the Jewish state be a normal state or an exceptional light unto the nations?

This first selection, Israel's Declaration of Independence, captures the two sides of Zionism—a movement that is both particular and universal, tempering ethnic nationalism with essential civic and democratic dimensions. The declaration also shows the two sides of the Herzlian dilemma—establishing a state that asserts its right to be normal while dreaming of opportunities to be exceptional.

This foundational document powerfully expresses the Zionist narrative—featuring the Jewish ties to the land, rights to the land, needs for the land, and the Jewish values expressed through the land. It opens with the kind of romantic history that shaped nineteenth-century European nationalism but with Jewish and Zionist twists emphasizing the richness of the biblical heritage, the anguish of exile, the continuing ties to the land, and the recent redemption.

Simultaneously, offering peace, promising "full . . . equality," and envisioning a state that can be "for the benefit of all" the land's "inhabitants," demonstrates Zionism's universal dimension. Expansive democratic values were entwined in the Jewish state's DNA. Promising that the state "will be based on the precepts of liberty, justice and peace taught by the Hebrew Prophets," honors those ancient preachers as the architects of modern democracy. Substituting for a constitution, these ideals have not just been aspirations, but legal guarantees.

Balancing religious and non-religious, then as now, the final paragraph trusts in *Tsur Yisra'el*. Some translate the phrase into English as "the Almighty" or "Almighty God," but the words mean "the Rock of Israel." This phrasing acknowledges the spiritual power behind Judaism without mentioning "God."

Zvi Berenson of the Histadrut prepared the first draft. A committee consisting of Moshe Shertok (Sharett), David Remez, Pinhas Rosenblueth (Rosen), Moshe Shapira, and Aaron Zisling then edited it. A second committee of Shertok, Zisling, Rabbi Yehudah Leib Fishman (Maimon), and David Ben-Gurion reworked it. Ben-Gurion annoyed Shertok by making the document less legalistic. The vote to declare the state divided the provisional government. Representatives debated for twelve hours before voting six to four in favor. When Chaim Weizmann, the World Zionist Organization chairman who would become the country's first president, heard about the hesitations, he muttered, "What are they waiting for, the idiots?"

Israel's Declaration of Independence (May 14, 1948)

This right is the natural right of the Jewish people to be masters of their own fate, like all other nations, in their own sovereign State.

The Land of Israel was the birthplace of the Jewish people. Here their spiritual, religious and political identity was shaped. Here they first attained to statehood, created cultural values of national and universal significance and gave to the world the eternal Book of Books.

After being forcibly exiled from their land, the people kept faith with it throughout their Dispersion and never ceased to pray and hope for their return to it and for the restoration in it of their political freedom.

Impelled by this historic and traditional attachment, Jews strove in every successive generation to reestablish themselves in their ancient homeland. In recent decades they returned en masse. Pioneers, defiant returnees, and defenders, they made deserts bloom, revived the Hebrew language, built villages and towns, and created a thriving community controlling its own economy and culture, loving peace but knowing how to defend itself, bringing the blessings of progress to all the country's inhabitants, and aspiring towards independent nationhood.

In the year 5657 (1897), at the summons of the spiritual father of the Jewish state, Theodor Herzl, the First Zionist Congress convened and proclaimed the right of the Jewish people to national rebirth in its own country.

This right was recognized in the Balfour Declaration of the 2nd November, 1917, and re-affirmed in the Mandate of the League of Nations which, in particular, gave international sanction to the historic connection between the Jewish people and *Eretz Yisra'el* and to the right of the Jewish people to rebuild its National Home.

The catastrophe which recently befell the Jewish people—the massacre of millions of Jews in Europe—was another clear demonstration of the urgency of solving the problem of its homelessness by reestablishing in *Eretz Yisra'el* the Jewish state, which would open the gates of the homeland wide to every Jew and confer upon the Jewish people the status of a fully privileged member of the community of nations.

Survivors of the Nazi holocaust in Europe, as well as Jews from other parts of the world, continued to migrate to *Eretz Yisra'el*, undaunted by difficulties, restrictions and dangers, and never ceased to assert their right to a life of dignity, freedom and honest toil in their national homeland.

In the Second World War, the Jewish community of this country contributed its full share to the struggle of the freedom- and peace-loving nations against the forces of Nazi wickedness and, by the blood of its soldiers and its war effort, gained the right to be reckoned among the peoples who founded the United Nations.

On the 29th November, 1947, the United Nations General Assembly passed a resolution calling for the establishment of a Jewish state in *Eretz Yisra'el*; the General Assembly required the inhabitants of *Eretz Yisra'el* to take such steps as were necessary on their part for the implementation of that resolution. This recognition by the United Nations of the right of the Jewish people to establish their State is irrevocable.

This right is the natural right of the Jewish people to be masters of their own fate, like all other nations, in their own sovereign State.

Accordingly we, members of the People's Council, representatives of the Jewish Community of *Eretz Yisra'el* and of the Zionist Movement, are here assembled on the day of the termination of the British Mandate over *Eretz Yisra'el* and, by virtue of our natural and historic right and on the strength of the resolution of the United Nations General Assembly, hereby declare the establishment of a Jewish state in *Eretz Yisra'el*, to be known as the State of Israel. . . .

The State of Israel will be open for Jewish immigration and for the Ingathering of the Exiles; it will foster the development of the country for the benefit of all its inhabitants; it will be based on freedom, justice and peace as envisaged by the prophets of Israel; it will ensure complete equality of social and political rights to all its inhabitants irrespective of religion, race or sex; it will guarantee freedom of religion, conscience, language, education and culture; it will safeguard the Holy Places of all religions; and it will be faithful to the principles of the Charter of the United Nations.

The State of Israel is prepared to cooperate with the agencies and representatives of the United Nations in implementing the resolution of the General Assembly of the 29th November, 1947, and will take steps to bring about the economic union of the whole of *Eretz Yisra'el.*

We appeal to the United Nations to assist the Jewish people in the building-up of its State and to receive the State of Israel into the community of nations.

We appeal—in the very midst of the onslaught launched against us now for months—to the Arab inhabitants of the State of Israel to preserve peace and participate in the upbuilding of the State on the basis of full and equal citizenship and due representation in all its provisional and permanent institutions.

We extend our hand to all neighboring states and their peoples in an offer of peace and good neighborliness, and appeal to them to establish bonds of cooperation and mutual help with the sovereign Jewish people settled in its own land. The State of Israel is prepared to do its share in a common effort for the advancement of the entire Middle East.

We appeal to the Jewish people throughout the Diaspora to rally round the Jews of *Eretz Yisra'el* in the tasks of immigration and upbuilding and to stand by them in the great struggle for the realization of the age-old dream—the redemption of Israel.

Placing our trust in the Rock of Israel, we affix our signatures to this proclamation at this session of the provisional Council of State, on the soil of the Homeland, in the city of Tel Aviv, on this Sabbath eve, the 5th day of Iyar, 5708 (14th May, 1948).

David Ben-Gurion (1886–1973)

The new Jew builds *Am Segula*.

Israel's bold, brilliant, combative, controversial first prime minister, David Ben-Gurion (1886–1973), was born David Gruen in Plonsk, Poland. A Socialist Zionist, and leader in Poalei Zion, the Social-Democratic Workers of Zion, he arrived in Palestine in 1906, inspired by "the positive purpose of rebuilding a homeland." He farmed and fought in Petah Tikva and the Galilee, joining the Jewish defense organization HaShomer. He wandered and studied in Thessaloniki,

Constantinople, Jerusalem, Cairo, and New York, then served in the Jewish Legion during World War I.

By 1919 he returned to now-British-controlled Palestine and headed the centrist Socialist Zionist group Ahdut HaAvoda, which formed the nucleus of his Mapai party in 1930. He chaired the executive committee of the Jewish Agency, Israel's government-in-formation, starting in 1935. He served as prime minister from 1948 to 1953, and from late 1955 until 1963. Most of that time he doubled as defense minister, making tough decisions as the young state developed.

In 1944 addressing a gathering of youth leaders in Haifa, Ben-Gurion emphasized the Zionist revolution's unique dual mission. It's easier, he argued, to unseat governments than to transform oneself and one's people, especially after the perverse impact of exile. Ben-Gurion's Zionist formula included: independence, unity, and pioneering.

Survival, however, came first. Speaking as violence mounted in the months before declaring independence, Ben-Gurion unleashed the Jews' "collective will" to make history as unrelenting if reluctant warriors. Fostering self-defense and self-reliance after millennia of oppression would launch the state and create proud New Jews.

Whenever possible, Ben-Gurion goaded his people to stretch, not just survive. In 1970 now living as a pioneering kibbutznik in the Negev desert, this scholar-statesman described Jews as uniquely idealistic. He anticipated that, increasingly, *aliyah* would not be about escaping "hardship." Distinguishing between true Zionists and mere "fans," Ben-Gurion appealed to Jews living in prosperity to sacrifice materialism for the spiritual payoffs living in Israel offered.

The Imperatives of the Jewish Revolution (1944)

The meaning of the Jewish revolution is contained in one word—independence! Independence for the Jewish people in its homeland! Dependence is not merely political or economic; it is also moral, cultural, and intellectual, and it affects every limb and nerve of the body, every conscious and subconscious act. Independence, too, means more than political and economic freedom; it involves also the spiritual, moral, and intellectual realms, and, in essence, it is independence in the heart, in sentiment, and in will. . . .

A revolution directed against a well-defined social structure is a one-time affair; it can succeed by seizing control of the government and wielding the newly seized power to change the existing social and economic order. The Jewish revolution against our historic destiny must be a prolonged and continuing struggle, an enlistment of our own generation and even of those to come, and its road to success is not through seizure of power but only by the gradual shaping of the forces, mentioned above, that lead to independence, by girding ourselves with unyielding tenacity for changing our national destiny. . . .

The second indispensable imperative of the Jewish revolution is the unity of its protagonists. This sharing together in a fate, a creative process, and a struggle is what unites this vanguard—the pioneers, the builders of the homeland, the workers of the land of Israel, who are inspired by the vision of a Jewish renaissance on humanistic, Zionist, and socialist foundations. The conquest of labor and the land, self-defense, the development of the Hebrew language and culture, freedom for the individual and the nation, cooperation and social responsibility, preparation for further immigration, and the welding of the arrivals from the various Diasporas into a nation—these fundamental purposes are held in common, both in theory and in practice, by all those who are faithful to our revolution. These values make it possible, and indeed mandatory, that they be united. . . .

Another kind of cooperation is required from those who are loyal to our revolution: the comradeship of Jewish labor with international labor. . . . The difficult task we are performing on the Jewish scene is part of a tremendous movement which involves all of humanity—the world revolution, whose aims are the redemption of man from every form of enslavement, discrimination, and exploitation, no matter whether the victims are nations, races, religions, or one of the sexes. . . .

The third—and perhaps the most important—imperative of the Jewish revolution is *chalutziut* [pioneering]. . . .

Now, more than ever before, we need a strong and devoted pioneering force. The desert area of our land is calling us, and the destruction of our people is crying out to us. In order to save the remnant—and all of us now constitute a remnant, including our own communities here in the Land of Israel—our work must proceed apace. . . .

The ingathering of the exiles into a socialist Jewish state is in fact only a precondition for the fulfillment of the real mission of our people. We must first break the constricting chains of national and class oppression and become free, enjoying complete individual and national independence on the soil of a redeemed homeland. After that we can address ourselves to the great mission of humanity on this earth—to master the forces of nature and to develop individuals' unique creative genius to the highest degree.

Speech to Mapai Central Committee (January 16, 1948)

There is now nothing more important than war needs, and nothing equal to war needs. And just as I don't understand the language of "state" right now, I don't understand the language of *aliyah* and the language of settlement and the language of culture. There is only one criterion: are these things needed for the war effort or not? If they are needed—let them be done. If they are unnecessary—let them wait until the crisis is past. There are no exceptions, that is the great terror and the great misfortune embedded in every war, that is a cruel and jealous Moloch [god that demands child sacrifice] who knows neither compassion nor compromise. . . .

It is necessary that we take up the yoke of war and show a greater will to win than those others. We shall do it, precisely because for us war is not a goal in itself, and we see war as a terrible accursed misfortune, and resort to war only from lack of choice—war and peace are nothing more than means to something else—that "something" will give us the advantage that our enemies do not have and that is denied to the followers of violence: a vision of life, a vision of national rebirth, of independence, equality and peace—for the Jewish nation and for all peoples of the world. . . .

Am Segula: Memoirs (1970)

What is Israel? It is two things: an Ark and a Covenant; in other words a refuge and a dynamic. I think the dynamic, the Covenant, takes precedence over the concept of refuge. . . . There are some who see Israel's importance primarily as an Ark, a place where the persecuted can go or hope to go. In Russia today, the harassed Jew looks secretly towards Israel. . . .

An Ark, however, is passive. We are a busy, forward-looking nation with much more work to accomplish. Israel cannot just be a refuge. If it is to survive as a valid nation it has to be much, much more. . . .

And our mission here? What have the Jewish people to accomplish in Israel? . . .

I have tried to find an adequate translation for the phrase *Am Segula* in any of several languages. . . . We might say that Moses's message from God could thus be summed up: "The Jews must be a unique nation in that they should embody the higher virtues." In other words, the uniqueness of the Jews is not that they consider themselves to be singled out for special status by God, to be his favored creatures or his super-race. . . . Rather *Am Segula* implies an extra burden, an added responsibility to perform with a virtue born of conscience and to listen to what Elijah later called "the still, small voice." . . .

I have always been very concerned, secularist though I am, with this country's spiritual state. . . .

You cannot reach for the higher virtue without being an idealist. The Jews are chronic idealists, which make me humbly glad to belong to this people and to have shared in their noble epic. . . .

Before the creation of the state two factors made for *aliyah*. One was the vision of national resurgence which had lived in the hearts of the Hebrew nation for thousands of years. . . . The second factor . . . was the political and economic hardship of the Jews in Eastern Europe, Asia, and Africa. But with the creation of the state a third factor came into being: the attractive force of the Jewish state. . . .

Herzl defines Zionism as "the Jewish people in the making," yet with few exceptions the Zionists of the United States, England, and other affluent lands did not consider themselves "in the making." They used their financial and political influence to help Jews in the lands of distress and aided in the settlement of Israel, but without being requested or volunteering (except for a small minority) to come and settle here. . . .

The main point is that they ignore the lessons of Jewish history: those who laid the foundations of the state from 1870 to 1948 came here not because under the Turks and the British the economic situation was more flourishing or the lives of Jews any safer than in the countries of their birth, but solely because of a vision of redemption which they wished to implement by pioneering zeal. . . .

After all, living conditions in the State of Israel are not all that much worse than in the lands of prosperity and there are young people, and not only young people, in those countries who feel a profound need for a life that involves more than movies, cars, and fancy apartments. What they are looking for is the satisfaction of moral and social needs and an historic vision. There are also Jews in the lands of prosperity who are deeply apprehensive about the growing assimilation and the fragmentation of the Jewish soul in the Diaspora, who are increasingly aware that only in Israel can a Jew live a full life, both as a Jew and as a human being. . . .

The Law of Return (1950)

Every Jew has the right to come to this country as an *oleh*, immigrant.

On July 5, 1950, Israel's First Knesset, elected with an 87 percent voter turnout, took a major step toward fulfilling Israel's basic Zionist mission. Passing the Law of Return, conferring automatic citizenship on any Jew choosing to move to Israel, meant that after thousands of years of homelessness, after millions of Jews were murdered, the homeless now had a home; the persecuted now had refuge. Subsequently, more than three million Jews have immigrated to Israel, many of them refugees with nowhere else to go, justifying Israel's existence—and its Law of Return.

Since 1950, the Knesset has tweaked the law, barring criminals in 1954 and, in 1970, expanding eligibility beyond Jewish law to anyone with a Jewish grandparent or Jewish spouse. Adolf Hitler and other oppressors had used such family ties to persecute people—now, these relationships became pathways to salvation.

Nations, even democracies, define borders and set boundaries, deciding who to let in—and keep out. International law recognizes the notion of achieving citizenship via ancestry, calling it *jure sanguinis*, Latin for "by the right of blood." In privileging Jewish immigrants, Israel's Law of Return fits democratic norms; others can achieve citizenship through a five-year procedure. Just as America's EB5-Visa program fast-tracks Green Cards for entrepreneurs who invest half a million dollars to create jobs and Italy's reunification program accepts anyone proving Italian ancestry, Israel fast-tracks citizenship for Jews, a people slaughtered when stateless.

The Law of Return (July 5, 1950)

Right of aliyah [immigration]: 1. Every Jew has the right to come to this country as an *oleh* [immigrant].

Oleh's visa: 2. (a) *Aliyah* shall be by *oleh's* visa. (b) An *oleh's* visa shall be granted to every Jew who has expressed his desire to settle in Israel, unless the Minister of Immigration is satisfied that the applicant (1) is engaged in an activity directed against the Jewish people; or (2) is likely to endanger public health or the security of the State.

Oleh's certificate: 3. (a) A Jew who has come to Israel and subsequent to his arrival has expressed his desire to settle in Israel may, while still in Israel, receive an *oleh's* certificate. (b) The restrictions specified in section 2(b) shall apply also to the grant of an *oleh's* certificate, but a person shall not be regarded as endangering public health on account of an illness contracted after his arrival in Israel.

Residents and persons born in this country: Every Jew who has immigrated into this country before the coming into force of this Law, and every Jew who was born in this country, whether before or after the coming into force of this Law, shall be deemed to be a person who has come to this country as an *oleh* under this Law. . . .

Isaiah Berlin (1909–97)

A Zionism of straight backs, normal life, and the power of choice

The brilliant philosopher and Oxford University don Sir Isaiah Berlin was known for his warmth and wit. For decades, his lectures and bon mots entranced the world's leading intellectuals. He taught the world two defining dualities that intellectuals invoke regularly: distinguishing between the monomaniacal hedgehog, who bores into one particular issue or skill set, versus the wide-ranging fox, who skates more broadly, thus superficially; and distinguishing between "negative liberty," freedom *from* oppression or state imposition, versus positive liberal freedom, the freedom *to* think, speak, and do. And he is best remembered for eloquently defending nationalism, liberalism, pluralism, individualism, and Zionism.

Born into a wealthy assimilated family in Riga, Latvia, on June 6, 1909, Berlin was a proud Jew and a "natural assimilator"—his maternal grandfather was a Lubavitch rabbi. Fleeing the Russian Revolution's chaos, he arrived in London with his parents in 1921. The man who would become "the last great Jewish intellectual of Czarist Russia," according to his biographer Michael Ignatieff, "became a master at fitting in, at the price of lingering self-dislike."

By 1932 Berlin was a lecturer in philosophy at New College, Oxford. His dispatches from America during World War II were so impressive that Winston Churchill insisted on meeting this mysterious Mr. Berlin—only to be sent Irving, the songwriter of "White Christmas." Postwar, after serving at the British embassy in Moscow, Isaiah Berlin—who eventually met and charmed Churchill—returned to Oxford, which became his permanent home.

In 1996, a year before he died at age eighty-eight, Sir Isaiah said in his high English accent that always retained just a touch of Latvia: "I can tell you why I'm a Zionist. . . . Assimilation might be a quite good thing, but it doesn't work. . . . There isn't a Jew in the world known to me who somewhere inside him does not have a tiny drop of uneasiness vis-a-vis 'them,' the majority among whom they live. They may be very friendly, they may be entirely happy, but one has to behave particularly well, because if they don't behave well they won't like us."

Paradoxically, Berlin also appreciated the Eastern European ghetto's insulation. He said it preserved Jewish civilization and provided the ideological, sociological, and political foundation for the state in ways the more tortured, ambivalent, yet supposedly sophisticated Western European and North American Jewish experience never could.

In an essay from 1953 and remarks in 1975, Berlin deftly summarized Israel's great contribution: solving the Jewish Problem, despite the problems arising with the state: by welcoming all Jews to live normally in their national homeland, Israel gave Diaspora Jews dignity and a shot at normalcy too.

Jewish Slavery and Emancipation (1953)

The creation of the State of Israel has rendered the greatest service that any human institution can perform for individuals—it has restored to Jews not merely their personal dignity and status as human beings, but what is vastly more important, their right to choose as individuals how they shall live—the basic freedom of choice, the right to live or perish, go to the good or the bad in one's own way, without which life is a form of slavery, as it has been, indeed, for the Jewish community for almost two thousand years. . . .

The communal Jewish future belongs to Israel. The Jewish religion will survive in the hearts of those who believe in it, wherever they may be. And individual Jews will surely claim their rights and perform their full duties as human beings and citizens in the communities in which, at last, they can freely choose to live—freely, because they are physically as well as morally free to leave them, and their choice whether to go or stay, being no longer forced upon them, is a genuine choice. . . .

A national problem—indeed a world problem—has been solved in our day. Surely, despite those who invent a hideous dilemma and demand all or nothing (all Jews to go to Israel, or in some other way to keep out of our sight), this is miraculous enough for one generation of men. Surely we are entitled to say *dayenu,* [enough]. . . .

The Achievement of Zionism (1975)

Nationalism often means a pathological condition of national consciousness when, for some reason, it becomes diseased and aggressive towards others. But in the Jewish case all I mean is awareness of oneself as a member of a community possessing certain internal bonds which are neither superior nor inferior to but simply different in some respects from similar bonds which unite other nations. It does not preclude holding a large area of ideals in common with everyone else. . . .

This is the normal national consciousness defined by German philosophers like Herder towards the end of the eighteenth century. They tried to say that, besides the basic desires of human beings for food, shelter, procreation and a minimum degree of liberty, there is also the desire to belong to a community which they can regard as their own, in which they feel comfortable and in which they do not feel stared at by others, in which they do not constantly have to justify their existence. This was all that Zionism in its beginnings amounted to—normalisation. . . .

Meanwhile, we have an Israeli nation, with its pros and its cons. The things being said against it are well known. The Israelis are accused of provincialism, of living on charity, of a certain degree of political tyranny, of some degree of corruption in their municipal and political life. All that may be so. But of course the experiment as an experiment was a success.

If its purpose was to straighten Jewish backs, to create a nation not suffering from the particular disease which brought the movement into being, not to create those insecure nervous types who did not know where they belong, who suffered from all kinds of suppressed and open inferiorities, who were constantly looking over their shoulders to see what other people thought of them; who were constantly nervous and being warned by their more cautious leaders of tactless behavior which must not irritate the neighbors—if that was the purpose, it was achieved. . . .

It is marvellous that Israelis have developed a normal life. They are perfectly ordinary human beings who do not suffer from the particular neuroses which the Zionist movement was intended to cure.

But the purpose of the movement was also to create a situation in which Jews, like other human beings, can make a free choice. . . .

Today, individual Jews have this choice. They can be passionate supporters of the State of Israel or they can ignore it. They can contribute to it, can live there, can visit it constantly, can regard themselves as its emissaries abroad. They can have any relationship they wish with it which is desirable in a free, open-textured liberal society. This was not open to them before. And this is the achievement.

Abba Eban (1915–2002)

The only state which has the same territory, speaks the same language and upholds the same faith as it did three thousand years ago.

By May 1967, the Egyptian dictator Gamel Abdul Nasser had united Egypt, Syria, and Jordan under his joint United Arab Republic military command. As Nasser led shouts on the Arab street to throw the Jews into the sea, Jews worldwide feared another Holocaust. After all, the impossible had already happened, barely two decades earlier. Then, the Israeli army won its six-day victory.

If the one-eyed warrior Moshe Dayan symbolized the New Jew as soldier, the silver-tongued diplomat Abba Eban symbolized the New Jew as statesman. Having Jews master both professions in defending their own country fulfilled Herzl's dream.

Abba Eban, born Aubrey Eban to Lithuanian Jewish parents in South Africa in 1915, was educated in England, earning a triple first—first class in all three parts—at Cambridge. A protégé of Chaim Weizmann and David Ben-Gurion, Eban became Israel's first permanent representative to the United Nations at age thirty-three. By thirty-five, he was also Israel's ambassador to the United States. Over the next decades Eban would become Israel's eloquent, elegant voice abroad.

By 1967 Eban, serving as foreign minister under Levi Eshkol, managed the excruciating negotiations between Israel and the United States as Israel prepared to defend against Nasser's genocidal threats. In articulating Israel's position before the Security Council on June

6, 1967, Eban refused to be defensive. Justifying Israel's actions, the dovish Labor Party loyalist who would accuse the Palestinians of never missing an opportunity to miss an opportunity for peace, used this opportunity to champion the three-thousand-year-old Zionist project. He also dreamed of "a brighter dawn" for Arabs and Jews.

Statement to the Security Council (June 6, 1967)

In short, there was peril for Israel wherever it looked. Its manpower had been hastily mobilized. Its economy and commerce were beating with feeble pulses. Its streets were dark and empty. There was an apocalyptic air of approaching peril. And Israel faced this danger alone. . . .

Now there could be no doubt about what was intended for us. With my very ears I heard President Nasser's speech on 26 May. He said: "We intend to open a general assault against Israel. This will be total war. Our basic aim will be to destroy Israel." . . .

I have said that the situation to be constructed after the cease-fire must depend on certain principles. The first of these principles surely must be the acceptance of Israel's statehood and the total elimination of the fiction of its non-existence. . . . After three thousand years the time has arrived to accept Israel's nationhood as a fact, for here is the only state in the international community which has the same territory, speaks the same language, and upholds the same faith as it did three thousand years ago.

And if, as everybody knows to be the fact, the universal conscience was in the last week or two most violently shaken at the prospect of danger to Israel, it was not only because there seemed to be a danger to a state, but also, I think, because the state was Israel, with all that this ancient name evokes, teaches, symbolizes, and inspires. How grotesque would be an international community which found room for 122 sovereign units and which did not acknowledge the sovereignty of that people which had given nationhood its deepest significance and its most enduring grace. . . .

But the central point remains the need to secure an authentic intellectual recognition by our neighbors of Israel's deep roots in the Middle Eastern reality. There is an intellectual tragedy in the failure of Arab leaders to come to grips, however reluctantly, with the depth and authenticity of Israel's roots in the life, the history, the spiritual experience, and the culture of the Middle East. . . .

Israel has in recent days proved its steadfastness and vigor. It is now willing to demonstrate its instinct for peace. Let us build a new system of relationships from the wreckage of the old. Let us discern across the darkness the vision of a better and a brighter dawn.

Teddy Kollek (1911–2007)

This beautiful golden city, the heart and soul, of Jewish history.

Teddy Kollek was Jerusalem's irrepressible mayor. Raised in Vienna, Kollek had helped found Kibbutz Ein Gev in 1937 two years after arriving in Palestine, was an intelligence officer for the Jewish Agency, and for twelve years had served as director general of Prime Minister David Ben-Gurion's office. When Ben-Gurion created the Raf"i party, he asked Kollek to run for mayor of Jerusalem. Although not excited to be mayor of this small town, Kollek always obeyed Ben-Gurion. In 1965 he ran, won, and first found the job boring. Once the lightning-quick 1967 victory reunited Jerusalem, Kollek discovered his life's mission.

Teddy Kollek became Jerusalem's master builder. As mayor from 1965 through 1993, he united and modernized an old, sleepy, fragmented city. Appreciating Jerusalem's centrality to three world religions, Kollek insisted the city's Arabs deserved equal services, even if they resented Israeli rule.

In this article in *Foreign Affairs*, Kollek never mentioned the word "Zionism." Yet his expansive, pluralistic, permeable vision for the Jewish people's capital, Jerusalem, realized Theodor Herzl's vision of the Jewish state as a progressive center for all. Ironically, Herzl articulated that vision in his novel *Altneuland*, which means "old new land," but was translated as "Tel Aviv." That city, springing from the ancient hill, the Tel, became Israel's modern metropolis and Jerusalem's urban rival.

Jerusalem (1977)

Let me be perfectly candid. The thing I dread most is that this city, so beautiful, so meaningful, so holy to millions of people, should ever be divided again; that barbed wire fences, minefields and concrete barriers should again ever sever its streets; that armed men again patrol a frontier through its heart. I fear the re-division of Jerusalem not only as the mayor of the city, as a Jew and as an Israeli, but as a human being who is deeply sensitive to its history and who cares profoundly about the well-being of its inhabitants....

The fact that all three great monotheistic religions find meaning in Jerusalem cannot be a random accident. I think the reason is clear. First of all, Jerusalem is a beautiful place set in the mystical Judean Hills, conducive to meditation and thought and wonder at the meaning of life. And secondly, for all their tensions and exclusiveness, the three great religions are historically deeply interrelated. Jesus came to Jerusalem because he was a Jew who made the pilgrimage to the City of David and the Temple. Mohammed, whose roots were in Mecca and Medina, is said to have visited Jerusalem during his night ride because his ideas and his vision were interrelated with Judaism and Christianity. We must live with the reality of these connections. For centuries men have fought and died because of them. But I am not alone in feeling intensely that men can also live in brotherhood because of them.

These very connections make any division of Jerusalem a senseless exercise. The remaining Western Wall of the Temple enclosure, the Church of the Holy Sepulchre, and the Dome of the Rock are all in the Old City within yards of each other. The Dome of the Rock is actually on top of the Temple Mount, the very site of the Temple of the Jews....

The religious tenets of the Muslims exclude internationalization because they reject the idea the Temple Mount—the Haram—should be ruled by infidels.... Moreover, it does not accord with their political aspirations. As to the Jews, the centrality of Jerusalem in Jewish faith and tradition and the intensity of Jewish feeling about Jerusalem are reflected in the two-thousand-year-old prayer repeated throughout the centuries, "Next year in Jerusalem." This symbolizes not only a religious hope but memories of ancient glories under Jewish rule and an unyielding struggle for their revival. All this is expressed for Jews in the word "Jerusalem." The Jewish people cannot give up Jerusalem, nor can or will they every again remove their capital from Jerusalem.

But independent of these intense feelings, internationalization will not work for pragmatic reasons. Past experience, whether in Trieste or in Danzig, has shown its unworkability. In the case of Danzig indeed it contributed to bringing on a world war. . . .

Tensions do exist today in the city and nobody can deny them. But it was a much less happy city when the walls and barbed wire divided it; and it was certainly a more violent city than it is today. We have made progress towards a city of tolerant coexistence in which common interests are emerging, and we have established crucial principles that make continuing progress possible. Four of these principles are:

There shall be free access to all the Holy Places and they shall be administered by their adherents.

Everything possible shall be done to ensure unhindered development of the Arab way of life in the Arab sections of the city and to ensure the Arabs a practical religious, cultural, and commercial governance over their own daily lives. The same holds true, of course, for the various Christian communities.

Everything possible should be done to ensure equal governmental, municipal, and social services in all parts of the city.

Continuing efforts should be made to increase cultural, social, and economic contacts among the various elements of Jerusalem's population.

And, in fact, civic affairs, law enforcement, infrastructure services, urban planning, marketing and supply, and to a great extent specialized medical services are centrally provided to all Jerusalemites. . . .

Within an undivided city, everything is possible, all kinds of adjustments can be made, all kinds of accommodations can be considered, all kinds of autonomy can be enjoyed, all kinds of positive relationships can be developed. . . .

I do not think you can find any Israelis who are willing to give up Jerusalem. They cannot and will not. This beautiful golden city is the heart and soul. If you want one simple word to symbolize all of Jewish history, that word would be Jerusalem.

Chaim Herzog (1918–97)

A vindication of the fundamental concepts of the equality of nations and of self-determination.

In November 1975, Chaim Herzog, a famous lawyer, radio commentator, and military intelligence officer recently appointed as Israel's ambassador to the United Nations, opposed the General Assembly's infamous "Zionism Is Racism" resolution 3379, with the following speech. The Jewish people were reeling, traumatized by the bloody Yom Kippur War of 1973, now hurt by the world's repudiation of their national movement. Zionism needed defending and reframing—a new justification in a changing world.

Herzog's restatement of Zionism's defining principles resonated widely, affirming the Zionist dream, nearly thirty years after Israel's founding. While opposition to antisemitism still fueled the movement, Herzog celebrated the young democratic and socialist state's accomplishments. Years later, Herzog, who would become Israel's president partially thanks to his UN efforts, joked that the fury the resolution provoked reinvigorated Zionism more than dozens of speeches ever could. If so, his speech helped provide the basic explanation and the ideological content many Jews and non-Jews needed to express their instinctive opposition to the UN's betrayal of the state it helped to establish.

Address to the United Nations General Assembly (November 10, 1975)

Zionism is the name of the national movement of the Jewish people and is the modern expression of the ancient Jewish heritage. The Zionist ideal, as set out in the Bible, has been, and is, an integral part of the Jewish religion.

Zionism is to the Jewish people what the liberation movements of Africa and Asia have been to their own people.

Zionism is one of the most dynamic and vibrant national movements in human history. Historically it is based on a unique and unbroken connection, extending some four thousand years, between the People of the Book and the Land of the Bible.

In modern times, in the late nineteenth century, spurred by the twin forces of antisemitic persecution and of nationalism, the Jewish people organized the Zionist movement in order to transform their dream into reality. Zionism as a political movement was the revolt of an oppressed nation against the depredation and wicked discrimination and oppression of the countries in which antisemitism flourished. It is no coincidence that the co-sponsors and supporters of this resolution include countries who are guilty of the horrible crimes of antisemitism and discrimination to this very day. . . .

The reestablishment of Jewish independence in Israel, after centuries of struggle to overcome foreign conquest and exile, is a vindication of the fundamental concepts of the equality of nations and of self-determination. To question the Jewish people's right to national existence and freedom is not only to deny to the Jewish people the right accorded to every other people on this globe, but it is also to deny the central precepts of the United Nations. . . .

Here you have a movement which is the embodiment of a unique pioneering spirit, of the dignity of labor, and of enduring human values, a movement which has presented to the world an example of social equality and open democracy being associated in this resolution with abhorrent political concepts. . . .

Zionism is our attempt to build a society, imperfect though it may be, in which the visions of the prophets of Israel will be realized. I know that we have problems. I know that many disagree with our government's policies. Many in Israel too disagree from time to time with the government's policies . . . and are free to do so because Zionism has created the first and only real democratic state in a part of the world that never really knew democracy and freedom of speech. . . .

I stand here not as a supplicant. Vote as your moral conscience dictates to you. For the issue is neither Israel nor Zionism. The issue is the continued existence of this organization, which has been dragged to its lowest point of discredit by a coalition of despots and racists. . . .

We, the Jewish people, will not forget.

For us, the Jewish people, this is but a passing episode in a rich and event-filled history. We put our trust in our Providence, in our faith and beliefs, in our time-hallowed tradition, in our striving for social advance and human values, and in our people wherever they may be. For us, the Jewish people, this resolution based on hatred, falsehood and arrogance, is devoid of any moral or legal value.

[Ambassador Herzog then ripped the resolution in half.]

Albert Memmi (b. 1920)

The Jew, oppressed as a people, must find his autonomy and freedom to express his originality as a people.

The Totalitarian Left's abandonment of Israel—and the libels accusing Zionism of racism, colonialism, and imperialism—devastated many liberal Jews. Some, like the Tunisian-born, French-based intellectual Albert Memmi, helped build the very ideological structure now being weaponized against them and the Jewish state.

Memmi's 1953 autobiographical novel, *Pillar of Salt*, introduced by the existential novelist Albert Camus, described growing up in the Tunisian Jewish ghetto before serving in a Nazi forced-labor camp. Documenting the Holocaust beyond Europe, Memmi felt enslaved yet liberated: "a half-breed of colonization, understanding everyone because I belonged completely to no one." He resented the Jews' double impotence: bullied by European colonial oppressors and neighboring Muslim Arab tormentors. "I'm a Jew!" he wrote. "My home is in the ghetto, my legal status is native African. I come from an Oriental background. I'm poor."

This understanding of marginalization, what academics call "liminality," shaped his 1957 classic, *The Colonizer and the Colonized*, introduced by the existential philosopher Jean Paul Sartre. Here, Memmi applied to the Jewish condition his insights into the codependent relationship between the oppressor and the oppressed. Though dispersed and not colonized, though a persecuted minority not a subjugated majority, Jews experienced similar powerlessness, conspicuous invisibility, and debilitating humiliations, personally and collectively.

This reluctant Jew flirted with socialism, hoping to bury his Jewish identity in "the honey of that universalist embrace." Caught between different classes, ethnicities, civilizations, he was playing musical chairs, the real-life edition: "In trying to sit on several chairs, one generally lands on the floor."

Memmi's 1962 book, *Portrait of a Jew*, denounced the incurable oppression of the Jew. His 1966 book, *The Liberation of the Jew*, championed the Zionist solution—as did his 1975 book *Jews and Arabs*. This reluctant Zionist still preferred universalism. The oppression of the Jew, however, was so total that it required an equally comprehensive solution. Zionism was a legitimate national liberation movement, comparable to other post-colonial movements. I "approve of the liberation and the national development of the Arabs," he wrote after the Yom Kippur War. "Why should I not wish for the same things for my own people?"

Subsequently, this courageous, increasingly iconoclastic and unpopular French intellectual resisted the post-modernist's prejudices. In his 1975 essay "Who Is an Arab Jew?" Memmi debunked the anti-Zionist myth that Muslims treated Jews well in North Africa and the Arabian Peninsula until Israel's founding soured everything. "Never, I repeat, never—with the possible exception of two or three very specific intervals such as the Andalusian, and not even then—did the Jews in Arab lands live in other than a humiliated state, vulnerable and periodically mistreated and murdered, so that they should clearly remember their place," he wrote. "The State of Israel is not the outcome only of the sufferings of European Jewry."

As an expert in colonialism and racism—*Racism* being the title of his 1982 book—Memmi rejected those labels for the Zionist project, even while sympathizing with Palestinians. Calling the Palestinian struggle against Israel a "convenient conflict," Memmi criticized the Arab world for creating "human time bombs" to distract from the region's real problems. The result, he argued, "has been stagnation in every field of life, the sidetracking of human endeavor toward the support of a myth."

The Liberation of the Jew (1966, 2013)

The Jew is not oppressed as a member of a class, which distinguishes him from the proletariat. . . . Nor is he oppressed as a member of a biological group, which distinguishes him from . . . women. He is affected as a member of a total, social, cultural, political, and historical group. In other words, the Jew is oppressed as a member of a people, a minor people, a dispersed people, a people always and everywhere in the minority. . . .

Therefore the Jew has to find a total solution, one which answers every aspect of his threatened existence, which guarantees his present but also rehabilitates his past and restores to him possession of his future. In other words, the Jew, oppressed as a people, must find his autonomy and freedom to express his originality as a people. . . .

Since a people cannot, even today, live and determine its destiny freely except as a nation, the Jews must be made into a nation. In short, the specific liberation of the Jews is a national liberation.

I did not suddenly become nationalistic as soon as [that] was in my own interest. . . . I continue to think that nationalism is far too frequently an alibi for hatred and domination. I cannot forget that the Jew was always one of the first victims of nationalist crises. But history has convinced me, at least twice, that a nation is the only adequate response to the misfortune of a people. In the case of the colonized I had already discovered that their liberation would be national before it could be social, because they were dominated as a people. The Jew too was oppressed as a member of a total society . . . considered and treated as a foreigner, or at best as a special kind of citizen. . . .

Jews and Arabs (1975)

I have not been more sparing in my criticisms of that young state [of Israel], of its political errors or its theocratic self-satisfaction. . . . All this, however, is merely a matter of criticizing details. The essential and undeniable fact is that from now on, the State of Israel is part of the destiny of every Jew anywhere in the world who continues to acknowledge himself as a Jew. No matter what doubts or even reproofs certain of Israel's actions may arouse, no Jew anywhere in the world can call its existence in question without doing himself grave harm. And the non-Jews, especially the liberals, must understand that Israel *represents the still-precarious result of the liberation of the Jew, just as decolonization represents the liberation of the Arab or black peoples of Asia and Africa.* . . .

I did not hide the fact that these new ties, this sentimental solidarity with the new state, were likely to intensify the climate of suspicion in which Jews everywhere have always lived. But we have always been in danger. I do not believe that we can be in greater danger. Let us at least face danger with dignity. . . . What they call our double allegiance was forced upon us. We would have liked nothing better than not to need it!

What exactly is a Zionist?

A Zionist is anyone, Jew or non-Jew, who, having found that the Jewish situation is a situation of oppression, looks upon the reconstruction of a Jewish state as legitimate: so as to put an end to that oppression and so that Jews, like other peoples, may retrieve their dimensions as free men.

Or again, anyone who considers the liberation of the Jews as a Jew desirable.

Yonatan (Yoni) Netanyahu (1946–76)

**I belong to Israel, the way Israel belongs to me
and to you and to every other Jew.**

Yoni Netanyahu was one of the many soldiers who fought valiantly in 1967. The son of the Revisionist intellectual, Professor Benzion Netanyahu, he and his two younger brothers, Benjamin and Iddo, were junior academic itinerants, hopping around the United States and Israel as their father built his scholarly career at Dropsie College in Philadelphia, University of Denver, and Cornell University. Despite many years in America, the brothers remained rooted in Israel. Ultimately, all three would serve in Israel's elite commando unit, Sayeret Matkal.

Starting as a paratrooper in 1964, Yoni sustained a wound near the elbow in the final hours of the 1967 war while saving another soldier on the Golan Heights. During the next nine years, he shuttled between studying at Harvard and serving in the Israel Defense Forces. Watching America during the 1960s filled him with "admiration" and "pity." "This country is colossal," he exclaimed, but lamented watching its "infantile," "lunatic," youth reject their country. He was more comfortable as a patriot—a Zionist in his own homeland.

On July 4, 1976, Netanyahu led Operation Thunderbolt, the raid on Uganda's Entebbe airport that freed 101 Jewish hostages and crew members from the hijacked Air France Flight 139 originating in Tel Aviv. The daring operation reinvigorated the Zionist superhero myths of 1967 that had been battered by Syria and Egypt's surprise attack on Yom Kippur 1973. Tragically, Israel's one military fatality during the operation was Yoni Netanyahu, epitomizing the Israel Defense Forces command ethos: "*acharei*," after me.

Subsequent books and movies about the renamed Operation Yonatan deepened the surge of Zionist euphoria. The subsequent publication of Yoni's letters made the story novelistic. His natural, passionate Zionism, his bond with Jewish history, his love of his people and their land, his willingness to sacrifice, and, in the last selection, the way his love of Israel interacted with his true love interest put into words the ideals he lived. The novelist Herman Wouk called these letters "a remarkable work of literature, possibly one of the great documents of our time." They stand four decades later as great expressions of post-1948 Zionism.

Letters from Yoni Netanyahu

JULY 22, 1968

Dear Father,

We must, we are obliged, to cling to our country with our fingernails, with our bodies and with all our strength. Only if we do that, if we give all we have for the well-being of our country, will Israel remain the State of the Jews. Only then will they not write in the history books that once indeed the Jews roused themselves to action and held on to their land for two decades, but then were overwhelmed and became once more homeless wanderers.

I belong to Israel, Father, the way Israel belongs to me and to you and to every other Jew. I belong to Israel now, at this moment, when everything points to a new explosion (although I fervently hope it will not come to pass), at this moment when every citizen who has served in Zahal [the Israel Defense Forces] is being called up for two and three months of reserve duty, when the whole House of Israel is united in its desire to continue its independent life, and in its conviction that this life is ours by right and depends on our will and our readiness to sacrifice our all for its sake. That is why I have to be here—now. It would be intolerable for me to be in Boston at this time. I can go back there a few years from now, when everything calms down, but not now. . . .

MARCH 25, 1975

My Bruria,

Tomorrow is Passover. I've always thought it the most wonderful of all our holidays. It's an ancient celebration of freedom—a thousands-of-years-old liberty. When I sail back over the seas of our history, I pass through long years of suffering, of oppression, of massacres, of ghettos, of banishments; of humiliation; many years that, in a historical perspective, seem devoid of any ray of light yet it isn't so. For the fact that the idea of freedom remained, that the hope persisted, that the flame of liberty continued to burn through the observance of this ancient festival, is to me testimony of the eternity of the striving for freedom and the idea of freedom in Israel. In this search through our past we come upon other periods—of tranquility and liberty, when we were the People of the Land as well as the People of the Book. . . .

My yearning for the past mingles with my longing for you, and because of you I find myself in my past, and find the time and the desire to reminisce in order to share my life with you. Yet by "past" I mean not only my own past, but the way in which I see myself as an inseparable part, a link in the chain of our existence and Israel's independence.

Elie Wiesel 1928–2016

The existential Zionist.

As Israel matured, making peace with Egypt and eventually prospering, the campaigns rejecting its right to exist persisted. Simultaneously, many Diaspora Jews, enjoying the dignity Isaiah Berlin credited Israel with mass-producing, wondered whether a touristy relationship with Israel was enough. This challenge particularly haunted Elie Wiesel, whose suffering and eloquence made him the voice of the Holocaust martyrs—and the world's Jewish conscience.

Born in 1928 in Sighet, Transylvania, Wiesel entered the Nazis' human hell when he was fifteen. "Life in the cattle cars was the death of my adolescence," he would recall. He survived Auschwitz and Buchenwald; his mother, father, and a sister did not.

After working as a journalist for Israeli and French newspapers, Wiesel settled in New York. He wrote more than sixty books, including the searing best-selling memoir *Night*. In 1986 he won the Nobel Peace Prize for crusading against oppression in South Africa, Cambodia, Argentina, and elsewhere in addition to his Holocaust testimony.

As the world's most prominent Holocaust survivor, Wiesel became one of Israel's leading defenders. He framed the Jewish people's understanding of Israel's founding and its campaign to free "the Jews of Silence"—Soviet Jewry. He hailed Israel's non-imperialist, necessary Six-Day War victory, having seen the paratroopers "as in a dream, jump two thousand years into the past," not "moved by a will for power," but with a will that "sprang from spirituality and the harrowing immediacy of their past." Alas, he understood, "the world begrudges Israel its victory."

Wiesel also repudiated the profane claim that Auschwitz spawned Israel. And exposing the singling out of Jewish nationalism as racism, he wrote: "To prepare 'solutions' to the 'Jewish problem,' the first step was to divorce the Jew from mankind."

Still, despite his passion for Israel, Wiesel struggled with the label "Zionist." He distrusted political slogans and parties, fearing their easy descent into fanaticism. He contrasted his comforts living in the West with the struggles Israelis experienced living on the front line. Ultimately, in 1975, to repudiate anti-Zionism, he embraced Zionism, affirming Jews' shared destiny.

Brandishing this "badge of honor" thirty-five years later, Wiesel defended Jerusalem against division in American's major newspapers, writing: "For me, the Jew that I am, Jerusalem is above politics. . . . It belongs to the Jewish people and is much more than a city; it is what binds one Jew to another. . . . When a Jew visits Jerusalem for the first time, it is not the first time; it is a homecoming." For Wiesel, Zionism was the movement expressing that homecoming.

One Generation After (1970)

Israel, an answer to the Holocaust? It is too convenient, too scandalous a solution. First, because it would impose a burden, an unwarranted guilt feeling, on our children. To pretend that without Auschwitz there would be no Israel is to endow the latter with a share of responsibility for the former. And second, Israel cannot be an answer to the Holocaust, because the Holocaust, by its very magnitude, by its essence too, negates all answers. For me, therefore, these are two distinct events, both inexplicable, unexplained, mysterious, both staggering to the mind and a challenge to the imagination.

We shall never understand how Auschwitz was possible. Nor how Israel, scarcely a few years later, was able to draw from itself the strength and vision to rebuild its home in a world adrift and in ruins. . . .

Let us be more specific: had Zionism and its demands not existed, what would have become of the survivors of the ghettos and the camps, the partisans emerging from the forests and mountains who, according to all logic, should have scorned the human race and dedicated themselves to hating and despising it? . . . They did not even take the opportunity to wreak vengeance on their avowed executioners.

Instead, they let themselves be caught up in the great political and messianic adventure held out by Palestine; they devoted to it all their energy, all their ambition. Nothing else mattered anymore. The struggle demanded all their passions, all their dedication. That is why there was no settling of accounts. . . .

I make mine Israel's determination to transform the hate imposed upon it into a craving for solidarity with the world. A world still dominated by hate. This is a miracle in itself, the only one perhaps.

A Jew Today (essay 1975; book 1978)

Reproaches, condemnations, indictments by other nations—the plot is clear. It leads to public humiliation, the forced isolation of a people whose suffering is the oldest in the world. . . .

To prepare "solutions" to the "Jewish problem," the first step was to divorce the Jew from mankind. . . . This is not the first time the enemy has accused us of his own crimes. Our possessions were taken from us, and we were called misers; our children were massacred, and we were accused of ritual murder. To weaken us they attempted to distort our self-image. No, the process is not new.

We are told that it is not about Jews, this is about Zionists. That, too, is hardly new. They try to divide us, to pit us one against the other after having pitted us against the world. . . .

Racists, we? How malicious and also how ignorant one must be to make such a statement. Messianic movement? Yes, Judaism is that. A movement of spiritual, national and political rebirth? Yes, that too. But racist, no—Judaism excludes racism. All men and all women of all colors and all origins are accepted as equals. If there is a tradition that is generous and hospitable toward the stranger, it is the Jewish tradition.

I have never been a Zionist, not in the formal sense of the word. I have never belonged to a political organization. But faced with the anti-Zionist attacks by those who corrupt language and poison memory, I have no choice but to consider myself a Zionist. To do otherwise would mean accepting the terms of reference used by Israel's enemies. I wish our non-Jewish friends would do the same, and claim Zionism as a badge of honor.

Natan Sharansky (b. 1948)

The call of the Shofar.

Anatoly Borisovich Scharansky was born in 1948 in the city of Stalino, in the Soviet Union—today, he is known as Natan Sharansky and his birthplace is known as Donetsk in the Ukraine. Those shifts reflect the revolution Scharansky helped lead—a peaceful revolution of ideas, identity, and internal resistance that defeated Soviet Communism.

In 1973 Scharansky, a chess prodigy and applied mathematician, sought an exit visa to Israel. The Soviets' refusal to allow him to emigrate made this newfound Zionist a human-rights activist too. By 1977 a kangaroo court sentenced him to thirteen years' imprisonment. He became the Soviet Union's most prominent political prisoner, symbolizing the Soviet Jewish demand to emigrate and the desire of many others simply to be free. This dual message of particularist Jewish solidarity linked to a broader campaign advancing universalist human rights against an evil oppressor galvanized the Zionist movement in the 1970s and 1980s. The Soviet secret policy dismissed the Jewish activists as "students and housewives." Meant as an insult, the label reflected the movement's global, grassroots nature as it united the Jewish world with Israel despite ongoing differences—affirming Zionism's continued relevance.

On February 11, 1986, the Soviets finally freed Scharansky, and he moved to Israel. Scharansky entered Israeli politics, serving as deputy prime minister, among other positions, and heading the Jewish Agency from 2009 to 2018.

His movement changed Israel too. Since the Soviet Union's collapse on December 25, 1991, more than one million immigrants have stabilized Israel's population; another 500,000 to 750,000 have reinforced American Jewry's commitment to peoplehood.

In his 1988 memoirs, Sharansky illustrates the robustness of the most successful Zionist movement in the Diaspora since 1948. Echoing Theodor Herzl and David Ben-Gurion, Sharansky's Zionism reflects the romance and idealism of liberal nationalism at its best—with a heavy Jewish accent and an inspiring human desire to turn from the suffering bigotry imposes to the possibilities freedom provides.

Fear No Evil (1988)

In those days the beginning and the end of my Jewishness was an awareness of antisemitism. As an adolescent I had come across some lines of Julian Tuwim, a Polish Jewish poet who wrote after the Holocaust that he felt himself Polish by virtue of the blood flowing in his veins (by which he meant Polish culture and literature), and Jewish by virtues of the blood that flowed out of his veins. . . .

Three years earlier, the Six-Day War had made an indelible impression on me as it did on most Soviet Jews, for, in addition to fighting for her life, Israel was defending our dignity. On the eve of the war, when Israel's destruction seemed almost inevitable, Soviet antisemites were jubilant. But a few days later even anti-Jewish jokes started to change, and throughout the country, in spite of pro-Arab propaganda, you could now see a grudging respect for Israel and for Jews. A basic, eternal truth was returning to the Jews of Russia—that personal freedom wasn't something you could achieve through assimilation. It was available only by reclaiming your historical roots.

By now the appeal of Zionism was growing stronger, and the authorities responded with a virulent anti-Israel campaign. The regime arranged press conferences, where tamed Jews declared that Soviet Jews wanted nothing to do with "fascist" Israel. But the louder they shouted, the more obvious it was that the Zionist movement was growing, especially when television brought the issue into every Jewish household. I was close with several families who started on the road to Zionism, and friends began giving me books about Israel, including the novel *Exodus*, which . . . had an enormous influence on Jews of my generation. By the time I graduated, I was ready to go on *aliyah*. . . .

While my own focus was on Jewish emigration, I was also active on behalf of people from many national and religious groups whose rights were brutally violated by the Soviet regime, including Pentecostals and Catholics, Ukrainians, and Crimean Tatars. The Helsinki Watch Group also produced documents about human rights violations in Soviet prisons, labor camps, and psychiatric hospitals. My interest in helping other persecuted people was an important part of my own freedom—a freedom that became real only after I returned to my Jewish roots.

For the activist Jews of my generation, our movement represented the exact opposite of what our parents had gone through when they were young. But we saw what had happened to their dreams, and we understood that the path to liberation could not be found in denying our own roots while pursuing universal goals. On the contrary: we had to deepen our commitment, because only he who understands his own identity and has already become a free person can work effectively for the human rights of others.

In Israel, while I was writing this book, I came upon an image by the American writer Cynthia Ozick that captures this idea perfectly. The shofar, the ram's horn that is sounded in the synagogue on the High Holidays, is narrow at one end and wide at the other. Nothing happens if you blow into the wide end. But if you blow into the narrow end, the call of the shofar rings loud and true. . . .

From an ocean of hatred I find myself in an ocean of love. Having left a country where only the government knows what must be done, I arrive in a society where everybody but the government knows what must be done. Here every taxi driver, every kibbutznik, every shopkeeper is, if not prime minister, then at least foreign and defense ministers combined. Having left a country in which criticizing the government can land you in prison, I now live in a society where the easiest thing in the world is to criticize the government, and the louder your criticisms the more popular you are. . . .

Emmanuel Levinas (1906–95)

Zionism as ethical particularism: The beyond of the state.

Emmanuel Levinas was born in Lithuania in 1906. He started studying in France in 1923, became a French citizen in 1931, and endured most of World War II in a special prisoner of war barracks for French-Jewish soldiers. Although a friend helped Levinas's wife and daughter hide in a monastery, the Nazis murdered his father, brothers, and mother-in-law. From these beginnings, he became a renowned intellectual who united East and West.

Levinas initially built his career as a *melamed*, a teacher running the Ecole Normale Israelite Orientale in Paris. For years he offered a weekly class on the medieval French Torah commentator Rashi. He entered academia in 1961, teaching in France and Switzerland. By his retirement in 1979, he was an academic pop star, selling as many as two hundred thousand copies of his books.

Levinas's life and thought affirmed the need for a Jewish state. But the philosopher-poet of the "other" linked this justification with Judaism's ethical grandeur, evoking Political Zionism at its Herzlian best.

Even as Israel became a state in a constant state of crisis, the Zionist quest for the Jewish state to be an ideal state persisted. Levinas explored Zionism's dual missions as political refuge and ethical model in the 1971 essay, "The State of Caesar and the State of David." He explained that the "State of Caesar," the conventional Western polity, often becomes "the place of corruption par excellence, and perhaps, the ultimate refuge of idolatry." By contrast, the rabbis' understanding of the State of David linked "the political order and the spiritual order" through its Messianic aspiration, resulting in a Jewish state perennially stretching for "the beyond of the State."

Levinas's protégé Jacques Derrida appreciated this Jewish communal attempt "to interpret the Zionist *commitment*, the promise, the sworn faith and not the Zionist *fact.*" Both thinkers saw the Zionist ideal going *"beyond* the political," hoping that Levinas's Davidic "messianic politics" could ennoble the Caesarian power politics.

Levinas toasted Israel's revolutionary ethical potential—"the possibilities of political invention that it opens up." He also proclaimed the moral grandeur of Zionism he believed even Egyptian president Anwar Sadat may have recognized by visiting Jerusalem in 1977.

Politics After (1979)

Zionism, supposedly a purely political doctrine, thus carries in the depths of its being the inverted image of a certain universality, while also correcting that image....

Oh, what bad negotiators the Israelis are! Whereas they are leading a struggle from which the memory of Masada is never absent, and which one dares to denounce as dependent on Western ideologies. Will one go so far in criticizing Israeli mistrust as to take the weapons from the defenders of the last ramparts? On the other hand, did not Sadat understand the opportunities opened up through friendship with Israel . . . and all the prophetic promises that are hidden behind the Zionist claims to historical rights. . . . All injustices, capable of being put right. All the impossible becoming possible. Which less lofty minds among Sadat's enemies in the Near East, or his friends in our proud West, have never sensed, plunged as they are in their political bookkeeping. . . .

Beyond the State of Israel's concern to provide a refuge for those without a homeland and its sometimes surprising, sometimes uncertain achievements, has it not, above all, been a question of creating on its own land the concrete conditions for political invention? That is the ultimate culmination of Zionism, and thereby probably one of the great events in human history.

For two thousand years the Jewish people was only the object of history, in a state of political innocence which it owed to its role as victim. That role is not enough for its vocation. But since 1948 this people has been surrounded by enemies and is still being called into question, yet engaged too in real events, in order to think—and to make and remake—a State which will have to incarnate the prophetic moral code and the idea of its peace. . . .

Assimilation and New Culture (1980)

Despite all the criticism levied against assimilation, we enjoy the enlightened ideas that it has brought, and we are fascinated by the vast horizons it has opened up for us. We breathe in deeply the air of the open sea, while Jewish peculiarity, which is a difficult destiny, constantly risks appearing to us as archaic and, in the growing ignorance of Hebrew's "square letters" and the inability to make them speak, as narrowing our vision. Nothing from now on would justify this in the modern world we have entered: a world belonging to all where, up until the Holocaust, nothing seemed to call our presence into serious question. . . .

[W]ho, within assimilated Judaism and among the nations, can still imagine that a peculiarity beyond universality is conceivable? That it could contain those Western values that cannot be repudiated, but also lead beyond them? . . . Up until now we have attempted only an apologetics, which, without great difficulty, was limited to modeling the truths of the Torah on the noble models of the West. The Torah requires something more. . . .

Only a Jewish culture called upon to develop out of a new life in Israel might put an end—for the Jews above all, but also for nations—to a persistent misunderstanding. It will make us open our closed books and our eyes. This is our hope. To that effect also, the State of Israel will be the end of assimilation. It will make possible, in its plenitude, the conception of concepts whose roots go right to the depths of the Jewish soul. The explication and elaboration of these concepts are decisive for the struggle against assimilation, and are preliminaries to all kinds of effort on the part of generous organizations, and all the self-sacrifices made by noble masters. . . .

Martin Peretz (b. 1938)

Zionism: The God that did not fail.

Despite so much enmity, Zionism blossomed. On the hundredth anniversary of the First Zionist Congress, the American publisher Martin Peretz put Zionism's success in historical perspective: Advancing a just cause through its characteristic pragmatic idealism had helped Zionism outlast communism, fascism, socialism, and other ideologies that seemed dominant at different times in the twentieth century.

Peretz brought the perspective of a left-wing activist and an academic—a fixture in Harvard's social studies program and the *New Republic's* editor-in-chief from 1974 through 2010. Born in New York City in 1938 and raised in a Zionist home, Peretz broke with the New Left over its growing anti-Zionism and antisemitism while retaining his progressive commitments to social and economic justice. Although critics complained that his Zionism shifted him to the right on foreign policy, his Zionism was more useful in maintaining the political iconoclasm and independence that made the *New Republic* a must read for thoughtful Democrats in the 1980s and 1990s. In marking the formal Zionist movement's centenary with a special *New Republic* issue, Peretz identified some of the secrets to Zionism's success, including morality, practicality, peoplehood, and an openness to modernity.

The God That Did Not Fail (1997)

If socialism was the God that failed, then Zionism was the God that did not fail....

Zionism was an ideology, emerging from among the high tide of ideologies; and its secular, worldly promise was certainly revolutionary. Of all the modern promises of transformation, Zionism is the only one to have accomplished what it set out to do—and to have done so with reasonable decency. The narrative of this century is cluttered with brutalized hopes, brutalized bodies, brutalized language. Socialism, communism, Third Worldism, pan-Arabism, even neutralism: all these isms, with their grandiose aims and their callous means, which conscripted many ordinary men and women and enticed so many intellectuals (and so many Jewish intellectuals), are already receding into the mists of time....

Zionism was an ideology unlike other ideologies, even if its decolonization struggle looks very much like other decolonizations, in the Indian subcontinent, for example. The State of Israel was born when the Zionists sent the British packing.... Israel was an anti-imperialist creation. . . . Is it still necessary to insist that the Jewish refugees who streamed into Palestine and later into Israel were not colonialists? Israel came into the world in the company of dozens of other states, some relatively homogeneous, some not, but all, unlike Israel, with their populations in place. The age of nation-building, of the great experiments in ethno-nationalism, had begun. . . .

There is no greater measure of the success of Zionism, finally, than the phenomenon of post-Zionism. What really gnaws at the post-Zionist scholars and writers is the spectacle of a Jewish society in which Jews are not always brooding about cosmic questions, in which they sit at cafes, dance in the moonlight, eat good food, make piles of money, chatter on cell phones, have film festivals—all of the activities of an unafraid and unanguished people. The post-Zionists claim that Israel is complacent, devoid of a self-critical temper. They want to deconstruct and to demythologize the old narrative of Zionism and its successes (the sort of narrative that I have just told). In their rage to modernize, didn't the Zionists offend the sensibilities of the Jews of the East? Didn't Jewish soldiers sometimes beat up on innocent Arab town-dwellers and even drive some of them into another part of historic Palestine? The answer to these questions, and to others, is "yes." Israel is a strong state, and it has fought wars, and it bears the responsibility of power—which is to say, Israel is not innocent. The Jewish state has committed acts that it should not have committed, just like every other country, including the United States. But Zionism permits us to admit this without flinching. Indeed, post-Zionism is a great tribute to Zionism, for it is the natural consequence of the open, wakeful, contrarian spirit that characterized Jewish nationalism from the start. Israel is not an evil state, and the post-Zionists are not prophets without honor: what we are witnessing is the continued "normalization of the Jewish people," to use the old Zionist slogan. Israel must feel pride where pride is right and regret where regret is right; but it must feel a tinge of pride also about its regret. . . .

The Zionists brought to Zion at least three advantages. The first was pragmatism, practicality, a willingness to compromise. . . . Second . . . the Zionists came with a confident notion of what their nation was, a confidence springing from the fact that this was the nation that more or less invented the idea of peoplehood. . . .

The third advantage of Zionism was the advantage of the modern. For this reason, Zionism was a genuine revolution in its region. Was modernity a foreign, Western import, as the critics like to say? Of course. That is why it worked. It did not mistake authenticity for backwardness. And so it traumatized its neighbors not only with nationalism, but also with science, with industry, with agriculture, with the whole gleaming consumerist oasis that it devised. . . . Herzl said that the Zionist goal was to have the Jewish people "live at last as free people on our own soil, and in our homes peacefully die." The first of these aims has been achieved. The second will be a long time in coming.

8

Builders

Labor Zionism

As a movement shaped by Jewish history and Western civilization, with many of its founders shtetl born, Zionism began with an Eastern European accent. As such, the Eastern European search for a classless society shaped early Zionism. Yet, in many ways it was a mismatch. Marxism, after all, rejected nationalism, Judaism, particularism, and Zionism itself.

Labor Zionism worked, however—more than most forms of socialism—because Zionists were not crusading communists seeking perfection, but pragmatic Jews accepting imperfect solutions to messy problems. David Ben-Gurion, Golda Meir, and their comrades were hard-nosed pragmatists more than pie-in-the-sky universalists. The early state's defining institutions reflected this Labor Zionist mix, especially the military elite unit, the Palmah; the agrarian commune, the kibbutz; and the mighty workers' union, the Histadrut. They got the job done.

Over the decades, however, persistent problems made these pragmatists look less effective and less romantic, especially as Marxist collectivism retreated globally. In Israel in the 1970s, the post-1967 euphoria faded. Menachem Begin's Likud party gained power. The complex Palestinian problem became incendiary. The pressing agenda—and overall vision—changed.

Increasingly, fighting the settlement movement and demanding land concessions defined the Israeli left. In addition, the spread of capitalism and individualism ended the Spartan conditions of early Zionism that nourished kibbutz and socialist ideals.

The feminist firebrand Shulamit Aloni helped shift Labor Zionism from "us" to "I," from instilling collective responsibility to protecting civil liberties. Aloni and her allies shared the Socialist Zionists' dreams of Israel teaching the world how to provide social justice for all. Yet they began their crusade by championing individual and minority rights, confident in the Zionist revolution's success in establishing a majoritarian Hebrew culture and sensibility. Golda Meir and Aloni were arch-rivals. Aloni once began a Mapai party convention speech by saying "I think . . ." Cutting her off, Meir snapped: "There is no 'I' here—only we.'" Meir stopped Aloni's speech that day—but couldn't stop the trend. [Amit Schejter, "Shulamit Aloni: Israel's Most Influential Woman Politician," *Ha'aretz*, January 26, 2014, http://www.haaretz.com/opinion/.premium-1.570613.]

Golda Meir (1898–1978)

**When Jews would return to their homeland . . .
they would make a better society.**

Golda Meir, Israel's fourth prime minister, was an activist and a quipster. In 1943 she said in her brusque "*doogri*" style: "There is no Zionism except the rescue of Jews." After 1948 remembering the pogroms of the Ukraine she was born into in 1898, she would say, "Above all, this country is our own. Nobody has to get up in the morning and worry what his neighbors think of him. Being a Jew is no problem here." A tough political operative, she said Israel's "secret weapon" was "*Ein Breira*," no alternative.

Her one-liners about the Arab-Israeli conflict still resonate. In 1957, speaking as Israel's foreign minister at the National Press Club in Washington, she said, "Peace will come when the Arabs will love their children more than they hate us." In 1969 speaking as Israel's prime minister in London, she observed: "When peace comes we will perhaps in time be able to forgive the Arabs for killing our sons, but it will be harder for us to forgive them for having forced us to kill their sons."

Golda Mabovitch's parents moved from Pinsk to Milwaukee in 1906. In 1917 she married Morris Myerson. The two moved to Kibbutz Merhavia in 1921. The marriage withered as Golda, who Hebraized her last name to Meir in 1956, became involved in Zionist affairs. She helped found Mapai, the Labor Party of the Land of Israel in 1930. In 1934 she was elected to the Executive Committee of another labor institution that would shape the state and define her life: the Histadrut, the General Federation of Labor.

Once the state was created, Meir served as ambassador to the Soviet Union, minister of labor, and foreign minister. In 1969 she succeeded Levi Eshkol as prime minister, becoming the third female prime minister in world history, and the first to emerge independently, not through family ties. To Meir, Labor Zionism offered a "better society" for all, even if toughness was required to make it happen. Her unique status, vision, wit, and Jewish grandmother affect made her one of the world's most admired women.

She was more controversial at home. Many Israelis blamed her for failing to prevent the Arabs' deadly surprise attack on Yom Kippur 1973. Still, thanks to her rock-star status worldwide, even after resigning as premier in 1974, Golda Meir remained a Zionist icon.

A Land of Our Own (1973)

Our pioneers interpreted *ata b'chartonu* [you have chosen us] to mean that when Jews would return to their homeland, and when they alone would be responsible for their home and society, they would make a better society. This is my explanation for their absolute devotion to the concept of Jewish peoplehood and the reestablishment of Jewish independence, combined at the same time with an equal fervor for the nature of the society which would emerge in this independent Jewish state: their desire that it should be something better than what had been known in most parts of the world. The pioneers believed that neither a social nor a national ideal was alien to Jewish thought, Jewish religion, or the vision of our prophets. Both had to be realized....

The pioneer settlers saved the Jewish people and the opportunity for the reestablishment of Jewish independence, because a simple, but basic principle became their bible: It was called *avodah atzmit*—self-labor.

Jews had to teach themselves to work with their hands. The Third Aliyah with its special Hashomer Hatzair group consisted of boys and girls who usually came from the homes of merchants, rabbis, scholars; many were from prosperous assimilated families. Yet they were the ones who built the first road between Tiberias and Nazareth. Labor was their creed. That was the faith each had to accept if he really wanted to build the country. We had to build it. The houses had to be built by us. The roads had to be built by us. The wheat had to be raised by us. The swamps had to be drained by us. This gave us a moral right to the land in addition to the historic right. If there are no more swamps in Palestine, it is because we drained them. If there are forests, it is because we planted the seedlings. If there are fewer deserts, it is because our children went to the arid areas and reclaimed them....

We are driven by the memory of the past, the responsibility for the future, and by the desire to live up to a sense of "chosenness"—not because we are better than others, but because we dream of doing better in building a society in Israel which will be a good society founded on concepts of justice and equality.

Address to the United Nations General Assembly (October 7, 1958)

None of us can object to a nationalism which is constructive and wholesome. The world is enriched by a nationalism only when that nationalism means that a people is achieving awareness of its unique national character; endeavors to give expression to its cultural heritage; strives for economic and social progress; seeks ways and means of broadening and deepening the ties of friendship and co-operation with other peoples, and when that nationalism is accompanied by the realization that every country is itself a part of the community of nations and that other peoples are also entitled to their nationalism. . . . This, it seems to me, is the test—the borderline—between acceptable nationalism and national aggressiveness. . . .

In the course of these ten years one million people, most of them refugees from scores of countries of the world, have come to our shores and have found new homes in their ancient homeland. They have come from over fifty countries with scores of different languages, cultures, and backgrounds. . . .

The people of Israel look back with pride on the crowded events of the past ten years, the absorption of this mass immigration, the establishment of a democratic society, the development of the country's neglected resources, the advancement made in the fields of education, learning and science, and not least the establishment of diplomatic relations with sixty-three other nations of the world. Moreover, the revived language of the Bible has replaced the many tongues formerly spoken by our people and has become a potent bond of union. . . .

Israel, I believe, has honorably striven towards a nationalism which is fruitful instead of sterile, creative instead of destructive. Though we have been obliged to defend ourselves against invasion and attack, our purposes since the establishment of our state have remained unaltered: to rebuild a poor, barren land, to enable the return of an ancient people to its source, to regain our independence and national self-expression, to live in peace with all peoples near and far, and to take our place in the community of free nations.

Muki Tsur (b. 1938)

**We fight, for we have no choice—while
dreaming of being able to stop one day.**

Israel's Six-Day War win produced a remarkable document. Shortly after the 1967 war, as the streets still rang with songs of victories, kibbutznikim shared their mixed feelings about fighting. Eventually, four hundred veterans submitted to interviews in what was supposed to be an internal kibbutz movement document. When published, *Siach Lochamim*—literally "the soldiers' chats"—had an initial print run of 150,000. Eventually it would be translated into half a dozen languages, including English, with the title *The Seventh Day*.

Publishing the book then was like setting off a mortar shell during Independence Day celebrations. Tough Israelis, protecting the image of the hardened "sabra," dismissed it as "Shooting and Crying." Some considered it hostile to what was considered a just war, or treasonous.

Yet the book resonated globally. It perpetuated the stereotype of the prickly sabra, the native-born Israeli who, like the fruit, was hard on the outside, but soft, sweet, contemplative within. The testimonies also highlighted contradictions within contemporary Zionist ideology. The Holocaust's shadow hovered above, as the fighters swore "Never Again" would they be victims—while fearing they might become victimizers. As pride in winning clashed with regret over fighting, these New Jews revealed much of the Old Jew's sensibility, for better and worse. Finally, this was a document of the kibbutz movement at its height—the quintessential Labor Zionist institution, producing the stereotypically Israeli sabras, proud of their characteristically kibbutz-like idealism.

As observer and ideologue, Muki Tsur has tracked the changes within kibbutzim and helped shape them. Born in Jerusalem in 1938, he was raised mostly in Argentina as his father represented the Yishuv there. Tsur joined Kibbutz Ein Gev in 1956, eventually serving as secretary general of the kibbutz movement. He has spent decades studying kibbutz-written *Haggadot* and other updated rituals, demonstrating that "secular" does not mean belief in nothing or not being Jewish, and emphasizing how kibbutz ideas still influence Israel.

Tsur eloquently captured the rollercoaster feelings linking the catastrophe of the Holocaust with the miracle of 1967. The pragmatic Zionist's understanding of the war's necessity nestled uncomfortably, creatively, with the Socialist Zionist's dream of a better world.

The Soldiers' Chat (1967)

We tend to forget those days before the war, understandably. Yet those trying moments propelled us back toward the gruesome Jewish destiny we had repressed like traumatized burn victims since 1945. Suddenly, everyone's talking Munich, the Holocaust, the Jewish people's fate. Unlike the Europeans, we didn't fear a new Holocaust; we feared an enemy victory—and vowed to do everything possible to prevent it.

We know what genocide is: whether we witnessed the Holocaust or were born right after it. And that's probably why the world will never understand us, never fathoming our courage, our hesitations, or our pangs of conscience, while fighting the war—or recovering from it. We all survived the Holocaust: whether we still try picturing Father and Mother, whether we hear our relatives crying out in their sleep, or whether we just heard stories. We all know that no other nation shoulders such ghastly images. These phantoms embolden us in combat yet shame us too.

The saying, "Excuse us for winning" isn't ironic, it's true. Of course, one might dismiss our hesitations as hypocritical, our moral pretensions and behaviors as downright paradoxical. But isn't war one big contradiction?

When the fighting erupted, as the mountains encircling Ein Gev began donning ominous combat gear while spitting fire, a squad of our reconnaissance fighters on one hill by the Syrian border was busy—extinguishing a fire in an Arab peasant's little field. "A field is a field," one scout insisted. Could behavior get more ridiculous? Yet it seems to me that such behavior really captures our fate. Our feelings are mixed. We swore never to return to the Europe of the Holocaust; yet we refuse to lose that Jewish sense of identifying with victims.

We, perhaps, are the ultimate contrast to the ghetto Jew, who witnessed the slaughter, felt utterly helpless, heard the cries, yet could only rebel at heart while dreaming about gaining the strength to react, to strike back, to fight. We actually do react, strike back, fight, for we have no choice—while dreaming of being able to stop one day, and live in peace.

Amos Oz (b. 1939)

I believe in a Zionism that faces facts, that exercises power with restraint, that sees the Jewish past as a lesson . . . that sees the Palestinian Arabs as Palestinian Arabs.

One of the veterans, subjects, and interviewers in *The Seventh Day*, Amos Oz, was then a young teacher on Kibbutz Hulda. Today, Oz is Israel's literary lion. Feted worldwide, he remains controversial at home, a proud member of the Zionist left. He repeatedly confronts opponents of the two-state solution to his right and anti-Zionists to his left.

Oz was born in 1939 in Jerusalem, the city where everyone, is "half prophet and half prime minister," he once wrote. His grandfather, the businessman and poet Alexander Klausner, "believed wholeheartedly that the time had come for the Jews to return to the Land of Israel, so that they could begin by becoming a normal nation like all the rest, and later perhaps an exceptional nation." His great uncle was the Revisionist Zionist Joseph Klausner. His father was a frustrated academic forced to work in the Hebrew University library, while his mother committed suicide when he was twelve. Oz would write: "I was destined to be a new chapter, a plain, tough Israeli, fair-haired and free from Jewish neuroses and excessive intellectualism."

Oz—who changed his name from Klausner after he fled Jerusalem and settled on Kibbutz Hulda—boils down his Zionism to one fact: Jews have nowhere else to go. He explained in 2008, in *How to Cure a Fanatic:* "When my father was a little boy in Poland, the streets of Europe were covered with graffiti, 'Jews, go back to Palestine,' or sometimes worse: 'Dirty Yids, piss off to Palestine.' When my father revisited Europe fifty years later, the walls were covered with new graffiti, 'Jews, get out of Palestine.'" In his monumental memoir, *A Tale of Love and Darkness,* he remembers the night the United Nations partition plan passed, November 29, 1947, as the only time he saw his father cry. His cerebral, bird-like father described the antisemitic humiliations Poles imposed, then said: "From now on, from the moment we have our own state, you will never be bullied just because you are a Jew."

Oz also respects Palestinian rights, calling the conflict "a clash between right and right." Despite seeking Zionist normalcy, in the 1980s he frequently chided American Jews for casting themselves as spectators watching this historic Jewish drama unfold on "center stage"—Israel. He insisted that only in Israel could Jews and Judaism flourish creatively.

In this spirit, Oz has long celebrated the kibbutz as what Martin Buber called "an exemplary non-failure." Oz appreciates it as a Socialist Zionist phenomenon, the "only attempt to establish a collective society, without compulsion, without repression, and without bloodshed or brainwashing."

His famous essay, "The Meaning of Homeland," showcases Oz's quiet, passionate, but ever reasonable and rational liberal Zionism; he identifies the basis, and the limits, of his Zionism as a non-religious, left-wing Jew. Oz's ability to digest and dissect contradiction so precisely makes him a great writer—and a mainstream Zionist.

The Meaning of Homeland (1967)

I am a Jew and a Zionist. In defining the nature of my identity, I do not rely on religion, for I stand outside it. I have not learned to have recourse to verbal compromises like "the spirit of our Jewish past" or "the values of Jewish tradition," for values and tradition alike derive directly from tenets of faith in which I cannot believe; and I am incapable of separating Jewish values and Jewish tradition from their source, which is commandment, revelation, and faith. Nouns like "mission," "destiny" and "election," when used with the adjective "Jewish," only embarrass me and worse. A Jew, in my vocabulary, is someone who regards himself as a Jew, and also someone who is forced to be a Jew. . . .

Further: To be a Jew means to relate mentally to the Jewish past, whether the relation is one of pride or of oppression or of both together, whether it consists of cultural and linguistic or of emotional participation.

Further: To be a Jew means to relate to the Jewish present, whether by action or inaction; to take pride and participate in the achievements of Jews as Jews, and to share responsibility for injustice done by Jews as Jews (responsibility—not guilt!).

And last: To be a Jew means to feel that where a Jew is persecuted because he is a Jew—that means you. . . .

Therefore, being a Jew in the Diaspora means just that one terrible thing: Auschwitz is meant for you. It is meant for you because you are a symbol. The symbol of the rightly persecuted vampire, or the symbol of the unjustly persecuted eternal victim, but always and everywhere, you are not an individual but a splinter of a symbol.

I am a Zionist because I will not and cannot exist as a splinter of a symbol in the consciousness of others. Not as the symbol of the shrewd, gifted vampire, and not as the symbol of the sympathetic victim who deserves compensation and atonement. Therefore, there is no place for me in the world other than in the country of the Jews. . . .

The country of the Jews could not have come into existence and could not have existed anywhere but here. Not in Uganda and not in Ararat and not in Birobidjan. . . . And on this point I commit myself to a severe, pitiless distinction between the inner motives of the return to Zion and its justification to others. The longings are a motive, but no justification. Our justification in respect of the Arab inhabitants of the country cannot base itself on our age-old longings. We have no other objective justification than the right of one who is drowning and grasps the only plank he can. (And let me anticipate here: there is a gap as wide as the abyss between the drowning man who grasps a plank and makes room for holding on by pushing the others that are sitting on it aside, and between pushing the others who sit on the plank into the sea. This is the difference between making Jaffa and Nazareth Jewish, and making Ramallah and Nablus Jewish).

I cannot use such words as "the promised land" or "the promised borders," because I do not believe in the one who made the promise. Happy are those who do: their Zionism is simple and self-evident. Mine is hard and complicated. I also have no use for the hypocrites who quickly resort to the promise and the promiser, whenever their Zionism runs into an obstacle and into the inner contradiction. I am a Zionist in all that concerns the redemption of the Jews, but not when it comes to the redemption of the Holy Land. . . .

Why here of all places? Because here, and only here, is where the Jews were capable of coming and establishing their independence. Because the establishment of the political independence of the Jews would not have come about in any other territory. Because here was the focus of their longings. . . .

I do not regard myself as a Jew merely by virtue of "race" or as a "Hebrew" merely because I have been born in the Land of Canaan. I choose to be a Jew. As a Jew, I would not and cannot live anywhere but in a Jewish state. The Jewish state could only come into being in the Land of Israel. That is as far as my Zionism goes. . . .

The new State of Israel is not tied by an umbilical cord to Jewish religion and history, but also not completely detached from them. It is in the curious and fascinating situation of "facing." The Bible and the Mishnah, the prayers and the *piyyutim, halakhah,* and *aggadah* do not dominate the State of Israel, but they are present in it and indirectly shape its everyday and spiritual life.

"Facing" means neither uninterrupted continuity, nor a new start. "Facing" means continuous reference to the Jewish past. The Hebrew language, law and justice, customs, stories, lullabies, literature—all refer continually to the heritage of Jewish culture. It is not merely a new interpretation of an ancient culture, as the disciples of Ahad Ha'am would have it, but also no leap across the past to link up with ancient pre-Judaic strata, as the school of Berdichevsky claims. It is an indirect, tortuous, dialectic reference, burdened with conflicts and tensions, saturated with the confusion of revolt and the emotionalism of nostalgia, full of contradictions and contrasts. . . .

I believe in a Zionism that faces facts, that exercises power with restraint, that sees the Jewish past as a lesson, not as a mystical imperative or as an insidious nightmare; that sees the Palestinian Arabs as Palestinian Arabs, not as the camouflaged reincarnation of the ancient tribes of Canaan or as a shapeless mass of humanity waiting for us to form it as we see fit; a Zionism *also* capable of seeing itself as others may see it; and finally, a Zionism that recognizes both the spiritual implications and the political consequences of the fact that that this small tract of land is the homeland of two peoples fated to live facing each other, willy-nilly, because no God and no angel will come to judge between right and right. The lives of both, the lives of all of us, depend on the hard, tortuous, and essential process of learning to know each other in the curious landscape of the beloved country.

Roy Belzer (1953–93)

**It takes more than spirit alone to build a living
community out of rock and soil. What is required is
a deep love for this dynamic homeland of ours.**

Although the kibbutz experience was not for everyone, it enchanted a passionate minority of American baby boomers. These activists fused Zionist ideology with the ideology of "*the* movement," the Sixties rebellion against the Vietnam War, racism, sexism, and corporate capitalism. Roy Belzer exemplified this phenomenon.

Belzer was born in 1953 in middle-class suburbia—Culver City, California. While raising money for Cesar Chavez's United Farm Workers campaign, Belzer filled his parents' garage with so many donated cans, they had to find trucks to pick up and distribute the food. At age sixteen, after a summer experiencing kibbutz living organized by the Habonim youth movement, he became a Zionist. Enrolling in San Diego State University in 1971, he decided to recruit other veterans of these kibbutz summers to create a *garin*, a nucleus, of immigrants to settle the Golan Heights. He made *aliyah* with ninety young Americans and Canadians a year later. Supplemented by a *garin* from the Tsofim, the Israeli Scouts movement, Belzer and his comrades founded Kibbutz Kfar Haruv and Kibbutz Afik. Today, the two kibbutzim combined have more than six hundred members.

Belzer died when he was only forty, in a plane crash in Los Angeles. The writings from the *garin's* mimeographed anthology of original writings and inspirational Zionist texts illustrate his idealism, and his resonant synthesis of Zionism with America's counterculture.

Garin HaGolan Anthology (December 1972)

"*Garin*" is singular—but the components of *garin*, or seed, are many—being that they are all of us. We, the land, the people, the culture, the idea, the spirit, the pain, the joy, the tears, the births, the deaths, the plowing, the showing, the harvesting, the hating, the loving, the fearing, the dancing, the growing, and the living, are all inextricably bound and our existences interlocked.

The success of our kibbutz will not be determined by how many specialists and experienced or educated members join us, but rather by the inner strength contained by all of us—and our ability to learn with each other.

We must never let ourselves surrender, or feel condemned to failure. But our success depends heavily on our insight into the causes of failure of those who have preceded us. I pray that we have [this] ability. . . .

It might be a good time for all of us to take a deep breath and truly examine what we have before us. The *garin* now has fifty strong and dedicated *chevre* [comrades] who have made the decision that Israel will become the benefactor of their billowing spirit. It takes more than spirit alone to build a living community out of rock and soil. What is required is a deep love for this dynamic homeland of ours. You must feel for Israel and feel for humanity and out of this love comes a raging commitment—a commitment which transcends personal ambition.

The decision to live in Israel, the Jewish State, among the Jewish People, is not an arbitrary one. It is not because there are things wrong with America that I want to escape. It is not because I want an alternative with the possibilities of a socialistic environment which could be Cuba or Sweden or some other place, but happened to be in Israel.

It is because I am Jewish. I need to be with my *chevre*, as they need me. We will work the land—not as laborers for others—but for ourselves, for our children, and our people.

Why will we succeed? Because the land which awaits our labor is the land of the Jewish people. And under Jewish hands it blossoms like no other land before, for any other people at any other time, in any other place in the history of humanity.

Before we take this journey let's search our motives and objectives. We are young serious adults who are going to put our life's energies into this monumental undertaking. We ask that all of your visions and hopes be focused on a rich piece of land in the Southern Golan Heights. A piece of land which has been barren for thousands of years—and which we will build for ourselves and our children.

So please, before you decide to join Garin Hagolan, see very clearly that your own failure can have a devastating effect on the rest of your *chevre*. The success of our kibbutz depends entirely on each one of us. To our future together ...

The Members of Kibbutz Ketura (founded 1973)

**We see ourselves as a community leading a
unique, all-encompassing lifestyle.**

As Israel changed, so, too, did the kibbutz. Pummeled by the Great Inflation and some bad investments in the 1980s, the kibbutz movement also could not adjust to the spreading individualism—and materialism. As the modest, self-sacrificing, and constrained culture of *tsena* (limits) succumbed to the bold, expansive, and affluent culture of Start-Up Nation, many kibbutzim privatized. Those that didn't, like Kibbutz Ketura in the Arava desert, reaffirmed their ideologies, with a modern, more individualistic, New Agey accent.

Ketura was not a typical kibbutz. Founded by countercultural Americans in the 1970s when the state was relatively stable, it fused an American-style openness to traditional Judaism with a first-generation immigrant's commitment to the ideological pulls of Israel, the kibbutz movement, and Israel's south—its final frontier. In the founding document, kibbutz members sought to fulfill the general Zionist principles of their youth movement, Young Judaea/Hashachar. In the kibbutz's updated vision two decades later, in 1994, the founding ideals remain—alongside the emphasis to respect the individual within the group.

The Kibbutz Ketura Vision (accepted by the Aseifa, October 9, 1994)

We see ourselves as a community leading a unique, all-encompassing lifestyle, which, while not stagnant, emphasizes these core ideas:

A tight connection between economics and ethics: Economic equality among the members, mutual assistance, and self-sufficiency, along with economic responsibility and morality within our community, and beyond.

Vibrant interaction and interconnection among members, and with that, preventing any one individual from dominating others.

The ideals of equality of labor and gender equality, in all their manifestations, at work, in education, and within the community.

Nurturing the individual to flourish in the community and at work, culturally and spiritually, while valuing creative self-expression.

A deep connection to Jewish tradition that nevertheless allows the individual a wide range of approaches, including innovative ones. Our kibbutz is a critical part of the Zionist enterprise, whose central mission is the Jewish people's national, spiritual, and cultural renewal. Our identities, as Jews, as individuals, as a kibbutz and as a nation, are all part of a dynamic growth process. We encourage active participation in this great adventure.

This is a call to members, and to those interested in joining our community, to embrace these ideals, for they define us as Kibbutz Ketura.

Yaakov Rotblit (b. 1945)

A song for peace

Beyond the question of the kibbutz and the broader issues of social justice, the Zionist discourse increasingly focused on the question of how to achieve peace, what true peace entailed, and what Israel's borders should be. Ironically, Menachem Begin's openness to Anwar Sadat's peace initiative encouraged more voices, heretofore silenced, pushing for peace.

In March 1978, when the Egyptian negotiations seemed bogged down, a group of peace activists, some of whom had previously launched HaTnua LeTzionut Acheret, the Movement for a Different Zionism, took action. They drafted a letter demanding that Begin pursue peace more proactively, asserting "A government that prefers the existence of the State of Israel within the borders of 'Greater Israel' to its existence in peace with good neighborliness will be difficult for us to accept." Limiting its signatories to combat veterans, they recruited 348 soldiers and reservists. The letter attracted much attention, and hundreds more signatures, ultimately resulting in the founding of Shalom Achshav, (Peace Now).

In 1969, Yaakov Rotblit, who had lost part of his foot fighting for Jerusalem during the Six-Day War, composed the lyrics to "Shir LaShalom, A Song of Peace," the peace movement's unofficial anthem. The song expresses the bitterness of the dead, who cannot return; they prefer songs of peace not victory. Despite the critique, the Israel Defense Forces Infantry Ensemble performed "Shir LaShalom" first. Yitzhak Rabin sang it at a 1995 peace rally moments before he was murdered—

the bloodstained sheet of paper with the lyrics symbolizing the trauma of that awful moment.

Four decades later, Peace Now's members still sing "Shir LaShalom," and their organization remains the most prominent lobby pursuing a two-state solution. It emphasizes three principles: that the settlements threaten "the existence of Israel as a democratic and Jewish State," are "a main obstacle to any future peace agreement," and are "an element that harms the state on many fronts: security, nationally, economically, culturally, and morally. They also harm Israel's international standing." Calling itself a Zionist organization, Peace Now sees pursuing peace as central to the Zionist mission.

Shir LaShalom, A Song for Peace (1969)

Let the sun shine
Let the morning brighten,
Still, the purity in the prayers,
Will not bring us back.
Whoever's candle was snuffed out
And was buried in the dust,
Will not be awakened by bitter crying,
It won't bring him back.
No one can bring us back
from a deep and dark pit,
Nothing will help here . . .
Neither the joy of victory
Nor songs of praise.
So just sing a song for peace
Don't whisper a prayer
So just sing a song for peace . . .
in one loud shout.
Let the sun shine through the flowers,
Don't look back,

Let the dearly departed rest easily.
Lift your eyes in hope
Not through rifle sights
Sing a song for love
And not for wars
Don't say the day will come—bring on that day;
Because it is not a dream.
And in all the city squares cheer only for peace.

Leonard Fein (1934–2014)

The best defense we have is to look to the health of the Jewish soul.

Although this tradition has been largely abandoned, Progressive Zionists once criticized American Jewry even more lustily than they criticized Israel. They considered American Judaism staid, superficial, materialistic, and doomed. Leonard Fein challenged American Jewry on many fronts—while anticipating today's focus on Israel's failings by blasting Israeli policy equally. Known universally as Leibel, this academic turned journalist and social-justice crusader was a constructive critic. Perpetually in love with Israel and the Jewish people, he kept founding institutions to support—and save—both.

A Bronx-born graduate of the University of Chicago, with a political-science doctorate from Michigan State University, Fein taught at Massachusetts Institute of Technology and Brandeis University in the 1960s and 1970s. As the *Forward*—for which he was a longtime columnist—noted in its obituary: "In 1975, while a professor at Brandeis, he co-founded *Moment* magazine with Elie Wiesel. In 1985 he started Mazon: A Jewish Response to Hunger. In 1997 he set up the National Jewish Coalition for Literacy. Each of these organizations in its own way preserves his memory: without food we cannot live, without education we have no future and without thoughtful conversation we cannot thrive."

Fein spent decades trying to reconcile Jews with Judaism, reminding the community of its highest aspirations while confronting Israel's and

America's messy realities. Building toward the High Holidays of 1982, when many American Jews decried Israel's controversial invasion of Lebanon to destroy the Palestinian Liberation Organization ministate there, Fein captured many Zionists' ambivalence. Refusing to be an unrealistic dove insensitive to the threat the PLO posed in Lebanon, he also refused to excuse unrepentant hawks. Caught within the eternal Jewish and Zionist tension—the "is" and the "ought"—Fein described Zionism's often sobering realities and still soaring ambitions.

Days of Awe (September 1982)

There are two kinds of Jews in the world. There is the kind of Jew who detests war and violence, who believes that fighting is not "the Jewish way," who willingly accepts that Jews have their own and higher standards of behavior. And not just that we have them, but that those standards are our lifeblood, are what we are about. And there is the kind of Jew who thinks we have been passive long enough, who is convinced that it is time for us to strike back at our enemies, to reject once and for all the role of victim, who willingly accepts that Jews cannot afford to depend on favors, that we must be tough and strong.

And the trouble is, most of us are both kinds of Jew. . . .

There are two kinds of Zionists in the world: most of us are both. We want to be normal, we want to be special: we want to be a light unto the nations, we want to be a nation like all the others. We have still not figured out which we want more, and haven't figured out how to be both at once. And the circumstances of our lives don't give us much freedom of choice. They are nasty and brutish circumstances, and they require of us—or seem to—that we set aside our dreams of the heavenly Jerusalem, insure instead that the ramparts of the earthly Jerusalem are impregnable. Behind those ramparts, some day, perhaps, we shall dare to reach for the stars. For now, to turn our eyes toward the heavens is to risk not seeing the enemy as he approaches.

Yet the vision persists. We need to believe, for example, that the behavior of the Israel Defense Forces in the course of their movement through Lebanon was exemplary. . . .

There are those who believe only in the Zionism of the soul, in a disembodied Zionism that floats in abstract space. They prefer the Zionism of yearning, the rich imagining from Pinsk or from Boston, of what it might be like. A soul that has no body, no substance, is called a dybbuk, and is recognized as an untenable estate.

And there are those who believe only in the Zionism of the body, who have long since wearied of all this talk of "soul," who want us to be not an *Or la goyim*, a light unto the nations, but a *goy k'chul hagoyim*, a nation like all the others. A body without a soul. Normal. . . .

I vastly prefer a people that chooses to risk a collective nervous breakdown, as we do, by endorsing both visions, both versions. . . . Muscle and conscience, body and soul. . . . A people cannot live exclusively on its reactions. No, a people must stand for something, for something beyond its own survival. We live in a real world, and we cannot get by on dreams alone, but we cannot get by without dreams. Do we seek to protect and defend the Jewish body? The best defense we have—not the only defense, but the best defense—is to look to the health of the Jewish soul. For otherwise, will our children not be bound to ask why it is we care so much, what it is we seek so strenuously to preserve? . . .

Those who prefer "normalcy" will be deaf to that prayer. But . . . if it's normalcy we want, being Jewish is a very roundabout way to get there. . . .

Yitzhak Rabin (1922–95)

From nationalist fighter to warrior for peace

The first "sabra"—native born—prime minister, Yitzhak Rabin made his reputation as a warrior. Born in Jerusalem in 1922 and raised mostly in Tel Aviv, Rabin joined the Palmah during the pre-state period and directed operations in both Jerusalem and the Negev in 1948. Early in his career, this tough, taciturn, chain-smoking, Scotch-drinking soldier could have been voted least likely to appear in an anthology of Zionist thought.

Rabin was a reluctant solider who dreamed of a career in agricultural engineering but felt duty bound to become a soldier—working his way up to chief of staff in 1964. As a result, he experienced the crushing burden of determining Israel's fate in May 1967, as Egypt's strong man Gamel Abdul Nasser rallied Egypt, Syria, and Jordan to threaten Israel with destruction. The tension was so great during those crucial days that by June a severely stressed Rabin left center stage to Israel's defense minister, Moshe Dayan.

The Six-Day War victory was so impressive, and the generated myths so starry-eyed, that Rabin's reputation recovered quickly. A critical moment in his rehabilitation occurred on June 28, 1967, when Hebrew University granted him an honorary doctorate. Accepting the degree for all his soldiers, celebrating "their human values, their moral values," Rabin found the victory "exalted" but refused to exult over the enemies' defeat. "It may be that the Jewish people never learned, never accustomed themselves, to experience the thrill of conquest and victory," Rabin asserted, "and so we receive it with mixed feelings." Zionist soldiers, he said, were defined "by virtue of their moral stature and spiritual readiness in the hour of need." This ambivalence, paralleling the feelings the tortured kibbutznik-soldiers of *The Soldiers' Chat* would echo, reflected a new, made-in-Israel, forged-in-battle Zionist value.

Rabin entered politics shortly thereafter. He served as prime minister from 1974 to 1977, then again from 1992 to 1995. In 1993 he signed the Oslo Accords, channeling Israel's ambivalence about negotiating with Yasir Arafat along with the growing excitement about the chance for peace.

During this "battle without cannons in a war without fire," Rabin found his voice—articulating a Zionist vision of peace making after nearly a century of war making. In uncharacteristically eloquent speeches, Rabin oscillated between realism and idealism, acknowledging the challenges and celebrating the possibilities. Out of this tension came a message of hope and healing, of wariness and willingness, of still-unsheathed swords and newly lowered drawbridges. This hard-bitten twentieth-century general became the harbinger of twenty-first-century peace.

In November 1995, just moments after a peace rally in central Tel Aviv that culminated with Rabin awkwardly but earnestly singing

"Shir LaShalom," a song he didn't seem to know, a right-wing religious zealot shot him. Dozens of world leaders gathered in Jerusalem to bid farewell to Rabin, now Israel's martyr for peace.

Our Tremendous Energies from a State of Siege (Address at Levi Eshkol Creativity Awards Ceremony, October 6, 1994)

These days we are in the midst of a battle without cannons in a war without fire, which may turn out to be perhaps one of the most significant and decisive battles in the annals of the Jewish people in recent generations: the war over the nature of the State of Israel. We will have to choose, on the one hand, between the road of zealousness, the tendency towards dreams of grandeur, the corruption of ethical and Jewish values as a result of ruling over another people, the blind faith, the hubris of "I am, and there is no one else beside me"; and, on the other hand, the road of maintaining a Jewish, democratic, liberal way of life, with consideration for the beliefs of others, even among ourselves, as well as side by side with us, with everyone living their lives according to their own faith.

The battle over the nature of the Jewish state in the twenty-first century has begun. In this battle we return to the cemeteries, this time to bury old concepts, to bury a way of life in a state under siege. In this battle there will also be tactical withdrawals in order to achieve a strategic goal, and the strategic goal today is peace. Everything is measured against it. We take our leave, therefore, without great pain, from the realm of victory albums—even though we have not yet formed our own new world view. . . .

The coming years will be overshadowed by questions. Following the signing of peace, following the border that will open, following the walls that will tumble down, essential questions will arise: Who are we? Towards what are striving? What is our new character? What kind of nation do we want to be? How shall we live with those who surround us? Shall we be "a light unto the nations," or shall we be "a nation like all the nations"? Will religion continue to preserve Judaism? Preserve the Chosen People? And what is the place of secularism in it all? Will a new Jew arise, a new Zionist, a new Israeli?

Shimon Peres (1923–2016)

Today, as in my youth, I carry dreams.

Yitzhak Rabin's successor, Shimon Peres, was also his longtime rival. Their prolonged, dysfunctional enmity frequently paralyzed the Labor Party. Intensifying the battling egos, the petty intrigues, the conflicting claims to David Ben-Gurion's mantle was a clash of Zionist typologies. Rabin stirred Israelis' pride as a straight-shooting sabra warrior born into a dangerous situation yet always fighting for normalcy. Peres invited more ambivalence as a wily yet urbane Eastern European intellectual, more Abba Eban than Moshe Dayan.

Born in 1923 in White Russia, Poland (Belarus today), Peres arrived in Israel in 1934. Unlike many of his political peers, he did not make his reputation as a dashing fighter in the field, but as an ace weapons procurer in the Ministry of Defense and an aide to David Ben-Gurion. This difference, along with his lingering Polish accent and elegance, undermined his popularity for decades.

During the Oslo period Rabin and Peres finally seemed to have developed a workable dynamic: Peres was the idealist and Oslo enthusiast to Rabin's cautious but willing skeptic. As the excerpt from Peres's Nobel lecture reveals, while Rabin was not yet ready to sheathe his sword, Peres was updating Herzl's early dream of Arab-Jewish cooperation and shared redemption within a New Middle East.

Following Rabin's assassination, Peres ended up cast as his longtime rival's less-popular successor. He lost the follow-up elections to Benjamin Netanyahu due to a spate of terrorism and his stumbling in a pre-election debate. But, proving that a politician who lives long enough becomes a statesman, Peres became a beloved president.

Suddenly, he was no longer Ben-Gurion's hidden henchman or Rabin's manipulative challenger or the pie-in-the-sky-dreamer or the Israeli public's unrequited suitor. Instead, Shimon Peres became the last of the Founders. This living link to the great generation that established the state articulated a Zionist vision of "an Israel whose moral code is old as the Ten Commandments tablets, and whose imagination as new as the digital tablets as well."

Floating, finally, on this sea of public affection—and worldwide popularity—Peres became a great Zionist cheerleader in an age flirting with post-Zionism. His celebration of Jewish creativity, joy in the Jews' "dissatisfaction gene," and hopes for a modern, peaceful, high-tech Israel as a model of what he called the New Middle East cut through Israelis' usual cynicism—and even resonated among many skeptics abroad.

Nobel Lecture (1994)

From my earliest youth, I have known that while one is obliged to plan with care the stages of one's journey, one is entitled to dream, and keep dreaming, of its destination. A man may feel as old as his years, yet as young as his dreams. The laws of biology do not apply to sanguine aspiration.

I was born in a small Jewish town in White Russia. Nothing Jewish now remains of it. From my youngest childhood I related to my place of birth as a mere way station. My family's dream, and my own, was to live in Israel, and our eventual voyage to the port of Jaffa was like making a dream come true. Had it not been for this dream and this voyage, I would probably have perished in the flames, as did so many of my people, among them most of my own family. . . .

Today as in my youth, I carry dreams. I would mention two: the future of the Jewish people and the future of the Middle East. . . .

Jewish history presents an encouraging lesson for humanity. For nearly four thousand years, a small nation carried a great message. Initially, the nation dwelt in its own land; later, it wandered in exile. This small nation swam against the tide and was repeatedly persecuted, banished, and downtrodden. There is no other example in all of history, neither among the great empires nor among their colonies and dependencies—of a nation, after so long a saga of tragedy and misfortune, rising up again, shaking itself free, gathering together its dispersed remnants, and setting out anew on its national adventure. Defeating doubters within and enemies without. Reviving its land and its language. Rebuilding its identity, and reaching toward new heights of distinction and excellence.

The message of the Jewish people to humanity is that faith and moral vision can triumph over all adversity. . . .

In the five decades of Israel's existence, our efforts have focused on reestablishing our territorial center. In the future, we shall have to devote our main effort to strengthen our spiritual center. Judaism—or Jewishness—is a fusion of belief, history, land, and language. Being Jewish means belonging to a people that is both unique and universal. My greatest hope is that our children, like our forefathers, will not make do with the transient and the sham, but will continue to plow the historical Jewish furrow in the field of the human spirit; that Israel will become the center of our heritage, not merely a homeland for our people; that the Jewish people will be inspired by others but at the same time be to them a source of inspiration. . . .

Israel's role in the Middle East should be to contribute to a great, sustained regional revival. A Middle East without wars, without enemies, without ballistic missiles, without nuclear warheads. . . . A Middle East which will serve as a spiritual and cultural focal point for the entire world.

Shulamit Aloni (1928–2014)

The shift from the collective to the individual search for justice.

When the State of Israel was established in 1948, Socialist Zionism—with its collective sensibility—dominated, politically and ideologically. Labor's subsequent loss of power to the Likud in the Menachem Begin revolution of 1977 set the stage for two critical turning points. Over the next decades, Labor learned how to be in the opposition. At the same time, individualism eclipsed Socialist Zionist collectivism—even on the left.

The fiery feminist lawyer Shulamit Aloni embodied both these trends. Although she occasionally served in government, most famously as minister of education from 1992 to 1993, she succeeded Menachem Begin as Israel's ultimate opposition politician. Deploying her sharp tongue and intense passion, she championed individualism, pushing a more Americanized rights-based discourse. Although she was too much the firebrand to merit full credit, the Basic Law of 1992, "to protect human dignity and liberty, in order to establish in a Basic Law the values of the State of Israel as a Jewish and democratic state," resulted directly from the Aloni revolution.

Born in Tel Aviv in 1928, Aloni was a member of the left-wing Hashomer Hatzair youth movement and fought for the Palmah. She would fondly recall being a "Zionist from the age of 12" in a Zionist youth movement, "and swearing allegiance to the Bible, the gun, and the flag, in the ninth grade." In 1948 she fought to free the Jewish Quarter of Jerusalem and was imprisoned briefly by its conquerors, the Jordanian Foreign Legion.

After the war, she attended law school. In 1965 she was elected to the Knesset as part of a broad Labor Alignment coalition. In 1973 she bolted, founding the Citizen Rights Movement, Ratz. An outspoken critic of the status quo long after retiring from politics in 1996, she never stopped pursuing peace, human rights, democracy, and the election of a leader who could rejuvenate Israel. Nevertheless, she declared herself "very proud of what we have achieved as a country," remembering that "the Zionist movement arose to establish a sovereign nation of Israel in the Jews' homeland." That goal made the movement "an amazing success," creating "a flourishing and progressive state offering a home to every Jew who wants to live there." Proud of being "an Israeli without hyphens," she explained: "The sovereignty of the people and its connection to its past, its land and its culture is of supreme importance. Here, there is no duality of identity like that among Jews abroad."

I Cannot Do It Any Other Way (1997)

Let's consider the term that has become so cliché, "a Jewish and democratic state." I hate applying the notion of "Jewish" to my identity as a citizen. For that, I prefer the term "Israeli," because Israeli is both Jewish and sovereign, with the notion of sovereign entailing responsibility and commitments. . . . Not just power but also responsibilities to the individual and to minorities. The concept of Israeliness expresses an expansive, sovereign citizenship, while the term "Jewish identity" reflects a closed clannishness. I am shocked that we abandon the Israeli identity so easily, rather than appreciating it for expressing the sovereign Jewish nationalism flourishing here. . . .

There doesn't have to be contradiction between a Jewish approach and a democratic approach. They can overlap. In the same way that I cannot separate my identity as a human being and as a woman, I am not ready to separate my being a woman and my being a daughter of the Jewish nation. I therefore prefer the phrase "An Israeli democratic state," because Judaism is a three-thousand-year-old tradition and culture. Within that tradition, within that heritage, in Jewish sources, we can find "seventy faces," meaning many contradictory values. . . .

I am in favor of Israel being a state for all its citizens. In order to be such a state, and if we are true democrats, Israel's laws must apply universally to all. . . .

England has many minorities; does that stop her from being English? Is France not France because Jews live there? We are the majority here, and the majority determines the rhythms of life. From the cultural, religious, social perspective, we are a pluralistic society. Nevertheless, Saturday is the Sabbath, even as the Christians and the Muslims have the right to rest on their own Sabbaths. Arabic is the second official language. . . .

I don't need Arabs celebrating the Jewish liberation from Egypt with me on Passover. I do want us all to share the universal value of freedom. I don't want people's non-Jewish status preventing them from sharing equally in all our rights as citizens—they don't have to eat matzah with me for that to happen. . . .

The ancient aspiration to be an exemplary society, to be an enlightened democracy, is still widely shared. That is not merely the fantasy of the founders' generation; it's central to the Israeli ethos. So we have to roll up our sleeves, steel ourselves, and help.

9

Builders

Revisionist Zionism

Ze'ev Jabotinsky, the Israeli right's ideological father, was a complex thinker with a rich legacy. His ideological heir, Menachem Begin, maintained Jabotinsky's mix of individualistic, rights-oriented democracy and proud nationalism, although other followers rejected this balance. Moreover, the Labor Party's dominance during the state's first three decades embittered the displaced Jabotinskyites.

Three key moments reflecting Menachem Begin's democratic restraint, triumph, and deployment of power shaped the Israeli right during Israel's first five decades. First, Prime Minister David Ben-Gurion's sinking of the *Altalena*, an Irgun-commissioned ship laden with weapons in June 1948, demonstrated Ben-Gurion's ruthlessness, and Begin's self-control. Worried that, untamed, the rival paramilitary groups Irgun and Lechi would undermine the rule of law, Ben-Gurion asserted the new state's authority. Exhibiting class and patriotism, Begin acquiesced, averting civil war. Meanwhile his respect for the new state's power demoralized many Revisionists, who insisted he resist.

Begin seemed doomed to perpetual opposition, forever alienated from the ruling Labor Zionist *branja*, elite, even though he joined the National Unity government shortly before the Six-Day War. Yet in 1977 Begin rode the shock waves from the 1973 Yom Kippur War into power. Suddenly, the outsiders were in—and have dominated Israeli politics since.

Finally, Begin demonstrated that power in a democracy often proves moderating. The fiery nationalist became an unexpectedly flexible statesman, inviting Egyptian president Anwar Sadat to Israel after Sadat indicated a willingness to come. Sadat's visit in November 1977 was historic, euphoric. Less than a year later, Menachem Begin returned to Israel from

Jimmy Carter's presidential retreat, Camp David, with a surprising peace agreement with Egypt.

Begin's willingness to trade land for peace, including uprooting Sinai settlements such as Yamit, devastated many long-suffering loyalists. Yet as Begin evolved from doctrinaire naysayer to subtle statesman and Nobel Peace Prize–winning peacemaker, he taught the right about power's tradeoffs and possibilities.

Uri Zvi Greenberg (1896–1981)

Israel without that Mount is—not Israel

The nationalist poet Uri Zvi Greenberg reflects the post-1948 Revisionists' intense Jewish fluency, rich Zionist passion, conflicted patriotism, and undiluted bitterness. Born in Galicia in 1896, raised in a prominent Hasidic family, he served in the Polish army during World War I. Polish soldiers celebrating the war's end nearly killed him and his parents.

This pogrom convinced him that European Jewry was doomed, as he warned in his 1923 Yiddish poem, "In the Kingdom of the Cross." That year, he immigrated to Palestine and began writing in Hebrew, heralding a Hebrew revolution.

Initially a Labor Zionist, Greenberg went Revisionist after Arab rioters massacred his Jewish neighbors in Hebron in 1929. The "Oration to the Nation" he published four years later glorified the Revisionist New Jew with images so vivid they evoke the propaganda posters of the 1930s. "O Nation, You're awesome!" he exclaimed, delighting how this shattered people raised a new generation of "sons, their spirits as broad as their shoulders, flexing arms of iron, thighs of steel," and "daughters, healthy and lovely, primed to work the towns and villages." Honoring and honing their battle cry, he exulted: "They will burst forth as rebels and you will hear them bursting into their song: Of freedom, conquest, redemption, expansion, majesty!"

Despite his collectivist zeal, Greenberg nevertheless mocked naïve Socialist Zionists. "Decay of the House of Israel" (1936) rejected his old Socialist Zionist comrades' "sick bureaucratic-literary-philosophical Judaism." He hated the "stench of their reasonableness," that they came not "to build a State, only a haven"—a central Jabotinsky complaint. A land, Greenberg preached, "is conquered in blood."

In the 1940s Greenberg joined Revisionism's military organization, the Irgun. When his prophecies proved correct—the "*Churban*," the destruction, occurred—he was devastated. His rage bled through his anguished 1951 poem "Under the Tooth of Their Plough," imagining that a farmer churning up "a skeleton of mine. . . . will grin," rejoicing with Europe's Christians that "the Jews are no more." The Zionist implications were clear: only Israel is our home.

While Greenberg's Zionism was simple and pure, his relationship to modern Israel was complex. The spilling of more Jewish blood in 1948 broke his heart; the loss of Jerusalem's Jewish Quarter tortured his soul. Such sentiments made him resent Labor's dominance. Greenberg served in the first Knesset, allying with Menachem Begin.

Rooted in traditional texts, Greenberg's poetry also toasted Israel's glorious past. "The Man Who Stepped out of His Shoes," a 1953 poem generations of Israeli schoolchildren memorized, warned Israelis not to step away from tradition, to remain rooted. "Israel without the Mount" contains what became a popular Revisionist slogan: "Israel without that Mount is Not Israel."

Those Living-Thanks to Them Say (1948)

They were the chosen ones, joyfully singing . . their voices now
    silenced.
Sons of the seed of David who fell with their sword in their hand.
They were as simple and adorable as David the youth from the
    family of shepherds . .
And, they bless You from the earth, Lord!
The earth now encasing them is not the earth of death . .
From this very soil You long-ago created humanity.
From this strain comes the Temple Mount, the soil, and the rock.
Those who bless you from such earth . . they are immortal!
There is no truth except theirs and no glory without them.
And we in this universe--without them-are merely
Living-thanks-to-them,. And their radiance also rewards us.
Those who look toward their graves cease to be slaves—

Israel without the Mount (1948–49)

Don't hang out in Eilat and plant your flag in the Red Sea
There-you'll just get Reeds.
You've betrayed your Mount, the world's loftiest
The holiest mountain of any in the world.
You'll never sit proudly among the nations without that mountain
 of mountains
that props you up in the world.
You can sit among the nations, once that Mount props you up.
The Mount will sit in concealed glory, just as you lived in alien
 lands with eclipsed strength.
And even your foes knew you as the children of the loftiest Mount.
And your kings' psalms spring forth from their mouths
when they mourn or when they crown their kings..
Without that glory, what is your value in the universe?-:
Take North from world and become-a triangle.
Take East from world and become-nothing.
Israel without that Mount is-not Israel.

Geulah Cohen (b. 1925)

A Zionist maximalist.

As hard as it was for Begin and his Irgunists to accept post-1948 realities, those to their right suffered more. The Lechi or Stern Group had found the Etzel (or Irgun) too accommodating, insisting on fighting the British during World War II. Like many Lechi members, Geulah Cohen, born in 1925, joined the Irgun in 1942 and migrated to the Lechi a year later. An editor and radio announcer, she broadcasted Lechi's viewpoint before the British imprisoned her in 1946—and after escaping prison too.

Cohen's autobiography, *Woman of Violence: Memoirs of a Young Terrorist, 1943–1948,* appeared in Hebrew under the neutral title "Story of a Fighter." The book poignantly described her shift from the purity of fighting the British and the Arabs to the complexity of supporting a state whose leaders disdained you and your comrades, despite your sacrifices to establish that state.

In the 1960s and early seventies, Cohen worked as a journalist for *Ma'ariv.* In 1973 she joined the Knesset as a member of Menachem Begin's Herut party. She led the purists' fight against Begin's Camp David agreement with Egypt. Ultimately, she formed a breakaway party, Tehiya, in 1979, renouncing all territorial compromises. Nevertheless, Cohen stayed in Begin's coalition, serving in the Knesset until 1992.

Memoirs of a Young Terrorist (1943–48)

The British were leaving, but somehow it wasn't the way we had expected. . . . Break up and go home. We weren't ready for that. Where was there to go? In our ecstatic vision of Redemption, it had always seemed to us that victory in war would coincide with the fulfillment of the dream of ages. Somewhere beyond the realms of cold reason, we had believed that, when the last British soldier left the country, messianic times would arrive. Now, however, the British were going home; the veil had fallen, but no Messiah stood behind it. . . .

With their typical opportunism and their ingenious ability for adjusting to any situation, they [the Labor Zionists] were already moving to fill the power vacuum that the British would leave. They enjoined us to dissolve.

"Come back home," they requested, in a tone that left little doubt whose home it was.

No, it was not the home we had envisioned and yearned for. It was not so much the house itself, narrow and cramped though it was, which made us feel ill at ease. It was the character of our landlords. We knew them well and had known them since we first left them and their docile masses to go to war. They were not great architects of aspiring temples hewn out of rock. They were designers of apartment houses built on sand, strictly functional structures whose sole purpose was to keep away thieves, highwaymen, high winds, and dreams. We undergrounders felt more at home in prison than in such houses, for in a cell at least we could dream as we pleased. We were requested to come home. They did the requesting. Somehow the rudder of history had slipped from our hands. . . . Victory over the British had brought about the liberation of a portion of the Jewish homeland, but at the same time it had vanquished Lechi completely. . . .

I felt only the infinite grief of a slaughtered dream, a dream that could not be divided without being mutilated at the same time. Anyone could draw boundaries in the ground, but a land that had a soul of its own and had been sanctified from above had its frontiers not on earth but in Heaven. Heaven had made those frontiers and Heaven alone could change them.

The Tehiya Party Platform (1988)

The exclusive and eternal right to the Land of Israel lies with the Jewish people. That right is anchored in the heritage of the Jewish People and the Zionist vision.

This right cannot be surrendered, abrogated, or transferred under any condition. No government has the authority to yield up any portion of the Land of Israel whatsoever.

Any political solution that includes the withdrawal from portions of the Land of Israel under our control is summarily invalid. We will oppose all forms of territorial compromise or plans for autonomy.

Tehiya will continue to struggle in the Knesset as in the past to legislate the Law of Sovereignty that will apply Israel's sovereignty over Judea, Samaria, and Gaza.

On that day that the Law of Sovereignty will be passed the name of the state will be changed from "Israel" to "*Eretz-Yisra'el*"—the Land of Israel.

Moshe Shamir (1921–2004)

We commit fully and steadfastly to the fullness of our land—uniting the Jewish people's past with the Jewish people's future.

David Ben-Gurion's passionate Labor nationalism, paralleled by many Revisionists' estrangement, sometimes blurred lines between left and right, especially in the Zionist discourse. Key figures zigzagged ideo-logically as circumstances changed.

The novelist Moshe Shamir became one of the most famous Labor turncoats. Born in Safed in 1921, a leader of the left-wing movement Hashomer Hatzair, Shamir helped romanticize the Palmah. His 1947 novel *He Walked through the Fields* and his 1951 memoir about his brother Eli who had died in the War of Independence, *With His Own Hands*, popularized the stereotype of the diffident but heroic sabra soldier who yearned to farm. Shamir beautifully memorialized his brother with "his fair hair, his easy laughter, his warmth, his fine strong hands that bespoke activity, and his ready repartee." Alas, Eli knows that "Each bullet has a name on it." Indeed, one arrives with "the three small letters: ELI."

Shamir's importance in creating the Labor mythology made his shift right—when he helped launch the Land of Israel Movement—all the more painful. Just days after the Six-Day War, David Ben-Gurion's ally Zvi Shiloah had responded to a Natan Alterman column rejoicing that, finally, the Land of Israel and the people of Israel were reunited. Alterman involved Shamir, who was equally excited. Together, the three Labor Zionist stalwarts recruited fifty-three other intellectuals, authors, activists, and politicians to sign their manifesto, "For a Greater Israel."

Joining a Likud faction, Shamir was elected in 1977, with Menachem Begin. Still, Shamir was too iconoclastic to be a loyalist. Objecting to withdrawing from any inch of territory, he broke with Begin over the 1979 Israel-Egypt Peace treaty. Beyond politics, defining Zionism as "national, political, military, and economic liberation." Shamir pronounced the Zionist movement "the twentieth century's greatest success story."

For a Greater Israel (September 22, 1967)

The IDF victory in the Six-Day War has catapulted the people and the state into a new and portentous period. Greater Israel is now in the Jewish people's hands. Just as we dare not abandon the State of Israel, we are commanded to perpetuate what is now in her hands: the Land of Israel.

We commit fully and steadfastly to the fullness of our land—uniting the Jewish people's past with the Jewish people's future. No government has the right to relinquish that wholeness.

The current borders of our state guarantee security and peace while expanding the horizons that once were missing, encouraging a thorough national renewal, physically and spiritually.

Within these borders, all will enjoy freedom and equality: the fundamental rights the State of Israel provides all of its inhabitants, with no distinctions.

Our future depends on the two principles of continuing *aliyah*, immigration, and settling the land. A mass migration from all over the Jewish Diaspora is an essential condition for fulfilling the Land of Israel's full national destiny. The new missions and possibilities this era evokes will trigger a new awakening and focus for the People of Israel and the Land of Israel....

The Green Space: Without Zionism, It'll Never Happen (1991)

The Green Space is *Eretz Yisra'el*, the Land of Israel....

Amid the constant sense of flashing red lights signaling danger, defying all the world's warning signs and stop signs, Jewish history has been progressing for over a hundred years in this Green Space. When the Zionist movement first launched its quest, this place was a yellow wasteland. Zionism in its glory surmounted all the obstacles it faced, making the wasteland a flourishing green field....

As we approach the first Zionist Congress's hundredth anniversary, it should be clear that the Zionist movement is the twentieth century's greatest success story. The dynamic, cutting-edge power that teaches and fulfills, that revolutionizes and builds, that saves and creates, as a unique force in contemporary Jewish history has been and still is the Zionist idea. A mark of the idea's triumph comes by recalling its early foundational stages, then seeing its realization: the Jewish people returned and built an independent and sovereign home in the Land of Israel....

Open an Israeli newspaper today or tomorrow or any day—see the litany of all the wounds and woes. . . . Take every problem that ails us. We will always arrive at one answer: Without Zionism, it'll never happen. . . .

It will be nice and fitting, for both the government and the settlements, if the government of Israel will finally implement its settlement plans, and mobilize the necessary manpower for it. But without Zionism, it'll never happen. . . .

The great misfortune generated by our current diplomatic and security status is our loss of autonomy. The meaning of Zionism, at its most basic, is national, political, military, and economic liberation. . . . and without Zionism, it'll never happen.

Menachem Begin (1913–92)

The fighting Jew . . . whom the world considered dead and buried never to rise again, has arisen.

When Menachem Begin became Israel's sixth prime minister in 1977, many Revisionists now accustomed to the political wilderness were even more surprised than displaced Laborites. Begin's tenure would recalibrate Zionist ideology and Israeli historiography. Finally, Israelis—and the Israeli establishment—would recognize Revisionist ideas—and Revisionists' historical contributions.

Born in Brest-Litovsk, Poland, (now Russia) in 1913 to a Zionist family, Begin learned in yeshiva and attended secular high school. At sixteen, after first joining the Socialist Zionist youth movement Hashomer Hatzair, he joined Jabotinsky's Betar. He studied law at the University of Warsaw while becoming Betar's leader.

During World War II, Begin's father led hundreds of Jews in singing "Ani Ma'amin" ("I Believe") and "Hatikvah" ("The Hope") before the Nazis drowned them. Begin fled to Vilna, where the Soviets arrested him in the middle of a chess game on September 20, 1940. Although sentenced to eight years in Siberia, he was freed in May 1942 with 1.5 million other Poles, then joined the Polish Free Army. The army brought him to Palestine in 1942. While others fled, he remained enlisted until properly released.

Begin became the new commander of the Irgun Zvai Leumi, the National Army. On February 1, 1944, using the nom de guerre Ben Ze'ev, he issued the "Proclamation of the Revolt" "Every Jew in the homeland will fight," he declared. "There will be no retreat. Freedom or death!"

Under Begin, the Irgun attacked the British, determined to expel them from Palestine. For the next four years, until the British departed in May 1948, Begin was a hunted man, with a fifty-thousand-dollar bounty on his head.

Running in Israel's first Knesset elections as the leader of the Herut (Freedom) Party, Begin endorsed Jabotinsky's vision of individual freedom, capitalism, a strong defense, and a refusal to relinquish Jews' ancestral rights to the entire Land of Israel. Herut eventually expanded to become Gahal—then, in the 1970s, Likud.

In 1952 Begin, always a fiery orator, rejected German war reparations. In 1967 Begin, always a patriot, joined the National Unity Government before the Six-Day War. As minister without portfolio, Begin emboldened the government to reunite Jerusalem.

Begin was pushing sixty-four when he became prime minister in 1977. Surprisingly, he accepted Egyptian president Anwar Sadat's demand that Israel return the entire Sinai, including thriving settlements, for peace. Begin explained to his furious comrades that peace was also a Jewish national value—and the Sinai was not part of the Biblical Land of Israel.

Begin was more ambivalent about Israel's presence in what he always called Judea and Samaria. He initiated much settlement building there while encouraging Palestinian autonomy. The deposed Labor prime minister Yitzhak Rabin noted Begin's great "advantage—that as prime minister he doesn't have Begin in the opposition."

Begin's tenure ended tragically, with the Jewish unity he treasured collapsing over Israel's war in 1982 against Palestine Liberation Organization's terrorism in Lebanon. Many Israelis and Diaspora Jews criticized this operation as the country's first optional war. Taking every soldier's loss personally—more than most leaders in history—broke Begin. He resigned from office in 1983 and withdrew from public life. He died in 1992.

Begin's writing illustrates his many identities: Zionist activist, Holocaust survivor, guerilla fighter, opposition firebrand, prime minister. These selections trace Begin's evolution from uncompromising opposition leader to prime minister—leading a nation toward compromise, no matter how difficult, for a shot at peace.

The Revolt (1951)

I have written this book primarily for my own people, lest the Jew forget again—as he so disastrously forgot in the past—this simple truth: that there are things more precious than life, and more horrible than death.

But I have written this book also for Gentiles, lest they be unwilling to realize, or all too ready to overlook, the fact that out of blood and fire and tears and ashes a new specimen of human being was born, a specimen completely unknown to the world for over eighteen hundred years, "the Fighting Jew." That Jew, whom the world considered dead and buried never to rise again, has arisen. For he has learned that "simple truth" of life and death, and he will never again go down to the sides of the pit and vanish from off the earth. . . .

It is axiomatic that those who fight have to hate—something or somebody. And we fought. We had to hate first and foremost, the horrifying, age-old, inexcusable utter defenselessness of our Jewish people, wandering through millennia, through a cruel world, [exposed to the masses for whom] . . . the defenselessness of the Jews was a standing invitation to massacre them. We had to hate the humiliating disgrace of the homelessness of our people. We had to hate—as any nation worthy of the name must and always will hate—the rule of the foreigner, rule, unjust and unjustifiable per se, foreign rule in the land of our ancestors, in our own country. We had to hate the barring of the gates of our own country to our own brethren, trampled and bleeding and crying out for help in a world morally deaf. . . .

And in our case, such hate has been nothing more and nothing less than a manifestation of that highest human feeling: love. For if you love Freedom, you must hate Slavery; if you love your people, you cannot but hate the enemies that compass their destruction; if you love your country, you cannot but hate those who seek to annex it.

Broadcast to the Nation (May 15, 1948)

The State of Israel has arisen. . . . It has been difficult to create our state. But it will be even more difficult to keep it going. We are surrounded by enemies who long for our destruction. . . .

Now, for the time being, we have a Hebrew rule in part of our homeland. And as in this part there will be Hebrew Law—and that is the only rightful law in this country—there is no need for a Hebrew underground. In the State of Israel, we shall be soldiers and builders. And we shall respect its government, for it is our government. . . .

The State of Israel has arisen, but we must remember that our country is not yet liberated. . . . Our God-given country is a unity, an integral historical and geographical whole. The attempt to dissect it is not only a crime but a blasphemy and an abortion. Whoever does not recognize our natural right to our entire homeland does not recognize our right to any part of it. And we shall never forego this natural right. We shall continue to foster the aspiration of full independence. . . .

We cannot buy peace from our enemies with appeasement. There is only one kind of "peace" that can be bought—the peace of the graveyard, the peace of Treblinka. Be brave of spirit and ready for more trials. We shall withstand them. The Lord of Hosts will help us. . . .

Statement to the Knesset upon the Presentation of His Government (June 20, 1977)

By virtue of this age-long heritage, I wish to declare that the Government of Israel will not ask any nation, be it near or far, mighty or small, to recognize our right to exist. The right to exist? It would not enter the mind of any Briton or Frenchman, Belgian or Dutchman, Hungarian or Bulgarian, Russian or American, to request for his people recognition of its right to exist. Their existence per se is their right to exist. The same holds true for Israel. We were granted our right to exist by the God of our fathers, at the glimmer of the dawn of human civilization, nearly four thousand years ago. For that right, which has been sanctified in Jewish blood from generation to generation, we have paid a price unexampled in the annals of the nations. Certainly, this fact does not diminish or enfeeble our right. On the contrary. Therefore, I re-emphasize that we do not expect anyone to request, on our behalf, that our right to exist in the land of our fathers, be recognized. It is a different recognition which is required between ourselves and our neighbors: recognition of sovereignty and of the mutual need for a life of peace and understanding. It is this mutual recognition that we look forward to.

And now, members of the Knesset, the appeal to ourselves, to our people. I call on all citizens of Israel who have left the country, to return home.... The Government will act to ease matters for the returning families. We shall not address these people by derogatory terms. Insults solve no problem. We shall say to them simply: the time has come to return home.

We call on the young generation, in the homeland and in the Diaspora, to arise, go forth and settle. Come from east and west, north and south, to build together the Land of Israel. There is room in it for millions of returnees to Zion. We do not wish to evict, nor shall we evict, any Arab resident from his land. Jews and Arabs, Druze and Circassians, can live together in this land. And they must live together in peace, mutual respect, equal rights, in freedom and with social-economic progress.

Yitzhak Shalev (1918–92)

Ignite the flame of resistance to the horrible amputation of the land of Israel against her will and against her grain.

A talented man of letters, the father of the contemporary novelist Meir Shalev, Yitzhak Shalev was born in 1919 in Tiberias. After serving with Begin in the Irgun, this ardent Zionist and Bible enthusiast lamented Israel's establishment on only part of its homeland. His book *Songs of Jerusalem* envisioned the future "one day after Jerusalem is redeemed."

In his most famous novel, *The Gavriel Tirosh Affair* (1964), a history teacher fights against the British and the Arabs in 1936 and, invoking the Crusaders, insists that unlike the Christian interlopers, Israel is here to stay. That same sentiment animates Shalev's 1975 poem, "The Crusaders," a powerful affirmation of Zionist staying power in a multilayered land. Returning today, the Crusaders discover the Jew's "flag is on the fortress and ours has been lowered." All that remains of their former ferocity are ruins and some "blond hair here and there" in Arab villages.

We Shall Not Give Up Our Promised Borders (1963)

First of all, the Jewish people [outside Israel] must face the simple truth: if they will continue to send only their money and not the best of their sons and daughters, we are destined to the same fate as that of the Crusaders who suffered, among other things, from lack of sufficient reinforcements from Europe. Whether we shall live here as lords or as the Crusaders is dependent entirely on the Jewish people....

Do the Jewish people understand the events in the Middle East or do they not? This is the main problem, not that which is called the "Arab problem." The Arab problem is one that is entirely Jewish and it is possible to solve it only through the flow of Jewish force which is aware of the vision. People. Materials. Scientific and industrial brains. Everything that can be sent will be sent. And in the name of God, these things must be sent before it will be necessary to send to Israel boats to carry the Jewish refugees from their homeland....

And at last, we must educate our youth towards *Eretz Yisra'el* in its entirety. This education should be performed by the parent, the kindergarten teacher, the teacher, the leader of the youth movement, and the commander in the army....

The Armistice Agreement became the final word, not only in military movement, but also in the movement of literary imagination. The borders of the Armistice Agreement became our emotional borders, and the borders of our desires and wishes. Further than these borders we have no requirements, no desires, no dreams, no song....

The destiny of literature in connection with youth should be entirely different. It must protect the spark of longing for all that we have lost and for our ancient sites which are spoken of in the Bible. It must ignite the flame of resistance to the horrible amputation of the land of Israel against her will and against her grain. It must teach the sons of Judah a theory of a vast and complete country and prepare them for the important revision in the future. . . .

Such a future cannot be achieved by the Israeli ghetto in whose borders we are trapped today. Sooner or later we will have to break out of this trap towards the two rivers in order to reach our destiny in the land which was given to Abraham.

Eliezer Schweid (b. 1929)

Aliyah: the essence of the dynamic contact between Diaspora Jewry and the State of Israel.

Even as wielding power sullied their ideological purity, Revisionists have stood out as passionate Jewish nationalists and zealots of the Land—not just the State—of Israel.

The Jerusalem-born philosopher and Israel Prize–winner Eliezer Schweid has spent most of his career at Hebrew University. Although his academic greatness transcends particular partisan affiliation, and he began his life as a kibbutznik, he eloquently explains two central tenets of modern Revisionism: Zion's ongoing mission and the Promised Land's enduring power.

Schweid argues that without a sense of mission Israel will wither: Zionism must be an ongoing "project" educating toward *aliyah* and absorbing Jewish immigrants. Rather than viewing Jews as the specially Chosen People, he believes the Israeli people themselves must be special. He is also famous for noting that those dissatisfied with any aspect of Israeli life should redouble efforts to fix it, not dodge responsibility by rejecting Israel itself.

Schweid pinpoints an even more central Zionist fundamental: the bond linking the Jewish people with their homeland, generating values, shaping identity. His vision transcends the equation of Israel's providing spiritual and ideological goodies as the Diaspora responds financially and politically. He sees great spiritual payoffs for Israel, too.

Israel as a Zionist State (1970)

As a Zionist state, the State of Israel, contrary to other states, must regard itself as the state of a people the majority of which is not concentrated within its borders. As a Zionist state, it must bear the responsibility for the security, well-being, unity and continuous cultural identity of the Jewish people. . . .

Aliyah constitutes the essence of the dynamic contact between Diaspora Jewry and the State of Israel. It is clear, therefore, that the State of Israel as a Zionist state must prepare itself for *aliyah*. Israel should encourage education towards *aliyah* and readiness to absorb the immigrants. This should be emphasized in particular: an immigrant-absorbing state is not only a state ready to receive immigrants, but a state that is prepared to attract them and to organize its economy and patterns of social life, particularly in the field of education, in a manner which will make possible their absorption in the most effective way. . . .

Secondly, a Zionist policy must be one of fostering the Jewish identity of the state as such and of the people living in it. The Jewish identity of the state as such means on the external front that the Jewish state should not agree in any way to a solution of the Israel-Arab conflict which would entail jeopardizing its Jewish majority and undermining its sovereignty. Moreover, the State of Israel, even though it contains national minorities whose rights as citizens of a democratic state should not be affected in the slightest degree, must define itself as a Jewish state. That is to say, as a state that embodies Jewish nationalism and serves the national interest of the Jewish people.

On the internal front, this means that the State of Israel should concern itself with educating its younger generations in the cultural legacy of the Jewish people and fostering its ties with the Jewish people and its history; its Jewish character should also find expression in its legislation and ceremonies. . . .

Finally, a Zionist policy means a project-oriented policy: the State of Israel, insofar as it remains loyal to its mission, should not regard its existence and present achievements as an end in themselves but rather as a means to fulfilling its role which lies mainly in the future. This is not mere rhetoric nor a demand for general awareness. It has to do with the everyday life of Israel's citizens, since it determines the basic orientation of Israeli society and every single member of it. . . .

Why is the abandonment of a Zionist policy tantamount to destruction for the State of Israel? First of all, if there is no moral justification for its existence, a state tends to lose its moral strength to stand up to the pressures of its surrounding. He who has not had to struggle for a very long time for his survival can take this argument as mere abstraction which does not count in real life. He who has had to stand in such a struggle knows very well that moral strength is the basis of physical strength. Israel would not have come into being, nor survived up to now, were it not for the awareness of the significance of its existence of its mission, and of its just goals. Israel will not be able to persist even for a short time without this moral conviction. . . .

The Promise of the Promised Land (1988)

The Land of Israel is . . . the land that was promised as a national homeland, the basis of the nation's economic weal and state power, but at the same time it symbolizes the Torah's universal moral and religious meaning. . . .

What is there about this land in particular for it to be made the homeland of the chosen people?

The Bible sings the praises of the land's abundance and its beauty, but there is nothing religious in that. A theological dimension appears in the Book of Deuteronomy, where a point is made about the difference between Egypt, which drinks river water, and the Land of Israel, which drinks rainwater. Rainfall is a symbol of divine providence. Furthermore, according to the biblical stories, in the great riverine countries a nation's sense of ownership of its land and mastery of its destiny is reinforced, leading to the development of tyrannical regimes and slavery.

In lands that drink rainwater, on the other hand, man constantly senses his dependence on God, and for that reason such a land will sustain a regime of justice free of subjugation. . . .

Later in Prophets we find a somewhat different variant of this theme. The land is located between the great river powers (Egypt, Babylonia) and between the desert and the sea. It is a middle land. It attracts all nations and is a pawn in the hands of the powers who fight for world dominion.

Those who live in the land are tempted to take part in the struggle between the powers as a way to aggrandize power for themselves. But the only way to live in the land peacefully and to bring a vision of peace to the world is by refraining from participation in those pagan power struggles and by living a life of justice and truth in accordance with the Torah. In a word, then, the nature and status of this land embodies the conditions of the covenant made between the nation and God as expressed in the Torah.

Benjamin Netanyahu (b. 1949)

The incomparable quest of a people seeking, at the end of an unending march, to assume its rightful place among the nations.

The son of a leading Revisionist scholar, Professor Benzion Netanyahu, Benjamin Netanyahu was born in Tel Aviv in 1949. Although initially raised in Jerusalem, he had two extended family stays in the Philadelphia suburbs when his father taught at Dropsie College. Enlisting after graduating from Cheltenham High School in 1967, he served as an elite commando in Sayeret Matkal until 1972.

That year, he enrolled at Massachusetts Institute of Technology but rushed back in October 1973 to serve in the Yom Kippur War. Afterwards, he completed degrees in architecture and business, then worked at the Boston Consulting Group.

From 1978 to 1980, Netanyahu ran the Jonathan Netanyahu Anti-Terror Institute, named after his older brother Yoni, who died rescuing hostages in Entebbe in 1976. He subsequently served as deputy chief of mission at the Israeli Embassy in Washington. In 1984, at age thirty-five, he was already Israel's ambassador to the United Nations. He became one of Israel's most effective spokespeople: confident, unapologetic, nimble, and eloquent. Four years later he joined the Likud Party and was elected to the Knesset.

His book, *A Place among the Nations* (1993), combined Netanyahu's love of history and political combat. Embracing the heritage of both Jabotinsky and Begin, Netanyahu defended Israel's rights, while striking a balance between affirming its normalcy and celebrating its uniqueness.

Three years later, amid the turmoil following Yitzhak Rabin's assassination and the first waves of Palestinian suicide bombings, Netanyahu was elected prime minister. He served from 1996 until 1999, left politics briefly after a rocky term, then returned in 2002. He continued to serve in a variety of positions, most notably as prime minister since 2009.

A Place among the Nations (1993)

In the case of the Jewish national claim, the central issue is this: Does a people that has lost its land many centuries ago retain the right to reclaim that land after many generations have passed? And can this right be retained if during the intervening years a new people has come to occupy the land? Advocates of the Arab case commonly present these questions, and they answer both of them in negative. Further, they add, if the Jews have a historical "quarrel" with anyone, it is not with the Arabs but with the Romans, who expelled them from their land in the first place. By the time the Arabs came, the Jews were gone.

How, then, were the Jews finally forced off their land? The most prevalent assumption is that the Jewish people's state of homelessness was owed solely to the Romans. It is generally believed that the Romans, who conquered Palestine and destroyed Jewish sovereignty, then took away the country from the Jews and tossed them into exile that lasted until our own century. However common this view is, it is inaccurate. . . .

In 636, after a brief return of the Byzantines under Heraclius, the Arabs burst into the land—after having destroyed the large and prosperous Jewish populations of the Arabian Peninsula root and branch. The rule of the Byzantines had been harsh for the Jews, but it was under the Arabs that the Jews were finally reduced to an insignificant minority and ceased to be a national force of any consequence in their own land. . . . In combination with the turmoil introduced into the land by the Arab conquest, these policies finally succeeded in doing what the might of Rome had not achieved: the uprooting of the Jewish farmer from his soil. *Thus it was not the Jews who usurped the land from the Arabs, but the Arabs who usurped the land from the Jews.*

The question of Jewish powerlessness is central to the traumatic experience of the Jewish people, and it is the obverse side of the question of Jewish power. It is between these two poles that Jewish history has oscillated in modern times. . . .

The first result of the atrophy of Jewish resistance was physical destruction on an unimaginable scale. No other people has paid such a price for being defenseless. But there was a second fateful consequence: Slowly and surely, through the centuries of exile, the image and character of the Jew began to change. For non-Jews, the glorious Jewish past faded into dim memory and irrelevance. The word *Jew* became an object of contempt, derision, at best pity. It became synonymous with the word *coward* in a hundred different tongues. The adjective *wandering* was affixed to it, signifying the rootlessness and precariousness of Jewish existence. . . .

Worse, a substantial segment of Jewish opinion assimilated this disparaging image of the Jew, and many Jews came to view themselves as other had come to view them. This took on a particularly pernicious twist in the modern era. As the doctrines of modern pacifism emerged, many Jews rushed to embrace them, pretending they could transform into a universal virtue what had always been a unique vulnerability of the Jews. That the Jews "would not" (could not) resort to arms, that they would not "demean" themselves by "stooping to violence," was taken to be a clear sign of their moral superiority over other peoples who were not similarly constrained. Once leading segments of Jewish opinion in Europe had transformed Jewish weakness into positive good, the Jewish people's chances of escaping its fate reached a new low. . . .

With the founding of the State of Israel, the majority of Jews quickly came to understand the critical importance of military power—a change far more abrupt and spectacular than the gradual loss of this understanding had been. For if the rendering of the Jews from a militant to a docile people had taken place over many centuries, here in the space of only a few years a reborn Jewish sovereignty rediscovered the art of soldiering. . . .

But the change in the way the Jews viewed themselves was even more dramatic. It had begun as early as the 1890s. Visitors to Palestine at the time noted a change in the first generation of Jewish youngsters who had been raised on the land outside the enclosed ancient Jewish quarters of Safed and Jerusalem. Unlike their Orthodox brethren, these young Jews, mostly sons and daughters of recent immigrants, cultivated the land, rode horses, learned to shoot, spoke a revived Hebrew, and were capable of befriending or confronting the Arabs, earning their respect if not their love.

Israel encounters difficulties in explaining its position that no other nation encounters. No other country faces both constant threats to its existence *and* constant criticism for acting against such threats. . . .

This is an important part of the secret of the success of Arab propaganda: It appeals to a world that has not yet accustomed itself to the sight of Jewish strength, military and political. It implicitly urges philo-Semites to yearn for a "purer" age when Jews were beyond reproach because they were beyond succor.

But now the Jews have entered a new phase in their history. Since the rise of Israel, the essence of their aspirations has changed. If the central aim of the Jewish people during exile was to retrieve what had been lost, the purpose now is to secure what has been retrieved. It is a task that has barely begun, and its outcome is of profound import not only for the fate of the Jews but for all mankind. . . .

The rebirth to Israel is thus one of humanity's great parables. It is the story not only of the Jews, but of a human spirit that refuses again and again to succumb to history's horrors. It is the incomparable quest of a people seeking, at the end of an unending march, to assume its rightful place among the nations.

10

Builders

Religious Zionism

The State of Israel's founding transformed the Religious Zionist discussion. Underlying practical questions about riding buses on the Sabbath and selling bread on Passover were deeper questions about this new state's meaning and Judaism's new opportunities to thrive back home in its natural habitat, the Land of Israel. Even for secular Jews, the debate about the Jewishness of the state pitted the Zionist quest for normalcy against the Jewish mission seeking universal justice. And, if Religious Zionists first tried explaining how Jewish tradition justified creating a modern Jewish state, after 1948 they tried interpreting the state's spiritual significance, especially following the Holocaust.

Many rabbis reexamined the nature of God's covenant with the Jewish people while rethinking God's role in human affairs. Rabbi Joseph Ber Soloveitchik, among others, deemed the Holocaust a time of *hester panim*, literally the hiding of the face. God was obscured from humanity as people exercised their free will, even to do evil.

The miracle of 1967, with the switch from fearing destruction to celebrating Jerusalem's liberation, intensified the debate about Israel's spiritual meaning as even many secular Jews treated the triumph as a modern miracle. Religious Zionists focused on settling the biblical lands now under Israel's control. In non-Orthodox circles, many liberal Zionist rabbis reexamined their movement's relationship with Zionism. Most dramatically, Reform Judaism Zionized, embracing the great modern Jewish peoplehood project in ways that would have scandalized the Reform movement's founders.

Ben-Zion Meir Chai Uziel (1880–1953)

Nationalism is a worldview committed to improving our human life on earth.

Born in 1880 to a leading Sephardic family in Jerusalem, by 1911 Uziel had become the *hakham* (sage) of Jaffa's Sephardic community. With his colleague Abraham Isaac Kook, he worked on uniting Ashkenazi and Sephardi communities while establishing Yeshivot and other communal institutions. Eventually, he served as the *Rosh Yeshiva* (dean) of Yeshivat Tiferet Yerushalayim, the Old City's leading Sephardic institution.

In 1917 the Ottoman Turks exiled Uziel with other leaders to Damascus. When he returned in 1920, he joined the Religious Zionist organization Mizrachi. Serving for three years as rabbi of Salonika, then as chief rabbi of Tel Aviv, he became chief Sephardic rabbi of *Eretz Yisra'el* in 1939. Nine years later, that made him the first chief Sephardic rabbi of the new State of Israel. He served until his death in 1953.

As a religious nationalist, Uziel understood Zionism's success as a first step in fulfilling Israel's redemptive mission in the world. Nationalism was a tool toward greater spirituality. The Jewish people's values took precedence over land, state, or government, which were means to the broader goal. In that spirit, as early as 1947, he emphasized the Jews' and Muslims' shared religious origins when appealing to Muslim leaders for peace.

In September 1948, Uziel and the Ashkenazi chief rabbi Yitzhak Halevi Herzog published a prayer for the new state in the Religious Zionist newspaper *HaTzofeh* and the general paper *Ha'aretz*. Apparently, the author S. Y. Agnon helped, possibly contributing the famous line characterizing the state as *resheit tzmeechat geulateinu*, the first flowering of our redemption. The incongruity of a prayer that rabbis wrote, a novelist edited, and daily newspapers published, suited the complexity of a secular democratic state's chief rabbis praising its religious meaning after many decades of secular Zionists having rebelled against the rabbis.

Prayer for the State of Israel (1948)

Our Father in Heaven, Rock and Redeemer of Israel, bless the State of Israel, the first flowering of our redemption. Shield it with Your loving kindness, envelop it in Your sukkah of peace, and project Your light and truth upon its leaders, ministers, and advisors, and grace them with Your wise counsel. Strengthen the hands of our Holy Land's defenders, rescue them, and adorn them in a mantle of victory. And You shall bestow peace in the Land and grant its inhabitants eternal happiness.

And our brothers and sisters, the entire House of Israel, protect them in all the lands of their Diaspora, and lead them quickly upright to Your city Zion—to Jerusalem, Your name's dwelling place, as is written in the Torah of Moses your servant: "If you will be scattered to the ends of the heavens, from there the Lord your God will gather you and from there he will take you. And the Lord your God will bring you to the land that your ancestors inherited and you shall inherit it; and He will be good to you and expand you more than your ancestors. And the Lord will sculpt your hearts and the hearts of your descendants, so that you will love the Lord your God with all your heart and all your soul, for the sake of your lives."

Unite our hearts to love and revere Your name, and to follow all the words of Your Torah. And quickly send us the son of David your righteous Messiah, to redeem those waiting for the era of your salvation. Reveal gloriously the genius of your strength to all the inhabitants of Your physical world and all who have breath in their nostrils shall say: "The Lord the God of Israel is King and his sovereignty reins over all," Amen Selah.

On Nationalism (ca. 1940–50)

Nationalism is not about a common race, it is not homeland or government or monarchy and it's not about leaders or shared obligations or literature or a common culture. All these are expressions of the collective or the state. But nationalism in the strict sense is a worldview committed to improving our human life on earth. It's about achieving the peak of human consciousness and success, by imparting the truths about goodness and law and morality to our descendants and spreading these spiritual ideas and ethics "not by power and not by force" but with explanations and insights that foster appreciation of these attitudes' spiritual power and truth, and that cultivate goodness within all those who follow their ways. . . .

With Israel's righteous nationalism preceding its politics, the noble idea of *tikkun olam*, fixing the world through the kingdom of God, takes precedence over nationhood and statehood. This primacy orients and shapes Jewish politics. The father of our nation Abraham was commanded by the Lord, who said: "Go forth from your land and your birthplace and your father's house to the land that I will show you" (Gen. 12:1). Jacob the father to God's tribes also lived a nomad's life. From this you learned: neither patrimony nor the customs of the country created Jewish nationalism. Rather, God's will in beneficently guarding over us chose our nation's ancestors and their descendants to be an *Am Segula*, a righteous people. . . .

Israel is a patriotic nation deeply connected to its land and homeland, even when distanced from it. This commitment stems from a sincere understanding that its Exile was neither natural nor accidental, but a divine decree to test it and spread its Torah among the masses. Israel remains loyal to its land as a commandment. . . . This nation preserves its nationalism and its love and hope for its homeland. This duality does not fracture its soul, just the opposite. From a deep love of the land of Israel it adds love and loyalty to the lands of its exile.

David Edan (1872–1955)

**We need to celebrate her holidays and enjoy her joys,
by immigrating en masse to this new place.**

Rabbi Yosef Kapach (1917–2000) once asked, "If Zionism is the cure, what is the disease?" This Yemenite wise man noted that for most Jews—he was too polite to say especially Ashkenazim—choosing to be Zionist and move to Israel was an exceptional act. By contrast, his

Yemenite community was waiting to move, and thrilled when granted the opportunity.

The Wise One, HaChacham David Edan, was among many *Mizrahi* Jews who took Zionism personally, experiencing the call to *aliyah*, to settle the land. A cantor, *mohel*, and shofar blower in the great synagogue of Djerba, Tunisia, he also established Djerba's first Hebrew printing press, the Zionist Press.

Despite Edan's yearning to fulfill the Zionist dream, ill health kept forcing him to defer his move. He died before immigrating. Nonetheless, his writing captured the excitement many *Mizrahi* Jews felt when embracing a personal challenge—"risking it all, physically and materially," to "ascend there."

A Call for *Aliyah* (ca. 1950)

Behold, I want to talk to and rouse our brothers the children of Israel to wave the Israeli national flag, the flag of our country and our patrimony, and to offer some words of praise. . . .

It is not only our duty to love Israel from a distance, we also need to celebrate her holidays and enjoy her joys, by immigrating en masse to this new place, and joining in the novel and practical task of settling the land. This is our goal and it's good for us. Thus, those blessed by God with wealth and assets and clear vision should prepare themselves to ascend there, and, quite quickly, to start building and planting to settle the Land.

This is what the great human and Zionist effort will yield: God Almighty will bless those who arrive and work hard for many years. All our efforts should be devoted to settling the Land by planting and other initiatives that will persist for generations. . . .

And despite all we have donated to be planted in Israel via the Zionist movement, we still have not fulfilled our personal religious obligation, because each of us is commanded to try, to band together and unite in this regard, to build, to plant, and to envision this great new society, risking it all, physically and materially.

Joseph Ber Soloveitchik (1903–93)

Listen! My beloved knocks!

Rabbi Joseph Ber Soloveitchik validated Zionism as a political phenomenon bursting with spiritual meaning. Interweaving religious and political language, he rejoiced in the modern miracle of Israel's founding on Israel Independence Day 1956—and challenged Jews to move from their covenant of Egypt, their shared fate, to the mission-oriented covenant forged at Sinai. His sermon—published as *Kol Dodi Dofek, (Listen! My Beloved Knocks!)*—thus charged the Jewish people to become a "holy nation," striving to ennoble humanity by living exemplary ethical and religious lives.

Born in 1903 in Pruzhan, Poland, into a distinguished rabbinic line, Soloveitchik earned a doctorate in 1931 from the University of Berlin. Arriving in Boston in 1932, he became chief rabbi in the city, founded the Maimonides Day School and, starting in 1941, headed Yeshiva University's Rabbi Isaac Elchanan Theological Seminary in New York. Carefully navigating the modern world, he opposed mixed seating of men and women in synagogues and dialogues with liberal denominations but fought stubbornly to teach women Talmud. Similarly, his Zionism balanced his daily life in Boston with his yearnings for the Promised Land, and his hard-headed assessment of the need for a Jewish state with his soft-hearted vision of that state as a light unto the nations.

Listen! My Beloved Knocks! (1956)

Eight years ago, amid a night of terror filled with the horrors of Majdanek, Treblinka, and Buchenwald; in a night of gas chambers and crematoria; a night of absolute divine self-concealment; a night ruled by the devil of doubt and destruction which sought to sweep the maiden from her house into the Christian church; a night of continuous searching, of yearning for the Beloved—that very night the Beloved appeared. "God who conceals Himself in his Dazzling hiddenness" suddenly manifested

Himself and began knocking at the tent of His despondent and disconsolate love, twisting convulsively on her bed, suffering the agonies of hell. Following the knocks on the door of the maiden, enveloped in mourning, the State of Israel was born!

How many times did the Beloved knock on the door of the tent of His Love? It appears that we can count at least six knocks.

First, the Beloved's knock was heard in the political arena. No one can deny that from the standpoint of international relations, the establishment of the State of Israel, in a political sense, was an almost supernatural occurrence. Russia and the Western countries jointly supported the state's establishment. This was perhaps the only resolution that united East and West [during the Cold War].... If John Doe had chaired the United Nations' session, the State of Israel never would have been born. The Beloved knocked on the chairman's podium, then the miracle occurred. Listen! My Beloved Knocks!

Second, the Beloved's knocking resounded on the battlefield. The small Israeli Defense Forces defeated the mighty Arab armies.... Listen! My Beloved Knocks!

Third, the Beloved also began knocking on the door of the theological tent. This may be the strongest knock of all.... The establishment of the State of Israel has *publicly refuted* all the Christian theologians' claims that God deprived the Jewish people of its rights in the Land of Israel, and that all the biblical promises regarding Zion and Jerusalem refer, in an allegorical sense, to Christianity and the Christian church....

I always derive a particular sense of satisfaction from reading in a newspaper that the State of Israel's reaction is not yet known since today is the Sabbath and government offices are closed.... Listen! My Beloved Knocks!

Fourth, the Beloved is knocking at the hearts of the perplexed and assimilated youth. The era of self-concealment—*hester panim*—at the beginning of the 1940s sowed great confusion among the Jewish masses and, particularly, among young Jews. Assimilation grew, becoming even more rampant, as the impulse to flee from Judaism and the Jewish people peaked. Fear, despair, and sheer ignorance caused many to spurn the Jewish community. . . .

Many of those who, in the past, were alienated from the Jewish people are now tied to the Jewish state by a sense of pride in its outstanding achievements. . . . The very fact that "Israel" always is on everyone's lips reminds Jews in flight that they cannot abandon the Jewish community to which they have been connected from birth. . . . Listen! My Beloved Knocks!

The fifth knock of the Beloved is perhaps the most important. For the first time in the history of our exile, divine providence has surprised our enemies with the sensational discovery that Jewish blood is not cheap, not *hefker*—open season is over! . . . Blessed are You for granting us life and bringing us to this moment, when Jews have the power, with God's help, to defend themselves.

Let us not forget that the venom of Hitlerian antisemitism, which made the Jews like the fish of the sea to be preyed upon by all, still infects many in our generation who viewed the horrific spectacle of the gassing of millions with indifference, as an ordinary event barely requiring notice. The antidote to this deadly venom that poisoned minds and numbed hearts is the State of Israel's readiness to defend the lives of its children, its builders. Listen! My Beloved Knocks!

The sixth knock, which we must not ignore, was heard when the Land of Israel's gates opened. A Jew who flees from a hostile country now knows that he can find safe refuge in the land of his ancestors. . . . Listen! My Beloved Knocks! . . .

The individual is tied to his people through the chains of fate and the bonds of destiny. . . . The covenant in Egypt was a covenant of fate; the covenant at Sinai was a covenant of destiny. . . .

The Camp emerges from a desire for self-defense and is nurtured by fear. The Congregation reflects longing to fulfill an exalted ethical idea, nurtured by the sentiment of love. Fate reigns, in unbounded fashion, in the Camp; destiny reigns in the Congregation. . . .

With Israel's establishment, secular Zionism declares we have become a people like all peoples. . . . Only the religious *shivat Zion* movement, with its traditional, authentic approach, can rectify these distortions. . . .

The mission of the State of Israel is neither to terminate the unique isolation of the Jewish people nor abrogate its unique fate—in this it will not succeed! Rather, the mission is to elevate a Camp-people to the rank of a holy Congregation-nation, transforming shared fate to shared destiny. . . .

Our historic obligation, today, is to raise ourselves from a people to a holy nation, from the covenant of Egypt to the covenant at Sinai, from an existence of necessity to an authentic way of life suffused with eternal ethical and religious values, from a Camp to a Congregation. . . .

Yeshayahu Leibowitz (1903–94)

We brought this state about by dint of our common efforts as Jewish patriots.

Just as the Puritan Roger Williams called for separation of church and state in Rhode Island to protect the church from the state's impurities, the Orthodox intellectual virtuoso and political provocateur Yeshayahu Leibowitz tried protecting the purity of Judaism from the messiness of the Jewish state—and its politics.

Born in Latvia in 1903, educated in Berlin, he moved to Israel in 1935. A chemist and physician, he also edited the *Encyclopedia Hebraica* and became a controversial philosopher who called settlers the reprehensible term "Judeo-Nazis."

Leibowitz noted that "of all the political movements that arose during the nineteenth century, only Zionism fulfilled its goals." Still, he refused to consider Israel's founding redemptive, or spiritually significant. And he insisted that religion required protection from the state.

For decades, Leibowitz's bracing rhetoric and iconoclastic approach to religion, nationalism, diplomacy, and security vexed Israel's leaders and Zionism's greatest thinkers. Nevertheless, appreciating Zionism as a "political program" that meant "national independence for the Jewish people in its own country," Leibowitz wanted that independence to liberate the Jewish people's moral energies in this real-world test of Jewish ethics.

A Call for the Separation of Religion and State (1959)

From a religious viewpoint . . . the present relations between the state and the Torah appear as *hillul ha-Shem*, contempt of the Torah, and a threat to religion. . . .

The State of Israel that came into being in 1948 by the common action, effort, and sacrifices of both religious and secular Jews was an essentially secular state. It has remained essentially secular and will necessarily continue to be such, unless a mighty spiritual and social upheaval occurs among the people living here. The secularity of this state is not incidental but essential. . . .

Whether we are religious or secular, we brought this state about by dint of our common efforts as Jewish patriots, and Jewish patriotism—like all patriotism—is a secular human motive not imbued with sanctity. Holiness consists only in observance of the Torah and its Mitzvoth: "and you shall be holy to your God." We have no right to link the emergence of the State of Israel to the religious concept of messianic redemption, with its idea of religious regeneration of the world or at least of the Jewish people. There is no justification for enveloping this political-historical event in an aura of holiness. Certainly, there is little ground for regarding the mere existence of this state as a religiously significant phenomenon. . . .

There is no greater degradation of religion than maintenance of its institutions by a secular state. Nothing restricts its influence or diminishes its persuasiveness more than investing secular functions with a religious aura; adopting sundry religious obligations and proscriptions as glaring exceptions into a system of secular laws; imposing an arbitrary selection of religious regulations on the community while refusing to obligate itself and the community to recognize the authority of religion; in short, making it serve not God but political utility.

This is a distortion of reality, a subversion of truth, both religious and social, and a source of intellectual and spiritual corruption. The secular state and society should be stripped of their false religious veneer. Only then will it become possible to discern whether or not they have any message as a Jewish state and society. Likewise, the Jewish religion should be forced into taking its stand without the shield of an administrative status. Only then will its strength be revealed, and only thus will it become capable of exerting an educational force and influencing the broader public. . . .

Zvi Yehuda Hakohen Kook (1891–1982)

Where is our Hebron—have we forgotten her?!
Where is our Shehem, our Jericho,—where?

For some Religious Zionists, as with some Revisionists, Israel's founding was bittersweet. Losing Old Jerusalem tempered their joy. In May 1967, celebrating Israel's nineteenth Independence Day, the head of Mercaz HaRav, Zvi Yehudah Hakohen Kook, articulated those mixed emotions, calling for "our Hebron . . . our Shehem, our Jericho." The son of the Religious Zionist Abraham Isaac Kook, he maintained his father's patriotism. He encouraged his students to serve in the army and became even more of a maximalist regarding settling the Land of Israel.

After the Six-Day War triumph weeks later, Kook's Independence Day address seemed clairvoyant. Hearing of Jerusalem's liberation, Kook rushed to the Western Wall and participated in the *Minha* afternoon service. Years later, he recalled: "It was the first national prayer at the Kotel after a nineteen-hundred-year separation! A prayer which was utter cleavage to God. Every eye was filled with tears. Soldiers prostrated themselves on the ground of the square. Others wedged their fingers between the stones of the Wall. Everyone chanted the Psalm, 'A Song of Ascent; When the Lord brought back the exiles of Zion, we were like dreamers.'" Interviewed on radio and television, Kook declared: "Behold. We announce to all of Israel, and to all of the world, that by a Divine command, we have returned to our home, to our holy city. From this day forth, we shall never budge from here! We have come home!" This fiery nationalism inspired Gush Emunim and the broader settlement movement. Rav Zvi Yehudah served as the settlers' spiritual grandfather until his death in 1982.

On the 19th Anniversary of Israel's Independence (1967)

Nineteen years ago, on the night when news of the United Nations decision in favor of the reestablishment of the State of Israel reached us, when the People streamed into the streets to celebrate and rejoice, I could not go out and join in the jubilation. I sat alone and silent; a burden lay upon me. During those first hours I could not resign myself to what had been done. I could not accept the fact that indeed "they have ... divided My land." (Joel 4:2)! Yes [and now after nineteen years] where is our Hebron—have we forgotten her?! Where is our Shehem, our Jericho,—where?

Have we forgotten them?! And all that lies beyond the Jordan—each and every clod of earth, every region, hill, valley, every plot of land, that is part of *Eretz Yisra'el*? Have we the right to give up even one grain of the Land of God? On that night, nineteen years ago, during those hours, as I sat trembling in every limb of my body, wounded, cut, torn to pieces. I could not then rejoice. . . .

The question has been asked, "Is this the state that our prophets envisioned?" And I say: This is the state that the prophets envisioned. Of course, it has not yet attained perfection. But our prophets, our sages and those who followed them, said: "The seed of Abraham, Isaac, and Jacob will return and will reestablish settlement and independent political rule in the Land." We were not told whether those who return will or will not be men and women of righteousness. . . .

Indeed, surely as a result of the return of Israel to their Land there will come about the increase of Torah and its glorification. But the first step is the settlement of Israel on their land! . . . [T]he order of Redemption is: agricultural settlement, the establishment of the state, and as a consequence—to follow—the uplifting of that which is sacred, the dissemination of the teaching of Torah, its increase and glorification. . . .

The true Israel is Israel redeemed, the kingdom of Israel and the armies of Israel, a people in its wholeness and not a diaspora in exile. . . .

Abraham Joshua Heschel (1907–72)

The State of Israel is a spiritual revolution, not a one-time event, but an ongoing revolution.

The Polish-born American rabbi, Abraham Joshua Heschel, is remembered today as a mystic, social activist, friend to Martin Luther King Jr. and the entire civil rights movement, and an inspiration to Jewish environmentalism. But Heschel was also a Zionist, profoundly connected to Israel and Jerusalem.

Born in Warsaw in 1907, yeshiva trained and raised within the Hasidic tradition, he earned a doctorate at the University of Berlin and a liberal rabbinic ordination too. Fleeing the Nazis, he arrived in New York City, teaching at the Conservative Movement's Jewish Theological Seminary until his death in 1972.

Mourning the Nazi murders of his mother and three sisters, he wrote, "If I should go to Poland or Germany, every stone, every tree, would remind me of contempt, hatred, murder, of children killed, of mothers burned alive, of human beings asphyxiated." By contrast, visiting Jerusalem shortly after its liberation in 1967 enraptured him. In his subsequent book, *Israel: An Echo of Eternity*, a lyrical celebration of Jerusalem, Israel, and Zionism, he viewed Israel's rebuilding as promising humanity's redemption.

Israel: An Echo of Eternity (1969)

Jerusalem, you only see her when you hear. She has been an ear when no one else heard, an ear open to prophets' denunciations, to prophets' consolations, to the lamentations of ages, to the hopes of countless sages and saints; an ear to prayers flowing from distant places. And she is more than an ear. Jerusalem is a witness, an echo of eternity.

Jerusalem was stopped in the middle of her speech. She is a voice interrupted. Let Jerusalem speak again to our people, to all people. . . .

The State of Israel is not only a place of refuge for the survivors of the Holocaust, but also a tabernacle for the rebirth of faith and justice, for the renewal of souls, for the cultivation of knowledge of the words of the divine. By the power and promise of prophetic visions we inhabit the land, by faithfulness to God and Torah we continue to survive. The land presents a perception which seeks an identity in us. Suddenly we sense coherence in history, a bridge that spans the ages. . . . A land that was dead for nearly two thousand years is now a land that sings. . . .

We have been beset by a case of spiritual amnesia. We forgot the daring, the labor, the courage of the seers of the State of Israel, of the builders and pioneers. We forgot the pain, the suffering, the hurt, the anguish, and the anxiety which preceded the rise of the state. We forgot the awful pangs of birth, the holiness of the deed, the dedication of the spirit. We saw the Hilton and forgot Tel Hai. The land rebuilt became a matter of routine, the land as a home was taken for granted. . . . The State of Israel is a spiritual revolution, not a one-time event, but an ongoing revolution. . . .

However, it was not justice as an abstract principle which stirred us so deeply [in 1967]. Auschwitz is in our veins. It abides in the throbbing of our hearts. It burns in our imagination. It trembles in our conscience. We, the generation that witnessed the Holocaust, should stand by calmly while rulers proclaim their intention to bring about a new Holocaust?

A new life in Israel has bestowed a sense of joy upon Jews everywhere, by creating a society based on liberty, equality and justice, by the great moral accomplishments, by their scientific, technical and economic contributions. In the Land of Israel those rescued from the Holocaust of Europe and the refugees from persecution in Arab lands have found a home and are able to renew their lives. A well which had been blocked and sealed in some deep corner of the soul was suddenly opened. What sprang forth was the realization that while we may be extending our lives in so many different directions, our secret roots are near the well, in the covenants, with the community of Israel. This is not an ideology, a matter of choice, it is an existential engagement, a matter of destiny. We may not all understand the meaning of the divine but to us our relationship to the community of Israel can never be detached from our gropings for the divine. . . .

One of the insights learned from the great crisis in May 1967, is the deep personal involvement of every Jew in the existence of Israel. It is not a matter of philanthropy or general charity but of spiritual identification. It is such personal relationship to Israel upon which one's dignity as a Jew is articulated. . . . The Lord's compassion is over all that He has made (see Psalm 145:9). We mourn the loss of lives, the devastation, the fruits of violence. We mourn the deaths of Jews, Christians, Moslems. The screams of anguish are not to be lost to our conscience. . . .

The six days of war must receive their ultimate meaning from the seventh day, which is peace and celebration. . . .

What is the meaning of the State of Israel? Its sheer being is the message. The life in the Land of Israel today is a rehearsal, a test, a challenge to all of us. Not living in the land, nonparticipation in the drama, is a source of embarrassment. Israel is a personal challenge, a personal religious issue. It is a call to every one of us as an individual, a call which one cannot answer vicariously. It is at the same time a message of meaning, a way of dealing with the monsters of absurdity, a hope for a new appreciation of being human. The ultimate meaning of the State of Israel must be seen in terms of the vision of the prophets: the redemption of humanity. The religious duty of the Jew is to participate in the process of continuous redemption, in seeing that justice prevails over power, that awareness of God penetrates human understanding.

Esther Jungreis (1936–2016)

How will the Jews in exile answer to future generations when they ask, "Where were *you*?"

The 1973 Yom Kippur War frightened Jews all over the world who once again feared Israel's destruction. It triggered an outpouring of financial support—and guilt. The gap between the comforts of the Diaspora and the travails Israelis faced daily, even without war, generated a constant undercurrent in Zionist discourse. Some Israelis specialized in making Diaspora Jews feel guilty—and many Diaspora Jews internalized and echoed it. Today, the older generation's guilt tripping has made a younger generation of Diaspora Jews particularly resistant to such an approach. But in the 1960s and 1970s, especially among Holocaust refugees, this quite literal survivors' guilt could be scorching.

The Hungarian-born *rebbetzin* Esther Jungreis, a survivor of the Bergen-Belsen concentration camp, was a charismatic practitioner of Orthodox outreach. Known as "the Jewish Billy Graham," she stayed in America to fight what she called the growing "spiritual Holocaust" of assimilation and mass Jewish illiteracy. The organization she founded, Hineni (Here I am), mounted mass rallies to stir Jewish consciousness, hosted once-alienated Jews for Sabbath getaways, and broadcast weekly television programs teaching Torah in the 1980s.

In one of her trademark parables, Jungreis wondered how someone standing by an enchanting violinist could resist such hypnotic sounds. Those are the Jews who failed to return to the restored Jewish homeland, she concluded. Imagine, having "been given *Eretz Yisra'el* and to be indifferent to it." Her 1977 pamphlet, *Zionism: A Challenge to Man's Faith,* similarly chiding American Jewish softness and self-absorption, is also laden with the non-*aliyah*-making Zionist's guilt.

Zionism: A Challenge to Man's Faith (1977)

In the Holy City I met a woman. . . . She related a tale to me . . . which reflects the agony of Zionism in the twentieth century.

This woman of Jerusalem had a son by the name of David. He was twenty years old. She also had a sister who lived in New York. She too had a son of the same age. His name was Chaim.

The American cousin came to Jerusalem for a year of study. Then suddenly, the Yom Kippur War broke out. Both boys were in the synagogue praying side by side. David, still wrapped in his tallit [prayer shawl], without pausing for food or water, ran to answer the call of his people. He bid farewell to his cousin, to his mother, to his father, and to his young bride. He had no choice but to go forth to defend his people.

The following day, the mother in Jerusalem received an emergency call from the United States. "Please, please," a near hysterical voice called across the great ocean, "Where is my Chaim? Please do not let him do anything rash . . . you must find him and get him out on the first plane to safety. We are sick with worry. I want him home!"

The mother in New York was overcome by fear and somehow in her agitation she forgot to ask about David, her sister's son, the son of Jerusalem, whose heart at that very moment was pierced by a shell in the Golan. . . .

The story haunts me. It leaves me no peace. . . . For indeed, if the Land of Israel has been given by God as an inheritance to all Jews, then by what right do we in the United States go to sleep in security, knowing that our sons are well and sound, while our sisters lie awake with a gnawing fear gripping their hearts . . . asking the question, "Where is he now?" and whispering a silent prayer, "Hashem, Almighty G-d watch over him. . . ."

No matter how much the American Jew has given and will give on behalf of Israel, he will never equal the sacrifice of those who live there and offer their very lives for the land.

No matter how much the American Jew continues to give, he will never be able to justify the fact that he belongs to the generation that was given Jerusalem yet opts for New York or Los Angeles.

To have waited 2,000 years, to have suffered the agonies of exile, to have dreamt and hoped, to have been given the land only to reject it. How will the Jews in exile answer to future generations when they ask, "Where were *You*?"

Talma Alyagon-Roz (b. 1944)

**To a people who will not go unheard, /
Who will not abandon their sons to others.**

Just three years after the horrors of the Yom Kippur War—which Israel won in an impressive military comeback—the mythic hostage rescue at Entebbe restored the country's reputation. As part of the subsequent mythmaking, the Israeli actor and singer Yehoram Gaon starred as the martyr Yoni Netanyahu in the movie celebrating the event, *Operation Thunderbolt*. The producers commissioned the Israeli author, television writer, librettist, and songwriter Talma Alyagon-Roz to write a song Gaon would sing in the movie.

Alyagon-Roz's composition, "Eretz Tzvi / The Land of Beauty" she later wrote, "symbolizes our symbiotic relationship with the land of Israel, with her people, her landscapes, her history . . . our mutual responsibility for one another as a people." The song became a popular anthem in the religious community, especially with members of the B'nai Akiva youth movement. As a result, the non-religious Alyagon-Roz has shaped modern religious Zionism.

In 2006 during the Second Lebanon War, Major Roi Klein threw himself on a grenade to save his men—yelling as he died, "*Sh'ma Yis-ra'el*," "Hear O'Israel," a Jew's final words. At Klein's sister's request, "The Land of Beauty" was played on radio in his memory. Eight years later, Klein's family attended an Alyagon-Roz concert. After singing the song for them, she wrote a new stanza, in Klein's memory, included here.

Eretz Tzvi, The Land of Beauty (1976; updated May 12, 2014)

In the middle of the night they rose,
Striking the edge of the world.
Like angels of fire, they flew skyward,
Restoring the dignity of man.

To Eretz tzvi,
To the honey of its fields,
To the Carmel and the desert,
To a people who will not go unheard,
Who will not abandon their sons to others,
To Eretz tzvi which in its mountains,

Pulses a city from generation to generation,
To a motherland whose sons are attached to her
For better and for worse.

In the middle of the night a scorching wind
Blows through our fields,
And the mute willow bows her head
For those who did not return at sunrise.

To Eretz tzvi,
To the honey of its fields,
To the Carmel and the desert,
To a people who will not go unheard,
Who will not abandon their son to others,

To Eretz tzvi whose tears
Drop onto a field of sunflowers,
Whose sadness and joy are woven into her gown.

*

When sunrise cut through the dark,
He rescued the injured from fire.
He lay his body on a thrown grenade,
To protect his comrades is what he craved.

So Eretz tzvi—
conquered her tears in the face of martyrdom,
And when he called out—"Sh'ma Israel!"
The wind silently carried his name.

Roi, may God protect you,
Your way of innocence, your courage,
May God protect Eretz tzvi—which your soul
Weaves forever into her gown.

Eliezer Berkovits (1908–92)

The great spiritual tragedy of the exile consists in the breach between Torah and life, for exile means the loss of a Jewish-controlled environment.

Born in Oradea, Transylvania, in 1908, Eliezer Berkovits became a leading theologian and philosopher while living the life of wandering Jew and academic troubadour. Fleeing Berlin in 1939 after having received rabbinical ordination and earning a PhD there, he ministered in Australia, England, and the United States, eventually chairing the department of Jewish Philosophy at the Hebrew Theological College in Skokie, Illinois. In 1976, at age sixty-seven, he made *aliyah*, writing and teaching in Israel until his death in 1992.

Berkovits emphasized the Jewish religion's unique relationship to the Jewish nation. While most people are born into their nation, anyone could convert to Judaism and join the Jewish nation. Those who denied Judaism's national dimension, he argued, were rejecting the Torah itself, whose natural habitat was the Land of Israel. Zionism, therefore, and the new state, enabled Judaism to grow organically again, repairing the Exile's anomalies.

Rejecting the Zionist push for normalcy, Berkovits claimed it produced Jewish pagans aping American values. He also criticized Orthodox colleagues who neutered Judaism by cutting it off from the land or imported the Diaspora version back to Israel. *Halakhah*, Jewish law, Berkovits insisted, is a way of life, requiring a Jewish context to thrive. In Exile, be it forced or voluntary, *halakhah* became defensive, a bastion against assimilation rather than a dynamic system.

On Jewish Sovereignty (1973)

The rabbis in the Talmud declared that a Jew who lives outside the Holy Land is to be considered as if he were an idolater. This rather startling pronouncement flows from their understanding of Judaism. . . . It links the importance of the land not so much to the Jew as to the realization of Judaism. . . .

Israel alone is a people made to fulfill a God-given task in history; the people whom, as Isaiah expressed it, God "formed" for himself. Normally, religion follows nationhood; for the Jew, his peoplehood flows from his religion. This is not only an accurate account of the emergence of Israel; in a sense, it is valid to this day. An Englishman might accept Hinduism or Buddhism in London; it will not make him Indian or Burmese. He will remain an Englishman.

If, however, the people of Israel is the instrument of realization, there must be a Land of Israel as the place of realization. There must be a place on earth in which the people are in command of their own destiny, where the comprehensive public deed of Judaism may be enacted. Individuals may live in two cultures; but no distinctive culture may grow and flourish authentically in an area already preempted by another one. The individual Jew may well find a home in any democratic society; Judaism must remain in exile anywhere outside the Land of Israel. Outside the Land of Israel, Judaism is capable of partial realization only. . . .

Those Jews who separate Judaism from Zion, Torah from the Land of Israel, give up both Torah and the land. Judaism without the opportunity for its comprehensive fulfillment is a spiritual tragedy. For the longest period of its history, Jews have lived with it. But to embrace the tragedy as a desired form of Jewish existence is a falsification of the essence of Judaism. Those who sever Zion from the Torah have severed Judaism from its authentic realization. They have surrendered, as a matter of principle, Judaism's *raison d'etre*, which is fulfillment in history. They have transformed its character by reducing it to the level of religion. They have reduced it to a credo, a regimen of worship, and some customs in the home. All this may well be accompanied by fine, humanitarian resolutions; but the unique significance of the Judaism of history will have been abandoned. . . .

Halakhah, in its authentic function, must address itself to the Jewish people and not to members with congregational ideologies. What we have in Israel today is an understanding of *halakhah* and its application to an exilic reality that no longer exists. It is the *halakhah* of the shtetl, not the *halakhah* of the state; it is not the Torah of the Land of Israel. . . .

There is widespread secularism in Israel today. But there is also an awakening to the truth that, especially in Israel, secularism is leading the people toward a spiritual and moral dead end. There are many who search for a Jewish way. The people will not be the Jewish people and the state not a Jewish state without Judaism, and Judaism will not be true to itself without finding the way to the people . . .

And yet, this is the land and this the people. It is here, in the Land of Israel, that the destiny of all Israel will be decided for all generations to come. Thus, the problems of this land become the problems of the Jewish people the world over. Their solution is the responsibility of us all.

Gush Emunim

Come, let us go up and settle the land!

The opportunity to resettle the biblical Lands of Israel revitalized Religious Zionism—but also distracted it. Increasingly, the political, diplomatic, and military dimensions of the settlement question blurred with its theological and ideological aspects. In February 1974, students of Zvi Yehuda Kook founded Gush Emunim—Bloc of the Faithful—a term one of them, Haim Drukman, suggested. He, along with Hanan Porat, Moshe Levinger, Yoel Bin-Nun, and others, hoped "to bring about a major spiritual awakening in the Jewish people for the sake of the full realization of the Zionist vision, in the knowledge that this vision's source and goal in the Jewish heritage and in Judaism's roots are the total redemption of both the Jewish people and the whole world." The movement deteriorated in the 1980s, after Zvi Yehuda's death, though its ideology remains influential. In speeches and publications, the organization's leaders have rejected any peace plan involving withdrawal from the territories won in 1967.

Friends of Gush Emunim Newsletter (January 1978)

The hope for peace has captured the people of Israel of all ages. The people of Israel—its blessing is peace, the end of its prayers is for peace, and even upon leaving for battle it calls out to its enemies for peace.

But just because of our strong desire for peace, we need great strength of wisdom and courage not to mistake a deceitful peace for a real peace, a weak peace for a peace of honor and strength, a peace of crisis and retreat for a peace of renewal and creation. . . .

Our sages have said, "A bit of light pushes much of the darkness aside," and we will proceed likewise. We will raise the light of revival; we will arouse the power of Israel through great public outcries of honor and strength; we will rejoice in the land with settlements and waves of immigration; we will, through education and information, open our eyes to see what is this peace we are yearning for, and what the difference is between true peace and a deceitful peace. Rav [Abraham Isaac] Kook of Blessed Memory, said, "The truth is not shy or cowardly." We shall follow in his footsteps and not be deterred from stating loudly the truth of renaissance, even if it is not the kind of peace that can be attained from one day to the next, one that is all lies and illusion.

We believe that the people will yet awaken from the illusion of this imaginary peace and will strengthen itself in its onward struggle.

We pray that this awakening will not be accompanied by the sufferings of despair and as a result the hope for true peace, of strength, brotherhood, honor and light will not be lost.

God will grant His people strength!

God will bless His people with peace!

Come, let us go up and settle the land!

David Hartman (1931–2013)

Living in total exposure to integrate the moral seriousness of the prophet with the realism and political judgment of the statesman.

The traumatic months before the 1967 war, followed by Israel's near-death experience in the 1973 Yom Kippur War, stirred long repressed feelings about the Holocaust. For many, Rabbi Emil Fackenheim's 614th Commandment "Don't let the Nazis win" soon became the most important commandment. David Hartman resisted a Holocaust-centered Jewish identity. To invigorate Israel and Judaism, he emphasized his teacher Joseph Soloveitchik's notion of uniting Jews thanks to the inspiring mission passed on at Sinai—not the horrors visited upon them at Auschwitz.

Born in Brooklyn in 1931, Hartman received ordination at Yeshiva University and served as a congregational rabbi in the Bronx before moving to Montreal. There, he completed a PhD in contemporary philosophy at McGill University, becoming a popular professor while leading a growing congregation. In 1971 he moved with his family to Israel, quipping that he finally took his own *aliyah* sermons seriously. Five years later, he established the Shalom Hartman Institute, a think tank working on reinvigorating Judaism and Zionism.

Hartman agreed with mainstream Orthodox thinkers that Israel's establishment had religious, even messianic, significance, triggering great debates with his occasional sparring partner, Yeshayahu Leibowitz. But rather than seeing the state as proving God's return to directing history after hiding during the Holocaust, Hartman embraced the religious opportunity Israel's establishment presented to the Jewish people. "Israel can be a profound instrument serving the renewal of Jewish spirituality," he explained, "because it forces individual Jews to become responsible for a total way of life in a land that anchors them to their biblical and talmudic historical roots." Hartman taught that the State of Israel is "the main catalyst to rethinking the meaning of God as the Lord of History. The future of Judaism depends on our ability to discover meaningful ways of relating to God's love and power in a world where history, and not only Torah, is not in heaven."

Auschwitz or Sinai (1982)

One of the fundamental issues facing the new spirit of maturity in Israel is: Should Auschwitz or Sinai be the orienting category shaping our understanding of the rebirth of the State of Israel? . . .

Israel is not only a response to modern antisemitism, but is above all a modern expression of the eternal Sinai covenant that has shaped Jewish consciousness throughout the millennia. It was not Hitler who brought us back to Zion, but rather belief in the eternal validity of the

Sinai covenant. . . . It is dangerous to our growth as a healthy people if the memory of Auschwitz becomes a substitute for Sinai.

The model of Sinai awakens the Jewish people to the awesome responsibility of becoming a holy people. At Sinai, we discover the absolute demand of God; we discover who we are by what we do. Sinai calls us to action, to moral awakening, to living constantly with challenges of building a moral and just society which mirrors the kingdom of God in history. Sinai creates humility and openness to the demands of self-transcendence. In this respect, it is the antithesis of the moral narcissism that can result from suffering and from viewing oneself as a victim. . . .

Sinai requires that the Jew believe in the possibility of integrating the moral seriousness of the prophet with the realism and political judgment of the statesman. Politics and morality were united when Israel was born as a nation at Sinai. Sinai prohibits the Jewish people from ever abandoning the effort of creating a shared moral language with the nations of the world.

The rebirth of Israel can be viewed as a return to the fullness of the Sinai covenant—to Judaism as a way of life. The moral and spiritual aspirations of the Jewish tradition were not meant to be realized in Sabbath sermons or by messianic dreamers who wait passively on the margins of society for redemption to break miraculously into history. Torah study is not a substitute for actual life, nor are prayer and the synagogue escapes from the ambiguities and complexities of political life.

The Jewish world will have to learn that the synagogue is no longer the exclusive defining framework for Jewish communal life. Moral seriousness and political maturity and wisdom must come to our nation if we are to be judged by the way we struggle to integrate the Sinai covenant with the complexities of political realities. . . .

We will mourn forever because of the memory of Auschwitz. We will build a healthy new society because of the memory of Sinai.

The Third Jewish Commonwealth (1985)

When Jews live in their own environment and are responsible for the unfolding of the spirit of Judaism in a total society, they must also link their covenantal religious identity to the mitzvot, commandments, through which they share in the universal struggle to uphold human dignity. The normalization of the Jewish people brought about by Zionism makes possible a new appreciation of the mitzvot, whereby the social, ethical, and political attain their full covenantal place. In the messianic society, a total way of life and the society's entire social and economic structure have to mirror God's covenantal judgment. When that is so, the social, moral, and political status of the society becomes a religious issue. The Sabbath in a messianic society is not only the Sabbath of the seven-day week but also the Sabbatical and Jubilee years. The egalitarian spirit of the laws of those years should move the society and its political leaders to a concern with greater degrees of social and economic equality. How the laws of the Sabbatical and Jubilee years can be expressed in a modern economic system is a serious hal'akhic question that many have tried to answer in different ways. One thing, however, is clear. Something radical will happen to Judaism when we are challenged to have our economic and social order mirror the Sabbath's celebration of the world as a creation and of human beings as creatures and not absolute masters over nature or other human beings. . . .

The rebirth of Israel marks the repudiation of the hal'akhic ghetto as the means for guarding Jewish survival in history. Israel not only argues against the ghettoization of Judaism, but is also a rejection of the mistaken universalism that characterized the assimilationist tendencies that affected many Jews as a result of the breakdown of the ghetto. The birth of the third Jewish commonwealth teaches all of Jewry that being rooted in a particular history and tradition need not be antithetical to involvement and concern with the larger issues affecting the human world. . . .

Commission on the Philosophy of Conservative Judaism (1985–88)

Israel should reflect the highest religious and moral values of Judaism and be saturated with Jewish living to the fullest extent possible in a free society.

Of American Jewry's three major denominations, the Conservative movement has consistently seen itself as the most Zionist. Many Orthodox rabbis disliked Zionism's secularism. Many Reform rabbis once disdained Zionism's particularism. Conservative Jews traditionally loved Zionism's expansiveness as a grand Jewish peoplehood project. In 1973 the newly appointed Jewish Theological Seminary chancellor, the historian Gerson D. Cohen, emphasized Israel's unique role in uniting Jews worldwide as they hadn't been united in millennia through this notion of *am*, people.

Twelve years later, Cohen helped establish a Commission on the Philosophy of Conservative Judaism, charged with developing an official statement articulating Conservative Judaism's philosophy. Chaired by Rabbi Robert Gordis and involving leaders from all of the Conservative movement's institutional arms, the commission issued the Conservative platform, *Emet V'Emunah*, (Truth and faith) after meeting regularly for three years, in 1988. The forty-six-page Statement of Principles of Conservative Judaism began with "God in the World," ended with "Living a Life of Torah," and within the middle section, "The Jewish People," articulated a nuanced, profound Zionist vision.

In discussing Israel, the statement demonstrated how central Zionist ideas were to the movement—and how vexing the state could be. Conservative leaders rejoiced "in the existence of *Medinat Yisra'el* (the State of Israel) in *Eretz Yisra'el* (the Land of Israel) with its capital of Jerusalem, the Holy City, the City of Peace. . . . We consider it to be a miracle, reflecting Divine Providence in human affairs." Yet the manifesto, excerpted here, condemned the religious coercion of Israel's Orthodox monopoly and affirmed the spiritual and ideological significance of the Diaspora where the overwhelming majority of Conservative Jews live.

Emet V'Emunah: Statement of Principles
of Conservative Judaism (1988)

The State of Israel . . . is and ought to be a democratic state that safeguards freedom of thought and action for all of its citizens. On the other hand, it is and ought to be a distinctively Jewish state, fostering Jewish religious and cultural values. . . .

The Jewish religion as reflected in the Jewish way of life constitutes the most significant factor that identifies, distinguishes, unites, and preserves the Jewish people. Consequently, we believe that the State of Israel must encourage Jewish patterns of life in all of the agencies of the state and its political subdivisions. . . . Israel should reflect the highest religious and moral values of Judaism and be saturated with Jewish living to the fullest extent possible in a free society. Hence, we welcome the reality that Shabbat, Yom Tov, kashrut, and other mitzvot are officially upheld by the civilian and military organs of the state, and that the Jewish calendar is in general use. Even in secular schools, classical Jewish sources such as Bible and rabbinic literature are taught, and Jewish observances are at least acknowledged.

While we strongly endorse the need to maintain the Jewish character and ambience of the State of Israel, we regard it as an overriding moral principle that neither the state nor its political subdivisions or agencies employ coercion in the area of religious belief and practice. . . .

The Conservative movement has not always agreed with Israel's positions on domestic and foreign affairs. We have often suffered from discriminatory policies, but we remain firm and loving supporters of the State of Israel economically, politically, and morally. . . .

Israel and the Diaspora enjoy different advantages while facing unique challenges. Only in Israel may a Jew lead an all-encompassing Jewish life. There, Shabbat, Yom Tov, and kashrut are officially observed in varied degrees by the civilian organs of state and by the military; there Hebrew is the nation's language and the Bible is studied in every school. Paradoxically, the very ease with which Jewish identity may be expressed in the Jewish state may give the false impression that religion is not needed in Israel for Jewish survival as it is in the Diaspora. We do not believe that Jewish identity can be replaced by Israeli identity or the ability to speak Hebrew. We are convinced that Jewish religion is essential as a source of ethical and moral values.

Both the State of Israel and Diaspora Jewry have roles to fill; each can and must aid and enrich the other in every possible way; each needs the other. It is our fervent hope that Zion will indeed be the center of Torah and Jerusalem a beacon lighting the way for the Jewish people and for humanity.

Richard Hirsch (b. 1926)

The testing grounds for keeping the covenant between God and God's people.

Israel's founding challenged Reform as much as Orthodox theology. Although by 1948, the Reform movement had largely come to accept Zionism, still the destruction of European Jewry and the establishment of the Jewish state demanded a more thorough embrace—and spiritual reckoning.

One of the major catalysts in what he called "Zionizing" Reform Jewry was Rabbi Richard Hirsch. Born in Cleveland in 1926, ordained by Hebrew Union College, he founded the Reform movement's Religious Action Center in Washington DC in 1962. After an intense decade of social activism that included lending his offices to Martin Luther King Jr., when the reverend was in town, Hirsch moved to Jerusalem in 1973. There, he built the ideological and institutional infrastructure of Reform Zionism, helping to establish the World Union for Progressive Judaism's headquarters in Jerusalem, to create the Association of Reform Zionists of America, and to found two Reform movement kibbutzim (Yahel in 1976 and Lotan in 1983).

As a Religious Zionist attuned to the Jewish and Zionist imperative *Na'aseh v' nishma*, "We will do and we will listen," Hirsch said that in establishing the Reform seminary's magnificent campus overlooking Jerusalem's Old City, the movement was marrying history. In 2000 he articulated Reform Jewry's "Declaration of Interdependence": "of people and faith, of Jewish tradition and contemporary needs, of the universal and the particular, of Israel and the Diaspora, of each Jew with all Jews."

Toward a Theology of Reform Zionism (2000)

The establishment, protection, and development of the State of Israel are integral premises of Progressive Jewish belief. . . . In making this statement, it is essential to delineate between two distinct realities, at times conflicting and at times confusing. The first reality: the State of Israel is a state like all other states. As a modern political movement, Zionism parallels the other movements of national renaissance that sprouted in the nineteenth and twentieth centuries. To be sure, the Jewish people's political claim to national independence was reinforced by a moral appeal to the world's conscience following the Holocaust. However, to the extent that the Jewish state is one among many states, it is to be judged by the same criteria of international law and democratic values as all other states. . . .

The second reality: the State of Israel represents the return to the Land of Israel and the restoration of the Jewish people's sovereignty. As such, its very establishment fulfills sanctified religious aspirations, even as its continued existence attests to profound religious convictions. These aspirations and convictions are rooted in the Jewish concept of the covenant between God and Israel. The covenant is the central theme of the Bible, indeed of all Jewish history. God and the Jewish people have made an eternal pact that obligates the people to serve God by preserving distinctive patterns of life, worship, and morality. This eternal covenant between God and the people of Israel is inseparable from the Land of Israel. . . .

In the Diaspora, Jewish life is voluntary. A person is free to decide on Jewish identity and the extent of participation in, and support of, the Jewish community. In Israel, Jewish identity is compulsory. By virtue of living in a Jewish state, the individual Jew is obligated to identify as a Jew, pay taxes to the Jewish state, and fight in the army to defend the Jewish state. In the Diaspora, Jewish activity is confined to what is defined as the private sector: the home, the synagogue, the Jewish community. Judaism is a private experience observed in life-cycle events, the Sabbath and holidays. . . . In Israel, the Jews are not afforded the luxury of selecting favorite issues and noble causes. All issues are Jewish and all are denominated as Jewish, both by those who live in the state and by those who live outside it. Both the private and the public sectors are Jewish. Indeed, everything is Jewish: from economy to culture, politics, the army, and the character of society. In the Diaspora, Jews tend to distinguish between universal and particular concerns. In Israel, every issue is both universal and particular. It is impossible to separate between humanness and Jewishness. . . .

The State of Israel is the testing grounds for keeping the covenant between God and God's people. How do Jews as a people create a just society when they are given responsibility? How do Jews use political power? How do Jews apply Jewish values in everyday conditions of a Jewish society? How do Jews relate to issues of poverty, unemployment, health care, and the aged? How does a Jewish government relate to a host of other issues that affect every society? . . .

In sum, how do Jews keep the covenant in the open, visible, volatile crucible called the State of Israel? . . .

The State of Israel is the Jewish people's symbol of hope in its own future and in the future of all humankind. It . . . will always be confronted by the tension between the holy and the secular, the potential and the actual, the vision and the reality.

Ovadia Yosef (1920–2013)

Atchalta d'geula: **The beginning of the redemption.**

Given the intense traditionalism of most Sephardic Jews who moved to Israel, many considered them "born Zionists." So, perhaps, was the great hero of *Mizrahi* Jewry, Rabbi Ovadia Yosef. Born in Iraq in 1920, he moved with his family to Mandatory Palestine in 1924. From 1973 to 1983 he served as Sephardic chief rabbi but was most influential as the spiritual leader of the Shas Party and the iconic leader of the *Mizrahi* community. His attempt to align Ashkenazic and Sephardic customs in Israel—guided by the medieval rabbi from Safed Joseph Caro—expressed Religious Zionism at its most unifying and constructive. When he died in 2013, supporters claimed that 850,000 people came to his funeral, which would make it the largest gathering in modern Israeli history.

Yosef agreed with Religious Zionists like Abraham Isaac Kook that Zionism was the *atchalta d'geula*, the beginning of the redemption. He did not go as far as others who, already tasting salvation, called Israel the first flowering of our redemption. Still, teaching that living in the Land of Israel fulfilled the ultimate commandment, Yosef was frustrated that Jews now remained in exile voluntarily.

Simultaneously, however, contrary to his hardliner image—and placing him to the left of many Ashkenazi rabbis—Yosef was willing to consider relinquishing territories if it preserved Israeli lives, invoking the religious imperative *piku'ah nefesh*—to save lives above all.

When secular Jews frustrated by the Shas party's ultra-Orthodoxy disparaged Yosef as "anti-Zionist," he bristled. He approved Shas's membership in the World Zionist Organization in 2010, creating the first ultra-Orthodox Zionist party. "It is a lie . . . a term which they have concocted themselves," he responded. "I served for ten years as a Chief Rabbi—a key public position in the State of Israel. . . . We pray for Zion, for Jerusalem and its inhabitants, for Israel and the Rabbis and their students. . . . By our understanding, a Zionist is a person who loves Zion and practices the commandment of settling the land. Whenever I am overseas I encourage *aliyah*. In what way are they more Zionist? . . ."

Oral Torah 14 (1979)

The primacy of the commandment to live in *Eretz Yisra'el* according to our sages:

I begin by emphasizing the rabbis' teachings about the primary importance of living in the Land of Israel, about the land's holiness, and about the magnitude of the mitzvah, the commandment, to live in the land. . . .

The Sages even said: A person should always dwell in *Eretz Yisra'el*. Even if living in a city inhabited mostly by Jews, he should not dwell outside the land. Anyone dwelling in *Eretz Yisra'el* is like one who has a God, for Leviticus teaches: "I give you this land of Canaan so that I can be your God. And anyone who dwells outside the Land is like one who has no God. . . ."

The value of saving a life *piku'ah nefesh*: We learn that if doctors disagree about a sick person fasting on Yom Kippur, even a hint of danger compels the person to eat. Even if only two say the person must eat and one hundred say the person doesn't need to eat, we ease the restrictions to preserve life. Because we give the benefit of the doubt, the two witnesses can outweigh one hundred if it comes to preserving life.

So Jewish law is clear here. If some security experts say this is not a matter of preserving life, but others say not returning territories risks war and could endanger lives, because we give the benefit of the doubt . . . territories should be returned to avoid the risk of death from the danger of war.

The overall conclusion, beyond any doubt, emerges. . . . If there is a chance of a genuine peace between us and our Arab neighbors by returning territories, because nothing is more important than preserving life, the territories must be returned.

11

Builders

Cultural Zionism

The State of Israel's establishment proved Ahad Ha'am doubly wrong. The visionary Cultural Zionist could not imagine the Jewish people creating a state. Nor could he appreciate just how creative and inspiring that political act would be.

In fact, the resulting Jewish renewal revived the national spirit with Israel at the center radiating toward the other Jewish communities. Cultural Zionism not only survived; it became the defining ideology for many Diaspora Jews, especially Americans. At the same time, a Jewish cultural renaissance flourished in Israel. By the 1980s, Professor Arnold Eisen would say Ahad Ha'am "triumphed in large measure because he failed."

Beyond conveying the excitement of the Jewish return to statehood, these excerpts illustrate the ongoing debate about what that state can and should mean to this new historical phenomenon—the Israeli—and to that much older phenomenon, the Jew.

Haim Hefer (1925–2012)

On the command post sits a city, perhaps, thanks to those times.

By winning its War of Independence in 1949, Israel solidified the image
of the New Jew personified by the Palmah, the elite strike force of the
Haganah, and the socialist kibbutzim. Poets like Haim Gouri and
Haim Hefer, along with singers like Shoshana Damari and Yaffa Yar-
koni, sang their way into the hearts and souls of Jews—and democracy lovers—worldwide. Supplementing poignant songs such as the
War of Independence favorite "Hen Efshar" / "Yes It's Possible," Hefer
contributed funny songs and skits to the Palmah's merrymaking—and
mythmaking—choir, the Chizbatron, literally the Tall-Tale-Machine.
Such bluster and humor made the New Jew a Zionist success story.

Born in Poland in 1925 as Haim Feiner, the son of a chocolate sales-
man, Hefer arrived in Israel with his family at age eleven. Six years
later, he was already a Palmahnik. His classic 1947 song celebrating the
coffee pot, "HaFinj'an," epitomized the new outdoorsy Jews forced to
fight but able to laugh at themselves too. As "the coffee pot, the finj'an,
goes around and around," the friends kibitz, telling a "story that's so
aging in years / It is very quickly sprouting a beard."

One of Hefer's many War of Independence ballads, "HaYu Zmanim"
/ "There Were Times," is a stunningly wise work for a twenty-three-
year-old. The song—translated here to emphasize Hefer's vision more
than his poetry—imagines looking backward, from the vantage point
of years, to that portentous moment, capturing the normal, thriving,
delightfully boring life every fighter—and Zionist—hoped to have.
Similarly, another classic he wrote two decades later, "To the Life of
This People," celebrating how this crazy people "politically fragmented
all year long," suddenly coalesces when it sees "trouble," spoke deeply
to Israelis. Both works are rooted in the Zionist narrative: an eternal
people, a scattered people, but nevertheless a united people determined to defend their new state in their old homeland.

In 1956 Hefer and the author Dan Ben Amotz celebrated the
Palmahnik and the Sabra with their best-selling collection of tall tales,
A Bag of Fibs. Hefer then became a columnist and a playwright. He

turned his 1954 play rhapsodizing about the emerging multicultural Israel, *Kazablan* into a musical in 1966. It was filmed in 1974, shortly after Hefer's Yom Kippur instant classic, *HaMilchama HaAchrona*, had a soldier, speaking for all soldiers, promising his little girl that "this will be the last war." When Hefer died in 2012, this troubadour of Zion with joy in his heart and lyrics on his tongue was celebrated as "personifying the words and the tune of the Zionist enterprise."

There Were Times (1948)

The day will come, and you'll sit by the fireplace,
And your back will be a big hump,
And then you'll remember your days in the Palmah,
And recall it while smoking a pipe.

And around, and around, the children shall sit,
And your wife will also be advanced in years,
You'll shed a tear and wipe your nose,
And sigh: Once Upon A Time, Once Upon A Time. . . .

There were times,
That we sat at the command post,
there were times,
We fought and we loved,
But now there's nothing to recognize,
On the command post sits a city,
Perhaps, thanks to those times. . . .

And then tell of the conquests and the battle,
And the youngest of the children will wake and whisper:
Well, it was grandpa who saved the day!
From such a grandfather one can really, really, be proud.

Then you'll expose your bare arm,
The one with a scar encrusted over the years

And you'll smile, saying grandma healed this back then,
Oh, and since . . . there were times, there were times. . . .

And if you continue and elaborate a bit,
And also, preach morality hoarsely, in a voice thinned by age,
Suddenly, the oldest among them will shake it off,
And answer, o, grandpa, what do you know. . . .
And then you will understand that this is a contagious disease,
And then you'll think, maybe the boys are right,
Back in the day, I too was correct,
But now . . . , there were times, there were times. . . .

A. M. Klein (1909–72)

They showed the shaping Hebrew imagination to be alive again.

Israel's founding drew the Canadian lawyer, poet, and activist A. M. Klein to the Middle East. The trip inspired his extraordinary novel, *The Second Scroll* (1951), organized along the lines of the First Scroll, the Five Books of Moses.

Born in Ratno, Poland, in 1909, Abraham Moses Klein grew up in Montreal, served as national president of Canadian Young Judaea, and studied at McGill University. While practicing law, advising the liquor magnate Samuel Bronfman, and editing the *Canadian Jewish Chronicle*, Klein produced vivid, often satirical poetry. Critics and readers rejected his poem *The Hitleriad* in 1944, feeling Adolf Hitler's murders were too dark a subject for Klein's dark humor.

Alas, his impressive successes were never impressive enough for him. Klein became depressed while writing *The Second Scroll* and attempted suicide in 1954. He died in 1972, never having published anything again.

Klein's novel was partially a travelogue based on his 1949 visit to Europe, North Africa, and Israel and, partially, a quintessentially Jewish act of time travel, conveying the sweep of Jewish history. Capturing one of Zionism's greatest cultural accomplishments—reviving

Hebrew—he celebrated the cerebral and political act of forging a new language as an achievement of proletarians naturally living their daily lives.

The Second Scroll (1951)

And then—it was after I had returned from Tiberias to Tel Aviv to attend a literary soiree—then the creative activity, archetypical, all-embracing, that hitherto I had sought in vain, at last manifested itself. Not at the soiree. In the streets, in the shops, everywhere about me. I had looked, but had not seen. It was all there all the time—the fashioning folk, anonymous and unobserved, creating word by word, phrase by phrase, the total work that when completed would stand as epic revealed!

They were not members of literary societies, the men who were giving new life to the antique speech, but merchants, tradesmen, day laborers. In their daily activity, and without pose or flourish, they showed it to be alive again, the shaping Hebrew imagination. An insurance company, I observed as I lingered in Tel Aviv's commercial center, called itself Sneh—after Moses' burning bush, which had burned and burned but had not been consumed. Inspired metaphor, born not of the honored laureate, but of some actuary, a man of prose! A well-known brand of Israeli sausage was being advertised, it gladdened my heart to see, as Bashan—just tribute to its magnum size, royal compliment descended from Og, Bashan's giant king. A dry-cleaner called his firm Kesheth, the rainbow, symbol of cessation of floods! An ice-cream organization, Kortov, punned its way to custom fissioning kortov, a drop, to kor-tov, cold and good! In my student days I had been fascinated always by that word which put an end to the irreconcilable controversies of the House of Hillel and the House of Shammai: the House would maintain "Permitted," that House would insist "Prohibited"; a deadlock would ensue. Came then the Talmud editor and wrote taiku, stet, the question abides. My teacher would go on to explain that taiku was really a series of initials that stood for *Tishbi yetaraitz kushioth v'abayoth*, the [messianic prophet, Elijah the] Tishbite would resolve all problems and difficulties. Now the magic cataleptic word was before me again, in a new context, in a newspaper, the report of a football game where the score had been tied. Taiku!

There were dozens, there were hundreds, of instances of such metamorphosis and rejuvenation. Nameless authorship flourished in the streets. It was growth, its very principle, shown in prolific action! Twigs and branches that had been dry and sapless for generations, for millennia, now budded, blossomed—and with new flowers.

It was as if I was spectator to the healing of torn flesh, or heard a broken bone come together, set and grow again. . . .

And this discovered poetry, scattered though it was, had its one obsessive theme. It was obsessed by the miraculous. . . . Little David had slain Goliath? The miracle had again been repeated; against great odds, the little struggling state had withstood the onslaught of combined might. . . .

Leon Uris (1924–2003)

This land is mine / God gave this land to me /
This brave and ancient land to me.

Seven years after *The Second Scroll*, another novel bridging the Bible and Israel's founding became a blockbuster, defining Zionism for Jews and non-Jews. Published in 1958, by 1965 *Exodus* had already sold over five million copies, become a movie starring the heartthrob Paul Newman, and inspired the Christian singer Pat Boone's hit song, "The Exodus Song." Boone would call the song Israel's "second national anthem," and in many ways it was.

The unlikely author of this and a dozen other best-sellers was Leon Uris. Born in Baltimore in 1924, he failed English three times and dropped out of high school to join the Marines after Pearl Harbor. He financed the writing of *Exodus* by selling the film rights in advance. Uris then read three hundred books, completed 1,200 interviews, and traveled twelve thousand miles, after first completing an intense physical training program to prepare himself for the grueling mission.

Exodus romanticized and Americanized Zionism, describing the New Jews as combining the virtue of Lincoln, the wisdom of Einstein, the toughness of Patton, and the goodness of Jesus himself. Read in comfortable American homes, smuggled into cramped Soviet apartments, quoted widely, it would be translated into fifty languages and be reprinted nearly ninety times. "As a literary work it isn't much," David Ben-Gurion quipped. "But as a piece of propaganda, it's the best thing ever written about Israel."

The magic of 1948, aided by the pixie dust of *Exodus*, had American Jews enthralled with the plucky pioneers who made the desert bloom. Life was often tough in Israel in the 1950s and 1960s. With Israelis struggling to survive economically, Arab armies and guerillas threatened the state constantly, refugees from Arab lands faced harsh conditions stoically, and Israeli Arabs suffered under military rule, often unfairly. Nevertheless, many American Jews viewed Israel as a Zionist paradise where New Jews lived noble ideas.

Exodus captured the texture, the emotions, of the Jewish return: the trauma of the Holocaust, the joys of the kibbutz, the thrill of rebuilding, the anguish of the Arab fight, the sweetness of idealism, the wonder of mass migration. Uris's book—even its movie version—also tackled serious ideological issues within Zionism. When Ari Ben Canaan drives his non-Jewish love interest Kitty Fremont north, they stop to look at the Valley of Jezreel. They marvel at seeing the "same paving stones that Joshua walked on when he conquered" the land, along with "every clump of trees" Ari's father planted in rebuilding himself and his land. Ari rejoices that the valley is becoming Jewish once again. He tells Kitty: "I'm a Jew. This is my country." When Kitty dismisses differences between people as artificial, Ari makes the particularist case against universalism: "People are different. They have a right to be different." They suspend the debate, Hollywood style, with their first kiss.

In print, on screen, and in song, *Exodus* cast Zionism in such glowing terms that, it condemned Israel to the inevitable comedown. Decades later, the *New York Times* columnist Thomas Friedman, trying to justify his anger as Israel's popularity flagged, would define this mythic place he missed as "your grandfather's Israel." In fact, Israel today—Friedman's Israel—is more compassionate, just, equitable, and democratic.

Concerned to appear tough yet smart, thoroughly normal yet proud of his heritage, Leon Uris asked that his epitaph read: "American Marine/Jewish writer." Despite this expression of deep Zionist ambivalence, Uris's book captured the heroism of the ingathering of the exiles, which proved the need for a Jewish state. Uris wrote: "From the moment the downtrodden set foot on the soil of Israel they were granted a human dignity and freedom that most of them had never known, and the equality fired them with a drive and purpose without parallel in man's history."

The Exodus Song / This Land Is Mine (Pat Boone, 1960)

This land is mine
God gave this land to me

This brave and ancient land to me
And when the morning sun
Reveals her hills and plains
Then I see a land
where children can run free.

So take my hand
And walk this land with me
And walk this lovely land with me
Tho' I am just a man
When you are by my side
With the help of God
I know I can be strong.

So take my hand
And walk this land with me
And walk this golden land with me.
Tho' I am just a man

When you are by my side
With the help of God
I know I can be strong.

To make this land our home
If I must fight
I'll fight to make this land our own.
Until I die this land is mine!

Shmuel Yosef Agnon (1888–1970)

**Granted the privilege of living in the land which
God promised our forefathers to give us.**

Still considered by many to be the greatest modern Hebrew writer,
Shmuel Yosef Agnon was yet another living bridge between Eastern
Europe and Israel, between the traditions of the shtetl and the shocks
of the homeland. As Israel's Shakespeare, he developed a layered, modern Hebrew style deep in conversation with the Bible, the Talmud,
and the rabbinical sources, as well as European thought, Zionist ideology, and the emerging realities in Palestine then Israel. Many Israelis
perceived Agnon's greatest Zionist achievement—being awarded the
Nobel Prize for Literature in 1966—as the world's validation of their
entire national project.

Born in 1888 in Buczacz, Eastern Galicia, today's Ukraine, Agnon
grew up steeped in the Jewish sources he would later wield as literary
tools. He first moved to Palestine in 1907, staying for six years. After an
eleven-year-stint in Germany from 1913 to 1924, he settled in Jerusalem.

Agnon set most of his short stories and novels in the Galician shtetl
or in Palestine. His great novel *T'mol Shilshom / Only Yesterday* (1945)
captured the excitement and strain of life in Palestine as the Second Aliyah confronted the Old Yishuv. A keen observer who came
from the religious world, Agnon depicted the awkwardness of yeshiva
boys turned secular pioneers. First, they broke commandments of

commission—"thou shalts," such as attending synagogue and putting on tefillin; then those of omission—"thou shalt nots," such as not working on the Sabbath and shunning unkosher food. With their old identities rejected and new ones still fluid, they compensated by swapping traditional tales, singing traditional songs, and even speaking in Yiddish—secretly.

Two decades later, the Nobel Prize committee honored Agnon "for his profoundly characteristic narrative art with motifs from the life of the Jewish people." When accepting the award, Agnon said his birth in Eastern Europe was accidental, due to the exile following the Second Temple's destruction; he truly was born in Jerusalem. His speech, like most of his writing, broadcast his gratitude to be living—and writing—in the Jewish homeland.

Nobel Prize Speech (December 10, 1966)

As a result of the historic catastrophe in which Titus of Rome destroyed Jerusalem and Israel was exiled from its land, I was born in one of the cities of the Exile. But always I regarded myself as one who was born in Jerusalem. In a dream, in a vision of the night, I saw myself standing with my brother-Levites in the Holy Temple, singing with them the songs of David, King of Israel, melodies such as no ear has heard since the day our city was destroyed and its people went into exile. I suspect that the angels in charge of the Shrine of Music, fearful lest I sing in wakefulness what I had sung in dream, made me forget by day what I had sung at night; for if my brethren, the sons of my people, were to hear, they would be unable to bear their grief over the happiness they have lost. To console me for having prevented me from singing with my mouth, they enable me to compose songs in writing. . . .

I was five years old when I wrote my first song. . . . The young artisans, tailors, and shoemakers, who used to sing my songs at their work, were killed in the First World War, and of those who were not killed in the war, some were buried alive with their sisters in the pits they dug for themselves by order of the enemy, and most were burned in the crematories of Auschwitz with their sisters, who had adorned our town with their beauty and sung my songs with their sweet voices. . . .

At the age of nineteen and a half, I went to the Land of Israel to till its soil and live by the labor of my hands. . . . After all my possessions had been burned [a second time], God gave me the wisdom to return to Jerusalem. I returned to Jerusalem, and it is by virtue of Jerusalem that I have written all that God has put into my heart and into my pen. . . .

If I am proud of anything, it is that I have been granted the privilege of living in the land which God promised our forefathers to give us. . . .

Naomi Shemer (1930–2004)

Jerusalem of gold, and of bronze, and of light.

The People of the Book's great revolution was not just spoken but sung, making Zionists the People of the Songbook too. Popular songs such as "Palmah Anthem" in the 1940s and "Tsena" in the 1950s propelled Zionist ideas—and feelings—straight into Jewish hearts. This newly resounding soundtrack helped personalize, romanticize, and immortalize what began as a heady, manifesto-heavy movement.

Decades later, in 1971, Tel Avivi Arik Einstein, the First Hebrew City's Hip Hebrew Rock Superstar, released "Me and You." With his silky-smooth Frank Sinatra-like voice, reinforced with a Bob Dylan–type edge and depth, Einstein expressed the universal yet deeply Zionist faith in the power of *ani veata*, "me and you," to change the world.

This Zionist music magic worked most dramatically in May 1967, when Naomi Shemer's euphonic ode to the Jew's historic capital, "Jerusalem of Gold," premiered. The audience went wild, insisting she play the song again. Three weeks later, she added a verse celebrating what had been inconceivable weeks before: the city's reunification. When she met the paratroopers who sang her song after liberating Jerusalem, she said: "Actually, I should be applauding you, since it is much easier to change a song than to change a city."

"Jerusalem of Gold" captured the power of the moment and solidified the unity of the time. However differently the religious and non-religious, the left and right, related to Jerusalem, they could all sing Shemer's magical lyrics together. It was truly a national anthem.

Born on the classically Zionist kibbutz Kinneret in 1930, Naomi Shemer demonstrated a remarkable ability to intuit the Israeli mood. Her heartbreaking song, "We Are Both from the Same Village," written shortly after 1967, encapsulated the great cost of war, balancing any national jingoism with collective mourning for many lost lives. The lyrics speak of "Yosele" and "Zevele," two soldiers from Nahalal whose friendship inspired Shemer. In fact, both Yosef Regev and Ze'ev Amit survived the 1967 war—but Zevele was killed during the Yom Kippur War six years later.

In 1973 Shemer illuminated the sense of loss balanced by determination triggered by the Yom Kippur War with "Lu Yehi" / "May it Be." In 1991 the song she wrote to comfort her sister after her brother-in-law's death, "Al Kol Eileh" / "Over All This," illustrating the rollercoaster of Israeli life, also took on national significance. Her phrase urging personal continuity, "Do not uproot what's been planted," became a rallying cry for settlers opposing territorial withdrawals.

In 1983 Shemer won the Israel Prize for her "poetic and musical" songs that "express the emotions of the people." Indeed, her death in 2004, and Arik Einstein's in 2013, triggered outpourings of love—and nostalgia—for a time when, despite all the problems, the right song really did help.

Jerusalem of Gold (1967)

As clear as wine the wind is flying
Among the dreamy pines
As evening light is slowly dying
And a lonely bell still chimes
So many songs, so many stories
The stony hills recall . . .
Around her heart my city carries
A lonely ancient wall.

Yerushalayim all of gold
Yerushalayim, bronze and light
Within my heart I shall treasure
Your song and sight.

Alas, the drying wells and fountains,
Forgotten market-day
The sound of horn from Temple's mountain
No longer calls to pray
The rocky caves at night are haunted
By sounds of long ago
When we were going to the Jordan
By way of Jericho.

Yeruhsalayim all of gold . . .

But when I come to count your praises
And sing Hallel to you
With pretty rhymes I dare not crown you
As other poets do
Upon my lips is always burning
Your name, so dear, so old:
If I forgot Yerushalayim
Of bronze and light and gold . . .
Yerushalayim all of gold . . .

Back to the wells and to the fountains
Within the ancient walls
The sound of horn from Temple mountain
Loudly and proudly calls
From rocky caves, this very morning
A thousand suns will glow
As we shall go down to the Jordan
By way of Jericho.

Yerushalayim all of gold . . .

Yehudah Amichai (1924–2000)

**All the generations before me contributed
me little by little .... It obligates.**

Dubbed by the critic Robert Alter as "the most widely translated
Hebrew poet since King David," Yehudah Amichai was a Palmah
commando turned man of letters. Born into a religious family in Germany in 1924, Amichai arrived in Palestine in 1936 and, after fighting
in World War II, fought in three Israeli wars. Despite being neither a
native-born Hebrew speaker nor a native Jerusalemite, his eloquence,
wryness, and passion for his city, language, and homeland made him
beloved in Israel and world famous.

Amichai's Jewish tribalism was ingrained in him. Even in Germany,
he explained, "We were so strong in our beliefs and dreams and imagi-
nations, we felt we could live with the others because we were so deeply
different." Like Amos Oz, Amichai recalled that in Germany, "They
threw stones at us and shouted, Go to Palestine. Then in Palestine we
were told to leave Palestine—history juxtaposed can be very ironic."
He added: "Irony is for me a kind of cleaning material."

Amichai celebrated the great accomplishment of daily life in Israel
using the kind of biblically infused language Shai Agnon had mastered. A time traveler, Amichai navigated the daily challenges of life
in a city where the most important numbers are historical dates—"70
After, 1917, 500 B.C." His Zionism was assumed, not proclaimed; its
impulse was toward normalcy. His poem "Tourists" urges tourists
to see his shopping in Jerusalem's old-new land as more significant
than any ruins.

Yet Amichai also articulated a Zionist exceptionalism—appreciating
the historic achievement of executing the most mundane tasks in this
exalted place, this "port city on the shores of forever." Amichai's sometimes lyrical, sometimes cutting, always clever phrasing still helps
Israelis frame their country's constant flickering between historical
profundity and modern triviality.

All the Generations before Me (1968)

All the generations before me contributed me
Little by little so that I will arise here in Jerusalem
All at once, like a synagogue or a charitable institution.
It obligates. My name is my donor's name.
It obligates.

I approach the age of my father's death.
My will is patched together with numerous patches,
I must change my life and my death
day by day to realize all the prophecies
that prophesied me. So they won't be lies.
It obligates.

I've passed the age of forty. There are
professions that won't accept me
because of that. Had I been in Auschwitz,
they wouldn't have sent me to work,
they would have incinerated me instantly.
It obligates.

Tourists (1980)

Condolence calls are all they grant us,
Sitting in Yad Vashem, looking grave at the Western Wall
and laughing behind heavy curtains in hotel rooms,
Taking photos with important corpses at Rachel's Tomb
and Herzl's grave and on Ammunition Hill,
Crying over our young men's lovely heroism
And lusting after our young women's prickliness
and hanging their underwear
for a quick dry
in a cool, blue bathroom.

Once I sat on the steps by the gate at David's Tower, having laid two heavy baskets by my side. A group of tourists stood there surrounding the guide and I served as their reference point. "You see that guy over there with the baskets? A little to the right above his head is a Roman arch. A little to the right of his head." But he moved, he moved! I said to myself: Redemption will come only when they say to them: You see that Roman arch over there? Insignificant. But next to it, a little to the left and below, sits a man who just bought fruit and vegetables for his family.

Gershon Shaked (1929–2006)

There is no other place.

The destruction of six million Jews almost crushed the Jewish people. Some Jews abandoned Judaism. Some Zionists shifted focus: Hitler proved the need for a state of Jews, more than a Jewish state.

At first glance, Gershon Shaked's down-to-earth, *ein breira,* there's-no-other-place Zionism encapsulated political Zionism at its rawest: They hated us, they persecuted us, we're lucky to get out and be here. But, in his most famous essay, this leading Israeli literary critic recalled his brutalization as a nine-year-old in Vienna—turning it into an equally devastating critique of his fellow high-falutin' European refugee colleagues and of Israeli culture itself. Unlike the survivors who yearned for the culture that exorcised them, Shaked refused to be Lot's wife, looking back at a world that was so vicious beneath its veneer. Recoiling from Europe propelled him toward Zion.

The child born as Gerhard Mandel in Vienna in 1929 made it to Palestine in 1939. He changed his name to Gershon Shaked—"Mandel" is almond in German, "Shaked" is almond in Hebrew. Eventually, he earned his PhD at Hebrew University. As a revered academic and prolific literary critic, he shaped the conversation about Hebrew literature for decades. He won the Israel Prize in 1993 for his Janus-like, eminently Zionist, ability to look back, rooting Israeli literature in Jewish civilization, while looking forward, challenging Israeli writers to be innovative and authentic.

No Other Place (originally written 1980; book 1987)

On 10 November 1938, a nine-year-old boy was alone in a large apartment on a respectable street in Vienna. His mother had gone out. His father had been deported to a concentration camp in April. The boy did not know that there was rioting outside. Sensing the approaching dusk by the shadows on the city walls, he crawled under the piano in a corner. To calm his fear he played. He tried to take refuge in fantasy; but his fear overwhelmed him. There was shouting on the floor above. He turned on all the lights and put two chairs against the front door. Soon there was knocking. The boy was afraid to open the door. When the men came bursting in, he did not know where to hide. None of the tricks he had learned from his books were of any help. Finally, he crawled back under the piano.

The boy never saw the men's faces, only their five pairs of boots. Taking no interest in him, they emptied the apartment of its contents—rugs and paintings, silver, and finally furniture, piece by piece. It was only when they turned to the piano that they noticed the child clinging to one of its legs. They worked him over with their boots; they said and did things that the boy does not want to remember.

When it was all over, the boy curled up within himself, surrounded by the bare walls of the now empty apartment. He could not turn on the lights because the raiders had taken all the bulbs. Huddled in that darkness, mortified and alone, the boy discovered his own private kind of Zionism. How different it was from the Zionism of those pioneers in the sunny fields of the Jezreel Valley.

It was Tolstoy who said that all happy families are alike and that only miserable families differ from one another. The normal lives of children, from Switzerland to New Zealand, are all alike; the fate of Jewish children in the 1940s, from the banks of the Volga to the English Channel, differ. Each has his or her own tragic tale.

The answer to this question is to be found by asking a larger question: What is *Eretz Yisra'el* to those cultured European Jews for whom history has decreed exile? Is it not some kind of Devil's Island to which history expelled them while they, like Dreyfus in his time, long to get back to the European motherland, to have their honor restored, to regain their positions in the cultural avant-garde? Is the scale of our tiny country not drawn to their cultural dimensions? Even the trauma of the Holocaust has not led this group (which includes the cream of German Jewry and the intellectual elite of European immigrants) to prefer a life of independence in the jungle to one of slavery in the Academie Francaise. . . . Y. H. Brenner, in *From Here and From There* (1911), wrote in pessimistic tones of the Jewish people, *Eretz Yisra'el*, and their interrelations. He was forced to conclude, nevertheless, that although "it may be that it is impossible to live here . . . there is no other place." . . .

I too lost the foundations of my existence. Yet despite my own ambivalences—the longings for the West, the love for and aversion to the *Eretz Yisra'el* of today—it seems to me that the commitment must be unequivocal. . . . I would argue that once the ground is destroyed there is no recovering it. . . .

[T]o the extent that identity depends on consciousness . . . a person has no choice but to decide. And if one has fled the ruins of Sodom, there is no other place but here.

Letty Cottin Pogrebin (b. 1939)

I am a feminist Zionist.

The New Left was, as the cliché goes, good for the Jews and bad for the Jews. Good, in that it energized young, proud, creative Jews to reform and renew Judaism. Some synthesized feminism and other new phenomena with traditional Judaism and Zionism; others stayed more traditional and found the authenticity American Judaism often lacked.

But the New Left also turned anti-Zionist, not just criticizing Israeli policies but rejecting Israel's existence. Fueled by rage over Palestinian statelessness, feeling legitimized by the United Nations' Zionism-is-racism resolution, encouraged by the systematic Arab campaign against Israel, the radical left started competing with the far right as the central headquarters for antisemitism and anti-Zionism.

Watching the hatred against Israel boil over into hatred against Jews was particularly painful for Jewish activists, especially those in the women's movement. Since so many Jews helped launch feminism—including Betty Friedan, Gloria Steinem, and the Hebrew-speaking Bella Abzug—it was a family feud. Another Jewish activist, Letty Cottin Pogrebin, a founding editor of *Ms.* magazine and a co-founder of the National Women's Political Caucus, wrote "Antisemitism in the Women's Movement" for *Ms.* in 1982, prompting lengthy pro and con responses.

In her 1991 memoir, *Deborah, Golda, and Me: Being Female and Jewish in America,* Pogrebin blasted the anti-Zionism and antisemitism she first noticed in 1975 when the International Women's meeting in Mexico City denounced Zionism as racism. She rebuilt her identity, balancing the universal impulses she cherished with the particular Jewish and Zionist identity she loved. Fusing Theodor Herzl and Ahad Ha'am, she taught Jews that the best way to counter the Jew hatred they encounter is to deepen their encounters with Judaism.

Pogrebin explained Zionism in feminist terms. "To my mind, Zionism is to Jews what feminism is to women—an ongoing struggle for self-determination, dignity, and justice," she wrote. Yet, for decades now, she has been "struggling to be a feminist among Zionists and a Zionist among feminists. . . . split at the root, one side of me struggling against the hijacking of feminism for anti-Israel aims (with an occasional dash of Jew-hating thrown in), the other side resisting the institutionalized patriarchy and entrenched sexism of Jewish institutions." Her eloquence remains the standard—referred to whenever radical voices within feminism try turning this movement to empower women against Zionism's movement to empower Jews.

Deborah, Golda, and Me (1991)

Thinking one's gender or peoplehood irrelevant does not for a moment change what *is*. Ultimately, somewhere down the line, the world will not allow a woman to say, "Being female doesn't matter," nor a Jew to say "I used to be a Jew." The Jewish woman who does not take possession of her total identity, and make it count for something, may find that others will impose upon her a label she does not like at all.

That is what I discovered in 1975, when the delegates meeting in Mexico City at the first of three United Nations International Woman's Decade Conferences passed a resolution that effectively identified all Jews as "racists." . . .

Although it was ostensibly the Israelis who had been attacked as racists, I knew the arrow also was meant for me. I could stand under any damn sign I pleased, but to feminists who hate Israel, I was not a woman, I was a *Jewish* woman. The men of the minyan might not consider me a Jew among Jews, but to many of those delegates at Mexico City, that's all I was. Now the question I had to answer was, *Why be a Jew for them if I am not a Jew for myself?* . . .

Zionism is to Jews what feminism is to women. Zionism began as a national liberation movement and has become an ongoing struggle for Jewish solidarity, pride, and unity. Similarly, feminism, which began as a gender-liberation movement, has become an ongoing struggle for women's solidarity, pride, and unity. Just as feminism has been maligned and misunderstood by those who do not bother to understand it, so, too, Zionism has been maligned and misunderstood by its enemies. . . .

Both movements are fueled by the fires of self-determination. Calling Zionism racism makes Jewish self-determination sound like an attack on non-Jews . . . as if female self-determination were an attack on men. . . .

Emotionally, I grew to accept my Otherness as a Jew, the way I had accepted my Otherness as a woman—with pride and purpose, and a willingness to create a positive "we" where no category had existed before. . . .

I saw the importance of being a public, affirmative Jew—even when ethnicity or religion "didn't matter." As much as I might wish for a world of universalist values and deemphasized differences, I would no longer tolerate a Women's Movement in which Jews are the only group asked to relinquish their own interests while other women were allowed to push their private agendas, and subvert feminist ideals when it suited them. I would no longer assume all women were my sisters. . . .

I still have universalist dreams—visions of one world without the rancors of nationalism, tribalism, and patriarchy—but now I dream them only when fully awake, and I take my inspiration not from some naive UNICEF greeting card but from a pluralist feminism founded on a mutual respect for each other's "identity politics," which include the particularities of culture, peoplehood, and history. . . .

If feminists can understand why history entitles lesbians to separatism, or minorities and women to affirmative action, we can understand why history entitles Jews to "preferential" safe space. To me, *Zionism is simply an affirmative action plan on a national scale.* Just as legal remedies are justified in reparation for racism and sexism, the Law of Return to Israel is justified, if not by Jewish religious and ethnic claims, then by the intransigence of worldwide antisemitism. . . .

Andrea Dworkin put it brilliantly: "In the world I'm working for, nation states will not exist. But in the world I live in, I want there to be an Israel."

Anne Roiphe (b. 1935)

A Judaism that does not involve new commitments, work for others, will melt away in the heat of the barbecue on the patio, the light of the TV.

Ahad Ha'am was right: the Jewish people craved a cultural renaissance. For all its complexities, Israel steeped its citizens in a rich, multidimensional, deeply Jewish experience. One way of appreciating this great success of Cultural Zionism is by viewing it from afar.

In 1981 the feminist essayist and novelist Annie Roiphe provided that perspective in what emerged as a surprisingly Zionist critique of her bourgeois liberal Upper West Side life. Born in 1935, educated at Sarah Lawrence, swimming in the universalism of the sophisticated, self-satisfied New York Jewish liberal, Roiphe backed into what ended up being a long career as a commentator on Jewish issues. Her *New York Times* op-ed in 1978 about her family's Christmas celebration, tree and all, infuriated so many Jews, she decided to explore her own Jewish identity. The resulting book, *Generation without Memory* (1981), lamented the thinness of the Jewish identity she gave her children— and admired Israelis' rich Jewish identity.

Roiphe's analysis proved prescient. A decade before surveys alarmed the Jewish community about the "continuity crisis" evidenced by an intermarriage epidemic, she warned about American Judaism's cultural and demographic sterility. And two decades before American Jews started shutting down such critiques of American Jewry, this all-American insider was able to look outside—toward Zion—and pine for Israeli culture's democratic fecundity and Jewish vitality.

Generation without Memory (1981)

All Jewish rivers run toward Israel. . . . Zionism is then the yearning for completion—for the righting of a historical injustice—a response to the everpresent insanity of antisemitism. Zionism is the logical response to the unavoidable knowledge that Jewishness appears indigestible to other countries. Jews have never been permitted, except for brief moments, to settle comfortably in the Christian or Moslem countries of their adoption.

Zionism is also the religious response to the Holocaust. The redemption of the Holy Land and its return to the Jews allows faith to spring like the phoenix from the ruins of Dachau and Auschwitz. But Zionism, religious or political, is still mystical in nature. It requires a passionate emotional commitment to the redemption—it is not a position of rationalists, for universalists. It requires unthinking commitment to one side of the story. It grants the rewards of togetherness. . . .

A fear of tribalism is part of being humanist. Another authentic response to the Holocaust is to resist all efforts to separate human beings into categories of greater or lesser value—to use culture, or skin color, or blood type to select one life over another is to dishonor those who died in the ovens and the trains and the ditches—the victims of ss and Einsatzgruppen—the victims of nationalism (tribalism) gone amok. . . .

This assimilation process is a little like a parade, a long, huge parade with the German Jews in the front and the Sephardic Jews in the reviewing stands and the long, long line of Ostjude stretching back a way. . . . I slip slided, I inched, I backed up into the intellectual, left-wing, primarily Jewish (though for most the Jewish part is not very consciously relevant) class. My children went on peace marches as babies. . . . They are concerned with problems of energy, ecology, race relations. In part due to the Vietnam War they consider themselves as nationless, as unattached souls, as involved in the drama of South America as in the injustices in South Africa. . . .

Approximately thirty-five percent of young Jewish people may be intermarrying. The attendance at synagogues steadily declines except for a small group of returnees. . . . Judaism and Jewishness in America (with some exceptions) appear to be thinning. (Along with the loss of Yiddish comes a loss of the Jewish ethnicity.) The parade narrows at its front end.

But when I think of our traditions of the family, traditions that are electric, thin, without magic or destiny of time, I can see that we have made an error. I appreciate our Thanksgiving and Christmas. I know that I will make beautiful weddings for our daughters and that our funerals will serve well enough. But I do believe that the tensions of the ancient ways, the closeness of primitive magic, the patina of the ages and the sense of connection to past and future that are lacking in our lives are serious losses. Our morality is only as tarnished as most earth creatures' by our style of living in which we celebrate no ancient victories, in which we atone for nothing and are thankful for little, in which we have no group cultural past and no group cultural future—this is not adequate. . . .

I believe on balance that the wellbeing and happiness of my family would have been better supported within the wealth of a Jewish past. . . . In their universalism will the furnishings of their souls look like Olympic stadiums? The idea makes me anxious for my children. . . .

A Judaism that does not involve new commitments, work for others, will melt away in the heat of the barbecue on the patio, the light of the TV, the warmth of the variety of comforts now available. Reform Judaism has been the easy way out for a generation of comfortable, nearly assimilated Jews. In many affluent communities it somehow has often lost the mystery and drama, the terror of the burning bush, the excitement in the bondage of the covenant. If one modernizes Judaism too far it becomes like a TV game show as compared to a fine Shakespeare performance (a Doris Day film as compared to a Fellini or Bergman). Indifferently the next generation is tempted to drift away, to turn it off.

12

Builders

Diaspora Zionism

American Zionism's grand synthesis worked. Justice Louis Brandeis Americanized Zionism by imbuing it with progressivism and treating it as mass philanthropy to save other Jews. By the early 1940s, most American Jews had embraced Political Zionism, albeit belatedly. The Holocaust proved that Jews needed a state in Palestine, not just a restored homeland. The Biltmore Program, endorsed by six hundred Zionist delegates from eighteen countries in May 1942 at New York's Biltmore Hotel, urged "that the gates of Palestine be opened" to some two million Jews and that "Palestine be established as a Jewish Commonwealth, integrated in the structure of the new democratic world" [Biltmore Program, May 11, 1942, MidEast Web, http://www.mideastweb.org/biltmore_program.htm].

After the war, American Jews joined the fight for Israel—which they viewed as at least partial redemption following Auschwitz. In lobbying for the state, some displayed a ferocity most of the community lacked when Europe's Jews burned.

Once Israel emerged, American Jews approached the Jewish state defensively. They demanded respect from Israeli Zionists who believed in negating all Diasporas, even the one in the Golden Medina (land). Gradually, American Jewry, inspired by Israel's political rise, mastered American power politics. As the United States emerged as an embattled Israel's closest friend, these empowered American Jews became more secure in the relationship.

The narrative of an Israel in crisis desperately needing Diaspora support became so widespread, especially among American Jews, that Israeli leaders occasionally needed to remind everyone that the relationship was mutual. True, Diaspora support for Israel was more easily quantified, counting money raised, votes passed, arms shipped. Israel's support for Jews worldwide was less tangible but no less potent. It involved pride, culture, and Jewish identity building. This inspiration was most evident following Israel's Six-Day War triumph.

Arthur Hertzberg (1921–2006)

I am a Zionist because I am a citizen of world Jewry, of Am Yisra'el.

Although the fight to establish the state galvanized American Jewry, and those years are now enshrouded in myth, American Zionists sank into crisis soon after Israel's founding crisis. Trying to burst through American Zionism's "impasse," the young Zionist firebrand Arthur Hertzberg would quote Oscar Wilde in *Commentary* in 1949: "There are two tragedies in the world—one is not getting what you want and the other is getting it."

American Zionists faced two ideological riddles. Israelis, led by David Ben-Gurion, negated all Diasporas' legitimacy. At the same time, as committed as American Jews were to helping the new state survive, most sought an Ahad Ha'am–style spiritual and cultural revival centered on the Jewish homeland. Caught between what felt like Zionist fanaticism in Israel and rampant assimilation in America, American Zionists tried legitimizing their personal choice to live in America while deploying Zionism to revitalize American Jewry. In a career combining impressive scholarship and communal leadership, academic posts and rabbinical pulpits, Arthur Hertzberg tackled these tensions.

Born in Poland into the Belzer Hasidic rabbinic dynasty, he arrived in America with his family when he was five. He earned rabbinical ordination from the Conservative movement's Jewish Theological Seminary and a history PhD from Columbia University. As a community leader who marched on Washington with Martin Luther King Jr. in 1963, Hertzberg insisted that "a rabbi should be where the real issues of society are, not where the safe platitudes are to be preached."

Hertzberg challenged American Jews to live more meaningful Jewish lives. He chided congregants for using the synagogue as "a personal decoration" while warning them not to make support for Israel their religion. He also criticized the Israeli government for not declaring a Palestinian state immediately after the 1967 war.

Writing in 1976 as a leading Zionist, having published his 1959 magnum opus *The Zionist Idea*, Hertzberg despaired about communal drift and assimilation. He imagined a vast Zionist educational initiative to raise a new generation of Jewish citizens. His essay proved prescient, as identity building through Israel experiences became mainstreamed more than two decades later, thanks to Taglit-Birthright Israel and other programs. And his collection of essays, *The Zionist Idea,* proved enduring, providing generations of Jews and non-Jews with the foundational texts of a movement Hertzberg helped shape—and always challenged to grow.

Impasse: A Movement in Search of a Program
(*Commentary*, October 1, 1949)

As a Zionist, I face an impasse. Without passing moral judgment on either myself or Israel, I know that I am something other than the Israeli, by upbringing, by my allegiance to America, and by my desire to be part of the cultural traditions of the Western world. . . . Inevitably, as a Zionist, I will look for content in the direction of cultural endeavor. The homeland has always been envisaged by an important body of Zionist theory as the center which would feed the spiritual energies of Jews the world over. The Hebraic values being revitalized and created by the renascent national culture would provide stimulation for all the Jewish world. This was the emphasis of Ahad Ha'am. . . .

There is no great likelihood that for Jewish national reasons American Jewry will swim upstream and steep itself in Hebrew language and Hebrew culture. Israeli national culture will be admired by world Jewry, but not really shared, for we are not in the mood for becoming artificial cultural irredentists. . . .

The experience of Israel, a nation in the making, is complex on the surface but in reality simple—it is the problem of getting on with the job. The problems of the Diaspora, under the tension of both Jewish and general spiritual allegiances, are rather less precise and more difficult. The Diaspora has chosen to live on as such. How to make it live on creatively and how to maintain inner identity between it and Israel—these are the most important questions that face us today. . . .

The only image that has not tarnished for me is my grandfather. My Palestine-born cousins have inherited from him his strength in the face of hardship and adversity, his capacity to start over again after failure, his ingenuity. What remains to me is the echo of his piety, the tefillin he sent me for my bar mitzvah and the books of homilies and tales of Hasidic saints that came in the same package. . . . Perhaps all of us, Israelis and the rest, should start over again from our grandfathers to make of our Jewish experience the deepest of all emotions and the greatest of all ties. Perhaps together we might all become what we ought to be, their grandchildren.

Some Reflections on Zionism Today (1977)

In America, Zionism has contributed not to the discomfort of the Jews in the Diaspora, but rather to the acceptance of themselves and their acceptance by others. It has provided the Jews of America with a set of mitzvot, the labors for Israel. The only offense for which Jews can be "excommunicated" in the U.S. today is not to participate in those efforts. Intermarriage, ignorance in the Jewish heritage, or lack of faith do not keep anyone from leadership in the American Jewish community today. Being against Israel or apathetic in its support does.

What we have today, and for at least a generation to come, is a Jewish World which our Zionist fathers imagined not, in which the largest Diaspora, that in the U.S., derives much of its sense of security out of working to lessen the insecurities of Israel. . . .

At this moment, the prime task of Zionism in the Diaspora is to mount a rescue operation so that every Jewish child receives some kind of Jewish education, some direct experience of Israel early in his life, and is challenged with the possibility of opting himself for *aliyah*. In this endeavor the preeminence of Israel is clear. I must add that it is a tragic sign of the weakness of Zionism in the U.S. that it has had so little cultural impact. . . . Today there is no Zionist education in the U.S., no schools, no teaching seminaries, no commitment by Zionists to the notion that the education of a Zionist kind of Jewish personality is of prime concern. . . .

Of course Israel is in danger and defending it is the prime objective of world Jewry, but strengthening and preserving Jewishness, wherever it might be, is an almost coequal purpose.... I cannot see radical solutions to make an end to the problems of the Jews of the world, either with the Gentiles or with ourselves. To be utterly candid my sense of three generations of Zionist achievement, including the state, is that some very fundamental new things are present in the Jewish world. We now do battle in our own name; we have the capacity to receive Jews into a Jewish state if that need should arise; and, above all, Israel is the magnet to draw Jews toward their own center. On the other hand, we are not "like all the other nations." Our uniqueness has not ended. It has only been recreated through different means, both in tragedy and in triumph, and as far as the eye can see that uniqueness will remain.

I am a Zionist not because I may carry an Israeli passport, but because I am a citizen of world Jewry, of *Am Yisra'el*. The task of Zionism in our time is to educate our children for that pervasive citizenship, and to create the modes of joint endeavor, with Israel as the center, which will create and retain that citizenship.

Heinrich Graetz defined Jewish history, in a phrase which has often been mocked, as being the history of literature and suffering. By that he meant that what has united the Jews throughout the ages, amid all kinds of political and social changes, was their joint commitment to a spiritual heritage and their joint involvement in each other's problems. Pragmatically, which is the only way Zionism can be defined for all Jewry today, it seems to me that it is these two motifs which both unite us and which are our present tasks.

Mordecai M. Kaplan (1881–1983)

Zionism is contemporary Judaism in action.

Israel's founding thrilled, then dismayed, one of Arthur Hertzberg's teachers: the pioneering rabbi and educator Mordecai Kaplan. Kaplan resented *shlilat hagalut*, the Zionist negation of the "exile," meaning

Diaspora Jewry, especially when it came from Ben-Gurionite secular Israelis who were hostile to Judaism. Kaplan also found Israel's religious establishment too authoritarian, and Israelis overall too brusque and scarred by the brutal fight for independence.

While accepting the Herzlian responsibility to support the Jewish state. Kaplan preferred the Ahad Ha'am model of an innovating, inspiring, Cultural-Spiritual Zionism. He envisioned American Jews serving as Israel's supportive "home front," just as civilians supported Allied soldiers during World War II. But he also sought more.

Born in Lithuania, Kaplan arrived in the United States when he was eight. He received his secular education at the College of the City of New York and Columbia University, and his rabbinic degree in 1902 from the Conservative movement's Jewish Theological Seminary. Eventually, he broke with Conservative Judaism by reimagining what an American Jewish religion should be. In 1916 he organized the Jewish Center in Manhattan, spearheading a new model for the synagogue: as cultural center. In 1922 Kaplan's daughter Judith became the first "bat mitzvah," another of his many innovations. His ground-breaking work, *Judaism as a Civilization* (1934), articulated a new philosophy of Judaism, Reconstructionism, viewing Judaism as an evolving civilization rooted in art, culture, and peoplehood.

As the ultimate Jewish peoplehood person, Kaplan described Jewish civilization with a hyphenated adjective—religio-national. Like any complex of rituals and values constituting a way of life, Judaism had to answer genuine spiritual, cultural, and communal needs. In his 1959 volume, *A New Zionism*—the enlarged edition of a work first published in 1954—Kaplan defined Zionism as "contemporary Judaism in action." Injecting his religious innovations into his Zionist dreams, Kaplan wanted Zionism to create an expansive, abundant Judaism. He affirmed the homeland and those who chose to live outside it. He asked secular Israelis to be more open to tradition, and traditional American Jews to be more open to change. In short, Mordechai Kaplan synthesized a new, American, identity-based Zionism. Today, from peoplehood talk to social action, Kaplan's ideas have permeated so fully that what were once his outlaw innovations have become American Zionism's defining assumptions.

A New Zionism (1954, 1959)

Without a Jewish people regenerated in spirit, no matter how successful the state it would establish, and how large a population that state could muster, Zion will continue to be unredeemed. . . .

As long as Zionism was merely a dream, it suffered none of the disheartenments which have come with its realization. Like a newborn infant, the State of Israel was no sooner born than it contracted all the possible diseases of an infant state. To cure those ills, Zionism has to enlarge its vision and to broaden the scope of its interests and activities. . . .

Actually there have been two Zionisms, a European and an American. The European Zionism has as its avowed aim the ingathering of all Jews from the various lands of their dispersion. American Zionism is merely a philanthropic movement to secure a haven of refuge for harassed and persecuted Jews. . . .

To expect American Jews to subscribe to this narrow interpretation of Zionism is quixotic and harmful. . . . No American Jew will subscribe to any cause that may cast serious doubt on the wholeheartedness of his Americanism. . . .

Zionism is contemporary Judaism in action. Judaism in action means that the Jewish people is actively engaged in an effort to adjust itself creatively to the contemporary world. . . .

All this leads to one inescapable conclusion: Zionism should henceforth treat the establishment of the State of Israel only as the first indispensable step in the salvaging of the Jewish people and the regeneration of its spirit. Actually to attain these objectives, Zionism has to be viewed not merely as a cultural and political movement, but also as a religious movement for our day. . . .

To live a more abundant Jewish life, whether in Israel or outside, Jews will have to foster a form of religion which will be relevant both to the past career of the Jewish People and to the spiritual needs and world outlook of the modern man. It will have to be a religion free from both creedal and clerical authoritarianism, and able to meet the moral and spiritual needs of our day. Such a religion will necessarily have to allow for diversity of belief and practice. . . .

It must not have political ties with government, either in Israel or in the Diaspora. A movement like Zionism should not bring it about that Jews who have won the right to live should lose the right to live according to the dictates of their conscience. . . .

Diaspora Jewries are in a state of moral and spiritual crisis, and their drift to assimilation is being daily accelerated. That fact is quite patent, except to those who deliberately shut their eyes to what is taking place about them. . . .

The New Zionism. . . . should relate the Jewish people, the Jewish religion, and the Jewish way of life to *Eretz Yisra'el* as the alpha and omega of Jewish existence. *Eretz Yisra'el* has to be reclaimed as the only place in the world where Jewish civilization can be perfectly at home. But also other lands where Jews have taken root have to be rendered capable of harboring that civilization. The one purpose cannot be achieved without the other. Should Jewish civilization fail to be at home in *Eretz Yisra'el*, it will disappear everywhere else. . . .

As Zionists, we have to reconstitute our peoplehood, reclaim our ancient homeland and revitalize our Jewish way of life. Each of these three objectives should be pursued with the end in view, both in Israel and in the Diaspora, of developing such interpersonal and intergroup relations as are likely to help us become more fully human. That is to be our religion and our mission.

Rose Halprin (1896–1978)

The more-than-platonic Zionist.

The Zionist identity crisis following the state's founding was particularly relevant to Hadassah. The formidable Women's Zionist Organization of America epitomized the American Zionist model of supporting the Jewish State while remaining patriotic Americans. Although Hadassah's founder Henrietta Szold had moved to Palestine in 1933, Hadassah's signature program, its Jerusalem Medical Center, relied on generous American funding to serve Israeli patients.

Hadassah's national president at the time was Rose Halprin. Born Rose Luria in New York in 1896, and educated at the Jewish Theological Seminary, Hunter College, and Columbia University, she would go on to engage with Hadassah and the Jewish Agency executive committee on every major Zionist controversy, from the Arab riots of the 1930s through the UN's Zionism-is-racism resolution of 1975.

Having lived in Palestine after her first term as national president, and appreciating the pioneering ideal, Halprin understood the American Zionist's deep commitment—and limits. In 1950 when Israel's minister of religion, Rabbi Judah Leib (Fishman) Maimon, avowed, "We must educate the Jewish youth abroad for many years, until it understands that the Land of Israel is the only place for the Jewish people," Halprin bristled. Simultaneously, however, she defined "*chalutziut,*" pioneering, as Jewish, Zionist, and American, and rejected the notion that to be a Zionist a Jew needed to live in Israel. Halprin's balance was the Hadassah balance—welcoming millions of American Jewish women over generations into a passionate, pioneering, state-transforming, Zionist mission that made them proud Americans and Zionists.

Speech to the Zionist General Council (April 24, 1950)

The American Zionist movement did not see itself as a great *halutz* [pioneering] movement. Nor indeed was the Zionist call addressed to it in these terms by the leaders of the movement who are now members of the government. Did they appeal to us as a *halutz* movement? They appealed for many things, they appealed for mass support, for political work and political support and they made appeal for funds. They made that appeal on the basis of the great need for these things and of our capacity to work in these spheres. That was the appeal that we tried to answer.

Then, at the last General Council meeting and during the past twelve months, many leaders in Israel began to define Zionism as synonymous with the *halutziut* concept. They defined the task of the Zionist Movement not as *"kibbutz galuyot"* [ingathering exiles] but *"kibbutz **hagaluyot**"* [ingathering *all* the exiles]. Here is the difference between us. We say: *kibbutz galuyot,* yes, but *kibbutz **hagaluyot,*** at this time, no.

And it does not change the situation if some of you consider us not Zionists but merely Friends of Israel. There is no question that Israel needs *halutziut* also from the Western world, but the question is: *halutziut* how? Under what slogans and under what terms? We say: *halutziut* in the Jewish spirit, in the Zionist spirit, but also in the American spirit. We will say to American young people, "There is the State of Israel, which needs your strength and knowledge; go there; give it what you can in the best tradition of the country where you were born and of the country which needs you." There will come people to whom a completely free Jewish life is essential. A completely free Jewish life you can have only here and not in America. *Halutziut—yes,* but the conception that at this moment no one can be considered a Zionist who does not come to *Eretz Yisra'el* is false. . . .

The question has been raised: what is Zionism, or rather, what is a Zionist? I could not give you a dictionary definition of a Zionist. But emotionally, I know the answer . . . A Zionist has more than platonic feelings. You are in his blood and bones, and he cannot get rid of you. . . .

Jacob Blaustein (1892–1970)

Bound to Jews the world over by ties of religion, common historical traditions and by a sense of common destiny.

American Jewry's *aliyah* anxieties also reflected fears that the Jewish state would stir American antisemitism, with Jew haters accusing American Jews of having dual loyalties. By the 1950s, leaders of the American Jewish Committee (AJC), the Jewish communal defense organization founded by well-bred German Jews, had accepted the need for a Jewish state, but remained worried about the implications. David Ben-Gurion's call for mass *aliyah,* and his claims to represent every Jew, infuriated them.

Ben-Gurion knew he could not alienate this most influential organization in this most influential Jewish community. In formal correspondence with the American Jewish Committee's president Jacob Blaustein, with Blaustein treating Israel's prime minister as his equal, Ben-Gurion tried reassuring these high-church American Jews.

Born in Baltimore to Lithuanian Jewish immigrants, Jacob Blaustein and his father would found a number of lucrative businesses, including the American Oil Company, which was eventually incorporated into Amoco. As AJC leader, Blaustein played a central role in the diplomatic negotiations regarding Palestine in the 1940s. In the Ben-Gurion exchanges, first in 1950, clarified in 1956, then formally refreshed and reaffirmed in 1961, he helped define American Jews' relationship to Israel. In treating Israel's prime minister as a peer and setting clear limits, Blaustein emphasized the American dimension in American Zionism. The American Zionist consensus accepted Israel's significance, not its centrality—as other Zionists did.

Statements by Prime Minister David Ben-Gurion and Mr. Jacob Blaustein on the Relationship between Israel and American Jews (1950, 1956)

Ben-Gurion: The Jews of the United States, as a community and as individuals, have only one political attachment and that is to the United States of America. They owe no political allegiance to Israel. . . . We, the people of Israel, have no desire and no intention to interfere in any way with the internal affairs of Jewish communities abroad. The government and the people of Israel fully respect the right and integrity of the Jewish communities in other countries to develop their own mode of life and their indigenous social, economic and cultural institutions in accordance with their own needs and aspirations. Any weakening of American Jewry, any disruption of its communal life, any lowering of its sense of security, any diminution of its status, is a definite loss to Jews everywhere and to Israel in particular. . . .

We should like to see American Jews come and take part in our effort. We need their technical knowledge, their unrivalled experience, their spirit of enterprise, their bold vision, their "know-how." We need engineers, chemists, builders, work managers and technicians. The tasks which face us in this country are eminently such as would appeal to the American genius for technical development and social progress. But the decision as to whether they wish to come—permanently or temporarily—rests with the free discretion of each American Jew. . . . The essence of *halutziut* is free choice. They will come from among those who believe that their aspirations as human beings and as Jews can best be fulfilled by life and work in Israel.

Blaustein: What you are doing and creating in this corner of the Middle East is of vital importance not only to you and to Jews, but to humanity in general. For I believe that the free and peace-loving peoples in the world can look upon Israel as a stronghold of democracy in an area where liberal democracy is practically unknown and where the prevailing social and political conditions may be potential dangers to the security and stability of the world. . . .

Important to your future, as you recognize, is the United States of America and American Jewry. Israel, of course, is also important to them. . . .

As to Israel, the vast majority of American Jewry recognizes the necessity and desirability of helping to make it a strong, viable, self-supporting state. This, for the sake of Israel itself, and the good of the world. . . .

Israel's rebirth and progress, coming after the tragedy of European Jewry in the 1930s and in World War II, has done much to raise Jewish morale. Jews in America and everywhere can be more proud than ever of their Jewishness. . . .

I would be less than frank if I did not point out to you that American Jews vigorously repudiate any suggestion or implication that they are in exile. . . .

To American Jews, America is home. There, exist their thriving roots; there, is the country which they have helped to build; and there, they share its fruits and its destiny. They believe in the future of a democratic society in the United States under which all citizens, irrespective of creed or race, can live on terms of equality. . . .

American Jews feel themselves bound to Jews the world over by ties of religion, common historical traditions and in certain respects, by a sense of common destiny. We fully realize that persecution and discrimination against Jews in any country will sooner or later have its impact on the situation of the Jews in other countries, but these problems must be dealt with by each Jewish community itself in accordance with its own wishes, traditions, needs and aspirations.

Jewish communities, particularly American Jewry in view of its influence and its strength, can offer advice, cooperation and help, but should not attempt to speak in the name of other communities or in any way interfere in their internal affairs. . . .

Simon Rawidowicz (1897–1957)

The people of Israel, the sum of all Jewish communities.

The pride, power, and stability of the newly Zionist American Jewish community required new paradigms for envisioning modern Zionism. The Russian-born Hebraist Simon Rawidowicz believed a united Jewish people could thrive in both Israel and the Diaspora. Rawidowicz, who spent a rich academic career teaching in Germany, England, and the United States, became best known for calling the Jews "the ever-dying people," emphasizing Jewish perseverance amid seemingly perennial crises. His model of Jerusalem and Babylon nicely articulated what emerged in these, more stable, times.

Rejecting Ahad Ha'am's metaphor of the Jews as a wheel with Israel at the center, Rawidowicz imagined "an ellipse with two foci, the Land of Israel and the Diaspora of Israel." Celebrating the two as Jerusalem and Babylon—"every place that is not Jerusalem"—he advocated a mutual partnership with authentic cultural expression from each.

Rawidowicz died young. His posthumously published book *Babylon and Jerusalem* was mostly ignored when published—too scholarly and too ahead of its time for a popular audience. Today, his notion of "two that are one" prevails, in many ways.

Babylon and Jerusalem (1957)

The face of Israel has two profiles—Babylon and Jerusalem. . . .

By Jerusalem, we mean Jerusalem as a symbol of the Land of Israel in its entirety. By Babylon, we mean not only that territory that lies on the banks of the Tigris and Euphrates, but every place that is not Jerusalem. . . .

Jerusalem is the point of destination, the end of the journey; Babylon is transition, the journey itself. . . .

Shabby and threadbare is the cloak in which our Westernized "theologians" and European and America assimilationists have dressed themselves, rejecting any genuine Jewish existence and declaring that Judaism is a "religion—only a religion." This emaciated and emasculated "religion" of theirs . . . is merely a subterfuge for denying Israel as a living and vital people. . . .

Jerusalem remains isolated, surrounded by enemies on all sides who are ready to pounce upon her at every opportunity. Babylon, for her part, is insecurity incarnate. . . .

Two That Are One (Speech at Yiddish Language Symposium in New York, 1949)

"Two that are one" . . . must not be understood as a one-sided obligation; each must mutually recognize the other. The Diaspora of Israel must build the State of Israel with all its strength, even more than it has in the past seventy years, and the state must recognize the Diaspora as of equal value, and an equally responsible co-builder and co-creator of all Jewish life. . . .

The Land of Israel in and of itself has an exceptional, unique place in the Jewish soul, in Jewish history, and in Jewish reality, that no other piece of earth has yet had or will ever have, so far as we can foresee. But I am calling for the recognition of full moral and practical equal right and value between Jews in the Land of Israel and Jews outside of it. . . . Every Jewish community, large or small, must, so long as it exists, be recognized as an equal partner in the people of Israel, which is the sum of all Jewish communities.

I reject also the entire notion and terminology of "giving" and "taking" between the State of Israel and the Diaspora. There are not, nor should be, absolute givers and takers among Jews. I do not want to try to calculate who gives more, and who will give more in the future; that is not important. What is important is the independent spontaneous creativity of each center of Jewish life, "each man in his own camp," each community where it lives, be it heaven or hell.

Irving "Yitz" Greenberg (b. 1933)

The revival of the space dimension of holiness in Judaism.

The terrifying May of 1967, followed by that exhilarating June, transformed Diaspora Jewry. Relieving Auschwitz's traumas and 1948's redemption amid the 1960's rebellion centered Israel in Jewish consciousness. Assimilated Jews discovered how deeply Jewish they were, especially as Christian friends and the United Nations stayed silent. Pride in Israel surged, as did guilt regarding American Jewish silence during the Holocaust, boldness in asserting Jewish political power, activism to save Soviet Jewry, comfort in being publicly Jewish, and the creative synthesis of Judaism and Americanism.

Irving "Yitz" Greenberg defined many of these trends. Trained as an American historian at Harvard and an Orthodox rabbi, Greenberg began as a congregational rabbi. In the 1960s and 1970s, he helped launch the Student Struggle for Soviet Jewry, helped establish Jewish Studies as an academic discipline, and founded Clal the National Jewish Center for Learning and Leadership—which included Zachor, America's first Holocaust-education resource center. Subsequently, he chaired the United States Holocaust Memorial Council Museum and helped Taglit-Birthright form.

This activism publicized his theology, building on his teacher Rabbi Joseph Soloveichek's covenant of fate and destiny. Auschwitz and Israel had reaffirmed the Jews' common fate, the "covenant of Egypt," now expressed through donating to Israel and other new mitzvot.

With Israeli triumphs reinforcing his American-infused optimism, Greenberg encouraged a positive Jewish revival reinforcing the "covenant of Sinai," of destiny—an affirmative "Judaism or Jewishness" celebrating "voluntary *aliyah*" over ingathering by oppression. Greenberg also exulted that new festive days like Israel's Independence Day and Jerusalem Day had started balancing out the litany of exilic suffering clouding much of the Jewish calendar. Ironically, Greenberg's legacy entails strengthening American Jewish consciousness about the Holocaust, while using Israel to inspire American Jews to build positive Jewish identities without being imprisoned by that consciousness.

Twenty Years Later: The Impact of Israel on American Jewry (A symposium sponsored by the American Histadrut Cultural Exchange Institute, 1968)

The true impact of the events of the Six-Day War has been on the unconscious levels of Jewish psyche and imagination. Moreover, the State of Israel itself has asserted a new centrality in the minds and hearts of Jews. . . .

One of the victims of this shift, I hope, will be the idolatry of universal idealism which often obscures Jewish capacity to protect the legitimate rights of particular groups—most of all, of Jews. . . . The inaction of the American Jewish community during the days of the Holocaust was in major part due to the fear of being identified as a particular group with special needs. . . .

The reality of the state, almost lost and remarkably restored to us intact, also is going to intensify Jewish awareness that we are living through the end of "Golus Judaism" [the oppressed Judaism of exile]. The major focus is shifting from the dignity of powerlessness and the significance of spirit to the dilemmas of power. . . . In the helplessness of the Diaspora existence, the religious equilibrium was knocked askew. The primary concern became to give dignity and moral significance to passivity, powerlessness, and internal freedom. The restoration of power need not—

should not—involve a new idolatry of power. Rather, if we are faithful to a new healthy condition, Jews can strike a morally significant balance in the relationship of ideals and means. Religion and morality will again focus on the legitimate and illegitimate uses of power. . . .

Another effect of life in Israel on the faith of Israel may well be specific to Jews living in the land. It is the revival of the space dimension of holiness in Judaism. During its relatively disembodied existence in the Diaspora the Jewish people has pretty much lived in the dimension of time. . . . We have forgotten—and as modern culture denizens are unsympathetic to—the holiness of specific space. If anything, such concepts are suspect for their association with blood and soil. Yet physical roots and the sense of organic existence on the land does affect human perception and the psyche of those dwelling on the land. There is little doubt then that this awareness is in for a significant revival in Israel. The obvious example of this is the cult of the Wall. But I refer simply to the historical and existential concerns which seem to grow out of the sense of rootedness. . . . It is likely to lead to an Israeli religious tone more nationalistic and particularistic than the universal focus which suffuses Judaism in the exile. . . .

One should also take note of the extraordinary response of Jews to the needs of the state during the crisis. It suggests that Israel is deeper in the Jewish psyche than had been recognized. This points to a strategy of making Israel central in religious and Jewish educational life—if only because thereby we can tap strong loyalties and deep feelings.

The crisis response proves also that the Holocaust is burned more deeply into the minds and hearts of our Jews than we can possibly imagine. There is little doubt in my mind that much of the worldwide Jewish response was based on the conviction that Auschwitz must not happen again. To this one might add the general feeling that Jews in the Diaspora may yet need a place to go to if this threat looms over them again. Finally it dramatized the old Kabbalistic idea that there is a spark in the soul of every Jew waiting to be fanned into a flame of devotion and commitment. . . .

After the events of the war, *aliyah* has become more of a live option for a limited but definite additional group of Jews in America. For the seriously religious fraction of American Jewry, and for Jews whose Judaism or Jewishness is of fundamental priority overriding all other concerns, *aliyah* always is and will be a real possibility. . . .

Voluntary *aliyah* will depend on the extent to which more Jews, out of love and new depth of understanding, come to see their Judaism or Jewishness as the concern of their lives. . . .

Yom Yerushalayim: Jerusalem Day (*Jewish Way*, 1988)

For nineteen hundred years, as the role of Jewish suffering unfolded, the Jewish calendar expanded with days of sadness. Grief so dominated the calendar (three weeks in the summer; several weeks of Sefirah [counting of the Omer] in the spring; Monday and Thursday in the fall; the eve of the new moon every month; the four fast days) that there was fear additional days might tip the balance of the year into excessive mourning.

The climax of these nineteen hundred years of growing gloom and pain came in the Holocaust. . . . Jewish suffering could go no further without ending the very existence of the Jewish people. The sheer magnitude of the Holocaust dictated the inclusion of another mourning day, Yom ha-Shoah. But the bulk of the Jewish people declared that Jewish suffering should go no further. "Never again!" meant no more permanent grief days as well. In Israel's War of Independence an aroused Jewry beat back the invaders by the narrowest of margins. The victory upheld the state, and the celebration of that redemption added Yom Ha'atzmaut—a happy day—to the calendar. Since Independence Day fell during the Sefirah Period, the modern Exodus reclaimed one day from the ranks of the days of sorrow and added it to the days of joy.

But a question remained: Was this merely a respite, a short-term upturn from an unchanged long-term trend of oppressive sorrow, or was this the beginning of a major reversal of historic proportions from sorrow to joy? This question was answered in the Six-Day War. By a far greater margin, would-be destruction was turned back. The margin of victory made clear the incredible accomplishment of two decades of state-building. . . . A second day of celebration was added—Yom Yerushalayim.

Since Jerusalem Day occurs in the Sefirah Period, another calendar day was shifted from the side of sorrow to the side of joy. As the security and peace of Israel's establishment sinks in, one can project a pattern: In time, the day of concluding the peace treaty of Camp David (and the day of the signing of the final total peace) will be added to the holidays of celebration. Eventually, the three weeks between Yom Ha'atzmaut and Yom Yerushalayim will be filled in as days of joy and celebration. . . . Step by step, victory by victory, the Jewish people are reversing the tide of Jewish history from mourning to celebration, from death to life.

Eugene Borowitz (1924–2016)

**The sense of that rootedness in the soil
has forced that particularity on me.**

The Reform theologian Eugene Borowitz agreed with his Orthodox colleague Yitz Greenberg that the Six-Day War validated Jewish particularity and stirred surprisingly deep feelings about land and place among normally cosmopolitan Jews. Born in Columbus, Ohio, in 1924, ordained at Hebrew Union College in Cincinnati in 1948, Borowitz articulated a post-Holocaust and postmodern covenantal relationship with God. Such ideas pushed the Reform movement toward a rigor and mysticism few of its founders imagined.

Borowitz's Zionism was unconventional too. Rejecting the usual Zionist building blocks, he discounted Hebrew as a force in building identity. He disdained what the political scientist Daniel J. Elazar called "Israelolotry" following 1967, insisting "We cannot function as Jews by trying to live a vicarious Israeli existence on American soil." And by emphasizing a Jew's covenant of faith more than a Jew's ethnic ties—or covenant of fate—he questioned the nationalist consensus about Zionism's core. Borowitz's traditionalist Reform approach could easily justify "non-Zionism," the leading Reform Zionist rabbi Richard Hirsch warned.

Still, as a master teacher at Hebrew Union College's Manhattan campus for half a century and the founder of the Jewish journal for ideas, *Sh'ma*, Borowitz affirmed Israel's centrality in modern Jewish identity. Addressing the same 1968 conference as Yitz Greenberg, Borowitz articulated an Americanized Zionism, championing the "desirability of a strong Zionist attitude on the part of Jews." He also encouraged thoughtful criticism of Israel despite its many enemies. Altogether, Borowitz was a pioneer in anticipating today's robust Reform criticism of Israeli policies while teaching how this deeply American, profoundly liberal, and proudly Jewish movement could remain thoroughly Zionist.

Twenty Years Later: The Impact of Israel on American Jewry (A symposium sponsored by the American Histadrut Cultural Exchange Institute, 1968)

I understand myself as person and as self-participating on the very deepest level in the covenant relationship between God and the people of Israel. . . . I find that covenant to be true in my own personal life and in the lives of the American Jewish community and if that is so . . . that covenant is made . . . with a people or folk or, in a more European sense, a nation. The Jews are obviously all of that, and in order to carry out their covenant responsibilities for God, as the Torah indicates, as the historical record makes perfectly clear, the Jewish people is obligated to live out in a communal and social way on its own land the life of the covenant. I am therefore, if such a thing is imaginable to you, a Reform Jewish Zionist. I am a religious Zionist, of non-Orthodox religious persuasion, and the religious foundation to my understanding of the necessity and the desirability of a strong Zionist attitude on the part of Jews has as its adjunct the notion that one can live out that covenant relationship elsewhere than on the Land of Israel. I understand my presence where I am as being of appropriate derivation from the roots which I have.

There has been a tremendous positive, constructive, worthwhile impact of the State of Israel on Jews of my persuasion and on myself. That specific impact . . . has been a general sense of positive Jewish self-acceptance and . . . to help the synagogue point to a place where being a Jew is not only real, but visible. In the United States it's sometimes difficult to understand what the visibility of being a Jew is, where one actually sees it, how that Jewishness affects one's life. The [1967] Arab-Israeli war did something to us that no one, I think, could have known in advance. In my own case, what has strengthened and deepened has been a very personal existential sense of the particularity of what it is to be a Jew, the specificity of being a Jew as a member of an ethnic community.

We were always aware of our people's fervent association with the land; but they are far deeper than we thought, those ties with the land. . . . I had not heard anybody talk very much about the religious importance or significance of Old Jerusalem before last June. So that when Old Jerusalem was captured and was somehow, to use that marvelous word, "ours," it hit us with an impact which we couldn't imagine, and suddenly we realized the depths of roots we had in a very specific place. . . . Now what can it mean that Jews who have never been near the Wall, who haven't heard about the Wall, who haven't talked about the Wall, who have no theoretical relationship to the Wall are suddenly moved to tears by its being in Jewish hands, moved to the depths of their being by the possibility of themselves going to the Wall, perhaps even to pray, which it would seem to me is the only proper and reasonable response to the Wall? So there is something about its being tied very specifically, not only to that tradition, but to the religious roots of that tradition. . . .

I think the worst thing that Zionism and the State of Israel have done for us is to give us another topic in America which cannot be debated. We now have a subject on which no arguments are allowed, no criticism. A new sacred cow is introduced. Open your mouth in a Jewish audience to raise a question critical of the State of Israel, critical of Zionism, and if you're talking with Israelis, that's all right; if you're in the State of Israel and getting into an argument, that's all right; but to an American Jewish audience you are not allowed to say anything bad about the State of Israel. . . .

It seems to me that the State of Israel is sufficiently secure that American Zionists should be sufficiently secure to allow for the normal kind of intellectual give-and-take over the issues of the State of Israel. . . . I am for the kind of freedom and openness among ourselves in the American Jewish community which would allow us to face some of our problems with the State of Israel, and out of that kind of more mature self-understanding . . . we would have a much better chance of communicating, not only with ourselves, but with our brothers (and sisters) of the State of Israel as well.

Herman Wouk (b. 1915)

A single long action of lifesaving.

The American novelist Herman Wouk captured the shift in consciousness after the Six-Day War when revising his best-selling introduction to Orthodox Judaism, *This Is My God*. The first edition, published in 1959, affirmed Zionism's "lifesaving action," but sagged with the burden of Holocaust victimhood and the engaged Jew's fears of assimilation. The tenth anniversary edition, in 1969, brimmed with the war's redemptive energy, offering the "radical" conclusion that Israel had become the center of world Jewry. As Wouk explained: "The thunder of the Six-Day War was the heartbeat of Old Jewry, starting up again after the paralytic shock of the Holocaust."

Still, Wouk couldn't comprehend why anyone, especially his own son, would abandon the comforts of America for the wilds of Israel. Born in the Bronx, Wouk had a golden career in the Golden Medina. A Columbia University education, naval service, work as a radio dramatist, led to a Pulitzer Prize, theatrical release, and movie version of his 1951 best-seller *The Caine Mutiny*, starring Humphrey Bogart. Subsequent works included the culturally influential tale of a young Jewish American princess, *Marjorie Morningstar* (1955), and the majestic World War II novels, *The Winds of War* (1971) and *War and Remembrance* (1978). Both became blockbuster TV miniseries, introducing millions to the horrors of the Holocaust in 1983, then 1988. While editing the letters of Entebbe's fallen hero, Yoni Netanyahu, published in 1980, Wouk came to appreciate Israel's "irrepressible" spirit. This conclusion helped him understand the meaning his son and others derived from living in Israel.

This Is My God (1969, 1974)

In the categories of Hebrew law, modern Zionism is a single long action of lifesaving, of snatching great masses of people out of the path of sure extinction....

The special feeling that comes to one who has been a member of a minority all his life, and now finds himself in a place where everybody is like him—this extraordinary shift which changes the very nerve signals, as it were—must be a sensation that only a Diaspora Jew who comes to Israel can know. Born Israelis cannot imagine it....

A taxi driver courteously and ably explained to me where I had gone wrong in writing *The Caine Mutiny*, in terms not much different from the first American reviews. I was his cousin, you see; he could speak freely....

There will be no death camps in the United States that we live in. History is a phantasmagoria, and anything can happen. But the civilization we know will have to be obliterated before a Hitler can sit in Washington. The threat of Jewish oblivion in America is different. It is the threat of pleasantly vanishing down a broad highway at the wheel of a high-powered station wagon, with the golf clubs piled in the back.... "*Mr. Abramson left his home in the morning after a hearty breakfast, apparently in the best of health, and was not seen again. His last words were that he would get in a round before going to the office....*" Of course Mr. Abramson will not die. When his amnesia clears, he will be Mr. Adamson, and his wife and children will join him, and all will be well. But the Jewish question will be over in the United States....

Seventy years ago, Herzl's great opponent, Ahad Ha'am, foresaw the new Jewish state as the spiritual center of a regenerated Diaspora. For this moderate claim he was attacked and scorned by the all-out Zionists. Now he appears to have been a prophet. The return of all Jewry to the Holy Land remains a messianic vision, but Israel already exists as our new spiritual center....

We Jews have had our age of ash, and we have survived, barely, but we have survived. With struggles and dangers that still mount, we have found our way to Jerusalem the Golden, and we are rebuilding it. From this wonder of history, all men can take hope.

Arnold Jacob Wolf (1924–2008)

Did Zionism mean to create an American-style supermarket on the Mediterranean built by Arab masons and carpenters?

Even amid the Jews' post-1967 euphoria, some American Jewish radicals began criticizing Israel, tackling unaddressed concerns about Palestinian nationalism, Orthodox hegemony, and Israeli militarism. These critiques launched intense debates that sound all too familiar. One organization in particular, Breira (Alternative), challenged American Jews to express their Zionism by dissenting, anticipating the New Israel Fund, J-Street, and other contemporary organizations.

Breira's founder, Arnold Jacob Wolf, was a Chicago-born Reform rabbi who boasted about becoming "more traditional theologically than my family and more radical politically." He revered Abraham Joshua Heschel, consorted with the Chicago Seven radicals, and marched with Martin Luther King Jr.

In March 1973, Wolf published an essay in *Sh'ma: The Journal of Jewish Responsibility* he helped found, asserting that an increasingly militaristic, expansionist, theocratic, Jabotinskyite Israel was making him a disappointed Zionist. Later that year, resisting the American Jewish "consensus" on many issues, including Palestinian rights, he started Breira: A Project of Concern in Diaspora-Israel Relations. The organized Jewish community and the Israeli government counterattacked. After four tumultuous years, with some members' radical statements increasing Breira's vulnerability to scorching mainstream criticism, Wolf closed the organization, citing lack of funds.

Nevertheless, Wolf's precedent gradually changed Jewish communal norms. Today's American Zionist conversation is far livelier than it was in the 1970s, even if many debates still trigger mutual indignation, with critics inflamed by the particular issue and defenders offended by the critics' disrespect for Israel's particular predicament. Breira's contention that "Israel and the communities of the Diaspora are strong enough to accept or reject others' suggestions on their merits" turned out to be true—even if today the dialogue largely remains brittle.

Wolf spent his last decades as a rabbi and rabbi emeritus in Hyde Park, Chicago. One neighbor, Barack Obama, eulogized him in 2008 as "a titan of moral strength and a champion of social justice."

Will Israel Become Zion? (*Sh'ma*, March 30, 1973)

Zionism, as I understand it, meant and means primarily the end of subservience to other men's determination. It meant the fulfillment of God's promise (Lev. 26) to "break the bonds of your yoke and make you walk upright," *kom'miyut*. Zionism promised and promises a new, organic authenticity, a Jewish life lived out of inner standards, in dialogue with Jewish sources, speaking the Hebrew language, without the circumlocutions and the evasions of all our fearful ghettos. Zionism opposed and opposes that comfortable liberalism which substitutes premature utopianism for patient Jewish Messianism and which asks us to become part of the nations instead of a nation dwelling alone. Zionism opposed and opposes that Orthodox petrifaction which treated the *halakhah* as a fortress to be defended and not a life to be lived....

Revolutionary Zionists like Hess and A. D. Gordon and Rav Kook and Martin Buber superbly refracted these traditional Jewish norms until they shone forth with a profoundly innovative communitarianism in the kibbutz, and a brave new Exodus from lands where Jews could no longer live or could not live like Jews. The conquest of the land and the conquest of labor and the conquest of self-hating atavisms were all achievements of Zionism as the authentic and unique national movement of the Jewish people everywhere....

The Jewish state is a fact, ineluctable and glorious, but it is not and may never be the Zion desired by the Movement or foreshadowed by the Tradition.

There has been in Israel a steady retreat from socialist and religious egalitarianism. The *kibbutz* is isolated and diminished and, if it is the glory of our propaganda, it is also a vulnerable island in a sea of capitalist encroachment—and now knows it is. Where Pro-Palestinian Zionism was open, the State of Israel has become triumphalist and often also expansionist....

Israel colonizes the "administered" territories without regard to international law or to the rights of the indigenous Palestinian nationality. . . .
Few Israeli soldiers die now (thank God!) but, as in Vietnam, its pilots can rain death from skies which they and they alone control.

Zionism opposed Orthodox unilateralism, but in the Jewish state, Orthodoxy is empowered, entrenched, established and corrupt. . . .

Zionism spoke movingly of *kibbush avodah* (the dignity of work) but, increasingly, in the Jewish state, hard work is done by Arab hirelings. . . .
Did Zionism mean to create an American-style supermarket on the Mediterranean built by Arab masons and carpenters? . . .

Jabotinsky, the life-long *bete noire* of the Zionist movement, is now posthumously rehabilitated, to become a Hero of the Jewish State with his name on a hundred street signs and his face on thousands of stamps. . . .
Israel sends to America not her scholars or her farmers or her singers, but generals and strategists, as if the Six-Day War were her finest hour and *Tsahal* (the Israeli Army) her greatest accomplishment. . . .

Israel may be the Jewish state; it is not now and perhaps can never be Zion, the Zion of scripture or the Zion of the Movement, in Moses Hess's words "the historic ideal of our people, none other than the reign of God on earth."

Breira National Platform (February 21, 1977)

We are committed to Jewish life—its resilient ethical principles, its moving spiritual and aesthetic achievements, its cultural heritage, its inspiring, evolving history. We affirm that Jews throughout the world and throughout the ages constitute one people. The State of Israel is a particular manifestation of this peoplehood; the communities of the Diaspora form an equally vital element. We believe that the continuity of Jewish life now rests on the interdependence of the Jewish people in both Israel and the Diaspora.

We love Israel. We cherish the cultural treasures and the many moral examples it has given us. And we similarly affirm the richness of the Jewish experience in North America and are eager to explore and extend its possibilities.

The primary decisions of Israel's life and policy must be made by the Israelis, as the many decision of Diaspora life must be made by each Jewish community for itself. Nonetheless, we must communicate our feeling to each other, as a reflection of our mutual responsibility, support, and concern. Israel and the communities of the Diaspora are strong enough to accept or reject others' suggestions on their merits; neither should attempt to manipulate or intimidate the other.

We affirm *aliyah* as a positive act, but we also affirm the right of Israelis to take up residence elsewhere. We . . . advocate direct political, moral, and financial support of those forces within Israeli society which promote the principles of peace, social equality, democracy, civil rights, and other values consistent with the Jewish prophetic tradition. An important expression of this tradition includes safeguarding the rights of Arab and other non-Jewish minorities within the State of Israel. . . .

Hillel Halkin (b. 1939)

A great adventure. I wouldn't have missed it for the world.

The rebels of the 1960s and 1970s enjoyed exposing "Establishment" hypocrisies, while ignoring their own. Inevitably, the American Zionist's ambivalence about *aliyah* made for a delicious target.

In 1977 the translator and essayist Hillel Halkin published one of the most controversial Zionist tracts in the post-1948 period. *Letters to an American Jewish Friend* imagined a literary ping-pong match. The chapters pitched him, a new immigrant who had moved to Israel in 1970, against an unnamed friend "A.," a composite who exemplified the literate American Jew deeply concerned about the Jewish future. Halkin shrewdly ignored the indifferent Jew who would have been easily trounced in such a debate.

Justifying life in Israel—now without having to justify being Jewish—Halkin's unapologetic, in-your-face portrayal praised Israel's authentic, compelling Jewish life, blessed by the "vital spark" of living on the Jewish people's own land and speaking its own language.

This contrasted with his depiction of American Jewry's mediated, diluted, and ultimately conflicted existence. Polarizing, offending many, the book nonetheless elegantly explained the Zionist case. As Halkin proudly reported in the preface to his second edition released in 2013, it even inspired some to make *aliyah*.

Letters to an American Jewish Friend: The
Case for Life in Israel (1977, 2013)

American Jews, though sympathetic, were detached. Israel was no longer the can-do-no-wrong country it had been for them in 1967. It was certainly no longer a country to consider living in. When friends visited from the States, the subject wasn't raised. They came for their summer vacation, or part of it, and went home while I went back to another month in the army and the worry of paying the bills. I was bearing a burden they weren't; more and more, it felt like the burden of Jewish history. I didn't say this to their faces. I should be grateful, I told myself, that they bothered to visit at all. But had I been truthful, I would have said other things. And so I wrote *Letters to an American Jewish Friend....*

What I was asking for was honesty—the honesty to face a historical situation and draw the right conclusions....

My quarrel was with American Jews who did care deeply about being Jewish. I didn't doubt that they were as committed to their Jewishness as I was to mine. I didn't think that living in Israel made me a better Jew. I thought it made me a more logical one. It gave my life as a Jew its maximal value....

And yet there were moments in which I needed firming up. Talking with my American Jewish friends, I sometimes felt a twinge of envy. Life was so damned easy for them. The second car they thought nothing of owning. (We could barely afford a first one.) The weekend house on ten acres in the country. (Ten acres? We were considered the owners of a latifundium for having bought three-quarters of one acre.) The vacations abroad. (In Israel there was something called a "travel tax" that charged you a fortune just for the right to buy a ticket to anywhere.) Things like that. I needed to reassure myself, not that I had good reasons for being where I was, but that I had better reasons than they had for being where they were. . . .

I had no trouble putting myself in A.'s place. I knew his arguments. They were, allowing for the changed times, the same arguments American Jews had always used to explain why life in Israel wasn't for them. I thought these were evasions, rationalizations. But then American Jewish life had always seemed to me one big rationalization. It had always struck me as a kind of play-acting, even as a boy. Israel was genuine. Jews were fighting there for a country of their own, living in it, building and defending it. In America, they were listening to sermons. . . . I loved America for many things, but not for its Jewish life, to which I couldn't see myself belonging if I remained an American. . . .

A great adventure. I wouldn't have missed it for the world.

There's been nothing like it in human history. A small and ancient people loses its land and forgets how to speak its language; wanders defenselessly for hundreds, thousands, of years throughout the world with its God and sacred books; meets with contumely, persecution, violence, dispossession, banishment, mass murder; refuses to give up; refuses to surrender its faith; continues to believe that it will one day be restored to the land it lost; manages in the end, by dint of its own efforts, against all odds, to gather itself from the four corners of the earth and return there; learns again to speak the language of its old books; learns again to bear arms and defend itself; wrests its new-old home from the people that had replaced it; entrenches itself there; builds; fructifies; fortifies; repulses the enemies surrounding it; grows and prospers in the face of all threats. Had it not happened, could it have been imagined? Would anyone have believed it possible?

Would anyone believe it possible that one could belong to this people, value one's connection to it, even construct one's life around it, but have no interest in taking part in such an adventure? Would anyone believe that one could repeatedly declare how much this people means to one but think the adventure is entirely for others?

Yet this describes the average "committed" American Jew. . . .

Dennis Prager (b. 1948) and Joseph Telushkin (b. 1948)

The essence of Judaism since before the Bible was written.

The Six-Day War energized Zionists worldwide, fashioning an image of the New Jew as a great fighter. By 1969 *The Encyclopedia of Jewish Humor* included a chapter on Israeli jokes celebrating Israeli military prowess intensified by traditional Jewish cleverness. The crooner Frank Sinatra quipped, "I'm going to Israel to see the pyramids," as Jews joked that the Cairo Hilton was taking bar mitzvah reservations.

Yet, as the columnist George Will would later note, Israel did a terrible thing in 1967—it won, just as the world started loving underdogs. Although Israel remained embattled and outnumbered, although Israel remained a democracy surrounded by autocracies, the Six-Day War—and Israel's new control over the West Bank, the Sinai, and the Golan—stirred up the anti-Zionists. By 1975 when two Columbia University classmates, Dennis Prager and Joseph Telushkin, published a nine-question primer about Judaism, their sixth question was "Is there a difference between anti-Zionism and antisemitism." Increasingly, the answer was "no."

Nine Questions People Ask about Judaism became a canonical text, a mainstay of most American Jewish libraries. The authors' economical, surgical, treatment of the distinction between anti-Zionism and antisemitism illustrates why—and inspired their 1983 blockbuster *Why the Jews? The Reason for Antisemitism.*

The two still lecture and publish extensively, now separately. Telushkin's books teach about Jewish texts, ethics, and theology, with Israel often framed as a pillar of Jewish identity and civilization. A popular talk radio host and television commentator, Prager has been more involved in public debates, readily defending Israel and Zionism as the attacks have morphed over the decades.

Nine Questions People Ask about Judaism (1975)

"Is there a difference between anti-Zionism and antisemitism?"

Anti-Zionism differs from other expressions of antisemitism only in which aspect of the Jewish identity it chooses to hate. Those medieval Christians who burned Jews alive also claimed (and perhaps sincerely) that they did not oppose all Jews, only those Jews who insisted on retaining their Jewish faith and practices. . . .

Can someone deny that Italians are a nation, work to destroy Italy, and all the while claim that he is not an enemy of the Italian people because he does not hate all Italians? The question is obviously absurd. If you deny Italian nationhood and any Italian rights to their homeland, and seek to destroy Italy, no matter how sincerely you may claim to love some Italians, you are an enemy of the Italian people. The same holds true for those who deny Jewish nationhood and the Jews right to their state, and who advocate the destruction of Israel. Such people are enemies of the Jewish people, and the term of their attitudes, even when espoused by people who sincerely like some Jews, is antisemitism. . . .

The Jews' self-definition as a nation with a homeland in Israel is not merely some new political belief of contemporary Jews, but the essence of Judaism since before the Bible was written. . . .

Those who believe that they can deny Jewish nationhood and advocate the elimination of the Jewish state without being antisemitic, must do so out of a willful ignorance about Jews, Judaism, Jewish history, the Middle East, and the Arab and Muslim worlds. . . .

Should *aliyah* prove to be impossible for you at this time, we urge you to take the following actions to solidify your ties with the Jewish state:

1. *Visit Israel as often as you can.* Travel around the country and meet its people. Come to feel at home in Israel. You are.

2. *Live for a year in Israel.* . . . Everyone, no matter what his or her work, should live a year or more in the one Jewish country in the world and the one which has the potential to create a society based on Judaism. You need Israel as much as it needs you.

3. *Learn Hebrew.* . . .

4. *Learn about the issues in the Middle East conflict.* . . .

5. *Appeal to all the American people for support for Israel.* . . .

6. *Support political candidates who show concern for Israel and other moral issues.* . . .

Alex Singer (1962–87)

I can do more for the body of Jews from its heart than from its toenails.

Ultimately, the American *aliyah* was limited. While the Zionist youth movements may have celebrated *aliyah* as their highest ideal, they produced few immigrants—and continued to shrink. This failure defused the ideological tension around *aliyah*. Many Israelis also became less judgmental, especially as hundreds of thousands of their fellow citizens left Israel.

In this less-charged atmosphere, the occasional immigrant's perspective could be welcomed as an often admirable, occasionally illuminating, yet clearly quirky take on the Zionist or Jewish norm in America. So it was that the sweet, straightforward, patriotic Zionism of Alex Singer inspired American Jews without threatening them.

A suburban New Yorker born in 1962, a Cornell graduate, fluid writer, and talented painter, Singer was the kind of superstar overachiever the American Jewish community loved. But Singer, whose family had spent four years in Israel when he was young, wanted to join the Israel adventure, improving Israel from within. He believed he could "do more for the body of Jews from its heart than from its toenails." After graduating, he moved to Israel and enlisted, eventually becoming an officer.

Alex Singer died in battle in Lebanon in 1987—on his twenty-fifth birthday. Nine years later, his parents Max and Suzanne Singer published *Alex: Building a Life*, a collection of his letters and drawings which have inspired thousands since.

Alex: Building a Life (letters from 1983 and 1986, published in 1996)

APRIL 17, 1983, KIBBUTZ EIN TZURIM

Dear Saul,

It seems that the irony of the Torah is that the closer you follow it the less of a burden it becomes. But then again maybe that's the difference between life in the Diaspora and in Israel: It's much harder to say that the more observant you are in Silver Spring, let alone in a non-Jewish neighborhood, the less burdensome your Judaism becomes. Torah can be a joy for some people everywhere but in Israel it can more easily be a joy for more people. . . .

The purpose of my *aliyah* will be a combination of wanting a greater chance to make my Judaism one of joy rather than one of burdens, of wanting to be part of Israel's development as both a state and a beacon, and of the feeling that it is the duty of the individual Jew to help the Jewish People. Ahad Ha'am wrote that the Jew's relation to his people was like that of the limb to the body and that the "actions of the individual have their reward in the good of the community." It is when reward is described this way that *aliyah* begins to seem the right word to describe a Jew's move to Israel because it is indeed "going up" when the hand decides to live for the body rather than for itself alone. And, while it seems silly to talk about a hand living for itself, such talk is not much sillier than talk of the individual who denies being part of a larger body. . . .

It certainly is not an easy country. But, maybe that is the real attraction of *aliyah*—Just as I feel (sacrilegiously, I guess) that I prefer the challenges of a messed-up world to the utopia of a messianic age, I also prefer the challenges of Israel to the ease of America. I guess I should start a new movement . . . "Jews for a masochistic *aliyah*." . . .

JUNE 21, 1983 LONDON

Dear Josh,

I just feel too much a part of the Jewish community to become (albeit blissfully) unaffiliated. Even if I didn't believe that the Jews have a purpose—the purpose of working to make the world a place where all behave as if they believe in a God who is just (or, for that matter, as if the whole world were like northwestern Scotland)—I would not be able to "drop" the Jews. The Jew who says that he is contributing to the growth of his people from Scotland is like the child who moves across the world from his family and says that he is still contributing to the unity of the family. And, even if this analogy seems weakened by the saying "absence makes the heart grow fonder," it must be remembered that fondness doesn't contribute anything to the well-being of its object unless it leads to commitment.

My thinking about moving to Israel is somewhat related to this. Once the lone Jew on the moors sees that his contribution to his people cannot be as great as that of a Jew in a large community of Jews in London or even Glasgow, he will also see that the contribution of the London Jew is rarely as great as that of the Jew who lives in Israel. The Jew in Jerusalem is far more likely to shape the health of Jews and Judaism than the Jew in London, New York, or Washington. I can do more for the body of Jews from its heart than from its toenails. . . .

DECEMBER 20, 1986

Dear Katherine,

This country is my home emotionally, religiously, and in every other way except for the location of my family. When I say that Israel is my home religiously, I mean that as a Jew I should live in the Jewish state, the only Jewish state, the Jewish state which Jews for 2,000 years prayed to return to, and died for, and dreamed of. . . .

Don't read any of the above as blind nationalism. It is not. There are many things about this country which I truly hate (others hate them enough to be driven to leave). I hate the economic idiocy; I hate the way the PLO is allowed to determine the anti-Israeli education of Arab children (this may surprise you but it is true); I hate the fact that members of Parliament are exempt from all the disgusting taxes they impose on the rest of us; I hate the way talent is wasted. There is a long list. But, because I see this place as my home, I don't pile the cons on one side of the scale, and the pros on the other, and come to a conclusion about whether it was "worth" staying here. Home is home and it will take more than irritations to force me to leave. I want to make this place better.

Blu Greenberg (b. 1936)

**I celebrate the cosmic significance of Israel
at the very core of my being.**

With Israel increasingly embedded as a cornerstone of modern Jewish identity, by the end of the twentieth century, the more engaged Jews were with Judaism, the more engaged with Israel they tended to be. The Orthodox Jewish feminist writer Blu Greenberg, for one, identified Israel as being of "cosmic significance" to her, at the core of her identity. This framing was particularly illuminating given her role as one of the great American Jewish bridge builders: creating Jewish-Palestinian dialogues, leading Jewish-Christian interfaith encounters, and, most famously, reconciling not just Judaism and feminism, but Orthodox Judaism and feminism.

As the keynote speaker at the first National Jewish Women's Conference in 1973, and the chair of the first two International Conferences on Feminism and Orthodoxy, Greenberg spearheaded what may be the most influential change agent in Jewish life since Zionism: the women's movement in Judaism. Born in Seattle in 1936, but a lifelong New Yorker with advanced degrees in clinical psychology and Jewish history, she coined the phrase: "Where there's a rabbinic will, there's a halakhic way." The quip reflected her demand that even traditional Judaism had to adjust and empower women. In the following excerpt, she demonstrated, that, usually, where Judaism treads, Zionism follows.

Greenberg's quest to make visible even the most traditional, and traditionally invisible Jewish women has reached into some of Israel's most insular Orthodox communities. The notion from her now-classic work *On Women and Judaism* that Jewish women must stop being "inside persons," parallels the Zionist mission to be Jews comfortably on the street, not just in their homes. Thanks to Diaspora Zionists like Greenberg—and the newfound pride Israel radiated—that Zionist confidence now empowers Jews on the streets of Miami, Montreal, and Melbourne as well as Jerusalem, Haifa, and Tel Aviv.

What Do American Jews Believe? A Symposium (1996)

Living in America, an open society, with every choice to be made; the opportunity to live openly as a Jew without repression or antisemitism, to feel freedom and acceptance so profoundly that you take it for granted—this has made it easier to be a Jew.

But it has also made it harder, for the forces that impelled Jewish identity in the past no longer operate. The underbelly of an open society is an attitude of "Why bother?" Without the tools—knowledge, ties to community, some formal religious expression—it becomes very difficult to hold on. . . .

Israel has done more to reconfirm my faith and identity and gratitude than I could have ever imagined. In no other issue am I more engaged. Though I am an Orthodox Jewish feminist living in America, when I awake each morning the first thing I look for in the paper is news about Israel. But it is more than the immediate urgencies. Simply to think about the miracles of Israel—I must say it—thrills me. Oh, I have my anxieties about the other stories of '48, about integrating the claims of Palestinians to the land, about world opinion, and most of all, about peace that seems so elusive. But I also celebrate the cosmic significance of Israel at the very core of my being.

PART THREE

Torchbearers

Reassessing, Redirecting,
Reinvigorating

13

Torchbearers

Political Zionism

By 1948 the West had endorsed the Zionist idea. A Jewish state giving refuge to Nazism's survivors made sense to many. Most Westerners now considered the Jews a stateless people looking for a home while acknowledging that an ethnic group could have a religious identity too.

Today, many Western intellectuals reject both assumptions. Many European and American progressives repudiated ethnic nationalism following the Holocaust, the sixties' ideological rebellion, the rise of the European Union, then, the Trump-Brexit-Le Pen counterreaction. Most Europeans also downgraded the religious dimension of their national identities, although crosses remain on the flags of Sweden, Norway, the United Kingdom, and twenty-seven other, mostly European, countries.

These ideological shifts made Zionism unpopular, especially amid the Palestinians' accusations of dispossession and some Jews' return to defining Judaism solely as a religion. The United Nations' Zionism-is-racism resolution in 1975 intensified the tendency to single out Israel as an anachronism in the modern world—an imperialist, colonialist, and racist holdover. None of those terms apply. Israel lacks an empire, has historic and security claims to neighboring disputed territory, and is fighting a national (not racial) conflict with Palestinians—whose ethnic-based nationalism with religious overtones these radicals champion.

Beyond the dispute, many Israelis found the terms "Jewish" and "democratic" to be in conflict, despite the biblical roots of core democratic ideas including equality, liberty, and individual dignity.

As a result, in the twenty-first century, the debate about Theodor Herzl's original vision continued. Discussions around Political Zionism focused on justifying the Jewish state against the delegitimizers, while still trying to create a Jewish democracy welcoming to religious and non-religious Jews, to Jews and Arabs, to majority rule and minority rights.

Michael Oren (b. 1955)

Delmore Schwartzian Zionism: "In dreams begin responsibilities."

The life story of the author, diplomat, and centrist politician Michael Oren parallels the Jewish people's story. Born a scrawny New Jersey kid bullied by antisemites, Oren became an Israeli paratrooper in the 1980s, then represented Israel as a politician two decades later. In going from powerlessness to power, Oren—and the Jews—embraced new responsibilities and encountered new dilemmas, especially because of ongoing hostility from the Palestinians and much of the Arab world.

Born in 1955, educated at Columbia University and Princeton, Oren made *aliyah* in 1979. His 2002 blockbuster, *Six Days of War: June 1967 and the Making of the Modern Middle East,* launched him as one of the leading Middle East historians. He followed with the 2007 bestseller, *Power, Faith and Fantasy: The United States in the Middle East, 1776–2006.* He represented Israel in Washington from 2009 to 2013, sacrificing his American citizenship to serve as ambassador.

In his controversial 2015 memoir, *Ally: My Journey across the American-Israel Divide,* Oren attributed the "drift away from an Israel-centric American Jewish identity" to the distancing from Jewish concerns in non-Orthodox Jewish communities with intermarriage rates averaging 70 percent. Unfortunately, a partisan fight over Oren's criticism of President Barack Obama's Israel policies upstaged Oren's challenges regarding modern Jewish identity and Israel affiliations.

Joining the centrist Kulanu Party, Oren was elected to the Knesset in 2015. In 2016 he became deputy minister in the Prime Minister's Office and head of public diplomacy. Having diagnosed Jews' tortured relationship to power, he now witnesses it daily—and tries healing it.

Jews and the Challenge of Sovereignty (*Azure,* 2006)

Ben-Gurion . . . understood that the transformation from a people recoiling from power to a people capable of embracing it would be the single greatest challenge facing Israel. "We must adopt a new approach, new habits of mind," he told listeners shortly before the state's founding. "We must learn to think like a state."

He even coined a Hebrew word for that challenge, *mamlachtiyut*, a neologism which eludes English equivalents but which roughly translates as "acting in a sovereign-like manner." By *mamlachtiyut*, Ben-Gurion meant the Jews' ability to handle power—military power as well as democratic and political power—effectively, justly, responsibly. The Jews of Israel, Ben-Gurion knew, might succeed in repelling Arab armies, in absorbing many times their number of new [Jewish] immigrants, and in creating world-class governmental and cultural institutions, but without *mamlachtiyut*, without the ability to deal with power and take responsibility for its ramifications, they could not ultimately survive. . . .

Arab Muslims . . . have a problem with a palpably powerful Jewish state, and in recent years they hit upon the ideal solution. Terrorism not only requires little by way of technical sophistication or capital outlays, but by forcing Israel to fight back in densely populated areas . . . [thus] drawing international wrath toward Israeli policies, it thrusts to the fore the deepest Jewish ambivalence toward power. . . .

Mamlachtiyut, in fact, was what drew me to Israel in the first place. I grew up just about the only Jewish kid on the block, and the almost daily trouncing I took from the neighborhood gang taught me a great deal about power and the hazards of lacking it. . . .

There followed the Six-Day War—the only event in history in which Jews have been powerful and appreciated for it. I was fascinated by the notion of Jews taking responsibility for themselves as Jews—for their taxes and their sewers and their lampposts. My Zionism was less Herzlian than Schwartzian—as in the beat generation poet Delmore Schwartz. If Herzl said, "If you will it, it is no dream," then Schwartz said (as the title of his 1937 short story put it), "In dreams begin responsibilities." I wanted the responsibility. So I moved to Israel, became a citizen, and joined the army. I put on those red paratrooper boots the first time and was overwhelmed by the realization that I was a member of the first Jewish fighting force in 2,000 years, a Jew from New Jersey lucky enough to live at a time when I could serve a sovereign Jewish state. . . .

Today, as an Israeli, I must confront questions that derive from having power. I had to decide, for instance, whether to support the construction of a fence which may provide greater security against terrorist attacks, but which evokes the very ghetto walls that Zionism aspired to topple. . . .

Yet, in spite of the immense forces arrayed against it, Israel has not only stood up to the test of power . . . it has presented to the world a model of balance between the requirements of justice and morality and the requisites of power. . . . Israel does not evict a people that threatens its existence—and the last century is rife with such expulsions, especially in the West—but rather offers that people an opportunity to live with it side by side, even offering large parts of its own historical and spiritual homeland.

Israel's soldiers go into battle armed not only with guns and grenades but with pocket-size, laminated cards containing the IDF code of ethics. . . . Israelis fight, asking themselves at every stage whether in fact they are doing the right thing, the moral thing, the Jewish thing. . . .

Our responsibility today is to prove to ourselves, and the world, that the phrase "Jewish state" is not in fact a contradiction in terms. Let us remain cognizant not only of our great achievements—the Nobel Prizes our scientists are awarded or the European championships our basketball players win—but also of the weighty responsibilities we bear: the responsibilities of reconciling our heritage with our sovereignty, our strength with our compassion, and our will to survive with our desire to inspire others.

Tal Becker (b. 1974)

**Zionism was never only a response to crisis—
it was a values project from its inception.**

Herzl's calculation that a Jewish state would normalize Jewish life has, so far, proven only half right. While the Jewish experience in Israel has been naturalized, freed of exilic doublethink, the Jewish Problem persists. "Zionists" replaced Jews as targets.

Conditioned to fight oppression, many Jews rally around Israel when it's attacked. To Tal Becker, this Crisis Zionism blocks the Aspirational Zionism this "Values Nation" deserves. After endorsing Political Zionism, justifying Israel's rights as a normal nation state, Becker wants Israel to be an exceptional state too.

A scholar diplomat, Becker has combined senior fellowships at the Shalom Hartman Institute and the Washington Institute for Near East Policy with serving as a legal adviser in Israel's foreign ministry. Born to a Moroccan father and Australian mother, raised in Melbourne, a national leader of the Religious Zionist youth movement B'nai Akiva, Tal made *aliyah* in 1994. Trained in law and international relations, he served in the United Nations and endured the daily grind of negotiations with Palestinians. Nevertheless, Becker remains idealistic, pushing the Zionist debate beyond survival to fulfilling a "common moral calling."

Beyond Survival: Aspirational Zionism (2011)

For many years now, the conversation about Israel in the Jewish world has taken a familiar form. With rare exceptions, our sovereign project is spoken of in Jewish communities across the globe with pride about the past and anxiety about the future. . . .

Unlike the Political Zionism that underpins [this] crisis model . . . promoting a state that defines its Jewishness in minimalistic and, largely if not exclusively, survivalist terms . . . [is] a discussion about Israel founded on values . . . the unique opportunity and responsibility that come with belonging to a people 3,500 years old. The question it seeks to address is not "How do we survive?" It is this: As custodians of an ancient story, as bearers of a particular moral tradition, and as a people shaped by particular historical experience, what form and nature should a Jewish sovereign society take? . . .

Israel is Jewish in the sense that it has a Jewish majority to maintain Jewish political self-determination, the Law of Return enables all Jews to find refuge here, the state feels an obligation to protect Jews worldwide, and the state's public symbols and days of rest have Jewish origins. But in what ways can it be said that Israel's policies or society reflect Jewish values or aspirations? By this, I do not mean the way in which Israel meets Torah standards or approaches theocracy. I mean . . . the kind of Zionism that a values narrative engenders: one which imagines Israel not as a "normal state" but as a state which gives public expression to the unique history and tradition of the Jewish people. It argues that the "Chosen People" in the Holy Land need to ... debate, articulate, and ultimately seek to implement what the prophetic vision of a sovereign nation that lives in righteousness means in modern times. ...

This Aspirational Zionism would ask more aggressively how we create a society that is both Jewish and democratic—recognizing both as values that need to live in harmony with one another. It would examine options for a responsible and lasting peace not only through the prism of Israel's basic need and right for security and stability, but also through a Jewish prism that sees the relentless and genuine pursuit of a responsible peace as a moral and quintessentially Jewish obligation. And it would examine Israel's social and economic challenges by asking not only how to enhance prosperity and reward excellence, but also by honoring the supreme Jewish obligation to care for the needy and vulnerable. ...

Indeed, Zionism was never only a response to crisis—it was a values project from its inception. In fact, many current Israeli policies and the debates around them can be understood on moral grounds, even if they are more often couched today in survivalist terms. ...

Conducted responsibly, [today's] values-driven conversation creates a bigger tent in which our differences are less rancorous and divisive. Such a conversation has the potential to transcend political divides, not because it resolves disputes, but because it recognizes that what ultimately connects the Jewish people to Israel is not a shared fate or policy position, but a common moral calling. ...

Michael Walzer (b. 1935)

Universal statism: I want the state to be as good as it can be, but above all I want it to be.

As some radical leftists turned on Israel and Zionism, garnering most of the headlines, others remained Zionist. The political philosopher and co-editor of *Dissent* for decades, Michael Walzer, was an early critic of Israel's control of the West Bank while steadfastly championing the

Zionist Idea. He continues to balance his policy critiques with support for the state, explaining: "We can accept severe standards so long as the severity isn't designed, as it often is, just for us." He also refuses to apologize for the antisemite's confusion about the Jewish mix of religion and nation, writing, "We should not take responsibility on ourselves for the hatred we inspire among (some) of our neighbors."

In an academic career at Harvard and Princeton, Walzer wrote landmark works on Just War theory, the search for economic justice, the justification of the modern nation-state, and the balance between majority rule and minority rights in multicultural democracies. His most influential Jewish book, *Exodus and Revolution* (1985), sees the Jews' liberation from Egypt as the template for many freedom quests. This "Exodus politics," balancing "political Messianism" with "this-worldly complexity," identified a key source of vertigo in Zionist and Israeli politics: The constant toggling between the petty and the profound, the reductionist and the redemptive, often escalates minor issues into existential crises, while trivializing consequential debates.

In 2012 Walzer described his "half-*aliyah*," his intimate connection with Israel while living in America. He started with the Jewish nation-religion anomaly, having written elsewhere that "The constant mixing of incongruous elements *is* our history, and this is what I would teach our children." As he explained, his political Zionism expresses his commitment to "universal statism," that peoples best flourish with national sovereignty. Thus, he supports Israel's existence and Law of Return, along with Palestinians' right to a state and right of return. In addition to being a noteworthy Progressive Zionist, reconciling liberalism and Zionism, Walzer is a leading Political Zionist, understanding Zionism in the context of liberal nationalism as normative philosophically, and admirable historically.

The State of Righteousness: Liberal Zionists
Speak Out (*Huffington Post*, 2012)

I have been a Zionist ever since the year of my bar mitzvah, 1948, when I sought out every possible piece of news (that was available in Johnstown, Pa.) about Israel's war of independence and covered my school notebooks with hand-drawn maps of the new state and its battlefields. But I never went to live in Israel. In 1957, right after we were married, my wife and I spent a summer there, thinking about *aliyah*, but we came back to the States for graduate school and soon had children and a life here in the U.S. We chose instead what Shlomo Avineri calls *hatzi aliyah*—literally, "half-immigration"—so that now, nearing the end of our lives, we have spent years in Israel, over some 40 visits and several sabbaticals, and we probably have more friends there than here. So what is this half-way Zionism?

It is first of all the emotion-laden belief of someone who grew up during World War Two that the Jews need a state, and that this need is so critical and so urgent that it overrides whatever injustices statehood has brought. We still have to oppose the injustices with all the resources we can muster, but we can't give up the state. So I participate vicariously in Israeli politics by supporting my social-democratic and peacenik friends. I want the state to be as good as it can be, but above all I want it to be.

My Zionism is also a universal statism. I think that everybody who needs a state should have one, not only the Jews but also the Armenians, the Kurds, the Tibetans, the South Sudanese—and the Palestinians. The modern state is the only effective agency for physical protection, economic management, and welfare provision. What the most oppressed and impoverished people in the world today most need is a state of their own, a decent state acting on their behalf. I feel some hostility, therefore, toward people who want to "transcend" the state—and I am especially hostile toward those who insist that the transcendence has to begin with the Jews.

My Zionism is a secular nationalism. The Jewish people have a two-fold character: We are a nation—*Am Yisra'el*, the people Israel—and we are what Americans call a "community of faith." This is not a common combination; it is shaped by the peculiar history of the Jews. But statehood requires separation: the Jewish state should be an expression of the people, not of the faith (which many of our people don't share, at least not in its Orthodox form)....

The Zionist project is central to Jewish life because it has led to the revival of the Hebrew language and the creation of a modern Hebrew culture—novels, poems, plays, and films of remarkable power—and because it makes possible the enactment of what many of us have always imagined to be Jewish values: justice, above all. . . . Needless to say, we are not there yet, not even close. High ambition requires a long life, and Israel is a very young state.

Aharon Barak (b. 1936)

There are many democratic states in the world. But only the State of Israel is a democratic, Jewish nation.

The passing of Israel's Basic Laws in 1992 and 1994 empowered its Supreme Court to take the lead in the tug of war between Zionism's Jewish and democratic heritages. "The purpose of this basic law," the Knesset declared, "is to protect human dignity and liberty so as to anchor in a basic law the values of the State of Israel as a Jewish and democratic state." Aharon Barak, the president of Israel's Supreme Court from 1995 to 2006, used the laws to expand the judiciary's role in multiple areas of Israeli life.

Barak's self-proclaimed "Constitutional Revolution" included dramatic new choreography in Israel's delicate dance between Judaism and democracy. Barak entered the debate with explicitly Zionist, meaning nationalist, assumptions. He explained, in an oft-quoted lecture, that "The state is 'Jewish' not in a halakhic-religious sense, but in the sense that Jews have the right to immigrate to it, and their national experience is the experience of the state," expressed through speaking Hebrew as the official language and publicly observing Jewish holidays, for example.

To critics like Justice Menachem Elon, a Religious Zionist, Barak's approach "abstracted" the word Jewish "of all independent and original meaning," treating it "as an artificial attachment that is subordinate to the concept of 'democracy,'" even though "the expression 'democratic' . . . appears second, after the expression 'Jewish.'" One of Barak's most controversial decisions, *Katz v. Regional Rabbinical Court*, found in 1995 that Knesset law and common law treating marriage as a legal contract between equals trump the Rabbinical Court's reading of Jewish marital law.

Barak recalled learning to love democracy the hard way—missing it while suffering in Lithuania's Kovno ghetto during the Holocaust. Having also "learned the extent to which racist treatment, dictated by religious or national belonging, can degrade human character," Barak insists Zionism was born to negate racism.

After the war, his family wandered through Europe, arriving in Palestine in 1947. Barak worked to combat "any patterns of discrimination on the basis of religion or nationality," first as a Hebrew University law student, professor, and dean; as Israel's attorney general from 1975 through 1978; and as a Supreme Court justice from 1978 through 2006.

Barak's revolution continues every time Israelis—and Palestinians—turn to Israel's increasingly activist Supreme Court to check the decisions of the government or even the Knesset. His influence on Zionism continues to resonate in Court decisions that follow Barak's logic in defining Zionism as having a "decisive—if not exclusive—influence in forming . . . the 'heritage of Israel,'" and among those for whom those Zionist and democratic values take precedence over Jewish legal precedents.

Address to the 34th World Zionist Congress in Jerusalem (June 18, 2002)

A "Jewish state" is a state whose history is bound up with the history of the Jewish people, whose principal language is Hebrew, and whose main holidays reflect its national mission. A "Jewish state" is a state which counts the resettlement of the Jewish people in its fields, its cities, and villages among its highest concerns. A "Jewish state" is a state that embodies the memory of the Jews who were slaughtered in the Holocaust, and whose purpose is [in Ben-Gurion's words] to be a "solution to the problem of the Jewish people lacking a homeland and independence through the renewal of Jewish statehood in the Land of Israel."

A "Jewish state" is a state that fosters Jewish culture, Jewish education, and love of the Jewish people. A "Jewish state" is a state whose values are the values of freedom, justice, righteousness, and peace within the Jewish heritage. . . . A "Jewish state" is a state in which the values of the Torah of Israel, the values of the Jewish tradition, and the values of *halakhah* [Jewish law] are among the basic values. . . .

In truth, Jews are given a special key to enter the State of Israel. This is the essence of Zionism, and this the essence of our Jewish tradition. This need not entail discrimination against those who are not Jewish. Indeed, when an essential goal embodied in the founding of the state is that it will serve as a national home to Jews wherever they are, giving the right of *aliyah* to Jews does not entail discrimination against those who are not Jews. It entails recognition of difference without discrimination. . . .

Yael "Yuli" Tamir (b. 1954)

Liberal nationalism and the power of home.

While some religious and conservative critics blasted Aharon Barak for privileging democratic values over Jewish ones, some from his left believed that in "abstracting" core Jewish values, Barak had minimized the tensions between the two. Other Israelis, such as Yael "Yuli" Tamir, have acknowledged the tensions and believe that democratic values must dominate. Tamir nevertheless justifies incorporating a Jewish dimension into the Israeli public sphere, as long as the Israeli majority desires it.

Rejecting modern liberals' push for neutral states and against nationalism, Tamir argues that "every nationalism privileges a group." She appreciates nationalism because, she says, she was "born into" Zionism. Tami helped found Peace Now in 1978 and served in Israel's cabinet and Knesset on and off between 1999 and 2009. "My Zionism defines my identity," she writes, "my core beliefs, my historical perspective, my own private history, the language I speak, my way of life, the place I live in, the issues that irritate me, my hopes, my fears, my pride and shame, as well as my dreams."

Tamir's 1993 book *Liberal Nationalism* prioritized "liberalism" over "nationalism," while justifying nationalism. "Underlying nationalism is a range of perceptive understandings of the human situation," she wrote, "of what makes human life meaningful and creative, as well as a set of praiseworthy values" including "belonging, loyalty, and solidarity." In 2000 she explained how the "ideal state of neutrality misconstrues the role of culture in public life," failing to create a "home" for a majority of its citizens. A pillar of what critics dismiss as "The Republic of North Tel Aviv," the caricature of Israel's metropolis as too cosmopolitan and unpatriotic, Tamir continues her Zionist twist on modern universalism, insisting that the world can be bettered by deepening liberals' connections to their democratic communities and cultures.

A Jewish and Democratic State (2000)

This ideal state of neutrality misconstrues the role of culture in public life. Trying to restrict culture to the private sphere, it empties the state of its symbolic role. The result is a state that can serve all its citizens impartially but cannot be a home to any of them. A home is not an institution, not even a fair and efficient one, but a place to which one is tied emotionally, which reflects one's history, memories, fears, and hopes. A home cannot have merely universal features; it must always be embedded in the particular.

So here is the source of the tension: if Israel is a home to the Jewish people, its non-Jewish citizens will feel estranged from it. Must it then shed its particularist nature, be a state like all others? Israel should indeed aspire to normality. But every state must operate within a cultural-historical context; it must have an official language(s), a flag, an anthem, public holidays, and public celebrations. It must build monuments, print money and stamps, adopt a historical narrative and a vision of the future. As feminists and members of national and racial minorities discovered long ago, the idea that a state can be void of any cultural, historical, or linguistic affiliation is a misleading illusion—which is not only naive but also oppressive.

It is therefore one of Israel's advantages that it openly declares its cultural national bias. This allows those who are harmed by this bias— mainly its Palestinian citizens, but also other non-Jews—to explain the source of their grievances. . . .

Democratic life constantly produces losers, and is always a source of discontent. The modern conception of democracy is, in many ways, majoritarian. It assumes that all citizens must be allowed to participate in an open democratic process, and then the majority wins. . . .

Israel can be a Jewish and democratic state if its citizens aspire that it be one, and if Judaism and democracy concur on a wide enough range of practices to allow such a state to function. At present, both conditions are fulfilled.

Ze'ev Maghen (b. 1964)

The power of preferential love.

Yuli Tamir felt compelled to defend liberal nationalism in part because since the 1960s the universalist impulse had grown throughout the West. For Jews, though, it was not a new phenomenon: Jewish fascination with universalism dates back to the Enlightenment, when many assimilated European Jews aspired to become citizens of the world.

Many Zionists from right to left reject this cosmopolitanism, believing with Theodor Herzl that humans can join together, living good lives and doing great things through particular, tribal affiliations. Among them is Ze'ev Maghen, a professor of Persian language and Islamic history at Bar-Ilan University and Shalem College, an Israeli tank-corps veteran, and a former International Frisbee Gold Champion. His 2010 "philosophical rampage," *John Lennon and the Jews,* endorses "an all-out campaign on every front imaginable to unseat Universalism in favor of Preferential Love, and to subject Rationalism to the sovereignty of Romance." His launching pad: attacking John Lennon's renowned ode to universalism, "Imagine." Thanks to Maghen's charming, coruscating, cascading tirades, more and more Zionists find themselves singling out Lennon's "Imagine" as the false god of faux cosmopolitanism that aspirational Zionists counter with their faith in achieving universal-good-through-particularist affiliations.

John Lennon and the Jews: A Philosophical Rampage (2010)

I *don't* want John's vision [in his song "Imagine"] to be fulfilled speedily and in our days. I don't want it to be fulfilled—*ever*. . . . John's beautiful ballad is in reality a death march, a requiem mass for the human race. His seemingly lovely lyrics constitute in truth the single most hideous and unfortunate combination of syllables ever to be put to music. The realization of *his* dream—even in large part—would inevitably entail the wholesale and irreversible destruction of the dreams, hopes, happinesses, and *very reason for living* of yourself and every single person you know. If we—who for so long unthinkingly admired and warbled-off Lennon's words, were to live to see his wish come true, the result would be more staggeringly horrific and more devastatingly ruinous than you could ever possibly—*imagine*. . . .

It's time to propose. Down I go on one knee. I look dreamily up into your eyes. I reach deftly into the pocket of my Giorgio Armani blazer and pull out a rock the size of Venus. I take your two hands in mine, and, gently caressing them, I coo: "My darling, I love you. I love you *soooo* much. I love you as much as I love . . . as much as I love . . . as much as I love that *other* woman, the one walking down the street over there. See her? Oh, and *that* one, too . . . I love you as much as I love *everybody else* on this planet, and for that matter, I love you as much as I love the animals, too, and the weeds, and the plankton and—Oh *God*! What's that searing, indescribable pain in my groin? Hey, where are you going, my *daaaaarliiiiing*?"

No one gets turned-on by "universal" love. It doesn't get you up in the morning, it doesn't give you goose-bumps or make you feel all warm and tingly inside. . . .

Because love means preference. The kind of love that means anything, the kind of love we all really want and need and live for, the kind of love that is *worth* anything to anyone—that is worth *every*thing to *every*one—is love that by its very nature, by its very definition, distinguishes and prefers. . . .

We Jews are and have always been not primarily adherents to a set of spiritual dogmas, but *members of an extended family*, of a nation, and of a "tribe." ...

You are a Jew, and *another* Jew—the heart that was huge enough to imagine the State of Israel and then bring that imagination down here to earth, Dr. Theodor Herzl—once declared plainly: "The greatest happiness in life, is to be that which one is." I couldn't agree more. . . . So I figure, if you *are* going to be who you are—a Jew—*do it up*. Don't be a "by-default Jew," a "checkbook Jew," a "High-Holiday Jew," a "peripheral Jew" or a "marginal Jew"—*Yuk!* Be a "bold, breathless" Jew, be a "wild, wanton" Jew, be an "I'm going to milk this cultural identity thing for *everything it's got*" Jew—be a knowledgeable, thirsty, caring, daring, *actively involved* Jew. . . .

Tapping into this vast and plumbless resource is not an ability acquired solely through learning or reading (although this is a *major* ingredient, I hasten to emphasize); it is first and foremost a function of connection, of belonging, of powerful love. If you reach out and grasp your people's hands—*you were there*. . . . You participated in what they did . . . fought their battles, felt their feelings and learned their lessons. You tended flocks with Rachel, and slaved in Potiphar's house with Joseph; you sang in the wilderness with Miriam, and toppled the walls of Jericho with Joshua. . . . You were shot with your family in the forests of Poland, and dug a mass grave and perished there at Babi Yar; you revived your dead language, you resurrected your sapped strength, you returned to yourself and renewed the lapsed covenant, you arose like a lion and hewed out your freedom on the plains and the mountains of your old-new land. . . .

Daniel Gordis (b. 1959)

People thrive and flourish most when they live in societies in which their language, their culture, and their history, and their sense of purpose are situated at the very center of public life.

Ironically, Zionist particularism and Ze'ev Maghen's notion of preferential love should resonate with many who hate Israel. According to the senior vice president and Koret Distinguished Fellow at Shalem College, Daniel Gordis, Israeli democracy offers a template for Arab reformers. As American progressives and European Union postmodernists dream of universalism, Israeli democracy reflects a Herzlian, *altneuland* approach: synthesizing tradition with modernity, and group prerogatives culturally, even religiously, with individual rights. Expectations that any democratic successor to the Arab Spring would try implementing an American model of civic nationalism overlook Islam's centrality as an identity anchor in most Arab countries. More realistic is Israel's model guaranteeing individual rights for all while treating a nation's cultural heritage as relevant, and worth preserving.

The founding dean of the Ziegler School of Rabbinic Studies at the University of Judaism, Gordis arrived with his wife and three children in Jerusalem for sabbatical in 1998. Deciding that, "on many levels, Israel felt like home in ways that America never had," they decided to stay, and enjoy their "chance to be at center stage during one of the most dramatic episodes of Jewish history—the creation of the first modern Jewish state."

Gordis published selected emails from his transition year in 2002. The book title, *If a Place Can Make You Cry,* refers to his grandfather's tears in New York when Anwar Sadat flew to Jerusalem in 1977 and his own tears in Baltimore when Yitzhak Rabin was assassinated in 1995. In time, Gordis came to understand "everything I never let those memories teach me. After all, if there's a place in this world that can make you cry, isn't that where you ought to be?"

In *The Promise of Israel: Why Its Seemingly Greatest Weakness Is Actually Its Greatest Strength* (2012), Gordis explained why Israel should not only be an inspiration to the Jewish people, but also to its Arab neighbors—and the West. Obviously, the promise of Israel has not yet turned into the salvation of the Middle East. But the analysis reflects Zionism's continuing ambition to harmonize with its environment—and contribute to humanity.

The Promise of Israel (2012)

Israel is marginalized and reviled because of a battle over the idea of the nation-state. . . . Israel, the quintessential modern example of the ethnic nation-state, came on the scene just as most of the Western world had decided that the time had come to be rid of the nation-state. . . .

The conflict in the Middle East is about borders and statehood. But the conflict *about* the Middle East is over universalism versus particularism, over competing conceptions of how human beings ought to organize themselves. . . .

Imagine a world in which instead of maligning Israel, the international community encouraged emerging ethnic nations to emulate Israel. Egyptians, for example, may have demonstrated for regime change and for democracy, but they did not gather to demonstrate against Islam or their Arab identity. They have no plans to become the "America" of Africa, secular and heterogeneous. They wish (or so the most Western of them claim) to celebrate their Muslim heritage and thousands of years of Egyptian history and to join the family of modern, democratic nations. As they do so, to whom can they look for a model of a stable, prosperous, and open state based on a shared religion and heritage? There is no denying that Egypt, Syria, Pakistan, and many other Muslim countries would benefit from being more like Israel instead of hoping for its destruction. . . .

The whole world would benefit from thinking in terms of the questions Israel raises. . . . All citizens of every nation would benefit from asking themselves, explicitly, what values they hope their nation will inculcate in its citizens, what culture they are committed to preserving and nourishing. . . .

Battered by Europe and by history, the Jews emerged from the Shoah with a sense that more than anything, they needed a state of their own. Just as some of the world thought that it might move beyond nations, the Jews (who had dreamt of a restored Zion for two millennia) now intuited that nothing could be more urgent than finally re-creating their state. Zionism and post-war Europe were thus destined for conflict.

Zionism was not a matter of mere refuge; it was a matter of breathing new life into the Jewish people.... of re-imagining Judaism for a world post-destruction....

Israel is a country based on a belief that human beings live richer and more meaningful lives when those lives are deeply rooted in a culture that they have inherited and that they can bequeath. Human life flourishes most when a society's public square is committed to conversations rooted in that people's literature, language, history, narrative, and even religion....

The Zionist experiment . . . has been a matter of cherishing the Jewish roots of the Jewish state, and at the same time, forcing them to participate in a free market of ideas with competing notions from the Western world. It has been about giving the Jewish tradition a privileged place in the public square while preserving the rights of those who do not wish to observe Jewish law. For instance, intercity buses do not run on the Sabbath and holidays, the food in the army is kosher, and bread cannot be legally displayed for sale during the week of Passover. But local Tel Aviv buses, for example, *do* run on the Sabbath, non-kosher restaurants can be found all over the country, and bread is still obtainable during Passover if one wants it.

The mélange of views that is Zionism simply states unabashedly that Israel is a country, to paraphrase Abraham Lincoln, "by the Jews, of the Jews, and for the Jews," while . . . also working to guarantee the rights of non-Jews in its society....

Leon Wieseltier (b. 1952)

Bitzu'ism: **Pragmatic Zionism.**

In an age of delegitimization, some academics targeted Zionism as proof of the illegitimacy of nationalism—even while supporting Palestinian and other "politically correct" nationalisms. When in 2003, the Jewish historian Tony Judt declared Israel "an anachronism" and endorsed a "bi-national state," the *New Republic's* literary editor Leon

Wieseltier eloquently rebutted his arguments, calling Judt's bi-national state "not the alternative *for* Israel" but "the alternative *to* Israel." Recognizing that "Judt and his editors have crossed the line from the criticism of Israel's policy to the criticism of Israel's existence," Wieseltier deemed such attacks not only counterproductive—by emboldening Israeli and Palestinian rejectionists—but immoral.

The Brooklyn-born son of Holocaust survivors, educated at Columbia, Harvard, and Oxford, and author of moving musings on mourning, Kaddish, Wieseltier believes that American Jews have become "the spoiled brats of Jewish history," lucky to be free but shockingly "unlettered" in Hebrew—which he considers a portal into both Jewish civilization and fulfillment. "As a Jew," Wieseltier says, "I live in Hebrew. . . . The Jew's homeland is not only soil; it is the language. America has the first major Jewish culture to decide that it is possible to develop and bequeath the Jewish tradition without the Jewish language. It is a crime. [Jews] believe that any Jewish expression is equal to any other Jewish expression. . . . I study Maimonides and they cook chicken soup, and we are all Jews together—but it isn't true."

Here, Wieseltier celebrates the pragmatic, *y'alla,* let's-get-it-done, streak in Zionism that built the state and performed miracles, including saving thousands of Ethiopian Jews. That modern exodus marked the first time a majority white country willingly imported thousands of black immigrants into freedom.

Israel's actions not only refute the racism blood libel. They affirm the most basic, Herzlian Zionist mission: having one place where Jews in trouble can go.

Brothers and Keepers: Black Jews and the Meaning of Zionism (*New Republic*, 1985)

Operation Moses is an essential event, in that it discloses essences: the essence of the obligation to assist, and the essence of the national movement of the Jewish people. . . . This was in accordance with the Law of Return of July 5, 1950, that sublime symbol of Jewish self-help, which states that "every Jew has the right to immigrate to the country." . . .

There is a Hebrew term that is hard to translate. It is *bitzu'ism*. An accurate and awkward English equivalent would be "implementation-ism." During the 1930s and 1940s there was a notion called "practical Zionism," which conveys a bit of the temper of the term. It lies very deep in the psyche and the political culture of Israel. To call somebody a *bitzu'ist* is to pay him or her a very high compliment. The *bitzu'ist* is the builder, the irrigator, the pilot, the gunrunner, the settler. In the history of the Jewish state the *bitzu'ist* is really a social type: crusty, resource-ful, impatient, sardonic, effective, not much in need of thought but not much in need of sleep either. . . .

The intensity of the Israeli passion for activism undoubtedly owes something to the rather mixed consequences of Jewish quietism through the ages. For centuries the Jews had dreamed of deliverance, but they were not delivered. Now they would become deliverers. . . .

No explanation should be necessary for taking care of one's own. The community is not the only moral unit, but it is a moral unit. Moreover, the alternative is never between helping your own and helping every-body. Universalism, if the truth be told, is usually an alibi for inaction, accompanied by a moral thrill. In the real world the position of the uni-versalist usually comes to this: that nobody be saved unless everybody be saved. To be sure, it is neither easy nor enviable to choose from among the suffering. But practically speaking, there is no such thing as univer-salism. It is impossible to help everybody. A commitment on the part of many communities to help their own, on the other hand, adds up to many people helped. . . .

It was not religion that inspired Operation Moses. It was a strenu-ous sense of peoplehood. . . . The Israeli intervention on behalf of the *"falashas"* provides the most dramatic illustration since the early years of Israel, when virtually all the Jewish populations of the Middle East and North Africa were brought to Israel "on eagle's wings," of the funda-mental hypothesis of national Jewish identity: that a Jew from Ethiopia or Yemen has more in common with a Jew from Poland or France than with a non-Jew from Ethiopia or Yemen. It is a scandalous suggestion. It is both true and false, obviously. To the extent that it is false, Israeli society does not work. The brutal ethnic tensions of recent years are owed in good measure to the neglect of these differences among Jews. Still, they have not yet vanquished the similarities—or, more to the point, the sense of the similarities. It is the consciousness that counts. These Jews will live together exactly as long and as well as they feel that they should live together.

Irwin Cotler (b. 1940)

The original aboriginal people.

The attacks on Political Zionism often reduced it to Israel advocacy. But Theodor Herzl's Zionism sought not just to save the Jewish people, but to redeem the world. Canada's "Mr. Human Rights," Professor Irwin Cotler, epitomizes this dual mission.

Born in Montreal in 1940, educated at McGill University and Yale University, Cotler served as a professor of law at McGill and directed its Human Rights Program from 1973 until he was elected to the Canadian Parliament in 1999. For decades he crisscrossed the globe, defending Andrei Sakharov and Anatoly Scharansky in the Soviet Union, Nelson Mandela in South Africa, Jacobo Timmerman in Argentina, Muchtar Pakpahan in Indonesia, and many other dissidents.

Serving as Canada's minister of justice and attorney general from 2003 to 2006, Cotler championed indigenous rights. Once, when meeting with aboriginal—First Nations—law students, Cotler said the rabbis taught that true love comes from knowing what hurts the other. Coming from another indigenous people, the Jews, he said, he understood their pain. Moved, one student responded: "You know, we thought this was going to be another white man with the usual 'blah-blah.' Welcome—one aboriginal people to another." In this selection, adapted from a speech to the United Jewish Communities General Assembly, Cotler articulates his Zionist vision of the Jews as the original aboriginal people—an indigenous people returning to their old-new homeland not only to resist antisemitism but to pursue justice globally.

Speech to the United Jewish Communities
General Assembly (November 17, 2006)

Israel, rooted in the Jewish people's eternal story as an Abrahamic people, is a prototypical First Nation or indigenous people, just as the Jewish religion is a prototypical indigenous religion, the first of the Abrahamic religions.

In a word, the Jewish people is the only people that still inhabits the same land, embraces the same religion, studies the same Torah, hearkens to the same prophets, speaks the same indigenous language—Hebrew— and bears the same indigenous name, Israel, as it did 3,500 years ago.

Israel, then, is the aboriginal homeland of the Jewish people across space and time. It is not just a homeland for the Jewish people, a place of refuge, asylum and protection. It is the homeland of the Jewish people, wherever and whenever it may be; and its birth certificate originates in its inception as a First Nation, and not simply, however important, in its United Nations international birth certificate.

The State of Israel, then, as a political and juridical entity, overlaps with the "aboriginal Jewish homeland"; it is, in international legal terms, a successor state to the biblical, or aboriginal, Jewish kingdoms. But that indigenous homeland is also claimed by another people, the Palestinian/ Arab people, who see it as their place and patrimony.

The existence of a parallel claim does not vitiate that of the Jewish people or cause it to resonate any less as memory and memoir of homeland— where homeland represents history, roots, religion, language, culture, literature, law, custom, family, myth, and values. Rather, the equities of the claim mandate the logic of Israeli-Palestinian partition—a logic which in moral and juridical terms requires that a just solution be organized around the "principle of least injustice," and that includes mutual recognition of the legitimacy of two states for two peoples....

Israel is an antidote to Jewish vulnerability. It is not the case, as it sometimes said, that if there had been no Holocaust, there would not have been a State of Israel, as if a state could somehow even compensate for the murder of six million Jews. It is the other way around: If there had been an Israel, there would not have been a Holocaust, or other horrors of Jewish history. . . .

Today, Zionism doesn't just protect us from that which is inconceivable yet possible—it opens up all kinds of new possibilities.

We are . . . one people, with a common heritage and with a common destiny, and with values that underpin that common heritage and destiny, wherever we are. . . . We should always remember that this is the people that has "the rule of law" as our heritage, that has the notion of Jewish humanitarian law, as our doctrine, that has *"tzedek, tzedek, tirdof"*—"justice, justice, shall you pursue"—as a moral imperative, that has *"Shalom! Shalom!"*—"Peace, Peace"—as our abiding hope, as our abiding dream, as our abiding will.

Gadi Taub (b. 1965)

The Zionism of liberty.

Anti-Zionists and Greater Land of Israel enthusiasts agree on one thing: the settlement enterprise is the centerpiece of modern Zionism. The historian, screenwriter, and children's author Gadi Taub resists this land obsession of the right—rejecting the settlement enterprise without succumbing to the nihilism that is too pervasive among post-Zionist settlement critics. The son of a Czech immigrant who fled Bratislava shortly after the Nazis invaded Czechoslovakia and then wandered until arriving in Palestine, Taub starts by admitting "my own Zionism is instinctive. It precedes arguments. Because I cannot forget this picture: a Jewish boy, my father, who has only water under his feet, who has no piece of land under the sand to stand on."

Nevertheless, Taub has come to articulate the ideas behind the picture. His 2010 Hebrew manifesto, "What Is Zionism?" emphasizes that Zionism helped the Emancipated Jew achieve four key essentials: freedom, democracy, national self-determination, and the Land of Israel. His book, *The Settlers and the Struggle over the Meaning of Zionism,* also published in 2010, defends political Zionism's commitment to building a democratic national state, in contrast to the "religious movement" that put *"Eretz Yisra'el*—the Land of Israel" at "the center of the Zionist project." Taub also takes on the post-Zionists, whose fury at settlements has soured them on Zionism. "They only speak in terms of individual human rights," he says. "Their disgust with Jewish national sentiment has marginalized them."

In this selection, Taub distinguishes between this "Blood and Soil" Zionism "of land," which he finds abhorrent, and the "Zionism of liberty," which he understands as seeking a democratic Jewish state that allows the free, enlightened, humanist New Jew to flourish individually and collectively.

In Defense of Zionism (*Fathom*, Autumn 2014)

Zionism is seriously misconceived outside of Israel. It is identified to a large extent with support of the settlements. However, the settlements are an undermining of Zionism rather than a continuation of it; not just politically but also ideologically.

There are two different conceptions of Zionism which I call "the Zionism of liberty," which is about self-determination, and "the Zionism of land," which is about redeeming the old Jewish homeland. . . .

Zionism emerged in the best century for Jews in a long time, [the nineteenth century], certainly better than what came after it; it cannot be just a reaction to antisemitism. The conclusion was that if liberty is anchored in democracy, which is anchored in national identity, then the way to make people free was a democratic nation-state. Zionism was the application of this to the Jews. It's that simple; it's the application of the universal right to self-determination, even before the notion was popularized by Woodrow Wilson. . . .

[Once, in a documentary], Holocaust survivors answered the same question, "What was the happiest moment for you when the war ended?" . . . One woman said, "When I arrived at the ship (of the illegal *aliyah*) and I saw a sign saying *knisa* (entrance in Hebrew)." The interviewer was taken aback. "You were just liberated from Auschwitz and you were going to Israel, but that was the most exhilarating moment for you?" She answered, "You misunderstand; I had never seen Hebrew letters that size before."

My heart stopped. Most Israelis cannot understand this today: for her, Hebrew was something small, something you have to hide. To use the brilliant metaphor of the gay liberation movement, you can say that Jews had been "closeted" for centuries, denying their own identity. For her, here was the possibility of a public sphere in her own language, based on her own identity; this made her happier than anything else. This is the crux of Zionism: that you don't need to be a Jew in your own home and deny your Judaism outside it.

Therefore, if you are a true Zionist, you should support Palestinian self-determination; not just as a compromise or pragmatic consideration, but because at heart, this is your moral basis: the universality of self-determination. If you demand that people stop excluding Jews, you cannot exclude Palestinians.

Bernard-Henri Lévy (b. 1948)

The Rock of Israel: though I was then so tepidly Jewish, there I found the most unexpected of inner homelands, a rock on which I knew immediately that I would lean.

France's celebrity philosopher, Bernard-Henri Lévy, is a bold, thoughtful, provocative thinker whose approach to Zionism vividly captures Diaspora Jewry's many ambivalences. Although raised as a universalist Jew, he discovered the need for Jewish nationalism. While yearning for Israel to be an ideal state, he defends it as the only realistic response to millennia of hatred. And although happy to live very well in France, he nevertheless feels reassured by this inspiring Jewish insurance policy.

Levy argues that *The Genius of Judaism*, as his 2017 book is titled, lies in its "vaporous" qualities: its ability "to produce a little of the intelligence that will offer people, all people, a little of the teaching that they need to be different from others." Similarly, he uncovers a genius of Zionism in Israel's ability to live, flourish, and impress as a moral pluralistic democracy—amid all the abstractions and ambiguities.

Born in Algeria in 1948, raised in Paris, BHL—as he is widely known in France—built his reputation fighting human rights abuses in Bangladesh, Bosnia, and Darfur, while rejecting the totalitarian left's anti-Americanism and anti-Semitism. In 1967 he surprised himself "when the de-Judaized Jew that I was at that time began to fear for a country that meant nothing to him and about which he knew only that it had recently attained a national form that he thought outmoded." Arriving in Israel two days after the Six-Day War, he fell in love with the country—and the Zionist Idea. Now BHL fiercely combats antisemitism, Islamist jihadism, and anti-Zionism, which he points to as the new cloak for antisemitism and the new glue uniting the left, now that communism has failed. Israel, he concludes, "is a litmus test for Jews and non-Jews alike."

The Genius of Judaism (2017)

The question is to know where the Jewish state dreamed by Theodor Herzl and realized by David Ben-Gurion fits within the grammar not of being but of nations. And the answer is . . . that these dreamers gave birth to an unprecedented phenomenon, that of a revived land, a blooming desert, a miracle of rationality and hope under the stars. The answer is that this state has not reneged on its contract and has not, despite its flaws and errors, lost all the inspiration of its pioneers. That in a world so profoundly splenetic and disenchanted these beings have managed to survive, that they have had and retain a vitality and a passion both fanciful and practical—those achievements give Israel a dimension that escapes many contemporaries and makes its national epic an adventure in which, putting politics aside, a part of humanity's destiny is playing out. . . .

Zionism, which was, doctrinally, not my style, bowled me over when I encountered it. It is clear that a link was forged then between that nation and me, a link that nothing could break. . . . I remember stony landscapes in which I sensed the mysterious imprint left by eyes that had looked on them for centuries upon centuries before me. . . . I remember a country where everything whispered to my soul in its soft native tongue. And the truth is that, though I was then so tepidly Jewish, there I found the most unexpected of inner homelands, a rock on which I knew immediately that I would lean from that point forward.

The rock has two faces, of course. And since the existence of Israel is not the least of what fuels the new antisemitism, danger also emanates from the rock itself, completing a vicious circle that is central to the tragic aspect of Jewish destiny today. It is also complex. And the unique experience of Israel, the responsibility of a certain number of Jews over a land to which they have long been tied by memory, prayer, and longing, the embrace of politics and policy that they were paradoxically spared by ostracism and by the usurping kings that kept them in exile—all that constitutes one of the hardest and ultimately riskiest trials that the Jewish people have ever had to endure. And no one today can predict . . . whether this national gestation—the longest, bumpiest, and most chaotic in all human history—will produce an ordinary state or a return to Jacob, the man who earned the nickname Israel because he had struggled (with God and men). . . . In short, no one can predict whether or not Israel will turn from a fascinating country into an admirable or sublime one.

But one thing was apparent to me from that first trip, some part of which I have never let go. . . . If dark times, truly dark times, were to return . . . there would be, for imperiled and defenseless Jews, not a "solution" but a way out, which they so tragically lacked before. . . .

Oh, those self-shaming Jews! Those reluctant Jews whose mistrust regarding the subject of Israel is the correlate of the will to know nothing about outmoded Judaism, that residue of the ancient exiles, that remainder in the calculus of nations on an upward arc to victory, or that will to melt into the sort of world citizenship practiced in my family and, later, more radically, in the revolutionary circles of my youth. Well, even they prove the rule! Even for them the idea of Israel functions as the shelter I have described! I do not know of a single Jew in the world for whom the presence of Israel is not a promise—perhaps a promise deferred, but a promise nonetheless.

Asa Kasher (b. 1940)

**Writing a new chapter in the history of
Jewish power and powerlessness.**

In the shift from dreaming about a state to creating one, the ongoing military conflicts enmeshing Israel have challenged Zionism more than anything else. Along with the tragic loss of life, the unnerving threats of annihilation, and the horror of having to kill in self-defense have come challenges to Jewish morality and the Jewish self-image as a moral people. The conflict, thus, has not only threatened Jews physically but ideologically.

Amid such high stakes, the Israel Defense Forces code of ethics—which can have life-and-death consequences for Israelis and their enemies—may be the single most powerful distillation of Zionism in the modern era. Since 1994 the philosopher Asa Kasher has been most identified with writing, updating, and justifying the code.

Born in Jerusalem in 1940, the winner of the Israel Prize among many other honors, Kasher has devoted his career to helping Israel preserve its soul while protecting its people. He wants Zionism to be nurturing "the internal life of the country, which is democracy," and "the external life of the country, which is peace." He believes that modern Zionism entails not only removing "the Jewish people from the *galut*," but removing "the *galut*, Exile's mentality, from the Jewish people"—a process, he says, that requires "becoming more oriented toward long term planning rather than short term 'firefighting.' It means greater commitment to the values of personal and social responsibility in all dimensions of life."

Israeli soldiers constantly refer to the code of ethics, most especially during wartime. The frequent discussion about what they call in Hebrew "*dilemmot*," dilemmas, has soldiers preserving the code often by choosing to abort military operations or sacrificing the element of surprise to avoid endangering civilians. In shaping the conduct of Israel's Jewish, democratic army, Kasher emphasizes the Jewish, democratic values "of respecting and preserving human life and the

duty to retain 'purity of arms,' that is, to use the minimum force necessary to subdue the enemy." These values flow from the Bible—the
text quoted in almost every IDF ceremony to this day. What follows
are some of the underlying Zionist impulses that helped shape this
extraordinary Zionist document—which is taught not only to the
State of Israel's military forces but also at democratic military acade-
mies in the United States and elsewhere.

IDF Code of Ethics (1994, updated periodically)

IDF Mission: To defend the existence, territorial integrity and sovereignty
of the State of Israel. To protect the inhabitants of Israel and to combat
all forms of terrorism which threaten daily life.

The IDF Spirit: ... IDF soldiers are obligated to fight, to dedicate all
their strength and even sacrifice their lives in order to protect the State
of Israel, her citizens and residents. IDF soldiers will operate according
to the IDF values and orders, while adhering to the laws of the state and
norms of human dignity, and honoring the values of the State of Israel
as a Jewish and democratic state. . . .

The Spirit of the IDF draws on four sources:

The tradition of the IDF and its military heritage as the Israel Defense
Forces.

The tradition of the State of Israel, its democratic principles, laws and
institutions.

The tradition of the Jewish People throughout their history.

Universal moral values based on the value and dignity of human life.

Basic Values: Defense of the State, its Citizens and its Residents—The
IDF's goal is to defend the existence of the State of Israel, its independence and the security of the citizens and residents of the state.

Love of the Homeland and Loyalty to the Country—At the core of
service in the IDF stand the love of the homeland and the commitment
and devotion to the State of Israel—a democratic state that serves as a
national home for the Jewish People—its citizens and residents.

Human Dignity—The IDF and its soldiers are obligated to protect human dignity. Every human being is of value regardless of his or her origin, religion, nationality, gender, status or position.

The Values: Tenacity of Purpose in Performing Missions and Drive to Victory . . . Responsibility . . . Credibility . . . Personal Example . . . Human Life. . . .

Purity of Arms—The IDF servicemen and women will use their weapons and force only for the purpose of their mission, only to the necessary extent and will maintain their humanity even during combat. IDF soldiers will not use their weapons and force to harm human beings who are not combatants or prisoners of war, and will do all in their power to avoid causing harm to their lives, bodies, dignity and property.

Professionalism . . . Discipline. . . . Comradeship. . . .

Sense of Mission—The IDF soldiers view their service in the IDF as a mission; They will be ready to give their all in order to defend the state, its citizens and residents. This is due to the fact that they are representatives of the IDF who act on the basis and in the framework of the authority given to them in accordance with IDF orders.

14

Torchbearers

Labor Zionism

David Ben-Gurion's insight that the Jews were rebelling against their own personalities and not just political conditions continued to shape the Zionist mission in the twenty-first century. Zionism, the political scientist Shlomo Avineri explained, is a "permanent revolution," constantly seeking economic and social equality, not just national survival and dignity (Shlomo Avineri, "Zionism as a Permanent Revolution," in *The Making of Modern Zionism* [(New York: Basic, 2017), 227–39]). Even as Kibbutzim privatized and the Labor Party stopped dominating Israeli politics, Israel's leftists remained Labor Zionists at heart, the social justice seekers, the ones demanding compromises with the Palestinians while refusing to compromise in their quest for a free, fair, and egalitarian Israel.

These goals were easily articulated but difficult to implement. Israel's left faced the usual obstacles progressive reformers encounter, including an intractable status quo, complex and interlocking problems, unpredictable policy outcomes, and hostile rivals. Furthermore, the radical global left's alliance with pro-Palestinian forces to delegitimize Israel demoralized many Israeli leftists while emboldening Israeli right wingers to accuse the left of treason. Trying to transcend these histrionics, Professor Anita Shapira embraced Ben-Gurion's "Mapai'nik" mix of idealism and pragmatism, while Professor Ruth Gavison explained how particularist affiliations help advance her work for universal ideals. These idealists confirmed the assertions of left-wing Zionist organizations, like America's Ameinu, that "Progressive Zionism is not an oxymoron" ["Progressive Zionist Answers to the Anti-Israel Left," *Ameinu*, 2008, http://www.ameinu.net /wp-content/uploads/2012/06/Progressive-Zionist-Answers-to-theAnti -Israel-Left1.pdf].

Anita Shapira (b. 1940)

It is high time that we recapture the sense of togetherness we've lost, that was the cohesive power—and gift—of Zionism.

Professor Anita Shapira's greatest impact on Zionism has been as a thoughtful and eloquent teller of its tales—and analysts of its annals. Her biographies of Yigal Allon, David Ben-Gurion, Yosef Haim Brenner, and Berl Katznelson, along with more sweeping works such as *Israel: A History* (2012), have chronicled Zionism's achievements—and dreams—for the new generation of Torchbearers.

Born in Warsaw in 1940, she arrived in Tel Aviv with her family in 1947, then built her international reputation as a prize-winning historian at Tel Aviv University. Her fascination with Labor Zionist pioneers and Ben-Gurion's dominant Mapai Party shaped her own Zionist manifesto, articulated in 2012. As "the last of the Mapai'niks," members of Ben-Gurion's democratic socialist party, she, like her heroes, warned: if Zionism is too soft-hearted, it risks the Jewish state's survival, but if too hard-headed, it risks the state's Jewish soul.

The Abandoned Middle Road (April 25, 2012)

Sometimes I feel that I am the last of the Mapai'niks: a vanishing species of people who had deep convictions about identifying with the Jewish people, about taking responsibility for the destiny of the Jews; about mending themselves as part of a universal movement aimed at making the world a better place, taking care of the weak in society, striving for a more egalitarian society. This dual goal combined national redemption and world redemption, but it was never stated in absolute terms.... Mapai'niks were always wary of all-encompassing utopianism....

I believe in a social democratic Zionism in which the state does not shy away from its responsibility to its citizens, and its citizens feel committed to their state. My kind of Zionism would promote the feeling of social solidarity and the sense of community. As I see it, the pendulum between individual rights and the sense of collective has swung too far toward the individual, and the expansive individualism is overshadowing the obligation to the collective. But Zionism has always focused on the collective, its assumption being that national redemption would also promote personal redemption. It is high time that we recapture the sense of togetherness we've lost, the togetherness that was the cohesive power—and gift—of Zionism.

Ephraim Katchalski-Katzir (1916–2009)

**A pilot plant state in which dedicated people can
explore all kinds of imaginative and creative possibilities
aimed at improving society and the state.**

Many people today consider Israel's emergence as the Start-Up Nation as indicative of uber-individualistic capitalism, but Israel's hi-tech know-how and egalitarian aspirations are rooted in collectivist Zionist ideals. Labor Zionists believe that by combining scientific progress, social justice, democracy, and national pride, Zionism can improve individuals, Israeli society, and the world.

Israel's fourth president epitomized this defining Zionist dream. Born in Kiev, Ephraim Katchalski arrived in Jaffa at age six with his family. By the time he earned a PhD from Hebrew University, he and his older brother Aaron were developing explosives for the state in the making. They established the research group that eventually became the Israel Defense Forces's research and development unit and the billion-dollar weapons company Rafael.

Over the decades, Katchalski helped establish the Weizmann Institute of Science in Rehovot, developed the basic science behind the multiple sclerosis drug Copaxone, and became the father of Israeli biotech. A loyal Labor Party member, he served on national science commissions and created educational programs for talented Israeli high-school students to study science at universities. In 1973 a year after terrorists murdered his beloved brother Aaron in the infamous Lod Airport Massacre, Katchalski became president of the State of

Israel. Immediately, he Hebraized his name to Katzir, completing his evolution into a New Jew. As president, he continued boosting science, social welfare, and the state.

My Contributions to Science and Society (2005)

Not too many of my scientific colleagues have lived, as I have, through the birth pangs of a new state or felt the need to throw themselves into a lifestyle that is critical for their own survival and their nation's future. . . . Jews were returning to their ancient homeland after 2,000 years, filled with the desire to build a democratic state in which we could determine our own future, revive our original language, and revitalize our culture. We were ready to forge a new society which would be based on the principles of social justice defined by our biblical prophets and would offer a high quality of life enriched by the highest moral and spiritual values. In this exhilarating atmosphere, we threw ourselves with great enthusiasm into activities aimed at fulfilling the Zionist dream. . . .

While still a student, I had already formed quite a clear idea of my goals in life. I would do what I could to help establish the State of Israel and contribute to its security and its social and economic development. In addition, I would attempt to do some original research while at the same time playing my part in raising a new generation of Israeli scientists and helping to create the physical and intellectual conditions in which science and technology could flourish in this region. Like Chaim Weizmann, whose life and work served as an inspiration to many young scientists, I believed with all my heart "that science will bring peace to this country, renew its youthful vigor and create the sources for new life, both spiritually and materially." . . .

I have always thought of Israel as a pilot plant state in which dedicated people can explore all kinds of imaginative and creative possibilities aimed at improving society and the state. I feel certain that in the years to come we will continue to operate as a testing ground, drawing on the fruits of science and technology to determine the best and most satisfying ways of living in a country geared to the future. The highest standards of health care, educational practice, and cultural and recreational facilities will flow from research and development in the natural sciences, as well as in automation, computer science, information technology, communication, transportation, and biotechnology. I believe it is possible to create such a pilot plant state by encouraging the development of science-based high technology industry and agriculture. Once it gains momentum, this core of activity will contribute significantly to the economic growth and prosperity of the country. In this pilot plant state, I would like to see a free, pluralistic society, a democracy whose citizens live by the rule of law, and a welfare state in which public services are efficiently handled. Great emphasis will be laid on excellence in science and research, literature, and the arts, thus enriching the intellectual and cultural life of every citizen.

We Jews are eternal optimists. We have always believed, even in the depths of our despair, that the Messiah will come, even if he tarries a little. I am sure that ultimately we will create our model society geared for life in the twenty-first century and founded on the great moral and ethical tenets that we have held sacred since ancient times.

Ruth Gavison (b. 1945)

I reject the claim that there is a built-in contradiction between the Jewish nationalist movement, Zionism, and human rights.

Beyond the modern Israeli left's political challenges—peace, economic equality, religious coercion—it faced a major ideological challenge. An increasingly cosmopolitan global left viewed the Jewishness of the Jewish State as too narrow-minded at best, and undemocratic at worst.

The Hebrew University law professor and activist Ruth Gavison argues that Zionism can help make secular Jews—Americans and others—into better liberals and humanists. "American identity is broad but thin—you can't just be American, most people seek other affiliations as well," she explains. "Affirming the Jewish component of your identity permits you to become part of an ancient tradition that has miraculously survived and revived its independence."

Gavison notes that healthy democracies allow members of the "majority culture" to celebrate their heritage in public as a way of nurturing their souls and strengthening the body politic. Identifying as "a liberal Zionist secular Israeli Jew, committed to democracy and human rights," she demands individual equality for Israeli Arabs and respect for all expressions of Jewish identity in the democratic Jewish state.

Resisting Orthodox coercion as well as secular indifference to religious matters, in 2003 Gavison negotiated a covenant for coexistence with a leading rabbi, Ya'akov Medan. They endorsed ending the Orthodox rabbinate's monopoly on civil matters while still preserving a Jewish character in Israel's public sphere. Although it lacked legal power, the document had moral credibility with many secular and religious Israelis. It reflected the nuanced, consensus view that the state could have a Jewish cultural flavor expressed publicly and mostly voluntarily, with a minimum of Jewish legal obligations imposed through national legislation.

Statement of Principles, Gavison-Medan Covenant (2003)

I believe that a humanism or liberalism advocating a "thin person," limited only to one's self or one's family, is unnecessarily sterile. Affiliations with particular group identities offer individuals central foundational missions in their lives. Indeed, the human rights tradition recognizes freedom of religion and association along with a people's right to self-determination. There is, then, a general universal demand that individuals or groups be permitted to act on behalf of collective particularistic goals (within the operative constraints of the general humanistic framework). I, therefore, reject the claim that there is a built-in contradiction between the Jewish nationalist movement, Zionism, and human rights, which differs in some essential way from the perennial tension between universal values and a particular culture. It is interesting to note that many of those who insist on this alleged contradiction nevertheless champion other national movements enthusiastically, including Palestinian nationalism. . . .

I am a secular Jew who wants to feel fully free to seek inspiration, solutions, and elements of identity in every facet of human culture, while remaining aware that my unique culture is the Jewish-Hebrew one, in all its colors and components. A pluralistic framework enables me and others like me to engage in the urgent and vital task of infusing such a Jewish identity with meaning. To me, this process is part of the challenge of being a secular Jew. Those who reject the principle of observing Jewish law, along with substantial parts of the culture religious Judaism developed, risk ending up with a void, unless they start creating a new culture individually and collectively. . . .

Israel must be (and can be) a democracy that upholds human rights, including freedom of religion and conscience, along with the right to equality, while fulfilling the Jewish people's right to self-determination (a right similarly derived from the human rights tradition). I approach democracy in the relatively "thin" sense as a set of rules regulating how the relevant political community makes decisions, emphasizing the essential right of granting individual citizens full and equal participation in political decisions. . . .

Does the right to freedom of religion and conscience demand a regime of "separation of religion and state"? The answer to this question is "No." There are numerous models regarding possible relations between religion and state in liberal democracies, and each society should adopt the model best suited to its needs. . . . The Israeli reality supports the concept of a weak separation, enabling support for religion within a context nevertheless demanding equality. . . .

Einat Wilf (b. 1970)

Zionism: the most powerful force sustaining secular Judaism.

As the twentieth century ended, many young Israeli leftists became cynical about their country and about a Zionist movement identified with their parents and grandparents. Too many took Israel's founding for granted, considering its current problems unsolvable and its previous achievements intimidating. Dr. Einat Wilf responded by redefining Zionism for her "third generation," celebrating Israel's "grand story" of "tremendous suffering and remarkable renewal." Heroic stories, like this one of Israel's establishment, she argues in *My Israel, Our Generation,* "provide us with this thing we call meaning."

Unfortunately, the resurgence of Palestinian terrorism in 2000 gave Israelis an "existential struggle . . . no less important than the struggles of the previous generations." Yet Wilf—who advised Shimon Peres, served in the Knesset from 2010 to 2013, and is now an unofficial "roving ambassador," writing and lecturing independently—believes, "We want to sustain the State of Israel for positive reasons. We want to turn it into a country that we choose, not a country where we stay for lack of better alternatives."

A secular Israeli, Wilf has articulated for non-believers like herself new ways of inculcating deep connections to the Jewish community and tradition. Translating Zionist ideology into traditional Jewish concepts, she argues for "mitzvot of peoplehood"—new commandments to unite all Jews who accept that "If Israel is not the first home of all Jews, it should at least be their second."

Wilf notes that "this is not about real-estate, but about having a lifelong meaningful relationship with the country and its people." This relationship entails making Hebrew "a foundational mitzvah" which "connects Jews to their culture—ancient and modern, to their land, old and new, and to the millions of Jews who speak it."

Zionism: The Only Way Forward (*Daily Beast,* 2012)

I am a Zionist because I am an atheist and a Jew. Zionism has allowed someone like me to preserve my faith in the sovereignty of human beings over their fate, while maintaining a deep and continuous commitment to the Jewish people and its future. . . .

Of all the answers given to the challenges of modernization, only Zionism, by reformulating Judaism as a culture and civilization grounded in the ancient land and history of the Jews, allowed individuals to remain true to the ideas of the Enlightenment while contributing to a thriving Jewish life. Zionism has succeeded so much so that even religious and ultra-Orthodox Jews, who might not have needed national expression, have adopted and adapted Zionism into their religious identity. . . .

Even for those not living in Israel, Zionism is a powerful means of expressing Jewish identity. For many Jews, theists and atheists, engagement with Israel and Zionism, even without living there, is a fulfilling way of being Jewish. Israel and Zionism are so powerful that just a short visit to Israel (like Birthright) can have an effect on Jewish identification greater than years of Jewish education. Whether it is by advocating for Israel on campuses or the Hill, or whether it is (sadly) by engaging in anti-Israel activity, relating to Israel is how many Jews are Jewish. Both in Israel and the Diaspora, Zionism is the most powerful force sustaining secular Judaism.

Chaim Gans (b. 1948)

An egalitarian Zionism based on the primacy of the Land of Israel in the history and identity of the Jews.

By the twenty-first century, many of David Ben-Gurion's heirs on the left were souring on the state. Decades in opposition, combined with the Palestinian stalemate and the Western surge toward universalism, encouraged a post-Zionist rejection of the very idea of a Jewish state. Singing Ehud Manor's "Ein Li Eretz Acheret," I have no other homeland, was not enough. In *A Just Zionism: On the Morality of the Jewish State* (2008) and *A Political Theory for the Jewish People* (2016), the Israeli legal philosopher and law professor Chaim Gans justifies Zionism morally and philosophically even for those who detest Israel's post-1967 behavior.

Rejecting the "proprietary Zionism" of the Israeli right and center claiming the Bible as the Jews' deed to the Land of Israel, Gans endorses an "egalitarian Zionism" built on three pillars: 1. the Jewish people's universal right to self-determination; 2. Jews' longstanding, constructive, and organic connection to the Land of Israel; and 3. their historic right and need to find refuge from persecution, especially after the Holocaust. This "third way" analysis, Gans believes, validates Israel, repudiating post-Zionist rejections of the state's right to exist, yet supporting Palestinian claims to the 1967 territories.

The Zionism We Really Want (*Ha'aretz*, September 3, 2013)

Most nations claim a right to self-determination, and most of them realize this right (one way or another) in their homeland. However, the majority of the members of the other nations are concentrated in one place and share a history and culture in that particular place, which is also the birthplace of all the members of the group and indeed of the group itself. This was not the case with the Jews at the time of the inception of Zionism, and today it is only partially the case. More importantly, the particular place in question is the homeland of another group and the birthplace of the members of this group.

To overcome this difficulty, the Zionist movement and Israel's Declaration of Independence emphasized the persecution of the Jews and the Holocaust, which created an urgent necessity. This was used in addition to the Jews' historical ties to the Land of Israel in order to justify the choice of this particular place for the purpose of realizing Jewish self-determination despite the fact that it was inhabited by Arabs. This necessity argument is very similar to the necessity defense in criminal law.…

If the justification for the realization of the Jewish right to self-determination in Palestine despite its almost completely Arab character was the necessity created by the persecution of the Jews, then the territorial scope of this self-determination cannot exceed the boundaries that existed when that necessity existed: that is, the borders of Israel as set at the end of the 1940s, immediately after the Holocaust. These borders were initially demarcated in the Partition resolution adopted by the United Nations General Assembly in 1947, and at the end of the war that broke out following the Arabs' refusal to accept the Partition resolution.…

The post-1967 wrongs make it impossible to view the Zionist movement's deeds in this period as consistent with the original justness of the Zionist idea.…

In 1948–49, when the borders now called the "1967 borders" were set, Zionism realized the right of the Jews to self-determination in their historic homeland at the conclusion of centuries of persecutions. This form of Zionism could be deemed just, even sublimely just, even though it committed crimes along the way. It is impossible to say the same about the post-1967 settlements, since it is impossible to justify them on the basis of an imminent threat to human life and dignity. . . .

David Grossman (b. 1954)

Just as there is a war of no choice, there is also a peace of no choice.

As right-wing governments increasingly led the State of Israel, liberal Zionists developed an ethic of patriotic dissent. Perhaps the most prominent rebels, in a nation that esteems its cultural icons, were David Grossman, Amos Oz, and A. B. Yehoshua, Israel's prophetic troika.

Born in Jerusalem in 1954, the winner of the 2017 Man Booker International Prize, Grossman was a child radio star who then anchored the Israeli parallel to the *Today* show. In 1987 his searing book of reportage from the West Bank, *The Yellow Wind*, made him world famous. In 2006 as Grossman worked on a novel about an Israeli woman who takes a long hike to avoid the military chaplains who might tell her that her soldier son has been killed, Hezbollah terrorists surprised an Israeli patrol, inciting the Second Lebanon War. Initially Grossman supported the war. As it dragged on, he, Oz, and Yehoshua endorsed a cease-fire. The firing finally stopped—two days after a Hezbollah antitank missile had killed Grossman's youngest son, Uri.

The heartbroken father, aware that critics assumed he was "this naïve leftist who would never send his own children into the army," now symbolized the dissenting patriot, who is "very critical of Israel" yet is still "an integral part of it." Two months after Uri's death, Grossman delivered a speech at Rabin Square to one hundred thousand protestors demanding peace. His Zionism, his patriotism, his love of Israel, poked through his anguish, demonstrating a tenacious Zionist refusal to give up—or give into despair.

Speech at Rabin Square (November 4, 2006)

I am speaking to you this evening as someone whose love for this country is difficult and complicated, but nonetheless unequivocal. And as someone whose longstanding covenant with the country has become, tragically, a covenant of blood. I am a wholly secular man, yet to me the establishment and the very existence of the State of Israel are a sort of miracle that we as a people have experienced—a political, national, human miracle. I do not forget this even for a moment. Even when many things in the reality of our lives outrage and depress me, even as the miracle is broken down into tiny units of routine and misery, of corruption and cynicism, even when reality seems like a bad parody of the miracle, I always remember. And it is from this feeling that I speak to you tonight. . . .

The death of a young person is a terrible, shattering waste. But no less terrible is the sense that for many years the State of Israel has been criminally wasting not only the lives of its children, but also the miracle it experienced—the great and rare chance bestowed upon it by history, the chance to create an enlightened, decent, democratic state that would conduct itself according to Jewish and universal values. A state that would be a national home and a refuge, but not *only* a refuge: rather, a place that would also give meaning to Jewish existence. An essential part of the Jewish identity of this state, of its Jewish ethos, was to be thoroughly egalitarian, with a respectful attitude toward its non-Jewish citizens.

And look what has happened. . . .

And how, I ask you, is it possible that a nation with our powers of creativity and renewal, a nation that has managed to resurrect itself from the ashes time after time, finds itself today—precisely when it has such huge military power—flaccid and helpless? A victim once again—but this time, a victim of itself, of its own anxieties and despair, of its own nearsightedness.

Yitzhak Rabin turned to the path of peace with the Palestinians not because he felt any great affection for them or their leader. Then too, as we recall, the general opinion was that we had no partner among the Palestinians, and that there was nothing to talk about. Rabin decided to do something because he observed, wisely, that Israeli society could not continue to exist for very long in a state of unresolved conflict. He understood before many others did that life in a constant climate of violence, occupation, terror, anxiety, and hopelessness was taking a toll that Israel could not withstand. These things are still true today, even more sharply so. . . .

[Mr. Prime Minister:] Go to the Palestinian people. Speak to their deep wounds, recognize their continued suffering. Your status will not be diminished, nor will that of Israel in any future negotiations. But people's hearts will begin to open a little to one another, and this opening has huge power. Simple human compassion is as strong as a force of nature, particularly in a state of stagnation and hostility. . . .

Just as there is a war of no choice, there is also a peace of no choice. Because there is no choice anymore. We have no choice, and they have no choice. And a peace of no choice should be pursued with the same determination and creativity with which one goes to a war of no choice. . . .

Nitzan Horowitz (b. 1965)

Queer Zionism: People who stand up for their rights, who will not give up.

In the twenty-first century, the Shulamit Aloni Revolution, pushing the left from a socialist and Ben-Gurionite collectivism to a human-rights-based individualism, intensified. Meanwhile, ideological hurricanes sweeping the West, among them postmodernism, multiculturalism, and sexual liberationism, were altering Israeli society, although Israel remained more family oriented than most of the West.

The sexual conservatism of traditional Judaism, along with the macho culture of the Israeli farmer and soldier, initially silenced much discussion about gay and lesbian rights. Yet the Israel Defense Forces accepted openly gay soldiers long before the American military repealed "Don't Ask Don't Tell."

More recently, the publicity about Tel Aviv as a gay-friendly tourist mecca—and the irony that persecuted gay Palestinians sometimes find refuge in Israel—invigorated the conversation. Some LGBT Israelis found that Israel's characteristic openness helped them harmonize their Jewish and sexual identities. As the American dance critic and "Queer Zionist" Brian Schaefer explains about his experience living in Tel Aviv: "Israel allowed me to fully express every part of myself: my curiosity and my creativity, my adventurousness and my ambition, my spirituality and my sexuality."

Several years ago, the journalist Nitzan Horowitz decided to continue Shulamit Aloni's fight for individual freedom and champion Queer Zionism, cheering the "People who stand up for their rights, who will not give up." Joining the Knesset in 2009 for the first of two full terms with the leftist Meretz Party, he became only the second openly gay Knesset member in history. In 2015 after losing a 2013 mayoral campaign in Tel Aviv, Horowitz returned to broadcasting, becoming chief U.S. correspondent for Israel's Channel 2 News.

Pushing for marriage equality and civil marriage, in 2013 Horowitz officiated at an unofficial single-sex marriage ceremony outside the chief rabbinate's offices. Perched on what he called "the steps of boorishness," he championed "our struggle for the separation of religion and state, as central to our Zionist vision." Under the system operating since Ottoman rule, only religious authorities can perform marriages, meaning "Israel has no civil marriage, no marriage of same-sex couples." Horowitz sees Israel "as a Jewish and democratic state, but not necessarily a religious state. To me, the mixing of religious institutions in government and law violates the country's democratic character, without even strengthening its Jewish character."

One public protest will not end the rabbinate's coercive control. This symbolic ceremony, however, represented a broader shift that has more Israelis demanding more discretion in these personal matters.

On the Steps of Boorishness (*Horowitz* Blog, January 8, 2013)

Every year, thousands of Israeli couples do what we are doing—marry unofficially as couples who cannot or do not want to marry through the rabbinate's coercive establishment. Because Israel has no civil marriage, no marriage of same-sex couples, there is no freedom of choice in marriage here.

Hundreds of thousands of Israeli citizens are denied this basic right. They are forced to go abroad, to spend thousands of dollars, to struggle with legal headaches, to face the harassment of . . . bureaucrats and eventually someone has the audacity to accuse us of "destroying the Jewish people"—as some people from the right-wing parties have done.

The kind of person who speaks this way, someone who does this, is someone who actually rejects Judaism. These are people who spread hatred and evil.

So here we are, with couples who have chosen a different path, and say "no" to coercion. People who stand up for their rights, who will not give up, and are fighting, and are succeeding. And it's the most beautiful thing to see.

This joint wedding in my eyes symbolizes openness and tolerance, and especially a love that transcends all boundaries and breaks all the walls of indifference. . . .

Therefore, on this beautiful day, January 3, in the free city of Tel Aviv-Jaffa, I declare that:

In accordance with the authority and rights inherent in every person on the basis of the universal values of freedom, equality, and fraternity. . . .

On the basis of human rights and dignity—for all human beings—rights specified in Israel's Declaration of Independence, and in accord with the constitutional principles of the laws of the State of Israel and our Basic Laws. . . .

On the basis of pluralistic Judaism, of tolerant Judaism, of a Judaism of "love thy neighbor," a Judaism of healing the individual and healing the world [*tikkun olam*],

And of course based on the principles of Meretz, the party that always has and will fight for the rights of all humans and citizens,

I pronounce you, amid all of us gathered together here, as equal citizens enveloped within love's gates—hand in hand—

In good times, in happiness, and in health

Congratulations!

Alon Tal (b. 1960)

I am a green Zionist.

Israel modernized, evolving from being charmingly environmental, out of necessity, to distressingly dissolute, thanks to now-affordable luxuries. Back in the 1970s, part of the American's Israel experience involved visiting a less-developed country where you purchased loaves of bread off the shelves and carried them in reusable plastic baskets. By the late 1980s, as Americans starting conserving, Israelis started bringing pre-wrapped bread home in disposable plastic bags.

Amid this growing addiction to American consumerist imports, the Israeli environmental movement was an American import too. Many of its founders, like Alon Tal, made *aliyah* from America. Born in 1960, raised by academics in North Carolina, Tal settled in Israel in 1980. After fighting in the First Lebanon War, he earned a law degree from Hebrew University, then a PhD at the Harvard School of Public Health. Returning to Israel in 1989, he became an academic and activist, teaching at Ben-Gurion University and Tel Aviv University while founding significant advocacy groups, including the Israel Union for Environmental Defense.

For his 2002 book, *Pollution in a Promised Land: An Environmental History of Israel*, Tal interviewed hundreds of experts and activists determined to keep Israel's development sustainable. He recalled his own rude awakening when he embarked on "a unique historic opportunity" to "take good care of the astonishing historical and natural resources of our remarkable homeland." His 2016 prize-winning book, *The Land Is Full*, makes a Zionist case for a seemingly most un-Zionist cause—reducing population growth.

Pollution in a Promised Land (2002, updated 2017)

The day of my twentieth birthday I moved to Israel. Unlike the vast majority of *olim* [immigrants to Israel] who fled persecution or economic duress, I am an Israeli by choice. Even now I am frequently asked: "Just what were you thinking?!"

My answer hasn't really changed. I choose to live in Israel because it allows me to participate in a unique historic opportunity. After two thousand years, against all odds, Jews have the chance to reconnect and take good care of the astonishing historical and natural resources of our remarkable homeland. This seemed to be as close to a miracle as I have ever seen and it fired my imagination and spirit. It still does.

Yet, it didn't take long after I arrived to encounter the pollution in my promised land. It left me a little stunned and a little bit angry. I never imagined that after dreaming for so many years, and waiting so longingly to return, without even being aware of it, the people, the economy, and even the government would bring such ecological destruction to the Land of Israel: the damage to the open spaces and the vistas; the forests sullied by litter; the streams choking from toxic pollution or depleted waters; children sick because of the air that they breathed.

At the same time, I also knew that Zionism was a movement that historically had refused to accept conventional wisdom and helplessness. For the Jewish people, Zionism represented a profound revolution— politically and culturally. For Zionists, trend was not destiny. Scores of Israelis every day were bringing this restless temperament to the country's environmental challenges.

I was privileged to join the team. And so we have fought to make the air in Haifa cleaner; to stop the pollution in the Kishon and Yarkon rivers; to stop the decimation of the breathtaking Palmachim beach and dozens of other lovely places. And when we work hard enough, and when we are smart, and when we are lucky enough—we win these battles.

To be a Zionist not only means to join the fight to protect the borders. It also means joining the fight to preserve the environment in the only geographical home that the Jewish people will ever have for future generations.

Israel's environmental successes and failures are in fact opposite sides of the same coin. Both are symptoms of the powerful patriotism that characterizes the young state. Israelis gave up a national past time of picking wild flowers; they invested in water infrastructure, turned seawater into drinking water, set aside considerable public lands to preserve nature and planted trees because they were perceived as national objectives. Like the levying of outrageously big taxes or the rationing of food supplies, it was part of the price for restoring the ancient homeland, and most citizens willingly paid. . . .

More than any of their ancestors, the present generation stands at an ecological crossroads—offered the choice between life and death, or good and evil. This "last chance" to preserve a healthy Promised Land for posterity is a weighty privilege indeed. Surely . . . Israel will once again choose life.

Peter Beinart (b. 1971)

We won't check our liberalism at Zionism's door.

As frustrations grew with all-or-nothing support for Israel, educators and progressives juggled ironclad support for Israel's right to exist with a growing desire to criticize Israeli policies when necessary. Makom, the Education Lab of the Jewish Agency, popularized one metaphor for this new balance: "Hugging and Wrestling with Israel and the Jewish People."

A more famous—and controversial—formulation appeared in 2010 in Peter Beinart's *New York Review of Books* article, "The Failure of the American Jewish Establishment." Beinart, a Yale graduate and Rhodes scholar who had once edited the *New Republic,* called for "saving liberal Zionism in the United States"—by which he meant "talking frankly about Israel's current government"—so that "American Jews can help save liberal Zionism in Israel." He also reasoned that most young Jews are liberal; Israel's policies were anything but; thus, most young Jews must be rejecting Israel.

Rabbi Ammiel Hirsch, senior rabbi of New York's Stephen Wise Free Synagogue and former executive director of the Association of Reform Zionists of America, rejected Beinart's latter argument, saying: "Come on: You mean to tell me that if we only criticized Israel more our Jews would be less alienated from Israel?" Instead, Hirsch endorsed the "identity school" formulation, attributing any distancing between American Jews and Israel to assimilation, because "identification with Israel tends to be in direct proportion to identification with Judaism."

Two years later, in his book, *The Crisis of Zionism*, Beinart articulated a Zionist vision—which now endorses the identity school tenet that a positive Jewish nationalist vision is necessary to revive American Judaism. "We begin our stories with victimhood and end them with survival," Beinart protested. Such "perpetual victimhood" won't teach "how to sustain Judaism in America, a country that makes it easy for Jews to stop being Jews," nor "how to sustain democracy in Israel." Beinart's passion for creating a positive Jewish identity and for protecting human rights makes him particularly popular among Jewish millennials, who applaud his agenda and his candor.

The Failure of the American Jewish Establishment
(*New York Review of Books*, June 10, 2010)

Most . . . students, in other words, were liberals, broadly defined. They had imbibed some of the defining values of American Jewish political culture: a belief in open debate, a skepticism about military force, a commitment to human rights. And in their innocence, they did not realize that they were supposed to shed those values when it came to Israel.

The only kind of Zionism they found attractive was a Zionism that recognized Palestinians as deserving of dignity and capable of peace, and they were quite willing to condemn an Israeli government that did not share those beliefs. . . . The only kind of Zionism they found attractive was the kind that the American Jewish establishment has been working against for most of their lives. . . .

Particularly in the younger generations, fewer and fewer American Jewish liberals are Zionists; fewer and fewer American Jewish Zionists are liberal. One reason is that the leading institutions of American Jewry have refused to foster—indeed, have actively opposed—a Zionism that challenges Israel's behavior in the West Bank and Gaza Strip and toward its own Arab citizens. For several decades, the Jewish establishment has asked American Jews to check their liberalism at Zionism's door, and now, to their horror, they are finding that many young Jews have checked their Zionism instead.

Morally, American Zionism is in a downward spiral. If the leaders of groups like AIPAC [American Israel Public Affairs Committee] and the Conference of Presidents of Major American Jewish Organizations do not change course, they will wake up one day to find a younger, Orthodox-dominated, Zionist leadership whose naked hostility to Arabs and Palestinians scares even them, and a mass of secular American Jews who range from apathetic to appalled.

Saving liberal Zionism in the United States—so that American Jews can help save liberal Zionism in Israel—is the great American Jewish challenge of our age. And it starts . . . by talking frankly about Israel's current government, by no longer averting our eyes. . . .

In the American Jewish establishment today, the language of liberal Zionism—with its idioms of human rights, equal citizenship, and territorial compromise—has been drained of meaning. It remains the *lingua franca* in part for generational reasons, because many older American Zionists still see themselves as liberals of a sort. They vote Democratic; they are unmoved by biblical claims to the West Bank; they see average Palestinians as decent people betrayed by bad leaders; and they are secular. They don't want Jewish organizations to criticize Israel from the Left, but neither do they want them to be agents of the Israeli Right.

But there is a different Zionist calling, which has never been more desperately relevant. It has its roots in Israel's Declaration of Independence, which promised that the Jewish state "will be based on the precepts of liberty, justice and peace taught by the Hebrew prophets," and in the December 1948 letter from Albert Einstein, Hannah Arendt, and others to the *New York Times*, protesting right-wing Zionist leader Menachem Begin's visit to the United States after his party's militias massacred Arab civilians in the village of Deir Yassin. It is a call to recognize that in a world in which Jewish fortunes have radically changed, the best way to memorialize the history of Jewish suffering is through the ethical use of Jewish power.

Ari Shavit (b. 1957)

There is no Zionist future in this place that isn't liberal, and there is no liberal future in this place that isn't Zionist.

Largely because many read it as a Zionist *mea culpa*, Ari Shavit's *My Promised Land: The Triumph and Tragedy of Israel* (2013) became a bestseller. A veteran journalist, formerly a paratrooper, Ari Shavit called the Battle of Lydda "our black box. In it lies the dark secret of Zionism." He charged that Israel massacred two hundred Arabs as part of the Israel Defense Forces' uprooting of the Arabs from present-day Lod during the 1948 War. This "substantial contradiction" between Zionism's stated ideals and its ugly realities, Shavit asserted, created a situation in which "Israel is the only nation in the West that is occupying another people" and "the only nation in the West that is existentially threatened."

Some historians debunked Shavit's simplistic description of the battle, his exaggerated charge of mass murder, and his blaming of the Palestinian refugee problem on "Zionism" as if the movement were a character in a story. Nevertheless, the Lydda text resonated, especially among American Jewish liberals balancing concern for Palestinians with their love of Israel.

The controversy upstaged Shavit's broader Zionist vision. Embracing Israel as the one place where secular Jewish continuity is viable, Shavit doubts that his kids would have been Jewish had his great-grandfather remained in England. His passionate patriotism also leads him to denounce Israelis pursuing policy by extremist actions, explaining: "Only a progressive Israel that is also seen as a progressive Israel can survive."

Back to Liberal Zionism (September 11, 2014)

We've had it. We've had it with the delusional nationalists who are leading Israel to destruction, and we've had it with the visionary leftists who are stoning Israel. We've had it with the skullcap-wearing post-Zionists who are burying Zionism in the hills, and we've had it with the bespectacled post-Zionists who are depicting Zionism as a series of crimes. We've had it with the messianic believers in the entire Land of Israel, who don't understand that without dividing the land, there will be no state, and we've had it with the messianic believers in a perfect peace, who don't understand Hamas and the Islamic State and don't know where they are living.

We've had it with the racist Right, which destroys the image of the democratic Jewish state, and we've had it with the lamentations of the foolish Left, which has lost any feeling of blue-and-white pride. We've had it with those who live in an immoral world of being only for ourselves, and we've had it with those who live in a warped world of being only against ourselves. . . .

We've been broken by the stubborn refusal to understand that the occupation is killing us, diplomatically, morally, and demographically, and also by the refusal to recognize that Palestine isn't California. . . .

The nationalist Right has been acting for years in an anti-national fashion, weakening the Jewish nation-state and endangering the Zionist enterprise. The universalist Left has been acting for years in a non-universal fashion, adopting a particularistic approach that blames Israel (for everything) and forgives the Palestinians (for everything). The impassioned stupidity of both poles blinds us from seeing the fate of our generation, half of which was described by Moshe Dayan at Nahal Oz almost 60 years ago: to be prepared and armed and strong and hard, but also to be wise and moderate and just. The stupid spat between the blind zealots is preventing us from seeing a complicated but clear reality: There is no Zionist future in this place that isn't liberal, and there is no liberal future in this place that isn't Zionist. . . .

A Missed Funeral and the True Meaning of Zionism (December 12, 2013)

At base, the Jewish national movement was the most just liberation movement on the face of the earth. It was meant not only to free a nation, but to save a nation. Consequently, Theodor Herzl was always careful to be identified with progress.

The same went for his successors. The Labor Movement did this by adopting the values of socialism, and the Revisionist Movement by adopting liberalism. The Zionist Left and the Zionist Right upheld Herzl's legacy by ensuring that the movement he established would be committed to equality, peace, freedom, and nobility. . . .

It is a strategic necessity of the highest order for Israel both to be an enlightened state, and to be perceived as one. Benightedness is dangerous. It threatens Israel's ability to protect itself and maintain itself. . . .

To survive in a tough Middle East, we need the West's support, and therefore, we must be an inseparable part of the West. In order to have a future, we must renew our partnership with progressive Diaspora Jews and uphold the values in which they believe.

We must make Israel the moral state it was meant to be, and that it needs to be. We must not play into the hands of those who seek, unjustly, to push us into the world's dark corner. . . .

We cannot be viewed by the world as peace rejectionists. We must put forward a peace initiative that will serve us as a moral shield. We must make it clear to the world that we aren't a theocracy, we aren't an occupation state, and our hearts aren't closed.

To fulfill Herzl's dream, Israel must once again assume a Herzlian face. . . .

If we are not progressive and just and liberal, we will not be at all. . . . Only a progressive Israel that is also seen as a progressive Israel can survive.

Stav Shaffir (b. 1985)

Occupy Zionism!

Perhaps the most dramatic attempt by younger Israelis to revive a sense of Zionist mission occurred in tandem with the social protests and tent cities of the summer of 2011. A twenty-five-year-old video editor, Daphne Leef, received notice from her landlord that she had to move because her apartment was being renovated. Frustrated, she began a Facebook protest against Israel's high rents and high cost of living. Soon, hundreds had massed on Tel Aviv's Rothschild Boulevard to live in tents, wave placards, and demand government assistance for middle-class Israelis—not just the poor. Reflecting Israel's increasingly global perspective, the protesters modeled their grassroots campaign on the Arab Spring protests that tried democratizing Arab lands and America's anti-capitalist Occupy Wall Street movement, which also featured tent cities in town squares. Hundreds of thousands more joined the protest as it broadened from the actual cost of rent and cottage cheese to the social and ideological price of rampant capitalism. The 2011 movement peaked on September 3 with half a million Israelis rallying in Tel Aviv.

The protesters invoked Zionist symbols. Pictures and impersonators of Herzl and Ben-Gurion abounded, as did Herzl's phrase, "If you will it, it is no dream" and Ben-Gurion's supposed pronouncement, "I declare an *egalitarian* state." Addressing the crowd, Leef drew on one of the most powerful Zionist symbols, "Hatikvah," calling the summer of 2011 "the big summer of the new Israeli hope."

Some polls estimated that 87 percent of Israelis supported what many simply called "The Social Protest." And while it did not launch a movement and the government's reforms were limited, it did spawn a renewed progressive call for economic equality and social dignity rooted in Labor Zionism.

The protests also brought new leaders to power. Although Leef started the outcry, other protesters—like Stav Shaffir—ended up in the Knesset. A young journalist who became the movement's public-relations whiz, Shaffir had one "grandmother who escaped from Iraq" and a "grandfather who escaped during the Holocaust." Recruited by the Labor Party, she was elected to the Knesset in 2013, becoming at age twenty-eight the youngest female Knesset member ever. She remains a member as of this writing.

Insisting that "the Zionist dream will not be accomplished until Israel is equal as well as secure," Shaffir fights settlement subsidies for moral, political, and fiscal reasons. She believes "Zionism has been kidnapped by voices that are not ours." That, she explains, "is why I often use the terms 'occupy Zionism' or 'reclaim Zionism'—to say we still have to fight for security, democracy, and defined borders."

In her Knesset debut, Shaffir acknowledged her role as "the voice of this generation" and vowed to "act on behalf of the Zionism of this state's founders." Here, from a three-minute Knesset exchange that went viral, she confronts right wingers to offer her own Zionist hopes.

Knesset Speech (January 2015)

Don't preach to us about Zionism, because real Zionism means dividing the budget equally among all the citizens. Real Zionism is taking care of the weak. Real Zionism is solidarity, not only in battle but in everyday life, day to day, to watch out for each other. That is Israeliness. That is Zionism.

To be concerned about the future of the citizens of Israel. In the hospitals, in the schools, on the roads, on welfare. That is Zionism.

And you're taking it, and destroying it. You're taking it and turning the public purse into a license for your own political machinations, instead of worrying about the country.

You forgot about the Negev and the Galil to transfer 1.2 billion shekel bonuses to the settlements. You forgot Israel. You lost Zionism a long time ago.

Friends, when we sing "Hatikvah," we sing it in the fullest sense of the word, "Hope": a politics of hope, a politics that has a future, a politics that is forward-looking, that wants to make life here better, more secure, that wants to make peace, that wants to improve relations between the different sectors within Israeli society, that believes in equal rights, in budgetary equity, that thinks that every single Israel citizen deserves an equal portion, and deserves to live a truly good life here. That is the true Zionism. That's Hatikvah.

If Prime Minister Benjamin Netanyahu had written our national anthem, it would have been called "hopelessness" not hope. Against your politics, we fight. Against the slander and against the lies. And for a politics of hope.

15

Torchbearers

Revisionist Zionism

The right wing's dominance of Israeli politics demonstrated the many mismatches between the term "Revisionist Zionism" and the stream of Zionism it spawned. The label was always too reactive and too vague, obscuring Ze'ev Jabotinsky's liberal nationalist vision of a free nation with free enterprise balancing individualism and collectivism to restore the Jewish people's *hadar*, glory. At the same time, even as governing tensions splintered the right, that Jabotinsky-inflected, Menachem Begin implemented mix of democracy, dignity, with just a touch of demagoguery, reflected Revisionism's enduring power.

Ironically, Israel's maturation emphasized the similarities between the two rivals, David Ben-Gurion and Ze'ev Jabotinsky. In their day, Jabotinsky dismissed Ben-Gurion's socialist Zionism as *shatnes*, an unkosher mixing of two different ideologies that detracted from Zionism's purity. Ben-Gurion dismissed Jabotinsky as a demagogue—or worse. Yet both were, using Leon Wieseltier's apt term, *bitzu'ists*, pragmatists who envisioned a liberal nationalism prickly enough to survive while still idealistic enough to dream.

By the second decade of the twenty-first century, Benjamin Netanyahu's ideological plasticity to maintain power infuriated right-wing purists. Meanwhile, Netanyahu belonged to a dwindling band of traditionalist Revisionists often resisting right-wing assaults on democratic principles. As the right squabbled over its liberal legacy internally, the world's enmity and Israel's ongoing battle over the territories made Zionism's conservative camp appear united externally.

Ultimately, many of the Zionist right's debates have pivoted around issues that sound Jewish but are more broadly Western. The Oslo, then

Gaza, land concessions, reinforced by the post-Zionist demand that Israel be a "state for all its citizens," triggered passionate justifications of Israel as a Jewish state with rights to its biblical territories. At the same time, modern Revisionists worried about Jews' ability to exercise power effectively after millennia of powerlessness, and how to exercise it morally while living in a dangerous neighborhood.

These Jewish and Zionist dilemmas spilled over into the continuing Western debate about how democracies can fight terrorism effectively and ethically, and how democracies can sustain their distinctive national identities amid asymmetrical warfare, human-rights scrutiny, and post-modernist, universalist drift.

In this climate of political and ideological challenges, combined with ongoing challenges of antisemitism often masquerading as anti-Zionism, multiple players on the right often invoked their prolific founding hero Jabotinsky. President Reuven Rivlin employed Jabotinskyite individualism and nationalism to unite Israel's disparate Jewish and Arab sectors. Similarly, Israel's justice minister Ayelet Shaked tried harmonizing Israel's Jewish, democratic, and capitalistic legacies with a Jabotinskyite synthesis—and ambition.

Yoram Hazony (b. 1964)

**The Land of Israel is the historic inheritance
of only one people, the Jews.**

As Israel prospered in the 1990s, enjoying the hopes of peace and creating the financial and intellectual infrastructure for what would be celebrated as Start-Up Nation, a crisis of Zionist faith spread. In academia, New Historians, led by Benny Morris, disproved some of Israel's founding myths. In the arts, the post-1960s cynicism about nationalism and religion hit the Jewish state doubly hard. Perhaps most profoundly, the Oslo Peace Process challenged the original pioneering consensus about settling and keeping every accessible inch of the Land of Israel, no matter what. Many on the right feared Oslo's compromises compromised Israel's pre-1980s consensus that the Jews, not the Palestinians, had legitimate title to the land.

In 2000 Yoram Hazony's controversial assault against post-Zionism, *The Jewish State: The Struggle for Israel's Soul*, condemned those trying to create Israel's "post-Jewish state." Hazony eloquently reaffirmed "the most noble promise ever made": the "idea of the Jewish state." This counterattack galvanized Zionists who feared Israel was adrift and helped marginalize Israel's radicals, whom, Hazony charged, were "lost in a bitter sea of self-hatred."

Born in Rehovot in 1964, raised and educated in the United States, Hazony returned to Israel and in 1994 helped found a pro-Zionist think tank, the Shalem Center, in hopes of injecting "some ideas into the barren contests of ego and mediacraft of which so much of Israeli political life consists." Today, he is president of the Herzl Institute, a research center in Jerusalem.

The first selection exemplifies the argument against Oslo and for a continuing commitment to the Zionist idea. In the second, Hazony defends Benjamin Netanyahu's Jewish state bill by comparing Israel's political stability with that of its neighbors and arguing that those multicultural Middle Eastern countries united artificially by the British and other imperialists lack the cohesion Israel enjoys because of its Zionist character.

Hazony's broader mission to boost Israel's Jewish and democratic fiber resonated in a country seeking ideological renewal after Palestinian terrorism destroyed the Oslo hopes. Hazony understands that as a state founded by a pamphleteer, Theodor Herzl, Israel's strength stems from the vitality of that idea as a legitimizing force.

The End of Zionism? (*Weekly Standard*, October 9, 1995)

The reason that the Golan Heights, Bethlehem, and Jerusalem could be put on the negotiating block without pandemonium in the streets is the nearly total collapse of the Jewish nationalist ideology which built the state.... "Normal" people, so the argument goes, do not live in fear of being blown up on buses. They do not hold grudges over crimes committed years ago, and they do not spend their time fighting over real or imagined burial places of real or imagined ancestors. They just go to pubs and eat pasta.

The debate over the *normaliut* supposedly ushered in by Oslo underscores what has become evident to Israelis of all persuasions in recent months: That Oslo was not, like the peace agreements with Egypt and Jordan, a strictly political achievement whose desirability can be judged in terms of guns and butter. For "the handshake," as the deal with Arafat is known, sought to achieve the heart's desire of "normal" Israelis by renouncing precisely those emotional assets which allow "Jewish" Israelis to lead meaningful lives....

Zionism is Jewish nationalism—the belief that there should be a Jewish nation-state in the Land of Israel.... What took the teeth out of the anti-Zionism of the Jewish left and right was the Holocaust.... Yet Jewish and even Israeli intellectuals never became reconciled to the empowerment entailed in the creation of a Jewish nation-state....

Zionism was predicated on the idea that the Land of Israel is the historic inheritance of only one people, the Jews; that this right was recognized under international law by the League of Nations in 1920; and that the Arabs, having secured self-expression in twenty Arab national states, do not need one more. . . .

Nothing could be further from these original Zionist premises than the Oslo agreement, in which the government of Israel and the PLO agreed to recognize "their mutual legitimate and political rights"—a phrase usually glossed over as though it merely sets up Israeli concessions in the West Bank and Gaza. . . .

Which cuts to the heart of why Oslo has created such a sandstorm of opprobrium and horror in Israel: the recognition of such an Arab national right to the Land of Israel is a flagrantly post-Zionist proposition. It means that the PLO's carnival of carnage spanning three decades was a perhaps distasteful, but nevertheless justified, war of resistance. By the same token, all the lives lost in pursuing Zionism—from the draining of the malarial swamps to the raid on Entebbe—all were in the service of a morally questionable and perhaps even illegitimate enterprise. For under this rendering of history, the land never really belonged to the Jews. . . .

This means that, in spite of all the hardware procured over the last fifty years, the Jewish state will have to wage and win its next war, the war of ideas, outgunned again.

Yet in this fight Israel's Jewish nationalists have a hidden advantage: No people gives up its identity and life-meaning too easily, least of all the Jews. Indeed, it is just such conditions of intellectual wilderness and danger which bring the most creative and powerful aspects of the national character to the fore. . . .

The relentless trend towards a post-Zionist Israel must be reversed on the battlefield of ideas . . .

Israel's Jewish State Law and the Future of the Middle East (November 24, 2014)

On the face of it, Israel should not need a Jewish State Law. Until recently, Israel's status as the state of the Jewish people had never been seriously questioned. . . .

Of course, equality has always been a crucial value in Israel. But the disappearance of Jewish national self-determination from the [Israeli

Supreme] Court's list of the legitimate aims of Israeli policy called into question many of the most basic purposes for which the state had been founded. Would it soon be illegal to send Israel's security services to protect Jewish communities in other countries? To maintain a Law of Return offering automatic citizenship to Jews from other lands? To teach Judaism in the public schools? These and similar concerns are what stand behind [Israeli prime minister Benjamin] Netanyahu's present "Jewish State Law"—whose purpose is to reestablish the previous status quo on issues of Jewish national self-determination.

But there are deeper reasons for adopting the proposed Jewish State Law. The Herzlian political model has been a dramatic success. As the Jewish state, Israel has absorbed millions of destitute Jewish refugees from Arab lands and the former Soviet Union, offering them freedom from persecution, economic opportunity, and public schools where their children can learn Hebrew, Jewish history, and Bible (something available in the United States only to Jews who can afford private-school tuition). Far from creating a xenophobic and racist regime, the Jewish state has blossomed into a raucous liberal democracy—the only country in the Middle East in which Christians, Druze, and other minorities enjoy free worship and need not fear for their lives.

This success has not been in spite of Israel's character as the state of the Jewish people, but because of it. . . . Israel, built around a cohesive and overwhelming Jewish majority, was able to establish internal stability without repression, and quickly developed into a fully functioning democracy. . . .

We can hold off on reaching this conclusion as long as we please: But there will not be peace in Syria-Iraq until the borders are redrawn along ethnic and religious lines. In the end, Kurds, Alawites, Christians, Druze, Sunni Arabs, and Shiite Arabs must each have their own nation-state, each devoted to the well-being and interests of one people. And each must have its own "Law of Return," offering a place of refuge and automatic citizenship to the scattered and persecuted members of this one people. . . .

Shmuel Trigano (b. 1948)

A generic state exists nowhere in the world: No one asks whether France can be French and democratic.

To Shmuel Trigano, Paris University emeritus professor of sociology of religion and politics, the agonizing pitting "Jewish" versus "democratic" reflects the neurotic emancipated Jew's internalization of Marxist, now postmodernist, antisemitism. Every democracy, he argues, expresses a collective national identity. Polities that reject a particular peoplehood and seek a universalist utopia become dictatorships.

An Algerian-born Jew, Trigano spent most of his academic career as a sociologist and political philosopher in Paris before moving to Tel Aviv. From this outsider perspective, he has questioned some of the Western Enlightenment's governing assumptions, seeing its negation of genuine Jewish self-expression as exposing its narrowness. His "otherness" also helped him recognize the antisemitism in France at the start of the twenty-first century as an epidemic, when most French Jews and leaders still denied it. His cataloguing of hundreds of antisemitic incidents finalized his break with French leftists, who rejected his defenses of Israel and French Jewry. Trigano concluded that modern France is no longer a welcoming place for proud Jews.

Trigano's 1979 book, *The New Jewish Question*, rejected the Western obsession with normalization, replacing it with a *Mizrahi* reading of Zionism rooted in Jewish ethics and ideals. This analysis inaugurated his decades-long quest, in more than two dozen books, to articulate a Hebrew-based political theory endorsing particularist collective identities as keys to healthy democracies. To him, the post-Zionist cry for Israel to become a "state of all its citizens" shorn of its Jewishness threatens Israel's democratic character, as well as its national mission and identity. His fluency in postmodern theory and rootedness in his non-Western narrative makes Trigano a formidable advocate for Zionism as an authentic, truly postcolonial, movement.

There Is No "State of All Its Citizens"
(adapted from *New Jewish State*, Paris, 2015, 2017)

To become citizens and benefit from the French Revolution's "emancipation" in 1791, Jews had to renounce their specific collective status as a people. The birth of "antisemitism" forty years later proved that generic human rights don't work; without *national* civic rights, without a state, courts, and a military, individuals were unprotected.

The Dreyfus Affair taught Herzl that lesson. The Shoah and the expulsion of Jews from ten Muslim lands (1940–70) proved this later too: the Jewish fate is collective and therefore political. These historic events explain why a Jewish nation state responsible for the Jews' collective destiny had to be declared.

Who would have expected that in this Zionist state of Israel a new ideology would emerge, "post-Zionism," advocating the renunciation of *Jewish* national identity in Israel to create a "state of all its citizens"? This strange phenomenon stems from "post-modernism." This post-Marxist ideology inherited the Marxist hatred of any identity, especially Jewish identity.

Post-Zionism also stemmed from the impulse with Zionism that seeks "normalization." Even though Zionism tried correcting the Emancipation's approach of only granting Jews rights as individual citizens, this movement of Jewish "auto-emancipation" echoed the essential principle in creating a generic "Israeli," the product of a new state, not a three-thousand-year history. The citizens of this new state thus experienced the same condition modern Diaspora Jews experienced. The place of Jewishness, of Judaism, became the problem.

Today, a new version of "normalization" demands "a state for all its citizens." But this vision would again reduce Jews to being anonymous holders of rights in an exclusively constitutional state which undoubtedly would stop being called "Israel" soon enough.

Finally, post-Zionism reflects a weakness within modern democratic doctrine. If the nation simply results from a "social contract" among individuals, the collective identity disappears. Within this vacuum, modern national identities emerged—but so did the totalitarian movements praising a "universal" state, lacking any historical identity. Post-Zionism and postmodernism reflect a new, totalitarian, democratic utopianism claiming we have entered a post-national era: but it's just not true.

This background explains the typically "Israeli" dilemma: Can Israel be a Jewish and democratic state? Interestingly, such a question is asked only about the State of Israel. No one asks whether France can be French and democratic, or if the United Kingdom, whose Queen heads the Anglican Church, is really democratic. Behind the question about Israel lies the gnawing doubt—inherited from the now-obsolete Emancipation—about the Jews being a people. The title "Jew" indicates the collective, political, legal entity, which is what counts in a democracy. After all, "democracy" means "rule of the people." The Tower of Babel teaches there is no "universal" people. If there is a Jewish people there can be a Jewish democracy, without reservation.

Democracy developed only within the framework of the nation-state, tapping into the majority's historical identity. When a democracy goes from a national regime to a utopia promising a "universal democracy," or the universalist's democratic individualism causes some kind of social disintegration, it jeopardizes the collective's national identity—and totalitarianism erupts.

Viewed in this context, the post-Zionist slogan of a "state of all its citizens" is clearly demagoguery. A generic state, a universal society without a particular identity, does not exist anywhere in the world (and certainly not in the Muslim or broader postcolonial worlds). Obviously, the future of a country so "pure" is expected to be swallowed up by the Palestinian Muslim minority or a future Palestinian state—which, according to its planned constitution, will be declared as Muslim (its official religion), Arabic (belonging to the Arab nation/ "Ummah"), and Palestinian. The "monotheistic" religions would be reduced to the "dhimmi" status Jews already endured for centuries under Islam.

Multiculturalism, as well as the universal utopia of a state relying only on its constitution and not on a national identity, fails to address the problem of singular collective identity. No being can exist without an identity, even an alienated one. Every "universal" identity is an imperialist one. Today, postmodernism is the ideology of a new European empire, a truly non-democratic regime: the European Union.

This challenging dilemma concerns more than the Jewish case. Perhaps a creative Israeli solution allowing identity and justice to coexist can open horizons for European democratic regimes too.

Israel Harel (b. 1938)

We are here because this is the only place in the world where Jews are sovereign.

Increasingly, the dividing line between left and right in Israel and within the Zionist movement had to do with one four letter word: LAND. In the Jabotinskyite call for settlement on two sides of the Jordan, in the Revisionists' despair when the state began without the Old City of Jerusalem, the longstanding Jewish love affair with *Eretz Yisra'el* served as the central Zionist impulse. The need to settle the territories won in 1967 became an imperative, and the right to keep them sacrosanct. The ongoing security challenge—and the bloody deterioration of the Oslo Peace Process—added a safety dimension to the discourse. Still, as Israel Harel and others make clear in proclaiming. "We are here to stay," they care more about Jewish heritage and Jewish rights than geopolitics.

While Harel and many of these land zealots are religious, their nationalist fervor also has a kind of secular Zionist zeal. They see themselves as heirs to the mostly non-religious *halutzim*, the pioneers who settled the land kibbutz by kibbutz in the pre-state period.

Born in 1938 as Yisrael Hasenfratz, raised in Haifa, Harel transformed himself from refugee child to Israeli tough guy. He maintained his religious identity despite the challenges of growing up as a B'nai Akiva religious Zionist in a mostly secular city. An early settler in Ofra in 1976, he became a leading voice of the settler movement, justifying it in traditional Zionist terms more than religious terms.

While writing for the Land of Israel movement's newspaper, *This Is the Land,* and leading the Yesha Council, the Council of Jewish Communities in Judea, Samaria, and Gaza, Harel also worked for mainstream publications such as *Ma'ariv* and *Ha'aretz*. Here he describes his family's pilgrimage to Ofra, justifying this extension of Jewish sovereignty.

We Are Here to Stay (*Guardian*, August 16, 2001)

In 1976, a rickety lorry made its way from Petach Tikva, today a flourishing Tel Aviv suburb of some 200,000, towards the arid hills of Samaria. This land had been largely unfarmed since the expulsion of the Jews by the Romans some 1,900 years earlier.

The truck was carrying the belongings of my young family: we had decided to leave our pleasant apartment in Petah Tikva, our good jobs and promising studies, to build another gate of hope for the Jewish people. The truck came to a halt in Ofra, about a mile and a half west of Mount Baal Hatzor, the highest mountain in Samaria.

Ofra and Baal Hatzor, the Book of Joshua tells us, were settled by Jews. Just as Petah Tikva was the first Jewish settlement on the coastal plain, Ofra was the first Jewish settlement in the mountain area that was part of the tribe of Benjamin's inheritance. . . .

What do you need this for, ask journalists from abroad. There is only one answer: we are here because this is the only place in the world where Jews are sovereign; where, in their own country, they can take in other Jews, like those from Ethiopia, still suffering from persecution; where they can speak, study, and write in their own language; and where, without feeling like a minority, they can uphold the morality of the prophets. . . .

A negotiated agreement involving the removal of settlements will not end the conflict. As far as the Arabs are concerned, the conflict will only stop when the Jews of Tel Aviv or Petah Tikva are removed. This is Arafat's "strategy of stages."

Caroline Glick (b. 1969)

Renouncing rights to Judea and Samaria would mean denying Jewish history and heritage, and so emptying the Jewish state of meaning.

Jabotinsky's heirs were infuriated—yet oddly validated—by the continuing pressure on Israel to make concessions and establish a Palestinian state after so many peace initiatives had ended in terrorism and delegitimization. The pressure and the ideological attacks both confirmed Jabotinsky's sour assessment of the non-Jewish world and his teaching about the importance of defending the entire Jewish homeland.

Caroline Glick, a columnist for *Makor Rishon*, then the *Jerusalem Post*, defended Israel's attempts at self-defense and continuing control of the disputed territories unapologetically. Her 2014 book, *The Israeli Solution: A One-State Plan for Peace in the Middle East*, justified Israel's control of Judea and Samaria in Zionist terms, as part of the Jewish people's inheritance.

Born in 1969, raised in Chicago, Glick studied at Columbia University and Harvard's Kennedy School of Government. An Israeli since 1991, and later assistant foreign policy advisor to Benjamin Netanyahu, Glick presented herself as in recovery from the Oslo two-state illusion, having coordinated negotiations with the PLO from 1994 to 1996.

Glick believes that responding to terrorism revived mainstream Israeli pride in Zionism. Saying post-Zionism has become "so 1990s," she calls "Israel's return to its Zionist roots" the "greatest cultural event" of the decade. Through her weekly columns, frequent speeches, and clever use of social media, Glick effectively transcends the headlines, rooting her proudly nationalistic analysis in an enduring Zionist framework.

The Israeli Solution: A One-State Plan for Peace in the Middle East (2014)

Israel needs to control Judea and Samaria. It needs to be able to defend itself from the threats of Palestinian terrorism and external forces alike. Equally important, renouncing its rights to Judea and Samaria would mean denying Jewish history and heritage, and so emptying the Jewish state of meaning. Israel cannot do that. For more than twenty-five years, due to successive Israeli governments' preference for the ideal over the good, Israeli leaders have pursued chimerical peace processes with the PLO and doomed confederations with Jordan instead of considering the viability and the desirability of applying Israeli law to Judea and Samaria, and incorporating the areas and their Palestinian residents into Israel. . . .

By virtue of its sovereign rights since independence, its capture of the territory in a defensive war, and the limited nature of the right of self-determination (the Palestinians' strongest claim to sovereignty), Israel's legal claim to sovereign rights over Judea and Samaria is clearly stronger than that of the Palestinians. Despite the propaganda claims of Israel's detractors, there is no international legal obstacle to the application of Israeli sovereignty to Judea and Samaria. Israel, far from being a foreign occupier of Palestinian lands, is the legitimate sovereign. . . .

The people of Israel, and indeed the Jewish people worldwide, are a community of memory. The reconstitution of the Jewish state in the Land of Israel is an unprecedented historic accomplishment. No other indigenous people has preserved its national identity for so long and against such great odds, only to repatriate itself to its historic homeland—sometimes with the help of the nations of the world, sometimes in defiance of their collective will. The magnitude of the Jews' accomplishment in reestablishing their state is as remarkable as the Palestinians' obscene attempt to distort this accomplishment and destroy the historic record. Through their collective memory, and their tenacious, stubborn attachment to the Land of Israel, the Jews preserved their national rights. And it was in recognition of this remarkable feat that in 1922, the nations of the world determined that the legal right to sovereignty over the Land of Israel belongs to the Jewish people alone. . . .

The Israeli one-state plan provides an equitable, democratic means of resolving the conflict, and by safeguarding Israel's national and legal rights, it secures Israel's strategic posture. It neutralizes the Palestinians' capacity to destabilize Israel domestically and delegitimize it internationally, and it strengthens Israel militarily, both from foreign invasion and from terror assaults. . . .

Ruth Wisse (b. 1936)

The word goes forth from Zion: in defending themselves, Jews have been turned into the fighting front line of the democratic world.

In the 1990s, the scholar and Yiddish literature professor Ruth Wisse dismissed Israeli concessions as an illusion rooted in Jews' ambivalence toward power. Mocking "the Anti-Semite's Pointed Finger"—making accusations against Jews, and now Israel, to draw attention away from your own sins—she rejected the Jewish instinct to feel guilty and start appeasing to solve it. To her, "The Zionist misconception—namely, that actions on the part of the Jews would end antisemitism—found its apotheosis in the Oslo Accords of 1993." Calling the rehabilitation of Yasir Arafat "an absurd political decision," she mourned: "No threatened country has ever before armed its sworn enemy with the expectation of gaining security."

Wisse, who earned a 2007 National Humanities Medal for her distinguished scholarship and teaching of "Yiddish literature and Jewish culture," attributes the mounting Jewish criticism of Israel to Diaspora Jews' desire to be accepted by gentiles. She insists: "Doing justice to the story of modern Israel requires the moral confidence to distinguish between a civilization dedicated to building and one dedicated to destroying what others build." Underlying her fight for Zionism is a deep Jabotinskyite pride and a rejection of the "orthodox liberal belief in rational compromise, world peace, 'getting to yes,' and all the rest."

Born in the Ukraine in 1936, Wisse grew up in Montreal. She studied Yiddish literature at Columbia, then at McGill University, teaching there before moving to Harvard. Being raised in a *Folks Shule*, a Yiddish culture Jewish people's school, influenced her all-encompassing approach to Jewish and Zionist identity. "It was never a choice of Yiddish or Hebrew—it was Yiddish and Hebrew," she says. Similarly, "while you were dedicated to the rise of the State of Israel, there was no need to negate the Diaspora. It was clear to us that the Jewish people is this entity and everything Jewish belongs in it."

In *Jews and Power* (2007), Wisse celebrates a true Zionist inversion: the once powerless Jews now having a Jewish state that serves as a powerful ally to the United States, the leader of the free world, in the worldwide fight for democracy. Although too creative and iconoclastic to be defined by one political party or school of Zionist thought, Wisse has had a particular impact on Revisionist Zionists in her passionate advocacy of Zionism, incisive diagnosis of antisemitism, and ability to explain how the European Jewish cultural experience shapes contemporary Jewish attitudes toward the dual Zionist pursuits of individual dignity and national fulfillment.

Jews and Power (2007)

The creation of Israel solved the crisis of Jewish dispersion by resurrecting the Jewish homeland. But there were two problems it could not solve. The so-called Jewish problem was in reality the problem of nations that blamed their dysfunction on the Jews. . . . Just as no Jewish initiative could have solved the German problem that culminated in Nazism, no Israeli initiative could correct "what went wrong" in Arab societies. Jews could only hope to enhance their own security through the avoidance of fatal mistakes and nudge the Arab world to greater maturity by making it clear that Israel was in the region to stay.

The second—internal—problem that could not be alleviated by the creation of Israel alone was the relation of Jews to political power. Zionist thinkers had expected sovereignty to result in political normalization without being able to anticipate the role that a tiny Jewish state might play in the international struggle for power. In trying to withstand the Arab assault, Israelis, Jews, and concerned third parties tripped again and again over the same issue of power that had impeded the development of Jewish political history to begin with. If historians once mistook the absence of sovereignty to mean that Jews stood outside politics, modern students of the problem too often assumed that the resumption of sovereignty guaranteed political parity between Israel and the nations. Jews were said to have reversed their political fortunes once they began governing themselves and an Arab minority in a country of their own. Equating "statehood" with "power," the new experts confused Zionism's potential with its achievement, as if the acquired option of Jewish self-defense had erased Arab advantages of numbers, resources, and land. . . .

Far from exposing Jews to the temptations of might, the creation of Israel had inadvertently reproduced in the Middle East a political imbalance almost identical to the one that Jews had experienced in the Diaspora. Israelis were no more inclined or able to subdue the Arabs than the nations among whom Jews had sojourned in exile. . . .

Wielding military strength, Israel changed the Jewish political equilibrium in contradictory ways. The options of self-defense that Israel acquired by establishing its own military and intelligence made Jews for the first time in two thousand years a potentially valuable ally, including of the world's superpower, the United States. At the same time, Israel's susceptibility as a Jewish and democratic state greatly enhanced its utility as a political target for those who demonized both Jews and democracy These advantages and liabilities were inextricably linked, greatly magnifying Israel's prominence in the international arena and exaggerating the image of Jewish "power" without altering the radical imbalance between Arabs and Muslims on one side and Jews on the other. Already the world's most mythologized people, Jews acquired as the despised "Zionist entity" an international reputation greater than Jehovah's. . . .

The administration of George W. Bush articulated more clearly than any of its predecessors the strategic connection between Israel's security and its own. This, then, is the greatest difference for the Jews since the founding of Israel—that they have something to offer as an acknowledged ally, not merely as individual Jews behind the scenes, as bankers or scientists, cultural creators or impresarios, but collectively, because of the political role they have been forced to play. For the first time, the ability of Jews to withstand their assailants affects the security of other nations as much as their own. Jews always believed that they were meant to help repair the world, but now that belief has turned into plain political fact, albeit in the form they least expected and least desired. . . .

The word goes forth from Zion in ways that earlier Israelites never intended: in defending themselves, Jews have been turned into the fighting front line of the democratic world.

David Mamet (b. 1947)

Real life consists in belonging.

Ultimately, Revisionist Zionism was more tribal than most forms of Zionism, which explains many Revisionists' special fury against antisemitism and their strong sense of belonging. Echoing that approach, the Pulitzer Prize–winning playwright David Mamet says, "The world hates the Jews." This master of spare prose defines his identity simply: "To me, real life consists in belonging." In condemning antisemites and self-hating Jewish liberals, Mamet celebrates the Jabotinskyite ideal of freedom—those who denounce the Jewish state are free to denounce the state in that state.

Born in Chicago in 1947, Mamet, like many other playwrights, spent most of his life as an assimilated Jewish liberal. While courting his second wife Rebecca Pidgeon he became more interested in Judaism, then soured on liberalism. "My interest in Israel," he recalls, "came from discovering my vast interest in Judaism. It's hard for a Jew of my generation, an American Jew, who is philo-Zionistic, not to romanticize Israel. . . . Because, you know, two years before I was born, they were still burning Jews in ovens."

Mamet dedicates his 2006 book *The Wicked Son* with a Mametian, scorched-earth valentine: "To the wicked son who asks, 'What does all this mean to *you?*' To the Jews who, in the Sixties, envied the Black Power Movements; who, in the Nineties, envied the Palestinians, who weep at the *Exodus* but jeer at the Israel Defense Forces; who nod when Tevye praises tradition but fidget through the seder; who might take curiosity to a dogfight, to a bordello, or an opium den but find ludicrous the notion of a visit to the synagogue; whose favorite Jew is Anne Frank and whose second-favorite does not exist; who are humble in their desire to learn about Kwanzaa and proud of their ignorance of Tu B'Shvat; who dread endogamy more than incest; who bow the head reverently at a baptism and have never attended a bris—to you, who find your religion and race repulsive, your ignorance of your history a satisfaction. . . ."

Mamet's 2011 book, *The Secret Knowledge: On the Dismantling of American Culture*, continued his assault against the left's political correctness and anti-Zionism, maintaining his status as one of America's most famous—and toughest—Zionists.

Bigotry Pins Blame on Jews (August 10, 2006; May 25, 2011)

There is no "cycle of violence." Israel wants peace behind the 1949 armistice borders, with some relatively minor variation.... That the Western press characterizes the Israeli actions consistently as immoral is antisemitism. What state does not have the right to defend itself—it is the central tenet of statehood.

The Jews are not the victims of bad p.r. They are the victims of antisemitism....

No, we are told, it is not that Jews, somehow, need Christian blood for their nefarious ceremonies, they need Arab blood, and, for some reason, delight in murder. And much of the Liberal West, thrilled to have a Victim to worship, nods along.

To ask "must there not be a cause for this antisemitism?" is an outrage, similar to asking the rape victim "how short a skirt were you wearing?" The question cannot be posited without at least the implication of the victim "having, somehow, at least in part, 'brought it on yourselves.'"

Q. What is the cause of unrest in 1930's Europe? A. The Jews.

Absurd, one might say, how did "The Jews" cause Hitler to kidnap Europe? But see the same mechanism today. Israel (read "the Jews") we are told, has somehow so inflamed the Arabs, that they (Israel/the Jews) will bring the world to the brink of destruction. Arab Jihadists bomb the West and the West blames "the Jews."

But Israel's Jews are no more the cause of Arab Fundamentalist rage than they were the cause of European Fascism. We, as always, are the miner's canary, singled out as, and the first victims of, national or global unrest.

The Secret Knowledge: On the Dismantling of American Culture (2011)

We Jews live among ourselves. I love it. And all the carping about Israel, or mooing about the Palestinians, or about the emptiness of Religion, is a constant in Jewish life, and is, in fact, the descant of the Torah. The Jewish proclamation of disaffection is like the constant head and body movements of the blind called "blindisms." The blind use these to locate themselves in space. Our Jewish bitching is, similarly, a proprioceptive maneuver, used to locate in space our wandering, border culture.

Many Jews are confused about or opposed to the existence of the Jewish state, and, in their ignorance or muddleheadedness, wish it away. Much of this disaffection is laziness, for if Israel were gone, these anti-Zionist souls believe they might dwell in an unmitigated state of assimilation, any pressures of which might conceivably be combated by an effortless supineness. We were strangers in a strange land, and we are still strangers in a strange land—but the land is less strange than any in which we have dwelt. How to make it less strange still? To cease pretending and enjoy the benefits of liberty, security, and success, and defend them as an American, rather than posing as a "citizen of the World." For here the assimilated (Liberal) Jew simply expands the neurosis of Diaspora thinking: the United States offers Freedom to all, and there is no one here I need to placate; but this position suggests self-examination: "If this is so, why do I feel dislocated? Perhaps there is a wider polity whose 'Good wishes I must seek.' I will call it 'the World,' or 'World Opinion.' Or, 'What might I apologize for.'" . . .

Ze'ev B. "Benny" Begin (b. 1943)

The privilege of being part of a Jewish majority in our ancient homeland also gives rise to a duty . . . whatever the obstacles, to work for the equal rights of all Israeli citizens.

Menachem Begin's son Benny Begin often seemed ambivalent about following his father's career—but not his father's ideology. The younger Begin worked for the Geological Survey of Israel for two decades while simultaneously fighting for a Greater Israel, a vibrant democracy, and equal rights for all citizens, including Arabs. Starting from 1988 to 1999 he served in the Knesset, then from 2009 to 2013, and returned again in 2015. As the right fragmented, Begin quipped: "There is a moderate Right, an extreme right, and a stupid Right."

Noting that "we started in Oslo and got buses exploding in Tel Aviv," Benny Begin echoes his father's teaching that "the right of Israel's citizens to security is inextricably bound up with the right of the Jewish people to the Land of Israel." Nonetheless, aware that "life is truly complicated," he demands that Israel preserve Arab dignity.

"Is there a contradiction between my nationalism and my liberalism?" he asks rhetorically. "There might be. But I try to resolve the difficulties." Begin remains widely respected in Israel, a man of principle embodying the Begin-Jabotinsky tradition.

The Essence of the State of Israel (2015, 2017)

I am a Jew from *Eretz Yisra'el*, feeling that I identify with my people both in space and time: with all my brethren wherever they may be, and with my forefathers and the tradition they bequeathed to us. As such, I also bear responsibility toward the future of my people. And this is my approach: After 1,900 years of exile and subjugation, it is a wonderful gift to be a part of the Jewish majority in the State of Israel—the Jewish people's one and only homeland. . . .

Yet the privilege of being part of a Jewish majority in our ancient homeland also gives rise to a duty—that of the majority to reach out to the minority and, constantly and consistently, whatever the obstacles, to work for the equal rights of all Israeli citizens. Therefore, the character of our state comprises two complementary elements: it is at once the nation state of the Jewish people upholding equal rights to all its citizens.

When I say this, I am not closing my eyes to political platforms, proposed by some Arab leaders in Israel, that seek to fundamentally alter the character of the state of the Jews, or to viewpoints holding that Israel was conceived in sin and born in evil. I am not ignoring plans designed to transform Israel from being the nation state of the Jewish people to "a state of all its nations," that is, to empty it of its deep historical meaning and thereby to deny its raison d'être. But none of these exempt us, members of the Jewish majority, from the perpetual effort to improve the situation, to constantly and vigorously strive to realize the noble principle of equal rights for all Israeli citizens. In doing so, we are not acting generously, but rather perform our duty ... so that we may follow the verse in Leviticus, and the similar version in Numbers: *"You shall have the same rule for the sojourner and for the native."*

The essence of the State of Israel needs to be explicitly enshrined in law. Four hundred years ago, in France, Cardinal Richelieu, said: "If it is self-evident—write it down." ... In 2015, I proposed a bill in the Knesset entitled "The Essence of the State of Israel" affirming that "Israel is the nation-state of the Jewish people, based on the foundations of liberty, justice, and peace as envisioned by the prophets of Israel, and upholding equal rights for all its citizens." Together, the two principles conveyed in this sentence make a whole. They are both essential—not one without the other—and both are absent from our law book. The time has come for their legislation.

Reuven Rivlin (b. 1939)

We are all here to stay.

Reuven Rivlin, Israel's president as of this writing, seeks to preserve key Jabotinskyite liberal ideals despite pressures from an increasingly angry, chauvinist right. In defending democratic processes and minority rights while others on the right violate Jabotinsky's democratic commitments, Rivlin functions as the true Revisionist, the principled Jabotinsky heir.

Rivlin is an Israeli version of an aristocrat, meaning his distinguished family arrived in Jerusalem in 1809. A former intelligence officer who fought in the 1967 battle for Jerusalem and a lawyer, he was first elected to the Knesset in 1988; he became speaker in 2003.

Since 2014 as Israel's tenth president, his warmth and frankness as a Jabotinskyite contrarian have made him very popular. Rejecting appeals that French Jews should move to Israel to escape terrorism and antisemitism, Rivlin told them: "We want you to choose Israel, because of a love for Israel." Detesting the occasional outbursts of anti-Arab bigotry, Rivlin has embraced Israeli Arabs as equal citizens. He even apologized for the "brutal killing in Kafr Qasim" in 1956, calling it "anomalous and sorrowful." He has also expressed regret that *Mizrahi* immigrants experienced "exclusion" in Israel's founding years—a particularly tragic neglect, he notes, because these Jews in Arab and Muslim lands were "born Zionists of Zion." Rivlin's popularity, from left to right, reminds Jews in Israel and beyond of the enduring consensus ideals that unite, not just the passing political issues that divide.

Remarks of President Rivlin: Vision of the Four Tribes (Herzliya Conference, June 7, 2015)

We are all here to stay—*haredim* and secular Jews, National Religious Jews and Arabs. Now, if we truly want to deal with the significance of the "new Israeli order," then we must bravely face the issue, and ask ourselves some tough questions. Are we, the members of the Zionist population, able to accept the fact that two significant groups, a half of the future population of Israel, do not define themselves as Zionists? They do not watch the torch-lighting ceremony on Mount Herzl on Independence Day. They do not sing the national anthem with eyes glistening. . . .

Whoever is not willing to ask these questions today is not more or less of a Zionist or a Nationalist, but one who is ignoring the most significant challenge put before the Zionist enterprise today. . . .

Ladies and gentlemen, the "new Israeli order" now requires us to abandon the accepted view of a majority and minorities, and move to a new concept of partnership between the various population sectors in our society. . . .

I believe that there are four pillars on which this partnership must stand. The first is a sense of security for each sector, that entry into this partnership does not require giving up basic elements of their identity. The *haredi*, the secular, the National Religious, or the Arab individual must not feel that the issues most sensitive to them are in danger or under threat: whether this be the *haredi* way of education in the yeshivot [religious seminaries]; the national religious concept of redemption; the liberal lifestyle of a secular Jew, or the Arab-Palestinian identity. . . .

The second pillar is shared responsibility. When no tribe is a minority, no side can escape bearing responsibility for the destiny and the future of the State of Israel, and of Israeli society in general. So, no tribe is exempt from proposing solutions to deal with the challenge of defending the security of the state; from facing the economic challenges, or maintaining the international status of Israel as a member of the family of nations. Partnership demands responsibility.

The third pillar is equity and equality. In order to ensure the partnership between us, we must ensure that no citizen is discriminated against, nor favored, simply because they belong to a specific sector. . . . In order to create a strong basis for the partnership between us, we will have to ensure an accessible "Israeli dream" that can be realized by each and every young person, judged only on the basis of their talents, and not according to their ethnic or social origins.

The fourth, and the most challenging pillar, is the creation of a shared Israeli character—a shared "Israeliness." Despite the challenges the "new Israeli order" poses, we must recognize that we are not condemned to be punished by the developing Israeli mosaic—but rather it offers a tremendous opportunity. It encompasses cultural richness, inspiration, humanity and sensitivity. . . .

Only in this way, together and in partnership, shall we be able to rekindle the Israeli hope.

Ayelet Shaked (b. 1976)

We will be a more democratic country the more of a Jewish state we build, and we will be a more Jewish state the more democratic we become.

The new generation of Israeli-born Zionists often transcended the simple religious versus secular, capitalist versus collectivist, Ashkenazi versus Sephardi dualisms that defined the state's first half century. As a politician known as the "only secular woman" among the religious Jewish Home Party, Ayelet Shaked has bridged one of the great divides.

Even Shaked's "secular status" is blurry. She recalls growing up with Friday night dinners. She also challenges the rabbis who have questioned her high standing in the Jewish Home Party, saying that if she, Jewish Home Party leader Naftali Bennett, and others want a party "based on the Bible and Jewish values, then the party needs to be open to secular and traditional Jews who identify with the values of the religious Zionist community."

An ex-army instructor in the Golani Brigade, a former computer engineer, Shaked joined the Knesset in 2013 and became minister of justice in 2015. A fiery supporter of the Israeli settlements, Shaked rejects the claim that Israel's Jewish and democratic characters essentially represent an internal clash of civilizations. Her new integrative model, "A Thatcherite Manifesto" of October 2016, articulates a modern Jabotinskyite vision for Israel emphasizing free enterprise, individual freedom, and national solidarity. As the manifesto demonstrates, beyond her often combative positions as minister, Shaked has a deep reading of what Zionism is—and where it can take Israel in the twenty-first century.

Pathways to Governance (*HaShiloach*, October 2016)

The basic values of Judaism are the basic values of the state . . . loving humanity, the sanctity of life, social justice, doing the good and right thing, protecting human dignity, respecting the rule of law for all: these are values Judaism imparted to the world.

This reference to these values emphasizes their universal meaning compatible with the state's democratic character, without emphasizing the values of Israel as a Jewish state with Jewish law. After all, we cannot forget that Israel has a visible non-Jewish minority too. Ultimately, however, Israel's values as a Jewish state match the universal values shared by all democracies, which grew out of Jewish tradition and history. . . .

Against the theory of the relationship between "Jewish" and "democratic" as an eternal struggle and clash of civilizations, I think I can offer a different model. I refuse to be forced to side with one side and reject the other. Moreover, I do not accept the notion that these are incompatible traditions. . . .

On what did Thomas Jefferson . . . base himself when he drafted the Declaration of Independence and noted . . . "We hold these truths as self-evident, that all men are created equal. . . ."? What is the model that countless revolutionaries, justice seekers, and opponents of tyrannical regimes had in mind if not the image of the biblical prophet who bombards the king, despite his absolute power, with the bitter truth, with the uncompromising demand for justice that refuses to bow before his limitless power? . . .

In the previous Knesset I . . . submitted with my colleague, the Minister Yariv Levin, the "Basic Law: Israel as the nation state of the Jewish people." Before our very eyes we saw how the formulation of "Jewish and democratic" has been distorted. . . . We thought it appropriate to grant a special constitutional status defining Israel as a Jewish state. This time it would not be as a symbol, not as a flag or a sign, but as a serious matter bursting with various practical implications affecting the status of the Hebrew language, immigration to Israel and Jewish immigration, Jewish settlement, ties to the Diaspora, state symbols, the calendar and more. . . .

I believe we will be a more democratic country the more of a Jewish state we build, and we will be a more Jewish state the more democratic we become.

16

Torchbearers

Religious Zionism

Religious Zionists in the twenty-first century alternated between breast beating and chest thumping. Religious Zionists were far more mainstream and prominent in the state than they had been in 1948. From the network of Religious Zionist schools to the cadres of Religious Zionist Israel Defense Forces officers, Religious Zionists felt accepted, powerful, and proud of their place in Israel.

Yet, the Oslo withdrawals, the Yitzhak Rabin assassination, the Gaza Disengagement, and tides of secular postmodernism alienated many right-leaning Religious Zionists from the state. Meanwhile, left-leaning Religious Zionists felt distanced from their own movement, resenting a growing rigidity emphasizing individual religious practice rather than collective social-justice concerns, and an obsessiveness regarding keeping the Land of Israel rather than protecting the lives of Israelis—and Palestinians. In 2005 the journalist Bambi Sheleg chided her fellow Religious Zionists: "We fell in love with ourselves.... On the way to redeeming the land of our forefathers, we forgot our people. We looked out for ourselves and our children very well, and we forgot so many children of other people" ["Dear Friends—We Made a Mistake," *Jerusalem Post*, August 16, 2005]/ These concerns triggered vigorous debates about where the movement was going, what Zionism intended, how Israel should develop, and who would define traditional Judaism's future.

Daniel Polisar (b. 1964)

A democracy can flourish only if its people are steeped in religious traditions and values.

Just as nineteenth-century Zionism reflected a broader quest for self-determination, today's fight over Israel's character as a Jewish democratic state embodies the twenty-first century debate about whether liberal democracies should be neutral public spaces or tinted by particular cultures. Most defenses of Israel justify a democratic majority's right to express itself culturally, as long the state respects minority rights. Those explanations assume the Jeffersonian notion that a "high wall" must separate church from state.

Daniel Polisar embraces a different liberal and American tradition—that "a democracy can flourish over the course of generations *only* if its people are steeped in religious traditions and values." A Princeton and Harvard graduate who helped found Jerusalem's Shalem Center, Polisar identifies a "distinctive set of Jewish *ideas*." These include "belief in one God, the possibility of discovering moral truth, individual dignity, the centrality of the family, private initiative, communal responsibility, the rule of law, national independence, and the ideal of universal peace." These ideas, he argues, "which find their origin in the Hebrew Bible, have served to hold the Jewish people together through history," while shaping "the civilizations around us" too. Now, Polisar believes, those ideas should be the Zionist guideposts of Israel's modern Jewish democracy. Through his writings and through Shalem, Polisar has broadened the Zionist conversation beyond what American Jewish liberals define as liberal, using the range of American democratic ideas to cultivate modern Jewish nationalism.

Is Iran the Only Model for a Jewish State? (*Azure*, Spring 1999)

[O]ne of the most widely held myths of Israeli public debate [is] the belief that democracy is fundamentally at odds with religion, and that

Israelis must ultimately choose between a purely universal "state of its citizens" and an oppressive Khomeini-style regime. . . .

According to this model, which rejects not only religion but particularism more generally, there is no justification for Israel's acting to promote Judaism or the Jewish people; a state must be neutral on such issues, so that it can devote its resources solely to fulfilling the material needs of its citizens. . . .

But there is an opposing stream of Western thought—and an opposing conception of democracy—which rejects the radical impulse of the French Revolution to uproot all religious traditions and other particular attachments, and to paint them as the enemies of enlightenment and democracy. This stream is associated with thinkers such as Edmund Burke and Alexis de Tocqueville, and with political leaders such as George Washington and Alexander Hamilton in the United States, and Benjamin Disraeli in England. They believed that a democracy can flourish over the course of generations *only* if its people are steeped in religious traditions and values. Without the self-discipline and the commitment to the nation produced by particularist traditions, democratic freedoms will produce corruption and decay—and the destruction of the republic that offered those freedoms in the first place. . . .

It was also the basis for the vision of a Jewish nation-state. . . . Though neither Herzl nor Ben-Gurion were even remotely observant Jews, they never saw themselves as "secular" in the hard-core French Revolutionary sense this word has been given in Israel today. . . . Herzl tended to side with politically conservative attitudes towards religion, never deviating from the belief that Jewish religious tradition was the cornerstone of Jewish nationalism, and that it would continue to serve a critical function in maintaining the love and affection of the Jewish people once their state had been founded. Ben-Gurion turned dramatically towards an appreciation of the importance of religious tradition in the latter decades of his life, when he was forced actually to build a state. . . .

Israel needs . . . to return to the tradition of Herzl and Ben-Gurion, filling the void in the heart of the country by recognizing that we are most of us believers in the idea of Jewish nationalism, and that we want

Israel to continue building, refining and improving itself as a conservative democracy—and therefore as a Jewish state. . . .

What is needed is a new coalition, in which the leadership and philosophical basis come from a commitment to the conservative model of a democratic state: A constitution that balances the personal and universal with the Jewish and national; a public school system which rejects religious coercion, but aims at deepening the students' familiarity with the Jewish tradition; and an executive branch whose mandate includes pursuing the well-being of Jews and Jewish interests, not only in Israel but throughout the world. Such a state would give the lie to the current universalist demagoguery, reaffirming the vision of a thriving, democratic Jewish state set forth by Herzl a century ago.

Benjamin Ish-Shalom (b. 1953)

Toward a theology of sovereignty.

In harmonizing Israel's Jewish and democratic characters, many Religious Zionists apply traditional concepts to the Jewish people's modern state. Benjamin Ish-Shalom endorses a new theology of sovereignty, along with a new—or at least renewed—*halakhah* of sovereignty, which in part casts Israel as a model to other nations that also need ideological grounding in this confusing world.

A professor of Jewish thought and the founder of Beit Morasha, a center for Jewish leadership, Ish-Shalom helped found Gesher, to bridge the gap between religious and secular Jews; the Joint Institute for Jewish Studies, to educate immigrants about Judaism; Nativ, a program to instruct immigrant soldiers; and other initiatives to teach basic Judaism to a next generation. A consultant to the Israeli army, the Israeli Education Ministry, and various Jewish federations, Ish-Shalom has been instrumental in lobbying for a "friendly" and "considerate" conversion process. This devout Jew's openness reflects his community-minded "*halakhah* of sovereignty" in action, seeking reasonable applications of traditional Jewish law to modern problems.

Jewish Sovereignty: The Challenges of Meaning, Identity, and Responsibility (*Psifas*, August 2014)

Outside the land and without sovereignty, each person is responsible only for himself and his dependents. Inside the land with sovereign existence, responsibility becomes a national one, and an individual must choose the good of the collective over his own. This balance is expressed in Jewish law in other areas as well, such as the general prohibition against endangering oneself, as opposed to the obligation to engage in warfare to protect national life and protect others. . . .

We have then defined a revolutionary theological principle: identification with and responsibility toward the nation, and taking an active part in its national life are of monumental significance, since the lack thereof is equivalent to heresy. This radical position redefines our perception of Torah, nationalism, and of Judaism itself, informing a "theology of sovereignty." . . .

Development of a "*halakhah* of sovereignty," like that of a "theology of sovereignty," must consider the challenges of a sovereign state: development of ethical principles for a sound economy; ethics of diplomatic relations with other countries; formation of policy towards national minorities and other religions; and ethical standards and principles for military action. These areas have not been seriously developed in halakhic literature and religious thought over two thousand years of exile—however this literature can serve as the inspiration for a renewed creative effort to respond to the critical questions faced by a Jewish sovereign state. . . .

This approach forms the basis for a general Jewish political theology, and for a theology of sovereignty in particular. For although both the granting of political power to religion and attributing holiness to a secular polity have dangerous and destructive potential, both also have the capacity to create a distinct group identity, and foster identification and belonging. . . .

The ultimate goal of a Jewish theology of sovereignty is to articulate the many faceted character of Judaism in its fullest expression. Sovereignty creates opportunities for its theology to impact Jewish life dialectically in its spiritual and material, individual and communal, national and universal spheres. . . . [T]he ideal Jewish state [is] one that serves as a "Light unto the Nations," and that promotes mercy and justice toward all of humanity. This dialectic is one of the foremost challenges of Israel and for contemporary Jewish thought. . . .

Eliezer Sadan (b. 1948)

The State of Israel is not anyone's private property. It belongs not to the political right or the political left, the religious or the secular.

Just as Rav Kook struggled with the pioneers' secularism, Eliezer Sadan tempers his disappointment in Israeli secularism with faith in Israel's redemptive power. Sadan concentrated on educating a new generation of religious, patriotic soldiers. In 1988 he founded the B'nei David *mechina*, the first of now nearly fifty pre-military programs offering educational or volunteer programs, some religious, some secular, for more than three thousand Israelis annually before enlisting. Sadan's religious studies help religious Israelis study, then complete "a full and meaningful service"; by contrast, the Hesder yeshiva program shortens military service by mixing it with Torah study. An impressively high percentage of his academy alumni serve in elite combat units and as officers.

Born in Budapest on May 14, 1948, with the State of Israel, Sadan graduated from B'nai Akiva, served as a paratrooper, and spent fifteen years at Mercaz HaRav learning with Tzi Tau, the fiery rabbi who has radicalized the National Religious Right.

Tau rejects any land compromises over "God's inheritance," denouncing "the delusional butchers" who contemplate the "amputation of living limbs from the living body of our Holy Land, the land of our souls." Believing the "post-modernists in the IDF" are fighting a "culture war" against the religious community and the State of Israel, Tau has warned of the army's "self-destructiveness." While in line with Tau ideologically, Sadan has stayed more mainstream, especially because of his institutional ties to the army. Still, as his 2008 pamphlet articulating his Zionist vision demonstrates, Sadan—along with most of his colleagues—balances mounting fury over gays in the army and women in combat with a Kookian love for all Jews in the Holy Land, despite disdaining many of their values.

Religious Zionism: Taking Responsibility in the Worldly Life of the Nation (2008)

For some time now we have been going about with a feeling of dissatisfaction, even anger and harsh criticism of what has been happening in our country—beginning with the progressive loss of our national identity ... [within] the cultural and educational systems in the State of Israel, and ending with the surrender of parts of the Land of Israel to our worst enemies. . . .

[We experience] loss of faith in our uniqueness as a nation, which is necessarily also loss of confidence in our right to the land of Israel, and consequently appalling incompetence and powerlessness in defending our national interests, along with a cultural and spiritual process where the value of the individual is much greater than the value of the collective, where the national feeling is shunted aside in favor of globalization and cosmopolitanism, and the words "sacrifice" "selfless devotion" become archaisms that make way for words like "in" (that is, whatever the greater world out there happens to like), "getting ahead," and the like. All these are not just accidents but the direct consequence of the thoughts, ideas, and ambitions that shape the current elites who rule the state of Israel! . . .

The rebirth of the nation, in contrast to that, is first and foremost an expression of the profound desire to be a part of *tikkun olam* (reforming; improving the world) and to influence the workings of the world and of man. . . . This is also what gave rise to secular Zionism—the desire to improve the situation of the Jewish people who required a safe haven, and the creation of political instruments in order to bring that demand to fruition. And out of all this arose the desire to return to a life of toil, a life of creativity, to tilling the soil, to nature, health, and courage. These things are also sadly lacking inside the bunker, and so once again—the conventions are breached and the Torah is forsaken. . . .

Let us take responsibility . . . for rehabilitating society based on Torah values: let us have great forces in the army, in the court system, in the media, and the like—let all of these be built on a basis of sanctity and yet with full devotion and responsibility for building the national homeland of the Jewish people in the land of Israel! Let us raise the next generation which is full of the spirit of self-sacrifice in no way inferior to that of the defenders of Tel Hai and Deganya, of the Shomer and the Palmah—but all drawing inspiration from the life of holiness set forth in the Torah.

The establishment of the modern State of Israel is the most significant event in the past 2000 years of Jewish history. . . . Any act that protects and fortifies the State of Israel represents a positive scriptural commandment. . . .

Anyone in his right mind and with eyes to see knows that the so-called "secular" community, including those affiliated with the political left, make up an integral and essential part of the people that dwells in Zion. . . . The State of Israel is not anyone's private property. It belongs not to the political right or the political left, the religious or the secular. . . .

He who still has faith in the Jewish People knows that underneath the secular trappings there lies a pure Jewish heart, seeking justice and the right, value and the good, yearning to burst forth. Secular Jews, deep in their souls, are searching for the truth of Torah, the sanctity of the Land of Israel, the spiritual genius of the Jewish People and its prophetic mission of world-redemption and universal belief in God. . . .

Yaacov Medan (b. 1950)

The commandments we keep have a collective, not individual, significance.

In 2003, Yaacov Medan, a scholar at the Har-Etzion Yeshiva, produced a "covenant" with Ruth Gavison, a law professor (see "Torch Bearers: Labor Zionism), to mediate between secular and religious Israelis. Seeking Israeli unity during the Palestinian terror campaign, the covenant endorses Judaism and democracy. It perpetuates Rav

Kook's religious acceptance of secular contributions along with the State's secular acceptance of religious traditions.

In endorsing the covenant, Medan emphasizes a bedrock idea of Religious Zionism which many non-religious Jews miss: Responsibilities to follow the commandments are collective not individual, making Jewish piety—and unity—spiritually significant.

Statement of Principles, Gavison-Medan Covenant (2003)

Israel is a Jewish and democratic state. Israel will continue to respect the equal rights of all its citizens, Jewish and non-Jewish, along with freedom of religion and conscience, in the spirit of the Proclamation of Independence. . . .

A fundamental argument divides the Jewish public in Israel: Is the core principle we are called upon to uphold that of human freedom and dignity, the defense of which is the state's primary objective, or is it the preservation of the Jewish people and Jewish identity? These values may be compared to two carts, which on a broad flat plain can travel side by side in perfect harmony. On a steep and narrow incline, however, when one cart is forced to stand aside to make way for the other, liberals will prefer the cart bearing democratic values while the guardians of tradition will opt for the second cart. I count myself among the second group and the basic unit to which I belong, for better or worse, is that of the Jewish people.

The Jews are one family, the offspring of our three patriarchs and four matriarchs, a single historical unit. The Jewish people, delivered out of Egypt by the Almighty, joined in a mutual covenant with God on Mount Sinai. . . . The Jewish people entered this covenant as a people and not as individuals, and the commandments we keep have a collective, not individual, significance. This is the meaning of the mutual responsibility that connects all Jews, which refers not only to a shared struggle for existence and mutual aid, but also to the collective fulfillment of the commandments required to uphold the Sinai covenant. . . .

Mutual responsibility became even more powerful once a distinct association was established for the sake of a single purpose, a single ship:

the State of Israel. In my view, this association must be for the sake of Heaven. Numerous ultra-Orthodox (not all!) refused to participate in the establishment of the State of Israel and the creation of its laws. By comparison, those who considered themselves part of the state understood that its establishment included an important foundation that was for the sake of Heaven, even if not all its components were "kosher." This position ostensibly dictates a perpetual struggle over the character of the country's laws, in order to mold them as far as possible in the image of the Torah, or at least an imperative to do the utmost to preserve the status quo and prevent deterioration. . . .

The idea of "Israeliness," which posits the common denominator of our identity as members of the State of Israel rather than of the Jewish people, may ultimately prevail. The State of Israel, if not defined as the state of the Jewish people, will not be bound as a state to the Jewish tradition, and it will not be rooted in this land. The Jewish heritage will become a tribal legacy with no connection to the state, its laws, and institutions. The division between "Jews" and "Israelis," when juxtaposed against a large Arab population with a distinct national and religious identity having no connection to the State of Israel, will weaken us and jeopardize our existence here.

Yehuda Amital (1924–2010)

We must rejoice today just as we rejoiced in 1948.

Despite the growing impression of Religious Zionism as right wing, many religious thinkers resisted the political mold. Rav Yehuda Amital moved left politically, while retaining respect in the Religious Zionist world. Born on the Romanian-Hungarian border in 1924 as Yehudah Klein, by 1944 when he arrived in Israel, he was an orphan, having seen his parents and two sisters murdered. "I have no doubt that God spoke during the Holocaust," he later said. "I simply have no idea what He was trying to say."

Klein, who soon changed his name to Amital, fought in the 1948 war, later recalling the power of being a Jewish soldier in the first Jewish army in centuries. In 1959 he and his father-in-law, Rabbi Zvi Yehuda Meltzer, negotiated an arrangement, in Hebrew "*hesder*," with the army: The result was the popular Hesder yeshiva program rotating advanced Torah learning with army service that today involves approximately 8,500 student soldiers annually. After 1967, Amital led a new yeshiva in the restored Jewish settlement of Gush Etzion.

Unlike many of his peers and neighbors, Amital became increasingly open to territorial compromise. He was inspired by the Egyptian-Israeli peace treaty, disillusioned by Israel's mistakes during the 1982 Lebanon War, and skeptical of Religious Zionists' growing rigidity. He counseled that a student so immersed in Talmud who fails to hear a baby cry has sinned; this warning to manage your personal life also applied to communal and national responsibilities.

Amital also fought Israel's growing social alienation and economic gap. In 1988 he entered Israeli politics as the leader of Meimad, a moderate religious party. Although he didn't win a seat, he served as minister without portfolio in the government after Yitzhak Rabin's assassination in 1995. Believing that "only a Palestinian state will save us from losing the Jewish state," he nonetheless criticized the Gaza disengagement, fearing that it being a unilateral act "adds to the pain the evacuees feel, because in this situation they also do not understand why they have to undergo the pain."

In this excerpt, Amital sets priorities religiously, arguing that the act of becoming sovereign in the Land of Israel is far more significant than becoming sovereign over the entire Land of Israel. Such distinctions reflect the subtlety of Rav Amital's thought that makes him a rare figure revered by left- and right-leaning Religious Zionists.

Reishit Tzemichat Ge'ulatenu: What Kind of Redemption Does Israel Represent? (Yom Ha'atzmaut, 2005)

This year we are hearing, for the first time, some voices from within the Religious Zionist camp calling on us not to celebrate Yom Ha'atzmaut [Independence Day] and not to recite [the thanksgiving prayer] *Hallel*. . . .

The students of Rav Zvi Yehuda Kook . . . explained that the "begin-ning of the redemption" refers not to the Jewish nation dwelling in the Land of Israel, but rather to the absolute sovereignty of the Jewish nation over all parts of *Eretz Yisra'el*. . . . According to this understanding, if a major aspect of the purpose of the state is the fulfillment of the com-mand to exercise sovereignty over *Eretz Yisra'el*, then a state that hands over territories betrays its purpose, and we must question whether it is still "the beginning of the flowering of our redemption." . . .

I do not believe in this approach. I can testify concerning myself that I recited the blessing of "*She-hechiyanu*" [rejoicing in something new] and I danced on the 29th of November 1947, at [Kibbutz] Be'erot Yitzhak, even though the UN had partitioned the land, and likewise in 1948. Our feeling was one of elation; it was as though there was an intoxicating drug in the air—Israeli independence. We weren't rejoicing because of what the Ramban taught, but rather because of the fulfillment of Her-zl's vision. . . .

When the State was established, some of the greatest Torah Sages in the world—some of whom I was fortunate to know—declared that although we are not living in the time of the "revealed end" of the "foot-steps of the *Mashiach*," [the Messiah], there is still great importance to the political freedom of establishing a State. . . .

For these reasons, the Chief Rabbis, including Rav Herzog *zt"l*, ruled that the establishment of the State of Israel is "the beginning of the flow-ering of our redemption." A situation in which *Am Yisra'el* has "a king" (sovereignty) and freedom is a harbinger of redemption. . . .

At the same time, after the Six-Day War, some Jews—both religious and secular—. . . . began to speak about a vision of the complete *Eretz Yisra'el*, but they didn't notice the Arabs living within the borders of that "Whole Land of Israel." At the time of the establishment of the state, the Arab population within the borders of the country was relatively small, and there was a chance that the Jewish nation would remain the major-ity for the long term. Today, after our conquest of Judea, Samaria and Gaza, there arises a risk that the state will not remain Jewish. When the government agreed that marriage and divorce would be handled in this country in accordance with religious principles, and that public institutions would observe kashrut, this flowed from the sense that this is a Jewish country. But in a Jewish country there must be a Jewish majority, and this is diminishing with time. . . .

In any event, we must rejoice today just as we rejoiced in 1948. We must recognize that just as the Holocaust was a gargantuan *chillul Hashem*, [desecration] so the State of Israel is the greatest *kiddush Hashem* [sanctification]. We have a problem with giving away parts of *Eretz Yisra'el*, but let us look at what the Holy One has done for us! We have an independent state, we are a prosperous country, and we are militarily strong. . . .

Benjamin "Benny" Lau (b. 1961)

Zionist halakhic decision making should be guided by recognition of a duty to the public.

Religious Zionism does not just see itself as the Zionism of those who happen to be religious. Rooted in Rav Kook's teachings, Religious Zionism is a community-oriented ideology dedicated to building a Jewish state for all the Jewish people. As such, Religious Zionists do not cloister in the study hall avoiding Israel's real people and issues. They care about all Jews—and all Jews' piety. According to Rabbi Benjamin Lau, the patriotic, integrative "ethos of religious Zionism" rejects the ultra-Orthodox metaphor of an isolated ark. His operative metaphor is Abraham's message: "going forth throughout the land."

Lau refuses to see Religious Zionists as less devout than the ultra-Orthodox; nor will he abandon other Jews who are less devout. To him, the State of Israel provides an opportunity to apply Jewish law for the Jewish people in their modern Jewish state. Lau also criticizes the ultra-Orthodox monopoly on religious control, arguing in 2012 that Israel's religious status quo "encourages neither love of Torah nor respect for those that follow her." Believing that more Israelis will embrace religious practices and ideas voluntarily, he fights rabbinic coercion while popularizing Jewish learning.

Born in 1961, now the rabbi of Jerusalem's Ramban synagogue, Lau appears frequently in popular media, inviting Israelis to engage with tradition. His Project 929 encouraged tens of thousands of Israelis, including many famous intellectuals, to read five biblical chapters weekly, thus completing the Bible in a three-and-a-half year cycle. "It's sad to say, but today, our enemies around us make us one nation," Lau explains. "What the project says is the opposite: We need to find the shared language of one nation." This excerpt focuses on a seemingly minor problem of Jewish law to make that major point: Religious Zionism must take responsibility not only for religious Jews, but for all the Jewish people of Israel.

The Challenge of Halakhic Innovation (2010)

Many rabbis in the Haredi community see themselves as sacred guardians, standing on watch against any infiltration of external winds into the world of Torah-observant Judaism. . . .

The ethos of Religious Zionism was, for many years, just the opposite. Armed with great faith, the people of B'nai Akiva fostered the idea of being fully integrated into all aspects of public life—culture, education, security, and industry. If Haredi Judaism can be compared to the passengers on Noah's Ark, Religious Zionism adopted the image of the children of Abraham our father, acting with a sense of go forth (*lekh lekha*, God's charge to Abraham) to spread the great light of Torah as it reveals itself in all fields of life. . . .

The process can be seen as well in the context of *shemitah*, (the agricultural sabbatical year, when . . . land owned by Jews in the Land of Israel may not be cultivated and other restrictions apply). Since the early days of Zionism, the restrictions that apply during the *shemitah* year and the demands of modern agriculture have been reconciled by a sale of land to a non-Jew (a process termed *heter mekhirah*). Recently though, voices from within Religious Zionism have called for enhanced *shemitah* observance and have undercut *heter mekhirah*. The result, however, is an overall debasement of the sanctity of produce that grows during the *shemitah* year, for produce is sold in the normal way with only a small packaging notation that the product is subject to *shemitah*-sanctity (see, for example, the wines produced by Carmel Mizrahi).

Thousands of innocent Jews who are unaware of the product's *shemitah*-sanctity casually violate the prohibition, a transgression that could have been avoided through the use of *heter mekhirah*.

Religious Zionism is becoming like the religious courts on the Haredi street. Zionist halakhic decision making . . . should not be guided by an effort to satisfy the will of marginal groups. . . . It should be guided by a duty to the public at large and responsiveness to the needs of the majority. . . .

Yedidia Z. Stern (b. 1955)

A member of a minority group within the religious minority group whose members internalize simultaneously and without reservation both the Jewish world of values in its Orthodox religious version, and the humanistic liberal world of values.

While balancing loyalties to Judaism and the State, the Religious Zionist also balances modernity with tradition. Yedidia Stern, for one, happily juggles what he calls Israel's cultural duality rooted in Jewish tradition and Western ideas. He identifies himself as "a member of a minority group within the religious minority group whose members internalize simultaneously and without reservation both the Jewish world of values in its Orthodox religious version, and the humanistic liberal world of values." He agrees with Benjamin Lau that the Religious Zionist mission entails taking responsibility for the complexities arising from Western values and the challenges facing Israel's minorities.

Born in England and now a full professor at Bar-Ilan University Law School and the vice president of research at the Israel Democracy Institute, Stern has spearheaded efforts to draft a constitution for Israel. Although some religious Jews consider the Torah Israel's constitution, Stern and others seek to protect the government's defining arrangements and citizens' fundamental rights from legislative whimsy. Stern, along with Rabbi Benjamin Lau and others, fights to separate Judaism from rabbinic coercion so that Israeli Judaism can flourish naturally, organically, popularly.

Ani Ma'amin, I Believe (2005)

The Jewish sovereign existence, an exceptionally rare commodity in history, is the fundamental experience of my life. For me, the Jewish state is not just a socio-political framework which allows for the national group to organize conveniently—in terms of security, society, economics, or otherwise—but it is a prime component of identity, an important manifestation of my Judaism, of my existence, of who I am. . . .

[My] personal compass [consists of] four circles of identities which I share (and their respective values which I continually try to balance).

The first: as a citizen of the State of Israel I am very much aware of the unique character the only Jewish state in 2,000 years should have. Israel is simultaneously a link in the chain of Jewish existence, which ties it to its heritage in a diachronic axis, and a link in the chain of democratic existence, which ties it to its own period in a synchronic axis. It is dissimilar to the other links in each of the two chains: it is the sole appearance of a dominant democratic culture in the annals of the Jewish nation, while also being the only appearance of a dominant Jewish culture in the midst of the democratic nations. . . .

The second: being a member of the Jewish majority in Israel, I bear the responsibility for reining in the force of the majority in order to prevent it from aggressively promoting its particular interests while systematically harming "the stranger who dwells among us": the Israeli Arabs—as individuals and as a minority group. . . . The necessary balance requires recognition of the uniqueness of the Arab Israeli national community, without permitting it to exist as an independent entity (politically, geographically, or otherwise).

The third: being a member of the religious minority group which sees in Judaism not just a nation and culture but also a religion, I perceive it to be my duty to create a normative framework which will not foment continuous friction between state and religion. . . .

The great prominence of the struggle surrounding religious legislation has blurred the cultural value of the religious experience in all its nuances, a rich tapestry from which and within which it would have been possible to weave a Jewish Israeliness.

The struggle has not helped fortify the ramparts of Jewish law in the state, and, unfortunately, has contributed to transforming Jewish law, our national historic law, into a failed name brand in the Jewish state. Coercion of religious norms strengthens secular movements which are liable to be seduced to use the force of the majority in order to dictate arrangements which do not consider the unique needs of the religious minority. . . .

The fourth: I am a member of a minority group within the religious minority group whose members internalize simultaneously and without reservation both the Jewish world of values in its Orthodox religious version, and the humanistic liberal world of values. This dual obligation is not free of symbolic, principled, and practical difficulties. Yet, nonetheless, members of this group are always inescapably subject to two masters: the Sovereign of the World and the state sovereign; the King of Kings and the earthly kingdom. Two systems of law rule over their lives a priori and unconditionally: Jewish law and Israeli law. These two spheres of loyalties—like a pair of parents—guide them in existing in a cultural and normative duality. The central challenge for the members of this group is to create a harmonious and integrative existence bridging both worlds, and this is a task which few, far too few, in Jewish society in Israel confront seriously and with the necessary firmness. . . .

Leah Shakdiel (b. 1951)

Zionism was a big bet!

Contrary to public impressions, some Religious Zionists also support a Palestinian state. In 1978 Leah Shakdiel, a Religious Zionist peace activist, chose to move to Yerucham, a development town in the south, rather than the territories, where many of her childhood friends settled. Shakdiel was expressing the Zionist value of *hagshama* [fulfillment], "the realization of your ideals, the application of your ideals . . . on the ground." Looking back, she says that move spawned "Everything else . . . my involvement in politics, social action, social justice issues, peace, human rights, feminism."

In 1986 she was elected to the local Religious Council, only to have the appointment vetoed because of her gender. A two-year fight concluded with her landmark Supreme Court victory. Now Shakdiel challenges secular Jews who renounce their Judaism just as she challenges religious Jews who reject liberalism—calling for a Jewish state that fulfills the Torah's commitment to social justice and to the "other" as the ultimate fulfillment of Religious Zionism. Amid fears that many Religious Zionist rabbis are veering toward ultra-Orthodoxy, Shakdiel offers an alternative Religious Zionist vision—seeing modern progressive ideas as natural outgrowths of the Torah and the Zionist movement.

The Reason You Are Here Is Because You Are a Jew! (2004)

[M]y parents were part of a trailblazing generation. They broke new ground, they said, "Okay, we have this *historia lachrymosa* [history of weeping], but that's not all there is in life for us." It's not as if we forget anything, we don't. But while keeping account of our past, we also want to do the optimistic work of building a living, palpable future in the land.

You see, Zionism was a big bet! It's not as if anything was secured in advance, it was a very important bet to make that there's going to be a future—if we cast all our weight in one direction, it's going to happen. . . .

We have a state . . . a successful state . . . that's a major thing. . . . We all complain about it, it has many problems. . . . But . . . we have it. It's a fact. . . .

On the one hand, there is my people, the Jews, who are very ancient, have a very distinct identity . . . with its religion, language, ancient culture, rich literature, traditions, history. We can take pride in a lot of moral and ethical achievements, and this is our land. On the other hand, you have an entity [the Palestinians] that has been created on the same land . . . as a result of recent events in the history of this region—the European powers meddling with it and dividing it up. . . .

If you are religious you are supposed to be right-wing. If you are left-wing, you're supposed to be secular. Now, it's not just the fault of the religious that have moved so dramatically to the right, I think it's also the fault of the secular Israelis who have gotten it into their heads that they can do away with their Jewish identity, with their Jewish culture. This is ridiculous. I annoy my secular Israeli friends by telling them from every podium that if they do not see themselves as Jews that means that they are imperialists, colonialists, who have no business being here. They should leave the land to its native people. The indigenous people are Palestinians.

The reason you are here is because you are a Jew! . . .

The fact that the religious cling so much to right-wing politics also has to do with the fact that the leftists don't do very much about being Jewish, so we have a dichotomy where people feel pushed against the wall. Who are you? Are you a peacenik or a Jew? This dichotomy, as if being a peace seeker and being a good Jew are mutually exclusive, is a horrible thing. . . . Both sides sort of participate in the maintenance of that stupidity, which goes nowhere, because unless we can recruit self-identified Jews in this country to the peace camp, we'll get nowhere. . . .

I'm fifty-three years old. I want to see the two-state solution before I die. . . . If I get to see a Palestinian state in my lifetime, it's going to be a big thing, because it means an internal reorientation of the State of Israel, a complete reorientation, which was bound to happen. You take in the exiles, you do all those interesting experiments in populating the desert, you build an army, and then you have to reorient the whole thing by arranging it so that there is another state on the same piece of land. It's a tremendous thing.

Arnold Eisen (b. 1951)

Zionism must be a voice of aspiration that takes Jews higher, and a set of Jewish collective actions to bring the teachings of Torah to fulfillment.

Of the three major denominations in America, the Conservative movement has always been the most unambiguously Zionist. Orthodox rabbis disliked Zionism's secularism. Reform rabbis disdained Zionism's particularism. Conservative Jews loved Zionism's expansiveness as a grand Jewish peoplehood project. The chancellor of the Jewish Theological Seminary since 2007, Arnold Eisen, has championed that position. His Big Tent Judaism is political, committed to Jewish sovereignty; cultural, steeped in a love of Hebrew and Israeli civilization; and religious, rooted in Jewish texts and tradition, proving you don't have to be Orthodox to be a religious Zionist.

Eisen's 1986 book, *Galut: Modern Jewish Reflection on Homelessness and Homecoming,* examined many of Zionism's historical and ideological ambivalences. The book he co-authored with sociologist Steven M. Cohen fourteen years later, *The Jew Within: Self, Family, and Community in America,* identified the modern challenges stemming from the increasing privatization and iconoclasm of American Jewry, which undermines Conservative Jewry's love of Israel as peoplehood-central.

Born in 1951, Eisen taught at Columbia University, Tel Aviv University, and Stanford University before becoming only the second non-rabbi to lead the Conservative Movement's seminary in New York. He fears a growing rigidity and land idolatry among the most Orthodox Religious Zionists as he fears a growing chaos and self-worship among the least involved American Jews. He stakes his claim to a deep religious dimension to Zionism coexisting with other values, including democracy, loyalty, humility, that will help make Israel—and Zionism—great again, even in the eyes of disaffected American Jews.

What Does It Mean to Be a Zionist in 2015? Speech to the 37th Zionist Congress (October 20, 2015)

As a scholar of modern Judaism, I do not know a more powerful religious creed among Jews the world over, including among Jews who are disconnected from their local Jewish community, or who declare they are "definitely not religious"—than *Am Yisra'el Chai,* [the Jewish people live]. These words for them, as for me, combine longing, love, and faith. The people of Israel live in the face of enemies who have sought and still seek our destruction, and we as a people live most vividly, strive most boldly, in the State of Israel. That is why high-tech here matters more than it does in Silicon Valley, even to Jews who do high-tech in Silicon

Valley. *Am Yisra'el Chai* is why it is absolutely forbidden to Jews to despair of our Jewish future—whether in Israel or in Diaspora. . . .

Conservative Judaism Today and Tomorrow
(Jewish Theological Seminary of America, 2015)

Jews outside of Israel seem increasingly incapable of disagreeing about Israel with civility and respect. . . . That is why I've been urging Jews . . . to savor the blessing of being alive at this unique moment in Jewish history and experience. Jewish life and the practice of Judaism have become infinitely richer in our generation thanks to Israel. . . . I'd like us all to affirm clearly and without equivocation—no matter what our opinions about Israeli policy—that our connection to the State of Israel and its citizens is fundamental, nonnegotiable, and unbreakable. Israel is the single greatest project the Jewish people has going right now, and the most important arena that has been available to Jews in two millennia to put our values to the test and our teachings into practice. We need it. And it needs us.

That is the heart of the matter for me. I am a political Zionist who believes that the survival and thriving of Jews in the world, including here in America, depend upon the existence and vitality of the State of Israel. I am a cultural Zionist who believes that the flowering of Jewish civilization in the world depends upon close interaction with the "spiritual center" of the Jewish people in the Land of Israel. And I am a religious Zionist, convinced that Jews are heirs to a unique story that we are responsible for carrying forward, and—because of history, tradition, and faith—partners in a covenant aimed at bringing more justice and compassion to the world. The sovereign, democratic State of Israel affords unprecedented scope and responsibility for the fulfillment of covenant. It presents us with the chance to do what Conservative Judaism has always urged: adapt the teachings of Jewish tradition to unprecedented circumstances and join Torah with the very best of modern thought and expertise. In Israel, Jews can and must bring the Torah to bear on every aspect of society: health care and education, foreign policy and the welfare system, treatment of non-Jewish minorities and diverse streams of Judaism, relations of war and peace, and proper stewardship of the planet's resources. . . .

David Ellenson (b. 1947)

**The rebirth of Jewish life embodied in the State
of Israel is fraught with religious import: the
monism of universalism must be rejected.**

By the twenty-first century, the Reform movement, despite having
been "Zionized" post-1948, still housed many skeptics about Zionism. As American progressives veered toward universalism, the Jewish
left seethed about Israel's treatment of Palestinians; and Reform Jews
resented the Israeli rabbinate's mistreatment of liberal Judaism; Reform
Zionists felt embattled. Rabbi David Ellenson, for fourteen years the
president and then chancellor of the Reform seminary Hebrew Union
College–Jewish Institute of Religion, has pushed for a new synthesis.
Noting in 2007 that too many secular Israelis build their identities solely
on national and communal lines while too many American Jews build
their identities around "individual choice and religious voluntarism
above peoplehood and nationality," he challenges all Jews to forge "a
meaningful sense of Jewish identity established on both national and
religious foundations."

Ellenson calls himself a "failed Zionist" who only truly felt a "sense
of *shlemut*—not so much "wholeness" as "normalization" during his
year on Kibbutz Mishmar HaEmek. His balancing of universalism
and Zionist particularism, nation and religion, America and Israel,
individualism and communalism represents his understanding of the
Reform mission to live in the modern world enriched by tradition.
Having wondered "is Reform Judaism strong enough to promote an
ethos that constructs a sense of meaning in today's world?," Ellenson
sees Reform Zionism as a central repository of tradition, inspiration,
and values that will help him—and his fellow American Jews—say
"yes" and find that meaning.

Reform Zionism Today: A Consideration of First Principles (2014)

The legacy of our religious tradition's emphasis on justice as well as our
Reform commitment to morality and ethics make Israel the ultimate

testing ground for the truth of Jewish teachings and values. However, ... nothing should obscure or deny the religious significance the state possesses by virtue of the sheer fact of its existence....

Two decades ago I lived for a year at Mishmar HaEmek, a kibbutz of Hashomer Hatza'ir located in the Jezreel Valley next to Meggido. On many afternoons, after the day's work had been completed, I would walk up into the hills of the kibbutz. There, I would gaze out onto the valley below. And each time, when I looked, I would see the orchards and the irrigation pools, the cotton fields and the trees, the factories and the roads—and most of all, the people. And I would think of the words with which the prophet Amos concluded his preachments to the people Israel: "A time is coming—declares the Lord.... I will restore my people Israel. They shall rebuild ruined cities and inhabit them...." I would be deeply moved.

However, no blessing would emerge. For I was never sure, despite the prophecy, if what I saw was the work of God or of persons. Perhaps, I now think, it does not matter. For how, in assessing the meaning of Israel, can one distinguish between the sacred and the profane, the religious and the secular? Furthermore, why should one try?...

After some time on the top of the hill, I would return to the kibbutz, and there I would see families sitting together and talking on the lawn. I would watch little children tumble and run after one another, screaming all the time in Hebrew. At this point, the words of the *Sheheheyanu* [thanksgiving prayer for having lived to this moment] would silently form in my heart and escape from my lips.... In those moments my spirit moved me instinctively to thank God for the *kiddush ha-hayyim*, the sanctification of life, that the Jewish state and Jewish existence embody.

Our people's return to our land is not simply mythic. It has taken on flesh and blood, and to celebrate that fact is to applaud much more than "mythic renewal." It is to acknowledge that the rebirth of Jewish life embodied in the State of Israel is fraught with religious import and significance....

The Jewish people have "returned to history" with a degree of power unknown for the previous two millennia. Reform Zionism needs to know and affirm the religious significance of this fact. The monism of universalism must be rejected.

Our Zionism must be built upon the dialectical foundations of universalism and particularism and the interplay between them. Both poles must be accorded religious legitimacy by our movement, for only then can a platform be constructed in which each can inform and, at times, provide a corrective for the other. In so doing, a new ground for our Reform Zionism will be established. . . .

17

Torchbearers

Cultural Zionism

Israel in the twenty-first century was surprisingly modern. Gone were the days of endless waits on bank lines and for telephone lines. Delight in conveniences coexisted with nostalgia for simpler, more communal times. Both Ahad Ha'am and Theodor Herzl had won. The country was a center of Jewish spirituality, learning, and pride, with a rich Jewish culture that gave the most avowedly "secular" Israeli Jew a deep, normalized, 24–7 connection to the Jewish calendar, language, rituals, and values. The country was politically stable, socially progressive, and culturally creative; pioneering technologically, medically, academically, artistically.

Culturally, Israel echoed two major, albeit contradictory, Western trends. Individualism intensified, as did new forms of identity politics. Some categories were familiar to Westerners, as gays and feminists, among others, affirmed their identities. Others were particularly Israeli, as Ethiopians and *Mizrahim*, in particular, celebrated their rich, once-dismissed, heritages.

In this way, culturally, Zionists updated the pioneers' hyphenate Zionism. Early Zionists, from communist to religious, synthesized their particular worldviews with their Zionism. Their heirs now crossbred many other identities and affiliations with their Zionism. Ahad Ha'am's Cultural Zionism, therefore, is best understood today as Identity Zionism—a Zionism encompassing individual searches for meaning and different tribal identities intertwined with the Jewish people and the State of Israel.

Gil Troy (b. 1961)

**A century ago, Zionism revived pride in the label "Jew";
today, Jews must revive pride in the label "Zionist."**

The Palestinian turn from negotiations toward terror in 2000 traumatized the Jewish world. With many in the world blaming Israel even
as Palestinian terrorists were blowing up Israelis in cafés and buses,
many Diaspora Jews felt defensive—and angry at Israel too. For Israel
Independence Day 2001, six difficult months into the Palestinian terror
campaign, the American historian and McGill University professor
Gil Troy wrote "Why I Am a Zionist," for the *Montreal Gazette*. Some
anti-Zionists caricatured the op-ed as a confession: "I am a racist."
Troy responded that identity is not a zero-sum game; if Palestinians
and their supporters continue perceiving any affirmation of Jewish
nationalism as an attack, there will never be peace. He followed up
by writing, "Why I Am an Anti-anti-Zionist."

Simultaneously many people thanked Troy for affirming, during this
dark period that would ultimately kill over one thousand Israelis, how
lucky Jews were to have a thriving Jewish state. Inspired, he extended
his writing career to address Jewish issues. In 2002, he expanded the
essay into *Why I Am a Zionist: Israel, Jewish Identity and the Challenges
of Today*. This best-seller introduced the phrase "Identity Zionism" to
describe the emerging Zionist approach whereby Diaspora Jews draw
inspiration from Israel. The term explains the worldview of Taglit-
Birthright Israel, Masa, and other "Israel Experience" programs developed to build Jewish identity, especially since the 1990s.

Troy's 2013 book, *Moynihan's Moment: America's Fight against Zionism as Racism* explained the origins of the modern assault against
Zionism, while re-introducing a liberal American hero, Daniel Patrick
Moynihan, who resisted that pile-on. The book continued endorsing
a modern relegitimization of Zionism—rather than just opposing
delegitimization.

Born in Queens, New York in 1961, educated at Harvard University,
Troy was active in the Young Judaea youth movement in the 1970s

and the educational director of its national camp, Tel Yehudah, in the 1980s. An Israeli citizen since 2010, he lives in Jerusalem and writes regularly for the *Jerusalem Post,* the *Canadian Jewish News,* and the *Daily Beast.* The broad Zionist vision he articulates here reflects the "Big-Tent Zionism"—a phrase he coined in 2005—of Young Judaea and Hadassah, its sponsor for decades.

Why I Am a Zionist (2001, 2008)

A century ago, Zionism revived pride in the label "Jew"; today, Jews must revive pride in the label "Zionist." . . .

Zionists must not allow their enemies to define and slander the movement. No nationalism is pure, no movement is perfect, no state ideal. . . . Zionism remains legitimate, inspiring, and relevant . . . offering an identity anchor in a world of dizzying choices—and a roadmap toward national renewal.

I am a Zionist because I am a Jew—and without recognizing Judaism's national component, I cannot explain its unique character. Judaism is a world religion bound to one homeland, shaping a people whose holy days revolve around the Israeli agricultural calendar, ritualize theological concepts, and relive historic events. Only in Israel can a Jew fully live in Jewish space and by Jewish time.

I am a Zionist because I share the past, present, and future of my people, the Jewish people. Our nerve endings are uniquely intertwined. When one of us suffers, we share the pain; when many of us advance communal ideals together, we—and the world—benefit.

I am a Zionist because I know my history—and after being exiled from their homeland more than 1,900 years ago, the defenseless, wandering Jews endured repeated persecutions from both Christians and Muslims— centuries before this antisemitism culminated in the Holocaust.

I am a Zionist because Jews never forgot their ties to their homeland, their love for Jerusalem. Even when they established autonomous self-governing structures in Babylonia, in Europe, in North Africa, these governments in exile yearned to return home.

I am a Zionist because those ideological ties nourished and were nurtured by the plucky minority of Jews who remained in the Land of Israel, sustaining continued Jewish settlement throughout the exile.

I am a Zionist because in modern times the promise of Emancipation and Enlightenment was a double-edged sword, often only offering acceptance for Jews in Europe after they assimilated, yet never fully respecting them if they did assimilate. . . .

I am a Zionist because I celebrate Israel's existence. Like any thoughtful patriot, though I might criticize particular government policies I dislike—I do not delegitimize the state itself.

I am a Zionist because I live in the real world of nation-states. I see that Zionism is no more or less "racist" than any other nationalism, be it American, Armenian, Canadian, or Czech. All express the eternal human need for some internal cohesion, some tribalism, some solidarity among some historic grouping of individuals, and not others.

I am a Zionist because we have learned from North American multiculturalism that pride in one's heritage as a Jew, an Italian, a Greek, can provide essential, time-tested anchors in our me-me-me, my-my-my, more-more-more, now-now-now world.

I am a Zionist because in Israel we have learned that a country without a vision is like a person without a soul; a big tent Zionism can inculcate values, fight corruption, reaffirm national unity, and restore a sense of mission.

I am a Zionist because in our world of postmodern multidimensional identities, we don't have to be "either-ors," we can be "ands and buts"—a Zionist *and* an American patriot; a secular Jew *but* also a Zionist. Just as some people living in Israel reject Zionism, meaning Jewish nationalism, Jews in the Diaspora can embrace it. To those who ask "How can you be a Zionist if you don't make *aliyah*," I reply, "How will anyone make *aliyah* without first being a Zionist?"

I am a Zionist because I am a democrat. The marriage of democracy and nationalism has produced great liberal democracies, including Israel, despite its democracy being tested under severe conditions.

I am a Zionist because I am an idealist. Just as a century ago, the notion of a viable, independent, sovereign Jewish state was an impossible dream—yet worth fighting for—so, too, today, the notion of a thriving, independent, sovereign Jewish state living in true peace with its neighbors appears to be an impossible dream—yet worth seeking.

I am a Zionist because I am a romantic. The story of the Jews rebuilding their homeland, reclaiming the desert, renewing themselves, was one of the twentieth century's greatest epics, just as the narrative of the Jews maintaining their homeland, reconciling with the Arab world, renewing themselves, and serving as a light to others, a model nation-state, could be one of this century's marvels.

Yes, it sometimes sounds far-fetched. But, as Theodor Herzl, the father of modern Zionism, said in an idle boast that has become a cliché: "If you will it, it is no dream."

Yair Lapid (b. 1963)

I am a proud Zionist, I am a man of tomorrow but I also live my past.

Yair Lapid represents the sabra generation: committed to creating the new non-neurotic Jew, despite growing up under the shadow of the Holocaust—and waves of Israeli wars. This media star turned politician is the son of another media star turned politician, Tommy Lapid.

The elder Lapid was born in Novi Sad, Yugoslavia, present-day Serbia, in 1931 and watched the Gestapo take his father away. Tommy and his mother survived the Budapest Ghetto—but Tommy lost his faith in God there. He became a Herzlian Zionist, defining "the whole Zionist idea" as guaranteeing that "every Jewish child will always have a place to go." Forging the family path from journalism to politics, the elder Lapid led the reforming Shinui Party, serving in the Knesset from 1999 through 2006.

Born in Tel Aviv, Yair Lapid came to epitomize the trendy, breezy, easy Tel Avivi in his many public roles as columnist, children's author, actor, and television anchor. Bringing his new Yesh Atid party to a surprising second-place finish in the 2013 elections, made him the voice of Israel's political center.

Yair Lapid's Zionism is lighter, more lyrical, more Israeli, than his father's—and more textured, more experiential, than Gil Troy's. His "Cherry Tomato Zionism," appreciates the "intangible" advantages of Israel life. According to Harvard's James Kugel, the ideological Zionists "return to America": it's "only the tomato lovers who stay." In this prose poem from 2009, four years before joining the Knesset and Benjamin Netanyahu's cabinet as finance minister, Lapid offers an anthem of the sabra Zionist, that Zionist with a vivid love of the land, who echoes Ehud Manor's 1982 song, "I have no other country." The work captures Yair Lapid at his most archetypical: the Jew who has found his home after millennia of wandering, the total Jew immersed in a Jewish culture, the Jew also known as an Israeli.

I Am a Zionist (2009)

I am a Zionist.

I believe that the Jewish people established itself in the Land of Israel, albeit somewhat late. Had it listened to the alarm clock, there would have been no Holocaust, and my dead grandfather—the one I was named after—would have been able to dance a last waltz with Grandma on the shores of the Yarkon River.

I am a Zionist.

Hebrew is the language I use to thank the Creator, and also to swear on the road. The Bible does not only contain my history, but also my geography. King Saul went to look for mules on what is today Highway 443, Jonah the Prophet boarded his ship not too far from what is today a Jaffa restaurant, and the balcony where David peeped on Bathsheba must have been bought by some oligarch by now.

I am a Zionist.

The first time I saw my son wearing an IDF uniform I burst into tears, I haven't missed the Independence Day torch-lighting ceremony for twenty years now, and my television was made in Korea, but I taught it to cheer for our national soccer team.

I am a Zionist.

I believe in our right for this land. The people who were persecuted for no reason throughout history have a right to a state of their own plus a free F-16 from the manufacturer. Every display of antisemitism from London to Mumbai hurts me, yet deep inside I'm thinking that Jews who choose to live abroad fail to understand something very basic about this world. The State of Israel was not established so that the antisemites will disappear, but rather, so we can tell them to get lost.

I am a Zionist.

I was fired at in Lebanon, a Katyusha rocket missed me by a few feet in Kiryat Shmona, missiles landed near my home during the first Gulf War. I was in Sderot when the Color Red anti-rocket alert system was activated, terrorists blew themselves up not too far from my parents' house, and my children stayed in a bomb shelter before they even knew how to pronounce their own name, clinging to a grandmother who arrived here from Poland to escape death. Yet nonetheless, I always felt fortunate to be living here, and I don't really feel good anywhere else.

I am a Zionist.

I think that anyone who lives here should serve in the army, pay taxes, vote in the elections, and be familiar with the lyrics of at least one Shalom Hanoch song. I think that the State of Israel is not only a place, it is also an idea, and I wholeheartedly believe in the three extra commandments engraved on the wall of the Holocaust museum in Washington: "Thou shalt not be a victim, thou shalt not be a perpetrator, but above all, thou shalt not be a bystander."

I am a Zionist.

I already laid down on my back to admire the Sistine Chapel, I bought a postcard at the Notre-Dame Cathedral in Paris, and I was deeply impressed by the emerald Buddha at the king's palace in Bangkok. Yet I still believe that Tel Aviv is more entertaining, the Red Sea is greener, and the Western Wall Tunnels provide for a much more powerful spiritual experience. It is true that I'm not objective, but I'm also not objective in respect to my wife and children.

I am a Zionist.

I am a man of tomorrow but I also live my past. My dynasty includes Moses, Jesus, Maimonides, Sigmund Freud, Karl Marx, Albert Einstein, Woody Allen, Bobby Fischer, Bob Dylan, Franz Kafka, Herzl, and Ben-Gurion. I am part of a tiny persecuted minority that influenced the world more than any other nation. While others invested their energies in war, we had the sense to invest in our minds. . . .

I am a Zionist.

My Zionism is natural, just like it is natural for me to be a father, a husband, and a son. People who claim that they, and only they, represent the "real Zionism" are ridiculous in my view. My Zionism is not measured by the size of my *kippah*, by the neighborhood where I live, or by the party I will be voting for. It was born a long time before me, on a snowy street in the ghetto in Budapest where my father stood and attempted, in vain, to understand why the entire world is trying to kill him.

I am a Zionist.

Every time an innocent victim dies, I bow my head because once upon a time I was an innocent victim. I have no desire or intention to adopt the moral standards of my enemies. I do not want to be like them. I do not live on my sword; I merely keep it under my pillow.

I am a Zionist.

I hold on not only to the rights of our forefathers, but also to the duty of the sons. The people who established this state lived and worked under much worse conditions than I have to face, yet nonetheless they did not make do with mere survival. They also attempted to establish a better, wiser, more humane, and more moral state here. They were willing to die for this cause, and I try to live for its sake.

Micah Goodman (b. 1974)

I am a temperate Zionist, crystallizing the cold skepticism of secularism with the burning fire of religious fundamentalism.

The generation of non-religious Zionists following Yair Lapid, born in the 1970s and 1980s, often found themselves looking for something more spiritual than their elders. This yearning revived interest in traditional texts, in rituals such as the all-night Tikun Leil Shavuot learn-a-thon, and in syntheses between Jewish liturgy and popular music. Micah Goodman became a leading bridge builder, helping young secular and religious Israelis find a common language.

Raised in Jerusalem's German Colony as the son of American immigrants, Micah Goodman earned his PhD in Jewish thought from Hebrew University, where he teaches. He is the guiding light behind Ein Prat, a pluralistic Bet Midrash, center of Jewish learning, where religious and secular Israelis study Jewish and Western classics together. He has also written three bestsellers introducing the Israeli public to three great Jewish texts: one on Moses's final speech; one on Yehudah HaLevi's philosophical dialogue, the Kuzari; and one on Maimonides's *Guide for the Perplexed*.

In his 2018 book, *From the Secular and the Holy*, Goodman refutes all the talk about a seemingly impassable bridge between secular and religious Israelis. In this next stage of the Zionist revolution, "secular Israelis are becoming Jews," he says, and "a new-old paradigm is taking hold." This secularism is "based not on the repudiation of Judaism but on the willingness, and the desire, to be influenced by it. . . . The new Israeli paradigm embodies a more modest and less radical form of Zionism. . . . Embracing power, land, and language, it also welcomes and eagerly embraces Maimonides of Spain and Egypt, Rashi of France, and the talmudic sages of Babylonia."

From the Secular and the Holy (2018)

In the twentieth century the great Zionist challenge was for the Jews to ascend to Israel. In the twenty-first century, the challenge is for Judaism's status to ascend within Israel. In the twentieth century, the Zionist project expressed itself in *aliyah*, immigration, settlement, and security; in the twenty-first century the main Zionist achievement can be renewing Judaism. If the old Zionism tried repairing the damage from years of Exile, the new Zionism corrects the damage Zionism caused. . . . [T]he revival of Judaism is not only motivated by the desire to heal Judaism; it is also motivated by the desire to heal Westernism via Judaism.

The West is in distress. The West so cultivated individualism it found itself sinking in egoism, just as de Tocqueville envisioned. The first and biggest casualty of this transition from individualism to egoism is the family. Family life requires sacrificing individual prerogative daily. The family cannot function without taking the desires of others into account and sacrificing the full exercise of one's individual will. The data on the disintegration of the family unit in the West reveals that the individualism that undermined religion in the twentieth century is defeating the family in the twenty-first century. Moreover, virtual technology further draws individuals into themselves. Studies show that the hours young people fritter away in social networking erode their empathy and increase their narcissism. The technological processes and values dominating Western society compel humans to contract. . . .

As awareness of these major modern Western threats to consciousness, identity, and family grows, it triggers extreme reactions. Masses of people in the West, who are alarmed by modernity's psychological threats, flee in fear straight into tradition's warm protective bosom. This is why modernism fosters fundamentalism.

On the other hand, people who are appalled by how religious tradition fosters xenophobia, along with the accompanying male chauvinism and religious violence, escape into the modern liberal and secular vacuum, only to be swallowed by that. Just as religion is the first refuge from secularism, secularism is the last refuge from religiosity. These are the groups that not only radicalize religion and secularism; they are also the fundamental building blocks of Israeli society. . . .

The modern world suffers from the cold skepticism of secularism as well as the burning fire of religious fundamentalism. How does one know just what the happy and healthy temperature is for Jewish identity? . . . The secular skepticism that cut off the continuity between Jews and their past threatens the Jewish future. . . . Jewish religious fire, in its present constricted form, shuts itself off, negates the world, and, dressed in its fanatic garb, threatens to burn down the world. . . . Between the skeptical path that drains the world of meaning, and the fanatic path that threatens to destroy it, there is a very fragile border.

The heart of Israeli identity crystallizes on that very thin line. Those elements of the religious Zionist world that see Zionism as an opportunity for religious revival walk along that path, and those elements of the secular Zionist world that see Zionism as an opportunity to revive some connection to the past, also traverse that path. Meanwhile, the traditionalists who were always on that path and pointed to the Golden Mean remain there, patient as always.

Ronen Shoval (b. 1980)

I am a neo-Zionist building the culture of the Third Temple.

For many right-wing Zionists who were demoralized in the 1990s, infuriated by post-Zionism, and traumatized by the Oslo accords that granted the Palestinian Authority five-year governance over the West Bank and Gaza, the collapse of the peace process proved tragic but reenergizing. Yasir Arafat's wave of terror was pushing many Israelis right—souring on the Palestinians and rediscovering an old-fashioned Zionist idealism. The vicious attacks on the Jewish state reminded many Israelis why Jews still need one. The Israeli-born academic and journalist Dr. Ronen Shoval, among others, responded by articulating an updated Zionist vision for a maturing state.

Shoval initially led the Zionist non-governmental organization Im Tirtzu, "If you will it"—an echo of Theodor Herzl's slogan. Inaugurated in 2006, the organization became very controversial very quickly for denouncing left-wing artists, academics, and intellectuals harshly as traitors. Along with his activism, Shoval proffered a "neo-Zionist" vision—what he called "Herzl's Vision 2.0." In this excerpt, he identifies the values, the idealism, that give meaning to the state—with his Herzlian political vision clearly influenced by Herzl's culturally oriented rival Ahad Ha'am. Although often upstaged by anger against his allies' polarizing tactics, Shoval's broad vision gives meaning to Israel's daily life and Jewish quality of life, not just its big battles and major inventions.

Herzl's Vision 2.0 (2013)

The creation of a complex Israeli culture is the greatest and most far-reaching challenge facing Israeli society in the coming generations. It will lead to the continuing renewal of Zionist secularism and religiosity, modernity and Zionism combined and integrated. . . .

Integrating the values and abilities of the secular Jewish world with those of the religious Jewish world will result in extraordinary innovation and will usher in a new era in Israeli culture, an era worthy enough to be called "The Culture of the Third Temple." . . .

The connection between the Jewish people and Israeli culture is expressed in the special values that Israeli culture instills in the Jewish people, and vice versa. Neo-Zionist ideology aspires to realize these values in the State of Israel via the Jewish people, and throughout the world via the State of Israel. The spirit of the values Israeli culture imparts is embodied in such concepts as love, Shabbat observance, sanctity of life, liberty, equality, fellowship, mutual responsibility, hope, peace, justice, freedom, safeguarding nature, abolishing slavery, liberalism, and many more. Four of these values—belief in the freedom to choose, love, liberalism, and the Jewish moral approach—form the foundation of the connections between the Jewish people, Israeli culture and neo-Zionist ideology. . . .

The role of the State of Israel is to realize the internal ideals of the Jewish people for itself and for humanity as a whole.

In order to fulfill this tremendous task, the Jewish people must serve as personal examples by realizing a national, land-related, and historic life on a solid piece of land. Here, in the State of Israel, the Land of Israel achieves its full significance. The Israeli nation must live a full moral life within a political framework. Through the State of Israel, we have the ability to serve as a model that will instill a new consciousness within the nations of the world that will help humanity resolve most of the major spiritual problems of our times.

The central conflict today is the clash between different worldviews. This is the root of the controversy between Islam and the West: modernization versus tradition; the individual versus the community; science versus religion and the moral relativism of the Western world versus the totalitarian beliefs of the Islamic world. Israel is at the heart of this storm, both geographically and spiritually. . . .

There must be a suitable relationship between the State of Israel and the other nations of the world. First, we must create an original Israeli culture based on an awareness of Jewish culture, not only for the sake of the Jewish people. All of Western culture is presently mired in spiritual weakness and serious deterioration, and it is well aware of its inability to address life's essential questions. Western man lives an alienated and insufficiently meaningful life, in spite of all the technological and scientific advancements and all of the material and economic wealth he accumulates—or perhaps because of all this. Western moral values offer no hope of significant renewal and bear no moral message for Western society. . . .

The revival of an authentic Israeli culture would not only ensure our own continued national existence, but would benefit the entire Western world that awaits a positive moral message from the Land of Israel. . . .

Our aim is to turn the dream called the State of Israel into a more just, more modern, more democratic, and more Jewish state. It is our task to complete the historic and ethical enterprise of the return to Zion.

A. B. Yehoshua (b. 1936)

The pleasure of the freedom of being in your own home.

The great novelist, essayist, and provocateur A. B. Yehoshua has celebrated "*normaliut*," Israeli Jews' natural Jewish identities, while criticizing American Jews for "becoming detached" from Israel. Explaining that Israeliness is his "skin," not a "garment" he changes when convenient, Yehoshua proclaims: "A full Jewish life [can] only be had in the Jewish state."

Despite his frustrations with the Diaspora, Yehoshua's core Zionist belief is that "the State of Israel belongs not only to its citizens but also to the entire Jewish people." Being a *Mizrahi* Jew, something of an outsider, he says, intensified his awareness of how marginal the

Zionist movement was before World War II—and how integrated exile is into the Jewish DNA.

Born in Jerusalem in 1936 to a Moroccan mother and a father who was a fourth-generation *Mizrahi* Jerusalemite, Yehoshua served as a paratrooper from 1954 through 1957. He taught comparative and Hebrew literature at the University of Haifa for decades and started writing the prize-winning novels, plays, and essays that made him one of Israel's great seers. Viewing Yehoshua's extensive writings on Zionism in context, far beyond passing controversies with American Jews, three fundamental themes emerge. First, he emphasizes the importance of defining terms like "Zionism," "homeland," and "Israeli citizen" precisely, avoiding ideological and rhetorical inflation. Second, while mourning European Jews' failure to embrace Zionism before the Holocaust, he identifies Zionism's greatest accomplishment as saving Jews, not just from Hitler. Finally, his vision of Israelis as "total Jews" is carved not in opposition to American Jews, but as a corrective to the ideological confusion and suffering Jews endured for millennia in the Diaspora.

The Basics of Zionism, Homeland, and Being a Total Jew (adapted from various essays, 2017)

I deliberately adhere to the minimal true definition of the Zionist concept, a definition for which I have fought in many articles and countless lectures. Zionism is not an exclusive ideology, but has a common platform with various different and even conflicting ideologies. Different and contradictory philosophies were combined in Zionism, such as the socialist and even Marxist doctrines of the Hashomer Hatzair movement, the orthodox religious doctrines of *Agudat Yisra'el*, as well as the doctrines of the national religious, the bourgeois liberal, the social democrat and fascist nationalist parties, etc. The parties—in their various nuances—that participated in the Zionist Congresses were all Zionist. While their life programs were dissimilar, they had the common goal of establishing a sovereign Jewish state in the Land of Israel, open to every Jew wishing to come to it.

Ever since the State of Israel was founded in 1948, the definition of "Zionist" has been revised . . . as follows: A Zionist is a person who accepts the principle that the State of Israel doesn't belong solely to its citizens, but to the entire Jewish people. The practical expression of this commitment is the Law of Return. The state's affairs are indeed managed solely by its citizens, people who have an Israeli identity card, of whom 80 percent are Jews, while 20 percent are Israeli Palestinians and others. But only a person who supports and affirms the Law of Return is a Zionist, and anyone who rejects the Law of Return is not a Zionist.

To be a Zionist is not a badge of honor, or a medal a person wears on his chest. Medals are connected to actions, not to support of the Law of Return. Nor is there any connection between the size of the country and Zionism. The Law of Return is essentially the moral condition set by the countries of the world for the establishment of the State of Israel. The United Nations' partition of Palestine-*Eretz Yisra'el* in 1947 into a Jewish state and a Palestinian one was on condition that the Jewish state would not just be a state for the 600,000 Jews that lived there at the time, but would instead be a state that could resolve the distress of Jews all over the world, and would enable every Jew in the world to consider it home. Would it be moral for the hundreds of thousands of Jews who immigrated to Israel on the basis of the Law of Return to shut the door they entered through behind them?

The Zionist revolution created—or recreated—the "total Jew." We now have a Jewish identity in Israel, which we call Israeli identity (as distinct from Israeli citizenship, which is shared by Arab citizens who also live in the shared homeland, though their national identity is Palestinian). This Jewish-Israeli identity has to contend with all the elements of life via the binding and sovereign framework of a territorially defined state. And therefore the extent of its reach into life is immeasurably fuller and broader and more meaningful than the Jewishness of an American Jew, whose important and meaningful life decisions are made within the framework of his American nationality or citizenship. His Jewishness is voluntary and deliberate, and he may calibrate its pitch in accordance with his needs.

For me, Jewish values are not located in a fancy spice box that is only opened to release its pleasing fragrance on Shabbat and holidays, but in the daily reality of dozens of problems through which Jewish values are shaped and defined, for better or worse. A religious Israeli Jew also deals with a depth and breadth of life issues that is incomparably larger and more substantial than those with which his religious counterpart in New York or Antwerp must contend. Am I denouncing their incomplete identity? I am neither denouncing nor praising. It's just a fact that requires no legitimating from me, just as my identity requires no legitimating from them.

We in Israel live in a binding and inescapable relationship with one another, just as all members of a sovereign nation live together, for better or worse, in a binding relationship. We are governed by Jews. We pay taxes to Jews, are judged in Jewish courts, are called up to serve in the Jewish army, and compelled by Jews to defend settlements we didn't want or, alternatively, are forcibly expelled from settlements by Jews. Our economy is determined by Jews. Our social conditions are determined by Jews. And all the political, economic, cultural, and social decisions craft and shape our identity, which, although it contains some primary elements, is always in a dynamic process of changes and corrections.

While this entails pain and frustration, there is also the pleasure of the freedom of being in your own home. Homeland and national language and a binding framework are fundamental components of any person's national identity. Thus, I cannot point to a single Israeli who is assimilated, just as there is no Frenchman in France who is an assimilated Frenchman—even if he has never heard of Molière and has never been to the Louvre, and prefers soccer matches and horse races.

In a lecture Hayyim Nahman Bialik gave at Nahalal in 1932, he said: "It's very simple: The concept of culture for every people includes all elements of life, from the lowest to the most sublime. . . . Here in the Land of Israel the concept of culture assumes its full significance. Everything that is created in the Land of Israel by Jews becomes culture." Therefore, a Talmud lesson in a yeshiva or at an institute like Alma, the self-described home for Hebrew culture, has no more "Jewish identity" than a debate by the Committee to Prevent Road Accidents. Any differentiation between them is artificial and dangerous. Because Israeliness is what brings about a total integration between matter and spirit. . . .

The process of turning Israeli identity into a skin instead of a garment is a new and revolutionary process for the historic Jew, who for most of his history slipped in and out of the national clothes of others. . . . And once again, the fear returns. Will Jerusalem return to being an abstraction as it was for hundreds of years of Jewish history or will it remain a living entity? This will depend not on our Jewish identity, but on the Israeli identity alone.

If Israeliness is just a garment, and not a daily test of moral responsibility, for better or worse, of Jewish values, then it's no wonder that poverty is spreading, that the social gaps are widening, and that cruelty toward an occupied people is perpetrated easily and without pangs of conscience. . . . It will always be possible to escape from the reality to the old texts, and to interpret them in such a way that will imbue us with greatness, hope, and consolation.

Erez Biton (b. 1942)

I am a Zionist, a heavenly builder.

The social worker and poet Erez Biton built his career critiquing one of Zionism's early failures—and became an Israeli national asset thanks to one of Zionism's latest successes. Jews from Arab lands were not easily integrated into Israeli society, the Israeli narrative, or Zionist ideology. Now they are broadly accepted, in part because of Biton's bitter, biting, brilliant poetry, which mourns the many *Mizrahi* hearts broken by Ashkenazi arrogance, bureaucratic insensitivity, poverty, and sheer distance from the lands of their birth.

In lumping together Jews from Iraq, Morocco, Egypt, Algeria, and elsewhere into this artificial category of *Mizrahim*, mid-century Zionists dismissed and denigrated Sephardic traditions and many different Arab Jewish identities that had developed over centuries. The Hebrew University philosopher Meir Buzaglo identifies one of the great *Mizrahi* gifts to modern Israel as being traditionalists "devoted to the world of one's parents and teachers" but not "enslaved" to it. Erez Biton's poetry speaks to this juggling that so many Israelis master daily.

Born in Algeria in 1942, Biton made *aliyah* with his family in 1949. His parents' Zionism was that natural Sephardi Zionism; they didn't need much convincing from the emissaries who came to encourage *aliyah*, he says, because "They lived Jerusalem and the Land of Israel without living in Jerusalem and the Land of Israel—from the prayers." When they reached the Promised Land, they faced many hardships, including Biton's blinding, at age ten, by a discarded grenade he accidentally detonated in his new hometown of Lod.

When his poetry started gaining notice in the 1970s, Biton protested the disrespect *Mizrahim* experienced while celebrating the great heritage *Mizrahim* imported with them. His 1976 poem, "The Moroccan Wedding," sung by the rock group HaBreira Hativit on their first album in 1979, helped familiarize the Israeli mainstream with *Mizrahi* customs and pioneer what came to be known as *Mizrahi* Music, a fusion of East and West that revolutionized Israeli pop—and Israeli society. Biton's poem "Scaffolding" recalls his father's frustration at never really being accepted, and his own progress, which is impressive, albeit incomplete.

In 2015 the Israeli establishment signaled its acceptance of Biton—and his community—by granting Biton the Israel Prize. A year later, Biton chaired a commission to recommend how to better acknowledge *Mizrahi* identity in the classroom. In this excerpt, from an address he delivered at the president's residence, Biton reaches for the heavens—holding Israel to high moral, cultural, and social standards, by rooting the Zionist experience in those same heavens.

Address at the President's House on the Subject of Jerusalem (May 23, 2016)

The global vision of the prophet Isaiah bursts forth from a very constrained geographic space, very local, almost remote—the city of David, Jerusalem. It is reified not only on the level of moral energy but on a geographic level that develops and expands. Ultimately, this small space becomes a source of global energy that sustains the world.

Sometimes Jerusalem is within us, sometimes we are in Jerusalem, and sometimes it seems that everywhere is Jerusalem. . . .

This small provincial place becomes a source of spiritual energy for the entire world. The words of the prophet are like a small concentrated capsule that slowly releases its balm along the global spinal cord, first via individual consciousness, then through collective consciousness. Over the generations, the sensibility is expressed differently, but eventually the Prophet Isaiah's vision becomes the universal symbol of eschatological salvation. . . . that from Zion the Torah will emerge, and the word of the Lord from Jerusalem. . . .

The process of transforming the nation into a spiritual exemplar that justifies the title of "*Am Segula*," an enlightened nation, which will have a shot at influencing the world throughout the generations, can only occur with a society fully committed to achieving social justice.

As I wrote in my poem, "Scaffolding":

> On the threshold of half a house in the Land of Israel
> my father stood pointing to the sides and saying:
>> "On these ruins
>> we will build a kitchen some day
>> to cook a Leviathan's tail and a wild bull in it
>> And on these ruins
>> we will build a prayer corner
>> to make room
>> for some holiness."
>
> My father remained on the threshold
> and I, my whole life,
> have been erecting scaffolding
> reaching up into the heart of the heavens.

The debris becomes the foundation for a new building, and to take personal responsibility, to take the concrete action and not to remain stranded on the threshold of redemption, is not about something tangible and accessible; it's about vision.

The concrete act calls us to draw near, to build scaffolding for something even grander, that is thunderous and wonderful, from "the heart of the heavens." . . . The State of Israel, as an independent Jewish state, is the institution that allows us to create a society based on justice and generosity, on mutual engagement. The State of Israel is the infrastructure for fulfilling our commitment to perfect Israeli society, to repair our community, including each and every one of us, on our own path. The State of Israel is the land mass on which we can secure the scaffolding into the heart of the heavens and make our contribution to *tikkun olam*, repairing and perfecting the world.

And if we will eventually face the fact today that we are gathered in this same space, Jerusalem, nearly three thousand years since Isaiah's prophecy committed us to act ethically, how will we react to the elderly widow kicked out of her house because she didn't meet the bank's timetable for mortgage payments; how will we cope with the suffering of the handicapped and the weak? . . .

Judaism was also the place of yearnings in the map of global yearnings that looked toward Jerusalem, and we too come to her, those of us born on the borderline between exile and rebirth, with boundless courage to take on the disposable, the exceptional, the tenuous, the miraculous.

Bernard Avishai (b. 1949)

I am a Hebrew Culture Zionist.

While A. B. Yehoshua's "total Jew" finds identity reinforcement in all elements of Israeli culture taking place in Israel's Jewish surround sound, from cobbling shoes to tailoring Talmudic arguments, Bernard Avishai makes it all about language. Genuflecting toward Eliezer Ben-Yehudah, Avishai sees Hebrew as the passport that makes modern Israelis Israeli. Zionism's revived Hebrew language today provides entry, involvement, and ultimately, membership in what Avishai believes is the great Zionist enterprise—"Greater Israel's" great rival, "Global Israel." This expression of Cultural Zionism, what he calls Hebrew Culture, ultimately redeems Zionism for Avishai, despite his alienation from the post-1967 political status quo.

Avishai so abhors the religious right's dominance—and so shares the post-Zionist love of a neutral democratic square—that he flirts with rejecting the legitimacy of the Zionist project. His hard-hitting articles criticizing Israel's behavior in the territories culminated in the 1985 book *The Tragedy of Zionism*. Three decades later, he still believes that returning the territories remains Israel's only option. At the same time, his passion for the Jewish people and the Jewish state ultimately keep him inside the Zionist tent.

Born in Montreal in 1949, Avishai channels the multidimensional complexities of living in Quebec—and living through the French speakers' Quiet Revolution there—to advocate a more open approach to understanding Zionism and making Israel more democratic. Coming from a province so obsessed with language it defines its inhabitants as "Francophones," "Anglophones" and immigrant, non-combatant, "Allophones," Avishai builds his modern Zionism through shared mastery of a "transcendental instrument," Hebrew. Similarly, his Renaissance man career, ranging from a literary-historical treatise on the importance of Philip Roth's *Portnoy's Complaint* to Harvard Business School, digital-technology-oriented consulting gigs, deepens his passion for Israel as Start-Up Nation. For Avishai, fusing the modernized Holy Tongue with the old-new high tech revolution creates this Hebrew republic: a Zionism clearly rooted in Ahad Ha'am's republic of culture, while approaching yet not embracing post-Zionists' post-Jewish universal, neutered, citizenship.

The Hebrew Republic (2008)

Can a state for world Jewry be a republic of citizens, many of whom are not Jews? . . .

The great achievement of Zionism, the creation of the Hebrew-speaking nation, is a settled fact. The country that serves as its homeland might now adapt to any number of international political arrangements, while preserving its cultural distinction. The bloodshed between Israelis and Palestinians may not end anytime soon. Yet Greater Israel has a rival in Global Israel. Palestinians, Israeli Arabs, even the vast majority of Jews removed from settlements, could do worse than find themselves in the gravitational pull of Tel Aviv. . . .

The Israel [I] envision. . . . [is] a republic in which the Hebrew language predominates, partly through established legal protections, but also naturally, because the commercial hegemony of Israel's Jews will make Hebrew the language of work. It is a country already largely in existence. This Israel—this Hebrew republic—would be patently the state of the Jewish people, with voluntary links to Jews around the world, but it would be organized in a way that does not presume to straighten the crooked timber. Nor, I should emphasize, would it presume to replace Jews with Hebrews. A language is an ambience, not an indoctrination. Hebrew will provide a distinctly Israeli context in which its citizens—mainly Jews, but also Arabs, and others—work out their own lives. . . .

A Jewish state—it cannot be emphasized enough—does not have an identity like that of a Jewish person. A state is also not a family, or a club, or a congregation. It is a commonwealth, a social contract, in which individuals who are subject to equal rules of citizenship work out their lives—if they wish, in voluntary association with people, families, clubs, and congregations. Nor is this call for a Hebrew republic a desire to replace the Jewish people with a people called Hebrews or to impose Jewish identity on Israel's Arabs. On the contrary, I am just Zionist enough to believe that the Hebrew language is the best possible medium in which Jewish individuals, congregations, and so forth can try out whatever practical definitions of who is a Jew as they please. Hebrew is also spacious enough for Arabs to absorb its nuances and yet remain Arabs, at least in the hybridized way minorities everywhere adapt to a majority's language and the culture it subtends. Diaspora Jews are nothing if not proof of how this can work. . . .

Hebrew is the best possible context for communities to forge Jewish identities, secular and also religious. What a Hebrew republic does preclude is the monopoly that Orthodox rabbinic hierarchies have arrogated to themselves to define who is a Jew and Jewish values. A democratic state can tell you what to speak, not what to think....

With the important exceptions of nationalist Orthodox and Haredi folk, secluded in their spreading settlements and neighborhoods, nearly everybody in Israel—Ashkenazim, *Mizrahim*, Russians, and Arabs—is marinated in a popular Hebrew culture whose center is Tel Aviv. The English of international science and business is implanted here, yielding dozens of fertile hybrids. Younger Israelis are now accustomed to shuttling from nuanced Hebrew fiction to subtitled Hollywood movies, to the BBC, or a Lakers game; or from *Mizrahi* music, to sentimentalized Jewish holidays, to a Thai restaurant—and then to the beach.

Israel's Arabs, naturally enough, feel pulled by proximate currents, particularly in the Arab world, and even if the Arab world is skeptical of them. Yet even if they watch Al Jazeera at night, most Israeli Arabs read *Yediot Aharonot,* the popular Israeli tabloid, over lunch.... You can feel the integration most fully in Israeli medical facilities, where Jewish and Arab doctors and nurses deliver treatment, interchangeably, and without discrimination, to any patient....

Ahad Ha'am argued for a "spiritual center" in the national home which would revive the Diaspora....

Hebrew was a transcendental instrument. Like Emerson, Ahad Ha'am edited and mentored a generation of writers and activists who created the new country's DNA: not only Gordon, but Eliezer Ben-Yehuda, the creator of the modern Hebrew dictionary; Weizmann, the national home's first great diplomat; the poet H. N. Bialik; the writer Shmaryahu Levin; even, indirectly, David Ben-Gurion, who founded the *Histradut* in the 1920s. Weizmann wrote: "We were the spokesmen of the Russian-Jewish masses, who sought in Zionism self-expression and not merely rescue." It is Zionism's singular tragedy that all of these people are just street names in Israel today, while the term Zionism is applied to hilltop settlers with Uzis, flowing forelocks, and visits from Pat Robertson.

Saul Singer (b. 1961)

I am a Start-Up Zionist . . . the new *halutziut.*

Israel's shift from a poor socialist developing country to a high-tech power updated the Zionist vision and mission. The digital revolution showed that you don't have to be a socialist to be a Zionist—but a good Zionist cares about social concerns too. Moreover, as the Holocaust refugee turned real-estate developer David Azrieli insisted: "It is still possible to be a Zionist pioneer in Israel, a *halutz,* but the new *halutziut* is economic in nature." Just as President Ephraim Katzir—and Prime Minister David Ben-Gurion—connected Israel's scientific progress with Zionism's march toward Jewish self-determination and socialist fulfillment, a new generation of Start-Up Zionists connected Israel's hi-tech miracle making with Zionism's march toward Jewish greatness and individual fulfillment.

Along with his brother-in-law Dan Senor, Saul Singer helped name this most dramatic manifestation of the New Zionism—Israel as "Start-Up Nation." Their 2009 best-selling book, *Start-Up Nation* attributed Israel's outsized economic success to such phenomena as the army's culture of improvisation and self-criticism. Two years later, Singer wrote that Israel's high-tech success is a key building block in creating a new Jewish narrative—with a dynamic business vision updating the Zionist vision.

Singer was born and educated in the United States. He moved to Israel in 1994, seven years after his brother Alex Singer was killed in action in Lebanon. Echoing some of the moving letters that Alex Singer sent and the family published, Saul Singer also sees the Jewish state as a values nation, embodying a moral as well as business vision. He calls for "updating the narrative" of the Jewish people from one of survival to purpose: "They tried to kill us, we won, now we're changing the world!" Translated into multiple languages, including Polish, Korean, and Mongolian, *Start-Up Nation* takes Ahad Ha'am's Cultural Zionism on the road, showing that modern Zionism can not only energize Jews in the Jewish state, can not only inspire Jews throughout the world,

but can truly be a cutting-edge, energy-efficient, life-enhancing LED
light to the nations.

They Tried to Kill Us, We Won, Now We're Changing
the World (*Jerusalem Post*, April 1, 2011)

We need to update our narrative. The Jewish narrative has changed over
the years. We need to enter the 3.0 era.

1.0 was the era of the Bible. What we Jews were about then was purpose. And our purpose was to transform the pagan world—the world
of child sacrifice and extreme immorality. Along with Christianity and
Islam, we succeeded in spreading a message of one God and of ethics.
The pagan world was transformed. Mission accomplished. And we grew
as a people. But then we faced the destruction of the Temple and exile.

And that took us into the 2.0 era. 2.0 was the era of survival. In that
mode, what we Jews were about was survival, and the dream of a return,
and messianism. We were hoping we'd be around to see the future.

That 2.0 period lasted 2,000 years. Today, we've still got this narrative: They tried to kill us, we won, let's eat. That's how we still think of
our narrative.

That's a narrative of survival. That's not a purpose. Unless you call
survival a purpose. . . .

We must update the narrative to: They tried to kill us, we won, now
we're changing the world! . . .

When I moved here sixteen years ago, we thought that the dream of
being a light unto the nations probably had to wait for peace. We were
busy surviving.

That challenge is still there. But . . . the light unto the nations dream is
already happening. We are saving lives though medicine—through medical innovation. . . . Almost every technology you look at—computers,
cellphones, Internet—has a piece of Israel in it. . . . Yet that's not what
we talk about when we talk about Israel. It's not what we show when we
bring people to Israel. It's not integrated into the way we think about our
purpose as a people in the world. Not yet. . . .

If we focus on purpose, derivative concerns—such as "relevance," "identity" and "continuity"—will automatically be addressed. . . .

So what is our modern purpose? The context of our ancient purpose was the global struggle to conquer adversity. Though tyranny and poverty are still with us, the challenge of the modern world is increasingly to cope in a world that lacks physical adversity and faces instead a crisis of meaning and community in the face of frayed societal bonds. If the Jews can show that they produce more ethical people, more cohesive families, and the only religion that is also a·coherent people (there is no Christian people or Muslim people, but Christians and Muslims), I believe we will be able to attract both disaffected born Jews and a small but significant fraction of non-Jews to join our cause. If we continue to let our enemies fool us into thinking we are only about survival, the only "continuity" we will experience is on a path toward obscurity and decline.

Sharon Shalom (b. 1973)

Ethiopian Zionism: The moment he set foot on the ground of Jerusalem, he began to count the years of his life anew.

The tensions between Zionist ideals and Israeli realities played out dramatically with Ethiopian immigration. Zionism still proved relevant—and far from racist—as Israel welcomed yet another oppressed Jewish population, becoming the only non-African country to seek out thousands of black Africans. Nevertheless, Ethiopian Jews faced a difficult adjustment to a modern country complicated by manifestations of crass racism.

Born Zaude Taspei, Sharon Shalom arrived in Israel in 1982 as one of eight thousand Ethiopian Jews Operation Moses brought to Israel; Operation Solomon would bring fourteen thousand more in 1991.

Shalom went on to become a leader in the Religious Zionist youth movement B'nai Akiva, study at the Har Etzion Hesder Yeshiva, serve as an army officer, earn his rabbinic ordination, and receive a PhD in Jewish philosophy. Today, he is a rabbi in Kiryat Gat, and part of the Tzohar movement nurturing responsive and inspiring rabbis.

As a leading Ethiopian Israeli, Shalom looks back—telling the inspiring story of his Zionist journey to salvation—while looking forward—building a Zionism that has left Ben-Gurion's zeal for sameness behind. He believes that Israeli Jews should keep juggling pride in their country with pride in the particular Jewish heritage that nurtured them. In *From Sinai to Ethiopia*, his 2016 exploration of Ethiopian Jewry's "halakhic and conceptual world," Shalom calls for a pluralism that endorses "preservation of uniqueness" along with "mutual personal responsibility" and "mutual respect." He understands the words "as yourself" in the Torah's dictum, "Love your neighbor as yourself" to mean that "You should be capable of looking at the world through the eyes of the other." And "uniqueness," he insists, "is not the opposite of unity, but rather its synonym."

A Meeting of Two Brothers Who Had Been Separated for Two Thousand Years (2017)

As a child in Ethiopia, I thought that Jerusalem was made of gold. I dreamed of a land of milk and honey, in which everyone was Jewish and the gentiles did not hate them. In the village, we continued dreaming of Jerusalem.

Rumors began to fly around our village and others that Jews from Jerusalem had come to Sudan in order to help the Ethiopian Jews, the Beta Israel community, to go to Israel. . . . After two thousand years, we began to internalize the idea that the road to Jerusalem was open. . . .

We walked for over two months from Ethiopia to Sudan, exposed to the dangers of the road. People were certain they would reach Jerusalem within a short time, but in reality, some of them were forced to wait in the Twawa refugee camp in Sudan for as long as six years. Conditions in the camp were harsh. . . .

The mortality rate among children in the camp was particularly high, so some of the parents decided to send their children ahead of them to Israel, to try to save their lives. . . . Along with hundreds of other children, adults, and elderly, I was packed into a crowded truck. . . . Conditions inside the truck were foul. . . .

Finally, the truck stopped, and we heard a powerful racket outside. . . .
I saw an amazing sight [the sea], something I had never seen before. I
saw water, more and more water that erupted and writhed fearfully. . . .
Then suddenly a miracle happened. From out of this nowhere, from deep
within the darkness and the fog, the tumult and the confusion, comman-
dos from Unit 13 of the Israeli Navy rose up out of the sea. They shed
tears, and we cried along with them. It was a meeting of two brothers
who had been separated for two thousand years. . . .

In January 1982, I stood in front of an Immigration Ministry clerk at
Ben-Gurion Airport. . . . I barely managed to pronounce my name in
a whisper. For over two thousand years, our people recited the prayer
"May our eyes behold Your return to Zion in mercy." After an absence
of 2,500 years, the Ethiopian Jewish community has merited the return
to our homeland. We have returned to our home. . . .

I discovered that my Ethiopian name, Zaude, had been changed to the
Israeli name of Sharon. I was pleased to have this name, because people
explained to me that this was a new name from Jerusalem. Wonderful,
I thought, but that led me to ask: Who am I, an Israeli or an Ethiopian?
What does it mean to change your name to an Israeli one? Or on the
contrary, to keep your Ethiopian name? Was society a factor that pulled
me down and kept me back, or was it a motivating factor that pushed me
forward? I also asked, why am I different? Is difference a blessing or a
handicap? Is this society racist or not? I had to reformulate my identity—
how should I go about it? I was confused.

Furthermore, I constantly heard conflicting voices. Some said that
Israeli society was racist, while others said it wasn't. Some said we had to
throw our Ethiopian identity out the window, but some said we should
preserve our traditions. I heard these two voices even within my own
family. One day I asked my grandfather, Abba Dejen Mengashe, of blessed
memory, "Grandfather, how old are you?" He replied, "I'm eight years
old." I was astonished. "Eight years old? How can that be?" He answered
that the moment he set foot on the ground of Jerusalem, he began to
count the years of his life anew. I was thrilled. With all the complex reality of life after *aliyah*, my grandfather still saw the light of Jerusalem. . . .

I, like my grandfather, have chosen to emphasize the good side of Israeli society, and I have found much to appreciate. . . .

After over two thousand years of exile and wanderings, we are proud to live in Kiryat Gat in the Holy Land. It is truly a miracle, a miracle of the revival of the Jewish people, and a sign that the redemption will soon be coming.

Einat Ramon (b. 1959)

My particularist perspectives: I am a Womanist and a Zionist.

Increasingly, Zionism felt countercultural in the twenty-first century. Radical activists tried turning progressive movements like feminism against Israel because many of Zionism's philosophical underpinnings were no longer trendy. Einat Ramon became the first Israeli-born woman rabbi in 1989, and the first woman and first sabra to head a Conservative rabbinical school, the Schechter Rabbinical Seminary in 2005. Today a scholar and a pioneer in pastoral care, she endorses Zionism and feminism as counters to contemporary identity politics. Resisting postmodernism's homogenizing cosmopolitan identity soup, she stands for Jews—and women—standing out and standing strong.

Born in 1959 to a family steeped in Labor Zionism, Ramon appreciates that, for the pioneers, Zionism was "a personal, existential redemption, a one-time opportunity to endow their lives with meaning . . . reclaiming their souls from assimilation, emptiness, decadence and alienation." Hoping to renew that old-new existential vision, Ramon champions "Torah learning with modern Hebrew culture" to access "the stories of Jewish inner, spiritual strength."

Ramon represents a broader Zionist impulse to liberate Jewish learning and ideas from the ghetto. Studying Jewish texts in different contexts, applying them to everyday life, living them—and sometimes ignoring them—has invigorated religious and secular Jewish culture. The sovereign state has taken Ahad Ha'am's cultural revolution further than he imagined, expanding the range of cultural expressions

and intensifying Zionism's cultural impact, in the Land of Israel—
and beyond.

Zionism: A Jewish Feminist-Womanist Appreciation (2017)

Living in the Land of Israel grants Jews the opportunity to indulge their
particularism at its best, expressing Jewishness every moment. We are
just learning how to master this huge spiritual challenge. A. D. Gordon
explained that here was our chance to follow the Torah's philosophical
teachings fully, naturally. We not only celebrate the Sabbath and the
holidays on Jewish time and in our Jewish space, but, today, we run
Israeli military, agriculture, industry, and economics on Torah time and
in the Torah's sacred space. These wonderful opportunities also offer
daily challenges for a young state struggling with the curse of terror and
facing the blessed challenge of absorbing Jews from so many different
countries and cultures.

Both nationhood and Womanist perspectives are particularistic perspectives. The term "womanist" was coined originally by African American women seeking an alternative to the feminism that strives to blur and
ignore "essentialist" differences between men and women. Post-gender
feminists are not even allowed to speak about "men" and "women" anymore, as these are regarded as "compulsive" terms. By the same token,
the postmodern and post-Zionist climate rejects any affirmation of the
uniqueness of any people, let alone the Jewish People.

In the same way that I long for the moment when women and men,
once again, will not be ashamed to speak about their concrete female or
male experiences, encouraging discussions about how to create the conditions of covenant between them, I long for the moment when all Jews
can again revel in their uniqueness, as we did when the State of Israel was
declared. Jewish uniqueness is rooted in the Torah's ancient traditions
translated into secular realities in daily Jewish life. Celebrating the plu-
rality of human experiences, we must promote just enough pluralism—
but not too much as to create chaos by denying a common denominator.

We Israeli Jews are the "dry bones" that came to life (Ezek. 37). We
become a living people as we gather here in Israel from our different

diasporas and as we (re)discover our common denominator rooted in the Hebrew Bible and made relevant through our learning and actions. Yes, we are not yet the holy "kingdom of priests" that God and the world expect us to be. There is much to learn, much to improve. We do not always succeed in defeating all the patriarchal ills that affect the rest of the world: sexual abuse, pornography, economic and cultural discrimination, etc. But following the Zionist thinker, Ahad Ha'am, we trust that we will eventually find our own unique Jewish moral voice and wisdom in the face of modern and postmodern challenges.

Our modern experience teaches us that when Jews gather as a sovereign nation in the Land of Israel, they bestow many blessings to the world. Today, we proud Zionist men and Zionist women hope to bring even more, through innovations in all fields of life, through fulfilling the vision and the goals set out for us when we stood thousands of years ago at Mount Sinai.

Adam Milstein (b. 1952)

Israeliness provides a powerful reminder about where our people have come from, and an inspiring vision of where the Jewish people is going.

The hundreds of thousands of Israelis who left Israel threatened Zionism ideologically. It was hard to see the state as a refuge or peddle *aliyah*—ascending to the land—when so many seemed to be making *yeridah*—descending from the land. Meanwhile, initially, Israelis cursed their fellow citizens abroad—Yitzhak Rabin dismissed them as the "droppings of weaklings." Stung by such contempt, and confused themselves, many Israelis insisted the only left temporarily, condemning their identities to a kind of suspended animation.

In our age of multiple identities and allegiances, such judgments and insecurities seem as anachronistic as Ben-Gurion's insistence that all Jews live in Israel. A turning point occurred in 2007, when Adam and Gila Milstein founded the Israeli Leadership Club in Los Angeles. This nationwide Israeli-American council defines its mission as "building an active and giving Israeli-American community in order to strengthen the State of Israel, our next generation, and to provide a bridge to the Jewish American community." In this excerpt, Adam Milstein, a sabra who fought in the Yom Kippur War, studied at the Technion, and became a real-estate investor and philanthropist in Southern California, offers a vision of Israeliness to invigorate Zionism and Jewish identity—in Israel and abroad.

Israeliness Is the Answer (2016, 2017)

Israeliness incorporates many elements, including Israeli culture, Jewish values and Hebrew, the language of our Bible; extraordinary pride in Jewish tradition and our history; a deep belief in Zionism; an incredible connection between Israelis and the Land of Israel; and a commitment to the idea *"Kol Yisra'el areivim zeh lazeh,"* "All the children of Israel are responsible for one another."

Israeliness provides a powerful reminder about where our people have come from, and an inspiring vision of where the Jewish people is going. It makes complete strangers feel like family. It gives young men and women the courage and conviction to fight against evil and for what is right, to defend our Jewish homeland, our Jewish values, and the Jewish people.

Israeliness reminds us about the many contributions to the world that have been born in the Land of Israel, from the advent of Judeo-Christian values to the creation of the Start-Up Nation. In Israel, young people see a country that has more companies listed on the Nasdaq exchange than Africa, Germany, France, the Philippines, Japan, Russia, Singapore, Korea, and India combined, a country whose research has been instrumental in developing pivotal technologies used all around the world from voice mail to computers to text messaging and Waze.

Israeliness opens up a whole new world for young American Jews, many of whom have been conditioned to believe that Jewish identity must be centered around attending synagogue. In discovering their homeland, young Jews are able to discover a piece of themselves, connect with young Israelis, and find new ways to express their Judaism through an Israeli lens.

The obsolete call for all Jews to immigrate to Israel doesn't work anymore. A changing paradigm for understanding the relationship between Israel and the Jewish world now rests on Jewish peoplehood. Jews should build Jewish communities all over the world that embrace a strong Jewish heritage and a strong connection to the State of Israel. If people want to move from Israel to the Diaspora they should be welcome, and vice versa.

Israeli Americans and Israelis share the same identity, which is a combination of culture, language, Jewish heritage, Zionism, a feeling of responsibility for standing up for the Jewish people and the State of Israel, and the values of brotherhood, sisterhood, and family. Israeli Americans are a strategic asset for our families back in Israel, and we stand here to fight against the antisemites and anti-Israel hate groups. Our Israeliness strengthens our Jewish identity, and our unique character—forged by living in Israel—enables us to fight back effectively against those that seek us and the Jewish people harm. In so doing, we are enriching and strengthening the broader Jewish-American community.

Israeliness, thus, is a twenty-first century manifestation of the Zionist dream.

Rachel Sharansky Danziger (b. 1986)

As we participate in civil society, as we interact with each other, as we do our jobs well, we are building Israel from within.

What the educator Micha Goodman calls the "Zionist Beauty Myth" has often immobilized the new generation of Israelis. Naomi Wolf's book *The Beauty Myth* describes how comparing themselves to models makes many women feel inadequate. The Zionist Beauty Myth describes how comparing their prosaic lives to their parents' heroism demoralizes young Israelis.

Nevertheless, many young Israelis are articulating updated Zionist visions. "I find Zionism today still a dynamic word we can actually use," one Israeli fighter pilot turned high-school teacher recently proclaimed. "Judaism and Israel are too solid. Zionism [invites me to] create what I think Israel should be." Another activist invokes the word to distinguish himself from other leftists who seek a one-state solution. Using the "Z-word" broadcasts his commitment to a Jewish state.

The Zionist Beauty Myth could easily paralyze Rachel Sharansky Danziger. One of two daughters of Natan and Avital Sharansky, she grew up in the Jerusalem home of two Zionist icons: the Soviet dissident who resisted the KGB, and his equally indomitable wife who fought ferociously for his freedom. Every February 11, the family celebrates what Danziger calls "a private 'seder' of sorts," marking the day her father was freed after nine years' imprisonment and arrived in Israel. Her father, she writes, "wears the *kippah* a fellow inmate made for him. He pulls out the little Psalms book that was his companion in prison. And like the children on Pesach, we ask questions to celebrate this exodus." The family remembers Rabbi Tzvi Yehuda Kook pronouncing, "Our brothers in Russia are in danger, we must fight for them," and the Jews whose yells worldwide "broke through the Iron Curtain" and "broke into my father's cell long before they broke him out of it." Blessed—yet burdened—with this heritage, Danziger, a *Times of Israel* blogger, celebrates the "New Kind of Zionist Hero" she believes she and her peers must become.

A New Kind of Zionist Hero (*Times of Israel,* April 23, 2015; adapted in 2017)

In Israel, we grow up in the shade of bigger-than-life heroes. Our teachers instill in us the ideal of *shlichut,* a sense of mission. Our national holidays remind us that independence requires sacrifices. The army and its legacy await us. But once we enter our twenties, the minutiae of daily life take central stage. From heroes in training we turn into students and professionals, spouses and parents. We, who grew up preparing to save the world, find ourselves worrying about exams and the cost of cottage cheese.

Why, I thought then, can't I have a proper challenge?

Many of us share this frustration. We dream of being trailblazing leaders and modern-day Abrahams, but history chose to give us Isaac's lot.

Like Isaac, we inherited a path from our parents, and the glory of their heroism is beyond our reach.

But is Isaac's lot any less important than Abraham's? If our generation doesn't maintain our predecessors' achievements, what will remain of their efforts? Furthermore, an established state requires different ideals than a state in the making. It is our lot to maintain Israel; it is our "*shlichut*," our mission, to improve it.

It is our *shlichut* as citizens to strengthen civil society by creating opportunities for dialogue on the local and national level.

It is our *shlichut* as parents and educators to break down the founders' grand ideals into ideas that our kids, growing up free and comfortable, can relate to and embrace.

It is our *shlichut* as young professionals to ensure that our various fields contribute to a just society, instead of breaking it apart on the altar of individual ambition.

It is our *shlichut* as Zionists to stand guard and thrive, not merely survive, making sure that the very prosperity and freedom our parents dreamed of won't blind us to each other's needs, to the bigger purpose of being a model society, or detract from the communal values that inspired the state's founding in the first place.

As we face Isaac's path, the routines of daily life become important. "We brought you here," my father said at my wedding, "but it is up to you to build a life here." Our parents' heroism enabled us to establish a living, happy society in Israel. As we participate in civil society, as we interact with each other, as we do our jobs well, we are building Israel from within.

18

Torchbearers

Diaspora Zionism

As Israel approached its fiftieth birthday in 1998, the conversation about Israel and the Diaspora changed dramatically. With the launching of the Oslo Peace process, the first stirrings of what became Start-Up Nation, and the emergence of its Jewish community as nearly half the world's Jewish population, Israel seemed increasingly stable. The Soviet Union's collapse and the airlift of Ethiopian Jews to Israel had saved the two Jewish communities most endangered physically by antisemitism. American Jews, looking at spiking intermarriage rates, increasingly worried about "continuity," meaning the Jewish future. With most Jews living in democratic countries, enjoying relative freedom and prosperity, Zionism was no longer a matter of life and death. Zionism became a choice, a voluntary expression of identity.

Ultimately, American Zionism, the Zionism of helping others live better lives in Israel from afar, became the Zionism of most Diaspora countries. Differences of nuance were evident here and there. Some communities were more embattled, as in France, or more united, as in Canada, or more Hebrew oriented, as in Argentina. At the same time, starting in the 1990s, Diaspora Zionism also became Identity Zionism, with Diaspora Jews turning to Israel to help them build more inspiring and lasting Jewish identities. This educational mission reinforced the Americanization of Diaspora Zionism, a movement more focused on saving the Jewish soul and supporting the State of Israel rather than saving Jewish lives by settling them in Israel.

Jonathan Sacks (b. 1948)

Once, Israel saved Jews. In the future, it will save Judaism.

In his 1994 work, *Will We Have Jewish Grandchildren? Jewish Continuity and How to Achieve It*, Lord Rabbi Jonathan Sacks, who served as chief rabbi of the United Hebrew Congregations of the Commonwealth from 1991 to 2013, anticipated Zionism's shift toward identity building. He proclaimed: "The role of Israel in an era of continuity is not the same as in an era of survival." Starting with the central Zionist assumption—"Jewish life cannot be sustained without Israel at its core"—Sacks argued: "Once, Israel saved Jews. In the future, it will save Judaism."

Characterizing Israel as the home of Total Judaism built on A. B. Yehoshua's Total Jew. Sacks observed that "Only in Israel can Jews live Judaism in anything other than an edited edition." Jews in modern democracies were living the life that Moses Mendelssohn dreamed of in the 1700s, limiting their Jewishness to their homes and synagogues. Israel's Judaism was one of the street too. Sacks explained that those public, full-time, Jewish dimensions made visiting the Jewish state so compelling to Diaspora Jews.

Born in 1948, trained in philosophy and rabbinics, knighted in 2005, welcomed into the House of Lords in 2009, now Baron Sacks of Aldgate in the City of London, Sacks emphasizes two central Zionist ideas. He brands anti-Zionism "the new antisemitism." Acknowledging that not all criticism of Israel is antisemitic, he targets the obsessive, irrational scapegoating, noting that "In the Middle Ages, Jews were hated because of their religion. In the nineteenth and twentieth centuries they were hated because of their race. Today, they are hated because of their nation-state, Israel."

Second, Sacks celebrates Israel's many human achievements, which Jews often take for granted. An early voice in the movement to view Israel as identity builder, he continues to shape this ongoing educational revolution in his writings. He toasts Israel as "the home of hope," an "everlasting symbol of the victory of life over death." Sacks inspires audiences worldwide, rejoicing that Israel has "taken the West's oldest faith and made it young again. . . . taken a tattered, shattered nation and made it live again."

Will We Have Jewish Grandchildren? (1994)

Jewish life cannot be sustained without Israel at its core. That was true for nineteen hundred years when there was no Jewish state. It is no less true now that the state exists. One of the most profound turning points in the history of a community is when it declares that it has no interest in the return to Zion. That occurred among Reform Jews in nineteenth-century Germany. Similarly, there are people today who claim that twentieth-century America is not *galut*. It has none of the characteristics of exile. Jews are equal, respected, and secure. They identify with the American dream. Indeed Jews have been the authors of some of its most famous expressions. The inscription under the Statue of Liberty was written by Emma Lazarus. Irving Berlin wrote "God Bless America." As Israel is to Israeli Jews, so America is to American Jews: home.

Sooner or later, such a view spells the end of Jewish life. To be a Jew means to live between two different worlds: the finite and the infinite, the particular and the universal, here and elsewhere. Once that tension is broken, the dissolution of Jewish identity follows as inevitably as night follows day. The process takes on average four generations. But it is inexorable. A Diaspora that turns in upon itself and severs its connection with Israel is a community which, wittingly or otherwise, is breaking its links with Jewish tradition and the Jewish people and taking the first step on the path to complete assimilation. . . .

Both Jewries are beginning to see that *how* we live as Jews may be as important as *where* we live as Jews. . . . The Israel of survival was Jewry's "city of refuge," what A. B. Yehoshua called the Diaspora's insurance policy. The Israel of continuity must become Jewry's classroom, the Diaspora's ongoing seminar in Jewish identity. Once, Israel saved Jews. In the future, it will save Judaism. . . .

Israel is now the only place in which a total Jewish experience is possible. It is the one country where Jews constitute a majority of the population. It is the only context in which they exercise political sovereignty.

It is the sole place where Judaism belongs to the public domain, where Hebrew is the language of everyday life and where the Sabbath and the festivals form the rhythm of the calendar. It is the land of our origins, the terrain on which Joshua and David fought and Amos and Isaiah delivered prophecies. It is the birthplace of Jewish memory and the home of Jewish destiny.

It is impossible to overestimate the impact of Israel on the formation of Jewish identity. Jewish existence, which in today's Diaspora may appear random, arbitrary, and disconnected, in Israel takes on coherence. There the Bible comes alive against the backdrop of its own landscape and its own language, once again a living tongue. There, too, the concept of the Jewish people becomes vivid in the visible drama of a society gathered together—as Moses said it would be—"from the ends of the heavens." Above all, it is in Jerusalem that the mystery of Israel becomes tangible. Here is the old-new heart of the old-new people, the place from which, said Maimonides, the Divine presence never moved. . . .

Judaism was never the private faith of isolated individuals. Its entire pulse is collective, societal, communal. From the destruction of the second Temple until the end of the eighteenth century, Jews lived in self-governing communities. Exiled from their land, they took a fragment of Israel with them. In each locality they had their own language, customs, and culture; their collective life. In the modern Diaspora, however, Judaism has been confined to the private domain of the home, school, and synagogue. Israel restores to Jewish life what it has lost elsewhere: a public dimension. Within its borders, Jewishness is *out there* in the street as well as *in here,* in the home. That is why spending time in Israel is today essential to a full understanding of what it means to be a Jew anywhere in the world.

So we arrive finally at the third policy option for the Jewish future. The Diaspora will no longer use its funds to support Israel. Nor will it use them to support itself alone. It will use them to resource Israel to strengthen the Diaspora, since this is in their joint best interests. It will fund Israel experiences for young Jews. It will make it a goal that every Jewish teenager should spend time in Israel. The Israel-based year of study or service will become normative. The Diaspora's teachers will be part-trained in Israel. Its rabbis, youth leaders, and outreach workers will study there. There will be more exchanges between Israeli and Diaspora teachers and academics. The entire relationship between Israel and the Diaspora will shift from dependence to reciprocity. . . .

Israel, surely, is our ultimate destination. But the immediate question is less whether Jews are at home in London or Jerusalem than whether they are *at home in their Jewishness*. . . .

Alan Dershowitz (b. 1938)

Israel—like Judaism itself—must remain a positive option to be freely chosen out of love, not merely a negative response to hatred and fear.

As Jonathan Sacks spoke of Israel and Diaspora needing to strengthen one another, many Diaspora Jewish leaders feared Diaspora Jewry's deterioration. In *The Vanishing American Jew: In Search of Jewish Identity for the Next Century* (1997), Alan Dershowitz worried that with intermarriage, American Jews were being loved to death.

Born in Williamsburg, raised in Borough Park, the youngest-ever Harvard Law professor at age twenty-eight, and a celebrity lawyer who also defended celebrities, Dershowitz sought to motivate the next generation of disaffected and unaffiliated Jews. He called for a new Jewish state of mind centered on Israel, as a mostly secular, values-oriented, Jewish civilization.

Playing the role of Israel's master advocate, Dershowitz has demonstrated how to fight against Israel's delegitimization effectively. He has also shown that defending Israel's right to exist will not stop him from criticizing Israel's ongoing presence in the West Bank—or any other particular policies or strategies he cannot abide.

While best known for his involvement in the public controversies surrounding Israel, Dershowitz has also advocated an important Diaspora mission for Israel: inspire secular American Jews through the vitality of Israeli culture. In doing so, Dershowitz is helping push the American Jewish community from only reading Israel through the lens of crisis to seeing it through the prism of opportunity.

The Vanishing American Jew (1997)

I am a committed Zionist. I believe passionately in the Jewish state. If I had several lives to live, one of them would be as an Israeli. I hope to continue to spend a considerable amount of time, even more as I approach retirement, in Israel. But I am an American, and I love America and believe in its future. I am thankful that as a Jew I always have the Israeli option available to me and my family if the militia, the skinheads, or the Farrakhans were ever to come to power here. I know that it is unfair for American Jews to regard Israel as the provider of an insurance policy, to whom we pay premiums but with whom we refuse to share the risks and burdens of being a direct part of the Jewish state. . . .

The time has come to articulate a new, more positive Zionism, responsive not to the anachronistic realities of the late nineteenth and early twentieth centuries but to the new realities of the (hopefully) post-antisemitic era of Jewish life in the twenty-first century. We must, of course, never forget the recent pervasiveness of antisemitism and the possibility of its recurrence, in either an old or a new incarnation. That is one of the reasons the Law of Return should never be abrogated. But we must also prepare ourselves for the prospect, admittedly unique in Jewish history, of an era without external enemies. . . .

Israel—like Judaism itself—must remain a positive option to be freely chosen out of love, not merely a negative response to hatred and fear, as Herzl characterized both Zionism and Judaism a century ago. As Israel and the Jewish communities around the world strengthen and mature, a new, more symbiotic relationship must develop among them. . . . As Israel grows stronger both militarily and economically, it will become less dependent on Jewish communities around the world. . . .

We will continue to send our children to Israel for visits from all parts of the Jewish world. Israel will continue to produce Jewish literature, Jewish music, Jewish art, and Jewish philosophy, as the rest of world Jewry gravitates more closely to the national characters of its adoptive homes.

Yes, a divided Israel may divide world Jewry in the short term, as it appears to be doing today, but as Israel becomes stronger, it will help to unite us by becoming the place where the elusive Jewish character is defined and perpetuated, especially for more secular Jews.

Yossi Beilin (b. 1948)

Israel: the solution for the continuation of a secular Jewish life.

In the late 1990s, the conversation about Israel's contribution to Jewish identity was shifting in Israel too. One Labor politician, Yossi Beilin, declared that Israel no longer wanted Diaspora funding, only Diaspora friendship. To him, the Jewish National Fund's Blue Box, once embodying proud Jewish solidarity, now symbolized humiliating Israeli dependence. Most Jewish leaders in Israel and abroad, addicted to this funding model, rejected his analysis. They feared Beilin's push for Zionist autonomy threatened Zionist unity.

Beilin, a political science PhD, served in various governmental positions, including justice minister. In 1994, as a deputy foreign minister seeking more mutuality by emphasizing how Israel helps Diaspora Jews, Beilin proposed to give young Jews a voucher promising a free trip to Israel. This idea blossomed into the Taglit-Birthright Israel program, which flourished when the philanthropists Charles Bronfman and Michael Steinhardt realized Beilin's dream.

Beilin's *His Brother's Keeper: Israel and Diaspora Jewry in the Twenty-First Century* (2000), envisioned a healthy mutual relationship devoid of old-fashioned stereotypes, such as Israel Independence Day celebrations revolving around camels and Jaffa oranges. Instead, he proposes drawing inspiration from modern Israel, from high-tech, hip Tel Aviv.

A proud secular Jew, Beilin observes that while Israel is not "the most secure place for Jews ... it is the most secure place for being Jewish." Going beyond his Zionist hero Ahad Ha'am, Beilin trusts Israel's everyday culture—not just its high culture—to be a transformational agent. He sees the casual Judaism of the Israeli street and home as the most powerful, grounding, modern force for most Jews who are not religious and who need this Israeli model.

His campaigns against religious coercion and for peace take on added urgency for him because he wants Israel to inspire the very Jews liable to be alienated by Israel's religious establishment and ongoing wars. If Jonathan Sacks has given rabbinic blessing to the Zionist shift toward appreciating Israel as identity builder for Diaspora youth, Beilin, another in a long line of Zionist philosopher kings, has given the Zionist thinkers' blessing to this new model shifting from pushing *aliyah* to seeking inspiration.

His Brother's Keeper: Israel and Diaspora Jewry in the Twenty-First Century (2000)

Israel at the beginning of the twenty-first century is not a "normal state," nor is it the most secure place for Jews, but it is the most secure place for being Jewish. From this perspective, it goes a long way toward fulfilling Ahad Ha'am's somewhat nebulous vision of a Jewish spiritual center.

Jews may continue to thrive in the secular world of the twenty-first century, but this does not guarantee a Jewish future. In order for the Jewish people to continue to exist, young Jews must actively prefer marriage partners who will join them in maintaining Jewish family values. The best venues for this preference exist among Orthodox Jews in the Diaspora and among all Jews in Israel, where potential Jewish spouses—religious and secular—are readily available. In Israel, it is possible to develop a Jewish future in a secular world.

Israel, then, is the solution for the continuation of a secular Jewish life, and since most of world Jewry is not religious, it is reasonable to conclude that Israel is the solution for Jewish life. Even if it is not a sufficient solution, and if it still needs many improvements, this fact has become self-evident in recent years. When Israel completes the circle of peace, it could indeed become the solution for Jews and Jewish life. . . .

What kind of dialogue can develop between someone rattling a cup and someone dropping coins into it? . . . Who can assess the price we have paid for perpetuating the image of "poor Israel" through the continued use of the Blue Box long after there was any need for it. . . .

Israel is an attempt to enjoy the advantages of the Jewish ghetto without paying the price. This experiment is being tested every day. Life in this framework is especially good for someone who does not want to worry when he leaves the room that someone may comment, "He's awfully nice—for a Jew." That rare Jewish feeling of belonging to a national majority is significant in an era in which nationalism still plays an important role. . . .

Most Diaspora Jews prefer assimilation to *aliyah*. . . . America is not the exile and Israel is not the desert. We need to get over this Jewish fear and replace it with a strong, ongoing, relevant, and institutionalized relationship. One of the things that this would enable is a new, nonreligious definition of who is a Jew in the twenty-first century. . . .

Israel must offer more Jewish content to the younger generation, devote more classroom hours to the study of Jewish thought, Bible, and Oral Law, while at the same time working to prevent religious coercion and the perception of such coercion. In an atmosphere free of religious legislation, young people will be more open to explore and choose from the treasure of the Jewish heritage.

A normal state, living at peace with its neighbors, whose existence is no longer threatened, where military service is not so long—and perhaps not compulsory—and whose law books are liberated from the invasion of religious legislation, would be much more attractive. . . .

Scott Shay (b. 1957)

The Land of Israel is integral to the Jewish national mission and the soul of every Jew.

The political storms around Israel largely clouded the conversation about Israel. Whereas Zionism started off by offering a solution to the Jewish Problem, many started seeing Zionism itself as the Jewish problem. Nevertheless, other American observers understood that

Zionism, while not a cure-all, could contribute to the intensifying conversation about how to build a thriving Jewish community.

In 2007 Scott Shay, an investment banker and New York Jewish community leader, came out swinging against American Jewish torpor. Shay was appalled by how many "customers" were abandoning American Judaism—especially Conservative Judaism. He endorsed a new relationship with Israel as part of the prescription. His provocative book, *Getting Our Groove Back: How to Energize American Jewry*, offered a ten-point program that included Diaspora Jews committing to spend more time in Israel. In "an age when everyone is interpreting their own meaning and their own individualistic way of tradition, Israel is our compass," Shay asserted. Only visiting Israel could give Diaspora Jews "that sense of Peoplehood" they need. Shay, who sat on the Birthright Israel Steering Committee, notes that "in terms of game changers . . . day schools and Birthright" have been the most "successful Diaspora initiatives since the end of World War II."

Getting Our Groove Back: How to Energize American Jewry (2007)

The principal cause of American Jewry's decline is its loss of a sense of wholeness and purpose. For a large number of American Jews, the future of American Jewry as a whole community is irrelevant. So what if the forces of assimilation, high intermarriage rates, low fertility rates and inadequate Jewish education cause the majority of American Jewry to dissolve into the American melting pot? So what if Orthodox, Conservative, Reform, and secular Jews each create their own exclusive enclaves? . . .

Israel must be a key component of reinvigorating American Jewry. The Land of Israel is integral to the Jewish national mission and the soul of every Jew. . . .

A trip to Israel is a unique way of awakening the Jewish connection in visitors. While there is no "magic bullet" to instill immediate and everlasting Jewish identity, trips to Israel are tremendously galvanizing and often lead to other Jewish experiences. . . . The impact of an organized Israel trip on fostering Jewish identity is spectacular. The reason for this is simple: trips to Israel bring Judaism and the land to life.

Trips to Israel impress upon young visitors the miracle of the modern state despite, or perhaps even because of, its present challenges. . . . Yet it is precisely the flourishing of Jewish life in the midst of all this difficulty that makes Israel so special. Furthermore, the ability to see issues first-hand allows young American Jews to engage with and connect to the real Israel and not the version portrayed on CNN. Trips to Israel challenge young American Jews to grapple with their identity and the experience of other Jews.

Trips to Israel also bring home the beauty of the land, the continuity of Jewish history and the diversity of Jewish life today. It is possible to miss these things if, for example, one were to take a direct flight to Eilat and spend a week on the beach, snorkeling and swimming with the dolphins. Yet such itineraries are rare. Most trips expose visitors to the Israel of the Bible, the Israel of the Second Temple and Talmudic periods, the context and complexities of the formation of the current state, the diversity of Jewish customs and the development of Israeli culture. An Israel trip also provides an excellent opportunity to experience the study of Jewish texts to savor the sacred time of Shabbat. Almost all Jewish visitors leave Israel with a heightened sense of Jewish peoplehood. For young American Jews, one trip to Israel sheds a new light on the risk and cost of breaking the 3,500-year chain that is the Jewish people.

Donniel Hartman (b. 1958)

Beyond Crisis Zionism to a values discourse for a "Values Nation."

Amid fears of a "distancing Diaspora," the Shalom Hartman Institute in Jerusalem began redefining Zionism. In 2009 its new president Donniel Hartman initiated the iEngage educational curriculum encouraging a mutual, critical, dynamic engagement between Israel and "world Jewry." Starting with what its liberal Jewish target audience could agree on before tackling tough issues, iEngage addressed peoplehood, then sovereignty or statehood, then power, then a Jewish-democratic state, concluding with Israel's aspirations as a "Values Nation." This five-part journey helped many communities that had avoided discussions about Israel as too polarizing start engaging again—and healing.

An American-born Israeli rabbi with a philosophy PhD who served in the Israel Defense Forces, as did his children, Hartman has been far more effective than most outside critics in balancing patriotism and dissent. In one widely-forwarded article during the stabbings in Jerusalem in fall 2015, "My Gun and I," he wrote movingly about detesting "the occupation" but detesting terrorists more, about defending himself while pursuing peace. In words that could have been written on a border kibbutz a century ago, he said: "I am grateful for my gun. I hate that I need it, but I am grateful for the fact that when I do, I have the ability to carry it. I hate the fact that the people I love are in danger, but I love the fact that neither I nor my people are helpless victims anymore. I love the gift of Israel, that if and when I need it, I do not merely have the right but the ability to protect myself."

Ultimately, Hartman tired of rallying Jews around threats to Jews. He advocates advancing the Israel-Diaspora relationship from a "crisis narrative" mired in judgmental notions of *galut*, exile, and *geulah*, redemption, to a refreshed, mutually respectful and inspirational— but nevertheless realistic—"values narrative." Through his writing and the Shalom Hartman Institute, particularly iEngage, Hartman has helped shape the North American Zionist conversation to start with the fundamentals that have long united us before jumping into a candid—and now contextualized—discussion about the flashpoints that occasionally divide us.

Israel and World Jewry: The Need for a New Paradigm (*Havruta*, August 24, 2011)

Today, we face a challenge: the crisis model may still have its place, but it is not as compelling or comprehensive as it used to be, and does not adequately reflect the new realities of Jewish life....

After the formation of the state, the two categories of *galut* and *geulah* continued to deeply influence the way the Diaspora and Israeli Jewish communities viewed themselves as well as each other. From the perspective of Israelis, the modern Diaspora remained the quintessence of *galut,* inferior to their own experience of *geulah.* . . . At the same time, many Jews around the world remained imprisoned within the categories of exile and redemption. Diaspora as *galut* was an appropriate perspective in a post-Holocaust world, and the crisis narrative framed the relationship to Israel. If Diaspora is *galut,* fraught with potential or imminent danger, then Israel is its *geulah,* a haven where all Jews could go in times of need. As such, Israel was worthy of one's support, both for its role in saving Jews at risk in the present and as one's own insurance policy for the future. . . .

We are living in a reality unprecedented in Jewish history, with two vital and powerful Jewish communities living side by side—one in Israel, and the other dispersed around the world, with its center in North America. A Jewish life built in isolation from either one will be impoverished. . . . We each have much to contribute to and learn from each other. . . .

We also strive for the opportunity to fulfill our purpose as a people—to live a life of value, meaning, and service. To do so, we need to cease to lean exclusively on the narrative of crisis and add to our vocabulary a narrative of values, whereby we work together as partners, Israel and world Jewry, to determine the moral principles which must govern our national and collective lives, and bring about their implementation. . . .

The first rule is that in this relationship, no one can claim seniority. In a crisis narrative, one side always has a greater voice, either because it is the one doing the saving, or because its life is on the line. In a relationship built on shared values, we must learn to see each other as equals, as partners with much to contribute to one another. . . .

Second, we will need to redefine our notion of loyalty. In a crisis narrative, loyalty means standing together against the enemy and advocating steadfastly for one's side. Criticism, in this context, is an act of treason. In a values narrative, where we work together to fulfill our mission as a people and a nation, loyalty may also express itself in disagreement and in healthy criticism that helps the other partner fulfill its potential. Far from being an act of betrayal, criticism aimed at helping the other is the ultimate act of love and respect.

Third, in a crisis narrative, differences are set aside for the sake of the ultimate concern, namely, survival. But in a values narrative, differences about values, and the ways to implement them, are a permanent feature. No single worldview or political position can be allowed to define the values and aspirations that shape the relationship, or define what it means to be a lover of Israel. The same pluralism which has become self-evident when it comes to the practice of Judaism must also apply to Israel and its policies. Only under these conditions will we be creating a wide enough tent under which all Jews can enter into the relationship.

Finally, in a crisis narrative, we must see each other as we are, in order to meet the real dangers that we face. In a values narrative, we must see each other for what we can become. The conversation is not about embracing and accepting what is, but rather about building a common vision of what ought to be. . . .

Yossi Klein Halevi (b. 1953)

Centrists know that a vital Jewish identity must express the uneasy interplay between our particularist Jewish commitments and our universalist human longings.

With extremists often defining the discourse about Zionism, being a centrist became countercultural. Although he called his first book *Memoirs of a Jewish Extremist,* the acclaimed journalist Yossi Klein Halevi has championed Zionism's reasonable center. Born in Borough Park in 1953, involved as a youth with the Jewish Defense League and the movement to free Soviet Jewry, Yossi Klein Halevi moved to Israel in 1982. Now a senior fellow at Jerusalem's Shalom Hartman Institute, he co-directs its Muslim Leadership Initiative. This outreach to American Muslim centrists could only come from a Yossi Klein Halevi–type centrist—one who understands that reaching out to others within your community or beyond can involve softening your language but must never involve sacrificing your principles.

His historical magnum opus, *Like Dreamers: The Story of the Israeli Paratroopers Who Reunited Jerusalem and Divided a Nation* (2013) described the young Israelis who reunited Jerusalem in 1967, crossed the Suez Canal in 1973, then splintered: founding the settlement movement on the right and the Peace Now movement on the left. This remarkably empathetic book helped critics of each extreme see each movement's idealism—and blind spots.

Klein Halevi seeks "partners in anguish," temperate, thoughtful Israelis and American Jews willing to see Israeli security concerns and Palestinian national ambitions, to appreciate the benefits of communal attachments and universal hopes. He hopes to reclaim the Jewish narrative and unite American Jews and Israelis—not in total agreement, but with awareness of common concerns and commitments. Through this welcoming vision—along with the vivid characters he introduced to bring Israeli history alive—Yossi Klein Halevi advances a Zionism of a vital Israel brimming in all its glory and complexity.

A Jewish Centrist Manifesto (June 5, 2015)

Our task in the twenty-first century is to defend the integrity of the Jewish story of the twentieth century—the return of the Jewish people home. . . . The most insidious threat of BDS [the Boycott, Divestment, Sanction movement] is not economic but ideological. On campuses around the world the very name "Zionism" is becoming tainted. Maddeningly, the more re-rooted we become as a people in our land, the more our indigenousness is being challenged. The growing counter-narrative to Zionism is that a Jewish state was forced on the Arab world by a guilty Europe—ignoring 4,000 years of Jewish connection to the land. . . .

We need to begin telling a story that is rooted not only in the European Jewish experience but in the Middle East—and more than half of Israel's Jews trace their origins to its ancient, uprooted Jewish communities. We need to tell the story of the forgotten refugees—the effective expulsion of the Jews of the Middle East. Theodor Herzl set out to save the Jews of Europe but for the most part failed. Yet the state he imagined into being did save the Jews of the Middle East—who are the region's only minority to attain sovereignty and self-defense. Who can imagine what the fate of the Middle East's Jewish communities would be today without the existence of a Jewish state? . . .

Israelis live in the most dangerous and inhospitable region on the planet and so must be tough. American Jews live in the most benign and welcoming environment Jews have ever known, and so must be flexible. . . .

I need American Jews to be actively involved in my society. The life and death questions of war and peace will be determined by Israel's citizens. Still, if we are serious about defining Israel as the homeland of the Jewish people, then every Jew not only has the right but the responsibility to critique Israeli policies. My plea to Israel's Jewish critics is, Don't underestimate the severity of Israel's dilemmas, the terrible choices we face in the Middle East between one form of vulnerability and another.

Most of all I need American Jews as partners in defending the achievements of Israeli democracy. Those achievements are miraculous. There is no other example of the persistence of vigorous democratic institutions in a country under relentless existential threat since its birth, and populated by waves of immigrants from countries without democratic traditions. . . .

I need the wisdom of American Jews in civil rights and minority relations. Israel needs to broaden its *Israeli* identity to embrace Arabs who are its citizens, even as it deepens its *Jewish* identity to include vigorous relationships with Diaspora Jews who are not its citizens.

I need your help in fulfilling Zionism's promise: to create a national identity that reflects the diversity of the Jewish people. Denying official recognition to entire Jewish denominations, while entrusting Judaism to a spiritually decadent rabbinic establishment, is a violation of the ethos of Jewish peoplehood—a profoundly anti-Zionist act.

I need your help in holding the Israeli center against the easy solutions of left and right, the purity of the extremes. I need partners in anguish, who share the two nightmares of centrist Israelis. The first nightmare is that there won't be a Palestinian state, and the status quo will continue indefinitely; the second nightmare is that there will be a Palestinian state, and we may not be able to adequately defend ourselves from the borders of June 4, 1967. . . .

The worldview of the Jewish center is commitment to *klal Yisra'el*, the entirety of the Jewish people, transcending the interests and ideologies of any of its constituent groups. Centrists know that a vital Jewish identity must express the uneasy interplay between our particularist Jewish commitments and our universalist human longings. Centrists are committed to an Israel that is alert to both security and morality; at once Jewish and democratic, the state of the Jewish people and the state of all its citizens; and modern and traditional, a secular state in a holy land. Indeed centrists embrace those paradoxes as the defining elements of our peoplehood and the animating force of Israeliness, transforming Israel into a laboratory for humanity's challenges in the twenty-first century.

Ellen Willis (1941–2006)

I am an anti-anti-Zionist.

Increasingly, leftist disdain for Israel muddled the Zionist discourse in the Diaspora. Although nearly three-quarters of American Jews supported Israel, it was easy to believe that "all young people," or "all intellectuals," or "all American Jews" had repudiated Zionism because those who did were so loud. But as anti-Zionism became a radical obsession, some leftists objected. Amid mass attacks against Israel in the early 2000s—from both Palestinian terrorists and self-righteous critics who never acknowledged Israel's generous concessions during the Oslo Peace Process—some on the left had enough.

Among them was the rock critic and self-described "rootless cosmopolitan" Ellen Willis. As a feminist who linked political authoritarianism—left and right—with male chauvinism, she branded the groupthink demonizing Israel irrational—and antisemitic. Demonstrating her own intellectual integrity, her analysis showed that while not calling herself a Zionist, she was one, accepting Jewish peoplehood, Israel's existence—and the Law of Return.

Cognizant that the threat of "anti-Jewish genocide" still lingers, Willis bravely insisted on having this difficult discussion with her allies. In fact, rather than accusations of antisemitism squelching leftist criticism of Israel, she showed that leftists were squelching any accusations of antisemitism.

Willis died at age sixty-four. Her essay on anti-anti-Zionism outlives her. It is frequently reprinted, often referenced, widely respected, as a clear-eyed iconoclastic statement exposing the irrational ancestral hatred inflaming—and ultimately obscuring—the critical scrutiny every country, including Israel, deserves and needs.

Is There Still a Jewish Question? I'm an Anti-Anti-Zionist (2003)

I'm not a Zionist—rather I'm a quintessential Diaspora Jew, a child of Freud, Marx, and Spinoza. I hold with rootless cosmopolitanism: from my perspective the nation-state is a profoundly problematic institution, a nation-state defined by ethnic or other particularist criteria all the more so. And yet I count myself an anti-anti-Zionist. This is partly because the logic of anti-Zionism in the present political context entails an unprecedented demand for an existing state—one, moreover, with popular legitimacy and a democratically elected government—not simply to change its policies but to disappear. It's partly because I can't figure out what large numbers of displaced Jews could have or should have done after 1945, other than parlay their relationship with Palestine and the (ambivalent) support of the West for a Jewish homeland into a place to be. (Go "home" to Germany or Poland? Knock, en masse, on the doors of unreceptive European countries and a reluctant United States?) And finally it's because I believe that anti-Jewish genocide cannot be laid to rest as a discrete historical episode, but remains a possibility implicit in the deep structure of Christian and Islamic cultures, East and West.

This last point is particularly difficult to argue on the left, where the conventional wisdom is that raising the issue of antisemitism in relation to Israel and Palestine is nothing but a way of stifling criticism of Israel and demonizing the critics. In the context of left politics, the dynamic is actually reversed: accusations of blind loyalty to Israel, intolerance of debate, and exaggeration of Jewish vulnerability at the expense of the real, Palestinian victims are routinely used to stifle discussion of how antisemitism influences the Israeli-Palestinian conflict or the world's reaction to it or the public conversation about it. Yet that discussion is crucial, for there is no way to disentangle the politics surrounding Israel from the politics of the Jewish condition. . . .

I reject the idea that Israel is a colonial state that should not exist. I reject the villainization of Israel as the sole or main source of the mess in the Middle East. And I contend that Israel needs to maintain its "right of return" for Jews around the world.

My inconsistency, if that's what it is, comes from struggling to make sense of a situation that has multiple and at times contradictory dimensions. Israel is the product of a nationalist movement, but it owes its existence to a world-historical catastrophe. The bloody standoff between Israelis and Palestinians is on its face a clash of two nationalisms run amok, yet it can't be understood apart from the larger political forces of the post–1945 world—anti-colonialism, oil politik, the Cold War, the American and neoliberal triumph, democracy versus authoritarianism, secularism versus fundamentalism.

Indeed, the mainstream of contemporary political anti-Zionism does not oppose nationalism as such, but rather defines the conflict as bad imperialist nationalism versus the good liberationist kind. Or to put it another way, anti-Zionism is a conspicuous feature of that brand of left politics that reduces all global conflict to Western imperialism versus Third World anti-imperialism, ignoring a considerably more complicated reality. But . . . at present, an end to nationalism in Israel/Palestine is not on either side's agenda. The question is what course of action, all things considered, will help in some way to further the possibilities for democracy and human rights as opposed to making things worse.

I support a two-state solution that in effect ratifies the concept of the original 1947 partition—bracketing fundamental questions about Jewish and Palestinian nationalism—out of the non-utopian yet no less urgent hope that it would end the lunacy of mutual destruction and allow some space for a new Middle Eastern order to develop. . . .

Leftists tend to single out Israel as The Problem that must be solved. That tropism is most pronounced among those for whom the project of a Jewish state is inherently imperialist, or an offense to universalist humanism, or both. . . . I've received countless impassioned e-mails emphasizing how imperative it is to show there are Jews who disagree with the Jewish establishment, who oppose [Prime Minister Ariel] Sharon. There is no comparable urgency to show that Jews on the left as well as the right condemn suicide bombing as a war crime.... At most I hear, "Suicide bombing is a terrible thing, but ..." But: if Israel would just shape up and do the right thing, there would be peace. Would that it were so....

Left animus toward Israel is not a simple, self-evident product of the facts. What is the nerve that Israel hits?

Underlining this question are the hyperbolic comparisons that animate the anti-Israel brief, beginning with the now standard South Africa comparison—the accusation that Israel is a "settler state" and an "apartheid state"—which has inspired the calls for divestment and for a boycott against Israeli academics. The South African regime, of course, was one whose essence was a proudly white racist ideology, a draconian system of legal segregation, and the denial of all political rights to the huge majority of people. To see Israel through this grid is to ignore a great many things: that Israel was settled primarily by refugees from genocide in Europe and oppression in Arab countries; that while Palestinian Israelis suffer from discrimination they are nevertheless citizens who vote, organize political parties, and participate in the government; that the occupation, while egregious, came about as a result not of aggressive settlement but of defensive war; that it continues because of rejectionism on both sides....

Even more fantastic is the Nazi comparison, often expressed in metaphors (Israeli soldiers as ss men, and so on). I imagine that most perpetrators of this equation, if pressed, would concede that Israel is not a totalitarian dictatorship with a program of world domination, nor has it engaged in the systematic murder of millions of people on the grounds that they are a subhuman race. But why do these tropes have such appeal? ...

It's impossible not to notice how the runaway inflation of Israel's villainy aligns with ingrained cultural fantasies about the iniquity and power of Jews; or how the traditional pariah status of Jews has been replicated by a Jewish pariah state....

The anti-Jewish temperature is rising, and has been for some time, in Arab and Islamic countries and in the Islamist European diaspora. I am speaking now not of the intemperate tone of left anti-Zionist rhetoric but of overt Jew hatred. . . . Many on the left view this wave of antisemitism as just another expression, however unfortunately couched, of justified rage at Israel—whether at the occupation and the escalating destruction of the West Bank or at the state's existence per se. In either case, the conflation of "Zionists" and "Jews" is regarded as a misunderstanding of the politically uneducated. . . .

If there should be a mass outbreak of anti-Jewish violence it will no doubt focus on Israel, but it will not, in the end, be caused by Israel, and the hatred will not disappear if Israel does. Nor will it disappear with an Israeli-Palestinian settlement. Still . . . an internationally brokered peace agreement is the first line of defense. And that agreement must allow Israel to retain its character as a haven for Jews, not as a validation of nationalism but as a gesture of international recognition that the need for such a haven has not yet been surpassed. It's not inconsistent to hope that this will not always be true.

Theodore Sasson (b. 1965)

From passive fans sitting in the bleachers to active players on the field of contentious Israeli politics.

The debate about American Jewry's relationship with Israel became both academic and political. Academics debated the "distancing thesis," the claim that young, liberal, American Jews were abandoning Israel. Scholars also analyzed different attachment models or understandings of nationalism and identity to explain American Jews' engagement—or disengagement—with a Jewish state six thousand miles away. Yet their arguments were ultimately ideological. The scholarly combatants often favored particular readings of Israeli politics, the American Jewish future, or the Zionist idea.

In 2013 the Brandeis and Middlebury sociologist Theodore Sasson analyzed the "new American Zionism." Using sociological analysis to move beyond speculation and finger-wagging, he refuted the distancing hypothesis statistically, noting that since the 1980s more than 60 percent of American Jews of all ages have found Israel at least "somewhat" important to them. He also contended that the various platforms for American Jews' interaction with their homeland reflected a robust multidimensional relationship.

Suggesting a way forward ideologically, Sasson now points to what could be called a doppelganger Zionism. This mirroring emerges most clearly in Birthright-style *mifgashim*, those popular encounters in which Israeli and Diaspora peers look at their intimate "other" closely and experience an intensity akin to a reunion with a long-lost relative. While that greater intimacy sometimes looks contentious because it generates greater intensity, the two groups appreciate enough similarities in each other's Jewish selves to feel comfortable enough to explore their differences. Sasson then points to a new, mobilized, Birthright-infused American Zionism that shifts from cheerleader to starring player, from Israel supporter to influencer.

The New American Zionism (2013)

In recent years, many journalists and social scientists have described American Jews as "distancing" from Israel. Yet . . . the evidence suggests something perhaps surprisingly closer to the opposite: Across multiple fields, including advocacy, philanthropy, and tourism, American Jews have stepped up their level of engagement with Israel. Attitudinally, they remain as emotionally attached to Israel as they have been at any point during the past quarter century.

Nonetheless, the relationship of American Jews to Israel has changed in several important ways. . . .

The mobilization model that characterized American Jewish engagement with Israel is in a state of decline. Alongside it, a new "direct engagement" model has emerged, especially among the most active segments of the community. . . . American Jewish engagement with Israel increasingly resembles the pattern established by other contemporary diasporas, a pattern characterized by diverse political and philanthropic projects, contentious politics, frequent homeland travel, high levels of consumption of homeland news and entertainment, and realistic rather than idealistic attitudes toward the homeland state and society. . . .

Today, American Jews are more likely to advocate politically on behalf of their own personal views and target their Israel-bound donations to causes they care about personally. They are also more likely to connect to Israel directly, through travel and consumption of Israeli news and entertainment, often through the Internet. . . . With these changes, American Jews are increasingly behaving like other contemporary diaspora communities—they are becoming a *normal* diaspora. As a result, Israel may become more personally meaningful for many American Jews even as, paradoxically, their capacity to influence Israeli policies diminishes. . . .

More American Jews care sufficiently about Israel to seek to influence its future. . . . For such individuals and the organizations they establish and support, mere support for Israel no longer reflects and expresses their deepest passions. Rather, they seek to mold, direct, shape, and influence Israel's future development. Moreover, they also seek to connect to Israel in a personal, direct, and experiential fashion. . . . They have gone from passive fans sitting in the bleachers to active players on the field of contentious Israeli politics.

Central Conference of American Rabbis

We affirm the unique qualities of living in *Eretz Yisra'el*, the Land of Israel, and encourage aliyah.

When the Central Conference of American Rabbis (CCAR), the world's oldest and largest rabbinic organization, issued its first mission statement in 1885, it echoed the Reform movement's German founders. "We consider ourselves no longer a nation, but a religious community," the "Pittsburgh Platform" declared, "and therefore expect neither a return to Palestine . . . nor the restoration of any of the laws concerning the Jewish state."

By 1937 Hitler's rise and Eastern European Jewry's growing influence on American Judaism led to a revolutionary "Columbus Platform." The rabbis still emphasized Judaism's religious nature and avoided the word "peoplehood," fearing charges of dual loyalty. Nevertheless, the CCAR proclaimed: "Judaism is the soul of which Israel is the body.... In the rehabilitation of Palestine, the land hallowed by memories and hopes, we behold the promise of renewed life for many of our brethren. We affirm the obligation of all Jewry to aid in its upbuilding as a Jewish homeland by endeavoring to make it not only a haven of refuge for the oppressed but also a center of Jewish culture and spiritual life."

In 1976, the CCAR continued transforming the movement's relationship with what was now the State of Israel. The "Centenary Perspective" pronounced: "We are bound to that land and to the newly reborn State of Israel by innumerable religious and ethnic ties.... We have both a stake and a responsibility in building the State of Israel, assuring its security, and defining its Jewish character. We encourage *aliyah* for those who wish to find maximum personal fulfillment in the cause of Zion."

The CCAR's "Pittsburgh Platform" below, urging Hebrew studies and Israel trips, reflects the ideological revolution the twentieth century wrought. While this 1999 manifesto—and others—emphasize the essential values informing Reform Zionism, the most recent statements are more detailed, political, and prickly. The December 2016 "Expression of Love and Support for the State of Israel" reaffirmed the Pittsburgh Platform, declaring, "Our love and support for the State of Israel are unconditional" while also quoting the notion of "disagreement for the sake of heaven." Tackling many controversial subjects including women's prayer at the Western Wall, liberal Judaism's status in Israel, civil rights in Israel, and the Palestinian conflict, this loving yet critical document reflects Reform Jewry's growing complexity and sensitivity in its relationship with Zionism, let alone Israel.

A Statement of Principles for Reform Judaism (1999)

We are Israel, a people aspiring to holiness, singled out through our ancient covenant and our unique history among the nations to be witnesses to God's presence. We are linked by that covenant and that history to all Jews in every age and place.

We are committed to the *mitzvah* of *ahavat Yisra'el*, love for the Jewish people, and to *k'lal Yisra'el*, the entirety of the community of Israel. Recognizing that *kol Yisra'el arevim zeh ba-zeh*, all Jews are responsible for one another, we reach out to all Jews across ideological and geographical boundaries.

We embrace religious and cultural pluralism as an expression of the vitality of Jewish communal life in Israel and the Diaspora. . . .

We are committed to *Medinat Yisra'el*, the State of Israel, and rejoice in its accomplishments. We affirm the unique qualities of living in *Eretz Yisra'el*, the Land of Israel, and encourage *aliyah*, immigration to Israel.

We are committed to a vision of the State of Israel that promotes full civil, human and religious rights for all its inhabitants and that strives for a lasting peace between Israel and its neighbors.

We are committed to promoting and strengthening Progressive Judaism in Israel, which will enrich the spiritual life of the Jewish state and its people.

We affirm that both Israeli and Diaspora Jewry should remain vibrant and interdependent communities. As we urge Jews who reside outside Israel to learn Hebrew as a living language and to make periodic visits to Israel in order to study and to deepen their relationship to the land and its people, so do we affirm that Israeli Jews have much to learn from the religious life of Diaspora Jewish communities. . . .

The World Zionist Organization

Zionism, the national liberation movement of the Jewish people . . . views a Jewish, Zionist, democratic and secure State of Israel to be the expression of the common responsibility of the Jewish people.

Theodor Herzl continued to symbolize all that Zionism accomplished—and all that remained to be done. At the 23rd World Zionist Congress in 1951, answering the challenge Arthur Hertzberg posed after Israel's founding—"What next?"—the Zionist Organization (ZO) Herzl founded now endorsed a new ideological platform: the Jerusalem Program. Herzl's Basel Program, which had aimed at "establishing for the Jewish people a legally assured home in Palestine," was retired. New verbs reflected new post-1948 realities. The movement committed to consolidating and in-gathering, while fostering unity and Jewish consciousness.

In 1960 the ZO became the World Zionist Organization (WZO), evolving from a mass movement of individuals who joined by paying a shekel into a coalition of Zionist organizations. Four decades later, the WZO updated its platform. While reaffirming the mission to build the state, including *aliyah*, settling the land, and the centrality of the land, the 2004 Jerusalem Program shifted ideologically too. First, by focusing on the Jewish state's character, the new platform demonstrated "that Zionism is about fashioning the Jewish state, not only defending it," WZO vice chairman Dr. David Breakstone explains. Beyond offering "a solution to the Jewish problem," Zionism offered an old-new "vision for Jewish life." Such aspirations, Breakstone says, fulfill Herzl's teaching that "A community must have an ideal, for it is that which drives us. . . . The ideal is for the community what bread and water are for the individual."

Second, calling Zionism "the national liberation movement of the Jewish people" debunked the libels against Zionism as colonialist and imperialist, "as an instrument of occupation and oppression," affirming what Breakstone calls its "fundamental nobility of purpose." Finally, transcending David Ben-Gurion's command-and-control, Diaspora-negating Zionism, the updated platform "emphasized the mutual responsibility the Jews in Israel and the Diaspora have in working together to assure their continuity." Today, reassessing this reconstructed platform, which 160 delegates from twenty-eight countries affirmed unanimously, Breakstone believes "it offers very relevant challenges that we have not done enough to meet since 2004."

Jerusalem Program (1951)

The task of Zionism is the consolidation of the State of Israel, the ingathering of exiles in *Eretz Yisra'el*, and the fostering of the unity of the Jewish people.

The program of work of the Zionist Organization is:

1. Encouragement of immigration, absorption, and integration of immigrants; support of Youth Aliyah; stimulation of agricultural settlement and economic development; acquisition of land as the property of the people.

2. Intensive work for *halutziut* (pioneering) and *hahsharah* (training for *halutziut*).

3. Concerted effort to harness funds in order to carry out the tasks of Zionism.

4. Encouragement of private capital investment.

5. Fostering of Jewish consciousness by propagating the Zionist idea and strengthening the Zionist Movement; imparting the values of Judaism; Hebrew education and spreading the Hebrew language.

6. Mobilization of world public opinion for Israel and Zionism.

7. Participation in efforts to organize and intensify Jewish life on democratic foundations, maintenance and defense of Jewish rights.

Jerusalem Program (2004)

Zionism, the national liberation movement of the Jewish people, brought about the establishment of the State of Israel, and views a Jewish, Zionist, democratic, and secure State of Israel to be the expression of the common responsibility of the Jewish people for its continuity and future.

The foundations of Zionism are:

1. The unity of the Jewish people, its bond to its historic homeland *Eretz Yisra'el*, and the centrality of the State of Israel and Jerusalem, its capital, in the life of the nation;

2. *Aliyah* to Israel from all countries and the effective integration of all immigrants into Israeli society.

3. Strengthening Israel as a Jewish, Zionist, and democratic state and shaping it as an exemplary society with a unique moral and spiritual character, marked by mutual respect for the multi-faceted Jewish people, rooted in the vision of the prophets, striving for peace, and contributing to the betterment of the world.

4. Ensuring the future and the distinctiveness of the Jewish people by furthering Jewish, Hebrew, and Zionist education, fostering spiritual and cultural values, and teaching Hebrew as the national language;

5. Nurturing mutual Jewish responsibility, defending the rights of Jews as individuals and as a nation, representing the national Zionist interests of the Jewish people, and struggling against all manifestations of antisemitism;

6. Settling the country as an expression of practical Zionism.

Source Acknowledgments

Smolenskin, Peretz

From *Maamarim* 2:141–47, 3:94–125, and 3:37–52, with cuts in all three sections (Jerusalem, 1925–26), reproduced from *The Zionist Idea*, edited by Arthur Hertzberg, by permission of the University of Nebraska Press, copyright © 1997 Arthur Hertzberg (Philadelphia: Jewish Publication Society), 145, 146–53, 154–57. Translated by Gil Troy.

Pinsker, Leon

"Auto Emancipation: An Appeal to His People By A Russian Jew," translated from the German by Dr. D. S. Blondheim, Federation of American Zionists, 1916, Essential Texts of Zionism, *Jewish Virtual Library*, jewishvirtuallibrary.org.

Herzl, Theodor

"The Jewish State" translated from the German by Sylvie D'Avigdor, this edition published in *Essential Texts of Zionism* (American Zionist Emergency Council, 1946).

The Complete Diaries of Theodor Herzl, edited by Raphael Patai, translated by Harry Zohn (New York: Herzl Press, 1960).

Nordau, Max

"Zionism" (1902) from *Zionistiche Schriften* (Berlin, 1923), 39–57 and 18–38, reproduced from *The Zionist Idea*, edited by Arthur Hertzberg, by permission of the University of Nebraska Press, copyright © 1997 Arthur Hertzberg (Philadelphia: Jewish Publication Society), 242–45, with cuts in both sections.

"Muskeljudentum, Jewry of Muscle" from *Juedische Turnzeitung*, June 1903. Republished in Max Nordau, *Zionistiche Schriften* (Cologne and Leipzig: Juedischer Verlag, 1909), 379–81. Translated by J. Hessing.

Klatzkin, Jacob

"Boundaries" reproduced from *The Zionist Idea*, edited by Arthur Hertzberg, by permission of the University of Nebraska Press, copyright © 1997 Arthur Hertzberg (Philadelphia: Jewish Publication Society), 314–25.

Weizmann, Chaim

"On the Report of the Palestine Commission" reproduced from *The Zionist Idea*, edited by Arthur Hertzberg, by permission of the University of Nebraska Press, copyright © 1997 Arthur Hertzberg (Philadelphia: Jewish Publication Society), 583–88.

Alterman, Natan

Song of the Homeland (Shir Moledet). Originally written for the film

The Land of Promise (L'Chayim
Hadashim), 1935.

The Silver Platter (Magash HaKesef)
(*Davar*, December 19, 1947).

Einstein, Albert (with Erich Kahler)

"Palestine, Setting of Sacred History
of the Jewish Race," *Princeton Herald*, April, 14, 1944.

Hess, Moses

Rom und Jerusalem, Leipsic 1862 (an
arrangement of passages culled
from all parts of the volume),
retranslated from the German by
Arthur Hertzberg on the basis of
an earlier translation by Meyer
Waxman, reproduced from *The
Zionist Idea*, edited by Arthur
Hertzberg, by permission of the
University of Nebraska Press,
copyright © 1997 Arthur Hertzberg (Philadelphia: Jewish Publication Society), 119–38.

Brenner, Joseph Hayyim

Excerpted from the essay "Haara-
hat Azmenu be-Sheloshet Ha-
Krahim" (1914), reproduced from
The Zionist Idea, edited by Arthur
Hertzberg, by permission of the
University of Nebraska Press,
copyright © 1997 Arthur Hertzberg (Philadelphia: Jewish Publication Society).

Syrkin, Nahman

Excerpted from the pamphlet *Die
Judenfrage und der sozialistische
Judenstaat* (1898), translated by
Arthur Herzberg, reproduced from
The Zionist Idea, edited by Arthur
Hertzberg, by permission of the

University of Nebraska Press,
copyright © 1997 Arthur Hertzberg (Philadelphia: Jewish Publication Society).

Borochov, Ber

"Our Platform (1906)" reproduced
from *The Zionist Idea*, edited by
Arthur Hertzberg, by permission
of the University of Nebraska
Press, copyright © 1997 Arthur
Hertzberg (Philadelphia: Jewish
Publication Society), 355–67.

Gordon, Aaron David

"People and Labor" and "Our Tasks
Ahead" both reproduced from
The Zionist Idea, edited by Arthur
Hertzberg, by permission of the
University of Nebraska Press,
copyright © 1997 Arthur Hertzberg (Philadelphia: Jewish Publication Society), 372–74 and
379–82.

Bluwstein, Rachel

From *Aftergrowth* (Safiah) (Tel Aviv:
Davar Press, 1927). Translated by
Gil Troy.

Katznelson, Berl

"Revolution and Tradition" reproduced from *The Zionist Idea*, edited
by Arthur Hertzberg, by permission of the University of Nebraska
Press, copyright © 1997 Arthur
Hertzberg (Philadelphia: Jewish
Publication Society), 390–96.

Ben-Zvi, Rachel Yanait

From Rachel Katznelson-Rubashow,
*The Plough Woman-Records of the
Pioneer Women of Palestine* (New
York: Nicholas L. Brown, 1932).

Union of Zionists-Revisionists
"Declaration of the Central Com-
mittee of the Union of Zionists-
Revisionists, Paris, 1925," file
Gimel 1–3, Hatzohar Paris Office,
Declarations.

Jabotinsky, Ze'ev
From the pamphlet *The Idea of Betar,
Lviv: The Betar Commission in
Poland, with the participation of
the Central Command of the Polish
Minority in Eastern Lviv* (1934),
World Zionist Organization,
http://www.wzo.org (London
1937), reproduced from *The Zionist
Idea*, edited by Arthur Hertzberg,
by permission of the University of
Nebraska Press, copyright © 1997
Arthur Hertzberg (Philadelphia:
Jewish Publication Society), 10–29.
"The Iron Wall (We and the Arabs),"
Jewish Herald, November 26, 1937
(first published in Russian as
"O Zheleznoi Stene," *Rassvyet*,
November 4, 1923).

Tschernichovsky, Saul
From *Melodies and Liturgy 1*
(Hezyonot Ve-Manginot Alef)
(Warsaw: Tushia,1898). Translated
by Gil Troy.
From *Collected Works, vol. 3* (Vilna:
Va'ad Hayovel, 1929). Translated by
Gil Troy.

The Irgun
Proclamation of the Irgun Zvai
Leumi, Jerusalem, June 1939.

Stern, Avraham (Yair)
"Eighteen Principles of Rebirth," *Ba-
Machteret*, November 1940.

Hazaz, Haim
The Sermon and Other Stories (Lon-
don: Toby Press, 2005), 231–49.
Translated by Hillel Halkin.

Alkalai, Yehuda
"The Third Redemption" reproduced
from *The Zionist Idea*, edited by
Arthur Hertzberg, by permission
of the University of Nebraska
Press, copyright © 1997 Arthur
Hertzberg (Philadelphia: Jewish
Publication Society), 105–7.

Mohilever, Samuel
"Message to the First Zionist Con-
gress" reproduced from *The Zionist
Idea*, edited by Arthur Hertzberg,
by permission of the University of
Nebraska Press, copyright © 1997
Arthur Hertzberg (Philadelphia:
Jewish Publication Society), 401–5.

Reines, Isaac Jacob
A New Light on Zion (Vilnius: Halmana Ve HaAchim Raem Press,
1901). Translated by Gil Troy.

Abraham Isaac Kook
"The Land of Israel," "The Rebirth of
Israel," and "Lights for Rebirth"
all reproduced from *The Zionist
Idea*, edited by Arthur Hertzberg,
by permission of the University of
Nebraska Press, copyright © 1997
Arthur Hertzberg (Philadelphia:
Jewish Publication Society), 419–
21, 424–26, and 427–30.

HaCohen, Moshe
"Mateh Moshe" in *MeHodu v'ad Kush:
Tzionut Mizrahit-Sepharadit: Yesh
Dvarim Kaela* [From India until
Kush: Mizrahi-Sephardic Zion-

ism: There are such things], edited by Adi Arbel (Jerusalem: Institute for Zionist Strategies and the Menachem Begin Heritage Center, 2016). Translated by Gil Troy.

Meir Bar Ilan
"What Kind of Life Should We Create in *Eretz Israel?*," reproduced from *The Zionist Idea*, edited by Arthur Hertzberg, by permission of the University of Nebraska Press, copyright © 1997 Arthur Hertzberg (Philadelphia: Jewish Publication Society), 548–54.

Ben-Yehudah, Eliezer
"A Letter of Ben-Yehudah (1880)" reproduced from *The Zionist Idea*, edited by Arthur Hertzberg, by permission of the University of Nebraska Press, copyright © 1997 Arthur Hertzberg (Philadelphia: Jewish Publication Society), 160–64.
"Introduction" in Ben-Yehuda Hemda, *HaMavo HaGadol* [The great introduction] vol. 1 (1948), in *The Complete Dictionary of Ancient and Modern Hebrew, 1908–1959*. Translated by Gil Troy.

Ahad, Ha'am
"On Nationalism and Religion" and "The Jewish State and the Jewish Problem" both reproduced from *The Zionist Idea*, edited by Arthur Hertzberg, by permission of the University of Nebraska Press, copyright © 1997 Arthur Hertzberg (Philadelphia: Jewish Publication Society), 261, 262–69.

Bialik, Hayyim Nahman
Complete Poetic Works of Hayyim Nahman Bialik vol. 1, translated from the Hebrew (New York: Histadruth Ivrith of America, 1948).
"At the Inauguration of the Hebrew University (1925)" reproduced from *The Zionist Idea*, edited by Arthur Hertzberg, by permission of the University of Nebraska Press, copyright © 1997 Arthur Hertzberg (Philadelphia: Jewish Publication Society), 281–87.

Berdichevski, Micah Joseph
"Wrecking and Building," "In Two Directions," and "On Sanctity" all reproduced from *The Zionist Idea*, edited by Arthur Hertzberg, by permission of the University of Nebraska Press, copyright © 1997 Arthur Hertzberg (Philadelphia: Jewish Publication Society), 293–94, 295–96, and 293–94.

Buber, Martin
"Hebrew Humanism" and "An Open Letter to Mahatma Gandhi" both reproduced from *The Zionist Idea*, edited by Arthur Hertzberg, by permission of the University of Nebraska Press, copyright © 1997 Arthur Hertzberg (Philadelphia: Jewish Publication Society), 453–56 and 463–65.

Schechter, Solomon
"Zionism: A Statement" from *Seminary Addresses and Other Papers*, translated by Arthur Hertzberg (New York: 1915), reproduced from *The Zionist Idea*, edited by Arthur

Hertzberg, by permission of the University of Nebraska Press, copyright © 1997 Arthur Hertzberg (Philadelphia: Jewish Publication Society), 91–104, 504–13.

Brandeis, Louis Dembitz

"The Jewish Problem and How to Solve It" reproduced from *The Zionist Idea*, edited by Arthur Hertzberg, by permission of the University of Nebraska Press, copyright © 1997 Arthur Hertzberg (Philadelphia: Jewish Publication Society), 517–22.

Szold, Henrietta

"Letter to Augusta Rosenwald" from *Henrietta Szold: Life and Letters* by Marvin Lowenthal, copyright © 1942 Viking Press, renewed copyright © 1970 Harold C. Emer and Harry L. Shapiro, executors of the estate. Used by permission of Viking Books, an imprint of Penguin Publishing Group, a division of Penguin Random House LLC. All rights reserved.

Kallen, Horace Mayer

"Zionism and Liberalism" reproduced from *The Zionist Idea*, edited by Arthur Hertzberg, by permission of the University of Nebraska Press, copyright © 1997 Arthur Hertzberg (Philadelphia: Jewish Publication Society), 528–30.

Wise, Stephen S.

Challenging Years: The Autobiography of Stephen Wise (New York: Putnam's Sons, 1949).

Steinberg, Milton

"The Creed of an American Zionist," *Atlantic Monthly*, February 1945.

Israel's Declaration of Independence

"The Declaration of the Establishment of the State of Israel," *Official Gazette* 1 (May 14, 1948). Official translation by the Israel Ministry of Foreign Affairs.

Ben-Gurion, David

"The Imperatives of the Jewish Revolution" reproduced from *The Zionist Idea*, edited by Arthur Hertzberg, by permission of the University of Nebraska Press, copyright © 1997 Arthur Hertzberg (Philadelphia: Jewish Publication Society), 606–19.

"Speech to Mapai Central Committee," January 16, 1948, translated by Ami Isseroff, accessed March 28, 2017, http://zionism-israel.com /hdoc/Ben_gurion_Speech_Jan _1948.htm.

From David Ben-Gurion, *Memoirs* (New York: World, 1970), 175.

The Law of Return

Passed by the Knesset July 5, 1950, and published in *Sefer Ha-Chukkim* 51 (July 5, 1950): 159. Official translation by the Israel Ministry of Foreign Affairs.

Berlin, Isaiah

Excerpted from "Jewish Slavery and Emancipation" in *The Power of Ideas*, 2nd ed., edited by Henry Harvey, foreword by Avishai Margalit, copyright © 1947, 1951, 1953,

or retransmission of this content without express written permission is prohibited.

Meir, Golda

A Land of Our Own: An Oral Autobiography, edited by Marie Syrkin (New York: Putnam's Sons, 1973).

Address to the United Nations General Assembly 13th Session, October 7, 1958.

Tsur, Muki

From Avraham Shapira, *Siach Lochamim* [Soldiers' chat] (Tfoos Co-op Achdut, 1967), 7–8. Translated by Gil Troy.

Oz, Amos

"The Meaning of Homeland," in *Under this Blazing Light*, translated by N. Lange Canto original series, 77–102 (Cambridge: Cambridge University Press, 1995). doi:10.1017/cbo9780511598173.010. Reprinted with the permission of Cambridge University Press.

Belzer, Roy

"Garin HaGolan Anthology," 1972, Belzer family private archive. Used with permission.

Members of Kibbutz Ketura

The Kibbutz Ketura Vision, October 9, 1994. Used with permission of the Ketura Community Administrator.

Rotblit, Yaakov

"Shir LaShalom, A Song for Peace." Copyright © Yaakov Rotblit and ACUM.

Fein, Leonard

"Days of Awe," *Moment* (September 1982).

Rabin, Yitzhak

"A Battle Without Cannons in a War Without Fire: Our Tremendous Energies from a State of Siege Address at the Levi Eshkol Creativity Awards Ceremony," October 6, 1994.

Peres, Shimon

"Nobel Lecture." Copyright © The Nobel Foundation (1994), http://nobelprize.org.

Aloni, Shulamit

I Cannot Do It Any Other Way, with Adit Zartel (Israel: Ma'ariv Book Guild, 1997).

Greenberg, Uri Zvi

"Those Living-Thanks to Them Say (1948)," copyright © Uri Zvi Greenberg, all rights reserved, and ACUM. Translated by Gil Troy,

"Israel without the Mount," copyright © Uri Zvi Greenberg, all rights reserved, and ACUM. Translated by Gil Troy and Dganit Mazouz Biton.

Cohen, Geulah

From *Woman of Violence: Memoirs of a Young Terrorist, 1943–1948*, translated by Hillel Halkin, copyright © Cohen Geulah (New York: Holt, Rinehart, and Winston, 1966).

The Tehiya Party Platform (1988). Government document.

Shamir, Moshe

The Green Space: Without Zionism, It'll Never Happen (Tel Aviv: Dvir Publishing House, 1991). Permission courtesy of Yael Shamir.

Begin, Menachem

The Revolt: Story of the Irgun, translated by Samuel Katz (1977). Steimatzky Agency, Ltd., reprinted by permission of the Begin Center.

"Broadcast to the Nation" (1948), courtesy of the Begin Center.

"Statement to the Knesset upon the Presentation of His Government" (1977), courtesy of the Begin Center.

Shalev, Yitzhak

"We Shall Not Give Up Our Promised Borders," in "How to Speak to the Arabs: A Maariv Round Table," edited by Geula Cohen, *Middle East Journal* 18, no. 2 (1964): 143–62, http://www.jstor.org/stable/4323700.

Schweid, Eliezer

"Israel as a Zionist State" (World Zionist Organization, 1970). Berman Policy Archives.

"The Promise of the Promised Land" (1988). www.myjewishlearning.com.

Netanyahu, Benjamin

Excerpt from *A Place Among the Nations* by Benjamin Netanyahu, copyright © 1993 Benjamin Netanyahu. Used by permission of Bantam Books, an imprint of Random House, a division of Penguin Random House LLC. All rights reserved.

Uziel, Ben-Zion Meir Chai

"Prayer for the State of Israel" (1948). Translated by Gil Troy.

"On Nationalism" in *MeHodu v'ad Kush: Tzionut Mizrahit-Sepharadit: Yesh Dvarim Kaela* [From India until Kush: Mizrahi-Sephardic Zionism: There are such things], edited by Adi Arbel (Jerusalem:

Institute for Zionist Strategies and the Menachem Begin Heritage Center, 2016). Translated by Gil Troy.

Edan, David

"A Call for *Aliyah*," in *MeHodu v'ad Kush: Tzionut Mizrahit-Sepharadit: Yesh Dvarim Kaela* [From India until Kush: Mizrahi-Sephardic Zionism: There are such things], edited by Adi Arbel (Jerusalem: Institute for Zionist Strategies and the Menachem Begin Heritage Center, 2016). Translated by Gil Troy.

Soloveitchik, Joseph Ber

Kol Dodi Dofek: Listen, My Beloved Knocks 1956, published as *Fate and Destiny: From the Holocaust to the State of Israel*, translated by Lawrence Kaplan (Hoboken: Ktav, 2000).

Leibowitz, Yeshayahu

Courtesy Leibowitz Family.

Heschel, Abraham Joshua

Israel: An Echo of Eternity (New York: FSG, 1969).

Jungreis, Esther

Zionism: A Challenge to Man's Faith (New York: Hinneni, 1977).

Alyagon-Roz, Talma

"Eretz Tzvi / The Land of Beauty," translation by Joanna Chen, music by Dov Seltzer, copyright © 1976 Talma Alyagon-Roz.

Berkovits, Eliezer

Essential Essays on Judaism, edited by David Hazony (Jerusalem: Shalem Press, 2002).

Emunim, Ohadei Gush

[Friends of Gush Emunim], January 1978, pp. 2–5.

Hartman, David
"Auschwitz or Sinai (1982)," Hartman blog, Shalom Hartman Institute, Jerusalem. Used by permission of the Hartman family.
"The Third Jewish Commonwealth," in *A Living Covenant: The Innovative Spirit in Traditional Judaism* (New York: Free Press, 1985). Used by permission of the Hartman family.

Commission on the Philosophy of Conservative Judaism
Emet V'Emunah: Statement of Principles of Conservative Judaism (1988).

Hirsch, Richard
"Toward a Theology of Reform Zionism," in *From the Hill to the Mount: A Reform Zionist Quest* (Jerusalem: Gefen Publishing House, 2000).

Yosef, Ovadia
"Mesirat Shtachim MeEretz Yisrael BiмКом Pikuach Nefesh" [Returning some of the Holy Land to preserve life] in *Remarks at the Conference on Oral Law at Merkaz HaRav Kook*, 1979.

Hefer, Haim
"Hayu Zmanim" [There were times], copyright © Haim Hefer and ACUM. Translated by Gil Troy.

Klein, A. M.
From *The Second Scroll* by A. M. Klein, annotated by Zailig Pollock and Elizabeth A. Popham, copyright © University of Toronto Press, 2000, 55–56. Reprinted with permission of the publisher.

Uris, Leon
"The Exodus Song or This Land Is Mine" (Pat Boone, 1960, based on the text by Leon Uris). Used with permission of Gold Label.

Agnon, Shmuel
"Banquet Speech," in *Nobel Lectures, Literature 1901–967*, edited by Horst Frenz (Amsterdam: Elsevier, 1969), copyright © The Nobel Foundation (1966). Source http://nobelprize.org.

Shemer, Naomi
"Jerusalem of Gold," copyright © Naomi Shemer and ACUM.

Amichai, Yehuda
"Tiyarim" [Tourists], in *Poems of Jerusalem* (New York: Harper & Row, 1988), 135. Translated by Gil Troy, with permission of Hana Amichai.
"Kol HaDorot SheLefanay" [All the generations before me], in *Poems of Jerusalem* (New York: Harper & Row, 1988), 3. Translated by Gil Troy, with permission of Hana Amichai.

Shaked, Gershon
Reproduced from *The Shadows Within: Essays on Modern Jewish Writers* by Gershon Shaked, by permission of the University of Nebraska Press, copyright © 1987 The Jewish Publication Society.

Pogrebin, Letty Cottin
Deborah, Golda, and Me: Being Female and Jewish in America (New York: Crown Publishers, Inc., 1991). Used with permission of the author.

Roiphe, Anne
From *Generation Without Memory* by Anne Roiphe, copyright © 1981 Anne Roiphe. Reprinted with the

permission of Touchstone, a division of Simon & Schuster Inc. All rights reserved. Reprinted by permission of ICM Partners.

Hertzberg, Arthur

"Impasse: A Movement in Search of a Program," *Commentary* (October 1, 1949): Used by permission of the Arthur Hertzberg Estate.

"Some Reflections on Zionism Today," *Congress Monthly* (March-April 1977): 3–7.

Kaplan, Mordechai

Toward a New Zionism (New York: Herzl Press & Reconstructionist Press, 1959). Used with permission from Reconstructionist Press.

Halprin, Rose

"Speech to the Zionist General Council," April 19–28, 1950, in *Session of the Zionist General Council, Jerusalem,* 110–13 (Jerusalem: Zionist Executive, 1950).

Blaustein, Jacob

"Statements by Prime Minister David Ben-Gurion and Mr. Jacob Blaustein on the Relationship Between Israel and American Jews," American Jewish Committee Archives, New York.

Rawidowicz, Simon

"Jerusalem and Babylon," in *Israel, the Ever-dying People, and Other Essays,* edited by Benjamin Ravid (Madison NJ: Fairleigh Dickinson University Press, 1986). Used by permission of Associated University Presses.

"Two That Are One," in *Israel, the Ever-dying People, and Other Essays,* edited by Benjamin Ravid (Mad-

ison NJ: Fairleigh Dickinson University Press, 1986). Used by permission of Associated University Presses.

Greenberg, Irving "Yitz"

"Twenty Years Later: The Impact of Israel on American Jewry," a symposium sponsored by the American Histadrut Cultural Exchange Institute (1968).

Yom Yerushalayim: Jerusalem Day (1988): in *The Jewish Way: Living the Holiday* (New York: Simon and Schuster, 1988), with the permission of Irving Greenberg.

Borowitz, Eugene

Twenty Years Later: The Impact of Israel on American Jewry (New York: American Histadrut Cultural Exchange Institute, 1968), 38–43.

Wouk, Herman

From *This Is My God: The Jewish Way of Life* by Herman Wouk, copyright © 1959, 1970, 1974, 1988 Abe Wouk Foundation, Inc., copyright © renewed 1987 Herman Wouk. Used by permission of Little, Brown and Company, All rights reserved. Copyright © 1959 Abe Wouk Foundation, Inc., copyright © renewed 1987 Herman Wouk.

Wolf, Arnold Jacob

"Will Israel Become Zion?" Reprinted with permission from *Sh'ma,* from an essay published March 30, 1973, http://forward.com/shma-now/.

"Breira's National Platform, February 21, 1977," in *American Jewish History: A Primary Source Reader,* edited by Gary Philip Zola and

Marc Dollinger, 385–86 (Waltham: Brandeis University Press, 2014),

Halkin, Hillel
Letters to an American Jewish Friend (Jerusalem: Gefen Publishing, 1977, 2013).

Prager, Dennis, and Joseph Telushkin
From *Nine Questions People Ask about Judaism* by Dennis Prager & Joseph Telushkin, copyright © 1981 Dennis Prager and Joseph Telushkin. Reprinted with the permission of Touchstone, a division of Simon & Schuster, Inc. All rights reserved.

Singer, Alex
Alex: Building a Life (Jerusalem: Gefen House, 1996).

Greenberg, Blu
"What Do American Jews Believe? A Symposium" (August 1, 1996).

Oren, Michael
"Jews and the Challenge of Sovereignty," *Azure* 23 (Winter 2006).

Becker, Tal
"Beyond Survival," Shalom Hartman Institute blog, June 5, 2011.

Walzer, Michael
"The State of Righteousness: Liberal Zionists Speak Out," *Huffington Post*, April 24, 2012, http://www.huffingtonpost.com/michael-walzer/liberal-zionists-speak-out-state-of-righteousness_b_1447261.html.

Barak, Aharon
"Jewish or Democratic? Israel's Former Top Judge Reflects on Values" (2012) from http://www.myjewishlearning.com/article/jewish-or-democratic-israels-former-top-judge-reflects-on-values/.

Tamir, Yael "Yuli"
Excerpt from "Jewish and Democratic State," in *The Jewish Political Tradition, vol. 1: Authority*, edited by M. Walzer, M. Lorberbaum, and N. J. Zohar (New Haven: Yale University Press, 2000).

Maghen, Ze'ev
Imagine: John Lennon and the Jews: A Philosophical Rampage (New York: Bottom Books, 2011).

Gordis, Daniel
The Promise of Israel: Why Its Seemingly Greatest Weakness Is Actually Its Greatest Strength (Hoboken NJ: John Wiley & Sons, 2012).

Wieseltier, Leon
The New Republic, February 11, 1985, copyright © 1985 New Republic. All rights reserved. Used by permission and protected by the copyright laws of the United States. The printing, copying, redistribution, or retransmission of this content without express written permission is prohibited.

Cotler, Irwin
Reprinted with permission from Irwin Cotler, adapted for this volume from Speech to the General Assembly of the United Jewish Communities, November 17, 2006 (2017).

Taub, Gadi
"In Defense of Zionism," *Fathom* (Autumn 2014), http://fathomjournal.org/in-defence-of-zionism/.

Lévy, Bernard-Henri
Excerpt from *The Genius of Judaism* by Bernard-Henri Levy, copyright © 2017 Bernard-Henry Levy. Used by permission of Random House, an imprint and division of Penguin Random House LLC. All rights reserved.

Kasher, Asa
IDF Code of Ethics, 1994, retrieved from https://www.idfblog.com /about-the-idf/idf-code-of -ethics/.

Shapira, Anita
"The Abandoned Middle Road: Liberal Zionists Speak Out," *Huffington Post*, April 25, 2012.

Katschaslki-Katzir, Ephraim
"My Contributions to Science and Society," *Journal of Biological Chemistry* 280, no. 17 (April 2005): 16529–541, copyright © 2005 American Society for Biochemistry and Molecular Biology.

Gavison, Ruth
"The Gavison-Medan Covenant: Main Points and Principles" (Israel Democratic Institute, 2003), https:// www.gavison.com/home.

Wilf, Einat
"Zionism: The Only Way Forward," *Daily Beast*, April 2, 2012, http:// www.thedailybeast.com/articles /2012/04/02/zionism-the-only -way-forward.html.

Gans, Chaim
"The Zionism We Really Want: A Third Way to Look at the Morality of the Jewish Nationalist Project," *Haaretz*, September 3, 2013. The full argument is included in Gans's *A Political Theory for the Jewish People* (Oxford University Press, 2016).

Grossman, David
Transcript of David Grossman's speech at the Rabin memorial— *Jewish Journal*. November 4, 2006, http://jewishjournal.com /news/world/13973/.

Horowitz, Nitzan
"On the Steps of Ignorance," על מדרגות הבערות, blog post August 1, 2013, www.nitzan.org.il.

Tal, Alon
"I Am a Green Zionist," adapted from *Pollution in a Promised Land—An Environmental History of Israel* (Berkeley: University of California Press, 2017).

Beinart, Peter
"The Failure of the American Jewish Establishment," from *The New York Review of Books*, June 10, 2010, http://www.nybooks.com/articles /2010/06/10/failure-american -jewish-establishment/, copyright © 2010 Peter Beinart.

Shavit, Ari
"Back to Liberal Zionism," *Haaretz*, September 11, 2014.
"A Missed Funeral and the True Meaning of Zionism," *Haaretz*, December 12, 2013.

Shaffir, Stav
"'Don't Preach about Zionism': Labor MK's Attack on Israeli Right Goes Viral," January 23, 2015, http:// www.haaretz.com/israel-news/1 .638670.

Hazony, Yoram
"The End of Zionism?," *Azure*, summer 1996.
"Israel's 'Jewish State Law' and the Future of the Middle East," in *Jerusalem Letters*, http://jerusalemletters.com/wp-content/uploads/2014/11/israels-jewish-state-law-future-middle-east.pdf.

Trigano, Shmuel
"There Is No 'State of All Its Citizens,'" adapted from *The New Jewish State* (Paris: Berg International, 2015).

Harel, Israel
"We Are Here to Stay," translated by Ruchie Avital, in Guardian, August 16, 2001, https://www.theguardian.com/world/2001/aug/16/comment.israelandthepalestinians.

Glick, Caroline
Excerpt from "The Israeli Solution: A One-State Plan for Peace in the Middle East" by Caroline Glick, copyright © 2014 Caroline Glick. Used by permission of Crown Forum, an imprint of the Crown Publishing Group, a division of Penguin Random House LLC. All rights reserved.

Wisse, Ruth
"Jews and Power," in *Jewish History* 22, no. 4 (New York: Schocken, 2007).

Mamet, David
"Bigotry Pins Blame on Jews," *Huffington Post*, August 10, 2006.
The Secret Knowledge: On the Dismantling of American Culture (Penguin Publishing Group, 2011).

Begin, Ze'ev B.
"The Essence of the State of Israel."
Used by permission of Ze'ev Begin.

Rivlin, Reuven
Remarks of President Rivlin at the Herzliya Conference, June 7, 2015. Used by permission of Reuven Rivlin.

Shaked, Ayelet
"Pathways to Governance," in *Hashiloach* 1 (October 2016).

Polisar, Daniel
"Is Iran the Only Model for a Jewish State?" *Azure* (Spring 1999).

Ish-Shalom, Benjamin
"Jewish Sovereignty: The Challenges of Meaning, Identity, and Responsibility," *Psifas* (August 2014).

Sadan, Eliezer
"Religious Zionism: Taking Responsibility in the Worldly Life of the Nation," in *Navigating a Direction for Religious Zionism* (Bnei David, 2008).

Yaacov Medan
"The Gavison-Medan Covenant: Main Points and Principles" (Israel Democratic Institute, 2003), https://www.gavison.com/home.

Amital, Yehuda
"Reishit Tzemichat Ge'ulatenu," in *The Israel Koschitzky Virtual Beit Midrash Yeshivat Har Etzion*, http://etzion.org.il/en/reishit-tzemichat-geulatenu.

Lau, Benjamin
"The Challenge of Halakhic Innovation," *Meorot* 8 (September 2010/Tishrei 5771): 36–50.

Stern, Yedidia Z.
"I Believe," in *Constitution by Consensus* (Jerusalem: Israel Democracy Institute [2007]: 86–100).

Shakdiel, Leah
Interview with Leah Shakdiel in *Just Vision* (2004).

Eisen, Arnold
"Speech to the 37th Zionist Congress in Jerusalem," October 20, 2015.
"Conservative Judaism Today and Tomorrow" (Jewish Theological Seminary of America, 2014).

Ellenson, David
Jewish Meaning in a World of Choice: Studies in Tradition and Modernity (Philadelphia: Jewish Publication Society, 2014).

Troy, Gil
"Why I Am a Zionist," May 7, 2008, *Jerusalem Post*, https:// giltroyzionism.wordpress.com /2008/05/07/why-i-am-a-zionist -2008/.

Lapid, Yair
"I'm a Zionist," 2009, http:// awiderbridge.org/yair-lapid-im-a -zionist/.

Goodman, Micah
Epilogue of *From the Secular and the Holy* (forthcoming).

Shoval, Ronen
Herzl's Vision 2.0: Im tirtzu: A Manifesto for Renewed Zionism (Jerusalem: Rubin Mass Publishers, 2013).

Yehoshua, A. B.
"The Basics of Zionism, Homeland, and Being a Total Jew," adapted from various essays of A. B. Yehoshua, 2017. Translated by Gil Troy.

Biton, Erez
"Address at the President's House on the Subject of Jerusalem" (May 23, 2016). Courtesy Erez Biton.

Avishai, Bernard
Excerpt from *The Hebrew Republic* copyright © 2008 Bernard Avishai, used by permission of Houghton Mifflin Harcourt Publishing Co., all rights reserved.

Singer, Saul
"They Tried to Kill Us, We Won, Now We're Changing the World," *Jerusalem Post*, April 1, 2011.

Shalom, Sharon
"My Story," https://www.brandeis .edu/israelcenter/pdfs/Shalom SharonStory.pdf.

Milstein, Adam
Updated (May 2017) from "Israeliness Is the Answer," *Jerusalem Post*, May 5, 2016.

Danziger, Rachel Sharansky
"Yom Ha'atzmaut 2015: A New Kind of Zionist Hero," first published in *Times of Israel*, April 23, 2015.

Sacks, Jonathan
Will We Have Jewish Grandchildren (1994). Reproduced by permission from Vallentine Mitchell & Co., Ltd., London.

Dershowitz, Alan M.
From *The Vanishing American Jew: In Search of Jewish Identity for the Next Century* by Alan M. Dershowitz, copyright © 1997 Alan M. Dershowitz. Used by permission of Grand Central Publishing. All rights reserved.

Beilin, Yossi

From *His Brother's Keeper: Israel and Diaspora Jewry in the Twenty-First Century* by Yossi Beilin, copyright © 2000 Yossi Beilin. Used by permission of Schocken Books, an imprint of the Knopf Doubleday Publishing Group, a division of Penguin Random House LLC. All rights reserved.

Shay, Scott A.

Getting Our Groove Back: How to Energize American Jewry (Jerusalem: Devora, 2007).

Hartman, Donniel

"Israel and World Jewry: The Need for a New Paradigm," Shalom Hartman Institute, August 24, 2011. https://hartman.org.il/Blogs _View.asp?Article_Id=1860&Cat _Id=273&Cat_Type=.

Klein Halevi, Yossi

"A Jewish Centrist Manifesto," *Times of Israel*, June 6, 2016.

Willis, Ellen

"Is There Still a Jewish Question? Why I'm an Anti-Anti-Zionist (*Wrestling with Zion*, edited by Tony Kushner and Alisa Solomon, 2003)," in *The Essential Ellen Willis*, 437 (Minneapolis: University of Minnesota Press, 2014), copyright © 2014 Nona Willis Aronowitz.

Sasson, Theodore

The New American Zionism (New York: NYU Press, 2014). Reprinted with permission.

Central Conference of American Rabbis

"A Statement of Principles for Reform Judaism," CCAR, May 1999.

World Zionist Organization

"The Jerusalem Program," The Jerusalem Program, June 2004, www .wzo.org.

Sources

Sources are arranged by individual thinkers' last names.

Agnon, Yosef Shmuel. "Banquet Speech." In *Nobel Lectures, Literature 1901–1967*, edited by Horst Frenz. Amsterdam: Elsevier, 1969.

Alkalai, Yehuda. "The Third Redemption." In *The Zionist Idea: A Historical Analysis and Reader*, edited by Arthur Hertzberg, 105–7. Philadelphia: Jewish Publication Society, 1959, 1997.

Aloni, Shulamit. *Ani Lo Yechola Acheret: Shulamit Aloni MiSochachat eem Adit Zartel* [I cannot do it any other way: Shulamit Aloni converses with Adit Zartel]. Translated by Gil Troy. Tel Aviv: Ma'ariv, 1997.

    "an Israeli without hyphens": "An Israeli without Hyphens," *Ha'aretz*, May 16, 2006.

Alterman, Natan. "Shir Moledet" [Song of the homeland], originally written for the film *The Land of Promise* [*L'Chayim Hadashim*] (1935), translated by Gil Troy; "Magash HaKesef" ["The Silver Platter"], *Davar*, December 19, 1947, translated by Gil Troy.

    "The Conscience": Vivien Eden, "Could an Older Man Have Written This?" *Ha'aretz*, March 25, 2014.

    "Alterman's bitter poem": Phyllis Chesler, "The Sublime Alterman," *Arutz Sheva*, July 10, 2011.

    "like massive-jawed": Natan Alterman, "The Killers of the Fields," translated by Lewis Glinert, http://www.poetryinternationalweb.net/pi/site/poem/item/3439/auto/0/The-Killers-of-the-Fields.

Alyagon-Roz, Talma. "*Eretz Tzvi* / The Land of Beauty." Translated by Joanna Chen. Music by Dov Seltzer. ©Talma Alyagon-Roz, 1976.

Amichai, Yehuda. "All the Generations before Me" ["Kol HaDorot SheLefanay"] and "Tourists" ["Tiyarim"]. Translated by Gil Troy.

    "the most widely translated": Robert Alter, "The Untranslatable Amichai," *Modern Hebrew Literature*, November 13, 1994.

    "We were so strong": Lawrence Joseph, "Interview: Yehuda Amichai, The Art of Poetry No. 44," *Paris Review* 122 (Spring 1992). https://www.theparisreview.org/interviews/2095/yehuda-amichai-the-art-of-poetry-no-44-yehuda-amichai.

Amital, Yehuda. *"Reishit Tzemichat Ge'ulatenu"* [The flowering of our redemption: What kind of redemption does Israel represent?]. *The Israel Koschitzky Virtual Beit Midrash, Yeshivat Har Etzion (Gush)*. Adapted by Shaul Barth with Reuven Ziegler. Translated by Kaeren Fish, May 12, 2005. http://etzion .org.il/en/reishit-tzemichat-geulatenu.

    "I have no doubt": Elyashev Reichner, *By Faith Alone: The Story of Rabbi Yehuda Amital* (New Milford CT: Maggid, 2011).

    "only a Palestinian": "The Rabbi of Intellectual Openness," *Jerusalem Post,* July 12, 2010.

    "adds to the pain": Yair Sheleg, "A Rare Breed, This Simple Jew," *Ha'aretz,* June 10, 2005.

Avishai, Bernard. *The Hebrew Republic: How Secular Democracy and Global Enterprise Will Bring Israel Peace at Last.* Orlando: Houghton Mifflin Harcourt, 2008.

Barak, Aharon. "Address to the 34th World Zionist Congress in Jerusalem," June 18, 2002.

    "The state is": Aharon Barak, "A Constitutional Revolution: Israel's Basic Laws," Yale Law School Faculty Scholarship Series 3697 (1993).

    "abstracted": Menachem Elon, *Human Dignity and Freedom in the Methods of Enforcement of Judgment: The Values of a Jewish and Democratic State* (Jerusalem: Magnes, 1999).

    "learned the extent": "The Values of the State of Israel as a Jewish and Democratic State," *Jewish Virtual Library,* Basic Law: Human Liberty and Dignity, passed by the Knesset on March 17, 1992, http://www .jewishvirtuallibrary.org/israel-studies-an-anthology-israel-as-jewish -and-democratic-state.

    "decisive—if not": Aharon Barak, *Jewish or Democratic? Israel's Former Top Judge Reflects on Values,* www.myjewishlearning.com; *Purposive Interpretation in Law,* translated by Sari Bashi (Princeton: Princeton University Press, 2011).

Bar-Ilan (Berlin), Meir. "What Kind of Life Should We Create in *Eretz Yisra'el?*" In *The Zionist Idea: A Historical Analysis and Reader,* edited by Arthur Hertzberg, 548–54. Philadelphia: Jewish Publication Society, 1959, 1997.

    "Our Zionism": "Mizrachi Biography Series—Rabbi Meir Bar-Ilan (Berlin) [1880–1949]," *Mizrachi World Movement.*

Becker, Tal. "Beyond Survival: Aspirational Zionism." Shalom Hartman Institute blog, June 5, 2011, https://hartman.org.il/Blogs_View.asp?Article_Id =711&Cat_Id=275&Cat_Type=.

Begin, Menachem. *The Revolt: Story of the Irgun.* New York: H. Schuman, 1951; "The State of Israel Has Arisen: Broadcast to the Nation," May 15, 1948 (Menachem Begin Heritage Center, 2001); "Statement to the Knesset upon the

Presentation of His Government," June 20, 1977 (Historical Documents of Israel Ministry of Foreign Affairs).

Begin, Ze'ev B. "The Essence of the State of Israel" (2015, 2017), provided by the author.

"we started in Oslo": Benny Begin, "Ari Shavit Interview with Benny Begin," *Ha'aretz*, December 2, 2009.

"There is a moderate": "Begin: Right-Wingers Who Support Liberman Are Fools," *Israel National News*, May 31, 2016.

Beilin, Yossi. *His Brother's Keeper: Israel and Diaspora Jewry in the Twenty-First Century*. New York: Schocken, 2000.

Beinart, Peter. "The Failure of the American Jewish Establishment." *The New York Review of Books*, June 10, 2010.

"Hugging and": Robbie Gringas, "Hugging and Wrestling: Alternative Paradigms for the Diaspora-Israel Relationship," *Makom*, 2004.

"Come on": Ammiel Hirsch, "Ammiel Hirsch's Response to Peter Beinart at the CCAR Convention," *We Are for Israel*, March 3, 2011.

"We begin": Peter Beinart, *The Crisis of Zionism* (New York: Times Books, 2012).

Belzer, Roy. "Garin HaGolan Anthology." Belzer Family private archive, 1972.

Ben-Gurion, David. "The Imperatives of the Jewish Revolution." In *The Zionist Idea: A Historical Analysis and Reader*, edited by Arthur Hertzberg, 606–19. Philadelphia: Jewish Publication Society, 1959, 1997; "Speech to Mapai Central Committee." Translated by Ami Isseroff, January 16, 1948 (Zionism and Israel Information Center); David Ben Gurion. *Memoirs*. New York: World, 1970.

Ben-Yehuda, Eliezer. "A Letter of Ben-Yehudah (1880)." In *The Zionist Idea: A Historical Analysis and Reader*, edited by Arthur Hertzberg, 160–64. Philadelphia: Jewish Publication Society, 1959, 1997; introduction to *Complete Dictionary of Ancient and Modern Hebrew—in Hebrew*, 8 vols., reprint. Excerpt translated by Gil Troy. Jerusalem: Makor, 1908, 1980.

Ben-Zvi, Rahel Yanait. Rachel Katznelson-Rubashow, *The Plough Woman—Records of the Pioneer Women of Palestine*. New York: Nicholas L. Brown, 1931, 1932, 137–45.

"its antiquities": Ruth Kark, "Not a Suffragist?: Rachel Yanait Ben-Zvi on Women and Gender," *Nashim: A Journal of Jewish Women's Studies and Gender Issues* 7 (April 2004): 9–10.

Berdichevski, Micah Joseph. "Wrecking and Building," "In Two Directions," and "On Sanctity." In *The Zionist Idea: A Historical Analysis and Reader*, edited by Arthur Hertzberg, 295–96, 301–3, and 293–94. Philadelphia: Jewish Publication Society, 1959, 1997.

Berkovits, Eliezer. "On Jewish Sovereignty (1973)." In *Essential Essays on Judaism*, edited by David Hazony, 177–90. Jerusalem: Shalem, 2002.

Berlin, Isaiah. "Jewish Slavery and Emancipation." In *The Power of Ideas*, 162–85, Vintage Digital, 2012; "The Achievement of Zionism." Transcript of remarks of June 1, 1975, *The Isaiah Berlin Virtual Library*. http://berlin.wolf.ox.ac.uk/.

"negative liberty": Isaiah Berlin, *Four Essays on Liberty* (New York: Oxford University Press, 1990).

"natural assimilator": Michael Ignatieff, *Isaiah Berlin: A Life* (Toronto: Penguin Canada, 2006).

"I can tell": "Isaiah Berlin, Philosopher and Pluralist, Is Dead at 88," *New York Times*, November 7, 1997.

Bialik, Hayyim Nahman. "The City of Slaughter." In *Complete Poetic Works of Hayyim Nahman Bialik Translated From the Hebrew*, vol. 1. New York: The Histadruth Ivrith of America, 1948; "At the Inauguration of the Hebrew University (1925)." In *The Zionist Idea: A Historical Analysis and Reader*, edited by Arthur Hertzberg, 281–87. Philadelphia: Jewish Publication Society, 1959, 1997.

"May they grow": Jonathan Mark, "The Six Wonders of Zion," *New York Jewish Week*, April 1, 2008.

BILU. Manifesto. "Israel Belkind." Jewish Virtual Library.

Biton, Erez. "On Jerusalem and on Isaiah the Prophet." May 23, 2016, the President's Residence, Jerusalem, Israel. Translated by Gil Troy.

Blaustein, Jacob. "Statements by Prime Minister David Ben-Gurion and Mr. Jacob Blaustein on the Relationship between Israel and American Jews." American Jewish Committee Archives, New York, 1950, 1956.

Bluwstein, Rachel. "My Country (1926)." In *Aftergrowth (Safiah)*. Tel Aviv: Davar, 1927. Translated by Gil Troy.

Borochov, Ber. "Our Platform (1906)." In *The Zionist Idea: A Historical Analysis and Reader*, edited by Arthur Hertzberg, 355–67. Philadelphia: Jewish Publication Society, 1959, 1997.

Borowitz, Eugene. *Twenty Years Later: The Impact of Israel on American Jewry.* New York: American Histadrut Cultural Exchange Institute, 1968, 38–43.

Brandeis, Louis Dembitz. "The Jewish Problem and How to Solve It." In *The Zionist Idea: A Historical Analysis and Reader*, edited by Arthur Hertzberg, 517–22. Philadelphia: Jewish Publication Society, 1959, 1997.

Brenner, Joseph Hayyim. "Self-Criticism (1914)." In *The Zionist Idea: A Historical Analysis and Reader*, edited by Arthur Hertzberg, 307–13. Philadelphia: Jewish Publication Society, 1959, 1997.

Buber, Martin. "Hebrew Humanism" and "An Open Letter to Mahatma Gandhi." In *The Zionist Idea: A Historical Analysis and Reader*, edited by Arthur Hertzberg, 453–56 and 463–65. Philadelphia: Jewish Publication Society, 1959, 1997.

Central Conference of American Rabbis. "A Statement of Principles for Reform Judaism," May 1999. http://www.jewishvirtuallibrary.org/reform -judaism-modern-statement-of-principles-1999; "The Columbus Platform," 1937. http://www.jewishvirtuallibrary.org/the-columbus-platform-1937; "A Centenary Perspective," 1976. http://www.sacred-texts.com/jud/100.htm.

"Expression of Love": "Central Conference of American Rabbis Expression of Love and Support for the State of Israel," December 16, 2015.

"The Pittsburgh Platform": *Jewish Virtual Library,* November 1885. http://www.jewishvirtuallibrary.org/the-pittsburgh-platform.

Cohen, Geulah. *Woman of Violence: Memoirs of a Young Terrorist, 1943–1948.* Translated by Hillel Halkin. New York: Holt, Rinehart and Winston, 1966; "The Tehiya Party Platform (1988)." In *The Israeli-Palestinian Conflict: A Documentary Record, 1967–1990,* edited by Yehuda Lukacs, 286–89. Cambridge: Cambridge University Press, 1992.

Commission on the Philosophy of Conservative Judaism. "Emet V'Emunah: Statement of Principles of Conservative Judaism (1988)." The Jewish Theological Seminary of America, by the Rabbinical Assembly and by the United Synagogue of America, 1988.

Cotler, Irwin. Adapted from "Speech to the General Assembly of the United Jewish Communities." November 17, 2006, 2017. Jpundit.org.

"You know": Andrew Cardozo and Dr. Maria Wallis, "Irwin Cotler Pursuing Justice," *Pearson Center,* April 15, 2016.

Danziger, Rachel Sharansky. "Yom Ha'atzmaut 2015: A New Kind of Zionist Hero." *Times of Israel,* April 23, 2015. Updated 2017.

"I find Zionism": Gil Troy, "Education towards 'Incredibles' Zionism: Both Normal and Special," *Jerusalem Post,* January 22, 2013.

"a private 'seder'": "Thirty Years after Glienicke Bridge," *Times of Israel,* February 11, 2016.

Dershowitz, Alan. *The Vanishing American Jew: In Search of Jewish Identity for the Next Century.* Boston: Little, Brown, 1997.

Eban, Abba. "Statement to the Security Council by Foreign Minister Abba Eban." June 6, 1967. *Israel Ministry of Foreign Affairs Historical Documents,* vol. 1–2, 1947–1974.

Edan, David. "A Call for *Aliyah.*" In *MeHodu v'ad Kush: Tzionut Mizrahit-Sepharadit: Yesh Dvarim Kaela* [From India until Kush: Mizrahi-Sephardic Zionism: There are such things], edited by Adi Arbel, translated by Gil Troy, 23. Jerusalem: Institute for Zionist Strategies and the Menachem Begin Heritage Center, 2016.

Einstein, Albert, with Erich Kahler. "Palestine, Setting of Sacred History of the Jewish Race." *Princeton Herald,* April 14, 1944.

"I am as": Walter Isaacson, *Einstein: His Life and Universe* (New York: Simon & Schuster, 2007).

"person of the century": Frederic Golden, "Person of the Century: Albert Einstein," *Time*, December 31, 1999.

"a pitiable attempt": "The American Council for Judaism," Albert Einstein Collection no. 42, *Philosophical Library* (2016).

"The Jews of Palestine": David Rowe and Robert Schulman, eds., *Einstein on Politics* (Princeton: Princeton University Press, 2007).

Eisen, Arnold. "What Does It Mean to Be a Zionist in 2015?: Speech to the 37th Zionist Congress in Jerusalem." October 20, 2015. http://www.jtsa.edu /About_JTS/Administration/Office_of_the_Chancellor/Eisen_in_the _News/What_does_it_mean_to_be_a_Zionist_in_2015.xml; "Conservative Judaism Today and Tomorrow." Jewish Theological Seminary of America, June 16, 2014.

Ellenson, David. "Reform Zionism Today: A Consideration of First Principles." In *Jewish Meaning in a World of Choice: Studies in Tradition and Modernity.* Philadelphia: Jewish Publication Society, 2014.

"individual choice": "Jewish Identity and National Strength," presented at Herzliya Conference on January 23, 2007, http://huc.edu/news/2007 /01/23/rabbi-david-ellensons-address-jewish-identity-and-national -strength-presented.

"sense of *shlemut*": *After Emancipation: Jewish Religious Responses to Modernity* (Cincinnati: Hebrew Union College, 2004).

"is Reform": "The Future of Reform Jewry," *Jerusalem Center for Public Affairs*, June 15, 2007, http://jcpa.org/article/the-future-of-reform-jewry/.

Emunim, Gush. Ohadei Gush Emunim [Friends of Gush Emunim]. *Newsletter*, January 1978. In Itamar Rabinovich and Jehuda Reinharz, eds, *Israel in the Middle East: Documents and Readings on Society, Politics and Foreign Relations*, 2nd ed. Waltham: Brandeis University Press, 2008.

Fein, Leonard. "Days of Awe." *Moment*, October 1982.

"In 1975, while a professor": "Leonard Fein, Progressive Activist and Longtime Forward Columnist, Dies," *Forward*, August 14, 2014, http:// forward.com/news/breaking-news/204134/leonard-fein-progressive -activist-and-longtime-for/.

Gans, Chaim. "The Zionism We Really Want: A Third Way to Look at the Morality of the Jewish Nationalist Project." *Ha'aretz*, September 3, 2013.

Gavison, Ruth, and Yaacov Medan. *The Gavison-Medan Covenant: Main Points and Principles.* Israel Democratic Institute. 2004.

"American identity": Gil Troy, "Reviving Liberal Zionism," *New York Jewish Week*, March 22, 2011.

Glick, Caroline. *The Israeli Solution: A One-State Plan for Peace in the Middle East.* New York: Crown, 2014.

"so 1990s": "Post-Zionism Is So 1990s," *Jerusalem Post*, April 27, 2012.

Goodman, Micah. "From the Secular and the Holy." *Lo BeShealah v' Lo BeTshuva* [Not in queries, not in answers]. Translated by Gil Troy. Kinneret Zmora-Bitan Dvir (forthcoming in 2018).

Gordis, Daniel. *The Promise of Israel: Why Its Seemingly Greatest Weakness Is Actually Its Greatest Strength.* Hoboken NJ: John Wiley & Sons, 2012.

"on many levels": *Home to Stay: One American Family's Chronicle of Miracles and Struggles in Contemporary Israel* (New York: Three Rivers, 2002).

"everything I never": *If a Place Can Make You Cry* (New York: Crown, 2002).

Gordon, Aaron David. "People and Labor" and "Our Tasks Ahead." In *The Zionist Idea: A Historical Analysis and Reader,* edited by Arthur Hertzberg, 372–74, 379–82. Philadelphia: Jewish Publication Society, 1959, 1997.

"Torah cannot": Samuel Hayyim Landau, "Towards an Explanation of Our Ideology," in *The Zionist Idea: A Historical Analysis and Reader,* edited by Arthur Hertzberg, 439 (Philadelphia: Jewish Publication Society, 1959, 1997).

Greenberg, Blu. "What Do American Jews Believe? A Symposium." *Commentary,* August 1, 1996.

"where there's a rabbinic": Blu Greenberg, *On Women and Judaism: A View From Tradition* (Philadelphia: Jewish Publication Society of America, 1981, 1996, 1998), 44.

Greenberg, Irving "Yitz." *Twenty Years Later: The Impact of Israel on American Jewry.* New York: American Histadrut Cultural Exchange Institute, 1968, 7–15; "*Yom Yerushalayim:* Jerusalem Day." In *The Jewish Way: Living the Holidays.* Simon and Schuster: New York, 1988.

Greenberg, Uri Zvi. "*HaChayim BeZchutam Omreem*" [Those living—thanks to them say]. January 23, 1948. In *Uri Zvi Greenberg: His Collected Works*, vol. 7. Translated by Gil Troy. Jerusalem: Bialik Institute, 1994; "*Yisrael Bli HaHar*" [Israel without the Mount]. 1948–1949. In *Uri Zvi Greenberg: His Collected Works,* vol. 7. Translated by Gil Troy and Dganit Mazouz Biton. Jerusalem: Bialik Institute, 1994.

Grossman, David. Transcript, speech at the Rabin memorial. *Jewish Journal,* November 4, 2006.

"this naïve leftist": "I Cannot Afford the Luxury of Despair," *Guardian,* August 28, 2010.

Ha'am, Ahad (Asher Zvi Ginsberg). "On Nationalism and Religion" and "The Jewish State and the Jewish Problem." In *The Zionist Idea: A Historical Analysis and Reader,* edited by Arthur Hertzberg, 262–69, 261. Philadelphia: Jewish Publication Society, 1959, 1997.

HaCohen, Moshe "Kalphon." *"Mateh Moshe."* In *MeHodu v'ad Kush: Tzionut Mizrahit-Sepharadit: Yesh Dvarim Kaela* [From India until Kush: Mizrahi-Sephardic Zionism: There are such things]. Edited by Adi Arbel. Translated by Gil Troy. Jerusalem: Institute for Zionist Strategies and the Menachem Begin Heritage Center, 2016, 13.

Halkin, Hillel. *Letters to an American Jewish Friend: The Case for Life in Israel.* Jerusalem: Gefen, 1977, 2013.

Halprin, Rose. "Speech to the Zionist General Council." Session of the Zionist General Council, Jerusalem, April 19–28, 1950. Jerusalem: Zionist Executive, 1950, 110–13.

Harel, Israel. "We Are Here to Stay." *Guardian,* August 16, 2001. Translated by Ruchie Avital.

Hartman, David. "Auschwitz or Sinai (1982)." Hartman blog. Shalom Hartman Institute. Jerusalem. https://hartman.org.il/Blogs_View.asp?Article_Id=394&Cat_Id=414&Cat_Type=; "The Third Jewish Commonwealth." In *A Living Covenant: The Innovative Spirit in Traditional Judaism.* New York: Free Press, 1985.

Hartman, Donniel. "Israel and World Jewry: The Need for a New Paradigm." Shalom Hartman Institute blog. https://hartman.org.il/Blogs_View.asp?Article_Id=1860&Cat_Id=273&Cat_Type= August 24, 2011.

"I am grateful": "My Gun and I," *Times of Israel,* October 14, 2015.

Hazaz, Haim. "The Sermon on the Failure of Jewish History." *Seething Stones* [Avanim Rotchot]. Am Oved, 1946. *The Sermon and Other Stories.* (London: Toby Press, 2005.), 231–39. Translated by Hillel Halkin

Hazony, Yoram. "The End of Zionism and the Last Israeli." *Weekly Standard,* October 9, 1995; "Israel's 'Jewish State Law' and the Future of the Middle East." In *Jerusalem Letters,* November 24, 2014, http://blogs.timesofisrael.com/israels-jewish-state-law-and-the-future-of-the-middle-east/.

"the most noble": *The Jewish State: The Struggle for Israel's Soul* (New York: Basic, 2001).

Hefer, Haim. "Hayu Zmanim" ["There Were Times"]. Song. 1948. Translated by Gil Troy.

"personifying the words": Israel Kershner, "Haim Hefer, Whose Songs Help Lift Israelis, Dies at 86," *New York Times,* September 23, 2012.

Hertzberg, Arthur. "American Zionism at an Impasse: A Movement in Search of a Program." *Commentary,* October 1, 1949. Used by permission of the Arthur Hertzberg Estate; "Some Reflections on Zionish Today," *Congress Monthly* (March-April 1977): 3–7.

"a rabbi should": Joe Holley, "Arthur Hertzberg, Rabbi Was a Scholar and a Social Activist," *Washington Post,* April 19, 2006.

"personal decoration": Joseph Berger, "Rabbi Arthur Hertzberg, Scholar and Blunt Advocate for Civil Rights, Dies at 84," *New York Times*, April 18, 2006.

Herzl, Theodor. "The Jewish State (1896)." *The Complete Diaries of Theodor Herzl,* vol. 1:4. Edited by Raphael Patai. Translated by Harry Zohn. New York: Herzl, 1960; "Third Letter to Baron Hirsch (Paris, June 3, 1895)." In Patai, *The Complete Diaries of Theodor Herzl* vol. 1:14; First Basle Conference. 1897.

"Zionism seeks": Retrieved from *Jewish Virtual Library*, http://www .jewishvirtuallibrary.org/theodor-binyamin-ze-rsquo-ev-herzl.

"the restoration": *Old New Land: AltNeuLand,* translated by David Simon Blondheim (New York: Federation of American Zionists, 1916), 107.

Herzog, Chaim. "Statement in the General Assembly by Ambassador Chaim Herzog on the Item Elimination of All Forms of Racial Discrimination." November 10, 1975. *Israel Ministry of Foreign Affairs Historical Documents,* vol. 3, 1974–77.

Heschel, Abraham Joshua. *Israel: An Echo of Eternity.* New York: Farrar, Straus, and Giroux, 1969, 1987.

Hess, Moses. "Rome and Jerusalem (1862)." In *The Zionist Idea: A Historical Analysis and Reader,* edited by Arthur Hertzberg, 119–38. Philadelphia: Jewish Publication Society, 1959, 1997.

Hirsch, Richard. "Toward a Theology of Reform Zionism." In *From the Hill to the Mount: A Reform Zionist Quest.* Jerusalem: Gefen, 2000.

Horowitz, Nitzan. *"Al Madreigot HaBa'orut"* [On the steps of boorishness]. Nitzan Horowitz blog post, January 8, 2013. Translated by Gil Troy. http:// nitzan.org.il/2013/01/%D7%A2%D7%9C-%D7%9E%D7%93%D7%A8 %D7%92%D7%95%D7%AA-%D7%94%D7%A8%D7%91%D7%A0%D7 %95%D7%AA/.

"Israel allowed me": Brian Schaefer, "Gay Pride 2015: Discovering My Queer Zionism," *Ha'aretz*, November 6, 2015.

"our struggle": Private communication to Gil Troy, December 1, 2016.

The Irgun. "Proclamation of the Irgun Zvai Leumi, Jerusalem: June, 1939." Eretz Israel Forever website, http://www.eretzisraelforever.net/IrgunZvaiLeumi /Principals.asp?bSearchOn=True&sKeyWord=fou.

Ish-Shalom, Benjamin. "Jewish Sovereignty: The Challenges of Meaning, Identity, and Responsibility." *Psifas*, August 2014.

"halakhah of sovereignty": "A Halakhic Conversion Process That Is Friendly," *Havruta*, January 8, 2009.

Israel's Declaration of Independence. The Declaration of the Establishment of the State of Israel. *The Official Gazette* 1 (May 14, 1948). Official translation, Israel Ministry of Foreign Affairs.

Jabotinsky, Ze'ev. "The Fundamentals of the Betarian Viewpoint. 1934." World Zionist Organization Website. http://www.wzo.org.il/index.php?dir=site &page=articles&op=item&cs=3360&langpage=heb&highlight=berterian +viewpoint; "Evidence Submitted to the Palestine Royal Commission, House of Lords." In *The Zionist Idea: A Historical Analysis and Reader,* edited by Arthur Hertzberg, 559–70. Philadelphia: Jewish Publication Society, 1959, 1997; "The Iron Wall (We and the Arabs)." *Jewish Herald,* November 26, 1937 (first published in Russian as "O Zheleznoi Stene" in Rassvyet, November 4, 1923).

"The aim": Walter Laqueur, *A History of Zionism* (New York: World Executive of Betar, 1975).

Jungreis, Esther. *Zionism: A Challenge to Man's Faith.* New York: Hinneni, 1977.

"the Jewish Billy Graham": William Grimes, "Esther Jungreis, the 'Jewish Billy Graham,' Dies at 80," *New York Times,* August 26, 2016.

Kallen, Horace Mayer. "Zionism and Liberalism." In *The Zionist Idea: A Historical Analysis and Reader,* edited by Arthur Hertzberg, 528–30. Philadelphia: Jewish Publication Society, 1959, 1997.

Kaplan, Mordechai. *Toward a New Zionism.* New York: Herzl, 1959.

Kasher, Asa. IDF Code of Ethics. 1994, "Zionism 2000." In *Zionism: A Contemporary Controversy*, edited by A. Bareli and P. Ginossar, 509–13. Sde Boqer: Ben-Gurion Research Center, 1996.

"internal life": "Zionism 2000," in *Zionism: A Contemporary Controversy.*
"of respecting": "The Ethics of Operation Protective Edge," *Jewish Policy Center,* spring 2016.

Katchalski-Katzir, Ephraim. "My Contributions to Science and Society." *Journal of Biological Chemistry* 280, no. 17 (April 2005): 16529–41.

Katznelson, Berl. "Revolution and Tradition." In *The Zionist Idea: A Historical Analysis and Reader,* edited by Arthur Hertzberg, 390–96. Philadelphia: Jewish Publication Society, 1959, 1997.

Klatzkin, Jacob. "Boundaries (1914–21)." In *The Zionist Idea: A Historical Analysis and Reader,* edited by Arthur Hertzberg, 314–25. Philadelphia: Jewish Publication Society, 1959, 1997.

Klein, A. M. *The Second Scroll.* Toronto: University of Toronto, 2000.

Klein Halevi, Yossi. "A Jewish Centrist Manifesto." *Times of Israel,* June 6, 2016. http://blogs.timesofisrael.com/the-state-of-the-jewish-world-2016/.

Kollek, Teddy. "Jerusalem." *Foreign Affairs,* July 1977.

Kook, Abraham Isaac. "The Land of Israel," "The Rebirth of Israel," and "Lights for Rebirth." In *The Zionist Idea: A Historical Analysis and Reader,* edited by Arthur Hertzberg, 419–21, 424–26, 427–20. Philadelphia: Jewish Publication Society, 1959, 1997.

"The entire debate": Chanan Morrison, "Rav Kook and the Balfour Declaration," *Israel National News*, May 15, 2014.

Kook, Tzvi Yehuda Hacohen. "On the 19th Anniversary of Israel's Independence." http://www.israel613.com/books/eretz_anniversary_kook.pdf.

"Maintain his fathers": HaRav Aviner and Shlomo Chaim Hacohen, *Torat Eretz Yisrael: The Teachings of HaRav Tzvi Yehuda HaCohen Kook*, translated by Tzvi Fishman (Jerusalem: Torat Eretz Yisrael, 1991).

Lapid, Yair. "I Am a Zionist." YNetNews.com, January 30, 2009, https://www.ynetnews.com/articles/0,7340,L-3664422,00.html.

"Tomato lovers": James Kugel, *On Being a Jew* (Baltimore: Johns Hopkins Paperbacks, 1998).

Lau, Benjamin (Benny). "The Challenge of Halakhic Innovation." *Meorot* 8 (September 2010, Tishrei, 5771): 36–50.

"encourages neither": "Who's Afraid of the Reform?" *Makom*, June 11, 2012.

"It's sad": Yair Rosenberg, "Left and Right, Secular and Religious, Brought Together by Bible Study," *Tablet Magazine*, January 9, 2015.

The Law of Return. Passed by the Knesset July 5, 1950. Published in *Sefer Ha-Chukkim* No. 51, July 5, 1950, 159. Translated by Israel Ministry of Foreign Affairs.

Leibowitz, Yeshayahu. "A Call for the Separation of Religion and State (1959)." In *Judaism, Human Values, and the Jewish State*, edited by Eliezer Goldman, 174–85. Cambridge: Harvard University Press, 1992.

Levinas, Emmanuel. *Beyond the Verse: Talmudic Readings and Lectures*. Translated by Gary D. Mole. Bloomington: Indiana University Press, 1982, 1994.

"to interpret the Zionist": Jacques Derrida, *Adieu to Emmanuel Levinas* (Palo Alto: Stanford University Press, 1999).

Lévy, Bernard-Henri. *The Genius of Judaism*. Translated by Steven B. Kennedy. New York: Random House, 2017.

Maghen, Ze'ev. *Imagine: John Lennon and the Jews, A Philosophical Rampage*. New York: Bottom Books, 2011.

Mamet, David. "Bigotry Pins Blame on Jews." *Huffington Post*, August 10, 2006; *The Secret Knowledge: On the Dismantling of American Culture*. New York: Penguin Books, 2011.

"The world hates": Aluf Benn, "An Interview with David Mamet on Israel and Zionism," *Ha'aretz*, January 13, 2012.

"To the wicked": *The Wicked Son: Anti-Semitism, Self-Hatred, and the Jews* (New York: Schocken, 2006).

Medan, Yaacov. Ruth Gavison and Yaacov Medan. "Statement of Principles." In *The Gavison-Medan Covenant: Main Points and Principles*. Jerusalem: Israel Democratic Institute, 2004.

Meir, Golda. Marie Syrkin, ed. *A Land of Our Own: An Oral Autobiography.* New York: Putnam's Sons, 1973; speech by Mrs. Meir (Israel), in *United Nations General Assembly Thirteenth Session, Official Records.* October 7, 1958.
  "There is no Zionism": "Golda Quotes," Golda Meir Center website, Metropolitan State University of Denver, https://msudenver.edu/golda /goldameir/goldaquotes/.
Members of Kibbutz Ketura. "The Kibbutz Ketura Vision, 1994." Kibbutz Ketura Archives.
Memmi, Albert. *The Liberation of The Jew.* New York: Orion, 2013; *Jews and Arabs.* Edited by Eleanor Levieux. Chicago: J. P. O'Hara. 1975; *Pillar of Salt.* Boston: Beacon, 1992; *The Colonizer and the Colonized.* London: Souvenir Press, 2016; *Who Is an Arab Jew?* Jerusalem: Israel Academic Committee on the Middle East, 1975; *Racism.* Minneapolis: University of Minnesota Press, 1999.
Milstein, Adam. "Israeliness Is the Answer." *Jerusalem Post,* May 5, 2016.
  "building an active": Sean Savage, "New Israeli-American Policy Group Seeks More Activity of State and Local Levels," *Jewish News Service,* February 23, 2016.
Mohilever, Samuel. "Message to the First Zionist Congress." In *The Zionist Idea: A Historical Analysis and Reader,* edited by Arthur Hertzberg, 401–5. Philadelphia: Jewish Publication Society, 1959, 1997.
Netanyahu, Benjamin. *A Place among the Nations: Israel and the World.* New York: Bantam, 1993.
Netanyahu, Yonatan. Binyamin Netanyahu and Ido Netanyahu. *The Letters of Jonathan Netanyahu: The Commander of the Entebbe Rescue Force.* Jerusalem: Gefen, 2001.
Nordau, Max. "Zionism." In *The Zionist Idea: A Historical Analysis and Reader,* edited by Arthur Hertzberg, 242–45. Philadelphia: Jewish Publication Society, 1959, 1997; "Muskeljudentum." Juedische Turnzeitung, June 1903. Translated by J. Hessing. Republished in *Max Nordau, Zionistische Schriften.* Cologne and Leipzig: Juedischer Verlag, 1909, 379–81.
Oren, Michael. "Jews and the Challenge of Sovereignty." *Azure* 23 (Winter 2006): 27–38.
  "drift away": *Ally: My Journey across the American-Israel Divide* (New York: Random House, 2015), 256.
Oz, Amos. "The Meaning of Homeland." In *Under this Blazing Light.* Translated by Nicholas Lange, 77–102. Cambridge: Cambridge University Press, 1995.
  "half-prophet": *The Amos Oz Reader,* edited by Nitza Ben-Dov (Boston: Houghton Mifflin Harcourt, 2009).
  "When my father": *How to Cure a Fanatic* (Princeton: Princeton University Press, 2010).

"From now on": *A Tale of Love and Darkness* (London: Vintage, 2005).

Peres, Shimon. Nobel Lecture. *Nobel Lectures, Peace 1991–1995,* edited by Irwin Abrams. Singapore: World Scientific, 1999.

"an Israel whose moral": Remarks by President Obama and President Peres of Israel at presentation of the Medal of Freedom, *White House Press,* June 13, 2012.

Peretz, Martin. "The God That Did Not Fail." *New Republic,* September 17, 1997.

Pinsker, Leon. "Auto Emancipation: An Appeal to His People by A Russian Jew." Translated from the German by D. S. Blondheim, Federation of American Zionists, 1916. Essential Texts of Zionism. Lightly edited from *Jewish Virtual Library.*

Pogrebin, Letty Cottin Pogrebin. *Deborah, Golda, and Me: Being Female and Jewish In America.* New York: Crown Publishers, 1991.

"Antisemitism": "Anti-Semitism in the Women's Movement," *Ms Magazine,* June 1982.

"to my mind, Zionism": "Zionism, Meet Feminism," *Daily Beast,* March 16, 2012.

Polisar, Daniel. "Is Iran the Only Model for a Jewish State?" *Azure* 7 (Spring 1999): 18–22.

"distinctive set": "Towards a Common Judaism," *Azure* 17 (Spring 2004): 23–24.

Prager, Dennis, and Joseph Telushkin. *Nine Questions People Ask about Judaism.* New York: Simon and Schuster, 1975.

Rabin, Yitzhak. "Our Tremendous Energies from a State of Siege" at the Levi Eshkol Creativity Awards Ceremony Tel Aviv, October 6, 1994. In Rabin, Yitzhak. *Rodef Shalom: Neumi HaShalom Shel Rosh HaMemshalah* [The pursuer of peace: The peace addresses of the prime minister]. Tel Aviv: Zemora-Baytan, 1995.

"their human values": Address by the chief of staff upon receiving the honorary doctorate of philosophy at Hebrew University of Jerusalem, June 28, 1967.

Ramon, Einat. "Zionism: A Jewish Feminist-Womanist Appreciation." Original essay for this volume, 2017.

"a personal": "(Post)Modern Alienation and Hope: Zionism as a Longing for Meaning," *Mercaz Olami Faculty Forum* 7:2 (November 1, 2008).

Rawidowicz, Simon. "Babylon and Jerusalem." In *Towards a Philosophy of Israel's Wholeness.* London, Ararat, 1957; "Two That Are One." In *Israel, the Ever Dying People,* edited by Benjamin C.I. Ravid, 145–49. Connecticut: Farleigh Dickinson University Press, 1986.

Reines, Isaac Jacob. "A New Light on Zion." Vilnius: Halmana Ve HaAchim Raem, 1901. Translated by Gil Troy.

"it is the duty": Rabbi Moshe Weiss, *Rabbi Isaac Jacob Reines: Founder of Mizrachi the World Religious Zionist Organization* (New York: Religious Zionist Organization of America, 1965).

Rivlin, Reuven. "Address to the 15th Annual Herzliya Conference: Vision of the Four Tribes," June 7, 2015. http://www.president.gov.il/English /ThePresident/Speeches/Pages/news_070615_01.aspx.

    "We want you": "President Rivlin Eulogizes Victims of Paris Attack," Israel Ministry of Foreign Affairs, January 14, 2015.

    "brutal killing": Batsheva Sobelman, "Israeli President Calls 1956 Massacre of Arabs a 'Terrible Crime,'" *Los Angeles Times,* October 26, 2014.

    "born Zionists": "President Rivlin Addresses the Ceremony Marking the First Day Commemorating the Expulsion and Exile from Arab Countries and Iran," retrieved from *President of the State of Israel,* November 11, 2014, http://embassies.gov.il/UnGeneva/NewsAndEvents/Pages /President-Rivlin-addresses-first-Expulsion-and-Deportation-of-Jews -from-Arab-Lands-Day-30-Nov-2014.aspx.

Roiphe, Anne. *Generation without Memory: A Jewish Journey in Christian America.* Boston: Beacon, 1981.

Rotblit, Yaakov. "Shir La Shalom, A Song for Peace," 1969. Translated by Gil Troy.

    "A government that prefers": "Peace Now Letter," in Reuven Kaminer, *The Politics of Protest* (Brighton: Sussex Academy, 1996).

Sacks, Jonathan. *Will We Have Jewish Grandchildren? Jewish Continuity and How to Achieve It.* London: V. Mitchell, 1994.

    "Only in Israel": *Future Tense: Jews, Judaism, and Israel in the Twenty-First Century* (New York: Schocken, 2009).

    "the new antisemitism": "The Mutating Virus: Understanding Antisemitism," speech given at the Future of the Jewish Communities in Europe Conference, Brussels, September 27, 2016, http://rabbisacks.org /mutating-virus-understanding-antisemitism/.

    "home of hope": "Israel-Home of Hope," *Office of Jonathan Sacks,* May 14, 2008, http://rabbisacks.org/israel-home-of-hope/.

Sadan, Eliezer. "Religious Zionism: Taking Responsibility in the Worldly Life of the Nation." In *Navigating a Direction for Religious Zionism.* Israel: Bnei David, 2008.

Sasson, Theodore. *The New American Zionism.* New York: New York University Press, 2014.

Schechter, Solomon. "Zionism: A Statement." In *The Zionist Idea: A Historical Analysis and Reader,* edited by Arthur Hertzberg, 504–12. Philadelphia: Jewish Publication Society, 1959, 1997.

Schweid, Eliezer. "Israel as a Zionist State." World Zionist Organization, 1970. Berman Policy Archives; "The Promise of the Promised Land." www.myjewishlearning.com.

Shaffir, Stav. "'Don't Preach about Zionism': Labor MK's Attack on Israeli Right Goes Viral." *Ha'aretz*, January 23, 2015. Translated by Gil Troy. http://www.haaretz.com/israel-news/1.638670.

"the big summer": Robbie Gringras, "Daphne Leef's Speech Translated," *Makom*, September 4, 2011, http://makomisrael.org/blog/daphne-leefs-speech-translated/.

"grandmother who escaped": Stav Shaffir, *Coisas Judaicas*, January 14, 2015, http://www.coisasjudaicas.com/2015/01/mk-stav-shaffir.html?m=1.

"the Zionist dream": "Occupy Zionism! Stav Shaffir on the New Politics of Patriotism and Protest," *Left Foot Forward*, May 7, 2013.

"Zionism has been kidnapped": Stav Shaffir, "Occupy Zionism," *Fathom Journal* (Summer 2013), http://fathomjournal.org/occupy-zionism/.

"the voice": Stav Shaffir, "Premiere Speech of Stav Shaffir," https://stavshaffir.co.il/?p=474.

Shakdiel, Leah. "Interview with Leah Shakdiel." *Just Vision*, 2004. http://www.justvision.org/portrait/836/interview.

Shaked, Ayelet. "Pathways to Governance." *Hashiloach* 1 (October 2016): 37–55. Translated by Gil Troy.

"based on": Yoel Meltzer, "An Interview with Ayelet Shaked," *Yoel Meltzer: Toward a New Jewish Mindset,* August 15, 2012, http://yoelmeltzer.com/an-interview-with-ayelet-shaked/.

"Thatcherite Manifesto": Mazal Mualem, "Can Israel's Becoming More Jewish Make It More Democratic?," *Al Monitor*, October 7, 2016.

Shaked, Gershon. "No Other Place: On Saul Friedlander's *When Memory Comes*, 1979." *The Shadows Within: Essays on Modern Jewish Writers*. Philadelphia: Jewish Publication Society, 1987, 181–89.

Shalev, Yitzhak. "We Shall Not Give Up Our Promised Borders." *Ma'ariv*, August 16, 1963.

"flag is on": "Crusaders," *Golden Drunkenness—Poems* (Tel Aviv: Levin-Epstein, 1975), 43–45.

Shalom, Sharon. "My Story." https://www.brandeis.edu/israelcenter/pdfs/ShalomSharonStory.pdf.

"halakhic and conceptual": *From Sinai to Ethiopia* (Jerusalem: Gefen, 2016).

Shamir, Moshe. "For a Greater Israel," *Ma'ariv*, September 22, 1967. Translated by Gil Troy; *The Green Space: Without Zionism, It'll Never Happen*. Or Yehuda: Dvir, 1991. Translated by Gil Troy.

"He Walked": *He Walked through the Fields* (Jerusalem: World Zionist Organization, 1959).

"his fair hair": *With His Own Hands* (Jerusalem: Israel Universities Press, 1970).

Shapira, Anita. "The Abandoned Middle Road: Liberal Zionists Speak Out." *Huffington Post*, April 25, 2012.

Sharansky, Natan. *Fear No Evil.* Translated by Stefani Hoffman. New York: Random House, 1988.

Shavit, Ari. "Back to Liberal Zionism." *Ha'aretz.* September 11, 2014; "A Missed Funeral and the True Meaning of Zionism." *Ha'aretz*, December 12, 2013.

"our black box": *My Promised Land: The Triumph and Tragedy of Israel* (New York: Spiegel & Grau, 2013).

Shay, Scott. *Getting Our Groove Back: How to Energize American Jewry.* Jerusalem: Devora, 2007.

Shemer, Naomi. "Jerusalem of Gold," 1967. Translation by Shemer Family.

"Actually, I should be applauding": Nathan Shahar, "Naomi Shemer," Jewish Women's Archive encyclopedia.

Singer, Alex. *Alex: Building A Life.* Jerusalem: Gefen House, 1996.

Singer, Saul. "They Tried to Kill Us, We Won, Now We're Changing the World." *Jerusalem Post*, April 1, 2011.

"new chalutziut": David Azrieli, *Rekindling the Torch: Story of Canadian Zionism* (Toronto: Key Porter, 2008).

Shoval, Ronen. *Herzl's Vision 2.0: Im tirtzu: A Manifesto for Renewed Zionism.* Jerusalem: Rubin Mass, 2013.

Smolenskin, Peretz. "It Is Time to Plant," "Let Us Search Our Ways," and "The Haskalah of Berlin." In *The Zionist Idea: A Historical Analysis and Reader,* edited by Arthur Hertzberg, 145, 146–53, and 154–57. Philadelphia: Jewish Publication Society, 1959, 1997.

Soloveitchik, Joseph Ber. *Kol Dodi Dofek, Listen! My Beloved Knocks* (1956), published as *Fate and Destiny: From Holocaust to the State of Israel.* Translated by Lawrence Kaplan. Hoboken: Ktav, 1992, 2000. Adapted by Gil Troy.

Steinberg, Milton. "The Creed of an American Zionist." *Atlantic Monthly,* February 1945.

Stern, Avraham (Yair). "Eighteen Principles of Rebirth." Ba-Machteret, November 1940.

"In days": "Unknown Soldiers: Anthem of the Fighters for the Freedom of Israel," in *The Origins of Israel, 1882–1948: A Documentary History*, edited by Eran Kaplan and Derek J. Penslar, 332–33 (Madison: University of Wisconsin Press, 2011).

Stern, Yedidia Z. "I Believe." In *Constitution by Consensus.* Jerusalem: Israel Democracy Institute, 2007.

Syrkin, Nahman. "The Jewish Problem and the Socialist Jewish State." In *The Zionist Idea: A Historical Analysis and Reader,* edited by Arthur Hertzberg, 333–50. Philadelphia: Jewish Publication Society, 1959, 1997.

Szold, Henrietta. "Letter to Mrs. Julius Rosenwald, January 17, 1915." In Marvin Lowenthal, *Henrietta Szold: Life and Letters.* New York: Viking, 1942.

Tal, Alon. *Pollution in a Promised Land—An Environmental History of Israel.* Berkeley: University of California Press, 2017.

Tamir, Yael "Yuli." "A Jewish and Democratic State." *The Jewish Political Tradition* vol. 1, edited by Michael Walzer, Menachem Lorberbaum, Noam J. Zohar, and Yair Lorberbaum, 523. New Haven CT: Yale University Press, 2000.

"every nationalism privileges": Roi Ben-Yehuda, "Peace Movement Has Become Powerless, Says MK Yuli Tamir," *Ha'aretz,* December 27, 2009.

"born into . . . My Zionism defines": "Estranged but Committed: Liberal Zionists Speak Out," *Huffington Post,* April 25, 2012.

"Underlying nationalism": *Liberal Nationalism* (Princeton: Princeton University Press, 1995).

Taub, Gadi. "In Defence of Zionism." *Fathom,* Autumn 2014.

"my own Zionism": "Gadi Taub's Euology for His Father, Yitzchak Taub," January 25, 2014, Gadi Taub blog, http://www.gaditaub.com/eblog/60/.

"religious movement": *The Settlers and the Struggle over the Meaning of Zionism* (New Haven CT: Yale University Press, 2010).

Tchernichovsky, Saul. "I Believe." Melodies and Liturgy I (Hezyonot Ve-Manginot Alef) Warsaw-Tushia, 1898. Translated by Gil Troy; "They Say There's a Land." *Collected Works,* vol. 3. Vilna: Va'ad Hayovel, 1929. Translated by Gil Troy.

Trigano, Shmuel. "There Is No State of All Its Citizens." Adapted from *The New Jewish State.* Paris: Berg International 2015. Translated by Gil Troy.

Troy, Gil. "Why I Am a Zionist." *Jerusalem Post,* May 7, 2008.

Tsur, Muki. Avraham Shapira, ed. *Siach Lochamim* [Soldiers' chat]. Tel Aviv: Tfoos Co-op Achdut, 1967. Translated by Gil Troy.

The Union of Zionists-Revisionists. Declaration of the Central Committee of the Union of Zionists-Revisionists, Paris, 1925. File Gimel 1–3. Hatzohar Paris Office, Declarations. Jabotinsky Institute in Israel. Tel Aviv, Israel.

"agrarian blind alley": Jan Zouplna, "Beyond a One Man Show: The Prelude of Revisionist Zionism, 1922–25," *Israel Affairs* 19 (2013): 410–28.

Uris, Leon. Pat Boone, "The Exodus Song, This Land Is Mine." 1960.

"second national anthem": David Brinn, "Pat Boone's Christmas Present to the Jews," *Jerusalem Post,* February 10, 2010.

"As a literary work": Adam Kirsch, "Macho Man," *Tablet,* February 1, 2011, http://www.tabletmag.com/jewish-arts-and-culture/books/57525/macho-man.

"the same paving stones": "Exodus-Script," Drew's Script-o-rama, http://
www.script-o-rama.com/movie_scripts/e/exodus-script-transcript-paul
-newman.html, 1960.

"your grandfather's Israel": Thomas Friedman, "Go Ahead, Ruin My Day,"
New York Times, March 18, 2015.

"from the moment the downtrodden": Leon Uris, *Exodus* (Garden City NY:
Doubleday, 1958).

Uziel, Ben-Zion Meir Chai. Uziel and Isaac Herzog. "Prayer for the State of
Israel." 1948. www.myjewishlearning.com; "On Nationalism." In *MeHodu
v'ad Kush: Tzionut Mizrahit-Sepharadit: Yesh Dvarim Kaela* [From India until
Kush: Mizrahi-Sephardic Zionism: There are such things]. Edited by Adi
Arbel. Jerusalem: Institute for Zionist Strategies and the Menachem Begin
Heritage Center, 2016, 8. Translated by Gil Troy.

Walzer, Michael. "The State of Righteousness: Liberal Zionists Speak Out." *Huffington Post,* June 24, 2012.

"We can accept": "Delegitimization and Dissent," *Makom*, September 20, 2011.

"Exodus Politics": *Exodus and Revolution* (New York: Basic, 1985).

"The constant": "The Anomalies of Jewish Identity," *Iyyun* 59 (2010): 24–38.

Weizmann, Chaim. "On the Report of the Palestine Commission." In *The Zionist Idea: A Historical Analysis and Reader,* edited by Arthur Hertzberg, 583–88.
Philadelphia: Jewish Publication Society, 1959, 1997.

Wiesel, Elie. *One Generation After*. New York: Random House, 1970; *A Jew
Today*. New York: Random House, 1978.

"Life in the": *Memoirs: All Rivers Run to the Sea* (Maine: Thorndike, 1994).

"the Jews of silence": *The Jews of Silence* (New York: Schocken, 2011).

"For me": "Elie Wiesel: Jerusalem is Above Politics," *Israel National News*,
April 17, 2010. http://www.israelnationalnews.com/News/News.aspx
/137057.

Wieseltier, Leon. "Brothers and Keepers: Black Jews and the Meaning of Zionism." *New Republic,* February 11, 1985.

"an anachronism . . . bi-national state": Tony Judt, "Israel: The Alternative,"
New York Review of Books, October 23, 2003.

"not the alternative": "What Is Not to Be Done.," *New Republic*, October
29, 2003.

"the spoiled brats": "Language, Identity, and the Scandal of American
Jewry," *My Jewish Learning.com,* http://www.myjewishlearning.com
/article/language-identity-and-the-scandal-of-american-jewry/.

"As a Jew . . . I live in Hebrew": Maya Sela, "Leon Wieseltier: 'I Am a
Human Being before I Am a Jew,'" *Ha'aretz*, June 14, 2013.

Wilf, Einat. "Zionism: The Only Way Forward." *Daily Beast*, April 2, 2012.

"third generation: *My Israel, Our Generation* (Jerusalem: Booksurge, 2007).

"mitzvot of peoplehood": "Mitzvot of Peoplehood," *YNET News*, February 6, 2005. https://www.ynetnews.com/articles/0,7340,L-3041999,00.html.

"this is not": "The Mitzvot of Peoplehood—Some Proposals," *Dr. Einat Wilf*, November 12, 2013, www.wilf.org.

Willis, Ellen, and Nona Willis Aronowitz. "Is There Still a Jewish Question? Why I'm an Anti-Anti-Zionist." In *The Essential Ellen Willis*, edited by Nona Willis Aronowitz, 437. Minneapolis: University of Minnesota Press, 2014.

Wise, Stephen S. *Challenging Years: The Autobiography of Stephen Wise*. New York: Putnam's Sons, 1949.

"The new world": "Zionist Congresses: The Biltmore Congress," *Jewish Virtual Library*.

"A people": "Rabbi Wise Defends Arms for Palestine," *New York Times*, October 27, 1945.

Wisse, Ruth. *Jews and Power*. New York: Schocken, 2007.

"the Anti-Semite's": "The Anti-Semite's Pointed Finger," *Commentary Magazine*, November 1, 2010.

"Doing justice": "Their Tragic Land," *Mosaic*, December 18, 2013.

"It was never": Ezra Glinter, "The Remarkable Career of Ruth Wisse, Yiddish Scholar and Political Firebrand," *Forward*, May 12, 2014.

Wolf, Arnold Jacob. "Will Israel Become Zion?" *Sh'ma*, March 30, 1973; "*Breira* National Platform, February 21, 1977." In *American Jewish History: A Primary Source Reader*, edited by Gary Philip Zola and Marc Dollinger, 385–86. Waltham: Brandeis University Press, 2014.

"more traditional theologically": Margalit Fox, "Arnold Jacob Wolf, a Leading Reform Rabbi, Is Dead at 84," *New York Times*, December 29, 2008.

"a titan": Letter from President-Elect Barack Obama read at funeral of Arnold Jacob Wolf, December 26, 2008.

World Zionist Organization. "The Jerusalem Program," 1951. https://www.azm.org/the-jerusalem-program-1951.

"the Jerusalem Program": The Jerusalem Program, June 2004, https://www.azm.org/the-new-jerusalem-program-adopted-june-2004.

"establishing": Jewish Virtual Library, http://www.jewishvirtuallibrary.org/first-zionist-congress-and-basel-program-1897.

"A community": David Breakstone, "Perspectives of Jewish Education," *Lookstein Center for Jewish Education*, http://www.lookstein.org/online_journal.php?id=233.

Wouk, Herman. *This Is My God*. New York: Pocket Books, 1974.

Yehoshua, A. B. Gil Troy. "The Basics of Zionism, Homeland, and Being a Total Jew." Adapted from various essays of A. B. Yehoshua, 2017: "Defining Who

Is an Israeli." *Ha'aretz,* September 12, 2013; "The Meaning of Homeland."
The A. B. Yehoshua Controversy, May 13, 2006; "Zionism Is Not an Ideology."
Ha'aretz, November 26, 2010; and "Defining Zionism: The Belief that Israel
Belongs to the Entire Jewish People." *Ha'aretz,* May 21, 2013.

Yosef, Ovadia. "Mesirat Shtachim MeEretz Yisrael Bimkom Pikuach Nefesh"
[Returning some of the Holy Land to preserve life]. In Remarks at the
Conference on Oral Law at Merkaz HaRav Kook, 1979. prdupl02.ynet.co.il
/ForumFiles/7522709.doc.

"It is a lie": "Rabbi Ovadia Yosef, 'Greatest Rabbi of the Generation,' Has
Died," *Israel National News,* October 7, 2013.

In the JPS Anthologies of Jewish Thought Series

Modern Conservative Judaism: Thought and Practice
Edited by Elliot N. Dorff
Foreword by Julie Schonfeld

Modern Orthodox Judaism: A Documentary History
Zev Eleff
Foreword by Jacob J. Schacter

A Kabbalah and Jewish Mysticism Reader
Daniel M. Horwitz

*The Growth of Reform Judaism: American and
European Sources*
W. Gunther Plaut
Foreword by Jacob K. Shankman
New introduction by Howard A. Berman
New epilogue by David Ellenson
With select documents, 1975–2008

*The Rise of Reform Judaism: A Sourcebook
of Its European Origins*
W. Gunther Plaut
Foreword by Solomon B. Freehof
New introduction by Howard A. Berman

*The Zionist Ideas: Visions for the Jewish
Homeland—Then, Now, Tomorrow*
Gil Troy

To order or obtain more information on these or other
Jewish Publication Society titles, visit jps.org.